The Mark of Nicholas Kegg

Volume III K-Z

Research and Compilation by

Debbie Alexander

Copyright © 2023, Debbie Alexander

ALL RIGHTS RESERVED.
No part of this publication may be reproduced, stored in a retrieval system, or transmitted in any form or by any means whatsoever, whether electronic, mechanical, magnetic recording, or photocopying, without the prior written approval of the Copyright holder or Publisher, excepting brief quotations for inclusion in book reviews.

Published by:

Janaway Publishing, Inc.
732 Kelsey Ct.
Santa Maria, California 93454
(805) 925-1952
www.janawaygenealogy.com

2023

Library of Congress Control Number: 2023941660

ISBN: 978-1-59641-475-4 Volume 3

Other volumes in this set:
978-1-59641-473-0 Volume 1
978-1-59641-474-7 Volume 2

Cover artist Chelan Hawk Shumacher (8th great grandson of progenitor Nicholas Kegg) artistically depicts the contents of this book. He includes the Mark of Nicholas Kegg carved into the family tree. The actual mark shown above was taken from a court document dated March 5, 1778 whereas Nicholas cursed the new law, damned the congress, money and those who made it. Unable to read or write, Nicholas made his mark with the letter N. It is all that remains by the hand of the progenitor.

Edited by Jenna Meeker Alexander Published by Janaway Publishing Inc., Publisher of Barbara Jean Walling Sistler (6th great granddaughter of Nicholas Kegg) along with her husband Byron H. Sistler, books.

Special thanks to more than 250 cousins who provided the photographs contained in this book.

DISCLAIMER: Within the following pages, the total number of children born to an individual includes only those who have been proven without a shadow of doubt. The utmost care has been taken to ensure the genealogical accuracy of this publication, however, that does not mean there can't be mistakes. You should always verify and do your own research.

Made in the United States of America

KEISER

DOROTHY JEANETTE KEISER [5054] (1908 – 1965) daughter of Floyd and Nellie (Wyckoff) Keiser, married Charles Malcolm Isaacson.
VIRGINIA WESLEY KEISER (1907 – 2005) daughter of Floyd and Nellie (Wyckoff) Keiser, married Richard Chas Hollinger with whom she was mother of (3).
JAIME R. KEISTER Sixth great granddaughter of progenitor Nicholas Kegg.
JODIE N. KEISTER Sixth great granddaughter of progenitor Nicholas Kegg.

KEITH

JACOB KEITH Seventh great grandson of progenitor Nicholas Kegg.
ROBERT KEITH Seventh great grandson of progenitor Nicholas Kegg.

KELLER

ANTHONY RAY KELLER Seventh great grandson of progenitor Nicholas Kegg.
AUDRIANNA RAY KELLER Seventh great granddaughter of progenitor Nicholas Kegg.
BENJAMIN KELLER Sixth great grandson of progenitor Nicholas Kegg. **BOBBI KELLER** Seventh great granddaughter of progenitor Nicholas Kegg. **EVA ROSE KELLER** Seventh great granddaughter of progenitor Nicholas Kegg. **HOLLY IRENE KELLER** Sixth great granddaughter of progenitor Nicholas Kegg. **ISABELLA KELLER** Seventh great granddaughter of progenitor Nicholas Kegg. **JASON KELLER** Sixth great grandson of progenitor Nicholas Kegg. **JASON LEE KELLER** Seventh great grandson of progenitor Nicholas Kegg. **JENNIFER LYNN KELLER** Sixth great granddaughter of progenitor Nicholas Kegg. **JEREMY KELLER** Sixth great grandson of progenitor Nicholas Kegg. **KYLE KELLER** Seventh great grandson of progenitor Nicholas Kegg. **LAUREN KELLER** Eighth great granddaughter of progenitor Nicholas Kegg. **MADISON KELLER** Seventh great granddaughter of progenitor Nicholas Kegg. **MCKENZIE KELLER** Seventh great granddaughter of progenitor Nicholas Kegg. **MICHELLE KELLER** Sixth great granddaughter of progenitor Nicholas Kegg. **MITCHELL KELLER** Seventh great grandson of progenitor Nicholas Kegg. **PATRICK SHANE KELLER** Seventh great grandson of progenitor Nicholas Kegg. **PATSY JO KELLER** Fifth great granddaughter of progenitor Nicholas Kegg. **RAYMOND KELLER** Sixth great grandson of progenitor Nicholas Kegg. **ROBERT KELLER** Sixth great grandson of progenitor Nicholas Kegg. **ROBERT KELLER** Sixth great grandson of progenitor Nicholas Kegg. **ROBERT KELLER** Seventh great grandson of progenitor Nicholas Kegg. **ROBERT KELLER** aka "Robbie", Eighth great grandson of progenitor Nicholas Kegg. **SCOTT KELLER** Sixth great grandson of progenitor Nicholas Kegg. **ZACKREY WAYNE KELLER** Seventh great grandson of progenitor Nicholas Kegg.

KELLEY

ALICIA KELLEY Fifth great granddaughter of progenitor Nicholas Kegg.
ALISA MICHELE KELLEY Seventh great granddaughter of progenitor Nicholas Kegg.
ANNETTE MARIE KELLEY Fifth great granddaughter of progenitor Nicholas Kegg.
AUGUSTINE BERNARD KELLEY Fifth great grandson of progenitor Nicholas Kegg.
BRENDAN KELLEY Fifth great grandson of progenitor Nicholas Kegg. **BRENTEN KELLEY** Eighth great grandson of progenitor Nicholas Kegg. **CALEB HENRY KELLEY** Sixth great grandson of progenitor Nicholas Kegg. **CATHERINE GAIL KELLEY** Sixth great granddaughter of progenitor Nicholas Kegg. **COLIN P. KELLEY** Fifth great grandson of progenitor Nicholas Kegg.

[5054] The Los Angeles Times (CA) April 13, 1965

DAVID KELLEY Fourth great grandson of progenitor Nicholas Kegg. **DAVID B. KELLEY** [5055] (1947 – 2008) son of Joseph and Annette (Beatty) Kelley, married Shirley A. Hayden with whom he was father of (2). David was employed by Fansteel Hydro Carbide in Youngstown and was a member of the Laurel Highlands Model Airplane Club at Mammoth Park. He was also a Vietnam War veteran, having served in the Air Force. **DONALD EDWARD KELLEY** Fourth great grandson of progenitor Nicholas Kegg. **ELLEN MARIE KELLEY** [5056, 5057] (1884 – 1980) aka "Sister Marcella", daughter of Abraham and Mary (Kegg) Kelley. Sister Marcella was above all a woman of prayer, a true Benedictine. She was a teacher in elementary and secondary school of the Dioceses of Pittsburgh, Greensburg and Altoona-Johnstown. She was witty, making her a good conversationalist. Sister Marcella enjoyed music, playing the piano and singing. She enjoyed literature. Her last assignments were to St. Benedict Academy where she taught French, and later operated the bookstore. **GARY J. KELLEY** Fifth great grandson of progenitor Nicholas Kegg. **HILARY KELLEY** [5058] (1968 – 2011) daughter of the Honorable James and Patricia (Phillips) Kelley, married Brian C. Querry with whom she was mother of (1). **JAMES R. KELLEY** Fourth great grandson of progenitor Nicholas Kegg. **JENNIFER KELLEY** Sixth great granddaughter of progenitor Nicholas Kegg. **JOHN A. KELLEY** Fifth great grandson of progenitor Nicholas Kegg. **JOHN JUDE KELLEY** Fifth great grandson of progenitor Nicholas Kegg. **JORDAN BERTRAND KELLEY** [5059] (1938 – 1953) son of Ralph and Josephine (Jordan) Kelley Jordan was a Junior High School pupil, he was a member of the Student Council, a Red Cross Representative and a member of the track team. **JOSEPH LAWRENCE KELLEY** Fifth great grandson of progenitor Nicholas Kegg. **JUSTIN A. KELLEY** Fifth great grandson of progenitor Nicholas Kegg. **JUSTYNA KELLEY** Sixth great granddaughter of progenitor Nicholas Kegg.
KATHERINE MARIE KELLEY aka "Kittie", Fifth great granddaughter of progenitor Nicholas Kegg.
KATHLEEN MARIE KELLEY Fifth great granddaughter of progenitor Nicholas Kegg.
LILLIA KELLEY Seventh great granddaughter of progenitor Nicholas Kegg. **LINDA KELLEY** Fifth great granddaughter of progenitor Nicholas Kegg. **MADELINE GRACE KELLEY** Sixth great granddaughter of progenitor Nicholas Kegg. **MARCELLA MARIE KELLEY** Fifth great granddaughter of progenitor Nicholas Kegg. **MARK KELLEY** Fifth great grandson of progenitor Nicholas Kegg. **MARTHA STONE KELLEY** Fifth great granddaughter of progenitor Nicholas Kegg.
MARY KELLEY Fifth great granddaughter of progenitor Nicholas Kegg.
MARY ELIZABETH KELLEY aka "Beth", Fifth great granddaughter of progenitor Nicholas Kegg.
MARY ELLEN KELLEY Fifth great granddaughter of progenitor Nicholas Kegg.
MARY LEA KELLEY Fifth great granddaughter of progenitor Nicholas Kegg.
MARY LYNNE KELLEY Fifth great granddaughter of progenitor Nicholas Kegg.
MARY MONICA KELLEY Fifth great granddaughter of progenitor Nicholas Kegg.
MATTHEW D. KELLEY Sixth great grandson of progenitor Nicholas Kegg. **MATTHEW KELLEY** Fifth great grandson of progenitor Nicholas Kegg. **MAURA KELLEY** Fifth great granddaughter of progenitor Nicholas Kegg. **MELISSA A. KELLEY** Fifth great granddaughter of progenitor Nicholas Kegg. **MICHAEL BERNARD KELLEY** Fifth great grandson of progenitor Nicholas Kegg.
NOLAN VANGILDER KELLEY Sixth great grandson of progenitor Nicholas Kegg.
OLIVER BENEDICT KELLEY (1888 – 1890) son of Abraham and Mary (Kegg) Kelley.
PATRICK LEONARD KELLEY Sixth great grandson of progenitor Nicholas Kegg.
PAUL CHRISTOPHER KELLEY Fifth great grandson of progenitor Nicholas Kegg.
PAUL GERARD KELLEY Fifth great grandson of progenitor Nicholas Kegg.
PETER THADDEUS KELLEY aka "Tad", Fifth great grandson of progenitor Nicholas Kegg.
RACHEL NICOLE KELLEY Sixth great granddaughter of progenitor Nicholas Kegg.
RALPH J. KELLEY Fifth great grandson of progenitor Nicholas Kegg.
RALPH JORDAN KELLEY [5060] (1936 – 2007) son of Ralph and Josephine (Jordan) Kelley, married and was father of (2). Ralph was employed as an attorney.

[5055] Greensburg Tribune Review (PA) May 13, 2008 [5056] ancestry.com/Funeral Eulogy shared by Mary K. Blendy [5057] p.10 Pittsburgh Post Gazette (PA) Sep 22, 1980 [5058] Greensburg Tribune Review (PA) Aug. 23, 2011 [5059] Tribune Review (PA) Aug 5, 1953 [5060] Detroit News (MI) Oct. 3, 2007

RICHARD BATES KELLEY Fifth great grandson of progenitor Nicholas Kegg. **ROBERT JAMES KELLEY** Fifth great grandson of progenitor Nicholas Kegg. **SARA JEAN KELLEY** Sixth great granddaughter of progenitor Nicholas Kegg. **SUSAN A. KELLEY** Sixth great granddaughter of progenitor Nicholas Kegg. **TIMOTHY GERARD KELLEY** Fifth great grandson of progenitor Nicholas Kegg. **VINCENT FRANCIS KELLEY** (1886 – 1980) son of Abraham and Mary (Kegg) Kelley. Vincent was a veteran of WWI. **WILLIAM F. KELLEY** Fifth great grandson of progenitor Nicholas Kegg. **ZACHARY BRYAN KELLEY** Sixth great grandson of progenitor Nicholas Kegg.

KELLY

CHAD MICHAEL KELLY Seventh great grandson of progenitor Nicholas Kegg.
CHRISTOPHER RONALD KELLY Seventh great grandson of progenitor Nicholas Kegg.
JANET L. KELLY Fifth great granddaughter of progenitor Nicholas Kegg.
MARK E. KELLY Sixth great grandson of progenitor Nicholas Kegg.
MICHAEL WILLIAM KELLY Seventh great grandson of progenitor Nicholas Kegg.
ROBERT KELLY Sixth great grandson of progenitor Nicholas Kegg.
SCOTT ALLAN KELLY Seventh great grandson of progenitor Nicholas Kegg.
THOMAS C. KELLY [5061] (1953 – 1979) son of Thomas and Dorothy (Thies) Kelly.

KELSO

BERTHA LOUISE KELSO [5062] (1933 – 2003) daughter of William Carl and Mabel De Hart (Beegle) Kelso, married David Murphin Bourne with whom she was mother of (4). Later, she married Malcom Harold Wilson. Bertha was a great fan of the outdoors and loved camping and fishing. Her family meant the world to her, and she had a way of showing it in everything she did for them. **DIANE KELSO** Sixth great granddaughter of progenitor Nicholas Kegg. **FLORENCE KELSO** Fifth great granddaughter of progenitor Nicholas Kegg. **GARY KELSO** Sixth great grandson of progenitor Nicholas Kegg. **HILDA KELSO** Fifth great granddaughter of progenitor Nicholas Kegg. **JOANNE KELSO** Sixth great granddaughter of progenitor Nicholas Kegg. **JODY SUSAN KELSO** (1970 – 1970) daughter of William and Anne Evelyn (Pastushuk) Kelso. **JORDAN KELSO** Seventh great grandson of progenitor Nicholas Kegg. **KAITLYN KELSO** Seventh great granddaughter of progenitor Nicholas Kegg. **KEVIN WILLIAM KELSO** [5063] (1960 – 2014) son of William and Anne Evelyn (Pastushuk) Kelso married Evelyn with whom he was father of (4). **KORY KELSO** Seventh great grandson of progenitor Nicholas Kegg. **KRISTAN KELSO** Seventh great granddaughter of progenitor Nicholas Kegg. **LACEY KELSO** Seventh great granddaughter of progenitor Nicholas Kegg. **MORGAN KELSO** Seventh great granddaughter of progenitor Nicholas Kegg. **NORMAN HAROLD KELSO** (1941 – 1989) son of William Carl and Mabel De Hart (Beegle) Kelso. **RANDY CARL KELSO** (1972 – 2007) son of William and Anne Evelyn (Pastushuk) Kelso. **RUSSELL GEORGE KELSO** (1937 – 1937) son of William Carl and Mabel De Hart (Beegle) Kelso. **WILLIAM KELSO** Fifth great grandson of progenitor Nicholas Kegg.

KEMP

DAVID KEMP Seventh great grandson of progenitor Nicholas Kegg.
DIANE KEMP Seventh great granddaughter of progenitor Nicholas Kegg.
JOSEPH KEMP Seventh great grandson of progenitor Nicholas Kegg.
TIMOTHY KEMP Seventh great grandson of progenitor Nicholas Kegg.

[5061] p.2C Plain Dealer (OH) Apr 12, 1979 [5062] Red Deer Advocate (Alberta, Canada) March 20, 2003 [5063] The Drayton Valley Western Review (Alberta, Canada) Sep 16, 2014

KEMPER

SHANE ANTHONY KEMPER Seventh great grandson of progenitor Nicholas Kegg.
SHAWN WAYNE KEMPER Seventh great grandson of progenitor Nicholas Kegg.

KEMPTON

BRADLEY G. KEMPTON Fourth great grandson of progenitor Nicholas Kegg.
MALINDA RENEE KEMPTON aka "Mindy", Fourth great granddaughter of progenitor Nicholas Kegg.   **SCOTT GRINNEL KEMPTON** Fourth great grandson of progenitor Nicholas Kegg.

KENDALL

ALEXANDER MASON KENDALL Seventh great grandson of progenitor Nicholas Kegg.
CORY KENDALL Sixth great grandson of progenitor Nicholas Kegg.   **JASON SCOTT KENDALL** (1970 – 1995) aka "Jase", son of Michael and Jan (Baughman) Kendall.   **JEANNE URLA KENDALL** [5064] (1917 – 2001) daughter of William and Alta (Turner) Kendall, married Wendell Walter Frederick with whom she was mother of (2). Jeanne was head librarian at the Crown Point Public Library, Indiana. She attended Evangelical Community Church of Bloomington. She was a member of the Order of the Eastern Star and the Indiana Library Association.   **KYLE KENDALL** Seventh great grandson of progenitor Nicholas Kegg.   **MARCY KENDALL** Sixth great granddaughter of progenitor Nicholas Kegg.   **MICHAEL KENDALL** Fifth great grandson of progenitor Nicholas Kegg.
RICHARD A. KENDALL [5065] (1946 – 1967) son of William and Margaret (Rife) Kendall. A Vietnam veteran discharged from the Army, was killed when his car crashed off the Milledgeville-Polo Blacktop.
RYAN KENDALL Seventh great grandson of progenitor Nicholas Kegg.   **TROY KENDALL** Seventh great grandson of progenitor Nicholas Kegg.   **WILLIAM FRANKLIN KENDALL** [5066] (1919 – 2008) aka "Frank", son of William and Alta (Turner) Kendall, married Margaret L. Rife with whom he was father of (2). Frank farmed in the Milledgeville area retiring.   **ZACHARY TAYLOR KENDALL** Seventh great grandson of progenitor Nicholas Kegg.

KENDELL

CONNIE ANN KENDELL Sixth great granddaughter of progenitor Nicholas Kegg.
KENNETH EUGENE KENDELL [5067] (1923 – 1994) son of Carl and Mabel (Schoettler) Kendell, married Concetta (Galatioto) Kendell with whom he was father of (2).   **KENNETH EUGENE KENDELL JR.** Sixth great grandson of progenitor Nicholas Kegg.   **SHELLEY ANNE KENDELL** Sixth great granddaughter of progenitor Nicholas Kegg.   **STEPHEN MICHAEL KENDELL** Sixth great grandson of progenitor Nicholas Kegg.   **WARREN KENDELL** Sixth great grandson of progenitor Nicholas Kegg.   **WARREN WAYNE KENDELL** [5068] (1929 – 1975) son of Carl and Mabel (Schoettler) Kendell, married Louise Ann (Dangelmair) Kendell with whom he was father of (2). Later, he married Lorraine Ann (Roth) McHatton Kendell with whom he was father of (1).   **WILLIAM ROBERT KENDELL** [5069] (1927 – 1989) son of Carl and Mabel (Schoettler) Kendell, married Christine Gmeiner. Following his time in the Army Air Forces and the Navy Air Corps, William became an engineer in Michigan Bell Telephone Co. and later obtained his law degree. He spent nearly half of his life working for K mart Corp., ending his career as an associate in real estate development at its international headquarters. According to those who knew him, William was a tireless worker who spent long hours in the office. He had a kind of an engineering mentality in that he was precise, organized with a good approach. William didn't leave anything on the table in respect to real estate development.

[5064] Stuart News/Port St. Lucie News Nov 27, 2001 [5065] p.D10 - Rockford Morning Star (IL) Dec. 24, 1967 [5066] Rockford Register Star (IL) May 25, 2008 [5067] Philadelphia Daily News (PA) Oct 4, 1994 [5068] Denver Post (CO) Nov 28, 1975 [5069] Oakland Press (MI) contributed by Mary Powell Phelps FindAGrave # 225798104

KENNEDY

ADELINE ELLA KENNEDY (1937 – 2002) daughter of Dewitt and Pearl (Hutton) Kennedy.
ALLISON KENNEDY Seventh great granddaughter of progenitor Nicholas Kegg.
AUSTIN KENNEDY Seventh great grandson of progenitor Nicholas Kegg.
BENNETT FARLIN KENNEDY (1888 – 1965) son of John and Adaline (Doak) Kennedy, married Pansy Leone Morrison with whom he was father of (2). **BENNETT K. KENNEDY** (1926 – 1944) son of John and Margaret (Cravens) Kennedy a member of the 309th Infantry died in Germany, WWII.
DEWITT CLINTON KENNEDY (1882 – 1977) aka "Dee", son of John and Adaline (Doak) Kennedy married twice; first to Belle Irene Carr with whom he was father of (2). Later, he married Pearl Lavesta (Hutton) Leitch with whom he was father of (2). **ELIZABETH KENNEDY** Seventh great granddaughter of progenitor Nicholas Kegg. **EMILY KENNEDY** Seventh great granddaughter of progenitor Nicholas Kegg. **EVA KENNEDY** (1871 – 1959) daughter of John and Adaline (Doak) Kennedy. **EVAN KENNEDY** Seventh great grandson of progenitor Nicholas Kegg.
FLORENCE JANE KENNEDY aka "Jane" Fifth great granddaughter of progenitor Nicholas Kegg.
ISABELLA KENNEDY Seventh great granddaughter of progenitor Nicholas Kegg.
JAMIE KENNEDY Sixth great granddaughter of progenitor Nicholas Kegg. **JANA KENNEDY** Seventh great granddaughter of progenitor Nicholas Kegg. **JARED KENNEDY** Seventh great grandson of progenitor Nicholas Kegg. **JASON KENNEDY** Fifth great grandson of progenitor Nicholas Kegg. **JASPER MICHAEL KENNEDY** (1920 – 2003) aka "Mike", son of John and Margaret (Cravens) Kennedy. **JEANNE KENNEDY** [5069A] (1915 – 2009) daughter of John and Margaret (Cravens) Kennedy married twice, first to Thomas Benton Hutton with whom she was mother of (1), later she married Roy William Reed with whom she was mother of (4). Jeanne worked hand in hand with her husband, Roy W. Reed and, though they started with nothing, together they went on to build a highly successful independent oil and gas company and established the Dog Creek Ranch, one of the largest cattle and real estate holdings in southeast Oklahoma and were original stockholders in the Poteau State Bank. Jeanne was a former youth Sunday School Teacher in Oklahoma City and a member of the First United Methodist Church in Poteau. She traveled abroad on numerous Missionary trips to help others and supported Project Compassion. She was selected as the Business and Professional Women's "Woman of the Year", received the Poteau Chamber of Commerce Lifetime Contribution Award, the Oklahoma City University Bishop Paul Millhouse Award, served as a Trustee of the Carl Albert State College Development Foundation, and was a member of the Carl Albert State College Hall of Fame. She also thoroughly enjoyed serving as Grand Marshall for the Poteau Frontier Days Rodeo Parade. She was a person that always put the needs of others before her own, never asking anything in return and one who always had a Christian attitude in all things and for all people. **JESSIE ADELINE KENNEDY** [5069B] (1896 – 1966) daughter of John and Adaline (Doak) Kennedy, married John L. Smith with whom she was mother of (1). Later she married Lewis Henry Dorey with whom she was mother of (4). Jessie was a past president of the American Legion Auxiliary. **JM KENNEDY** [5069C] (1935 – 2018) son of Dewitt and Pearl (Hutton) Leitch Kennedy, married Etta Lou Lance with whom he was father of (4). JM started his own successful business, Kennedy Dry Wall. He loved tending to his farm and raising a garden.
JOE KENNEDY Sixth great grandson of progenitor Nicholas Kegg. **JOHN H. KENNEDY** [5070] (1907 - 1974) son of Dewitt and Belle Irene (Carr) Kennedy married Mae Belle Kirk with whom he was father of (1). John was employed for six years by the Eudy Sheet Metal Co. He was a Baptist church member.
JOHN IRA KENNEDY (1890 – 1980) son of John and Adaline (Doak) Kennedy, married Margaret Marie Cravens with whom he was father of (7). **JOHN MICHAEL KENNEDY** (1847 – 1936) son of Michael and Sarah Ann (Cagg) Kennedy, married Adaline M. Doak with whom he was father of (7).
JOHNNY KENNEDY Fifth great grandson of progenitor Nicholas Kegg.
JORDAN KENNEDY Seventh great granddaughter of progenitor Nicholas Kegg.

[5069A] Evans Funeral Homes (OK) Aug 26, 2009 [5069B] The Wichita Eagle (KS) March 25, 1966 [5069C] King & Shearwood Funeral Home of Stigler [5070] The Arizona Republic (AZ) April 20, 1974

JUDITH ANN KENNEDY [5070A] (1941 –2006) daughter of Royce and Mary (Musser) Kennedy married twice, first to Wayne Fredrick Divis with whom she was mother of (2), later she married Walter Benton Willis with whom she was mother of (1).
JUSTIN KENNEDY Seventh great grandson of progenitor Nicholas Kegg.
LISA KENNEDY Seventh great granddaughter of progenitor Nicholas Kegg.
MARCI KENNEDY Sixth great granddaughter of progenitor Nicholas Kegg.
MARGARET AYN KENNEDY (1930 – 2004) daughter of John and Margaret (Cravens) Kennedy, married Russell David Madigan with whom she was mother of (3).
MIKE KENNEDY Sixth great grandson of progenitor Nicholas Kegg.
MILFORD GORDON KENNEDY [5070B] aka "Ted" (1922 – 2007) son of John and Margaret (Cravens) Kennedy was a retired realtor.   **MINNIE M. KENNEDY** [5071] (1884 – 1904) daughter of John and Adaline (Doak) Kennedy, married Clyde Kerwood.   **MORRISON KEITH KENNEDY** (1913 – 1978) aka "Morris", son of Bennett and Pansy (Morrison) Kennedy, married Esther Smith with whom he was father of (2).   **NANCY LOU KENNEDY** Fourth great granddaughter of progenitor Nicholas Kegg.
POLLY KENNEDY [5071A] (1917 – 2012) daughter of John and Margaret (Cravens) Kennedy, married Jesse Hales with whom she was mother of (2). Polly walked or rode her horse to Hickory Ridge School and in May of 1935 graduated from the High School Department at Connors in Warner, Oklahoma. Polly spent her entire adult life as an accomplished seamstress. Although being a seamstress was her occupation, she loved making the replicas of designer clothing for her Granddaughters and continued to provide her Great-Grandchildren with only the best in Christmas dresses and Halloween costumes. Her role as "MeeMa" was her most cherished. She attended First Baptist Church in Warner, Oklahoma where for many years she worked in the toddler nursery and taught Women's Senior Adult Sunday School well into her 80's. Polly especially enjoyed her travels abroad.
POLLY GERTRUDE KENNEDY [5072] (1893 – 1923) daughter of John and Adaline (Doak) Kennedy. At twenty years of age, she entered the M.O. & G. Hospital at Muskogee and graduated as a trained nurse in 1916 and has followed the profession of nurse since that time. She enlisted in the army as a Red Cross nurse in June 1918, served in Camps in Louisiana and Mississippi, and went overseas with the A.E.F. in September 1918. Since leaving the army she has worked at her profession in Oklahoma City and Wichita Falls, Texas. Polly possessed a beautiful Christian character. There was nothing lacking in her Christian faith or outlook. When death seemed inevitable, she faced it with calm resignation. She expressed a desire to be released from her suffering that she might enjoy the rest of eternity. Her trust in God prepared her for the end, and she met the close of life with the same courage with which she had met all the challenges of her life. She was faithful to the call of the sick and distressed, to the call of her country and to the call of her God. Her spirit abides with God. Could she but speak, she would gladly repeat the immortal words of Tennyson; "And after that the dark! And may there be no sadness of farewell. When I Embark; For tho' from out our bourne of Time and Place. The flood may bear me far. I hope to meet my pilot face to face. When I have crossed the bar."
PREMINA FRANCES KENNEDY (1844 – 1853) daughter of Michael and Sarah (Cagg) Kennedy.
RONDA KENNEDY Fifth great granddaughter of progenitor Nicholas Kegg.
ROSE GRACE KENNEDY [5073] (1911 – 2001) daughter of John and Margaret (Cravens) Kennedy married twice; first to Virgil Gilbert Long with whom she was mother of (3). Later, she married Robert L. Whitley. Rose was the founder and co-owner of Long's Paint and Body Shop.
RYAN KENNEDY Seventh great grandson of progenitor Nicholas Kegg.
SARAH KENNEDY Seventh great granddaughter of progenitor Nicholas Kegg.
SHANNON KENNEDY Fifth great granddaughter of progenitor Nicholas Kegg.
STELLA ANN KENNEDY (1891 – 1966) daughter of John and Adaline (Doak) Kennedy, married Roy L. Porter with whom she was mother of (1).
TRISTAN KENNEDY Seventh great granddaughter of progenitor Nicholas Kegg.

[5070A] The Chronicle (WA) Sep. 13, 2006 [5070B] Oklahoman (OK) Sep 23, 2007 [5071] The Bluff City News (KS) Apr 15, 1904 [5071A] Checotah Funeral & Cremation Service (OK) [5072] Okeene Record (OK) Aug 24, 1923 [5073] The Oklahoman (OK) Oct. 7, 2001

KENNELL

ALBERT KERR KENNELL (5074) (1927 – 1994) son of Albert and Josephine (Kerr) Kennell, married Helen Lounetta Kasecamp with whom he was father of (1); Albert retired with over 30 years of employment as a truck driver for the Interstate Motor Freight System. Prior to this, he was employed as a boilermaker at the Bolt and Forge Shops for the B&O Railroad in Cumberland, Md. He served in the US Navy aboard the destroyer USS Beatty as a Boilermaker 3rd Class during World War II. From 1946 to 1960, he was a catcher for the Barrelville and Wellersburg Pen Mar League baseball teams and the Wellersburg County League softball team. **ALICE LOU ELLEN KENNELL** (5074A) (1926 – 2003) daughter of Albert and Josephine (Kerr) Kennell married twice, first to Wilbert Eugene Harden with whom she was mother of (2). Later she married John R. Booth with whom she was mother of (1). Alice was a member of the Western Maryland Bowling Association. Her hobbies included bowling for over 20 years, cooking and making pies, putting puzzles together, rug making and shopping and lunch on Saturdays. She enjoyed watching deer, rabbits, and birds. - **JENNIFER KENNELL** Sixth great granddaughter of progenitor Nicholas Kegg. **JESSICA KENNELL** Sixth great granddaughter of progenitor Nicholas Kegg. **RANDY KENNELL** Fifth great grandson of progenitor Nicholas Kegg.

KEPHART

GARY ALLEN KEPHART Sixth great grandson of progenitor Nicholas Kegg.
MICHAEL NATHAN KEPHART Seventh great grandson of progenitor Nicholas Kegg.
ROBERT SHELDON KEPHART Sixth great grandson of progenitor Nicholas Kegg.
ANNE LOUISE KEPNER Sixth great granddaughter of progenitor Nicholas Kegg.

KEPNER

JANE ELLEN KEPNER Sixth great granddaughter of progenitor Nicholas Kegg.
JASON J. KEPNER Seventh great grandson of progenitor Nicholas Kegg.
RICHARD STEPHEN KEPNER (5075) (1946 – 1976) son of Richard and Miriam (Harclerode) Kepner, married Margaret E. Haley with whom he was father of (1). An Air force Captain, Richard had served at Moody AFB, Ga., George AFB, Calif., and in Iceland.

KEPPLE

JAMILA DAWN HULBERT KEPPLE Sixth great granddaughter of progenitor Nicholas Kegg.

KERN

ANN ELIZABETH KERN Fourth great granddaughter of progenitor Nicholas Kegg.
BLAIR NICOLE KERN Sixth great granddaughter of progenitor Nicholas Kegg. **BRIAN KERN** Sixth great grandson of progenitor Nicholas Kegg. **CARI BETH KERN** Sixth great granddaughter of progenitor Nicholas Kegg. **DUANE KERN** Sixth great grandson of progenitor Nicholas Kegg. **DUANE EUGENE KERN** (5076) (1947 – 2008) aka "Dooie", son of William and Arlene (Heffner) Kern, married Kay Woolheater with whom he was father of (2). **EMMA CATHERINE KERN** Seventh great granddaughter of progenitor Nicholas Kegg. **JENNIFER NICOLE KERN** Sixth great granddaughter of progenitor Nicholas Kegg. **KRISTIN CHARIETY KERN** Sixth great granddaughter of progenitor Nicholas Kegg. **LINDSAY JO KERN** Sixth great granddaughter of progenitor Nicholas Kegg. **PETER CARLSON KERN** (5076A) aka "Woody" (1947 – 2014) son of Peter and Dorothy

---

(5074) New Republic (PA) May 12, 1994, Meyersdale Library transcribed by Kerry L. Miller (5074A) Allegany County Public Library (MD) obituary clipping contributed by D. Sue Dible (5075) p.20 Air Force Times Jan 17, 1977 (5076) Pittsburgh Post-Gazette (PA) May 15, 2008 (5076A) Dallas Morning News (TX) Jan 10, 2014/ texasmonthly.com

(Rauch) Kern married four times, first to Sheila Duffy, then Donna J. Egli Oprandi with whom he was father of (2), 3rd he married Susan Beth Dearment with whom he was father of (3), later he married Sheri Dawn Robinson with whom he was father of (2). Woody was the sole owner of Texas Health Enterprises, the largest nursing home chain in the state of Texas with over 100 homes. Peter touted these homes as "a better place to live" for the elderly however, countless lawsuits tell a much different story, alleging one frail 97-year-old woman was found lying helplessly in her bed while fire ants crawled over her body, biting her on the face, chest, legs, and arms—an attack that a hospital report said contributed to her death. A woman with Alzheimer's disease wandered out of the home. She was struck and killed by a car on a nearby highway. DHS Investigators looked at the charts of sixteen residents and discovered that fourteen of them had developed multiple pressure sores (informally known as bedsores) since coming to the facility. If left untreated, these sores can turn deadly, burrowing toward the bone and causing infection. Investigators found that not only were the residents receiving little treatment for their sores but they were also not being adequately bathed or fed. Dried feces were spread over the buttocks of several residents. One woman was seen leaning against a bed's rails, trying to eat with her fingers, her bed padding soaked with urine. One man, left unattended, was seen trying in vain to cut his meat patty with a spoon. Many of the Texas Health Enterprises homes did meet government standards. 112 of his homes failed to meet licensing requirements when inspected. A Fort Worth attorney was quoted as saying "I don't think Peter sees his patients in his nursing homes as anything more than profit-making commodities," Woody never took responsibility for his understaffed and undersupplied homes that resulted in needless deaths. According to court testimony in one case of a sweet old lady who was underfed to the point of starvation. Her right leg turned black from gangrene, which went unnoticed by the nursing home's staff. Her own son discovered the gangrene when he pulled off one of his mother's socks, which smelled of urine. Peter insisted he had done nothing wrong. Woody was a lover of baseball and owned minor league baseball teams in North Carolina, Washington, California, New Jersey, and New York. The Ashville Tourist, an affiliate of the Colorado Rockies, was regarded as one of the best-run minor league franchises in the country. He began his career with the Arena Football League as the owner of the Fort Worth Cavalry in 1993. This team only operated for a single season. In 1994 he purchased the Arena Football team, Tampa Bay Storm, in Tampa Bay, FL. Under his watch the team won three championships. The Storm is noted as having won more games than any other team in AFL history. In 2010 he founded the Texas based Dallas Vigilantes Arena Football Team. The team played at American Airlines Center from 2010-2012. In 2012 he welcomed the addition of Cheer's Liquor and Spirits to his list of business ventures. Cheer's has many locations around Texas. **PETER CARLSON KERN** aka "Bo", Sixth great grandson of progenitor Nicholas Kegg. **RYAN CARL KERN** Sixth great grandson of progenitor Nicholas Kegg. **TANNER DEVIN KERN** Seventh great grandson of progenitor Nicholas Kegg.

KERNS

GINGER JEAN KERNS Sixth great granddaughter of progenitor Nicholas Kegg.

KERR

ADA MARGARET KERR [5077] (1901 – 1904) daughter of William Joshua and Sarah (Dibert) Kerr. Little Ada was a bright child and alike in the arms of strangers as well as acquaintances.
AMANDA KERR [5078] (1852 – 1923) daughter of George and Catherine (Turner) Kerr, married William Hillegass Mowry with whom she was mother of (4). No one ever came to Amanda in need of help and was denied. She was indeed a kind mother and a true friend. **AMY WATKINS KERR** Fifth great granddaughter of progenitor Nicholas Kegg. **ANNA ELNORA KERR** [5079] (1896 – 1962) daughter of John and Valeria (Mortimore) Kerr, married Rev. Frederick Marshall Grove. Anna was a member of Zion United Church of Christ and McKinley Chapter, Order of Eastern Star.

[5077] Bedford Gazette (PA) Jan 29, 1904 [5078] Bedford Gazette (PA) Feb 9, 1923 [5079] Cumberland Times (MD) March 21, 1962

ANNA MARY KERR [5080] (1862 – 1953) daughter of William and Anna (Turner) Kerr, married Joseph Bordner. **ANNE ABBITT KERR** Fifth great granddaughter of progenitor Nicholas Kegg.
AUDNA RUTH KERR [5081] (1891 – 1954) daughter of Henry and Theodosia (Moody) Kerr, married William Garland Overstreet with whom she was mother of (1). **BABY KERR** (1923 – 1923) daughter of Charles and Mary Ellen (Kerr) Kerr. **BEATRICE R. KERR** aka "Bette", Fourth great granddaughter of progenitor Nicholas Kegg. **BETTY CATHERINE KERR** Fourth great granddaughter of progenitor Nicholas Kegg. **BILL F. KERR** Fifth great grandson of progenitor Nicholas Kegg. **CHARLES EARL KERR** (1917 – 1998) son of Charles and Lillian (Gahlau) Kerr.
CHARLES ELBERT KERR [5082] (1892 – 1976) son of John and Valeria (Mortimore) Kerr married Lillian Gahlau with whom he was father of (2). Later he married Mary Ellen Kerr with whom he was father of (3). Charles was former chief engineer for FMC Corp. of Hoopeston, Ill.
CHARLES IRVIN KERR [5083] (1872 – 1937) son of William and Anna (Turner) Kerr, married Georgia Louise Anderson with whom he was father of (2). Charles entered the service of the railway as an operator on the Shenandoah division. Later, he was transferred to the Radford division where he was appointed dispatcher. **CLEO CATHERINE KERR** [5084] (1896 – 1985) daughter of Edward and Henrietta (Hillegass) Kegg. Cleo was a retired registered nurse having been night supervisor at Memorial Hospital in Cumberland for 18 years, and also a nurse at the former Timmons Hospital and Bedford County Memorial Hospital for many years. **DANIEL KERR** Fourth great grandson of progenitor Nicholas Kegg. **DAVID BRUCE KERR** [5086] (1928 – 1993) son of Earl and Marjorie (Baker) Kerr, married Nancy Jean Banks with whom he was father of (2). David served in the U.S. Navy during World War II. He has been an attorney in Southern California and later served as Municipal Court Judge in Westminster, California. He enjoyed football and fishing. **DONALD EUGENE KERR** [5087] (1928 – 1997) aka "Red", son of Geneva Kerr. Red had served in the U.S. Army for nine years, including tours in Korea and Japan during the Korean Conflict. He attended the Bible Gospel Church, Hyndman, and was a member of the Fort Bedford V.F.W. Post 7527 and the Bedford American Legion Post 113.
DOROTHY CLEO KERR [5088] (1918 – 2011) daughter of Charles and Lillian (Gahlau) Kerr, married Charles Eugene Walkley with whom she was mother of (2). Dorothy was an accomplished seamstress and a member of the Jensen Beach Community Church. She regularly volunteered at the church thrift store.
DOROTHY LOU KERR Fourth great granddaughter of progenitor Nicholas Kegg.
DOROTHY VIRGINIA KERR [5089] (1922 – 2002) aka "Patricia", daughter of Charles and Georgia (Anderson) Kerr, married James Edgar Wells.
EARL MORTIMER KERR [5090] (1894 – 1957) son of John and Valeria (Mortimore) Kerr married twice; first to Marjorie Lois Baker with whom he was father of (1). Later, he married Eva Thula (Jones) Luther. Earl served in the U.S. Navy. He was a member of Guardian Masonic Lodge and Hope Chapter Royal Arch Masons. **EBEN GOODWIN KERR** [5091] (1890 – 1958) son of Franklin and Delphia (MCIntire) Kerr married Nellie Irene (nee unknown). Eben was a retired optometrist who was employed as a salesman for Benson Realty.
EDWARD DANIEL KERR [5092] (1868 – 1954) son of George and Catherine (Turner) Kerr, married Henrietta Hillegass with whom he was father of (3). Edward was a member of the Reformed Church and Alpha Lodge 326. AF and AM of Green, Iowa. **EDWARD J. KERR** [5093] (1902 – 1973) son of George and Elizabeth (Bittner) Kerr. Edward was a retired salesman. **EDWARD J. KERR** Fifth great grandson of progenitor Nicholas Kegg. **EDWARD JOSEPH KERR** (1947 – 2000) son of William and Mary (Raymond) Kerr, a Vietnam Veteran was father of (2). **ELEANORA SUE KERR** [5093A] aka "Sue" (1935 – 2004) daughter of Mace and Catherine (Martz) Kerr. Sue had worked as an assembler at the Sheltered Workshop in Somerset, PA.
ESSIE M. KERR [5094] (1892 – 1966) daughter of William Joshua and Sarah (Dibert) Kerr, married

---

[5080] p.3 - Bedford Gazette (PA) Jan 12, 1953 [5081] Virginia Room Roanoke Public Libraries obituary obtained by D. Sue Dible [5082] Tampa Bay Times (FL) July 27, 1976 [5083] Roanoke Times (VA) Oct 29, 1937, obtained by D. Sue Dible [5084] Bedford County Genealogical Society obituary obtained by D. Sue Dible [5086] East Bonner County Library obituary obtained by D. Sue Dible [5087] Bedford Gazette (PA) June 19, 1997 [5088] The Stuart News (FL) June 19, 2011 [5089] Roanoke Times (VA) Oct 29, 2002 [5090] South Gate Press (CA) May 5, 1957 [5091] The Tampa Tribune (FL) April 26, 1958 [5092] Evening Times (MD) Nov 3, 1954 [5093] Cumberland Evening Times (MD) Dec 26, 1973 [5093A] p.3 - Bedford Inquirer (PA) Oct 29, 2004, contributed by Bob Rose [5094] Bedford Gazette (PA) March 7, 1966

George Maurice Geller with whom she was mother of (4). Essie was a member of St. Marks United Church of Christ in New Buena Vista and a member of the women's fellowship of the church.

FRANKLIN ELLSWORTH KERR (1865 – 1913) son of George and Catherine (Turner) Kerr, married Delphia Anna McIntire with whom he was father of (2).

FREDERICK H. KERR Fourth great grandson of progenitor Nicholas Kegg.

GENEVA KERR [5095] (1901 – 1988) daughter of Howard and Carrie (Tucker) Egolf Kerr was mother of (1). She married Robert Wilson Berkey with whom she was mother of (2). Geneva was formerly employed by the Amcelle Plant of Celanese Corp., Cumberland, and later as a domestic homemaker.

GEORGE E. KERR [5096, 5097] (1888 – 1939) son of William Joshua and Sarah (Dibert) Kerr. George was shot in the face by an Italian near Greensburg. After recovering he enlisted in the Army, serving in the Hospital Dept. in World War I. He was a member of Bedford Post 113, American Legion.

GEORGE HALLER KERR Fifth great grandson of progenitor Nicholas Kegg.

GEORGE W. KERR [5098] (1862 – 1939) son of George and Catherine (Turner) Kerr, married Mary Elizabeth Bittner with whom he was father of (6).

HARMAN HALLER KERR (1890 – 1963) son of George and Mary (Bittner) Kerr married twice; first to Mildred Jane Long with whom he was father of (2). Later, he married Mary Evelyn Brooks.

HARRIET MAY KERR Fourth great granddaughter of progenitor Nicholas Kegg.

HEATHER DYAN KERR Fifth great granddaughter of progenitor Nicholas Kegg.

HELEN MARIE KERR [5099] (1934 – 1967) daughter of John Mason and Catherine (Martz) Kerr, married Evan R. Hillegass with whom she was mother of (6). Helen was a member of the Lybarger Lutheran Church, Bedford Auxiliary VFW 7527 and Fort Bedford honor guard auxiliary.

HENRY CALVIN KERR [5100] (1862 – 1919) son of William and Anna (Turner) Kerr, married Theodosia Ernst Moody with whom he was father of (1).   **HOWARD SAMUEL KERR** [5101] (1865 – 1938) son of William and Anna (Turner) Kerr, married Carrie Myrtle (Tucker) Egolf with whom he was father of (5). Howard was a retired mining electrician and employed at Windber.

HOWARD WENDELL KERR (abt 1902 –?) son of Howard and Carrie (Tucker) Kerr.

JAMES GUY KERR [5102] (1897 – 1977) son of George and Mary (Bittner) Kerr married twice; first to Alice Marie Twigg. Later, he married Susan May (Gurtler) Crites. James was an Army veteran of World War I, he was a member of Fort Cumberland Post 13, American Legion, Senior Citizens and was a retired B&O Railroad conductor.   **JOHN CYRUS KERR** [5103] (1857 – 1940) son of William and Anna (Turner) Kerr, married Valeria Alice Mortimore with whom he was father of (7). A retired tannery worker, John was a member of the Reformed Church.   **JOHN MASON KERR** [5104] (1900 – 1962) aka "Mase", son of John and Valeria (Mortimore) Kerr married twice; first to Catherine Martz with whom he was father of (2). Later, he married Grace L. Klink with whom he was father of (2). A veteran of World War I, John was a member of Oscar Jordan Post 7375, VFW, life member of Bedford American Legion and of Hyndman Methodist Church.   **JORDON AMBROSE KERR** [5105] (1875 – 1961) son of George and Catherine (Turner) Kerr, married Anna Wiley Hausman with whom he was father of (2). Jordon was a lifelong member of Grace United Church of Christ, Manns Choice.

JOSEPHINE REBECCA KERR [5106] (1891 – 1942) daughter of John and Valeria (Mortimore) Kerr, married Albert Adam Kennell with whom she was mother of (2).   **KATHRYN L. KERR** [5106A] (1920 – 2012) daughter of Jordan and Anna (Hausman) Kerr married twice, first to John Job Sellers with whom she was mother of (1), she later married Ralph Victor Miller. Kathryn was co-owner of Sellers Jewelry Store in Hyndman and Sellers Cut Rate Merchandise Store in Schellsburg. Kathryn managed the first school cafeteria in Manns Choice and also worked at the Manns Choice Post Office. Kathryn and her first husband Jack were hired in 1962 as warden and matron of the Bedford County Jail. She worked at the jail

---

[5095] Bedford County Historical Society obituary obtained by D. Sue Dible [5096] Bedford Gazette (PA) Aug 23, 1912 [5097] Bedford County Historical Society (PA) obituary dated Mar 19, 1939, obtained by D. Sue Dible [5098] Bedford Gazette (PA) Aug 23,1955 [5099] Cumberland Times (MD) April 10, 1967 [5100] Roanoke Times (VA) Dec 23, 1919, obtained by D. Sue Dible [5101] Bedford County Historical Society, Bk 62, p 125 obtained by D. Sue Dible [5102] Cumberland News (MD) July 2, 1977 [5103] Cumberland Times (MD) May 13, 1940 [5104] Cumberland Times (MD) March 9, 1962 (5105) Bedford County Historical Society obituary obtained by D. Sue Dible [5106] Meyersdale Republican (PA) Feb 5, 1942 Myersdale Library transcribed by Richard Boyer [5106A] Mulkey Mason Family of Funeral Homes (TX)

for 17 years. Kathryn worked at the Bedford Arts Council for 15 years and then retired at the age of 89. She enjoyed gardening, cooking, reading and needlework. **KATHERINE VELONA KERR** [5107] (1903 – 1997) daughter of William and Ida (Bower) Kerr. Katherine retired from the accounting offices of Appalachian Power Company with 40 years of service. She was a member of First Presbyterian Church. **LYNN KERR** Fifth great granddaughter of progenitor Nicholas Kegg.
MAE ELIZABETH KERR [5108] (1904 – 1976) daughter of Jordon and Anna (Hausman) Kerr, married Carl Efradius Beltz with whom she was mother of (1). Mae was a member of the Limaville Methodist Church. **MARK KERR** Fifth great grandson of progenitor Nicholas Kegg.
MARY ELIZABETH JANE KERR [5108A] aka "Betty" (1922 – 2015) daughter of Harman and Mildred Jane (Long) Kerr, married Robert Garrett Keenan with whom she was mother of (5). Betty moved to Washington D.C. following college to help with the war effort. It was while she was working at the Pentagon that she met her future husband, an Army Air Force Second Lieutenant. Besides raising her family, Betty worked at various jobs in Ocean City over the years including at the Public Library, the Bayside Nature Center and as a realtor for Berger Realty. She was very active with the St. Frances Cabrini Catholic Church, including serving as Lector and participating in the Altar and Rosary Society. Her religion was a vital part of her life. She also made time for the Sunshine Foundation, Colony Club and the Democratic Club. She keenly enjoyed playing bridge and mahjong with her friends.
MARY ELLEN KERR [5108B] (1903 – 1998) daughter of Howard and Carrie (Tucker) Kerr, married Charles Elbert Kerr with whom she was mother of (3). **MARY VIRGINIA KERR** [5109] (1900 – 1981) daughter of William and Ida (Bower) Kerr, married Rev. Clarence Troxel Moyer.
MAX MITCHELL KERR [5110] (1894 – 1973) son of Franklin and Delphia (McIntire) Kerr, married Harriet Baker with whom he was father of (5). **MAXINE KERR** [5111] (1928 – 1995) daughter of Max and Harriet (Baker) Kerr, married Sherwood Clarence Boden with whom she was mother of (5). **MICHAEL KERR** Fifth great grandson of progenitor Nicholas Kegg. **MICHAEL KERR** Fifth great grandson of progenitor Nicholas Kegg. **NANCY EILEEN KERR** Fourth great granddaughter of progenitor Nicholas Kegg. **NELLIE SUSAN KERR** [5112] (1884 – 1954) daughter of William and Sarah (Dibert) Kerr, married James Ambrose Shook with whom she was mother of (3).
NORMA ELIZABETH KERR [5113] (1904 – 1993) daughter of George and Mary (Bittner) Kerr was a second-grade teacher in the Harrison-Manns Choice elementary school. **NORMA JEAN KERR** [5113A] (1928 – 2014) daughter of Charles and Mary Ellen (Kerr) Kerr, married George Eldon Lutz with whom she was mother of (3). Norma was Presbyterian by faith. Norma was a homemaker and loved taking care of her family. She also enjoyed sewing, knitting, playing piano and solving puzzle books.
OSCAR JACOB KERR (1894 – 1895) son of Edward and Henrietta (Hillegass) Kerr.
PAUL EDMUND KERR [5114] (1907 – 1975) son of William Joshua and Sarah (Dibert) Kerr, married Margaret Bernice Taylor with whom he was father of (3). Paul was a retired schoolteacher after having taught for 22 years in New Baltimore, Juanita Twp., and was the former principal of the Schellsburg Elementary School. He was a veteran of World War II, serving in the US Navy.
PAUL STATLER KERR [5115] (1943 – 1973) son of Paul and Margaret (Taylor) Kerr. Paul was employed by the Internal Revenue Service, Washington DC. He was a member of Bedford American Legion Post No. 113, and St. John the Baptist Catholic Church, New Baltimore. Paul served in the U.S. Army from 1966 to 1971. **PEARL CATHERINE KERR** [5116] (1894 – 1949) daughter of George and Mary (Bittner) Kerr. **PEARL D. KERR** (born abt.1894) daughter of William Joshua and Sarah (Dibert) Kerr married Mr. Cooper. **RICHARD HALLER KERR** [5116A] (1924 – 2014) son of Harman and Mildred Jane (Long) Kerr, married Lucille Perelman with whom he was father of (2). Richard spent three years in the Army Air Corps from which he was discharged as second lieutenant. He received his bachelor's degree from West Virginia University and a master's degree in hospital administration from the

---

[5107] p.B2 - Roanoke Times (VA) Dec 4, 1997 [5108] Bedford County Genealogical Society Spielman Obituary Book B Contributed by Annie Whiteman [5108A] Press of Atlantic City (NJ) March 12, 2015 [5108B] p.5- St. Petersburg Times (FL) Mar 11, 1998 [5109] Milton Standard (PA) Jan 22, 1979, obtained by D. Sue Dible [5110] Pittsburgh Press (PA) June 4, 1973 [5111] p.B6 Pittsburgh Post-Gazette (PA) Feb 6, 1995 [5112] Bedford Gazette (PA) Aug 17, 1911 [5113] p.2 - Bedford Gazette (PA) Sept 9, 1952 [5113A] Brewer Funeral Home (Brooksville, FL) [5114] p.3 - Bedford Inquirer (PA) Feb 14, 1975 [5115] p.5 - Bedford Inquirer (PA) Dec 7, 1973, obtained by Bob Rose [5116] Bedford Gazette (PA) March 25, 1949 [5116A] The Day (CT) Jan 13, 2014

Medical College of Virginia, School of Hospital Administration. His hospital career began as assistant administrator of Thomas Memorial Hospital in South Charleston, W.Va. followed by administrator of Laird Memorial Hospital in Montgomery, W.Va. At Lawrence + Memorial Hospital he was vice president of professional services, retiring after 22 years of service. Richard was a longtime member of the New London Kiwanis Club, the New London Country Club and the Niantic Community Church at which he served as deacon.

ROBERT A. KERR [5116B] aka "Bob" (1934 – 2017) son of Robert and Dorothy (Allen) Kerr. Bob spent his career working for the Pennsylvania Bureau of State Parks. He worked in numerous state parks and in Harrisburg, before retiring as Park Superintendent of Hickory Run State Park. He enjoyed reading, hunting, fishing and taking numerous hunting and fishing trips, including one to the Arctic Circle to harvest a Caribou. Bob enjoyed spending time outdoors, making woodworking gifts for his family, and volunteering at the Bedford Food Pantry.

ROBERT HILLEGASS KERR [5117] (1898 – 1946) son of Edward and Henrietta (Hillegass) Kerr, married Dorothy Allen with whom he was father of (3). Robert attended the University of Iowa and qualified as a mechanical draftsman. He worked for the State Highway Department in Bedford for some time. Later, he was employed by the Fairchilds Aircraft Company at Hagerstown, Md. Robert was a veteran of World War I and was a member of Bedford Legion Post No. 113 and of the Masons.

ROSS JOHN KERR [5118] (1909 – 1974) son of Howard and Carrie (Tucker) Kerr. Ross was a retired employee of Jones and Laughlin Steel Corporation, a member of the Hyndman United Methodist Church, United Steelworkers of America, Sons of Columbus and Hyndman VFW.

RUTH MARGARET KERR [5119] (1908 – 1994) daughter of George and Mary (Bittner) Kerr.

RYAN TAYLOR KERR Fifth great grandson of progenitor Nicholas Kegg.

SAMUEL KERR (1857 – 1872) son of George and Catherine (Turner) Kerr.

SANDRA ELIZABETH KERR [5119A] (1947 – 1991) daughter of Paul and Margaret (Taylor) Kerr, married Wayne Robert Shaffer with whom she was mother of (3). Sandra was a former employee of the Federal Bureau of Investigation in Washington, D.C. She also worked at the regional office at Shawnee State Park and as a waitress at Ed's Steakhouse, Bedford, and the Shawnee Inn, Schellsburg. She was a member of the Fishtertown Community Bible Church, the Bedford Chapter of the Daughters of the American Revolution and the Ladies Auxiliary of the Shawnee Valley Volunteer Fire Company. She was chairman of the Multiple Schlerosis Chapter for Bedford, Fulton and Blair counties and was instrumental in forming a local MS support group.   **SARAH MARGARET KERR** [5120] (1859 – 1949) daughter of George and Catherine (Turner) Kerr, married John Henry Markel with whom she was mother of (2).

THOMAS KERR Fifth great grandson of progenitor Nicholas Kegg.

WILLIAM BLAINE KERR [5121] (1895 – 1986) son of William and Ida (Bower) Kerr, married Geraldine Wise.

WILLIAM FRANKLIN KERR (1906 – 1972) son of Howard and Carrie (Tucker) Kerr, married Mary Magdeline Raymond with whom he was father of (2).   **WILLIAM J. KERR** [5122] (1897 – 1918) son of John and Valeria (Mortimore) Kerr served in the military C.O. 19th Tr. Co. 154th D.B. died at Camp Meade, Md. of the contagious Spanish Influenza.   **WILLIAM JOSHUA KERR** [5123] (1853 – 1915) aka "Joshua", son of George and Catherine (Turner) Kerr, married Sarah Elizabeth Dibert with whom he was father of (6). A highly esteemed resident of New Buena Vista owned and conducted the Juanita House for several years. He was a kind father, good neighbor and had a host of friends.

WILLIAM SCOTT KERR [5124] (1866 – 1947) son of William and Anna (Turner) Kerr, married Ida Kate Bower with whom he was father of (5). William was a retired baggage agent at the Norfolk and Western passenger station. He was first employed by the railway on the Radford division in 1893 and became baggage agent here in 1900, retiring in 1936 when he held the distinction of being the oldest person, in term of service, in the Roanoke terminal.

[5116B] Bedford Gazette (PA) Nov 10, 2017 [5117] Bedford Gazette (PA) Oct 31, 1946 [5118] Cumberland News (MD) May 29, 1974 [5119] Cumberland Times News (MD) July 23, 1994 [5119A] p.3 - Bedford Inquirer (PA) May 31, 1991, contributed by Bob Rose [5120] Baltimore County Public Library obituary obtained by D. Sue Dible [5121] p.C2 - Roanoke Times (VA) June 14, 1995 [5122] Bedford Gazette (PA) Oct11, 1918 obtained by Bob Rose [5123] Bedford Gazette (PA) Jan 7, 1916 [5124] Roanoke Times (VA) Jan 3, 1947, obtained by D. Sue Dible

KESLER

ADAM JOSEPH KESLER Eighth great grandson of progenitor Nicholas Kegg. **ALLISON MARIE KESLER** Eighth great granddaughter of progenitor Nicholas Kegg. **LAURA ANN KESLER** Seventh great granddaughter of progenitor Nicholas Kegg. **RICHARD JAMES KESLER** Seventh great grandson of progenitor Nicholas Kegg.

KESSELRING

JOY KESSELRING Sixth great granddaughter of progenitor Nicholas Kegg.
REBECCA A. KESSELRING, aka "Becky", Sixth great granddaughter of progenitor Nicholas Kegg.
STEVE H. KESSELRING Sixth great grandson of progenitor Nicholas Kegg.
TIMOTHY BRYAN KESSELRING Sixth great grandson of progenitor Nicholas Kegg.

KESSLER

MARK WILLIAM KESSLER Fifth great grandson of progenitor Nicholas Kegg.
SCOTT CURTIS KESSLER Fifth great grandson of progenitor Nicholas Kegg.

KEYS

ABIGAIL CATHERINE KEYS Sixth great granddaughter of progenitor Nicholas Kegg.
AMANDA WALLACE KEYS Sixth great granddaughter of progenitor Nicholas Kegg.
AMELIA BORTZ KEYS Sixth great granddaughter of progenitor Nicholas Kegg. **AUSTIN KEYS** Seventh great grandson of progenitor Nicholas Kegg. **BRANDON KEYS** Seventh great grandson of progenitor Nicholas Kegg. **BRIANNA VONDELL KEYS** Sixth great granddaughter of progenitor Nicholas Kegg. **CALEB KEYS** Seventh great grandson of progenitor Nicholas Kegg.
DARLENE MYRA KEYS [5125] (1938 – 1989) daughter of John and Leora (Rhoades) Keys married twice; first to Gerald Cooper with whom she was mother of (1). Later, she married George Henry Sapp. Darlene was solid as a rock. The beauty of her love and kindness was admired by everyone who knew her. Doctors and surgeons were always amazed by her considering her suffering. She surely taught them more about cancer for other people. **DAVID COLLEDGE KEYS** [5126] (1942 – 1991) son of Paul and Elsie (Bortz) Keys married Linda Kay Doughman with whom he was father of (3). David served in Vietnam, a SGT. US Marine Corps. **DIANE KEYS** Fifth great granddaughter of progenitor Nicholas Kegg. **FREDERICK JAMES KEYS** (1906 – 1906) son of John and Mintie (Colledge) Keys.
JACK KEYS [5127] (1932 – 1937) son of John and Leora (Rhoades) Keys. **JOHN WILLIAM KEYS** [5128] (1908 – 1964) son of John and Mintie (Colledge) Keys, married Leora V. Rhoades with whom he was father of (4). John was a member of Jehovah's Witnesses and German-Austrian Club.
JOHN WILLIAM KEYS [5129] (1921 – 2009) aka "Jack" son of Theodore and Helen (Hoover) Keys. Jack went by the surname Baughman, that of his mother's second husband. Jack married Martha Olympia Monteiro Dos Reis with whom he was father of (3). Jack was employed as a Purser for Pan American World Airways. **JOYCE MARIE KEYS** [5130] (1946 – 1949) daughter of Theodore and Florence (Heitchue) Keys; Joyce was stricken with the dreaded blood disease leukemia, and had spent two months in Children's Hospital, Pittsburgh, where she received treatments with the new drug, aminopterin. She returned home for Christmas and appeared to be gaining steadily for 5 months but early in June took a turn for the worst and died. **LOIS JEAN KEYS** [5131] (1924 – 2017) daughter of Theodore and Helen (Hoover) Keys. Lois went by the surname Baughman, that of her mother's second husband. Lois married

---

[5125] The Miami Herald (FL) June 29, 1989 [5126] The Cincinnati Enquirer (OH) Aug 18, 1968 (5127) Johnstown Tribune- Democrat (PA) Apr 12, 1937, obtained by D. Sue Dible [5128] Johnstown Tribune- Democrat (PA) Aug 25, 1964, obtained by D. Sue Dible [5129] The Union Democrat (CA) Jan 12, 2009 [5130] The Ligonier Echo (PA) June 17, 1949 [5131] Dignity Memorial/Mount Comfort Cemetery Alexandria, VA

Frank Daniel Barron with whom she was mother of (3). **PATRICIA ANNE KEYS** (1936 – 2001) aka "Patsy", daughter of John and Leora (Rhoades) Keys, married Mr. Gerard. **PAUL EUGENE KEYS** [5132] (1910 – 2007) son of John and Mintie (Colledge) Keys, married Elsie Eleanor Bortz with whom he was father of (3). **ROY D. KEYS** (1898 – 1918) son of John and Mornie (Finnie) Keys.
SCOTT MATTHEW KEYS Sixth great grandson of progenitor Nicholas Kegg.
THOMAS EUGENE KEYS (1935 – 2004) son of John and Leora (Rhoades) Keys.

KHOURI

JACK KHOURI Seventh great grandson of progenitor Nicholas Kegg.
RICHIE KHOURI Seventh great grandson of progenitor Nicholas Kegg.

KIDD

AMY NICOLE KIDD Seventh great granddaughter of progenitor Nicholas Kegg.
ANDREW S. KIDD Seventh great grandson of progenitor Nicholas Kegg. **ANNA DEAN KIDD** [5133] (1922 – 2004) daughter of William and Linnie (Naugle) Kidd, married Leo G. Bartholow with whom she was mother of (2). Anna had worked at Lions Manufacturing in Everett. She was a member of St. John's United Church of Christ and had been a member for many years of Friends Cove United Church of Christ. She was active in church activities, RSVP and the Hospital Auxiliary. **ASHLEY JOY KIDD** Sixth great granddaughter of progenitor Nicholas Kegg. **BRANDON WILLIAM KIDD** Seventh great grandson of progenitor Nicholas Kegg. **BRITTANY KIDD** Seventh great granddaughter of progenitor Nicholas Kegg. **CECIL E. KIDD** [5134] (1919 – 2012) son of William and Linnie (Naugle) Kidd married twice; first to Helen E. Amick with whom he was father of (2). Later, he married Janis L. Taft. Cecil was a member of the St. Marks Lutheran Church and was a World War II Army veteran serving in the Pacific Theatre. **CHRISTOPHER WAYNE KIDD** Fifth great grandson of progenitor Nicholas Kegg. **CINDY KIDD** Fifth great granddaughter of progenitor Nicholas Kegg. **DALE KIDD** Sixth great grandson of progenitor Nicholas Kegg. **DEBRA M. KIDD** Sixth great granddaughter of progenitor Nicholas Kegg. **DUSTIN KIDD** Sixth great grandson of progenitor Nicholas Kegg.
ERIC ZANE KIDD Sixth great grandson of progenitor Nicholas Kegg. **FREDERICK B. KIDD** (1928 – 1928) son of William and Linnie (Naugle) Kidd. **JACQUELINE J. KIDD** Fifth great granddaughter of progenitor Nicholas Kegg. **JANE L. KIDD** Fifth great granddaughter of progenitor Nicholas Kegg. **JEFF KIDD** Seventh great grandson of progenitor Nicholas Kegg. **JERRID M. KIDD** Seventh great grandson of progenitor Nicholas Kegg. **JOHN WILLIAM KIDD** (1917 – 1919) son of William and Linnie (Naugle) Kidd. **LAUREN KIDD** Seventh great granddaughter of progenitor Nicholas Kegg. **MARY EMMA KIDD** [5134A] (1915 – 2003) daughter of William and Linnie Mae (Naugle) Kidd, married Franklin C. Filler with whom she was mother of (4). Mary retired after 25 years of service as an LPN at the Hollidaysburg State Hospital. Mary was active in her church and enjoyed arts and crafts.
NANCY KIDD Sixth great granddaughter of progenitor Nicholas Kegg. **NIKOLE KIDD** Seventh great granddaughter of progenitor Nicholas Kegg. **PATTI KIDD** Sixth great granddaughter of progenitor Nicholas Kegg. **ROGER A. KIDD** Seventh great grandson of progenitor Nicholas Kegg. **RONALD P. KIDD** Sixth great grandson of progenitor Nicholas Kegg. **SAMUEL NEWTON KIDD** [5135] (1913 – 1997) son of William and Linnie (Naugle) Kidd, married Dorothy May Miller with whom he was father of (6). Samuel retired from Kilcoin Concrete Products. He was a member of the Trans Run United Methodist Church and Bedford County Sportsmen's Club.
SHANNA KIDD Fifth great granddaughter of progenitor Nicholas Kegg.
SHARON KIDD Fifth great granddaughter of progenitor Nicholas Kegg.
SHERRI DENISE KIDD Fifth great granddaughter of progenitor Nicholas Kegg.

[5132] p.3 The Daily Notes (PA) Nov 17, 1937 [5133] Bedford Inquirer (PA) Jan 9, 2004, obtained by Bob Rose [5134] Bedford Gazette (PA) Dec 12, 2012, obtained by Bob Rose [5134A] p.11 – Altoona Mirror (PA) Jan 1, 2004 [5135] Bedford Gazette (PA) June 18, 1997

THERESA KIDD Fifth great granddaughter of progenitor Nicholas Kegg.
TYLER KIDD Sixth great grandson of progenitor Nicholas Kegg.

KIDNEIGH

AYANNA KELLY KIDNEIGH Sixth great granddaughter of progenitor Nicholas Kegg.
KELLY ELIZABETH KIDNEIGH Fifth great granddaughter of progenitor Nicholas Kegg.
LIAM ANDREW KIDNEIGH Sixth great grandson of progenitor Nicholas Kegg.
MICHAEL PAUL KIDNEIGH Fifth great grandson of progenitor Nicholas Kegg.

KIDWELL

ROSE BERNADETTE KIDWELL Fifth great granddaughter of progenitor Nicholas Kegg.

KIEL

GERALD KIEL Fifth great grandson of progenitor Nicholas Kegg. **KAREN KIEL** Fifth great granddaughter of progenitor Nicholas Kegg. **TOM KIEL** Fifth great grandson of progenitor Nicholas Kegg.

KIFER

COLT KIFER Seventh great grandson of progenitor Nicholas Kegg. **TRISTAN EDWARD KIFER** Seventh great grandson of progenitor Nicholas Kegg.

KIGHT

BAILY KIGHT aka "Bai", Seventh great granddaughter of progenitor Nicholas Kegg.
BRYAN THOMAS KIGHT Sixth great grandson of progenitor Nicholas Kegg. **HANNAH KIGHT** Seventh great granddaughter of progenitor Nicholas Kegg. **MELODY AMBER KIGHT** Seventh great granddaughter of progenitor Nicholas Kegg. **RUSSEL J. KIGHT** Seventh great grandson of progenitor Nicholas Kegg. **RYAN KIGHT** Seventh great grandson of progenitor Nicholas Kegg.
TYLER KIGHT Seventh great grandson of progenitor Nicholas Kegg.

KIHN

BRADEN KIHN Seventh great grandson of progenitor Nicholas Kegg.

KILE

JASON KILE Seventh great grandson of progenitor Nicholas Kegg. **NOAH KILE** Seventh great grandson of progenitor Nicholas Kegg. **RYAN KILE** Seventh great grandson of progenitor Nicholas Kegg. **STEVEN B. KILE** Sixth great grandson of progenitor Nicholas Kegg.
TRACEY LYNNE KILE Sixth great granddaughter of progenitor Nicholas Kegg.

KIMBER

ANDREW MICHAEL KIMBER Sixth great grandson of progenitor Nicholas Kegg.
JOHN G. KIMBER Seventh great grandson of progenitor Nicholas Kegg.
REBECCA KIMBER Sixth great granddaughter of progenitor Nicholas Kegg.

KIMBLE

DEBORAH L. KIMBLE Fifth great granddaughter of progenitor Nicholas Kegg.
JEREMY LOUIS KIMBLE Sixth great grandson of progenitor Nicholas Kegg.
JUNE KATELYN KIMBLE aka "Kaytee", Sixth great granddaughter of progenitor Nicholas Kegg.
KELLY ANN KIMBLE Sixth great granddaughter of progenitor Nicholas Kegg.
LARISSA NICOLE KIMBLE Sixth great granddaughter of progenitor Nicholas Kegg.
MICHAEL LOUIS KIMBLE (1962 – 2019) son of Louis and Shirley (Hershiser) Kimble married Nancy A. Scherer with whom he was father of (1). He later married Brittni Ann Bailor with whom he was father of (2). **NICHOLAS SETH KIMBLE** Sixth great grandson of progenitor Nicholas Kegg.
RICHARD KELLY KIMBLE [5136] (1959 – 2019) aka "Kelly", son of Louis and Shirley (Hershiser) Kimble married Kathleen Lykins with whom he was father of (3). Kelly had a great sense of humor, always quick with a joke to make someone smile. Kelly was a pipe welder and fitter by trade and had a passion for tinkering and fixing things. He was a hard worker dedicated to providing for his family, but he also enjoyed playing as hard as he worked. He loved the outdoors and made memories taking family and friends out to Lake of the Ozarks on his boat. Kelly loved to travel the world, and thankfully he had a job that allowed him the opportunity. From deep sea fishing in Florida to helping build a gold mine in Nome, Alaska, Kelly always embraced and enjoyed life and the world around him.
TREVOR MICHAEL KIMBLE Sixth great grandson of progenitor Nicholas Kegg.

KIMERER

CHAD LESLIE KIMERER Sixth great grandson of progenitor Nicholas Kegg.
KEVIN B. KIMERER Sixth great grandson of progenitor Nicholas Kegg.

KIMMEL

CAROL KIMMEL Fifth great granddaughter of progenitor Nicholas Kegg.
JOLIE MICHELLE KIMMEL Seventh great granddaughter of progenitor Nicholas Kegg.
KAYLA MORGAN KIMMEL Sixth great granddaughter of progenitor Nicholas Kegg.
KELSEY R. KIMMEL Sixth great granddaughter of progenitor Nicholas Kegg.
NOELLE DAWN KIMMEL Seventh great granddaughter of progenitor Nicholas Kegg.

KING

BECKY S. KING Sixth great granddaughter of progenitor Nicholas Kegg. **CASSIE KING** Seventh great granddaughter of progenitor Nicholas Kegg. **CATHY J. KING** Sixth great granddaughter of progenitor Nicholas Kegg. **CODY KING** Eighth great grandson of progenitor Nicholas Kegg. **DANICA GRUYER MILLER KING** Sixth great granddaughter of progenitor Nicholas Kegg. **DARIN D. KING** Sixth great grandson of progenitor Nicholas Kegg. **DEREK R. KING** Sixth great grandson of progenitor Nicholas Kegg. **DEVIN C. KING** Sixth great grandson of progenitor Nicholas Kegg. **DEVLYN ALEXANDRA MILLER KING** Sixth great granddaughter of progenitor Nicholas Kegg. **DUANE E. KING** Sixth great grandson of progenitor Nicholas Kegg. **DYLAN KING** Seventh great grandson of progenitor Nicholas Kegg. **HENRY L. KING** (1941 – 1941) son of Leroy and Kathleen Emma (Stone) King. **JOSHUA DAVID KING** Seventh great grandson of progenitor Nicholas Kegg. **KALEB KING** Eighth great grandson of progenitor Nicholas Kegg. **KILEE KING** Seventh great granddaughter of progenitor Nicholas Kegg. **KYLE KING** Eighth great grandson of progenitor Nicholas Kegg. **LEROY ALEXANDER KING** [5137] (1920 – 2003) son of Ira and Mabel (Schoettler) King, married Kathleen Emma Stone with whom he was father of (5).
LEROY ALEXANDER KING JR. (1941 – 1941) son of Leroy and Kathleen Emma (Stone) King.

[5136] Pulaski County Daily News (MO) May 1, 2019, obtained by D. Sue Dible [5137] Detroit Free Press (MI) Sep 27, 2003

LEROY LEONARD KING Sixth great grandson of progenitor Nicholas Kegg. **LACIE RENA KING** Seventh great granddaughter of progenitor Nicholas Kegg. **LINDSAY JO KING** Seventh great granddaughter of progenitor Nicholas Kegg. **LISA DAWN KING** Seventh great granddaughter of progenitor Nicholas Kegg. **MARK A. KING** Sixth great grandson of progenitor Nicholas Kegg. **MARY JANE KING** Fifth great granddaughter of progenitor Nicholas Kegg. **MICHAEL J. KING** Sixth great grandson of progenitor Nicholas Kegg. **PATRICIA A. KING** Sixth great granddaughter of progenitor Nicholas Kegg. **ROBERT D. KING** Sixth great grandson of progenitor Nicholas Kegg. **SHERRY KAY KING** Sixth great granddaughter of progenitor Nicholas Kegg.

KINGERY

FRANCIS RUSSELL KINGERY [5137A] aka "Fran" (1938 – 2015) son of Albert and Helen (Richmond) Kingery, married Rita A. Prochaska with whom he was father of (1). Former owner of Fran's Body Shop in South Omaha, Fran was one of a kind, doing everything for everybody, always with a smile and love. **FREDA LUCILLE KINGERY** [5137B] (1936 – 2013) daughter of Albert and Helen (Richmond) Kingery married Darwin Long with whom she was mother of (3). Freda worked at the Linn County Courthouse and Long's Repair for many years. Freda was a member of Concordia Lutheran Church and Beta Sigma Phi. **ROSEMARY KINGERY** Fifth great granddaughter of progenitor Nicholas Kegg. **MASON KINGERY** Seventh great grandson of progenitor Nicholas Kegg. **MATTHEW D. KINGERY** Sixth great grandson of progenitor Nicholas Kegg.

KINGHORN

DAMON SCOT KINGHORN Seventh great grandson of progenitor Nicholas Kegg. **KIARA JUSTIN KINGHORN** Seventh great granddaughter of progenitor Nicholas Kegg. **SCOT D. KINGHORN** Sixth great grandson of progenitor Nicholas Kegg. **SEYCHELLE LORRAINE KINGHORN** Seventh great granddaughter of progenitor Nicholas Kegg.

KINGSLEY

BRYCE H. KINGSLEY Sixth great grandson of progenitor Nicholas Kegg. **HENRY KINGSLEY** Seventh great grandson of progenitor Nicholas Kegg. **KYLE J. KINGSLEY** Sixth great grandson of progenitor Nicholas Kegg.

KINNEY

BRIAN JAY KINNEY Sixth great grandson of progenitor Nicholas Kegg. **CECIL H. KINNEY** Sixth great grandson of progenitor Nicholas Kegg. **DONNA G. KINNEY** Sixth great granddaughter of progenitor Nicholas Kegg. **JASON KINNEY** Sixth great grandson of progenitor Nicholas Kegg. **JEFF KINNEY** Sixth great grandson of progenitor Nicholas Kegg. **JONATHAN L. KINNEY** (1985 – 2005) son of Cecil and Amanda (Meyers) Kinney. **JORY KINNEY** Sixth great granddaughter of progenitor Nicholas Kegg. **JOSEPH RALPH KINNEY** (1960 – 1985) son of H. Ralph and Miriam (Giffin) Kinney. **JOSHUA H. KINNEY** Seventh great grandson of progenitor Nicholas Kegg. **KATHERYN KINNEY** Seventh great granddaughter of progenitor Nicholas Kegg. **KISHA M. KINNEY** Seventh great granddaughter of progenitor Nicholas Kegg. **LYNDSEY KINNEY** Seventh great granddaughter of progenitor Nicholas Kegg. **PATTI L. KINNEY** Sixth great granddaughter of progenitor Nicholas Kegg. **RICHARD L. KINNEY** Sixth great grandson of progenitor Nicholas Kegg. **ROBERT HARRY KINNEY** aka "Bob", Sixth great grandson of progenitor Nicholas Kegg. **TIFFANY A. KINNEY** Seventh great granddaughter of progenitor Nicholas Kegg.

[5137A] Heafey-Heafey-Hoffmann-Dworak & Cutler Mortuaries and Crematory (NE) [5137B] The Gazette (IA) Jan 20, 2014

KINSER

RICK KINSER Seventh great grandson of progenitor Nicholas Kegg.

KINSEY

NICOLE RAE KINSEY Seventh great granddaughter of progenitor Nicholas Kegg.

KIRCHNER

BETH ANN KIRCHNER Seventh great granddaughter of progenitor Nicholas Kegg.
JILL C. KIRCHNER Seventh great granddaughter of progenitor Nicholas Kegg.

KIRK

MICHAEL RYAN KIRK Eighth great grandson of progenitor Nicholas Kegg.

KIRKPATRICK

ARLENE E KIRKPATRICK [5137C] aka "Pat" (1926 – 2016) daughter of John and Amy (Scharmen) Kirkpatrick, married Edwin Johnson with whom she was mother of (5). Arlene graduated high school as the class valedictorian. She was well known in the community for her gardening knowledge, bird watching and birding knowledge, expert bread making, and her wonderful sense of humor. Pat found her calling as a fiber artist, winning numerous ribbons and awards for her weaving. Pat was an active member of the Trinity United Methodist Church and a current member of Faith United Methodist Church
DARLENE KIRKPATRICK Fifth great granddaughter of progenitor Nicholas Kegg.
DENISE KIRKPATRICK Sixth great granddaughter of progenitor Nicholas Kegg.
GORDON WESLEY KIRKPATRICK (1928 – 1985) son of John and Amy (Scharmen) Kirkpatrick.
JAMES ALVIN KIRKPATRICK (1916 – 1997) son of John and Amy (Scharmen) Kirkpatrick, married Arlene Cook with whom he was father of (1). James was a WWII veteran having served as SGT. U.S. Air Corps.   **JOHN KIRKPATRICK** Fourth great grandson of progenitor Nicholas Kegg.
LYLE ERVIN KIRKPATRICK (1919 – 1975) son of John and Amy (Scharmen) Kirkpatrick.
MILDRED BLANCHE KIRKPATRICK [5138] (1913 – 2000) daughter of John and Amy (Scharmen) Kirkpatrick, married Elmer Clarence Eide with whom she was mother of (7). Mildred was known for her cooking and baking skills, having worked at several resorts, restaurants and schools in the area. She enjoyed gardening, walking and all outdoor activities.
MYRON EVAN KIRKPATRICK (1918 – 2005) son of John and Amy (Scharmen) Kirkpatrick.
ROLLIN WILBURN KIRKPATRICK (1931 – 1978) son of John and Amy (Scharmen) Kirkpatrick, married Goldie Virginia Miller.

KIRKSEY

COLTON KIRKSEY Seventh great grandson of progenitor Nicholas Kegg.
KAREN KIRKSEY Sixth great granddaughter of progenitor Nicholas Kegg.
SUSAN KIRKSEY Sixth great granddaughter of progenitor Nicholas Kegg.

KISCHE

KINDELL CHARLENE KISCHE Fifth great granddaughter of progenitor Nicholas Kegg.

[5137C] Downs Funeral Home & Cremation Services (WI) [5138] p. 5C - Duluth News-Tribune (MN) Jan18, 2000

KISNER

ABBY N. KISNER Seventh great granddaughter of progenitor Nicholas Kegg.
ADAM DALE KISNER Seventh great grandson of progenitor Nicholas Kegg.
ALLY M. KISNER Seventh great granddaughter of progenitor Nicholas Kegg.
ANNA KISNER Seventh great granddaughter of progenitor Nicholas Kegg.

KITCHEN

CHRISTINE FRANCES KITCHEN Sixth great granddaughter of progenitor Nicholas Kegg.
GEORGE ALLEN KITCHEN Sixth great grandson of progenitor Nicholas Kegg.
LISA NICOLE KITCHEN Seventh great granddaughter of progenitor Nicholas Kegg
SANDRA DENISE KITCHEN Seventh great granddaughter of progenitor Nicholas Kegg.

KITT

ABIGAIL KITT Seventh great granddaughter of progenitor Nicholas Kegg.
BENJAMIN ARTHUR KITT Sixth great grandson of progenitor Nicholas Kegg.
BRENDA LEE KITT Fifth great granddaughter of progenitor Nicholas Kegg.
CALEB KITT Seventh great grandson of progenitor Nicholas Kegg.
JOHN E. KITT Fifth great grandson of progenitor Nicholas Kegg.
MARK W. KITT Fifth great grandson of progenitor Nicholas Kegg.
PAUL ALLEN KITT Fifth great grandson of progenitor Nicholas Kegg.
SARA KITT Sixth great granddaughter of progenitor Nicholas Kegg.

KITTEL

ANNA LEE KITTEL Sixth great granddaughter of progenitor Nicholas Kegg.
BETTY KITTEL Fifth great granddaughter of progenitor Nicholas Kegg.
CALLIE L. KITTEL Sixth great granddaughter of progenitor Nicholas Kegg.
CHANCE JUSTIN KITTEL Sixth great grandson of progenitor Nicholas Kegg.
JAMES ORRIN KITTEL [5139] (1946 – 2010) son of John and Joyce (Rippetoe) Kittel. James was a Vietnam veteran, SP5 U.S. Army. **JERALD KITTEL** Fifth great grandson of progenitor Nicholas Kegg. **JESSE RICHARD KITTEL** Sixth great grandson of progenitor Nicholas Kegg.
JOHN JAMES KITTEL [5140] (1923 – 2006) son of John and Hazel (Beeber) Kittel, married Joyce Orrine Rippetoe with whom he was father of (3). While attending high school, John owned and operated the skating rink in Melvan, Kan., which he greatly enjoyed. During his senior year, he met his true love, Joyce Orrine Rippatoe -- the only girl he ever dated. After graduating, John joined the Army. He served in the Pacific Theater during World War II and received the American Service Medal, Asiatic-Pacific Service Medal, Philippine Liberation Ribbon, World War II Victory Medal and Good Conduct Medal. He received his honorable discharge in 1946. He was proud to have served his country. John attended Hartnell College in Salinas, Calif., where he received his degree in carpentry, which was his lifelong career. He worked as a building contractor, built a motel that he and his wife managed for several years. John later opened a cabinet and pre-hung door shop in Steamboat Springs that he managed until his retirement. John was an avid sportsman, collecting many trophies over the years. He enjoyed backcountry Jeeping and outings of any kind. John never met a stranger and was always willing to visit with or lend a helping hand to anyone he could. **JUDY KITTEL** Fifth great granddaughter of progenitor Nicholas Kegg. **LESLIE SPRING KITTEL** Sixth great granddaughter of progenitor Nicholas Kegg.
MOLLY KITTEL Seventh great granddaughter of progenitor Nicholas Kegg.

[5139] Steamboat Today (CO) Aug 27, 2010 [5140] Steamboat Today (CO) July 29, 2006

RANDAL LANE KITTEL aka "Randy", Fifth great grandson of progenitor Nicholas Kegg.
RICHARD LEE KITTEL Fifth great grandson of progenitor Nicholas Kegg.
ROBERT DEAN KITTEL (1950 – 1974) son of Robert and Vera (Duell) Kittel.
ROBERT R KITTEL [5140A] aka "Bob" (1927 – 2016) son of John and Hazel (Beeber) Kittel married Vera Lois Duell with whom he was father of (4). Bob enjoyed hunting, fishing and the great outdoors including being a Boy Scout Troop leader in Palisade. Cars and their history was also one of his passions. Other joys were board games, cards and watching sports from baseball to basketball. Robert was a born salesman and enjoyed helping people get the best deal possible, whether selling a gun at the old Montgomery Wards or later as a Real Estate broker helping a family find a house to make into a home. He loved to travel and had many adventures.

KLAMM

JONATHAN KLAMM Sixth great grandson of progenitor Nicholas Kegg.
KATIE KLAMM Sixth great granddaughter of progenitor Nicholas Kegg.

KLAVUHN

ALAINA KLAVUHN Eighth great granddaughter of progenitor Nicholas Kegg.

KLEINOSKY

CAMERON KLEINOSKY Seventh great grandson of progenitor Nicholas Kegg
CONNER KLEINOSKY Seventh great grandson of progenitor Nicholas Kegg.

KLESYK

EVALENE C. KLESYK Fourth great granddaughter of progenitor Nicholas Kegg.
PAULINE KLESYK Fourth great granddaughter of progenitor Nicholas Kegg. -
VIVIENNE KLESYK aka "Kitty", Fourth great granddaughter of progenitor Nicholas Kegg.

KLINE

BLANCHE ETTA KLINE (1879 – 1950) daughter of Daniel and Harriet (Kegg) Kline married twice; first to Albert Charles Wilhelm and later, to Amos A. Hobbs.
HARRY DANIEL KLINE, (1879 – 1968) son of Daniel and Harriet (Kegg) Kline married twice; first to Ocie P. Lint and later, to Elsie J. Wacker.   **MYRTLE ROSE KLINE** [5141, 5142] (1874 – 1955) daughter of Daniel and Harriet (Kegg) Kline married three times; first to August William Reyff with whom she was mother of (1). She married Clyde Vern Poyser and later married Irvin J. Bemiller.
TATIANA KLINE Seventh great granddaughter of progenitor Nicholas Kegg.

KLING

DONALD EUGENE KLING [5143] (1929 – 1999) son of Ernest and Vera (Davis) Kling, married twice. first to Delphia Gail Belcher with whom he was father of (1). Donald worked as a bartender at the Quality Inn on Capitol Hill for about 25 years. He served in the Army in 1947 and 1948 and was a past member of the D.C. Hotel and Restaurant Employee Local Union
DONELLA JEAN KLING Sixth great granddaughter of progenitor Nicholas Kegg.

[5140A] The Daily Sentinel (KS) May 22, 2016 [5141] p.8 - Elkhart Daily Review (IN) June 21, 1907 [5142] p.7 - Elkhart Truth (IN) Feb 10, 1922 [5143] Washington Post July 27, 1999

KLINKMAN

PAUL M. KLINKMAN Fifth great grandson of progenitor Nicholas Kegg.
RUTH A. KLINKMAN [5144] (1950 – 1995) daughter of Myron and Virginia (Kegg) Klinkman was a sales associate at Wal-Mart in Bellingham, Mass. She was a delivery worker for the U.S. Postal Service in the greater Providence area. Ruth sang with the Rhode Island Civic Choral and the Providence Singers.
SUSAN VIRGINIA KLINKMAN Fifth great granddaughter of progenitor Nicholas Kegg.

KLOKKENGA

BRITTANY RENEE KLOKKENGA Seventh great granddaughter of progenitor Nicholas Kegg.

KLOTZ

SALLY KLOTZ Fourth great granddaughter of progenitor Nicholas Kegg.
WILLIAM ELWOOD KLOTZ Fourth great grandson of progenitor Nicholas Kegg.

KLUSSENDORF

ARTHUR HUNTER KLUSSENDORF aka "Bud", Seventh great grandson of progenitor Nicholas Kegg.
KARLA JANE KLUSSENDORF Seventh great granddaughter of progenitor Nicholas Kegg.

KNAPP

JILLIAN KNAPP Seventh great granddaughter of progenitor Nicholas Kegg.

KNECHT

COLBY DAVID KNECHT Sixth great grandson of progenitor Nicholas Kegg.

KNEPPER

JUDITH ANN KNEPPER Fifth great granddaughter of progenitor Nicholas Kegg.
LINDA C. KNEPPER Fifth great granddaughter of progenitor Nicholas Kegg.
PAULA JEAN KNEPPER Fifth great - granddaughter of progenitor Nicholas Kegg.
REBECCA KAY KNEPPER Fifth great granddaughter of progenitor Nicholas Kegg.

KNIFFEN

DAVID KNIFFEN Fifth great grandson of progenitor Nicholas Kegg.
SUSAN LEE KNIFFEN Fifth great granddaughter of progenitor Nicholas Kegg.

KNIGHT

ADRIANNE KNIGHT aka "Ade", Seventh great granddaughter of progenitor Nicholas Kegg.
ANGELA KNIGHT aka "Angie", Seventh great granddaughter of progenitor Nicholas Kegg.
AUDREY LEE KNIGHT [5144A] (1924 – 2021) daughter of Robert and Virginia (Diehl) Knight, married Herbert Wilson Witt with whom she was mother of (2). Audrey was employed at the Celanese Plant and

---

[5144] Providence Journal (RI) Oct 7, 1995

Rosenbaum's Department Store. She was a volunteer at Sacred Heart Hospital in the gift shop and the information desk for many years. Audrey enjoyed the game of golf, gardening, working her daily puzzles in the newspaper, bowling, dining out with family and friends, watching the boats at the Jetty and just sitting around talking with her neighbors.

DANIEL KNIGHT Seventh great grandson of progenitor Nicholas Kegg.
DANIEL RUSSELL KNIGHT Sixth great grandson of progenitor Nicholas Kegg.
GRAYLEA KNIGHT Eighth great granddaughter of progenitor Nicholas Kegg.
KENNETH E. KNIGHT Sixth great grandson of progenitor Nicholas Kegg.
LANCELOT C. KNIGHT Sixth great grandson of progenitor Nicholas Kegg.
LINDA KNIGHT Sixth great granddaughter of progenitor Nicholas Kegg.
TRUDY KNIGHT [5144B] (1955 – 2016) daughter of Lancelot and Phyllis (Lutz) Knight married twice. Trudy was mother of (2) and later married Jeffrey Summers. Trudy possessed a vivacious and caring spirit.

KNIPPLE

BRIAN MICHAEL KNIPPLE [5145] (1975 – 1994) son of Michael and Bonnie (Arter) Knipple was a dock worker for Roadway Express in Carlisle, attended West Perry High School and was a member of Shermans Dale Community Fire Company.
EMILY L. KNIPPLE Sixth great granddaughter of progenitor Nicholas Kegg.
MICHAEL KAUFFMAN KNIPPLE Sixth great grandson of progenitor Nicholas Kegg.

KNISELY

ADA MAE KNISELY aka "Jackie", Sixth great granddaughter of progenitor Nicholas Kegg.
DEBRA L. KNISELY Sixth great granddaughter of progenitor Nicholas Kegg.
LISA A. KNISELY Sixth great granddaughter of progenitor Nicholas Kegg.
TERRY LEE KNISELY (1958 – 2021) son of Jackson and Ella Mae (Bollman) Knisely.

KNITTLE

CAROLEE KNITTLE Fifth great granddaughter of progenitor Nicholas Kegg.
DARRELL L. KNITTLE [5145A] aka "Rosy" (1912 – 2005) son of William and Mattie (Laird) Knittle, married Gretchen Engelke with whom he was father of (2). Darrell was proprietor of Knittle Grocery.
DOUGLAS SCOTT KNITTLE Sixth great grandson of progenitor Nicholas Kegg.
DUANE AUREL KNITTLE (1907 – 1998) son of William and Mattie (Laird) Knittle, married Doris Eleanor Denhart with whom he was father of (1).
DUANE DENHART KNITTLE [5146] (1947 – 2020) aka "Denny" son of Duane and Doris (Denhart) Knittle married and was father of (1). Denny earned his master's degree from George Washington University and worked his way up through several federal government jobs until he landed in Denver, Co. accepting the highest promotion ever given to a man of his tender years. Later, he moved to Omaha and began placing kids in training programs for Job Corps, which he continued to do until he retired. Denny was very involved in A.A., amassing over twenty years sober and helping many others towards their goal of sobriety. Denny loved Native American art, Siberian Huskies and reading. He had an unusual sense of humor and a brilliant mind. He helped change many lives for the better.
FANE KNITTLE (1910 – 1910) son of William and Mattie (Laird) Knittle.
JUDY KNITTLE Fifth great granddaughter of progenitor Nicholas Kegg. **KAY KNITTLE** Fifth great granddaughter of progenitor Nicholas Kegg. **MARJORIE PEARL KNITTLE** (1915 – 1999) daughter of William and Mattie (Laird) Knittle married Jack Weaver Embree with whom she was mother of (2).

[5144A] Cumberland Times-News (MD) March 21, 2021 [5144B] Lancasteronline (PA) Feb 17, 2016 [5145] Patriot-News (PA) Feb 18, 1994 [5145A] Funeral Plan Aurora Casket Co., Inc. (IA) [5146] Omaha World Herald (NE) Jan 26, 2020

RITA ETHEL KNITTLE [5147] (1903 – 1998) daughter of George and Grace (Laird) Knittle, married John Emlin Reynard with whom she was mother of (2).
SAMUEL KEITH KNITTLE [5148] (1906 – 2000) son of George and Grace (Laird) Knittle, married Maud Arline Whitehill with whom he was father of (2). Sam was vice president of City National Bank for 65 years in Shenandoah, IA. He was a member of the Masonic Lodge, Order of Eastern Star, Shenandoah Rotary Club, American Legion Country Club and Shenandoah Historical Society. Sam enjoyed golf and trout fishing. **STEVEN LAIRD KNITTLE** (1946 – 1995) son of Darrell and Gretchen (Engelke) Knittle. **VERA BEATRICE KNITTLE** [5149] (1900 – 1981) daughter of George and Grace (Laird) Knittle, married Lowell C. Hussey with whom she was mother of (2).

KNOLES

JENNIFER E. KNOLES Seventh great granddaughter of progenitor Nicholas Kegg.
MATTHEW T. KNOLES Seventh great grandson of progenitor Nicholas Kegg.

KNORI

MIKE S. KNORI Sixth great grandson of progenitor Nicholas Kegg. **RICHARD D. KNORI** aka "Rick", Sixth great grandson of progenitor Nicholas Kegg. **RICHARD LEROY KNORI** [5150] (1928 – 1958) aka "Buddy", son of Carl and Pansy (Clark) Knori married Dail Price with whom he was father of (2). Bud trained in the Army Medical Corp at Brooks Medical Center, Fort Sam Houston, Texas, and served eighteen months in Alaska. Later, he was employed by Clark's Construction Co. when he became ill. Buddy passed away before he met his 2nd child. **ROSEMARY KNORI** [5150A] (1927 – 2008) daughter of Carl and Pansy (Clark) Knori married Lenard Harry Mead with whom she was mother of (3).

KNOSP

MADISON KNOSP Eighth great granddaughter of progenitor Nicholas Kegg.
MORGAN KNOSP Eighth great granddaughter of progenitor Nicholas Kegg.

KNOUF

ALICIA NOEL KNOUF [5151] (1976 – 2018) daughter of Gary and Crystal (Haley) Knouf married twice; first to Mr. Enegren with whom she was mother of (3). Later, she married Eddie Swearengin. Alicia was a great singer, loved Starbucks, cupcakes and the color orange.
ALMONT KNOUF (1874 – 1875) son of Samuel and Iris (Cale) Knouf.
ANONA BELLE KNOUF (1923 – 1999) daughter of Seward and Maude (Wilson) Knouf, married Kenneth William Shaffer. **ARCHER ARTHUR KNOUF** [5151A] (1907 – 1939) son of John and Elnora (Dickey) Knouf married Louise Hildegarde Kluever with whom he was father of (2). Archer was employed in the Welcher meat market at Fontanelle.
AUGUSTUS BELL KNOUF [5152] (1859 – 1945) aka "Gus", son of John and Maria (Cook) Knouf.
BARBARA JEAN KNOUF (1926 - 2017) daughter of Harold and Ruth (Doud) Knouf married James Lee Godsey with whom she was mother of (2). **BENTON HENRY KNOUF** [5153] (1868 – 1938) son of George and Eliza (Myrick) Knouf, married Ida Rebecca Benesh with whom he was father of (9).
BESSIE MARIE KNOUF (1895 – 1987) daughter of Martin and Mamie (Miller) Knouf married Charles Brenton Brown with whom she was mother of (2).
BEVERLY KNOUF Fifth great granddaughter of progenitor Nicholas Kegg

---

[5147] p.275 Biography & Historical Record of Ringgold County, Iowa Lewis Publishing Company of Chicago 1887 [5148] p.B8-The Kansas City Star (MO) Nov 29, 2000 [5149] Los Angeles Times (CA) Nov 11, 1981 [5150] Jackson's Hole Courier (WY) April 17, 1958 [5150A] Antelope Valley Press (CA) March 18, 2008 [5151] John M. Ireland Funeral Home & Chapel. OK Obituary [5151A] p.3 Daily Nonpareil (Council Bluffs, Iowa) Feb 28, 1939 [5152] Des Moines Register (IA) March 4, 1945 [5153] p.2 -Wenatchee Daily World (WA) May 24, 1938

BLANCHE E. KNOUF (5154) (1914 – 1991) daughter of John and Lillian (Roberts) Knouf, married Homer C. Vinson with whom she was mother of (2).
BRENDA SUE KNOUF (5155) (1949 – 2020) daughter of Galen and Vera Mae (Brown) Knouf. The simple things in life made her happy. Brenda liked to stay busy, and she was always proud to share about her jobs cleaning and clearing tables. She had such a happy personality, and always had a smile on her face when she saw you. Brenda enjoyed life; despite the challenges she faced daily. She loved playing bingo, watching her favorite game shows, and going on outings with her fellow residents. A loved one shared what a treat it always was for Brenda when she took her for a Mountain Dew and a couple of scratch-offs at the local convenience store. **BURTON HOMER KNOUF** (5155A) (1903 – 1992) son of Guy and Dottie (Gill) Knouf married Margaret E. Hartung. Dr. Knouf a retired podiatrist was a member of Grace United Methodist Church and Masonic Lodge. Burton previously operated the Knouf & Livingston Orchestra and the former Sycamore Park Ballroom. Burton enjoyed Shooting and Photography as hobbies and won various honors in each. **CALEB KNOUF** Sixth great grandson of progenitor Nicholas Kegg. **CAROL KNOUF** Fifth great granddaughter of progenitor Nicholas Kegg.
CAROLINE KNOUF (1896 – 1969) aka "Carrie", daughter of William and Mary (Collins) Knouf, married Ralph Prescott Van Buskirk with whom she was mother of (1). **CARSON KNOUF** Sixth great grandson of progenitor Nicholas Kegg. **CATHERINE KNOUF** (1816 –?) aka "Katie", daughter of Jacob and Margaret (Kegg) Knouf, married William A. Hill with whom she was mother of (1).
CATHERINE KNOUF (1851 -?) daughter of Nicholas and Lidia (Lafferty) Knouf.
CATHERINE ANN KNOUF (5156) (1863 – 1933) aka "Cassie", daughter of Richard and Sarah (Riley) Knouf, married John F. Gillian with whom she was mother of (5). Cassie joined the Methodist Church and has remained a member until her death gave her entrance into the Church above. She always attended church until about five years ago, when her hearing got so bad that she could get nothing from the public services. But she continued to read her Bible much and commented in writing on a flyleaf of it as well as noting many passages of Scripture which were precious to her. Mrs. Gillilan was a kind, loving mother and wife, a good neighbor and a true friend. **CECIL E. KNOUF** (5157) (1900 – 1978) son of Vinton and Fanny (Simpson) Knouf, married Harmie L. Guzzle with whom he was father of (2). Cecil was employed as a freight inspector for the Chicago and Northwestern Railroad while in Cedar Rapids and operated a grocery store while in Urbana. **CHARLENE MAY KNOUF** Fourth great granddaughter of progenitor Nicholas Kegg. **CHARLES SHERMAN KNOUF** (5158) (1877 – 1959) son of William and Mary (Collins) Knouf married three times; first to Cora A. Lashell with whom he was father of (2). He married Rose Irene Gardner and later, married Lenna Elizabeth Green. **CHASITTY KNOUF** Sixth great granddaughter of progenitor Nicholas Kegg. **CHESTER WALLACE KNOUF** (1908 – 1979) aka "Chet", son of Benton and Ida (Benesh) Knouf. **CHRISTOPHER ANDREW KNOUF** Sixth great grandson of progenitor Nicholas Kegg. **CINDY L. KNOUF** 5th great granddaughter of progenitor Nicholas Kegg. **CLARA ELNORA KNOUF** (5159) (1891 – 1978) daughter of John and Elnora (Dickey) Knouf, married Wesley Ward Cline with whom she was mother of (1).
CLARA FLORENCE KNOUF (5160) (1892 – 1978) daughter of Jacob and Sarah Ella (Shafer) Knouf, married Paul Clifford Conant with whom she was mother of (2). **CLARE ELDON KNOUF** (5161, 5162) (1918 – 1958) aka "Scotty", son of Scott and Clara (James) Knouf, married Verna May Yetter with whom he was father of (4). Scotty received a commission in the U.S. naval reserves medical corps as ensign V.P.Later, a physician who had engaged in private practice became a member of the medical staff at Veterans hospital, was found dead of hanging in a closet of his bedroom at his home. Two other members of the hospital staff went to the home after Knouf failed to report to work. They found the lights burning and the doors locked. Police forced an entry. Police said that he had been dead about 12 hours before he was found. Police found no note and were unable to find any motive.

(5154) p.2D - Wichita Eagle (KS) Jan15, 1991 (5155) The Hays Daily News (KS) Nov 4, 2020, obtained by D. Sue Dible (5155A) p.18 The Des Moines Register (IA) Jan 15, 1992 (5156) Ainsworth Star Journal (NE) Nov 9, 1933, obtained by D. Sue Dible (5157) The Gazette (Cedar Rapids, IA) June 27, 1978 (5158) Hill City Times (KS) June 18, 1959, obtained by D. Sue Dible (5159) Atlantic News Telegraph (IA) Sept 9, 1978, obtained by D. Sue Dible (5160) Times-Advocate (Escondido, CA) Aug 22, 1978 (5161) p.6 Daily Nonpareil (Council Bluffs, Iowa) July 15, 1942 (5162) p.24 - Cedar Rapids Gazette (IA) June 5, 1958

CLARENCE ALLEN KNOUF [5163] (1923 – 1984) aka "Big Al", son of Nicholas and Mildred (Clark) Knouf married twice; first to Leona Mae Cameron with whom he was father of (4). Later, he married Sandra Kay (Kliem) Billings. Clarence had been employed by the J.H. Shears Company, Hutchinson, in construction work.
CLINTON BYRON KNOUF [5164] (1870 – 1955) son of George and Eliza (Myrick) Knouf, married Fannie Ester Southwick. Clinton and Fannie adopted a son. He was a retired fruit rancher from Washington State and a member of the Elks club. **CLYDE HOWARD KNOUF** [5165] (1881 – 1942) son of John and Elnora (Dickey) Knouf, married Vada W. Afflack with whom he was father of (1).
CORNELIA KNOUF (1879 – 1899) aka "Cora", daughter of John and Mollie (Brown) Knouf, married Jacob B. Raffensparger. **DAVID WILLIAM KNOUF** (1913 – 1944) son of John and Lillian (Roberts) Knouf, was a casualty of WWII. Killed in action. **DAVID MINTON KNOUF** Seventh great grandson of progenitor Nicholas Kegg. **DEBBIE KNOUF** Fourth great granddaughter of progenitor Nicholas Kegg. **DELLA I. KNOUF** [5166] (1884 – 1951) daughter of Samuel and Iris (Cale) Knouf, married Hausmer Edgar McCoy with whom she was mother of (1). Della was employed in the office of the Madison Coal Co. **DENISE RENEE KNOUF** Sixth great granddaughter of progenitor Nicholas Kegg.
DUSTIANN RANAE KNOUF [5167] (1979 – 1980) daughter of Robert and Cynthia (Weaver) Knouf.
EARLE KNOUF [5168] (1885 – 1938) son of Daniel and Eldora (McLain) Knouf, married Effie Louise Devine. Earle was associated with Hotel Fort Des Moines 13 or 14 years, had been assistant manager. Previously he had been associated with a rubber firm, worked in the post office and in insurance work.
EDITH IRENE KNOUF (1896 – 1937) daughter of John and Elnora (Dickey) Knouf, married Oliver E. Richmond with whom she was mother of (3). **EDYTHE MARIE KNOUF** [5169] (1902 – 1971) daughter of Warren and Mable (Harter) Knouf was a retired secretary for Aetna Life Insurance Co. She was a member of St. Ambrose Cathedral. **ELEANOR LOIS KNOUF** [5170] (1932 – 2016) daughter of William and Florence (Belveal) Knouf, married Larry Guthrie with whom she was mother of (2). Eleanor spent her life dedicated to growing a beautiful garden for her loved ones to bloom in.
ELIZABETH KNOUF (1820 -?) daughter of Jacob and Margaret (Kegg) Knouf, married Daniel W. Dean with whom she was mother of (10). **ELMER D. KNOUF** [5171] (1904 – 1973) son of Charles and Cora (Lashell) Knouf **ELNA L. KNOUF** [5172] (1915 – 2009) daughter of Benton and Ida (Benesh) Knouf, married Franklin Oscar Coonfield with whom she was mother of (1). Elna worked in numerous restaurants, at Mountain Products and the last years in the fruit industry at Cashmere Fruit Exchange and Columbia Fruit. **EMILY KNOUF** Sixth great granddaughter of progenitor Nicholas Kegg.
EMILY CHRISTINE KNOUF Seventh great granddaughter of progenitor Nicholas Kegg.
ETHEL L. KNOUF [5173] (1907 – 2004) daughter of Oscar and Vada (Owens) Knouf, married G. Albert Hazen. **EUNICE MINERVA KNOUF** [5174] (1917 – 2005) daughter of Oscar and Vada (Owens) Knouf, married Ernest Leroy Sandlin with whom she was mother of (2). Eunice enjoyed being a homemaker most of her adult life and was a caring and devoted wife and mother. Mrs. Sandlin was a long-time member of the First Presbyterian Church and Senior Adult Activity Center.
FLOYD CLAYTON KNOUF (1914 – 1916) son of Nicholas and Mildred (Clark) Knouf.
FRANCES LUCILLE KNOUF [5175] (1923 – 2012) daughter of Henry and Myrtle (Cunningham) Knouf, married Albert C. Stithem with whom she was mother of (2). Frances had a witty sense of humor and dedicated her life as a loving mother, grandmother and great-grandmother. She enjoyed cooking, baking, reading, playing cards, going to garage sales and most of all spending time with her family and friends. She also had an infinite love of animals and provided a loving home to many over the years. She was a stay-at-home wife until the mid-1980's when she took a position with the Plainville Laundromat.

[5163] p.11 -Salina Journal (KS) April 29, 1984 [5164] p.2 - Cedar Rapids Gazette (IA) Aug 22, 1955 [5165] Earlham Echo (IA) Apr 28, 1966, USGenWeb.org contributed by Pat Hochstetler [5166] Des Moines Tribune (IA) March 27, 1951 [5167] p.21 The Des Moines Register (IA) Feb 17, 1980 [5168] p.11 The Des Moines Register (IA) Aug 4, 1938 [5169] p.18 - Des Moines Register (IA) April 2, 1971 [5170] The Sacramento Bee (CA) Oct. 5, 2016 [5171] p.2 - Nampa Idaho Free Press Oct 1, 1973 [5172] Wenatchee World (WA) Oct 13, 2009 [5173] The Hays Daily News (KS) Oct17, 2004 [5174] East Bay Times (CA) Apr 5, 2005 [5175] Moore-Overlease Funeral Home (Plainville, KS)

Frances accepted a position with the Pony Express in the mid-1990's and traveled many miles around the Plainville/Hill City area. She enjoyed people and always had a quick smile or word of encouragement for anyone she met. **FRANKLIN PETER KNOUF** (1861 – 1873) son of John and Maria (Cook) Knouf drown in the Raccoon River west of Commerce, Iowa. **GABRIEL KNOUF** Fifth great grandson of progenitor Nicholas Kegg. **GABRIEL KNOUF** Sixth great grandson of progenitor Nicholas Kegg. **GABRIEL P. KNOUF** Sixth great grandson of progenitor Nicholas Kegg.
GALEN LAVERNE KNOUF [5176] (1921 – 1996) son of Nicholas and Mildred (Clark) Knouf, married Vera Mae Brown with whom he was father of (4). Galen was an Army veteran of World War II. He was a retired mechanic and a member of Veterans of Foreign Wars Post, WaKeeney.
GARY WAYNE KNOUF [5177] (1963 – 2001) son of Galen and Vera (Brown) Knouf married twice; first to Carla O. Moss with whom he was father of (3). Later, he married Karen Henke. Gary worked as a welder for Quinstar Equipment Company. Gary enjoyed hunting and fishing. **GEORGE KNOUF** [5178] (1830 – 1901) son of Jacob and Margaret (Kegg) Knouf, married Eliza Arvista Myrick with whom he was father of (7). George was a veteran of the Civil War; he enlisted in Company G, Iowa 24th Infantry Regiment on 03 Sep 1862. Mustered out on 17 Jul 1865 at Savannah, GA.
GEORGE BENTON KNOUF [5179] (1918 – 1992) son of Benton and Ida (Benesh) Knouf married twice; first to Delores McClellan. Later, he married Geraldine Lee Furguson with whom he was father of (2). George grew up on the family farm. He enlisted in the military in 1942 and served during World War II and the Korean Conflict. George was employed by Van Doren Inc. **GEORGE RUSSELL KNOUF** (1856 – 1923) son of John and Maria (Cook) Knouf. **GEORGE WILLIAM KNOUF** [5180] (1889 – 1983) son of Jacob and Sarah Ella (Shafer) Knouf, married Mabel Clara Conant with whom he was father of (2). Later, he married Emily Huff. George was a charter member of the Escondido First Church of the Nazarene and a member of the Retired Federal Employees Association. He attended elementary and high school in Kansas, and went to college in Pasadena, Calif. And was employed with the U.S. Postal Service. **GERALD LYNN KNOUF** Fifth great grandson of progenitor Nicholas Kegg. **GLADYS FERN KNOUF** [5181] (1905 – 1981) daughter of Scott and Clara (James) Knouf married three times; first to Ray E. Keating. Later, she married Kenneth Walter Bates with whom she was mother of (2). Then, married Glen Norval Ridout. **GRACE MARIAH KNOUF** Fifth great granddaughter of progenitor Nicholas Kegg. **GUY LEANDER KNOUF** [5182] (1880 – 1931) son of Samuel and Iris (Cale) Knouf, married Dottie Louise Gill with whom he was father of (3). Guy was a Mason and Woodman, and a member of the Typographical union and the Craftsman Club. He was employed for 35 years by the Homestead Company of Des Moines, Iowa. **HADEN KNOUF** Fifth great grandson of progenitor Nicholas Kegg. **HAILEY KNOUF** Fifth great granddaughter of progenitor Nicholas Kegg. **HATTIE JANE KNOUF** [5183] (1869 – 1899) daughter of Richard and Sarah (Riley) Knouf, married William W. Dwigans with whom she was mother of (7). **HELEN PEARL KNOUF** [5184] (1918 – 1991) daughter of Nicholas and Mildred (Clark) Knouf married twice; first to Walter Littlechild who was killed in a three-car pileup on U.S. Highway 40. Later, she married George Edward Herren. The couple ran the Fort Robinson Stage Lines and assisted at a Scout camp at Bozemont, Mont. After George died, Helen moved to Custer where she was an active member of the Church of Christ. **HENRY JACOB KNOUF** son of William and Mary (Collins) Knouf, married Myrtle O. Cunningham with whom he was father of (1). Henry served as a cook for Co. 18 Army Air Service returning to Stock Ranch farming. **JACOB KNOUF** [5185] (1848-1898) son of Nicholas and Lidia (Lafferty) Knouf, married Sarah Ella Shafer with whom he was father of (2). **JAMES MALCOM KNOUF** [5186] (1913 – 1993) son of Clyde and Vada (Afflack) Knouf, married Lillis Mae Imboden with whom he was father of (2). **JAMES MONROE KNOUF** (1863 – 1864) son of John and Maria (Cook) Knouf.

[5176] p.A7 - Salina Journal (KS) May 7, 1996 [5177] p.7 - Western Kansas World (KS) April 5, 2001 [5178] The Gazette (Cedar Rapids, IA) Nov 2, 1935 [5179] Wenatchee World (WA) Dec 29, 1992 [5180] Walla Walla Union-Bulletin (WA) Feb 6, 1983 [5181] p.D9 - San Diego Union (CA) May 7, 1981, obtained by D. Sue Dible [5182] p.15 The Des Moines Register (IA) Oct 11, 1931 [5183] p.409 History of Adair County, Iowa, and its people, Vol 2 [5184] Rapid City Journal (SD) Oct 20, 1991 [5185] The People's Reveille (Hill City, KS) April 28, 1898 contributed by Graham County Historical Society to Kansas Genealogy Trail [5186] p.3 Daily Nonpareil (Council Bluffs, IA) Nov 23, 1944

JANZEN L. KNOUF Sixth great grandson of progenitor Nicholas Kegg. **JEAN LOUISE KNOUF** (1933 – 1994) daughter of Harold and Ruth (Doud) Knouf, married Harvey Allen Hill. **JENNIFER KNOUF** Sixth great granddaughter of progenitor Nicholas Kegg. **JOHN ARTHUR KNOUF** [5187] (1925 – 1988) aka "Art", son of Nicholas and Mildred (Clark) Knouf, married Mable Elizabeth Brown with whom he was father of (3). Art worked for the Kansas Department of Transportation for 33 years and was World War II veteran. **JOHN BUDA KNOUF** [5188] (1857 – 1920) son of Richard and Sarah (Riley) Knouf, married Elnora Park Dickey with whom he was father of (7). **JOHN HENRY KNOUF** [5189, 5190] (1822 – 1896) son of Jacob and Margaret (Kegg) Knouf, married Maria Cook with whom he was father of (10). John was one of the first settlers in Iowa, arriving in the fall of 1876 where he owns a farm of 119 acres. **JOHN HENRY KNOUF** [5191] (1845 – 1909) son of John and Maria (Cook) Knouf, married Mary Lucina Brown aka "Mollie", with whom he was father of (4). **JOHN P. KNOUF** (1847 - ?) son of Nicholas and Lidia (Lafferty) Knouf. **JOHN PETER KNOUF** [5192] (1892 – 1965) son of William and Mary (Collins) Knouf, married Lillian M. Roberts with whom he was father of (5). John was a farm laborer. He was a member of the Christian Church. **JON KLINTON KNOUF** Fourth great grandson of progenitor Nicholas Kegg. **JOSEPH KNOUF** Sixth great grandson of progenitor Nicholas Kegg. **JOSEPH GAGER KNOUF** Fifth great grandson of progenitor Nicholas Kegg. **JOSEPH LEROY KNOUF** (1909 – 1980) son of Oscar and Vada (Owens) Knouf, married Irene Brandt with whom he was father of (2). Joseph had been employed as a machinist. **JOSHUA KNOUF** Fifth great grandson of progenitor Nicholas Kegg. **JOSHUA J. KNOUF** Sixth great grandson of progenitor Nicholas Kegg. **JOSIAH KNOUF** (1829 – 1831) son of Jacob and Margaret (Kegg) Knouf. **JOSIE KNOUF** Sixth great granddaughter of progenitor Nicholas Kegg. **JUSTIN KNOUF** Sixth great grandson of progenitor Nicholas Kegg. **JUSTINA MARIE KNOUF** Fifth great granddaughter of progenitor Nicholas Kegg. **KALISTA KNOUF** Sixth great granddaughter of progenitor Nicholas Kegg. **KAREN D. KNOUF** Sixth great granddaughter of progenitor Nicholas Kegg.
KATHRYN CHAPMAN KNOUF Seventh great granddaughter of progenitor Nicholas Kegg.
KAYLA KNOUF Sixth great granddaughter of progenitor Nicholas Kegg.
KENNETH GUY KNOUF Sixth great grandson of progenitor Nicholas Kegg.
KRISTAL KNOUF Sixth great granddaughter of progenitor Nicholas Kegg.
KRISTAL KNOUF Sixth great granddaughter of progenitor Nicholas Kegg.
KRYSTAL NICHOLE KNOUF Sixth great granddaughter of progenitor Nicholas Kegg.
KYLE KNOUF Sixth great grandson of progenitor Nicholas Kegg.
LARRY DEAN KNOUF 5th great grandson of progenitor Nicholas Kegg.
LELAND DALE KNOUF [5193] (1902 – 1993) son of Martin and Mamie (Miller) Knouf, married Melba Cleda Wolfe with whom he was father of (2). Leland was a retired yard foreman for Des Moines Steel Co. and was a member of the Christian Church of Norwalk. **LEONA MAXINE KNOUF** [5194] (1928 – 2008) daughter of Archer and Louise Hildegarde (Kluever) Knouf, married George Lester Shankle with whom she was mother of (3). Leona was a member of Fleming Island Baptist Church.
LESTER STEWART KNOUF [5195] (1881 – 1965) son of George and Eliza (Myrick) Knouf, married Estelle Margaret Slezak with whom she was mother of (2). **LLOYD L. KNOUF** (1897 – 1906) son of Vinton and Fanny (Simpson) Knouf. **LOUIS FRANKLIN KNOUF** [5196] (1921 – 1956) son of Benton and Ida (Benesh) Knouf, married Geraldine Lee Ferguson with whom he was father of (2). A truck driver, Louis was a member of the Teamsters Union and the Wenatchee Aerie No. 204, F.O.E.
LULU B. KNOUF (1887 – 1888) daughter of Samuel and Iris (Cale) Knouf.
LYDIA C. KNOUF daughter of William and Mary (Collins) Knouf married twice, first to Clyde Harrison Poffenberger with whom she was mother of (3). She later married Bert Bothwell Billings.
MACKENZIE LEA KNOUF Fifth great granddaughter of progenitor Nicholas Kegg.

[5187] p.11 - Salina Journal (KS) Sept 3, 1988 [5188] Iowa Library obituary clipping obtained by D. Sue Dible [5189] p.740 History of Warren County Iowa [5190] p.3 - Indianola Herald (IA) Nov 5, 1896 [5191] p.7 - Des Moines Daily News (IA) Mar 28, 1909 [5192] p.2 - Great Bend Daily Tribune (KS) Dec 17, 1965 [5193] p.19 The Des Moines Register (IA) Nov 14, 1993 [5194] Florida Times-Union (FL) Dec 28, 2008 [5195] Los Angeles Times (CA) Sep 2, 1965 [5196] p.14 - Wenatchee Daily World (WA) Aug 19, 1956, obtained by D. Sue Dible

MACY KNOUF Sixth great granddaughter of progenitor Nicholas Kegg. **MANYA I. KNOUF** Sixth great granddaughter of progenitor Nicholas Kegg. **MARCIA L. KNOUF** Fourth great granddaughter of progenitor Nicholas Kegg. **MARGARET KNOUF** (1923 – 1984) daughter of John and Lillian (Roberts) Knouf, married Harry D. Jeffries. **MARJORIE MARIE KNOUF** (1920 – 2000) daughter of William and Florence (Belveal) Knouf, married Carl Ferman Phillips. **MARLIN GAYLE KNOUF** Fifth great grandson of progenitor Nicholas Kegg. **MARTHA KNOUF** (1874 – 1888) daughter of Nicholas and Lidia (Lafferty) Knouf. **MARTIN VIRGIL KNOUF** [5197] (1900 – 1993) son of Martin and Mamie (Miller) Knouf, married Hazel Rosetta Baker with whom he was father of (3). Martin formerly worked for Iowa Power and the Des Moines airport. He was a member of the Norwalk Christian Church and the Eagles Lodge. **MATILDA MAY KNOUF** [5198] (1872 – 1958) aka "Tillie", daughter of George and Eliza (Myrick) Knouf was a member of Kenwood Methodist church and the WCTU. **MAUDE GERTRUDE KNOUF** [5199] (1878 – 1964) daughter of George and Eliza (Myrick) Knouf, married William James Pirie D.M.V., with whom she was mother of (5). Maude was active in the Methodist church. **MICHAEL KNOUF** Sixth great grandson of progenitor Nicholas Kegg. **MILDRED CAROLINE KNOUF** [5200] (1917 – 2006) daughter of George and Mabel (Conant) Knouf, married Lester Morris Ware. **MIDA KATHRYN KNOUF** (1903 – 1965) daughter of John and Eldora (Dickey) Knouf, married Clyde Milford Mean with whom she was mother of (2). **MYRTLE E. KNOUF** (1877 – 1952) daughter of Samuel and Iris (Cale) Knouf, married George A. Rye. **MYRTLE MAY KNOUF** (1880 – 1963) daughter of William and Mary (Collins) Knouf married twice, first to John Henry Chadsey with whom she was mother of (1). Later to a man with the surname Miller. **NANCY H. KNOUF** [5201] (1859 – 1900) daughter of Richard and Sarah (Riley) Knouf, married Hugh Gray with whom she was mother of (2). Nancy was only sick a couple of weeks with that dread disease-typhoid fever. She told her friends she was not going to recover and was prepared for death as her husband sat still at the bedside of their little daughter, Sarah, who also had typhoid fever was not expected to live. **NICHOLAS KNOUF** Sixth great grandson of progenitor Nicholas Kegg. **NICHOLAS ALEXANDER KNOUF** [5202] (1888 – 1970) son of William and Mary (Collins) Knouf, married Mildred Leona Clark with whom he was father of (8). **NICOLE KNOUF** Sixth great granddaughter of progenitor Nicholas Kegg. **NORMA KNOUF** (1910 – 1931) daughter of Benton and Ida (Benesh) Knouf, married Murrel Allen Morgan with whom she was mother of (1). **OPAL MARIE KNOUF** [5203] (1912 – 1990) daughter of Benton and Ida (Benesh) Knouf, married Vernon Morgan with whom she was mother of (3). **PAMELA KNOUF** Fifth great granddaughter of progenitor Nicholas Kegg. **PAUL KNOUF** Fifth great grandson of progenitor Nicholas Kegg. **PAUL DOUGLAS KNOUF** [5204] (1949 – 2011) son of Clare and Verna Mae (Yetter) Knouf married Karie Moulds with whom he was father of (4). Paul graduated from Simpson College with a Biology Degree. He then received his medical degree from the University of Iowa in Iowa City and did his residency in family medicine at the Iowa Lutheran Hospital in Des Moines. Later, Paul practiced medicine in Rockwell City for 32 years, and was also on staff at McFarland Clinics until his retirement. He was a member of St. Paul's Lutheran Church, Church Choir, Calhoun Co. Board of Health, Calhoun Co. Medical Director, and the Calhoun Co. Medical Examiner. Paul was also an avid reader, woodworker, and enjoyed singing and gardening. **PETER KNOUF** (1818 – 1839) son of Jacob and Margaret (Kegg) Knouf. **PHILIP ALAN KNOUF** [5205] (1948 – 2013) son of Clare and Verna (Yetter) Knouf, married Penny Wolff with whom he was father of (2). Phil had an enthusiasm for life, a passion for photography and the outdoors. **REBECCA KNOUF** (1858 – 1861) daughter of Nicholas and Lidia (Lafferty) Knouf. **RICHARD EMANUEL KNOUF** [5206] (1829 – 1902) son of Jacob and Margaret (Kegg) Knouf, married Sarah J. Riley with whom he was father of (4). Richard was a farmer.

[5197] Warren Town and Country News (IA) Mar 4, 1993, obtained by D. Sue Dible [5198] p.2 – Cedar Rapids Gazette (IA) March 15, 1958 [5199] p.2C - Cedar Rapids Gazette (IA) Dec 2, 1964 [5200] Walla Walla Union Bulletin (WA) May 3, 2006, obtained by D. Sue Dible [5201] Stuart Locomotive (IA) Jan. 26, 1900, obtained by D. Sue Dible [5202] Salina Journal (KS) Aug. 30, 1970 [5203] p.A2 -Skagit Valley Herald (WA) Mar 13, 1990, obtained by D. Sue Dible [5204] Palmers Wank Funeral Home (IA) [5205] Oregonian (OR) June 16, 2013 [5206] Greenfield-Democrat (IA) Nov 27, 1902, obtained by D. Sue Dible

ROBERT KNOUF Fifth great grandson of progenitor Nicholas Kegg. **ROBERT G. KNOUF** [5207] (1924 – 2007) aka "Bob", son of Benton and Ida (Benesh) Knouf, married Cheerful Watts. **ROBIN MARIE KNOUF** (1984 – 1993) daughter of Philip and Penny (Wolff) Knouf. **ROSE ELSORA KNOUF** [5208] (1885 – 1969) daughter of John and Mary (Brown) Knouf married Harvey M. Inman with whom she was mother of (3). Rose was a member of the Eagles Auxiliary. **RUSSELL KNOUF** (1880 - 1903) son of John and Mary (Brown) Knouf, married Jessie (nee unknown) with whom he was father of a son. Russell and his infant son were fatally injured from a tornado that hit Des Moines. **RUSTIN KNOUF** Sixth great grandson of progenitor Nicholas Kegg. **RUTH ETHEL KNOUF** (1897 – 1980) daughter of Martin and Mamie (Miller) Knouf, married Roy W. Stewart with whom she was mother of (4). **RUTH IRENE KNOUF** [5209] (1906 – 1976) daughter of Benton and Ida (Benesh) Knouf, married Paul Marcas Garrett with whom she was mother of (3). **RUTH PAULINE KNOUF** [5210] (1912 – 1987) daughter of Nicholas and Mildred (Clark) Knouf married twice; first to Francis Ivan Hetzel with whom she was mother of (5). Later, she married Jack Pillars. Ruth was a homemaker. **RYAN A. KNOUF** Sixth great grandson of progenitor Nicholas Kegg. **SABINA KNOUF** [5211] (1874 – 1962) aka "Vina", daughter of George and Eliza (Myrick) Knouf. Vina was a member of the Kenwood Methodist church. **SAMUEL WESLEY KNOUF** [5212] (1849 – 1913) son of John and Maria (Cook) Knouf, married Iris Gertrude Cale with whom he was father of (5). **SARAH A. KNOUF** (1878 – 1943) daughter of William and Mary (Collins) Knouf. **SCOTT KNOUF** Sixth great grandson of progenitor Nicholas Kegg. **SCOTT E. KNOUF** [5213] (1975 – 2003) son of Craig and Kristine (Schwartz) Knouf was a high school student who was in the Management Training Program at Wendy's. **SCOTT E. KNOUF** [5214] (1912 – 1985) son of Scott and Clara (James) Knouf, married Ina Malinda Katherine Truckenbrod. Scott was a barber, a member of the St. Paul Lutheran Church, American Legion, VFW, Kiwanis and Masonic Lodge. **SCOTT ELMER KNOUF** [5215] (1883 – 1936) son of John and Elnora (Dickey) Knouf, married Clara Belle James with whom he was father of (3). Scott was a barber, a member of the Woodman of the World and president of the Good Fellowship Sunday school class. **SHANNON KNOUF** Sixth great granddaughter of a progenitor Nicholas Kegg. **SHARON KNOUF** Sixth great granddaughter of progenitor Nicholas Kegg. **SHERRY KNOUF** Fifth great granddaughter of progenitor Nicholas Kegg. **SHIRLEY RAE KNOUF** [5216] (1934 – 2005) daughter of Harold and Ruth (Doud) Knouf married twice; first to Robert J. Post and later, to James E. Baratta with whom she was mother of (3). **SIMON PERRY KNOUF** (1865 – 1880) son of John and Maria (Cook) Knouf. **STANLEY JOE KNOUF** (1941 – 2005) son of Joseph and Irene (Brandt) Knouf married twice; first to Karen J. Clayton, later he married Mary Goreyko with whom he was father of (2). **STEVEN DOUGLAS KNOUF** Sixth great grandson of progenitor Nicholas Kegg. **SUSAN ELAINE KNOUF** Sixth great granddaughter of progenitor Nicholas Kegg. **SYBIL LOUISE KNOUF** [5217] (1927 – 1969) daughter of Nicholas and Mildred (Clark) Knouf, married Gilbert Leroy Bell with whom she was mother of (1). **THEODORE EDWARD KNOUF** (1928 – 1928) son of Benton and Ida (Benesh) Knouf. **THEODORE R. KNOUF** [5218] (1918 – 1988) aka "Ted", son of John and Lillian (Roberts) Knouf, married Lola M. Cartmell with whom she was mother of (2). A WWII veteran, Ted was a retired International Petroleum Service employee. **TONY R. KNOUF** Sixth great grandson of progenitor Nicholas Kegg. **TONY RAY KNOUF** Fifth great grandson of progenitor Nicholas Kegg. **VINTON W. KNOUF** [5219] (1868 – 1902) aka "Vint", son of George and Eliza (Myrick) Knouf married Fanny B. Simpson with whom he was father of (2). Vinton was a farmer. After nine years of illness, Vinton finally underwent an operation leaving him depressed. It wasn't long before he left the house to take a walk around the yard. He stepped into a buggy shed, presumably, to rest, and sat in a buggy, where he was

---

[5207] Arkansas Democrat Gazette (AR) Dec 8, 2007 [5208] p.14 – Des Moines Register (IA) Dec 27, 1969 [5209] p.9 - Wenatchee World (WA) Dec 27, 1976, obtained by D. Sue Dible [5210] p.B6 - Wichita Eagle (KS) Dec 7, 1987 [5211] p.3 - Cedar Rapids Gazette (IA) Nov. 5, 1962 [5212] Des Moines Register (MI) Jan 9, 1913 [5213] p.9C - The Columbus Dispatch (OH) Sept 4, 2003 [5214] Winterset Madisonian (IA) Jan 16, 1985 IA GenWeb transcribed by Treva Patterson [5215] p.6 Daily Nonpareil (Council Bluffs, IA) May 7, 1936 [5216] p. 6B - San Antonio Express-News (TX) Jan 2, 2006 [5217] p.5 - Hays Daily News (KS) Oct 27, 1969 [5218] p.4C - Wichita Eagle (KS) Jan 5, 1988 [5219] Cedar Rapids Gazette (IA) Apr 5, 1902

found some time after he had shot himself. No one saw him do the act or heard the report of the shot. **VIRGINIA P. KNOUF** [5220] (1905 – 2007) daughter of Oscar and Vada (Owens) Knouf, married Walter Abraham Brandyberry with whom she was mother of (4). A member of Hill City Christian Church, Virginia was a homemaker. **WARREN RUFUS KNOUF** [5221] (1882 – 1945) son of John and Mary (Brown) Knouf, married Mable Adelia Harter with whom he was father of (4). Walter was a retired sheet metal worker. He was a member of Fort Des Moines Presbyterian Church and charter member of the Moose lodge. **WESLEY JAMES KNOUF** (1958 – 2000) aka "Herky", son of Harry and Mary Louise (Gager) Knouf. **WILBUR CHESTER KNOUF** (1916 – 1982) son of Nicholas and Mildred (Clark) Knouf married twice; first to Margaret Elnora Sandlin and later, to Mabel Frances (Zade) Edmonds. **WILLIAM H. KNOUF** (1851 – 1851) son of John and Maria (Cook) Knouf. **WILLIAM MCKINLEY KNOUF** aka "Mack", son of William and Mary (Collins) Knouf, married Florence Edna Belveal with whom he was father of (3). **WILSON ALEX KNOUF** (1847 – 1848) son of John and Maria (Cook) Knouf.

KNOWLES

DAVID KNOWLES Fifth great grandson of progenitor Nicholas Kegg. **JOANN L. KNOWLES** Third great granddaughter of progenitor Nicholas Kegg. **SAMUEL RICHARD KNOWLES** [5222] (1929 – 2005) aka "Dick", son of Samuel and Lucylle (Kyner) Knowles, married Delores Marie Skelton with whom he was father of (2). Following high school Dick began working for Schmitten Lumber Company in the woods. In 1954, he enlisted in the U.S. Army, where he served as a Demolition Expert, and following his honorable discharge returned to Schmitten Lumber Company where he was employed as a logger. Later, Dick was employed by the Chelan County Road Department as an equipment operator until his retirement. Dick was an avid outdoorsman who loved his early morning rides, where most often he could be found cutting wood, hunting or fishing. His passion for trap shooting carried on throughout his life. He was a member of the National Rifle Association and had served as a volunteer for the Cashmere Fire Department from 1950, to 1958, and the Leavenworth Fire Department from 1958, until 1990. Dick also served six years as a councilman for the City of Leavenworth.

KNUTSON

KIM KNUTSON Seventh great granddaughter of progenitor Nicholas Kegg.
KRISTY KNUTSON Seventh great granddaughter of progenitor Nicholas Kegg.
TRACY KNUTSON Seventh great granddaughter of progenitor Nicholas Kegg.

KOCH

KEVIN KOCH Sixth great grandson of progenitor Nicholas Kegg.

KOCHEL

ASHLEY JO KOCHEL Sixth great granddaughter of progenitor Nicholas Kegg.
BENJAMIN EUGENE KOCHEL Fifth great grandson of progenitor Nicholas Kegg.
BRYAN KOCHEL Fifth great grandson of progenitor Nicholas Kegg.
CHARLES J. KOCHEL (1922 – 1977) son of Charles and Ida (Hershiser) Kochel.
DENNIS PAUL KOCHEL Fifth great grandson of progenitor Nicholas Kegg.
HAROLD L. KOCHEL [5223] (1923 – 2000) son of Charles and Ida (Hershiser) Kochel, married Patricia McClymonds with whom he was father of (3). Harold was employed as a maintenance worker.

[5220] Hays Daily News (KS) June 25, 2007 [5221] p.22 Des Moines Tribune (IA) Apr 5, 1945 [5222] The Wenatchee World (WA) July 6, 2005 [5223] The Ledger (Lakeland, FL) Feb 12, 2000

JOHNNY EUGENE KOCHEL Sixth great grandson of progenitor Nicholas Kegg.
JOYCE M KOCHEL (5223A) (1929 – 2015) daughter of Charles and Ida (Hershiser) Kochel, married George Yacob with whom she was mother of (2). Joyce retired from Pioneer Rubber Company in Willard, Ohio. She was a member of the First United Methodist Church in Willard and enjoyed playing cards.
KENNETH L. KOCHEL Fifth great grandson of progenitor Nicholas Kegg.
KIRSTEN IDA KOCHEL Sixth great granddaughter of progenitor Nicholas Kegg.
LORIE ANN KOCHEL Sixth great granddaughter of progenitor Nicholas Kegg.
LUKAS CHARLES KOCHEL Sixth great grandson of progenitor Nicholas Kegg.
MILDRED KOCHEL aka "Millie", Fifth great granddaughter of progenitor Nicholas Kegg.
PAMELA SUE KOCHEL Fifth great granddaughter of progenitor Nicholas Kegg.
PEGGY L. KOCHEL Fifth great granddaughter of progenitor Nicholas Kegg
RICHARD ALLAN KOCHEL Fifth great grandson of progenitor Nicholas Kegg.
RICHARD LOUIS KOCHEL Fourth great grandson of progenitor Nicholas Kegg.
RICHARD LOUIS KOCHEL (1956 – 1956) son of Richard and Marilyn (Marquart) Lochel.
RONALD EUGENE KOCHEL (5224) (1949 – 2002) son of Harold and Patricia (McClymonds) Kochel, married Carolyn Kay Hignite with whom he was father of (3).
SHERRY LYNN KOCHEL Sixth great granddaughter of progenitor Nicholas Kegg.
SONIA SUE KOCHEL Sixth great granddaughter of progenitor Nicholas Kegg.
TIMOTHY JAMES KOCHEL (5225) (1973 – 1988) son of Richard and Janet (Cornett) Kochel died from injuries sustained in an auto accident. The eighth-grade student was a member of the Pony League Farm Team, the VFW, Boy Troop 507 and the Junior High Football program.

KOENIG

LAWRENCE J. KOENIG Fifth great grandson of progenitor Nicholas Kegg.
MARGARET S. KOENIG Fifth great granddaughter of progenitor Nicholas Kegg.

KOENIGSEKER

ANN ELIZABETH KOENIGSEKER (5225A) (1929 – 2019) daughter of Sumner and Mary (Bradley) Koenigseker married Richard Edward Wieczorowski with whom she was mother of (2). Ann believed in community service, contributing to and helping direct a number of national and local non-profit organizations. Accomplished in both the visual and musical arts, she worked as a commercial illustrator, taught piano and voice, and performed as an organist and alto soloist in many venues. She earned a master's degree from Johns Hopkins late in life.
BRADLEY RICHARD KOENIGSEKER Sixth great grandson of progenitor Nicholas Kegg.
JENNIFER L. KOENIGSEKER Sixth great granddaughter of progenitor Nicholas Kegg.
MARY SUE KOENIGSEKER Sixth great granddaughter of progenitor Nicholas Kegg.
RICHARD BRADLEY KOENIGSEKER (5225B) aka "Dick" (1928 – 2012) son of Sumner and Mary Leona (Bradley) Koenigseker married twice, first to Mary Lou Shanahan with whom he was father of (3). Later he married Mary Ann Bubenzer. Dick attended Purdue University and served in the United States Army during WWII. He retired as marketing manager of United Hospital Services in Indianapolis. He was a member of the Masonic Lodge in Whitehouse, Ohio and a 32nd Degree Mason.
SARAH KOENIGSEKER (5226) (1991 – 2008) daughter of Bradley and Jane (Andersen) Koenigseker, graduated from St. Augustine School in Augusta and she was in her junior year at Cony High School. Sarah was a member of St. Augustine Catholic Church.

(5223A) secorfuneralhomes (OH) (5224) Lexington Herald-Leader (KY) June 11, 2002 (5225) News Journal (Mansfield, OH) July 20, 1988, obtained by D. Sue Dible (5225A) The Blade (OH) June 24, 2019 (5225B) Boone Funeral Home (Evansville, Indiana) (5226) Central Maine (ME) Mar. 7, 2008

KOERNER

IRENE KOERNER [5227] (1922 – 2013) daughter of Charles and Famie Leone (Rouzer) Koerner married Ronald Arthur Welch. Later, she married Porter Young Frazier. Irene attended Carnegie Tech, the University of Pittsburgh and the American University in Washington D.C. During World War II, she was employed by Westinghouse Electric in PA and U.S. Steel Research Lab in Monroeville, PA. Later she worked for the Pennsylvania Joint State Government Commission in Harrisburg, PA before moving to Alexandria, VA. She was employed by The Institute for Defense Analysis, The Police Foundation and The Urban Institute in Washington D. C. She retired from the American Statistical Association and moved to Tennessee. **KOLTEN KOERNER** Eighth great grandson of progenitor Nicholas Kegg.

KOHAN

GEORGE KOHAN Sixth great grandson of progenitor Nicholas Kegg.
LAURIE ANN KOHAN Sixth great granddaughter of progenitor Nicholas Kegg.

KOHER

JOSHUA LEE KOHER Sixth great grandson of progenitor Nicholas Kegg.

KOKAISEL

GARY ALLEN KOKAISEL Seventh great grandson of progenitor Nicholas Kegg.
TANYA RENEE KOKAISEL Seventh great granddaughter of progenitor Nicholas Kegg.

KOLLASZAR

JESSICA NICOLE KOLLASZAR Seventh great granddaughter of progenitor Nicholas Kegg.
NATHAN KOLLASZAR Seventh great grandson of progenitor Nicholas Kegg.

KONIGSMARK

ADAM SARO KONIGSMARK Sixth great grandson of progenitor Nicholas Kegg.
CRAIG EUGENE KONIGSMARK (1943 – 2001) son of Joseph and Evelyn (Callier) Konigsmark.
DAVID KONIGSMARK Sixth great grandson of progenitor Nicholas Kegg.
GARY LOYD KONIGSMARK Fifth great grandson of progenitor Nicholas Kegg.
JOHN JOSEPH KONIGSMARK Fifth great grandson of progenitor Nicholas Kegg.
KEEGAN KONIGSMARK Sixth great grandson of progenitor Nicholas Kegg.
KIRSTEN MARIA KONIGSMARK Sixth great granddaughter of progenitor Nicholas Kegg.
KOLBY BRANDON KONIGSMARK Sixth great grandson of progenitor Nicholas Kegg.
LUKAS GABRIEL KONIGSMARK aka "Luke", Sixth great grandson of progenitor Nicholas Kegg.

KONKLE

AVALEE KONKLE Eighth great granddaughter of progenitor Nicholas Kegg.

KONKOL

AMBER N. KONKOL Seventh great granddaughter of progenitor Nicholas Kegg.

[5227] Erwin Record (TN) June 10, 2013

DOUGLAS EDWARD KONKOL (5227A) (1949 – 2012) son of Edward and Janice (Wells) Konkol, married Donna L. Samuel with whom he was father of (2). **KIM RENEE KONKOL** Sixth great granddaughter of progenitor Nicholas Kegg. **LYNDA KONKOL** Sixth great granddaughter of progenitor Nicholas Kegg. **TIFFANY LYNN KONKOL** Seventh great granddaughter of progenitor Nicholas Kegg.

KOOISTRA

KATHRYN KOOISTRA, aka "Kate", Fifth great granddaughter of progenitor Nicholas Kegg. **KRISTIN KOOISTRA** Fifth great granddaughter of progenitor Nicholas Kegg.

KOONTZ

A.J. KOONTZ Eighth great grandson of progenitor Nicholas Kegg. **ADA ESTELLA KOONTZ** (5228) (1890 – 1989) aka "Stella", daughter of John and Margaret (Shoemaker) Koontz, married Israel Morris with whom she was mother of (1). **ANDREW JUSTIN JAMES KOONTZ** aka "Drew", Seventh great grandson of progenitor Nicholas Kegg. **ANGELA N. KOONTZ** Seventh great granddaughter of progenitor Nicholas Kegg. **ASHLAN MARGARET KOONTZ** Seventh great granddaughter of progenitor Nicholas Kegg. **AUDREY KOONTZ** Eighth great granddaughter of progenitor Nicholas Kegg. **BETTY JANE KOONTZ** (5229) (1931 – 1949) daughter of Dennis and Gladys (Morgart) Koontz. Betty was a member in the Cove Reformed church. **BARBARA JEAN KOONTZ** Sixth great granddaughter of progenitor Nicholas Kegg. **BRAD MATTHEW KOONTZ** Seventh great grandson of progenitor Nicholas Kegg. **BRADLEY RICHARD KOONTZ** Seventh great grandson of progenitor Nicholas Kegg. **BRANDON J. KOONTZ** Seventh great grandson of progenitor Nicholas Kegg. **BRAYDEN JOSHUA KOONTZ** Seventh great grandson of progenitor Nicholas Kegg. **BRIAN RICHARD KOONTZ** Sixth great grandson of progenitor Nicholas Kegg. **BRIAN RICHARD KOONTZ** Seventh great grandson of progenitor Nicholas Kegg. **BRUCE EDWARD KOONTZ** Sixth great grandson of progenitor Nicholas Kegg. **CAMDEN JOSEPH KOONTZ** Seventh great grandson of progenitor Nicholas Kegg. **CARL B. KOONTZ** (1896 – 1899) son of Nicholas and Pammie (Fickes) Koontz. **CAROL ANN KOONTZ** Sixth great granddaughter of progenitor Nicholas Kegg. **CHELSAE BETH KOONTZ** Seventh great granddaughter of progenitor Nicholas Kegg. **CHRISTY L. KOONTZ** Seventh great granddaughter of progenitor Nicholas Kegg. **CLARA KOONTZ** (5230) (1920 – 1992) daughter of Emanuel and Teena (Diehl) Koontz, married Donald R. Black with whom she was mother of (1). **DANIEL W. KOONTZ** Sixth great grandson of progenitor Nicholas Kegg. **DEBBIE KOONTZ** Fifth great granddaughter of progenitor Nicholas Kegg. **DENNIS EMANUEL KOONTZ** (5231) (1901 – 1970) son of Nicholas and Pammie (Fickes) Koontz, married Gladys Filler Morgart with whom he was father of (7). Dennis was a retired farmer and had been employed by Anderson Patrol. **DONALD EMANUEL KOONTZ** (1925 – 2016) son of Walter and Mildred (Pennel) Koontz married Linda Louise Hall. Donald was a WWII US Marine Corps veteran. **DONNA KOONTZ** Fifth great granddaughter of progenitor Nicholas Kegg. **DOROTHY L. KOONTZ** (5232) (1918 – 1979) daughter of Harry and Maude (Reininger) Koontz, married Edgar Frank Treese. **ELIZABETH MARLENA KOONTZ** (5232A) aka "Lizzy Ladybug" (2009 – 2017) daughter of Jeffrey and Concepta (Hall) Koontz. Lizzy was an identical twin attending Western Pennsylvania School for Blind Children. **EMILIA KOONTZ** Eighth great granddaughter of progenitor Nicholas Kegg. **FLORENCE EDNA KOONTZ** (5232B) aka "Flo" (1927 – 2019) daughter of Roy and Daisy (Nevett) Koontz married Joe C. Ritchey Jr. Flo was employed as a dental assistant for Dr. Brown. Flo enjoyed farming with her husband, gardening and had a passion for flowers. **FRANKLIN ANDREW KOONTZ** (5232C) (1921 – 2022) son of Walter and Mildred (Pennel) Koontz, married Mildred

---

(5227A) Plain Dealer (OH) March 3, 2012 (5228) Bedford Inquirer (PA) June 15, 1967 (5229) Bedford Gazette (PA) June 10, 1949 (5230) p.2 - The Daily News (Huntingdon, PA) Aug. 22, 1992 (5231) Cumberland News (MD) May 29, 1970 (5232) Altoona Mirror (PA) Dec 29, 2003obtained by D. Sue Dible (5232A) Bedford Gazette (PA) Nov 16, 2017, contributed by Bob Rose (5232B) Bedford Gazette (PA) July 19, 2019 (5232C) Bedford Gazette (PA) April 28, 2022

Pearl Koontz with whom he was father of (3). Franklin operated his own farm, and also worked for Westinghouse, from which he retired. **GARY DENNIS KOONTZ** Fifth great grandson of progenitor Nicholas Kegg. **GEORGE EDWARD CLYDE KOONTZ** [5232D] (1924 – 2005) son of Dennis and Gladys (Morgart) Koontz married Mildred Diehl with whom he was father of (3). George was a member and Sunday School teacher at Friends Cove United Church of Christ and had served on the Consistory for many years. He was on the Board of Directors at Pennknoll Village Nursing Home and was a former member of the Board of Directors at REA and Friends Cove Mutual Insurance Company. He was a member of the Fort Bedford Region Antique Car Club and was the former owner of Sunny Four Farms in Friends Cove. **GLENN CALVIN KOONTZ** [5233] (1968 – 1968) son of Glenn and Charlotte (Calhoun) Koontz. **GREGORY KYLE KOONTZ** Seventh great grandson of progenitor Nicholas Kegg. **GREGORY SCOTT KOONTZ** Sixth great grandson of progenitor Nicholas Kegg. **GRANT KOONTZ** Eighth great grandson of progenitor Nicholas Kegg. **HANNAH KOONTZ** Seventh great granddaughter of progenitor Nicholas Kegg. **HAROLD EUGENE KOONTZ** [5233A] (1929 – 2022) aka "Gene", son of Dennis and Gladys (Morgart) Koontz, married Rosemary Virginia Koozer with whom he was father of (4). Gene started his career hauling milk to Queen City Dairy with a milk can truck in 1952 as an independent hauler. In 1962, he attached a bulk tank to his truck, and continued to haul milk forming H. Eugene Koontz Trucking, Inc. in the late 1980s with his signature Mack trucks and bulk tanks. Gene enjoyed hunting and was a member of the Antique Car Club. He loved family picnics, helping people, and was a very kind and generous person with a great sense of humor. **HARRY ELLIS KOONTZ** [5234] (1888 – 1958) son of John and Margaret (Shoemaker) Koontz married twice; first to Maude Irene Reininger with whom he was father of (2). Later, he married Pearl Myers. Harry was a feed dealer in Curryville for many years before moving to Manns Choice where he conducted a grocery store. He was elected tax collector in 1957. Harry was a member of the Manns Choice Evangelical and Reformed Church and Schellsburg I.O.O.F. Lodge. **IZABELLA ZOE KOONTZ** Seventh great granddaughter of progenitor Nicholas Kegg. **JACK R. KOONTZ** Fifth great grandson of progenitor Nicholas Kegg. **JACOB KOONTZ** Eighth great grandson of progenitor Nicholas Kegg. **JAMES CLYDE KOONTZ** [5234A] aka "Jim" (1954 – 2013) son of George and Mildred (Diehl) Koontz married Cindy Walker with whom he was father of (2). Rev. Koontz was a former pastor of the First Brethren Church in Sarasota, Fla.; Fort Scott Brethren Church in Fort Scott, Kan., and the Beacon of Hope Community Church (First Brethren) in Louisville, Ohio. He was also a Vocational Agriculture teacher at Waynesburg High School in Waynesburg. Later, Jim was employed by Home Depot in Massillon, Ohio. **JANELLE KOONTZ** Sixth great granddaughter of progenitor Nicholas Kegg. **JANET LUCILLE KOONTZ** [5234B] (1926 – 2017) daughter of Dennis and Gladys (Morgart) Koontz married Warren Harding Lohr with whom she was mother of (3). Janet retired from the Allegany County Board of Education with 24 years of service driving school buses for special needs children. She was an avid card player and had a love for bowling, especially duck pin bowling. Janet had a strong passion for her job as a school bus driver and loved selling Avon. **JEFFREY KYLE KOONTZ** Seventh great grandson of progenitor Nicholas Kegg. **JEFFREY WAYNE KOONTZ** Sixth great grandson of progenitor Nicholas Kegg. **JOEL A. KOONTZ** Seventh great grandson of progenitor Nicholas Kegg. **JOEY KOONTZ** Eighth great grandson of progenitor Nicholas Kegg. **JOEL W. KOONTZ** Sixth great grandson of progenitor Nicholas Kegg. **JOHN NORMAN KOONTZ** [5234C] (1930 – 2017) son of Walter and Mildred (Pennel) Koontz, married Antonie Hogner with whom he was father of (1). John served in the U.S. Army. He was employed as a physical plant engineer in the state of Maryland. John was a member of the Free and Accepted Masons and had obtained entry into the Ancient and Accepted Scottish Rite of Freemasonry. **JOSEPH EDWARD KOONTZ** Fifth great grandson of progenitor Nicholas Kegg.

[5232D] p.3 - Bedford Inquirer (PA) Dec 2, 2005, contributed by Bob Rose [5233] Bedford County Historical Society Pioneer Library (PA), book 49, p.K40 obtained by D. Sue Dible [5233A] Bedford Gazette (PA) April 26, 2022 [5234] Altoona Mirror (PA) April 25, 1958 [5234A] Bedford Gazette (PA) Feb 28, 2013, contributed by Bob Rose [5234B] Bedford Gazette (PA) Oct 3, 2017 contributed by Bob Rose [5234C] Bedford Gazette (PA) April 12, 2017 contributed by Bob Rose

JOSHUA B. KOONTZ Seventh great grandson of progenitor Nicholas Kegg. **JULIE KOONTZ** Seventh great granddaughter of progenitor Nicholas Kegg. **KAITLIN JESSICA KOONTZ** Sixth great granddaughter of progenitor Nicholas Kegg. **KAREN KOONTZ** Sixth great granddaughter of progenitor Nicholas Kegg. **KASEY J. KOONTZ** Seventh great grandson of progenitor Nicholas Kegg. **KATHRYN VIOLA KOONTZ** [5235] (1915 – 1999) daughter of Emanuel and Teena (Diehl) Koontz, married William Gale Diehl with whom she was mother of (2). Kathryn was a member of Central Presbyterian Church in Chambersburg, Semper Fidelis Sunday School class and Lydia Circle of the Women's Association. She was a member of Christian Women and Greencastle-Antrim Women's Fellowship; Martha Custis Chapter 342 Order of Eastern Star; Falling Spring Court 139 Order of Amaranth; Menno Haven visitation volunteer, served meals on wheels; and Chambersburg Hospital Auxiliary. **KATIE JO KOONTZ** Seventh great granddaughter of progenitor Nicholas Kegg. **LANE EDWARD KOONTZ** Sixth great grandson of progenitor Nicholas Kegg. **LINDA KOONTZ** Fifth great granddaughter of progenitor Nicholas Kegg. **LINDA ANN KOONTZ** Sixth great granddaughter of progenitor Nicholas Kegg. **LINDA KAY KOONTZ** Sixth great granddaughter of progenitor Nicholas Kegg. **MAKAYLA KOONTZ** Ninth great granddaughter of progenitor Nicholas Kegg. **MARGARET KOONTZ** Fourth great granddaughter of progenitor Nicholas Kegg. **MARY CARLENA KOONTZ** (2009 – 2009) daughter of Jeffrey and Concepta (Hall) Koontz. **MAUDE M. KOONTZ** [5236] (1900 – 1938) daughter of Emanuel and Teena (Diehl) Koontz, married Rev. Roy Limbert with whom she was mother of (3). Maude was a life-long member of the Women's Missionary society and was vice president of the Dover Reformed Missionary group. Among the schools she attended was Lancaster Business College. **MELISSA SUE KOONTZ** Sixth great granddaughter of progenitor Nicholas Kegg. **MICHAEL J. KOONTZ** Sixth great grandson of progenitor Nicholas Kegg. **OLIVE MARGARET KOONTZ** [5237] (1913 – 1991) daughter of Harry and Maude (Reininger) Koontz, married Elmer Clair Dilling with whom she was mother of (2). Olive was a housewife and a lifelong member of the Church of the Brethren, which she attended regularly. **OLIVER KOONTZ** Eighth great grandson of progenitor Nicholas Kegg. **PALMER S. KOONTZ** [5238] (1908 – 1979) son of Emanuel and Teena (Diehl) Koontz was a guard at the state penitentiary in Baltimore, retiring. **PAUL VICTOR KOONTZ** [5239] (1923 – 1973) son of Walter and Mildred (Pennell) Koontz never married. **RAY E. KOONTZ** Fifth great grandson of progenitor Nicholas Kegg. **ROY VERNON KOONTZ** [5240] (1891 – 1966) son of John and Margaret (Shoemaker) Koontz, married Daisy Pearl Nevitt with whom he was father of (3). Roy was a lifelong resident of Friends Cove and was engaged in farming. **SAMUEL KOONTZ** Ninth great grandson of progenitor Nicholas Kegg. **SAMUEL WEHR KOONTZ** [5241] (1899 – 1982) son of Nicholas and Pammie (Fickes) Koontz, married Ethel Irene Swartzwelder with whom he was father of (2). Samuel operated a grocery store on King Street in Bedford for over 30 years until his retirement. He was a member of the Friends Cove United Church of Christ, member of Loyal Order of Moose No. 480 of Bedford, the Bedford County Sportsmen's Association, and the Friends Cove Sportsmen's Association. **SARAH PEARL KOONTZ** (1905 – 1919) daughter of Nicholas and Pammie (Fickes) Koontz. **SCOTT STEELE KOONTZ** Seventh great grandson of progenitor Nicholas Kegg. **SEWELL EDWARD KOONTZ** (1898 – 1907) son of Emanuel and Teena (Diehl) Koontz. **SOPHIA LUCILLE KOONTZ** [5242] (1903 – 1980) daughter of Nicholas and Pammie (Fickes) Koontz, married William Stanley Pennel with whom she was mother of (2). Lucille was a member of the Cove United Church of Christ. **STEPHANIE FILLER KOONTZ** Sixth great granddaughter of progenitor Nicholas Kegg. **TAYLOR ELIZABETH KOONTZ** Seventh great granddaughter of progenitor Nicholas Kegg. **THOMAS PENNELL KOONTZ** [5243] (1927 – 1933) son of Walter and Mildred (Pennel) Koontz who lived on a farm about one mile north of Rainsburg was sitting on one of the chairs his father was hauling in his Chevrolet truck, fell headlong from the side of the truck. His brother, Donald screamed as he saw his brother's fatal plunge from the chair. The father

---

[5235] The Herald Mail (Hagerstown, MD) Dec. 7, 1999 [5236] p.3 -The Star and Sentinel (Gettysburg, PA) May14,1938 [5237] p.3 -Bedford Inquirer (PA) Nov 1, 1991 [5238, 5239] Bedford County Genealogical Society obituary obtained by D. Sue Dible [5240] p.3 - Bedford Inquirer (PA) March 24, 1966 [5241] p.3 - Bedford Inquirer (PA) Jan 15, 1982 [5242] Bedford County Genealogical Society obituary obtained by D. Sue Dible [5243] Bedford Gazette (PA) May 12, 1933

heard this, and before they had gone far, he had stopped and went back to find his child dead from the fall. There was no evidence that the child was touched by any part of the truck as he fell. The truck was traveling at only about twenty miles an hour, about two and a half miles from home. The lurch from a sudden bump was sufficient to dislodge the little 6-year-old passenger. **TODD JOSEPH KOONTZ** Sixth great grandson of progenitor Nicholas Kegg. **VALERIE M. KOONTZ** Sixth great granddaughter of progenitor Nicholas Kegg. **VIRGINIA KOONTZ** [5244] (1920 – 2009) aka "Ginger", daughter of Walter and Mildred (Pennel) Koontz, married Paul Lesie Hendricks with whom she was mother of (1). Ginger was known for her love of baking, reading, birds, knitting, taking walks and enjoying a cup of black coffee any time of the day with good friends. **WALTER FRANKLIN KOONTZ** [5245] (1898 – 1972) son of Emanuel and Teena Diehl Koontz, married Mildred Leona Pennel with whom he was father of (9). **WILLIAM KOONTZ**, aka "Will", Eighth great grandson of progenitor Nicholas Kegg.

KOROS

SANDRA KOROS Sixth great granddaughter of progenitor Nicholas Kegg.

KORTAN

HAILEY ELISE KORTAN Seventh great granddaughter of progenitor Nicholas Kegg.
HILLARY KORTAN Seventh great granddaughter of progenitor Nicholas Kegg.
OLIVIA KORTAN Seventh great granddaughter of progenitor Nicholas Kegg.

KORZEC

AIDEN KORZEC Eighth great grandson of progenitor Nicholas Kegg.
DAKOTA KORZEC Eighth great grandson of progenitor Nicholas Kegg.

KOSER

CHLOE ASHTON KOSER Eighth great granddaughter of progenitor Nicholas Kegg.
JORDON KOSER Eighth great grandson of progenitor Nicholas Kegg.
KASEY KOSER Eighth great granddaughter of progenitor Nicholas Kegg.
KENNETH M. KOSER Seventh great grandson of progenitor Nicholas Kegg.
KEVIN M. KOSER Seventh great grandson of progenitor Nicholas Kegg.
KIMBERLY KAY KOSER Seventh great granddaughter of progenitor Nicholas Kegg.
KODY KOSER Eighth great grandson of progenitor Nicholas Kegg.
TYLER KOSER Eighth great grandson of progenitor Nicholas Kegg.

KOSKOSKI

ANGELA S. KOSKOSKI aka "Angie", Seventh great granddaughter of progenitor Nicholas Kegg.
JARROD FRANCIS KOSKOSKI Seventh great grandson of progenitor Nicholas Kegg.
REBECCA LYNN KOSKOSKI aka "Becky", Seventh great granddaughter of progenitor Nicholas Kegg.

KOST

JEFFREY GARRISON KOST Sixth great grandson of progenitor Nicholas Kegg.
JULIE ANN KOST Sixth great granddaughter of progenitor Nicholas Kegg.

[5244] p.3 - Bedford Inquirer (PA) June 5, 2009, obtained by Bob Rose [5245] The Cumberland News (MD) Aug. 12, 1972

KOTSALA

JACOB KOTSALA Eighth great grandson of progenitor Nicholas Kegg.
PAMELA KOTSALA Eighth great granddaughter of progenitor Nicholas Kegg.
SAMANTHA KOTSALA Eighth great granddaughter of progenitor Nicholas Kegg.

KOYM

SALLY ANN KOYM Fifth great granddaughter of progenitor Nicholas Kegg.

KOZAK

BERNARD J. KOZAK aka "Bernie", Fifth great grandson of progenitor Nicholas Kegg.
CONSTANCE KOZAK aka "Connie", Fifth great granddaughter of progenitor Nicholas Kegg.
HAILEY KOZAK Seventh great granddaughter of progenitor Nicholas Kegg.
KAITLIN KOZAK Seventh great granddaughter of progenitor Nicholas Kegg.
PATRICIA KOZAK aka "Pat", Fifth great granddaughter of progenitor Nicholas Kegg.

KOZLOWSKI

ALEXIA MARIE KOZLOWSKI Ninth great granddaughter of progenitor Nicholas Kegg.
ALEXIS ROSE KOZLOWSKI Eighth great granddaughter of progenitor Nicholas Kegg.
BLAKE KOZLOWSKI Eighth great grandson of progenitor Nicholas Kegg.
KARIE JEAN KOZLOWSKI Seventh great granddaughter of progenitor Nicholas Kegg.
TIFFANY KOZLOWSKI Eighth great granddaughter of progenitor Nicholas Kegg.

KRAJNAK

AMY A. KRAJNAK Sixth great granddaughter of progenitor Nicholas Kegg.

KRAMER

ADAM KRAMER Seventh great grandson of progenitor Nicholas Kegg.
ALEX KRAMER Seventh great grandson of progenitor Nicholas Kegg.
AMBER KRAMER Seventh great granddaughter of progenitor Nicholas Kegg.
ANDREA KRAMER Seventh great granddaughter of progenitor Nicholas Kegg.

KRAWCIW

ANDREA L. KRAWCIW Sixth great granddaughter of progenitor Nicholas Kegg.
HERBERT L. KRAWCIW Fifth great grandson of progenitor Nicholas Kegg.
TERESA ANN KRAWCIW Fifth great granddaughter of progenitor Nicholas Kegg.
TERRY LYNN KRAWCIW Fifth great granddaughter of progenitor Nicholas Kegg.

KREIDER

ELLIS KREIDER Seventh great grandson of progenitor Nicholas Kegg.
JONATHAN PEARSE KREIDER Sixth great grandson of progenitor Nicholas Kegg.
JOSIAH KREIDER Seventh great grandson of progenitor Nicholas Kegg.
NATHAN ALLEN KREIDER Seventh great grandson of progenitor Nicholas Kegg.
TIMOTHY ALLEN KREIDER Sixth great grandson of progenitor Nicholas Kegg.

KREITZ

ELIZABETH ANN KREITZ Seventh great granddaughter of progenitor Nicholas Kegg.
JOHN THOMAS KREITZ Seventh great grandson of progenitor Nicholas Kegg.

KREUTZ

DAVID MATTHEW KREUTZ Sixth great grandson of progenitor Nicholas Kegg.
JOSEPH E. KREUTZ Fifth great grandson of progenitor Nicholas Kegg.
JOSEPH EDWARD KREUTZ aka "Joey", Sixth great grandson of progenitor Nicholas Kegg.
TAMMY KREUTZ Sixth great granddaughter of progenitor Nicholas Kegg.

KREUTZPEINTNER

JOSEPH E. KREUTZPEINTNER (1938 – 1938) son of Joseph and Elizabeth (Smith) Kreutzpeintner.

KRIEGER

LOGAN KRIEGER Seventh great grandson of progenitor Nicholas Kegg.

KRIENER

JOHN KRIENER Sixth great grandson of progenitor Nicholas Kegg.

KRISTOVICH

JOSHUA KRISTOVICH Sixth great grandson of progenitor Nicholas Kegg.
RICHELE KRISTOVICH Sixth great granddaughter of progenitor Nicholas Kegg.

KRNACH

JEANNE L. KRNACH Fifth great granddaughter of progenitor Nicholas Kegg.
JEFFREY KRNACH Fifth great grandson of progenitor Nicholas Kegg.
SHANNON LEIGH KRNACH Sixth great granddaughter of progenitor Nicholas Kegg.
SUSAN KAY KRNACH Fifth great granddaughter of progenitor Nicholas Kegg.
TAYLER MICHAEL KRNACH Sixth great grandson of progenitor Nicholas Kegg.
TODD MICHAEL KRNACH Fifth great grandson of progenitor Nicholas Kegg.
ZACHARY QUINN KRNACH Sixth great grandson of progenitor Nicholas Kegg.

KRZANOWSKY

MICHAEL S. KRZANOWSKY Sixth great grandson of progenitor Nicholas Kegg.
STEVEN KRZANOWSKY Sixth great grandson of progenitor Nicholas Kegg.
SUSAN LYNN KRZANOWSKY aka "Suzy", Sixth great granddaughter of progenitor Nicholas Kegg.

KUCKUCK

EVA KUCKUCK [5246] (1901 – 1992) daughter of Charles and Carrie Ella (Kegg) Kuckuck, married Roy D. Hershberger. Eva had been employed as a secretary to Dr. J.D, Keiper.

[5246] Johnstown Tribune Democrat (PA) Sep 29, 1992, obtained by D. Sue Dible

KUEHL

HAIZLEE KUEHL Eighth great granddaughter of progenitor Nicholas Kegg.

KUEHNE

BRIAN CHRISTOPHER KUEHNE Seventh great grandson of progenitor Nicholas Kegg.
JEFFREY PAUL KUEHNE Seventh great grandson of progenitor Nicholas Kegg.
MYKEL ELIZABETH KUEHNE Seventh great granddaughter of progenitor Nicholas Kegg.

KUHN

AVERY ELAINE KUHN Seventh great granddaughter of progenitor Nicholas Kegg.
CYNTHIA KAY KUHN Fifth great granddaughter of progenitor Nicholas Kegg.
ELYSE KUHN Seventh great granddaughter of progenitor Nicholas Kegg.   **EMILY K. KUHN** Sixth great granddaughter of progenitor Nicholas Kegg.   **ERIC ALAN KUHN** Sixth great grandson of progenitor Nicholas Kegg.   **IRIS ARDEN KUHN** Seventh great granddaughter of progenitor Nicholas Kegg.   **JAMIE LOUISE KUHN** Fifth great granddaughter of progenitor Nicholas Kegg.
JUSTIN MICHAEL KUHN Sixth great grandson of progenitor Nicholas Kegg.
LYNN ELLEN KUHN Fifth great granddaughter of progenitor Nicholas Kegg.
MATHEW KUHN Sixth great grandson of progenitor Nicholas Kegg.   **MICHAEL KUHN** Seventh great grandson of progenitor Nicholas Kegg.   **NICHOLAS KUHN** Seventh great grandson of progenitor Nicholas Kegg.   **OLIVER KUHN** Seventh great grandson of progenitor Nicholas Kegg.
ROBIN ALAN KUHN Fifth great grandson of progenitor Nicholas Kegg.

KUKK

KATLIN ROSE KUKK Seventh great granddaughter of progenitor Nicholas Kegg.
STACY RENE KUKK Seventh great granddaughter of progenitor Nicholas Kegg.

KUKLA

NICHOLAS W. KUKLA Sixth great grandson of progenitor Nicholas Kegg.
STACIE A. KUKLA Sixth great granddaughter of progenitor Nicholas Kegg.

KUNS

JEREMY LEE KUNS Seventh great grandson of progenitor Nicholas Kegg.
MATTHEW KUNS Seventh great grandson of progenitor Nicholas Kegg.
TIFFANY KUNS Seventh great granddaughter of progenitor Nicholas Kegg.

KUNTZ

BONNIE LYNN KUNTZ Seventh great granddaughter of progenitor Nicholas Kegg.
BRUCE GLENN KUNTZ Sixth great grandson of progenitor Nicholas Kegg.
JOHN WALTER KUNTZ Seventh great grandson of progenitor Nicholas Kegg.
LYNN ANN KUNTZ Sixth great granddaughter of progenitor Nicholas Kegg.

KUONEN

ADDISON KAY KUONEN Eighth great granddaughter of progenitor Nicholas Kegg.

CONNER JAY KUONEN Eighth great grandson of progenitor Nicholas Kegg.

KURTZ

BRIAN KURTZ. Fifth great grandson of progenitor Nicholas Kegg.
JOHN MICHAEL KURTZ Fifth great grandson of progenitor Nicholas Kegg.
LYDIA D'ANNA KURTZ Fifth great granddaughter of progenitor Nicholas Kegg.
ROSALIND M KURTZ Fifth great granddaughter of progenitor Nicholas Kegg.

KUTSCHER

KENNETH FRANK KUTSCHER Fifth great grandson of progenitor Nicholas Kegg.
LAURA INGRID KUTSCHER Sixth great granddaughter of progenitor Nicholas Kegg.
PATSY RUTH KUTSCHER Fifth great granddaughter of progenitor Nicholas Kegg.
STEVEN RONALD KUTSCHER Sixth great grandson of progenitor Nicholas Kegg.

KVALHEIM

LILYANA PAMELA KVALHEIM aka "Lily" Ninth great granddaughter of progenitor Nicholas Kegg.
LUCAS JOAGUIN KVALHEIM Ninth great grandson of progenitor Nicholas Kegg.

KYNER

JULIE LUCYLLE KYNER [5247] (1968 – 2000) daughter of Paul and Shirley (Borg) Kyner, married Roland A. Schmitten. Julie graduated magna cum laude from Central Washington University with a B.S. degree in accounting. Following graduation, she worked at Stevens Pass and Cascade Medical Center and for the last four years had been employed in the Douglas County Auditor's Office in Waterville. Julie loved tending her flowers and working on craft projects. A kind, caring person, Julie had a great sense of humor. Julie was involved in a tragic and fatal auto accident returning from her honeymoon.
KRISTINE KYNER Fourth great granddaughter of progenitor Nicholas Kegg.
LUCYLLE M. KYNER [5248] (1898 – 1983) daughter of William and Mary Ellen (Kegg) Kyner married twice; first to Samuel D. Knowles with whom she was mother of (2). Later she married Stephen Leslie Knowles. Lucylle owned and operated a beauty salon. She was a member of the Cashmere Order of Eastern Star, Past Royal Matron, Past Worthy Matron of Amaranth and belonged to the Presbyterian Church. **PAUL R. KYNER** [5250] (1897 – 1988) son of William and Mary (Kegg) Kyner, married Mary Elizabeth Lingren with whom he was father of (3). Paul served in the Signal Corps in the U.S. Army during World War II. He then ran an orchard and was a state fruit inspector. Later, Paul owned and operated his own fruit ranch. He was past master of Mission Lodge No. 158 F. & A.M. of Cashmere; past commander of Cashmere American Legion Post No. 64; on Blue Star Growers board of directors and served as an officer from 1942 until 1983; a 30-year director of the Wenatchee Reclamation District; and served a term as president and was a member of the Wenoka Federation.
STEVE KYNER Fourth great grandson of progenitor Nicholas Kegg.
START PAUL KYNER Fourth great grandson of progenitor Nicholas Kegg.

LABO

DAVID DEAN WEIRICH LABO Seventh great grandson of progenitor Nicholas Kegg.
DUSTIN CHARLES LABO Seventh great grandson of progenitor Nicholas Kegg.

[5247] Wenatchee World (WA) Oct 30, 2000 [5248] Cashmere Valley Record Oct. 26, 1983, obtained by D. Sue Dible [5250] p.11 - Wenatchee World (WA) Jun 15, 1988, obtained by D. Sue Dible

LA PLANTE

DARRELL LA PLANTE Sixth great grandson of progenitor Nicholas Kegg.
KEVIN LA PLANTE Sixth great grandson of progenitor Nicholas Kegg.
PAULA LA PLANTE Sixth great granddaughter of progenitor Nicholas Kegg.
TINA LA PLANTE Sixth great granddaughter of progenitor Nicholas Kegg.

LACLAIR

AARON T. LACLAIR Seventh great grandson of progenitor Nicholas Kegg.

LACLAIRE

BRANDON JAMES LACLAIRE Seventh great grandson of progenitor Nicholas Kegg.
JAMES JOSEPH LACLAIRE Sixth great grandson of progenitor Nicholas Kegg.

LACROIX

AMBER LACROIX Sixth great granddaughter of progenitor Nicholas Kegg.
JOSHUA LACROIX Sixth great grandson of progenitor Nicholas Kegg.

LAFFERTY

BERNARD FRANKLIN LAFFERTY [5251] (1910 – 1984) son of Edward and Caroline (Ditch) Lafferty, married Adelia Defrancesco with whom he was father of (7). Bernard was a retired as a welder from Penn Central. **BERNARD FRANKLIN LAFFERTY** [5252] (1936 – 1983) son of Bernard and Adelia (Defrancesco) Lafferty, married Marjorie Jane Long with whom he was father of (3). Bernard was employed as a machinist at SKF. He was also a member of the Hollidaysburg Sportsmen's Club.
BRENDA M. LAFFERTY Fifth great granddaughter of progenitor Nicholas Kegg.
CHRISTOPHER LAFFERTY Sixth great grandson of progenitor Nicholas Kegg.
CINDY JO LAFFERTY Fifth great granddaughter of progenitor Nicholas Kegg.
COLE LAFFERTY Seventh great grandson of progenitor Nicholas Kegg. **DANIEL E. LAFFERTY** Fifth great grandson of progenitor Nicholas Kegg. **DARLENE D. LAFFERTY** Fifth great granddaughter of progenitor Nicholas Kegg. **DENISE D. LAFFERTY** Fifth great granddaughter of progenitor Nicholas Kegg. **DENNIS LAFFERTY** Fourth great grandson of progenitor Nicholas Kegg. **DENNIS E. LAFFERTY** [5253] (1971 – 1972) son of Dennis and Nancy (Baker) Lafferty. **DIANE LOUISE LAFFERTY** [5254] (1951 – 2003) daughter of Elmer and Winifred (Wolfram) Lafferty who was mother of (1). She married Thomas J. Sanker. Diane enjoyed reading, flower gardening and spending time with her pets. **DONALD LAFFERTY** aka "Jake", Fifth great grandson of progenitor Nicholas Kegg. **DONNA JEAN LAFFERTY** Fourth great granddaughter of progenitor Nicholas Kegg. **DYLAN LAFFERTY** Sixth great grandson of progenitor Nicholas Kegg. **EDWARD D. LAFFERTY** Fourth great grandson of progenitor Nicholas Kegg. **ELMER WILLARD LAFFERTY** [5255] (1901 – 1966) son of Edward and Caroline (Ditch) Lafferty married twice; first to Ferna Dora Black with whom he was father of (1). Later, he married Martha A. Kinsel. Elmer was employed as an electrician in the Juniata Diesel shop. **ELMER WILLARD LAFFERTY** [5256] (1927 – 1995) son of Elmer and Fern (Black) Lafferty, married Winifred S. Wolfram with whom he was father of (3). Elmer retired after 15 years of service from Blue & White Lines where he had been employed as a bus driver. Prior to that, he spent 18 years employed as a truck driver for Motor Freight Co. Elmer was a member of Catholic War

---

[5251] p.B3 - Altoona Mirror (PA) Mar 12, 1984 [5252] p.B3 - Altoona Mirror (PA) Dec 17, 1983 [5253] p.28 – Altoona Mirror (PA) Feb 5, 1972 [5254] Altoona Mirror (PA) Feb 25, 2003 [5255] Altoona Mirror (PA) Jan 6, 1966 [5256] p.B3 - Altoona Mirror (PA) Nov 9, 1995

Veterans, Altoona Lions Club and the Fort Fetter American Legion Post, Hollidaysburg. Elmer enjoyed fishing and hunting. He was a Navy veteran of World War II. **GAIL MARIE LAFFERTY** Fifth great granddaughter of progenitor Nicholas Kegg. **GEORGE EDWARD LAFFERTY** (1945 – 2009) son of George and Lorraine (Hunter) Lafferty married twice; first to Linda Carol Penner with whom he was father of (1). Later, he married Bonnie (Rodriguez) Delgado Davis.
GEORGE EDWARD LAFFERTY [5257] (1902 – 1954) son of Edward and Caroline (Ditch) Lafferty, married Lorraine Caroline Hunter with whom he was father of (2). A veteran of WWI, George was employed by the Lafferty Trucking Company. **GERRI A. LAFFERTY** Fifth great granddaughter of progenitor Nicholas Kegg. **GRACE ELEANOR LAFFERTY** [5258] (1904 – 1930) daughter of Edward and Caroline (Ditch) Lafferty, married William M. Irwin. Grace succumbed to injuries following a wild ride ending with a crash at Gardners Mill. A passenger in the car of intoxicated, Clyde Irvin, had sideswiped one motorist. Clyde failed to stop and render assistance after running down a pedestrian resulting in instant death. Others were seriously injured while two people escaped injury during Clyde's mad race escapade. Grace had been admitted to Altoona hospital, where to save her life, found it necessary to amputate her left leg above the knee. She failed to rally after the operation having suffered compound fractures of both legs, a fracture of the skull, body bruises and other severe injuries. **JON LAFFERTY** Sixth great grandson of progenitor Nicholas Kegg. **KATHLEEN LAFFERTY** [5259] (1949 – 1955) daughter of George and Lorraine (Hunter) Lafferty. **KENDRA A. LAFFERTY** Fifth great granddaughter of progenitor Nicholas Kegg. **KENDRICK LAFFERTY** Sixth great grandson of progenitor Nicholas Kegg. **KENYON LAFFERTY** Sixth great grandson of progenitor Nicholas Kegg. **KYLER LAFFERTY** Fifth great grandson of progenitor Nicholas Kegg. **LACI LANNE LAFFERTY** Sixth great granddaughter of progenitor Nicholas Kegg. **LIAM LAFFERTY** Seventh great grandson of progenitor Nicholas Kegg. **MELVIN LAFFERTY** aka "Barry", Fifth great grandson of progenitor Nicholas Kegg. **MELVIN E. LAFFERTY** [5259A] aka "Mel" (1949 – 2013) son of Bernard and Adelia (Defrancesco) Lafferty married Mary Ickes with whom he was father of (5). Mel served in the U.S. Army. He was employed with Lithcote, now Union Tank Car, and he enjoyed camping, hunting and working on cars and loved animals. **MILLICENT LAFFERTY** [5260] (1900 – 1947) daughter of Edward and Caroline (Ditch) Lafferty married twice; first to Lawrence Albert Dodson with whom she was mother of (1). Later, she married Charles Wade Huff who critically injured her during a family fight at their home. He pleaded involuntary manslaughter when Millicent never regained consciousness.
MINNIE C. LAFFERTY [5261] (1897 – 1967) daughter of Edward and Caroline (Ditch) Lafferty, married Elmer S. Dodson with whom she was mother of (4). Minnie had been employed for 50 years by the Schwarzenbach-Huber and Altoona Rayon Weaving Companies. She was a member of the 28th Street Church of the Brethren, the auxiliaries of the VFW, Military Order of the Purple Heart and the Lakemont American Legion. **PATRICIA A. LAFFERTY** Fourth great granddaughter of progenitor Nicholas Kegg. **PAUL L. LAFFERTY** Fourth great grandson of progenitor Nicholas Kegg.
PAUL L. LAFFERTY [5262] (1917 – 1969) son of Edward and Caroline (Ditch) Lafferty was a machinist for the Penn Central Railroad. He was a veteran of World War II and, a member the Duncansville VFW.
RANDY S. LAFFERTY Fifth great grandson of progenitor Nicholas Kegg.
RICHARD D. LAFFERTY Fourth great grandson of progenitor Nicholas Kegg.
RICKY JOE LAFFERTY Fifth great grandson of progenitor Nicholas Kegg.
ROBERT F. LAFFERTY Fifth great grandson of progenitor Nicholas Kegg.
ROBERT LEROY LAFFERTY Fourth great grandson of progenitor Nicholas Kegg.
ROBERT LEROY LAFFERTY Fifth great grandson of progenitor Nicholas Kegg.
SHELLI LYNN LAFFERTY Sixth great granddaughter of progenitor Nicholas Kegg.
SHERRI LAFFERTY Sixth great granddaughter of progenitor Nicholas Kegg.
STEPHANIE LAFFERTY Fifth great granddaughter of progenitor Nicholas Kegg.

[5257] Altoona Mirror (PA) Oct 19, 1954, obtained by D. Sue Dible [5258] Altoona Mirror (PA) Oct 14, 1930 [5259] p.21 – Altoona Mirror (PA) Sep 16, 1955 [5259A] Altoona Mirror (PA) Oct 25, 2013, contributed by D. Sue Dible [5260] Altoona Mirror (PA) Nov 12, 1947 [5261] Altoona Mirror (PA) Aug 21, 1967 [5262] Altoona Mirror (PA) Sep 22, 1969

WILLIAM ALAN LAFFERTY [5263] (1937 – 2011) aka "Bill", son of William and Beatrice (Gunnett) Lafferty married twice. He was father of (2). Later, he married Arlene Griffin Tillotson. Bill was a graduate of the former Williamsport Area Community College (now Pennsylvania College of Technology) and worked as an architect/engineer in the Pittston and Towanda areas. Later he was employed for a while as maintenance engineer at St. Joseph's Hospital in Elmira, and eventually as an architect with the Foors firm in Elmira, from which he retired. Following his retirement Bill continued to do consulting work. In his spare time Bill enjoyed golfing and rarely missed an opportunity to be out on the links. He was also a man of great faith in the Lord and expressed his love of Jesus through song. For many years Bill was a familiar face in the choirs of both the Alba Christian Church and the Grover Church of Christ. He also sang as part of the patriotic and spiritually uplifting "America" chorus which traveled the region in the days following September 11th, 2001. It was his way of helping to heal the broken hearts of the people following the events of that tragic day. A genuine "people person," Bill will always be remembered for his outgoing, friendly demeanor and keen sense of humor.

WILLIAM D. LAFFERTY [5264] (1914 – 1989) son of Edward and Caroline (Ditch) Lafferty, married Beatrice M. Gunnett with whom he was father of (3). William retired as a welder from the Samuel Rea Shops, Hollidaysburg of Penn Central. He was an Army veteran, serving in Panama.

LAFOLLETTE

THOMAS EDWARD LAFOLLETTE Sixth great grandson of progenitor Nicholas Kegg.

LAIRD

ALICE MARIE LAIRD [5265] (1929 – 2000) daughter of Guy and Mildred (Shannon) Laird, married Donald Eugene Wicker with whom she was mother of (4). Alice worked at the Mount Ayr cap factory and Clearview Nursing Home in Mount Ayr, Iowa in addition to farming. Alice was a member of the Kellerton Christian Church and the Ladies Aide. **ALMA LAVERN LAIRD** (1917 – 1997) daughter of Vernon and Laura (Maggard) Laird married twice, first to Haldon Dale Fugate with whom she was mother of (3). Later, she married Charles Northey. **AMANDA JANE LAIRD** Sixth great granddaughter of progenitor Nicholas Kegg. **ANN CATHERINE LAIRD** Seventh great granddaughter of progenitor Nicholas Kegg. **APRIL LAIRD** Seventh great granddaughter of progenitor Nicholas Kegg. **ARLENE B. LAIRD** [5266] (1913 – 2005) daughter of Freddie and Bertha (Vance) Laird, married James Oral Stanley with whom she was mother of (1). Arlene was employed as a cook at Mount Ayr Health Care Center. **BARBARA FAYE LAIRD** (1899 – 1981) daughter of William and Martha (McLaughlin) Laird, married Luther Lester Gartin with whom she was mother of (4).

BARBARA JANE LAIRD [5267] (1840 – 1912) daughter of Campbell and Cassander (Cagg) Laird, married John Wyckoff with whom she was mother of (5). Barbara was held by all in highest esteem, she lived with a confident faith in her Redeemer. **BERNICE BERLY LAIRD** (1892 – 1955) daughter of William and Martha (McLaughlin) Laird, married Everett Euritt with whom she was mother of (5). **BERTHA MATILDA LAIRD** [5268] (1901 – 1983) daughter of Herman and Myrtle (Shaner) Laird, married Robert Elroy Higday with whom she was mother of (2). **BEVERLY LOU LAIRD** (1935 – 1983) daughter of Guy and Mildred (Shannon) Laird, married Wayne Clifford Spriggs.

BLANCHE NEVERAH LAIRD [5269] (1843 – 1924) daughter of Campbell and Cassander (Cagg) Laird, married Joseph Wyckoff Sidders with whom she was mother of (11). **BRANDON LAIRD** Seventh great grandson of progenitor Nicholas Kegg. **BRENDON TAYLOR LAIRD** [5270] (1996 – 2014) son of Mike and Andrea (Soetmelk) Laird loved riding horses, especially his horse, Jewels, working on his Ford trucks, working outdoors and doing a man's job, being outdoors, hunting, fishing, welding, and

---

[5263] Daily Review (PA) Apr. 17, 2011 [5264] p.B3 - Altoona Mirror (PA) May 25, 1989 [5265] GenealogyBuff/Ringgold County, Iowa Obituary Collection - 12 [5266] Creston News Advertiser (IA) June 14, 2005 [5267] Bedford Free Press (IA) Oct 17, 1912, transcribed by Julie Johnson IAGenweb.org [5268] Library obituary clipping obtained by D. Sue Dible [5269] The Nance County Journal (NE) March 13, 1924 [5270] Grey Bull Standard (WY) June 12, 2014

spending time with his family and friends. The biggest thing he loved to do was to help others. Brendon was an AMAZING young man with a heart of gold, big brown eyes, a hardy laugh, and his smile that lit up a room. Brendon was creative and loved working with his hands and enjoyed helping everyone, never thinking twice and never expecting anything in return. He never knew a stranger! His future plans were joining the military and becoming a welder. Brendon left this earth too soon but will always be remembered for the remarkable way he made people feel and for the many lives he touched and continues to touch; **BRIAN DOUGLAS LAIRD** Sixth great grandson of progenitor Nicholas Kegg. **BRIANNA MARIE LAIRD** Eighth great granddaughter of progenitor Nicholas Kegg. **CHARLES WARREN LAIRD** [5271] (1863 – 1930) son of John and Matilda (Dobson) Laird married twice; first to Lavina Kinder with whom he was father of (6). Later, he married Anna Jane Bryan with whom he was father of (3). During his early manhood Charles was a prosperous farmer. **CLAUDE M. LAIRD** (1907 – 1907) son of Charles and Anna (Bryan) Laird. **CLEO MARIE LAIRD** [5271A] (1896 – 1925) daughter of William and Martha (McLaughlin) Laird married George Grigg with whom she was mother of (1). Cleo spent most of her short life in preparation for service. She graduated from the eighth grade in the country school at eleven years of age and then entered the Mount Ayr high school, where she took the normal training course and graduated with honor, being congratulated and notified by the State examination board that she had received the next highest average grade in the state, being excelled only by a girl from Manning, Iowa. She then taught for two years in country schools, after which she entered the State University in Iowa City, where she pursued her studies for one and one-half years. At this time humanity, and especially our own country, was calling loudly for help and service and, true to her aspirations, she answered the call by enlisting for service in June 1918, and enrolled in the army nurses' training school from which she graduated in June 1921, and was discharged from the army service December 13, 1921. She served in Camp Grant, Ft. Sheridan and Letterman Army Hospitals and also took affiliation work at the children's hospital and lying-in hospital, Chicago, and the Leland Stanford hospital in California, and, although neither shattered by shot nor shell, Cleo truly gave her life for her country as any martyr. **CLYDE ARTHUR LAIRD** (1899 – 1955) son of Herman and Myrtle (Shaner) Laird, married Ollie Bea Dady with whom he was father of (3). **CODY LAIRD** Seventh great grandson of progenitor Nicholas Kegg. **CRYSTAL LAIRD** Eighth great granddaughter of progenitor Nicholas Kegg. **DAISY EDNA LAIRD** (1915 – 1979) daughter of Rollie and Agnes (Tunney) Laird, married Alex A. Ulman. **DARCI R. LAIRD** Eighth great granddaughter of progenitor Nicholas Kegg. **DEAN J. LAIRD** Eighth great grandson of progenitor Nicholas Kegg. **DEBRA J. LAIRD** Sixth great granddaughter of progenitor Nicholas Kegg. **DENNIS ELVIN LAIRD** (1919 – 1993) son of Vernon and Laura (Maggard) Laird, married Cora Mae Wilson. **DONALD KEITH LAIRD** [5272] (1932 – 2006) aka "Pinky", son of Guy and Mildred (Shannon) Laird, married Helen M. Payton with whom he was father of (2). Pinky was a veteran of the Korean War. He was employed as a construction worker. **DOYLE DADY LAIRD** [5272A] (1924 – 1944) son of Clyde and Ollie Bea (Dady) Laird. Soundman 2C US Navy, a WWII Casualty, killed in action. **DUANE MELVIN LAIRD** [5273] (1932 – 2003) son of Russell and Winnie (Payton) Laird, married Merna Faye Mathany with whom he was father of (5). Duane worked as a truck driver for Spencer Foods for several years and for Midwest Coast until his retirement. He was a member of the Spencer Municipal Gold Course. **EARL EDWARD LAIRD** (1912 – 1973) son of Rollie and Agnes (Tunney) Laird. **EDNA MAUDE LAIRD** [5274] (1892 – 1922) daughter of Edward and Montana (Merritt) Laird, married William Thomas Timby with whom she was mother of (3). After the death of her parents, Edna found the home with which she is always associated under the roof of her father's friends, Mr. and Mrs. Frank Sheldon. In this home Edna blossomed into her attractive womanhood. She graduated from the Mount Ayr high school, then eager for higher training, twice entered the Rockford College for women at Rockford, Ill., and attended Monmouth College for a portion of one year. But ill health compelled her to abandon each of these attempts to complete her scholastic training. In

---

[5271] Mount Ayr Record-News transcribed by Sharon R. Becker IAGenWeb.org [5271A] Mount Ayr Record-News, 1925 contributed by Sharon R. Becker [5272] Creston News Advertiser (IA) Jan 4, 2006, transcribed by Sharon R. Becker IAGenWeb.org [5272A] ancestry.com Casualties from World War II for Navy, Marine, and Coast Guard Personnel [5273] p.2A Daily Reporter (IA) Apr 5, 2003 [5274] Mount Ayr Record-News, 1922 transcribed by Sharon R. Becker IAGenWeb.org

her girlhood Edna made confession of her faith in the Christian church of Kellerton, but when her home was established in Mount Ayr she entered the fellowship of the United Presbyterian church where she has since maintained her faith, serving loyally and efficiently. She was especially active, teaching in the Sabbath school and assisting in the Junior work, always alert and interested in the welfare of the church. **EDWARD HANSON LAIRD** (1863 – 1870) son of Campbell and Cassander (Cagg) Laird. **EDWARD PARKER LAIRD** (1869 – 1907) son of John and Matilda (Dobson) Laird married twice; first to Montana Lillie Bell Merritt with whom he was father of (1). Later, he married Jennie Lee Burchett. **EFFIE ENOLA LAIRD** [5275] (1890 – 1966) daughter of Herman and Myrtle (Shaner) Laird, married Clyde Clifton Small with whom she was mother of (7). **ELLADEEN RUTH LAIRD** [5275A] aka "Deannie" (1925 – 2017) daughter of Russell and Winnie (Payton) Laird married twice, first to Karl Layton McGahuey with whom she was mother of (2) Elladeen was a hard worker and did many things on the farm and for her family: she milked cows, drove the tractor, put up hay, and then fixed all of their meals. Elladeen may have driven all the tractors, but she never drove the corn planter or the combine! Elladeen had a strawberry patch, ducks and kittens. She loved to go mushroom hunting, ride the four-wheeler and check cows. In her spare time, she did embroidery. Elladeen and Karl enjoyed dancing, playing cards with friends. **ELMA R. LAIRD** (1891 – 1901) daughter of Charles and Lavina (Kinder) Laird. **ELVA LAIRD** (1891 – 1891) daughter of Charles and Lavina (Kinder) Laird. **ELZA ADELBERT LAIRD** [5276] (1871 – 1945) son of John and Matilda (Dobson) Laird married twice; first to Josie Merritt with whom he was father of (1). Later, he married Jennie May (Grindrod) Stuck with whom he was father of (2). Elza commenced farming and continued this occupation for 47 years. He was remembered as an honest, conscientious, hard-working father and neighbor. **EMILY LAIRD** Eighth great granddaughter of progenitor Nicholas Kegg. **EMMA ADELIA LAIRD** (1846 – 1907) daughter of Campbell and Cassander (Cagg) Laird, married Joseph H. Wyckoff with whom she was mother of (5). **ERIC LAIRD** Eighth great grandson of progenitor Nicholas Kegg. **ERIC BRUCE LAIRD** Sixth great grandson of progenitor Nicholas Kegg. **ERLIN E. LAIRD** (1871 – 1878) son of Samuel and Sarah (Caldwell) Laird. **ESTHER DERILLA LAIRD** [5277] (1910 – 1977) daughter of Rollie and Agnes (Tunney) Laird, married William Edward Hammel. **ETHAN LAIRD** Eighth great grandson of progenitor Nicholas Kegg. **EVA DELOME LAIRD** [5277A] (1919 – 2017) daughter of Clyde and Ollie Bea (Dady) Laird married Robert James Swift with whom she was mother of (2). Eva enjoyed reading, Canasta and Bingo. **EVA ETHEL LAIRD** [5278] (1886 – 1985) daughter of Samuel and Sarah (Caldwell) Laird, married Henry Harley Casady with whom she was mother of (4). **FLORENCE LAIRD** [5279] (1901 – 1964) daughter of Homer and Mary (Davis) Laird, married John Elmer Gray with whom she was mother of (3). **FLORENCE M. LAIRD** (1894 – 1901) daughter of Elza and Josie (Merritt) Laird. **FLOYD D. LAIRD** (1892 – 1971) son of Samuel and Sarah (Caldwell) Laird, married Laura M. Shiels with whom he was father of (1). **FRANK HERBERT LAIRD** [5280] (1860 – 1932) son of Campbell and Cassander (Cagg) Laird, married Emma Lucinda (Shaha) Giles. Frank was a member of the Salem Evangelical church for many years. He was quiet and unassuming he won the respect of his neighbors and friends and all with whom he came in contact by his everyday life. **FRANTIE LOUISE LAIRD** (1912 – 1991) daughter of Vernon and Laura (Maggard) Laird married Harold Melbourne Tarter with whom she was mother of (1). **FREDDIE EMERY LAIRD** (1893 – 1955) son of Herman and Myrtle (Shaner) Laird, married Bertha Vance with whom he was father of (5). **GAIL DEAN LAIRD** Sixth great grandson of progenitor Nicholas Kegg. **GARLAND LAIRD** Sixth great grandson of progenitor Nicholas Kegg. **GARNITA ELLOUISE LAIRD** [5280A] (1930 – 2014) daughter of Russell and Winnie (Payton) Laird married Bill Vere Ewart with whom she was mother of (3). After 34 years working for the Department of Agriculture, Garnita obtained her Real Estate Broker's License and sold real estate under Strictly Farm Realty. She served as Mayor for the City of Bedford, Iowa, a position she thoroughly

---

[5275] The Indianapolis News (IN) March 7, 1966 [5275A] Mount Ayr Record-News (IA) Jan 25, 2017 [5276] Mount Ayr Record News (IA) Oct 4, 1945 transcribed by Sharon R. Becker IAGenWeb.org [5277] IAGen Web.org posted by Errin Wilker from newspaper clipping hand dated 1977 [5277A] The Reporter (CA) July 6, 2017 [5278] St. Joseph Gazette (MO) Feb 22, 1985 [5279] Lenox Time Table (IA) Jan 12, 1964 transcribed by Lorelei Rusco IAGenWeb.org [5280] The Mount Ayr Record-News, 1932 transcribed by Sharon R. Becker IAGenWeb.org [5280A] Mount Ayr Record-News (IA) Dec 30, 2014

enjoyed. Garnita was a member of the Bedford American Legion Auxiliary, serving as President in the 1950s, the Order of Eastern Star, President of IASCO during her time with the ASCS office. Garnita enjoyed the outdoors and enjoyed boating and even owned her own jet ski. While living in Kimberling City, she enjoyed the entertainment in the Branson area. Over the years she enjoyed collecting porcelain head dolls. Later in life she was a member of the Red Hat Society. **GARY LEE LAIRD** [5280B] (1945 – 2010) son of Herman and Dorothy (Pyle) Laird married Linda Lee Erwin with whom he was father of (1). For nearly 20 years, Gary was employed as a meat cutter with Tyson Foods in Perry. He was an avid NASCAR Racing fan and enjoyed golfing, fishing and gardening. **GERALD DEAN LAIRD** (1921 – 1988) son of Guy and Mildred (Shannon) Laird. **GLEN LAIRD** [5281] (1954 – 2019) aka "Boss" son of Herman Eugene and Dorothy (Pyle) Laird married Nancy Summerson with whom he was father of (2). Boss was employed as a truck driver for various farmers in the area. **GOLDA LAIRD** (1900 – 1915) daughter of Samuel and Sarah (Caldwell) Laird. **GORDON LAIRD** Sixth great grandson of progenitor Nicholas Kegg. **GRACE BELLE LAIRD** (1878 – 1976) aka "Gracie", daughter of Samuel and Sarah (Caldwell) Laird, married George W. Knittle with whom she was mother of (3). **GREGORY STEVEN LAIRD** Sixth great grandson of progenitor Nicholas Kegg. **GREYSEN LAIRD** Eighth great grandson of progenitor Nicholas Kegg. **GUY FRANKLIN LAIRD** (1902 – 1979) son of Herman and Myrtle (Shaner) Laird, married Mildred Beatrice Shannon with whom he was father of (8). **HANNAH LAIRD** Seventh great granddaughter of progenitor Nicholas Kegg. **HELEN FRANCIS LAIRD** [5282] (1910 – 2006) daughter of Elza and Jennie (Grindrod) Laird, married Peres A. Tisdel with whom she was mother of (2). Helen managed the food services at the University of Northern Colorado for many years. She was a member of the First United Presbyterian Church, Greeley, the Knife and Fork Club and the Greeley Woman's Club. She enjoyed her family, travel, her church work, gardening and antique collecting and was an excellent tailor and seamstress. Helen was very proud of having climbed the Great Wall of China and Ayer's Rock in Australia. **HERMAN EUGENE LAIRD** [5283] (1923 – 2002) son of Guy and Mildred (Shannon) Laird, married Dorothy Mildred Pyle with whom he was father of (6). Herman was a farmer and had worked for Osmundson Mfg. Co. in Perry before retiring. **HERMAN LUCIUS LAIRD** (1867 – 1933) aka "Bud", son of John and Matilda (Dobson) Laird, married Myrtle Agnes Shaner with whom he was father of (6). **HOMER LLOYD LAIRD** [5284] (1875 – 1937) son of John and Matilda (Dobson) Laird, married Mary Lenora Davis with whom he was father of (1). Homer enlisted as a soldier in the U. S. army during the Spanish-American war but because of illness he was sent home and received an honorable discharge. Homer was a kind and loving husband and father and a friendly neighbor. **IRMA JEANNETTE LAIRD** [5284A] (1913 – 1989) daughter of Vernon and Laura (Maggard) Laird married twice. After a divorce, she married Maurice John Mondary with whom she was mother of (1). A registered nurse, Irma was a graduate of Cook County, Ill., Hospital School of Nursing and had worked at various military hospitals. **IVAH FERN LAIRD** (1889 – 1968) daughter of William and Martha (McLaughlin) Laird, married Walter Edgar Swank with whom she was mother of (6). **JAY SCOTT LAIRD** Sixth great grandson of progenitor Nicholas Kegg. **JAY SCOTT LAIRD JR.** Seventh great grandson of progenitor Nicholas Kegg. **JOHN WESLEY LAIRD** (1839 – 1916) son of Campbell and Cassander (Cagg) Laird, married Matilda Walker Dobson with whom he was father of (8). **JULIE LAIRD** Sixth great granddaughter of progenitor Nicholas Kegg. **KAREN LAIRD** Sixth great granddaughter of progenitor Nicholas Kegg. **KATHIE LAIRD** Fifth great granddaughter of progenitor Nicholas Kegg. **KEITH LAIRD** Sixth great grandson of progenitor Nicholas Kegg. **KENNETH LEE LAIRD** [5285] (1924 – 2003) aka "Ted", son of Guy and Mildred (Shannon) Laird, married Juanita Sevier with whom he was father of (3). **KEVIN RUSSELL LAIRD** [5285A] (1958 – 2007) son of Duane and Merna (Mathany) Laird married Jody Baldwin with whom he was father of (3). Kevin served in the United States Army. After his honorable discharge from military service, he lived in

---

[5280B] Des Moines Register (IA) July 13, 2010 [5281] The Perry News (IA) April 28, 2019, obtained by D. Sue Dible [5282] The Greeley Tribune (CO) Mar 1, 2006, obtained by D. Sue Dible [5283] p.26 Des Moines Register (IA) Nov 7, 2002 [5284] Lenox Time Table (IA) May 6, 1937 transcribed by Lorelei Rusco IAGenWeb.org [5284A] p.39- The Indianapolis Star (IN) May 9, 1989 [5285] Afton Star-Enterprise (IA) March 6, 2003 [5285A] Spencer Daily Reporter (IA) July 17, 2007

Colorado for a short while. He returned to the Spencer area and worked at Swift and Company in Worthington, Minn. **KRISTINA LAIRD** Sixth great granddaughter of progenitor Nicholas Kegg. **LADONNA LAIRD** Sixth great granddaughter of progenitor Nicholas Kegg. **LANNY LAIRD** Seventh great grandson of progenitor Nicholas Kegg. **LARRY LAIRD** Sixth great grandson of progenitor Nicholas Kegg. **LARRY LEROY LAIRD** [5285B] (1938 – 2006) son of Russell and Winnie (Payton) Laird married Lorrena McMains with whom he was father of (4). Larry retired from the Air Force in Cheyenne then, worked for DePaul Hospital, Warren Federal Credit Union and Unicover Corporation. Larry was active in St. Mary's Church and the Knights of Columbus. **LAURIE ANN LAIRD** Sixth great granddaughter of progenitor Nicholas Kegg. **LEE FRANKLIN LAIRD** Eighth great grandson of progenitor Nicholas Kegg. **LEE GRIFFIN LAIRD** Sixth great grandson of progenitor Nicholas Kegg. **LEO C. LAIRD** (1895 – 1968) son of William and Martha (McLaughlin) Laird married twice, first to Marie E. Wood with whom he was father of (1). Later, he married Vona Verta German Vaughn. **LILLIE ETNA LAIRD** (1882 – 1959) daughter of Samuel and Sarah (Caldwell) Laird, married Chris Wehrle with whom she was mother of (4). **LINDA I LAIRD** [5286] (1961 – 1998) daughter of Larry and Lorrena (McMains) Laird married twice; first to Mr. Donaldson with whom she was mother of (2). Later, she married Jeffrey M. Knapp with whom she was mother of (1). Linda was a pharmacist employed at Veterans Hospital in Des Moines, Iowa. She was a member of the Church of Jesus Christ of Latter-day Saints. **LOREN LAIRD** [5287] (1889 – 1955) aka "Ray", son of Samuel and Sarah (Caldwell) Laird. Ray had been involved in a tractor accident at the Elgie Drake farm where he was fatally injured. **LOUISE EVELYN LAIRD** [5288] (1927 – 1980) daughter of Guy and Mildred (Shannon) Laird, married Ralph Warren Ogier with whom she was mother of (2). Louise worked in the housekeeping departments of Story County Hospital and Mary Greeley Hospital. She was a member of the United Methodist Church. **LUELLA W. LAIRD** (1865 – 1928) daughter of John and Matilda (Dobson) Laird, married John L. Thompson with whom she was mother of (8). **LYLE VANCE LAIRD** (1920 – 1999) son of Freddie and Bertha (Vance) Laird, married Minnie L. Reed with whom he was father of (1). Lyle was a veteran of WWII. **LYLE VANCE LAIRD** aka "Butch", Sixth great grandson of progenitor Nicholas Kegg. **MABEL ANNA LAIRD** (1877 – 1961) daughter of John and Matilda (Dobson) Laird, married Emery A. Saltzman with whom she was mother of (3). **MARJORIE BEA LAIRD** (1921 – 1997) daughter of Clyde and Ollie (Dady) Laird, married William Warren Johnson with whom she was mother of (3). **MARK LAIRD** Sixth great grandson of progenitor Nicholas Kegg. **MARTHA LAIRD** Sixth great granddaughter of progenitor Nicholas Kegg. **MARY E. LAIRD** Fourth great granddaughter of progenitor Nicholas Kegg. **MARY MADELINE LAIRD** (1903 – 1988) daughter of William and Lottie (Swank) Laird, married Dr. Andrew Ritan with whom she was mother of (2). **MATTIE PEARL LAIRD** (1884 – 1973) daughter of Samuel and Sarah (Caldwell) Laird, married William Absolom Knittle with whom she was mother of (4). **MICHAEL LAIRD** Seventh great grandson of progenitor Nicholas Kegg. **MICHAEL DUANE LAIRD** (1954 – 1979) son of Duane and Merna (Mathany) Laird. **MYRTLE ENOLA LAIRD** (1871 – 1959) daughter of Samuel and Sarah Elizabeth (Caldwell) Laird, married Clarence Austa Jacobs with whom she was mother of (1). - **NEVA LAIRD** [5288A] (1920 – 1987) daughter of Rollie and Agnes Ella (Tunney) Laird married Roscoe Elmer Mosbarger. Neva was a homemaker and a member of St. Joseph's Catholic Church. **NORA E. LAIRD** (1887 – 1892) daughter of Charles and Lavina (Kinder) Laird. **NORMA ALICE LAIRD** [5289] (1928 – 2007) daughter of Vernon and Cora (Stewart) Laird married twice; first to Honor Monroe Tutwiler with whom she was mother of (2). Later, she married Everett Eugene Wagoner. Norma was a lifetime member of the Hoopeston Women's VFW Auxiliary. She was a caregiver to the elderly and to veterans. Norma also raised foster children for many years. **OWEN LAIRD** son of Charles and Lavina (Kinder) Laird. **OWEN EMERY LAIRD** (1917 – 1963) son of Rollie and Agnes (Tunney) Laird was a WWII, and Korea veteran having served in the U.S. Navy.

[5285B] Wyoming Tribune-Eagle (WY) Aug 10, 2006 [5286] Wyoming Tribune-Eagle (Cheyenne, WY) Aug 8, 1998 [5287] Mount Ayr Record-News (IA) Aug 18, 1955, transcribed by Sharon R. Becker IAGenWeb.org [5288] Nevada Journal (IA) Posted By: Linda H Meyers IAGenWeb.org [5288A] p.9A- The Des Moines Register (IA) June 15, 1987 [5289] Commercial News (IL) Mar 30, 2007

PAULINE ELLEN LAIRD (5290) (1925 – 2020) daughter of Fred and Bertha (Vance) Laird married Albert Morris Macauley with whom she was mother of (2). Pauline was a wonderful caretaker for her entire family. She babysat for years for a special family then worked at Dick's Laundromat. **RAYMOND CLAUDE LAIRD** (1922 – 2002) son of Freddie and Bertha (Vance) Laird, married Evonne Marie Davidson. **RICHARD EDMUND LAIRD** (5291) (1917 – 2010) son of Elza and Jennie (Grindrod) Laird married twice; first to Lena Waggoner. Later to Glatis. He was father of (3). **RICK LAIRD** Seventh great grandson of progenitor Nicholas Kegg. **ROLLIE FOREST LAIRD** (5292) (1885 – 1957) son of Charles and Lavina (Kinder) Laird, married Agnes Ella Tunney with whom he was father of (6). His lifetime occupation was farming. **ROSELEE ANN LAIRD** (1918 – 2004) daughter of Freddie and Bertha (Vance) Laird married twice; first to Dean Corman Whitson and later, to Carl Peter Brewer. **ROY C. LAIRD** (1880 – 1890) son of Samuel and Sarah (Caldwell) Laird. **RUBY DAYLE LAIRD** (1898 – 1982) daughter of William and Martha (McLaughlin) Laird, married Victor Rufus Skinner. **RUSSELL WALKER LAIRD** (1907 – 1985) son of Herman and Agnes (Shaner) Laird, married Winnie M. Payton with whom he was father of (5). **SAMANTHA LAIRD** Seventh great granddaughter of progenitor Nicholas Kegg. **SAMUEL A. LAIRD** (5292) (1853 – 1929) son of Campbell and Cassander (Cagg) Laird, married Sarah Elizabeth Ann Caldwell with whom he was father of (11). Samuel was converted in 1891 and united with the Salem United Evangelical church. He was a charter member of that organization and has since held membership there. He was not boastful of Christian graces but led a quiet, consistent Christian life, always standing for right and denouncing evil. He had told loved ones that he had put his trust and his all in the hands of the Lord and the end came peacefully. **SANDRA LAIRD** Sixth great granddaughter of progenitor Nicholas Kegg. **SARAH CATHERINE LAIRD** (5293) (1855 – 1882) aka "Sadie", daughter of Campbell and Cassander (Cagg) Laird, married William Perry Johnson with whom she was mother of (1). **SHANE LAIRD** Seventh great grandson of progenitor Nicholas Kegg. **SHIRLEY SUE LAIRD** (5293A) (1937 – 2004) daughter of Guy and Mildred (Shannon) Laird married Ivan C. Stephens with whom she was mother of (3). Shirley graduated from Mount Ayr High School in 1956 as valedictorian. She worked as a stenographer for Clyde Lesan and W. B. Cinning Company two years before becoming a homemaker. **SYLVIA LEOTA LAIRD** (1892 -?) daughter of Charles and Lavina (Kinder) Laird, married Martin Edward Davis with whom she was mother of (9). **TONY LAIRD** Sixth great grandson of progenitor Nicholas Kegg. **TRAVIS LAIRD** Seventh great grandson of progenitor Nicholas Kegg. **TRENT LAIRD** Seventh great grandson of progenitor Nicholas Kegg. **TROY DEAN LAIRD** Seventh great grandson of progenitor Nicholas Kegg. **VERLENE JANE LAIRD** (1922 – 1995) daughter of Leo and Marie (Wood) Laird, married Wilbur Lee Buck with whom she was mother of (1). **VERNON L. LAIRD** (5294) (1929 – 2014) son of Vernon and Cora (Stewart) Laird married twice; He was father of (6) and later, married Bessie L. (Sprague) Carlson. Vernon took a Business Course through LaSalle Extension University in Chicago, IL. He worked as the department manager at Montgomery Ward in Hoopeston for approximately 12 years. Later, he started working for Bohn Heat Transfer in Danville and other plant locations in Michigan and Atlanta. Vernon served in the United States Marine Corps for 2 years. He had also served on the Rankin High School Board and the Rankin Board of Trustees. He was a member of the American Legion and a past member of the Rankin Lions Club. Vernon was also the past coordinator of the Rankin Crime Watch Program. **VERNON LUTHER LAIRD** (1895 – 1971) son of Charles and Anna Jane (Bryan) Laird married three times; first to Laura Hazel Maggard with whom he was father of (5). Then, married Cora Alice Griffin Stewart with whom he was father of (2). Later, he married Inez L. Bird Thiess. **VICKI LAIRD** Sixth great granddaughter of progenitor Nicholas Kegg. **VIOLA VELMA LAIRD** (5294A) (1916 – 2000) daughter of Vernon and Laura (Maggard) Laird married twice, first to Glenn Leroy Godden with whom she was mother of (2). Later, she married William Peck. Viola's

---

(5290) Times-Republican (IA) Sep 26, 2020, obtained D. Sue Dible (5291) Denver Post (CO) June 16, 2010 (5292) Iowa obituary clipping transcribed by Mr. & Mrs. James F. (Jean) Fugate (5293) Ringgold Record, 1882 transcribed by Sharon R. Becker IAGenWeb.org (5293A) Creston News Advertiser (IA) Apr 30, 2004, contributed by Sharon R. Becker (5294) Anderson Funeral Home, Hoopeston, Ill. (5294A) Genealogy Buff Ringgold County, Iowa Obituary Collection - 19.

earlier years she worked in the Hyde and Vredenberg grocery store in Kellerton, Iowa. She worked in nursing for many years while living in Nebraska and worked for several years for Campbell Soup in Tecumseh, Nebraska. Viola was a person who enjoyed her home and the company of her grandchildren. She liked to keep up on the news whether local or worldwide and kept up on events with many hours watching CNN. **VIVIAN LAIRD** Sixth great granddaughter of progenitor Nicholas Kegg.
WAYNE EVERETT LAIRD [5295] (1919 – 1920) son of Rollie and Agnes (Tunney) Laird. **WILLIAM CAMPBELL LAIRD** (1857 – 1934) son of Campbell and Cassander (Cagg) Laird, married Martha Jane McLaughlin with whom he was father of (6). **WILLIAM LAWSON LAIRD** (1882 -?) son of John and Matilda (Dobson) Laird, married Lottie Ellen Swank with whom he was father of (1). **WINNIE LEONE LAIRD** (1894 – 1932) daughter of Samuel and Sarah (Caldwell) Laird, married William Norman Stanley with whom she was mother of (1). **WINONA LAIRD** (1910 – 1925) daughter of Charles and Anna Jane (Bryan) Laird.

LALLATHIN

BRITTANY DEANNE LALLATHIN Eighth great granddaughter of progenitor Nicholas Kegg. **JASON LEE LALLATHIN** [5296] (1972 – 2019) son of Gary and Janine (Smith) Lallathin was an adventurous man; he wasn't afraid of much. His favorite pastimes were all things nature, fishing, and being a collector of many things. **SERENITY F. LALLATHIN** Eighth great granddaughter of progenitor Nicholas Kegg. **LANA LALLATHIN** Eighth great granddaughter of progenitor Nicholas Kegg. **SHANE LALLATHIN** (1970 – 1971) son of Gary and Janine (Smith) Lallathin. **SHANNON SCOTT LALLATHIN** Seventh great grandson of progenitor Nicholas Kegg. **SHAWN LALLATHIN** Seventh great grandson of progenitor Nicholas Kegg.

LAM

ALEX LAM Eighth great grandson of progenitor Nicholas Kegg.

LAMBERT

AUSTIN TAYLOR LAMBERT Sixth great grandson of progenitor Nicholas Kegg.
MORGAN CHASE LAMBERT Sixth great grandson of progenitor Nicholas Kegg.

LAMP

JENA DIANE LAMP Seventh great granddaughter of progenitor Nicholas Kegg.
MATTHEW PAUL LAMP Seventh great grandson of progenitor Nicholas Kegg.

LANCELOTTI

BRADLEY LANCELOTTI Sixth great grandson of progenitor Nicholas Kegg.
DANIEL LANCELOTTI Sixth great grandson of progenitor Nicholas Kegg.

LAND

KAREN SUE LAND Sixth great granddaughter of progenitor Nicholas Kegg. **KENT LAND** Sixth great grandson of progenitor Nicholas Kegg. **KEVIN LAND** Sixth great grandson of progenitor Nicholas Kegg. **MALOREIGH LAND** Eighth great granddaughter of progenitor Nicholas Kegg. **SHELLEY LAND** Sixth great granddaughter of progenitor Nicholas Kegg.

[5295] Iowa obituary clipping transcribed by Mr. & Mrs. James F. (Jean) Fugate [5296] Advocate (OH) Aug. 27, 2019

THOMAS LAND Sixth great grandson of progenitor Nicholas Kegg.
TODD LAND Sixth great grandson of progenitor Nicholas Kegg.

LANDERS

ABIGAIL RENEE LANDERS Eighth great granddaughter of progenitor Nicholas Kegg.
BRITTANY LANDERS Eighth great granddaughter of progenitor Nicholas Kegg.
JONATHAN LANDERS Eighth great grandson of progenitor Nicholas Kegg.
MCKENZIE LANDERS Eighth great granddaughter of progenitor Nicholas Kegg.

LANDIS

KEITH A. LANDIS Fifth great grandson of progenitor Nicholas Kegg.
KIM LANDIS Fifth great grandson of progenitor Nicholas Kegg.
KRISTINE LOUISE LANDIS Fifth great granddaughter of progenitor Nicholas Kegg.

LANE

BRANDON JOSEPH LANE Sixth great grandson of progenitor Nicholas Kegg.
KAITLYN ANN LANE Sixth great granddaughter of progenitor Nicholas Kegg.

LANG

REAGAN LANG Eighth great grandson of progenitor Nicholas Kegg.
RILEY LANG Eighth great grandchild of progenitor Nicholas Kegg.

LANKEY

BRADLEY LANKEY Seventh great grandson of progenitor Nicholas Kegg.
ISAAC LANKEY Seventh great grandson of progenitor Nicholas Kegg.
JORDAN LANKEY Seventh great grandson of progenitor Nicholas Kegg.

LANNEN

JEREMY R. LANNEN Seventh great grandson of progenitor Nicholas Kegg.

LANNING

ANTOINETTE LANNING Sixth great granddaughter of progenitor Nicholas Kegg.

LANTHORN

BARBARA LANTHORN Fifth great granddaughter of progenitor Nicholas Kegg.
HEATHER LANTHORN Sixth great granddaughter of progenitor Nicholas Kegg.
THOMAS LANTHORN Fifth great grandson of progenitor Nicholas Kegg.

LAPLANTE

EVA ELIZABETH LAPLANTE Eighth great granddaughter of progenitor Nicholas Kegg.
JOSEPH MATTHEW LAPLANTE Eighth great grandson of progenitor Nicholas Kegg.

LARA

COURTNEY PATRICIA LARA Seventh great granddaughter of progenitor Nicholas Kegg.
LINDSEY ROSE LARA Seventh great granddaughter of progenitor Nicholas Kegg.

LASER

LISA LOUISE LASER Sixth great granddaughter of progenitor Nicholas Kegg.
VICKI ANN LASER Sixth great granddaughter of progenitor Nicholas Kegg.

LASHLEY

JAMES LASHLEY Seventh great grandson of progenitor Nicholas Kegg.
RICHELLE DENAE LASHLEY Sixth great granddaughter of progenitor Nicholas Kegg.

LASLEY

BEN LASLEY Eighth great grandson of progenitor Nicholas Kegg.
JOSHUA THOMAS LASLEY aka "Josh", Seventh great grandson of progenitor Nicholas Kegg.
ZACHERY W. LASLEY aka "Zac", Seventh great grandson of progenitor Nicholas Kegg.

LASTER

ALEX LASTER Seventh great grandson of progenitor Nicholas Kegg.
ZAK LASTER Seventh great grandson of progenitor Nicholas Kegg.

LATHAM

AMBRIE ROSE LATHAM Sixth great granddaughter of progenitor Nicholas Kegg.
KAYLIE ELIZABETH LATHAM Sixth great granddaughter of progenitor Nicholas Kegg.
ROWAN EMRYS LATHAM Sixth great grandson of progenitor Nicholas Kegg.
RYAN LATHAM Sixth great grandson of progenitor Nicholas Kegg.
SHANNON LATHAM Sixth great grandson of progenitor Nicholas Kegg.

LAURSEN

CONNER LAURSEN Seventh great grandson of progenitor Nicholas Kegg.
RYAN LAURSEN Seventh great grandson of progenitor Nicholas Kegg.

LAVOLD

MARIAH LYNN LAVOLD Seventh great granddaughter of progenitor Nicholas Kegg.

LAWLES

LEONARD R. LAWLES aka "Chuck", Sixth great grandson of progenitor Nicholas Kegg.

LAWRENCE

AUDREY MAY LAWRENCE Eighth great granddaughter of progenitor Nicholas Kegg.

GABRIAL DEAN LAWRENCE Eighth great grandson of progenitor Nicholas Kegg.
GORDON D. LAWRENCE Seventh great grandson of progenitor Nicholas Kegg.
JULIA KATHERINE LAWRENCE Eighth great granddaughter of progenitor Nicholas Kegg.
MIKAILA RENA LAWRENCE Eighth great granddaughter of progenitor Nicholas Kegg.
STACY LAWRENCE Seventh great granddaughter of progenitor Nicholas Kegg.

LAWSON

BETTY LAWSON Sixth great granddaughter of progenitor Nicholas Kegg. **BETTY JEANNE LAWSON** [5297] (1921 – 2013) daughter of Everett and Gladys (Wells) Lawson married twice; first to Kenneth Roger Davis with whom she was mother of (4). Later, she married Harold Lee Chandler. **CHRISTINA LYNNE LAWSON** Seventh great granddaughter of progenitor Nicholas Kegg. **DAVID LAWSON** Sixth great grandson of progenitor Nicholas Kegg. **DEBORAH LAWSON** Sixth great granddaughter of progenitor Nicholas Kegg. **DONNA KAYE LAWSON** [5298] (1956 – 2009) daughter of Everett and Virginia (Kilbury) Lawson was mother of (1). She married Robert E. Orsborn. Donna was employed at Goodyear. **EVERETT RAMON LAWSON** [5299] (1923 – 1978) aka "Ray", son of Everett and Gladys (Wells) Lawson, married Virginia Lee Kilbury with whom he was father of (10). **JEFFREY G. LAWSON** Sixth great grandson of progenitor Nicholas Kegg. **KATHY ELAINE LAWSON** Sixth great granddaughter of progenitor Nicholas Kegg. **LAURA DIANE LAWSON** (1949 – 1950) daughter of Everett and Virginia (Kilbury) Lawson. **MICHAEL B. LAWSON** Sixth great grandson of progenitor Nicholas Kegg. **MICHELE LAWSON** Sixth great granddaughter of progenitor Nicholas Kegg. **RICHARD WAYNE LAWSON** [5300] (1931 – 2005) son of Everett and Gladys (Wells) Lawson, married Jane Marie Wester with whom he was father of (3). Richard served with the 1st Marine Division in the Korean War, a member of the "Chosen Few." The conditions he encountered there affected his health for the rest of his life. Richard was a member of the Veterans of Foreign Wars and the American Legion of Bandon. In Tucson, he was a member of Pipefitters Local 741. **ROXANN LAWSON** Sixth great granddaughter of progenitor Nicholas Kegg. **SHERRY LAWSON** Sixth great granddaughter of progenitor Nicholas Kegg. **STACY RENEE LAWSON** Seventh great granddaughter of progenitor Nicholas Kegg. **STEVEN RAY LAWSON** (? – 1952) son of Everett and Virginia (Kilbury) Lawson. **SYLVIA ANN LAWSON** Fifth great granddaughter of progenitor Nicholas Kegg. **TERRY RAMON LAWSON** Sixth great grandson of progenitor Nicholas Kegg. **TIMOTHY RYAN LAWSON** Seventh great grandson of progenitor Nicholas Kegg.

LAY

BRIAN SCOTT LAY Sixth great grandson of progenitor Nicholas Kegg. **DAVID LEE LAY** Fifth great grandson of progenitor Nicholas Kegg. **FRANCIS MARTIN LAY** aka "Frank" [5301] (1940 – 2020) son of Cleo and Mary (Messinger) Lay married Cheryl K. Fredrickson with whom he was father of (1). Frank proudly served his Country in the United States Air Force during the Viet Nam Era. After his service he moved to the Hereford area and worked for Frito Lay and Hereford Bi-Products as a security guard. Frank was a kind and gentle man who would help anyone needing assistance.

LAYMAN

ALEXIS LEE-ANN LAYMAN [5302] (2013 – 2013) daughter of Wesley and Laura (Zeigler) Layman.
BETH ANN LAYMAN Sixth great granddaughter of progenitor Nicholas Kegg.
WESLEY JOHN LAYMAN Sixth great grandson of progenitor Nicholas Kegg.

[5297] Columbus Dispatch (OH) Oct. 1, 2013 [5298] p.4B-Columbus Dispatch (OH) Mar 18, 2009 [5299] Library obituary clipping obtained by D. Sue Dible [5300] Green Valley News & Sun (AZ) Feb 2, 2005 [5301] Parkside Chapel Hereford, TX

LAYTON

ANDREA DIANE LAYTON Seventh great granddaughter of progenitor Nicholas Kegg. **ANDREW D. LAYTON** Seventh great grandson of progenitor Nicholas Kegg. **ARIKA DANIELLE LAYTON** Seventh great granddaughter of progenitor Nicholas Kegg. **BENJAMIN ALBERT LAYTON** Sixth great grandson of progenitor Nicholas Kegg. **BETSY G. LAYTON** Sixth great granddaughter of progenitor Nicholas Kegg. **BETTY LAYTON** [5303] (1930 – 2020) daughter of Albert and Mabel (Hockenberry) Layton married Allen Andrew Akers with whom she was mother of (4). Betty was employed at Sunnyway Diner for 30 years and worked at the Family House in Breezewood for several years. She enjoyed spending time with her family, traveling, and completing word search puzzles. **CHRISTINA LOUISE LAYTON** [5304] (1971 – 2022) daughter of Anna Marie Trail together with Howard Josiah Corley was mother of (3). Christina was employed at Puff & Snuff in Everett. She enjoyed diamond art and collecting tiger memorabilia. **DANIEL E. LAYTON** Sixth great grandson of progenitor Nicholas Kegg. **DAVID E. LAYTON** Sixth great grandson of progenitor Nicholas Kegg. **DENISE E. LAYTON** Sixth great granddaughter of progenitor Nicholas Kegg. **DEREK LAYTON** Seventh great grandchild of progenitor Nicholas Kegg. **DEVON LAYTON** Seventh great granddaughter of progenitor Nicholas Kegg. **DOREEN EVONNE LAYTON** Sixth great granddaughter of progenitor Nicholas Kegg. **EDITH GRACE LAYTON** [5305, 5306] (1897 – 1904) daughter of Samuel and Minnie (Kegg) Layton was in the care of an aunt while her mother took care of her sick grandfather. While there Edith was attending school, being a member of Miss Michaels' A class. She contracted scarlet fever and seemed to rally from that dreadful disease, but rheumatism and blood poison set in, which was too much for her weakened condition to stand. Her suffering was intense, but she never murmured and at last fell calmly asleep in Jesus, there to join her little brothers who had gone on before. **GARY W. LAYTON** Fifth great grandson of progenitor Nicholas Kegg. **GUNNER LEE LAYTON** Sixth great grandson of progenitor Nicholas Kegg. **NATHAN ALAN LAYTON** Seventh great grandson of progenitor Nicholas Kegg. **OLIVIA LAYTON** Seventh great granddaughter of progenitor Nicholas Kegg. **RILEY LAYTON** Eighth great grandson of progenitor Nicholas Kegg. **STANLEY WEBSTER LAYTON** (1929 – 1929) son of Albert and Mabel (Hockenberry) Layton. **TIMOTHY LAYTON** Sixth great grandson of progenitor Nicholas Kegg. **WILLIAM ADAM LAYTON** Sixth great grandson of progenitor Nicholas Kegg.

LEACH

SHANE LEACH Eighth great grandson of progenitor Nicholas Kegg.
THOMAS CHARLES LEACH Seventh great grandson of progenitor Nicholas Kegg.

LEBLANC

MIKAYLA LEBLANC Eighth great granddaughter of progenitor Nicholas Kegg.

LECLAIN

ZACHARY LECLAIN Eighth great grandson of progenitor Nicholas Kegg.

LEDBETTER

BARBARA ELAYNE LEDBETTER Fifth great granddaughter of progenitor Nicholas Kegg.
GARY WATSON LEDBETTER Fifth great grandson of progenitor Nicholas Kegg.

[5302] p.5 Altoona Mirror (PA) July 22, 2013, obtained by D. Sue Dible [5303] Bedford Gazette (PA) May 28, 2020 [5304] Bedford Gazette (PA) March 17, 2022 [5305] Bloody Run Historical Society contributed by Regina Williams [5306] Martinsburg Herald (PA) Nov. 18, 1904

JACQUELINE LEE LEDBETTER aka "Jackie", Fifth great granddaughter of progenitor Nicholas Kegg.   **KATHERINE ELIZABETH LEDBETTER** [5307] (1945 – 2001) aka "Kathy", daughter of Watson and Lottie (Graham) Ledbetter married twice; first to Preston Dee Causey with whom she was mother of (1). Later, she married Leonard R. Mazzuca with whom she was mother of (1). Katherine was a member of the Simi Valley Quilt Guild and Christadelphian Esslesia of Reseda.
MARY S. LEDBETTER Fifth great granddaughter of progenitor Nicholas Kegg.

LEE

ANDREA LEE Sixth great granddaughter of progenitor Nicholas Kegg.   **ALFRED CHARLES LEE** Fifth great grandson of progenitor Nicholas Kegg.   **AUDREY E. LEE** (1963 – 1966) adopted daughter of William and Elaine (Randall) Lee.   **BOB LEE** Fifth great grandson of progenitor Nicholas Kegg.   **BONNIE JUNE LEE** Fifth great granddaughter of progenitor Nicholas Kegg.   **CAROL D. LEE** Fifth great granddaughter of progenitor Nicholas Kegg.   **CONNIE LUGENE LEE** Sixth great granddaughter of progenitor Nicholas Kegg.   **CLAUDIA LEE** Sixth great granddaughter of progenitor Nicholas Kegg (Adopted).   **DAVID LEE** Sixth great grandson of progenitor Nicholas Kegg (Adopted).   **DEBORAH LEE** Sixth great granddaughter of progenitor Nicholas Kegg.   **DIANA LEE** Sixth great granddaughter of progenitor Nicholas Kegg.   **DONALD ORVILLE LEE** [5308] (1920 – 2008) aka "Red", son of George and Minnie (Sidders) Lee married Dorothy Imogene Collins with whom he was father of (1). Later, he married Mary Mildred (Howell) Agnelly. Red was an orthopedist.   **DONNA GENE LEE** Sixth great granddaughter of progenitor Nicholas Kegg.   **DORIS ANN LEE** Fifth great granddaughter of progenitor Nicholas Kegg.   **FRANCES DELL LEE** [5308A] (1938 – 2012) daughter of Floyd and Hazel (Swank) Lee married Jerry Lee Bird with whom she was mother of (4). Frances had a strong Christian faith that she shared with her children. She was a stay-at-home mom and watched children in her home before going to work at a childcare facility. Later, she went to work at Greater Community Hospital in Creston in the Dietary Department. During her time working there, Frances went to school to further her education. After 20 years of service, she retired from GHC as Dietary Manager.   **GEORGE LEE** Fifth great grandson of progenitor Nicholas Kegg.   **GLADYS LEE** Fifth great granddaughter of progenitor Nicholas Kegg.   **JACKIE LEE** Seventh great granddaughter of progenitor Nicholas Kegg.   **JACKIE R. LEE** Fifth great grandson of progenitor Nicholas Kegg.   **JIMMIE LEE** Sixth great grandson of progenitor Nicholas Kegg.   **JIMMIE WAYNE LEE** Fifth great grandson of progenitor Nicholas Kegg.   **LINDA LEE** Fifth great granddaughter of progenitor Nicholas Kegg.   **LINDSEY C. LEE** Sixth great granddaughter of progenitor Nicholas Kegg.   **MACY ALEXANDRIA LEE** Seventh great granddaughter of progenitor Nicholas Kegg.   **MILDRED LEE** Fifth great granddaughter of progenitor Nicholas Kegg.   **NORA JAYNE LEE** Seventh great granddaughter of progenitor Nicholas Kegg.   **RICHARD DALE LEE** Fifth great grandson of progenitor Nicholas Kegg.   **RUBY GRACE LEE** Fifth great granddaughter of progenitor Nicholas Kegg.   **SHARI LYNETTE LEE** Sixth great granddaughter of progenitor Nicholas Kegg.   **SHIRLEY LEE** Fifth great granddaughter of progenitor Nicholas Kegg.   **SUSAN LEE** Sixth great granddaughter of progenitor Nicholas Kegg.   **TERESA LEE** Sixth great granddaughter of progenitor Nicholas Kegg.   **TIM LEE** Fifth great grandson of progenitor Nicholas Kegg.   **WILLIAM E. LEE** [5309] (1927 – 2016) son of George and Minnie (Sidders) Lee married Elaine Frances Randall with whom he was father of three adopted children and (1) natural. William joined the U.S. Air Force and served in the Korean War. Later, he managed Albion Co-op for 11 years. Moving to Falls City, Bill bought a gas station and ran it for seven years. In 1987, he began working for D&L in Columbus until retiring. Bill was a member of the American Legion. He led a prayer group and sang in a group at the Veterans Home. He enjoyed fishing, hunting and being around horses. He always had a joke to tell. Most of all, he enjoyed being with his grandchildren.

[5307] Los Angeles Daily News (CA) Aug. 21, 2001 [5308] The Nance County Journal (Fullerton, NE) Sep 7, 1944 [5308A] News-Leader (MO) July 17, 2012 [5309] The Grand Island Independent (NE) Jan 20, 2016

LEEKLEY

APRIL LYNN LEEKLEY Sixth great granddaughter of progenitor Nicholas Kegg.

LEESE

GARY LEE LEESE Sixth great grandson of progenitor Nicholas Kegg.
SHARON EMMY LEESE Sixth great granddaughter of progenitor Nicholas Kegg.
TIFFANY MARIE LEESE Seventh great granddaughter of progenitor Nicholas Kegg.
VICKIE MARIE LEESE Sixth great granddaughter of progenitor Nicholas Kegg.

LEETH

JASON ALAN LEETH Seventh great grandson of progenitor Nicholas Kegg.

LEGG

DREW LEGG Seventh great grandson of progenitor Nicholas Kegg.
IAN LEGG Seventh great grandson of progenitor Nicholas Kegg.

LEHMAN

BRIDGETTE KATHLEEN LEHMAN Sixth great granddaughter of progenitor Nicholas Kegg.
BRYN LEHMAN Sixth great grandson of progenitor Nicholas Kegg.
CAROLYN LEHMAN Fifth great granddaughter of progenitor Nicholas Kegg.
GEORGANNA CATHERINE LEHMAN Sixth great granddaughter of progenitor Nicholas Kegg.
GEORGE WILTON LEHMAN JR. [5310] (1930 – 1993) son of George and Nora (Conners) Lehman, married Edna Mae Cameron with whom he was father of (2). George retired from Clark Metal Products of Blairsville. He was a veteran of World War II, serving in the U.S. Army. He belonged to B.P.O.E. Lodge 406 of Blairsville.
GEORGE WILTON LEHMAN [5311] (1906 – 1971) son of Albert and Jessie (Rouzer) Lehman, married Nora Conners with whom he was father of (2).
KIERSTEN LEHMAN Sixth great granddaughter of progenitor Nicholas Kegg.
NICOLE LEHMAN Sixth great granddaughter of progenitor Nicholas Kegg.
ROBERT O. LEHMAN [5311A] (1960 – 2016) son of Jack and Dorothy (Biddle) Lehman, married Roxanne Funk with whom he was father of (1). Robert served in the United States Army form 1980-1988 where he was stationed in Germany. Later he was employed as a heavy equipment operator for Valley Quarries. He enjoyed hunting, watching NASCAR and spending time with his family.
SUE ELLEN LEHMAN Fifth great granddaughter of progenitor Nicholas Kegg.

LEHNHOFF

CHLOE LEHNHOFF Eighth great granddaughter of progenitor Nicholas Kegg
JOE LEHNHOFF Eighth great grandson of progenitor Nicholas Kegg.
KAYLIE LEHNHOFF Eighth great granddaughter of progenitor Nicholas Kegg
MARISSA LEHNHOFF Eighth great granddaughter of progenitor Nicholas Kegg
SAMI LEHNHOFF Eighth great granddaughter of progenitor Nicholas Kegg.

[5310] p.28 Indiana Gazette (PA) Aug 18, 1993 [5311] p.54 Pittsburgh Press (PA) Apr 24, 1963 [5311A] Public Opinion (PA) Sep 13, 2016

LEIBERT

CHRISTINE LEIBERT Seventh great granddaughter of progenitor Nicholas Kegg.
DEBBIE LEIBERT Sixth great granddaughter of progenitor Nicholas Kegg.
JON LEIBERT Sixth great grandson of progenitor Nicholas Kegg.
JUDITH LEIBERT [5311B] aka "Judy" (1952 – 2018) daughter of Rex and Ardell (Gibbens) Leibert married James Joseph Blaha with whom she was mother of (1). Judy was a Certified Surgical Technician at Lutheran Hospital in Omaha, NE, for 25 years and a Technician at Mercy Hospital in Council Bluffs, IA, for 15 years. Judith was a lifetime member of the Girl Scouts and a member of the Crescent, IA, Optimist Club. Judith was the first to volunteer for any tough, hard, or demanding job.
REX H. LEIBERT Sixth great grandson of progenitor Nicholas Kegg.
TROY PATRICK LEIBERT [5311C] (1977 – 1980) son of Debra Louise (Leibert) Ceder.

LEITCH

JAMES BRIAN LEITCH Sixth great grandson of progenitor Nicholas Kegg.

LEIMER

KIMBERLY LEIMER Seventh great granddaughter of progenitor Nicholas Kegg.
MEISHARA LEIMER Seventh great granddaughter of progenitor Nicholas Kegg.

LEINBACH

CARL LEINBACH Fifth great grandson of progenitor Nicholas Kegg.
DANIEL PIERCE LEINBACH Fifth great grandson of progenitor Nicholas Kegg.
DONNA SUE LEINBACH (1937 – 2000) daughter of Wayne and Martha (Whiting) Leinbach.
JOANN GRACE LEINBACH Fifth great granddaughter of progenitor Nicholas Kegg.
KELSEY LEINBACH Seventh great granddaughter of progenitor Nicholas Kegg.
LLOYD GLENN LEINBACH Fifth great grandson of progenitor Nicholas Kegg.
MARK ALLEN LEINBACH Sixth great grandson of progenitor Nicholas Kegg.
MICHAEL WAYNE LEINBACH Sixth great grandson of progenitor Nicholas Kegg.
RUTH MATILDA LEINBACH Fifth great granddaughter of progenitor Nicholas Kegg.

LEISTER

ELIZABETH GRACE LEISTER Seventh great granddaughter of progenitor Nicholas Kegg.
JILLIAN MICHELLE LEISTER Seventh great granddaughter of progenitor Nicholas Kegg.

LEISY

ANN PENNER LEISY Fifth great granddaughter of progenitor Nicholas Kegg.
JAMES PENNER LEISY Fifth great grandson of progenitor Nicholas Kegg.
MARY MONICA LEISY Fifth great granddaughter of progenitor Nicholas Kegg.
ROBERT H. LEISY Fifth great grandson of progenitor Nicholas Kegg.
WILLIAM BERNARD LEISY Fifth great grandson of progenitor Nicholas Kegg.

[5309] The Grand Island Independent (NE) Jan 20, 2016 [5310] p.28 Indiana Gazette (PA) Aug 18, 1993 [5311] p.54 Pittsburgh Press (PA) Apr 24, 1963 [5311A] Public Opinion (PA) Sep 13, 2016 [5311B] Roswell Daily Record (NM) Feb 3, 2018, contributed by D. Sue Dible [5311C] Omaha World Herald (NE) July 22, 1977

LEMAY

WILLIAM DEBRAL LEMAY (1890 – 1948) aka "Willie", son of David and Alice (Kegg) Lemay married three times; first to Lula Belle Le Blanch. He married Florence Streicher. Later, Willie married Margaret Leota (Dapller) Miller.

LEMERT

LOLA LU LEMERT [5312] (1944 – 1987) daughter of Charles and Nellie (Wyckoff) Lemert, married Gary Lee Moses with whom she was mother of (3).

LENDERINK

CHERYL LENDERINK Sixth great granddaughter of progenitor Nicholas Kegg. **HOLLY LENDERINK** Sixth great granddaughter of progenitor Nicholas Kegg. **KAYELA LENDERINK** Sixth great granddaughter of progenitor Nicholas Kegg. **KAYELA LENDERINK** Seventh great granddaughter of progenitor Nicholas Kegg. **SKYELAR LENDERINK** Seventh great granddaughter of progenitor Nicholas Kegg. **TAMMY LENDERINK** Sixth great granddaughter of progenitor Nicholas Kegg. **TARA LENDERINK** Sixth great granddaughter of progenitor Nicholas Kegg. **TATE LENDERINK** Sixth great grandson of progenitor Nicholas Kegg. **TAYLOR LENDERINK** Seventh great granddaughter of progenitor Nicholas Kegg. **TRACEY LENDERINK** Sixth great granddaughter of progenitor Nicholas Kegg. **TRENT A LENDERINK** [5312A] (1968 – 2001) son of Tom and Sallyanne (Lanthorn) Lenderlink married Tamara Renae Hill. An experienced free diver, Trent could dive without air and hold his breath for up to five minutes. He dove into the Blue Lagoon of the Caribbean waters where he took his last earthly breath. His body was found the next day with a gash in his head. He was home with Jesus. Troy's wife of 11 years, an accomplished Christian singer/songwriter known as Tammy Trent wrote the song "Stop the World" that played at Trent's funeral. She has used her talent to help others recover from tragedy by trusting God. **TROY AREND LENDERINK** [5312B] (1966 – 2009) son of Tom and Sallyanne (Lanthorn) Lenderlink married Denise Englehart with whom he was father of (3). Troy was funny, unpredictable and a bit outrageous. He was all about family and an example in teaching unconditional love. He fought his cancer with the same determination and endurance that helped him overcome the many other challenges of life. Though Troy loved life and wanted to live, he accepted and embraced that his healing would be when he entered into Heaven.

LENFERNA DE LA MOTTE

MARC ALEXA LENFERNA DE LA MOTTE Sixth great grandson of progenitor Nicholas Kegg.
PHILIPPE NOEL LENFERNA DE LA MOTTE Sixth great grandson of progenitor Nicholas Kegg.

LENGYEL

MEGAN LEIGH LENGYEL Sixth great granddaughter of progenitor Nicholas Kegg.
ROBERT S. LENGYEL Sixth great grandson of progenitor Nicholas Kegg.
SARAH BETH LENGYEL Sixth great granddaughter of progenitor Nicholas Kegg.

LENIGAR

ZACH LENIGAR Sixth great grandson of progenitor Nicholas Kegg.

[5312] p.3 Maryville Daily Forum (MO) Nov 10, 1962 [5312A] Cornerstone-Connection issue no. 1509 [5312B] Grand Rapids Press (MI) Aug 9, 2009

LENTZ

CARTER LENTZ Seventh great grandson of progenitor Nicholas Kegg. **JOHN SCOTT LENTZ** [5312C] (1958 – 1989) son of William and Carolyn (Hillegas) Lentz was a graduate of Grove City College with a bachelor's degree in political science. He was a member of the Episcopal Memorial Church of Our Father in Foxburg. **KASEN LENTZ** Seventh great grandchild of progenitor Nicholas Kegg. **KEIRA LENTZ** Seventh great granddaughter of progenitor Nicholas Kegg. **MARK E. LENTZ** Fifth great grandson of progenitor Nicholas Kegg. **STEVEN LENTZ** Fifth great grandson of progenitor Nicholas Kegg. **SHARON R. LENTZ** Fifth great granddaughter of progenitor Nicholas Kegg. **SUSAN LENTZ** Fifth great granddaughter of progenitor Nicholas Kegg. **WILLIAM S. LENTZ** Fifth great grandson of progenitor Nicholas Kegg.

LEONARD

KRISTY RENEE LEONARD Seventh great granddaughter of progenitor Nicholas Kegg. **MICHAEL DREW LEONARD** Seventh great grandson of progenitor Nicholas Kegg.

LEPLEY

ZACHARY LEPLEY Eighth great grandson of progenitor Nicholas Kegg.

LEPPERT

BRENDAN REILEY LEPPERT Fifth great grandson of progenitor Nicholas Kegg.
GORDON TODD LEPPERT Fifth great grandson of progenitor Nicholas Kegg.
KERRY SCOTT LEPPERT Fifth great grandson of progenitor Nicholas Kegg.

LESKINEN

AMANDA MAE LESKINEN Sixth great granddaughter of progenitor Nicholas Kegg.
KRISTINA MAE LESKINEN Sixth great grandson of progenitor Nicholas Kegg.
MICHAEL DONALD LESKINEN Sixth great grandson of progenitor Nicholas Kegg.

LESTOCHI

GEORGETTE LESTOCHI [5312D] (1934 – 2014) daughter of Albert and Mildred (Dodson) Lestochi married Henry J. Maccinile with whom she was mother of (2). Georgette retired as a dental assistant from Drs. Yovino and Lampard's office and was also the former owner of Al's Pizza. **ROBERT E. LESTOCHI** [5312E] aka "Bobby" (1936 – 2013) son of Albert and Mildred (Dodson) Lestochi married Tonia Figliorenzo. Bobby retired with 20 years of service from the U.S. Air Force as a master sergeant during the Korean and Vietnam wars. He and his sister, Georgette, also owned and operated Al's Pizza House in Altoona. He was a member of Our Lady of Mount Carmel Catholic Church and a life member of the Air Force Association, Air Force Sergeants Association, American Legion and Duncansville VFW. Bobby most enjoyed playing the lottery, cooking and taking care of his many cats.

LEVAN

KELLY JEAN LEVAN Fifth great granddaughter of progenitor Nicholas Kegg.
SUSAN RUTH LEVAN Fifth great granddaughter of progenitor Nicholas Kegg.

[5312C] p.14- Pittsburgh Press (PA) May 15, 1989 [5312D] Altoona Mirror (PA) Oct 14, 2014

LEVANDOSKI

LIBBY LEVANDOSKI Sixth great granddaughter of progenitor Nicholas Kegg.
LUKE LEVANDOSKI Sixth great grandson of progenitor Nicholas Kegg.
SOPHIE LEVANDOSKI Sixth great granddaughter of progenitor Nicholas Kegg.

LEVENTRY

BRANDON LEVENTRY Sixth great grandson of progenitor Nicholas Kegg.
JEAN ANN LEVENTRY Fifth great granddaughter of progenitor Nicholas Kegg.
JUSTIN LEVENTRY Sixth great grandson of progenitor Nicholas Kegg.
MISTY LEVENTRY Sixth great granddaughter of progenitor Nicholas Kegg.
SHELDON LEVENTRY Sixth great grandson of progenitor Nicholas Kegg.

LEWELLEN

ALEXANDER CHASE LEWELLEN Seventh great grandson of progenitor Nicholas Kegg.

LEWIS

ARA LEWIS Seventh great granddaughter of progenitor Nicholas Kegg.
ARTHUR RICHARD LEWIS Fifth great grandson of progenitor Nicholas Kegg.
CHRISTOPHER ANDREW LEWIS Sixth great grandson of progenitor Nicholas Kegg.
CLIFFORD F. LEWIS Sixth great grandson of progenitor Nicholas Kegg.
DONNA LEWIS Sixth great granddaughter of progenitor Nicholas Kegg.
GAIGE LEWIS Eighth great grandson of progenitor Nicholas Kegg.
GUY LEWIS Seventh great grandson of progenitor Nicholas Kegg.
HENRY WALTER LEWIS Sixth great grandson of progenitor Nicholas Kegg.
IRENE LUE LEWIS Sixth great granddaughter of progenitor Nicholas Kegg.
ISAAC LEWIS Seventh great grandson of progenitor Nicholas Kegg. **JAROD LEWIS** Seventh great grandson of progenitor Nicholas Kegg. **JASON L. LEWIS** Fifth great grandson of progenitor Nicholas Kegg. **JIMMY LEWIS** Fourth great grandson of progenitor Nicholas Kegg.
JOANNE R. LEWIS [5313] (1929 – 2009) daughter of Robert and Edith (Prentice) Lewis married twice; first to Richard Hadley Randolph with whom she was mother of (2). Later, she married Norman E. Travis. Joanne was employed by American States Insurance Company, where she served as an underwriter for 29 years. She was a member of Knightstown Christian Church and a former member of Knightstown United Methodist Church, where she was involved with the Methodist Women's organization. Joanne enjoyed needlework, gardening and feeding and watching birds.
JOHN K. LEWIS Fourth great grandson of progenitor Nicholas Kegg. **KRISTINA MARIE LEWIS** Sixth great granddaughter of progenitor Nicholas Kegg. **MARIE LEWIS** Sixth great granddaughter of progenitor Nicholas Kegg. **MARY ANNE LEWIS** Fifth great granddaughter of progenitor Nicholas Kegg. **MATTHEW ADAM LEWIS** Seventh great grandson of progenitor Nicholas Kegg.
MICHAEL LEWIS Sixth great grandson of progenitor Nicholas Kegg.
MICHAEL LEWIS Sixth great grandson of progenitor Nicholas Kegg.
MICHAEL R. LEWIS Sixth great grandson of progenitor Nicholas Kegg.
NICHOLAS TUCKER LEWIS Fifth great grandson of progenitor Nicholas Kegg. **RICHARD ARAM LEWIS** Fifth great grandson of progenitor Nicholas Kegg. **RUSSELL LEWIS** Sixth great grandson of progenitor Nicholas Kegg. **SHEILA MARIE LEWIS** Sixth great granddaughter of progenitor Nicholas Kegg. **VICKI LEWIS** Sixth great granddaughter of progenitor Nicholas Kegg.

[5312E] Altoona Mirror (PA) Aug. 24, 2013 [5313] Knightstown Banner (IN) Jan 23, 2008

LIEBERMAN

CELESTE LIEBERMAN [5314] (1959 – 1963) daughter of William and Kathryn (McMahan) Lieberman.

LIMBERT

CARRIE LIMBERT Seventh great granddaughter of progenitor Nicholas Kegg.
DELLA GRACE LIMBERT Seventh great granddaughter of progenitor Nicholas Kegg.
IVY LIMBERT Seventh great granddaughter of progenitor Nicholas Kegg. **LYNNE M. LIMBERT** Sixth great granddaughter of progenitor Nicholas Kegg. **MELANIE LIMBERT** Sixth great granddaughter of progenitor Nicholas Kegg. **NATHAN ROBERT LIMBERT** Seventh great grandson of progenitor Nicholas Kegg. **ROBERT S. LIMBERT** Sixth great grandson of progenitor Nicholas Kegg. **STEVEN DOUGLAS LIMBERT** Sixth great grandson of progenitor Nicholas Kegg.

LIMPER

HEATHER LIMPER Eighth great granddaughter of progenitor Nicholas Kegg.

LINDEMAN

CARTER LAWRENCE LINDEMAN [5315] (2010 – 2010) son of Todd and Stacie Jean (Calhoun) Lindeman. Carter was one of the triplet brothers. **COLIN STEVEN LINDEMAN** Eighth great grandson of progenitor Nicholas Kegg. **COY MARTIN LINDEMAN** Eighth great grandson of progenitor Nicholas Kegg. **NINA IRENE LINDEMAN** Eighth great granddaughter of progenitor Nicholas Kegg. **NOLAN WILLIAM LINDEMAN** Eighth great grandson of progenitor Nicholas Kegg.

LINDEN

CLAIRE ABIGAIL LINDEN Seventh great granddaughter of progenitor Nicholas Kegg.
OLIVER WILLIAM LINDEN Seventh great grandson of progenitor Nicholas Kegg.

LINDSTROM

GARY LEE LINDSTROM Sixth great grandson of progenitor Nicholas Kegg.
GAYLE LINDSTROM Sixth great granddaughter of progenitor Nicholas Kegg.
JOAN LINDSTROM Sixth great granddaughter of progenitor Nicholas Kegg.
RICHARD LINDSTROM, aka "Rick", Sixth great grandson of progenitor Nicholas Kegg.

LINE

ALEXA LINE Seventh great granddaughter of progenitor Nicholas Kegg.
OLIVIA LINE Seventh great granddaughter of progenitor Nicholas Kegg.

LINEBARGER

GEOFFREY LINEBARGER Seventh great grandson of progenitor Nicholas Kegg.
TYLER LINEBARGER Seventh great grandson of progenitor Nicholas Kegg.

[5214] Chicago Tribune (IL) Feb 23, 1963 [5315] The Plain Dealer (OH) Dec 4, 2010, obtained by D. Sue Dible

LINGENFELTER

BETHANY RHEA LINGENFELTER Sixth great granddaughter of progenitor Nicholas Kegg. **ETHAN THOMAS LINGENFELTER** [5315A] (1992 – 2023) son of Tom and Susan (Diehl) Lingenfelter was employed by CSX where he worked as an Electrician. Ethan was an entrepreneur owning Central Precast Concrete and along with being a collector of vintage lawn tractors he also owned Elwood's Vintage Lawn and Garden. He was a Sr. Guide for the Royal Ranger's, and a member, trustee, and treasurer of Shawnee Valley Fire Dept. **JACELYN LINGENFELTER** Seventh great granddaughter of progenitor Nicholas Kegg. **SETH WILLIAM LINGENFELTER** Fifth great grandson of progenitor Nicholas Kegg. **ZANE IRA LINGENFELTER** Fifth great grandson of progenitor Nicholas Kegg.

LINGREN

SAMANTHA LINGREN Sixth great granddaughter of progenitor Nicholas Kegg.

LINHART

KYLE LINHART Sixth great grandson of progenitor Nicholas Kegg.

LININGER

ALICE M. LININGER (born abt. 1872) daughter of Jacob and Julia (Wiley) Lininger. **EMMA LININGER** (born abt.1858) daughter of Peter and Caroline E. (Kegg) Lininger. **EVA A. LININGER** (1860 – 1929) daughter of Peter and Caroline E. (Kegg) Lininger, married Daniel Friend with whom she was mother of (1). Later, she married James W. Alderson. **FRANCES ELMORE LININGER** (1858 – 1923) aka "Frank", son of Peter and Caroline E. (Kegg) Lininger, married Elmira Catherine Rogers with whom he was father of (1). **FRANK LININGER** (1877 – 1966) son of Jacob and Julia (Wiley) Lininger was a Spanish-American War veteran. **GEORGIA LININGER** (1885 – 1936) daughter of Jacob and Julia (Wiley) Lininger, married George H. Burritt with whom she was mother of (4). Later Georgia married Charles A. Drake and Charles W. Hughes. **HARRIET LININGER** (born abt. 1814) aka "Hattie", daughter of Peter and Caroline E. (Kegg) Lininger, married David Cramer with whom she was mother of two adopted children. After her husband's tragic death, she married Daniel E. McKinzie. **HARRY HERSCHELL LININGER** (1886 – 1951) son of Frances and Elmira (Rogers) Lininger, married Mary Elizabeth Lorenz. **HENRY LININGER** (born abt. 1854) son of Peter and Caroline E. (Kegg) Lininger. **JACOB KENNETH LININGER** (born abt. 1845) son of Peter and Caroline E. (Kegg) Lininger. **JOHN LININGER** (born abt. 1850) son of Peter and Caroline E. (Kegg) Lininger. **MARGARET LININGER** (born abt. 1860) daughter of Peter and Caroline E. (Kegg) Lininger. **PERMELIA LININGER** (1843 – 1910) daughter of Peter and Caroline E. (Kegg) Lininger, married Frank McCullough.

LINK

EVAN ALEXANDER LINK Seventh great grandson of progenitor Nicholas Kegg.
SHANNON ALEXA LINK Seventh great granddaughter of progenitor Nicholas Kegg.

LINN

JESSE ROBERT LINN Seventh great grandson of progenitor Nicholas Kegg.
NICOLE RACHEL LINN Seventh great granddaughter of progenitor Nicholas Kegg.

[5315A] Bedford Gazette (PA) Apr 29, 2023

LINSCOTT

GARY LINSCOTT Fifth great grandson of progenitor Nicholas Kegg.
INFANT LINSCOTT (1950 – 1950) son of Howard and Margaret (Tennihill) Linscott.
KAY LINSCOTT Sixth great granddaughter of progenitor Nicholas Kegg.

LINTON

CHRISTINA SUE LINTON Sixth great granddaughter of progenitor Nicholas Kegg.
CRAIG ALLEN LINTON Sixth great grandson of progenitor Nicholas Kegg.
JAMES EDWARD LINTON [5316] (1939 – 1989) son of Paul and Florence (Cagg) Linton.
JAYSON LEE LINTON Sixth great grandson of progenitor Nicholas Kegg.
SHIRLEY LINTON Fifth great granddaughter of progenitor Nicholas Kegg.

LITTLE

AMBER LITTLE Seventh great granddaughter of progenitor Nicholas Kegg.

LITTLETON

JAKE LITTLETON Seventh great grandson of progenitor Nicholas Kegg.
KELLEY LITTLETON Seventh great granddaughter of progenitor Nicholas Kegg.

LIVENGOOD

ANNE LIVENGOOD Fourth great granddaughter of progenitor Nicholas Kegg.
ANNE LIVENGOOD Fifth great granddaughter of progenitor Nicholas Kegg.
BECKY SUE LIVENGOOD Fourth great granddaughter of progenitor Nicholas Kegg.
CHRISTOPHER LIVENGOOD Fifth great grandson of progenitor Nicholas Kegg.
DENVER LIVENGOOD Fifth great grandson of progenitor Nicholas Kegg.
HARPER JAY LIVENGOOD Ninth great grandson of progenitor Nicholas Kegg.
JAMES J. LIVENGOOD Fourth great grandson of progenitor Nicholas Kegg.
JERRY B. LIVENGOOD Fourth great grandson of progenitor Nicholas Kegg. **JOEL LIVENGOOD** Fifth great grandson of progenitor Nicholas Kegg. **JOHN LIVENGOOD** Seventh great grandson of progenitor Nicholas Kegg. **JULIE ROCHELLE LIVENGOOD** Eighth great granddaughter of progenitor Nicholas Kegg. **JYRI LIVENGOOD** Fifth great granddaughter of progenitor Nicholas Kegg. **LINDA LIVENGOOD** Seventh great granddaughter of progenitor Nicholas Kegg. **MARK SNIDER LIVENGOOD** Fifth great grandson of progenitor Nicholas Kegg. **MELVIN KREAMER LIVENGOOD** [5317] (1946 – 2013) son of Melvin and Wilma (Kreamer) Livengood, married Kathryn L. Sabin. Melvin was a businessman, a true patriot he served two tours in Vietnam. **SARA LIVENGOOD** Fifth great granddaughter of progenitor Nicholas Kegg. **SHANNON LIVENGOOD** Fifth great grandson of progenitor Nicholas Kegg. **TATYANA LIVENGOOD** Fifth great granddaughter of progenitor Nicholas Kegg. **TORRI LYNN LIVENGOOD** Fifth great granddaughter of progenitor Nicholas Kegg. **TRAVIS LIVENGOOD** Eighth great grandson of progenitor Nicholas Kegg.
TYLER J. LIVENGOOD [5318] (1998 – 1998) son of Todd and Ellen (Diehl) Livengood.

LIVINGSTONE

TEAGAN LIVINGSTONE Seventh great granddaughter of progenitor Nicholas Kegg.

[5316] Athens Messenger (OH) Jan 31, 1989, obtained by D. Sue Dible

LLOYD

ROBERT LLOYD Fifth great grandson of progenitor Nicholas Kegg.

LOCKHART

BARRY LOCKHART Sixth great grandson of progenitor Nicholas Kegg.
BRADLEY LOCKHART Sixth great grandson of progenitor Nicholas Kegg.
WILLIAM LOCKHART aka "Billy", Sixth great grandson of progenitor Nicholas Kegg.

LOFLAND

ALAN NED LOFLAND aka "Ned", Sixth great grandson of progenitor Nicholas Kegg.
AUDRAD MAUREEN LOFLAND Sixth great granddaughter of progenitor Nicholas Kegg.
VALERIE JEAN LOFLAND Sixth great granddaughter of progenitor Nicholas Kegg.
VIVIAN LOFLAND Sixth great granddaughter of progenitor Nicholas Kegg.

LOGAN

JACOB MICHAEL LOGAN Eighth great grandson of progenitor Nicholas Kegg.
JENNIFER MICHELLE LOGAN Sixth great granddaughter of progenitor Nicholas Kegg.
JOANN LOGAN Sixth great granddaughter of progenitor Nicholas Kegg.
MAYCIE MARIE LOGAN Eighth great granddaughter of progenitor Nicholas Kegg.
RYAN LOGAN Seventh great grandson of progenitor Nicholas Kegg.
SCOTT D. LOGAN Sixth great grandson of progenitor Nicholas Kegg.

LOHR

ANTHONY CRAWFORD LOHR Seventh great grandson of progenitor Nicholas Kegg.
BRENT DANIEL LOHR Seventh great grandson of progenitor Nicholas Kegg.
DANIEL WARREN LOHR Sixth great grandson of progenitor Nicholas Kegg.
DANNAH LEIGH LOHR Seventh great granddaughter of progenitor Nicholas Kegg.
ERIC RANDALL LOHR [5319] (1976 – 1976) son of Daniel and Debra (Walls) Lohr.
HEATHER RANAE LOHR Seventh great granddaughter of progenitor Nicholas Kegg.
JUDY DIANE LOHR Sixth great granddaughter of progenitor Nicholas Kegg.
JUSTIN WARREN LOHR Seventh great grandson of progenitor Nicholas Kegg.
MICHAEL WAYNE LOHR Sixth great grandson of progenitor Nicholas Kegg.

LONBERGER

GAIL JAMES LONBERGER aka "Jim", Sixth great grandson of progenitor Nicholas Kegg.
NANNETTE ELAINE LONBERGER Sixth great granddaughter of progenitor Nicholas Kegg.
RHONDA LONBERGER [5320] (1956 – 2007) daughter of Gail and Rona (Huddy) Lonberger, married William E. Rager with whom she was mother of (1). Rhonda had a deep relationship with her Savior, Jesus. **THOMAS E. LONBERGER** Sixth great grandson of progenitor Nicholas Kegg.

LONDON

JESSICA M. LONDON Fifth great granddaughter of progenitor Nicholas Kegg.

[5317] Sacramento Bee (CA) Jan 24, 2013 [5318] Bedford Gazette (PA) Oct 7, 1998 [5319] Cumberland News (MD) April 23, 1976

JUSTIN J. LONDON Fifth great grandson of progenitor Nicholas Kegg. **RICHARD LONDON** Fifth great grandson of progenitor Nicholas Kegg. **VICTORIA MARIE LONDON** [5321] (1968 – 2015) daughter of Richard and Victoria (Owens) London married Wayne Alvin Seymour, she later married Scott Ronald Eastwood with whom she was mother of (1). Lastly, she married Jacinto Lopez. **WENDELL ALVIN LONDON** Fifth great grandson of progenitor Nicholas Kegg.

LONG

AARON PATRICK LONG Sixth great grandson of progenitor Nicholas Kegg. **BRADFORD LONG** Sixth great grandson of progenitor Nicholas Kegg. **DANIEL EUGENE LONG** Seventh great grandson of progenitor Nicholas Kegg. **DEBORAH LONG** Sixth great granddaughter of progenitor Nicholas Kegg. **DEBRA LONG** Sixth great granddaughter of progenitor Nicholas Kegg. **GARY DOUGLAS LONG** [5322] (1938 – 2003) aka "Butch", son of Virgil and Rose (Kennedy) Long, married Marilyn Anne Brenner with whom he was father of (3). Gary was owner and operator of Long's Paint & Body Shop, which was started in 1946 by his mother, Rose Long, father, Virgil Long, & brother, John Long, all of whom preceded him in death. He served as Past President of ASA and was a veteran having served in the US Navy. **GAYLE LONG** Sixth great granddaughter of progenitor Nicholas Kegg. **GINGER ANN LONG** Sixth great granddaughter of progenitor Nicholas Kegg. **JACQUELYN LONG** Sixth great granddaughter of progenitor Nicholas Kegg. **JOANNE LONG** Sixth great granddaughter of progenitor Nicholas Kegg. **MICHELLE H. LONG** Seventh great granddaughter of progenitor Nicholas Kegg. **MORRIS EDWARD LONG** [5323] (1928 – 2002) son of Virgil and Rose (Kennedy) Long was father of (4). Morris retired from Tinker AFB in 1983. He had a passion for water skiing, motorcycles, and old cars. He was a kind, and generous soul, always extending a helping hand to the less "fun kid inside" and was onery to the end. **REBECCA LONG** Sixth great granddaughter of progenitor Nicholas Kegg. **SCOTT LONG** Seventh great grandson of progenitor Nicholas Kegg. **THOMAS BROOKS LONG** Sixth great grandson of progenitor Nicholas Kegg. **TREVOR MICHAEL LONG** Seventh great grandson of progenitor Nicholas Kegg. **VELVET LONG** Sixth great granddaughter of progenitor Nicholas Kegg. **VICKI LONG** Sixth great granddaughter of progenitor Nicholas Kegg.

LONGNECKER

JUSTIN LONGNECKER Seventh great grandson of progenitor Nicholas Kegg.
MICHELLE LONGNECKER Seventh great granddaughter of progenitor Nicholas Kegg.

LOPEZ

JOHNNY W. LOPEZ Sixth great grandson of progenitor Nicholas Kegg.

LOPITZ

ELIZABETH LOPITZ aka "Lizzy", Eighth great granddaughter of progenitor Nicholas Kegg.

LOPRESTI

ALIVIA LOPRESTI Seventh great granddaughter of progenitor Nicholas Kegg.
ANTHONY LOPRESTI aka "Tony", Sixth great grandson of progenitor Nicholas Kegg.
MELISSA LOPRESTI Sixth great granddaughter of progenitor Nicholas Kegg.

[5320] Columbus Dispatch (OH) Sep 12, 2007 [5321] The Palm Beach Post (FL) Nov 19, 2015 [5322] The Oklahoman (OK) Nov. 16, 2003 [5323] Oklahoman (OK) Dec 25, 2002

LOTHAMER

DAVID LOTHAMER Seventh great grandson of progenitor Nicholas Kegg.
HANNAH LOTHAMER Seventh great granddaughter of progenitor Nicholas Kegg.
JACOB LOTHAMER Seventh great grandson of progenitor Nicholas Kegg.
PAUL LOTHAMER Sixth great grandson of progenitor Nicholas Kegg.

LOUDERBACK

AARON LOUDERBACK Seventh great grandson of progenitor Nicholas Kegg.
KRISTEN LOUDERBACK Seventh great granddaughter of progenitor Nicholas Kegg.
LAUREN LAUDERBACK Seventh great granddaughter of progenitor Nicholas Kegg.
MORGAN LOUDERBACK Seventh great granddaughter of progenitor Nicholas Kegg.

LOUNDAS

CHRISTOPHER MICHAEL LOUNDAS [5324] (1967 – 2020) son of Marc and Margaret (Vlasaty) Loundas was father of (2). **ELIZABETH LOUNDAS** Seventh great granddaughter of progenitor Nicholas Kegg. **JORDAN LOUNDAS** Seventh great grandson of progenitor Nicholas Kegg.

LOVE

AMANDA MARIE LOVE Fifth great granddaughter of progenitor Nicholas Kegg.
MATTHEW JAMES LOVE Fifth great grandson of progenitor Nicholas Kegg.

LOVETT

CHRISTOPHER LOVETT Seventh great grandson of progenitor Nicholas Kegg.
CLIFFORD LOVETT Seventh great grandson of progenitor Nicholas Kegg. **JENNIFER LOVETT** Seventh great granddaughter of progenitor Nicholas Kegg. **JOANNE MARIE LOVETT** Sixth great granddaughter of progenitor Nicholas Kegg. **THOMAS E. LOVETT** [5325] (1988 – 2009) son of Thomas and Terri (Crose) Lovett was a senior at Harry S. Truman High School, participating in the Life Skills Program. **THOMAS EDMUND LOVETT** Sixth great grandson of progenitor Nicholas Kegg.

LOW

DOREEN A. LOW Fifth great granddaughter of progenitor Nicholas Kegg. **KENNETH W. LOW** Fifth great grandson of progenitor Nicholas Kegg. **TERRY LYNN LOW** Fifth great granddaughter of progenitor Nicholas Kegg.

LOWE

GEORGIA ANN LOWE Fifth great granddaughter of progenitor Nicholas Kegg. **SHARON LOWE** aka "Cherie", Sixth great granddaughter of progenitor Nicholas Kegg. **SHERRY LOWE** Fifth great granddaughter of progenitor Nicholas Kegg. **SUSAN LOWE** Fifth great granddaughter of progenitor Nicholas Kegg. **WESLEY LOWE** Fifth great grandson of progenitor Nicholas Kegg.

LOWERY

PAIGE MAIE LOWERY Seventh great granddaughter of progenitor Nicholas Kegg.

[5324] Baltimore Sun (MD) June 17, 2020 [5325] Bucks County Courier Times (PA) April 30, 2009

LOWMAN

SPENCER LOWMAN Seventh great grandson of progenitor Nicholas Kegg.

LOWRY

DAVID P. LOWRY Seventh great grandson of progenitor Nicholas Kegg.
GREGORY V. LOWRY Seventh great grandson of progenitor Nicholas Kegg.
JEFFREY CARL LOWRY Seventh great grandson of progenitor Nicholas Kegg.

LUCAS

CAROL LUCAS Fifth great granddaughter of progenitor Nicholas Kegg. **DIANE L. LUCAS** Fifth great granddaughter of progenitor Nicholas Kegg. **EDIE LUCAS** Fifth great granddaughter of progenitor Nicholas Kegg. **GEORGE FRANKLIN LUCAS** Fifth great grandson of progenitor Nicholas Kegg. **JAMES CRAIG LUCAS** (1948 – 2004) son of James and Roberta (Seese) Lucas, married Karen Louise (Seese) Rosin. **JOHN LESLIE LUCAS** Fifth great grandson of progenitor Nicholas Kegg. **PEGGY LUCAS** Fifth great granddaughter of progenitor Nicholas Kegg. **SHARON J. LUCAS** Fifth great granddaughter of progenitor Nicholas Kegg. **WAYNE LUCAS** Fifth great grandson of progenitor Nicholas Kegg.

LUCE

CHAUNCEY LUCE Seventh great grandson of progenitor Nicholas Kegg.
HARRISON LUCE Seventh great grandson of progenitor Nicholas Kegg.
RORY LUCE Seventh great grandson of progenitor Nicholas Kegg.

LUCITO

ALISHA DANIELLE LUCITO Seventh great granddaughter of progenitor Nicholas Kegg.
AMBER RENEE LUCITO Seventh great granddaughter of progenitor Nicholas Kegg.

LUCIUS

ALIVIA LUCIUS Sixth great granddaughter of progenitor Nicholas Kegg.
CONNER LUCIUS Sixth great grandson of progenitor Nicholas Kegg.
KAYLA LYNN LUCIUS Seventh great granddaughter of progenitor Nicholas Kegg.
MARSHALL LUCIUS Sixth great grandson of progenitor Nicholas Kegg.

LUCKETT

ALIVIA LUCKETT Seventh great granddaughter of progenitor Nicholas Kegg.
EMILY LUCKETT Seventh great granddaughter of progenitor Nicholas Kegg.

LUEBKE

MARIAN JANE LUEBKE Fifth great granddaughter of progenitor Nicholas Kegg.

LUFT

AARON LUFT Seventh great grandson of progenitor Nicholas Kegg.
JILLIAN NICOLE LUFT Seventh great granddaughter of progenitor Nicholas Kegg.

LUGRIS

AMY E. LUGRIS Sixth great granddaughter of progenitor Nicholas Kegg.
PHILIP STEPHEN LUGRIS Eighth great grandson of progenitor Nicholas Kegg.
WAYNE PHILIP LUGRIS Sixth great grandson of progenitor Nicholas Kegg.
ZACHARY LUGRIS Eighth great grandson of progenitor Nicholas Kegg.

LUKEN

ABBIE LUKEN (1885 – 1983) daughter of Edmund and Martha (Beaver) Luken, married Frederick William Helmering.   **CORA L. LUKEN** (1888 – 1983) daughter of Edmund and Martha (Beaver) Luken, married Sheldon C. Aaron.

LUKOWSKI

CHERYL J. LUKOWSKI Fifth great granddaughter of progenitor Nicholas Kegg.
TERRY G. LUKOWSKI Fifth great granddaughter of progenitor Nicholas Kegg.

LUNA

LINDA LUNA Seventh great granddaughter of progenitor Nicholas Kegg.

LUNDELL

JODY LUNDELL Seventh great grandson of progenitor Nicholas Kegg.
JON MARK LUNDELL Seventh great grandson of progenitor Nicholas Kegg.

LUNG

BARBARA ANN LUNG Fifth great granddaughter of progenitor Nicholas Kegg.
BRADLEY CLARENCE LUNG [5326] (1959 – 1979) son of Dallas and Bernice (Sacks) Lung.
COLIN LUNG Sixth great grandson of progenitor Nicholas Kegg.   **DOUGLAS A LUNG** [5327] (1951 – 1971) son of Dallas and Bernice (Sacks) Lung, a motorcycle enthusiast, who was killed instantly in a two-vehicle crash four miles northeast of South Bend. Police reported that Doug was westbound on Brick when it and a dump truck collided. After impact, the cycle burst into flames.
ELIZABETH ANN LUNG Sixth great granddaughter of progenitor Nicholas Kegg.
JAMES RICHARD LUNG Fifth great grandson of progenitor Nicholas Kegg.   **JAY LUNG** Sixth great grandson of progenitor Nicholas Kegg.   **JENNIFER NICOLE LUNG** Sixth great granddaughter of progenitor Nicholas Kegg.   **JONI LUNG** Sixth great granddaughter of progenitor Nicholas Kegg.
JULIE DENISE LUNG Sixth great granddaughter of progenitor Nicholas Kegg.   **KELLIE LUNG** Seventh great granddaughter of progenitor Nicholas Kegg.   **KEVIN LLOYD LUNG** Fifth great grandson of progenitor Nicholas Kegg.   **MARCUS LUNG** Seventh great grandson of progenitor Nicholas Kegg.   **MARY LUNG** Sixth great granddaughter of progenitor Nicholas Kegg.
MATTHEW M. LUNG Sixth great grandson of progenitor Nicholas Kegg.
MEGAN MICHELLE LUNG Sixth great granddaughter of progenitor Nicholas Kegg.
PHYLLIS LUNG (1931 – 1931) daughter of Clarence and Mary Ellen (Rice) Lung.
RANDALL KENT LUNG aka "Randy", Fifth great grandson of progenitor Nicholas Kegg.
RICHARD MATTHEW LUNG Fifth great grandson of progenitor Nicholas Kegg.

[5326] The South Bend Tribune (IN) Oct 15, 1979 [5327] The South Bend Tribune (IN) Nov. 13, 1971

STEPHEN L. LUNG Fifth great grandson of progenitor Nicholas Kegg.
TANNER LUNG Sixth great grandson of progenitor Nicholas Kegg.
TIMOTHY LUNG, aka "T. J.", Sixth great grandson of progenitor Nicholas Kegg.
TIMOTHY WAYNE LUNG Fifth great grandson of progenitor Nicholas Kegg.

LUNN

ANDREW LUNN Seventh great grandson of progenitor Nicholas Kegg.
BARBARA LUNN Sixth great granddaughter of progenitor Nicholas Kegg.
DANIEL JOSEPH LUNN Sixth great grandson of progenitor Nicholas Kegg.
DIERDRE LUNN Seventh great granddaughter of progenitor Nicholas Kegg.
GREGORY SCOTT LUNN Sixth great grandson of progenitor Nicholas Kegg.
MOLLY LUNN Seventh great granddaughter of progenitor Nicholas Kegg.
PATRICK LUNN Seventh great grandson of progenitor Nicholas Kegg.
SUSAN ELIZABETH LUNN Sixth great granddaughter of progenitor Nicholas Kegg.
WILL LUNN Sixth great grandson of progenitor Nicholas Kegg.

LUTZ

ALAN LUTZ Fifth great grandson of progenitor Nicholas Kegg. **BEVERLY A. LUTZ** Fifth great granddaughter of progenitor Nicholas Kegg. **CANDACE JOY LUTZ** Eighth great granddaughter of progenitor Nicholas Kegg. **GEORGE CLIFTON LUTZ** [5328] (1905 – 1994) aka "Cliff", son of George Ross and Eva Catherine (Beegle) Lutz, married Charlotte Esther Weaverling with whom he was father of (3). Cliff had formerly owned and operated Lutz's Garage in Bedford for many years. He then owned and operated Motel 30 in Everett until his retirement. **JASON LUTZ** Sixth great grandson of progenitor Nicholas Kegg. **JASON SCOTT LUTZ** Eighth great grandson of progenitor Nicholas Kegg. **JEFF LUTZ** Seventh great grandson of progenitor Nicholas Kegg. **JOSHUA RYAN LUTZ** Eighth great grandson of progenitor Nicholas Kegg. **JOYCE LUTZ** Fifth great granddaughter of progenitor Nicholas Kegg. **LINDA LUTZ** Fifth great granddaughter of progenitor Nicholas Kegg. **MARK LUTZ** Eighth great grandson of progenitor Nicholas Kegg. **MATTHEW LUTZ** Eighth great grandson of progenitor Nicholas Kegg. **NATASHA LUTZ** Sixth great granddaughter of progenitor Nicholas Kegg. **RONALD CLIFTON LUTZ** Fifth great grandson of progenitor Nicholas Kegg. **RYELYN DAWN MARIE LUTZ** Ninth great granddaughter of progenitor Nicholas Kegg. **SCOTT ALLEN LUTZ** Seventh great grandson of progenitor Nicholas Kegg.

LYBARGER

DEVON LYBARGER Sixth great grandson of progenitor Nicholas Kegg. **DUSTIN LYBARGER** Fifth great grandson of progenitor Nicholas Kegg. **TOBY LYBARGER** Fifth great grandson of progenitor Nicholas Kegg. **VENESSA LYBARGER** Sixth great granddaughter of progenitor Nicholas Kegg.

LYDA

LINDA LYDA Fifth great granddaughter of progenitor Nicholas Kegg.

LYDEN

KATHRYN MARIE LYDEN Sixth great granddaughter of progenitor Nicholas Kegg.

[5328] Bedford County Genealogical Society obituary obtained by D. Sue Dible

LYDY

ABIGAYLE MAE LYDY Sixth great granddaughter of progenitor Nicholas Kegg.
KRISTEN RENE LYDY Sixth great granddaughter of progenitor Nicholas Kegg.
MARIA LYNNE LYDY Sixth great granddaughter of progenitor Nicholas Kegg.
MATTHEW JOHN LYDY Fifth great grandson of progenitor Nicholas Kegg.
ROBERT BARTON LYDY Fifth great grandson of progenitor Nicholas Kegg.
STEVEN JAY LYDY (1955 – 2013) son of Barton and Janice (Hershiser) Lydy.
THOMAS DWIGHT LYDY Fifth great grandson of progenitor Nicholas Kegg.

LYNCH

CHLOE LYNCH Eighth great granddaughter of progenitor Nicholas Kegg.
KELLI LYNCH Sixth great granddaughter of progenitor Nicholas Kegg.
NATHAN LYNCH Eighth great grandson of progenitor Nicholas Kegg.
SARAH LYNCH Sixth great granddaughter of progenitor Nicholas Kegg.

LYTHGOE

SUSAN MARIE LYTHGOE Fifth great granddaughter of progenitor Nicholas Kegg.

MAASS

CALVIN MAASS Eighth great grandson of progenitor Nicholas Kegg.

MACAULEY

AMBER MACAULEY Seventh great granddaughter of progenitor Nicholas Kegg.
CONSTANCE JOY MACAULEY aka "Connie", Sixth great granddaughter of progenitor Nicholas Kegg.   **ELIZABETH MACAULEY** Eighth great granddaughter of progenitor Nicholas Kegg.
FRED MORRIS MACAULEY (1951 – 1987) son of Albert and Pauline Ellen (Laird) Macauley, married Anna Marie Lindsey with whom he was father of (1).
SCOTT JASON MACAULEY Seventh great grandson of progenitor Nicholas Kegg.

MACCAUSLAND

DONNA K. MACCAUSLAND [5329] (1952 – 2011) daughter of Douglas and Agnes (Sanders) Maccausland. Donna was an employee of Caremark in Monroeville and a former employee of Arden Courts in Monroeville.

MACCHIO

NICHOLAS MACCHIO Sixth great grandson of progenitor Nicholas Kegg.
VINCENT MACCHIO aka "Vinny", Sixth great grandson of progenitor Nicholas Kegg.

MACCINILE

KAREN ANN MACCINILE Sixth great granddaughter of progenitor Nicholas Kegg.
STEVEN H. MACCINILE Sixth great grandson of progenitor Nicholas Kegg.

[5329] Pittsburgh Post-Gazette (PA) Feb 28, 2011

MACCLANATHAN

DUNCAN MACCLANATHAN Seventh great grandson of progenitor Nicholas Kegg.
FINN MACCLANATHAN Seventh great grandson of progenitor Nicholas Kegg.

MACE

AMY B. MACE Sixth great granddaughter of progenitor Nicholas Kegg. **JEFFREY R. MACE** Sixth great grandson of progenitor Nicholas Kegg. **MICHAEL MACE** Sixth great grandson of progenitor Nicholas Kegg. **STEVEN MACE** Sixth great grandson of progenitor Nicholas Kegg.

MACHAN

JANICE MARIE MACHAN Sixth great granddaughter of progenitor Nicholas Kegg.
MICHAEL GENE MACHAN [5330] (1948 – 1999) son of Ralph and Vivian (Shafer) Machan was father of (1). Michael had been employed at Indiana Marine Products, as well as owning and operating Emcee Chimney Sweeps. He loved being outdoors as well as hunting and fishing.
MICHELLE MACHAN Seventh great granddaughter of progenitor Nicholas Kegg.

MACIOCE

DOMONIC MACIOCE Eighth great grandson of progenitor Nicholas Kegg.
TALIA MACIOCE Eighth great granddaughter of progenitor Nicholas Kegg.

MACINNIS

BRAXTON MACGINNIS Eighth great grandson of progenitor Nicholas Kegg.

MACK

ERIC MACK Fifth great grandson of progenitor Nicholas Kegg.
RYAN MACK Fifth great grandson of progenitor Nicholas Kegg.

MACKENS

ABIGAIL MACKENS Seventh great granddaughter of progenitor Nicholas Kegg.
AUSTIN WES MACKENS Sixth great grandson of progenitor Nicholas Kegg.
CHAD DILLON MACKENS Sixth great grandson of progenitor Nicholas Kegg.
KAYLYN MACKENS Seventh great granddaughter of progenitor Nicholas Kegg.
MADDIE MACKENS Seventh great granddaughter of progenitor Nicholas Kegg.
WILLIAM MASON MACKENS Seventh great grandson of progenitor Nicholas Kegg.

MACLEAN

ALISON MACLEAN Sixth great granddaughter of progenitor Nicholas Kegg.
GRAHAM THOMAS MACLEAN Fifth great grandson of progenitor Nicholas Kegg.
GRAHAM THOMAS MACLEAN Sixth great grandson of progenitor Nicholas Kegg.
SUEELLEN MACLEAN Fifth great granddaughter of progenitor Nicholas Kegg.
WILLIAM DOUGLAS MACLEAN Fifth great grandson of progenitor Nicholas Kegg.

[5330] Sturgis Daily Journal (MI) obituary Sturgis Library transcribed by Carole Lynn (Mohney) Carr

MACY

DIANE SUSAN MACY Fifth great granddaughter of progenitor Nicholas Kegg.

MADDOCKS

JENNA MADDOCKS Sixth great granddaughter of progenitor Nicholas Kegg.
JORDAN S. MADDOCKS Sixth great granddaughter of progenitor Nicholas Kegg.
JUSTIN LYLE MADDOCKS Sixth great grandson of progenitor Nicholas Kegg.

MADIGAN

BARBARA MADIGAN Fifth great granddaughter of progenitor Nicholas Kegg.
CHARITY AYN MADIGAN Sixth great granddaughter of progenitor Nicholas Kegg.
PATRICIA KAYE MADIGAN Fifth great granddaughter of progenitor Nicholas Kegg.
TERI LYN MADIGAN Fifth great granddaughter of progenitor Nicholas Kegg.

MADISON

JASON C. MADISON Sixth great grandson of progenitor Nicholas Kegg.

MAHAFFA

BRENDAN MAHAFFA Seventh great grandson of progenitor Nicholas Kegg.
BRITANY MAHAFFA Seventh great granddaughter of progenitor Nicholas Kegg.
MAYAH MAHAFFA Eighth great granddaughter of progenitor Nicholas Kegg.

MAGEE

JONATHAN MAGEE Sixth great grandson of progenitor Nicholas Kegg.
MICHAEL A. MAGEE Sixth great grandson of progenitor Nicholas Kegg.

MAHAN

MARY C. MAHAN [5331] (1955 – 2016) aka "Kitten", daughter of Clyde and Jean (Bowers) Mahan married twice; first to Robert J. Perdew with whom he was father of (1). Later, she married Jerry E. Carrier with whom she was mother of (2). Mary was a charter member of Dayspring Community Church; member of Franklin County Master Gardner Club; volunteer at Franklin Park Conservatory; 34-year employee with Discover Card; and a diehard Dallas Cowboys fan.

MAHNKE

CRYSTAL MAHNKE Sixth great granddaughter of progenitor Nicholas Kegg.
DARYL WILLIAM MAHNKE (1971 – 1994) son of Dale and Charlene (Stuckey) Mahnke.
DEDRA MAHNKE Sixth great granddaughter of progenitor Nicholas Kegg.

MAHONEY

BRIAN MAHONEY Sixth great grandson of progenitor Nicholas Kegg.

[5331] Columbus Dispatch (OH) Apr 21, 2016

MAIN

CHARLES WILLIS MAIN (1913 – 2006) son of Ray and Frances (Tracy) Main married twice; first to Ione Myrtle McMaster with whom he was father of (2). Later, he married Lorraine Johnson.
ERIK MICHAEL MAIN Seventh great grandson of progenitor Nicholas Kegg.
IVA MAIN [5331A] (1880 – 1975) daughter of Charles and Avia (Stuckey) Main married twice, first to John Ernest Lowe with whom she was mother of (2). Later she married John Walter Milne. Iva was active in the Presbyterian Church. She was also a member of the PEO and past president of the AQ & CY chapters. She was also a member of the Social Order of Beauceant and the Garden Club.
MATTHEW DAVID MAIN Seventh great grandson of progenitor Nicholas Kegg.
RAY WESLEY MAIN (1885 – 1964) son of Charles and Avis (Stuckey) Main, married Frances Lillian Tracy with whom he was father of (1).

MAJOR

AURELIA ALICE MAJOR [5331B] aka "Re" (1929 – 2008) daughter of George and Elizabeth (Burnham) Major, married Eldon Dale Toeller with whom she was mother of (2). Aurelia worked many years with her husband at Toeller's Market on Mission Avenue. She was a devoted wife and loving mother who's gentle and kind ways provided a constant example for her family and friends.
CATHERINE E. MAJOR [5332] (1880 – 1966) aka "Kate", daughter of George and Matilda (Knouf) Major.   **GERALDINE CATHERINE MAJOR** (1920 – 2009) daughter of Grover and Mary (Edsall) Major, married Joseph Carl Ferencz with whom she was mother of (3).
GROVER CLEVELAND MAJOR (1885 – 1928) son of George and Matilda (Knouf) Major, married Mary Lurena (Edsall) Nelson with whom he was father of (3).   **HENRY ALLEN MAJOR** [5333] (1874 – 1964) son of George and Matilda (Knouf) Major.   **IRENE F. MAJOR** [5334] (1883 – 1964) daughter of George and Matilda (Knouf) Major.   **LILLIE MAY MAJOR** [5335] (1875 – 1969) daughter of George and Matilda (Knouf) Major married three times; first to Thomas C. Jones with whom she was mother of (2). She married Clinton Charles Parsons and later, married Mr. Martin. Lillie was a member of Altadena Baptist Church. **LOUIS ARTHUR MAJOR** [5336] (1877 – 1972) aka "Art", son of George and Matilda (Knouf) Major.   **MABEL MARIA MAJOR** (1891 – 1978) daughter of George and Matilda (Knouf) Major, married Wallace Aaron Yeisley.   **PATRICIA JANE MAJOR** (1924 – 2005) daughter of Grover and Mary Lurena (Edsall) Nelson married Earl Robert Peterson.
RALPH J. MAJOR [5337] (1895 – 1945) son of George and Matilda (Knouf) Major, was a farmer.

MALCOLM

CHARLES SPENCER MALCOLM Eighth great grandson of progenitor Nicholas Kegg.
FAITH MALCOLM (2007 – 2007) daughter of Christopher and Ginger (Orr) Malcolm.
MOLLY ROSE MALCOLM Eighth great granddaughter of progenitor Nicholas Kegg.

MALDONADO

ABI MALDONADO Eighth great granddaughter of progenitor Nicholas Kegg.
BRENDA MALDONADO Sixth great granddaughter of progenitor Nicholas Kegg.
LUCAS MALDONADO Eighth great grandson of progenitor Nicholas Kegg.
MARI MALDONADO Sixth great granddaughter of progenitor Nicholas Kegg.
NIDIA MALDONADO Sixth great granddaughter of progenitor Nicholas Kegg.

[5331A] The Daily Sentinel (CO) Aug 17, 1975 [5331B] San Diego Union Tribune (CA) June 4, 2008 [5332] p.24 - Star News (CA) Oct 10, 1966 [5333] p.20 - Pasadena Independent (CA) Mar 16, 1964 [5334] p. 12 - Star News (CA) Jan 18, 1964 [5335] p.B6 - Star News (CA) Aug 21, 1969 [5336] p.B9 - Star News (CA) April 6, 1972

MALETICK

EMILY ROSE MALETICK Seventh great granddaughter of progenitor Nicholas Kegg.
STEVE MALETICK Seventh great grandson of progenitor Nicholas Kegg.
THOMAS MALETICK Seventh great grandson of progenitor Nicholas Kegg.

MALLOW

RAYLAN DWAYNE MALLOW Eighth great grandson of progenitor Nicholas Kegg.

MALLOY

LOGAN R. MALLOY Seventh great grandson of progenitor Nicholas Kegg.

MALONEY

ALISSA MICHELLE MALONEY Seventh great grandchild of progenitor Nicholas Kegg. **ANNETTE MALONEY** Sixth great granddaughter of progenitor Nicholas Kegg. **CELENA MARIE MALONEY** [5338] (1994 – 2009) daughter of Christopher and Annette (Maloney) See, came to be adopted by her aunt and now mother, Karen Maloney in Salem, Oregon at the age of 8. Celena was a beautiful, intelligent and creative young lady who loved the outdoors, the beach, reading, swimming and most especially being creative artistically. She collected frogs and loved stars, Harry Potter, Twilight, and was blessed with beauty and strength. Her amazing art showed layers of depth and attention to detail beyond her 16 years. **KAREN GRACE MALONEY** Sixth great granddaughter of progenitor Nicholas Kegg. **SAMANTHA MALONEY** Seventh great granddaughter of progenitor Nicholas Kegg. **WILLIAM JAMES MALONEY** aka "Bill", Sixth great grandson of progenitor Nicholas Kegg.

MALOSKY

BETTY LORRAINE MALOSKY Fourth great granddaughter of progenitor Nicholas Kegg.
DAVID GREGG MALOSKY Fifth great grandson of progenitor Nicholas Kegg.
EDWARD MALOSKY Fifth great grandson of progenitor Nicholas Kegg. **EUGENE A. MALOSKY** [5339] (1944 – 2011) aka "Gene", son of Eugene and Genevieve (Pennacchini) Malosky. 'Gene' was a teacher with Albert Gallatin School District. He was President of the Noah's Ark Humane Society and devoted his life to animals. **EUGENE L. MALOSKY** [5340] (1914 – 1955) son of Frank and Mabel (Ferrell) Malosky, married Genevieve Pennacchini with whom he was father of (1). Eugene was a veteran of World War II, a member of the Disabled American Veterans Assn. He was a former ballplayer of the American Legion and a graduate of Redstone township High School where he played football. **FRANK EDWARD MALOSKY** [5341, 5342] (1913 – 1984) son of Frank and Mabel (Ferrell) Malosky, married Sophia Zentarsky with whom he was father of (3). Frank was employed by the Pennsylvania Department of Highways. **FRANK EDWARD MALOSKY** [5343] (1940 – 1994) aka "Rock", son of Frank and Sophia (Zentarsky) Malosky married Nicolina Barbar Capriotti with whom he was father of (2). Rock received a bachelor's degree in business administration from Duquesne University in Pittsburgh, where he was a member of Alpha Epsilon fraternity. After beginning his career in accounting with the General Accounting Office in Pittsburgh, he joined the Army and rose to the rank of captain before being honorably discharged. He served in the Medical Service Corps with the 3rd Armored Division in Frankfurt, Germany, and with the 9th Infantry Division in Vietnam. He then served in the Army Reserves

---

[5337] Metropolitan Pasadena Star-News (CA) Sep 6, 1945 [5338] Statesman Journal (AK) Nov. 30, 2009 [5339] Herald-Standard (PA) Nov 6, 2011 [5340] p.6 - Evening Standard (PA) Nov. 10, 1955 [5341] p.3 Connellsville Daily Courier (PA) Oct 1, 1938 [5342] Stephen R Haky Funeral Home, PA [5343] Capital Gazette (DC) July 29, 1994

and was a member of the American Legion. He resumed his accounting career and worked for the Washington Post for 12 years. Later, he accepted a position with the University of Maryland, where he became the assistant director for hours and payroll. **FRANK EDWARD MALOSKY** Sixth great grandson of progenitor Nicholas Kegg. **GERALDINE JANE MALOSKY** [5343A] (1921 – 2014) daughter of Frank and Mable (Ferrell) Malosky married twice, first to Earl Edward Brockman with whom she was mother of (1). Earl was killed in action in Okinawa and Geraldine married again to Paul A. Artis with whom she was mother of (1). **KENNETH MALOSKY** Fifth great grandson of progenitor Nicholas Kegg. **MICHAEL MARSHALL MALOSKY** Sixth great grandson of progenitor Nicholas Kegg. **ROBERT LEW MALOSKY** [5344] (1920 – 1987) son of Frank and Mabel (Ferrell) Malosky. Robert attended Waynesburg College in Waynesburg, Pa., and then earned his degree from Columbia University in New York City. He moved to California in 1955 and taught school in several cities there. His last teaching job was at the Pebble Beach School for boys in Pebble Beach before he moved to Oregon in 1972. He became a social worker for the state of Oregon in the early 1970s and retired in 1985. Robert was a member of the Beaverton Elks. **SHIRLEY JUNE MALOSKY** [5345] (1928 – 2001) daughter of Frank and Mabel (Ferrell) Malosky married James Smith Fiedler with whom she was mother of (3). **TRACEY LEE MALOSKY** Fifth great grandson of progenitor Nicholas Kegg. **WENDELL J. MALOSKY** [5346] (1926 – 1973) aka "Bud", son of Frank and Mabel (Ferrell) Malosky was a veteran of World War II, he played sandlot baseball for many years and had taught school in Michigan. **WILLIAM MALOSKY** Fifth great grandson of progenitor Nicholas Kegg. **WILLIAM MALOSKY** Fifth great grandson of progenitor Nicholas Kegg. **WILLIAM RUSSELL MALOSKY** (1918 – 1995) son of Frank and Mabel (Ferrell) Malosky, married Marguerite Ann Houley. He was a veteran of WWII.

MANEELY

DORIS IDA MANEELY [5347] (1898 – 1960) daughter of John and Julia (Cagg) Maneely, married Alexander R. Pfaff. Doris was a member of the Meadow Farm Methodist Church and OES Chapter No. 52. Having no heirs, she requested that her estate be divided between Aid to Dependent Children, Aid to the Blind and Aid to the Disabled.

MANEVAL

ALLISON MANEVAL Sixth great granddaughter of progenitor Nicholas Kegg.
SAMANTHA DAWN MANEVAL Sixth great granddaughter of progenitor Nicholas Kegg.
ZACHARY MANEVAL Sixth great grandson of progenitor Nicholas Kegg.

MANGUS

JASPER MANGUS Sixth great grandson of progenitor Nicholas Kegg.
UNA MANGUS Sixth great granddaughter of progenitor Nicholas Kegg.

MANSPEAKER

BRIAN K. MANSPEAKER Sixth great grandson of progenitor Nicholas Kegg.
JAN ELAINE MANSPEAKER Sixth great granddaughter of progenitor Nicholas Kegg.
JOEL EDWIN MANSPEAKER Sixth great grandson of progenitor Nicholas Kegg.
JOHN WAYNE MANSPEAKER [5348] (1922 – 1989) son of Lewis and Mabel (Fickes) Manspeaker married twice, first to Dorothy Wigfield and later to Eva Hengst. J Wayne acted as sheriff for 20 years. He was also a member of the CB's, U.S. Navy, WWII; the American Legion Post 8, Everett; Pennsylvania

---

[5343A] Tampa Bay Times (FL) May 9, 2014 [5344] p.C8 - The Oregonian (OR) March 11, 1987 [5345] The La Porte County Herald-Argus (IN) Jun 7, 2001 [5346] p.10 - Evening Standard (PA) Jan 10, 1973 [5347] p.8B Times Recorder (OH) May 18, 1960 [5348] p.2 -The Daily News (Huntingdon, Pa) Apr 19,1989

Sheriff's Association; F and AM Lodge 524, Everett; Ancient Accepted Scottish Rite, Valley of Harrisburg; Jaffa Temple, Altoona, and the Tall Cedars of Lebannon. He also served as the Republican Chairman of Bedford County for many years. **PAUL L. MANSPEAKER** (5349) (1925 – 2003) son of Lewis and Mabel (Fickes) Manspeaker married Rilla Louise Kelly with whom he was father of (2). In his youth, Paul was a dressage horse trainer. He enjoyed raising quarter horses on his West Providence Township farm, where he was a specialized blacksmith with his own shop, having stud racehorses at Bedford Springs, and a championship bull at Falkland Farms. He was a judge for the American Quarter Horse Association. Later, Paul was employed for 40 years by the United States Postal Service. Initially, he worked as a clerk and assistant postmaster in Everett and was then financial examiner and floor supervisor in Johnstown. He was appointed as acting postmaster in State College, and in 1972, accepted the position of postmaster in Hollidaysburg. In 1977, he became postmaster of the Bedford office, where he served until his retirement. An avid pool player, Paul also enjoyed playing the 5-string banjo.
SUSAN ORICE MANSPEAKER Sixth great granddaughter of progenitor Nicholas Kegg.
THEOLA MAE MANSPEAKER (5350) (1923 – 2003) daughter of Lewis and Mabel (Fickes) Manspeaker married Ralph G. Adams with whom she was mother of (2). Theola was a homemaker who enjoyed flower gardening and caring for her family.
TOD W. MANSPEAKER Sixth great grandson of progenitor Nicholas Kegg.

MAPES

AARON CHARLES MAPES (1965 – 2004) grandson of progenitor Nicholas Kegg.
BRYAN EUGENE MAPES Sixth great grandson of progenitor Nicholas Kegg.
CHARLES EUGENE MAPES (5351) (1942 – 2020) son of Charles and Sarah Jane (Smith) Mapes married Pricilla Sue Vincent with whom he was father of (3). Charles was employed as a Machinist for over 60 years at Jessen Manufacturing and was a long-time member of St. Paul's United Methodist Church. He was an avid Bingo player, enjoyed visiting the casinos with Pat, and was a fan of westerns. Though he was often reserved in nature, he had a welcoming presence. His grandchildren and great grandchildren were his pride and joy.
CHRISTINA MARIE MAPES aka "Christy", Sixth great granddaughter of progenitor Nicholas Kegg.
DAVID ALLEN MAPES Fifth great grandson of progenitor Nicholas Kegg.
JOHN EDWARD MAPES (1941 – 2010) son of Charles and Sarah (Smith) Mapes, married Phyllis Lee (Houck) Mapes. John had been employed as a truck driver. He was a veteran of Vietnam.
KATHY ANN MAPES Fifth great granddaughter of progenitor Nicholas Kegg.
MCKINLEY MAPES Seventh great granddaughter of progenitor Nicholas Kegg.
RAYMOND L. MAPES (5352) (1945 – 2014) son of Charles and Sarah (Smith) Mapes.
ROBERT DEVON MAPES Fifth great grandson of progenitor Nicholas Kegg.
ROBIN SUNNY MAPES Sixth great granddaughter of progenitor Nicholas Kegg.
SASHIA ELIZABETH MAPES Seventh great granddaughter of progenitor Nicholas Kegg.
TANYA JANE MAPES Sixth great granddaughter of progenitor Nicholas Kegg.
VINNIA JEAN MAPES Fifth great granddaughter of progenitor Nicholas Kegg.

MARDIS

MARTI MARIE MARDIS Sixth great granddaughter of progenitor Nicholas Kegg.
ROBIN K. MARDIS Sixth great granddaughter of progenitor Nicholas Kegg.

MAREK

SHANE MAREK Seventh great grandson of progenitor Nicholas Kegg.

(5349) p.2 -The Daily News (Huntingdon, PA) Feb 3, 2003 (5350) p.3 – Bedford Inquirer (PA) July 4, 2003 (5351) Elkhart Truth (IN) Oct 28, 2020, obtained by D. Sue Dible (5352) Elkhart Truth (IN) Dec 15, 2014

MARGRAF

JACOB ANDREW MARGRAF Seventh great grandson of progenitor Nicholas Kegg.
JONATHAN MICHAEL MARGRAF Seventh great grandson of progenitor Nicholas Kegg.

MARINCHEK

CHRISTOPHER MARINCHEK Sixth great grandson of progenitor Nicholas Kegg.
ZACKARY MARINCHEK Sixth great grandson of progenitor Nicholas Kegg.

MARKEL

EDGAR GEORGE MARKEL [5353] (1889 – 1961) son of John and Sarah (Kerr) Markel, married Alice Elizabeth Scheib with whom he was father of (2). **HEATHER L. MARKEL** Sixth great granddaughter of progenitor Nicholas Kegg. **JANE MARKEL** Fifth great granddaughter of progenitor Nicholas Kegg. **JENNIFER SUSAN MARKEL** Sixth great granddaughter of progenitor Nicholas Kegg. **JOHN MARKEL** Sixth great grandson of progenitor Nicholas Kegg. **JOHN EDGAR MARKEL** [5353A] (1923 – 2020) son of Edgar and Alice (Scheib) Markel, married Elva Mae Jarvis with whom he was father of (3). A dentist, John was a dedicated husband and father. **JOHN STEVEN MARKEL** Fifth great grandson of progenitor Nicholas Kegg. **LYNDA SUE MARKEL** Fifth great granddaughter of progenitor Nicholas Kegg. **MARGARET LOU MARKEL** (1916 – 2001) daughter of Oscar and Mamie (Clay) Markel, married Howard Theodore Braecklein with whom she was mother of (1). **MOLLY MARKEL** Sixth great granddaughter of progenitor Nicholas Kegg. **OSCAR JOHN MARKEL** [5354] (1887 – 1954) son of John and Susan (Kerr) Markel, married Mamie Augusta Clay with whom he was father of (1).

RUTH CHARLOTTE MARKEL [5355] (1910 – 2001) daughter of Edgar and Alice (Scheib) Markel, married Thomas Lyell Owens with whom she was mother of (1).

MARLOWE

JAIME MARLOWE Sixth great grandson of progenitor Nicholas Kegg.
TROY MARLOWE Sixth great grandson of progenitor Nicholas Kegg.

MARQUARDT

MADDIE MARQUARDT Seventh great granddaughter of progenitor Nicholas Kegg.

MARSH

CRAIG MARSH Seventh great grandson of progenitor Nicholas Kegg. **DEBORAH L. MARSH** Seventh great granddaughter of progenitor Nicholas Kegg. **LANDON MARSH** Eighth great grandson of progenitor Nicholas Kegg. **LILLIAN MARSH** Eighth great granddaughter of progenitor Nicholas Kegg.

MARSHALL

LYN MARSHALL Fifth great granddaughter of progenitor Nicholas Kegg.

[5353] Baltimore County Public Library obituary obtained by D. Sue Dible [5353A] Baltimore Sun (MD) Dec 9, 2020, obtained by D. Sue Dible [5354] The Evening Sun (Baltimore, MD) June 1, 1956 [5355] Baltimore County Public Library obituary obtained by D. Sue Dible

MARSIGLIA

DANIEL JOHN MARSIGLIA Seventh great grandson of progenitor Nicholas Kegg.
MATTHEW MARSIGLIA Seventh great grandson of progenitor Nicholas Kegg.

MARTIN

AARON MARTIN Seventh great grandson of progenitor Nicholas Kegg. **ALICIA JANEE MARTIN** [5355A] (1983 – 2005) daughter of Kim and Verona (Tompsett) Martin. Alicia was a vibrant young woman with an enthusiastic spirit, touching all those around her. In high school she played basketball, volleyball and softball. She was also very active in the Madras FFA Chapter and MHS Forestry Club. While a student at COCC, she competed against 5,000 entrants for a position on the "Tough Enough" reality TV series, becoming one of the 10 contestants. She loved competing and excelled in whatever she did. She enjoyed sports, music and fishing. **AMBER LYNN MARTIN** Sixth great granddaughter of progenitor Nicholas Kegg. **ATTICUS LEWIS MARTIN** Eighth great grandson of progenitor Nicholas Kegg. **AUDRA ROSE MARTIN** Eighth great granddaughter of progenitor Nicholas Kegg. **BETH ANN MARTIN** Seventh great granddaughter of progenitor Nicholas Kegg. **BRET ANDREW MARTIN** Seventh great grandson of progenitor Nicholas Kegg. **CARL MARTIN** Sixth great grandson of progenitor Nicholas Kegg. **CATHLEEN MARIE MARTIN** aka "Cathy", Sixth great granddaughter of progenitor Nicholas Kegg. **CLARENCE WILLIAM MARTIN** Fifth great grandson of progenitor Nicholas Kegg. **CRYSTAL MARTIN** Sixth great granddaughter of progenitor Nicholas Kegg. **DAVID L. MARTIN** (1950 – 2021) son of Howard and Juanita (Keggs) Martin married Maureen Oyer with whom he was father of (3). Later, he married Bonnie Stock with whom he was father of (2). **DAVID WESLEY MARTIN** Seventh great grandson of progenitor Nicholas Kegg. **ELIZABETH SUSAN MARTIN** Fifth great granddaughter of progenitor Nicholas Kegg. **EMMA JANE MARTIN** [5356] (1865 – 1944) daughter of Squire and Sarah (Kegg) Martin, married Robert M. Elder with whom she was mother of (8). Emma was a member of the Baptist church. **EMMA JEAN MARTIN** Sixth great granddaughter of progenitor Nicholas Kegg. **ERIC A. MARTIN** Fifth great grandson of progenitor Nicholas Kegg. **EUGENE LEROY MARTIN** (1925 – 2004) son of Adam and Wilma (Kegg) Martin, married Bettie Jane Norman with whom he was father of (1). **FLORA EVELYN MARTIN** [5356A] (1922 – 2012) daughter of Adam and Wilma (Kegg) Martin, married Vancil Roy Gardner with whom she was mother of (5). Flora was a lifetime member of Moose Lodge No. 362, where she retired as a bartender. Flora also was a member of American Legion Post No. 44 and VFW Post No. 1062. She enjoyed Cleveland Indians baseball and camping. She was an avid card player and a prominent bowler. **GREGORY MARTIN** Sixth great grandson of progenitor Nicholas Kegg. **HANSON WESLEY MARTIN** Eighth great grandson of progenitor Nicholas Kegg. **HEATHER LEE MARTIN** Seventh great granddaughter of progenitor Nicholas Kegg. **JACOB MARTIN** Seventh great grandson of progenitor Nicholas Kegg. **JAYNE LOUISE MARTIN** Seventh great granddaughter of progenitor Nicholas Kegg. **JOAN ISABELL MARTIN** [5356B] (1929 – 2022) daughter of Adam and Wilma (Kegg) Martin married Glenn Creamer with whom she was mother of (4). Later, she married Harold Richard Triplett with whom she was mother of (1). Joan worked as a cook for the former Gary's Colonial House, College Inn, and deli clerk at Jay's. In addition, she was a volunteer at Alliance Community Hospital. **JOHANNA NICOLE MARTIN** Seventh great granddaughter of progenitor Nicholas Kegg. **JOYCE MARIE MARTIN** (1927 – 1930) daughter of Adam and Wilma (Kegg) Martin.
JULIE CHRISTINE MARTIN Seventh great granddaughter of progenitor Nicholas Kegg.
KELLY JO MARTIN Seventh great granddaughter of progenitor Nicholas Kegg.
LEONARD HARRY MARTIN Sixth great grandson of progenitor Nicholas Kegg.
LORI LYNN MARTIN Seventh great granddaughter of progenitor Nicholas Kegg.

[5355A] Portland Tribune (OR) Apr 17, 2005 [5356] The Courier (Findlay, OH) obtained by D. Sue Dible [5356A] Sharer-Stirling-Skivolocke Funeral Home (OH) [5356B] The Alliance Review (OH) Dec 9, 2022

MIKAYLA MARTIN Seventh great granddaughter of progenitor Nicholas Kegg. **NICOLE LEE MARTIN** Fifth great granddaughter of progenitor Nicholas Kegg. **PAUL ERWIN MARTIN** [5357] (1934 – 2005) son of Adam and Wilma (Kegg) Martin, married Irene Ann Duchon with whom he was father of (1). Paul was a Millwright for Carpenters and Millwright Local 69 of Canton. He later retired from American Steel Foundries. A U.S. Navy veteran, Paul served during the Korean War. **PAUL WARREN MARTIN** (1949 – 1993) son of Leonard and Helen (Calhoun) Martin, married Jackie Lynn Carson. Paul was a veteran of Vietnam having served in the U. S. Army. **PERRY SIMPSON MARTIN** (1920 – 1993) son of Adam and Wilma (Kegg) Martin, married Yvonne Isabel Rowan. **SEBASTIAN THOMAS MARTIN** Eighth great grandson of progenitor Nicholas Kegg. **SORIN CHRISTOPHER MARTIN** Eighth great grandson of progenitor Nicholas Kegg. **VIRGINIA M. MARTIN** [5358] (1919 – 1997) daughter of Adam and Wilma (Kegg) Martin, married Herbert L. Betts with whom she was mother of (2). Virginia retired as a cashier from the former J. C. Murphy Company and was a member of the Women of the Moose Lodge No. 362.

MARTINET

PAULA YVONNE MARTINET Fifth great granddaughter of progenitor Nicholas Kegg.
ROBERT WAYNE MARTINET Fifth great grandson of progenitor Nicholas Kegg.

MARTINEZ

CORA MARTINEZ Seventh great granddaughter of progenitor Nicholas Kegg.
OLIVIA MARTINEZ Eighth great granddaughter of progenitor Nicholas Kegg.

MARTY

DYLAN MARTY Seventh great grandson of progenitor Nicholas Kegg.
ROGER M. MARTY Fifth great grandson of progenitor Nicholas Kegg.
STACEY MARTY Sixth great granddaughter of progenitor Nicholas Kegg.

MASELLI

GABRIELLA MASELLI aka "Gabby", Seventh great granddaughter of progenitor Nicholas Kegg.
GIOVANNI MASELLI Seventh great grandson of progenitor Nicholas Kegg.

MASON

ETHAN MASON Seventh great grandson of progenitor Nicholas Kegg.
ISABELLE MASON Seventh great granddaughter of progenitor Nicholas Kegg.
JACK MASON Seventh great grandson of progenitor Nicholas Kegg.

MAST

CHARLENE ANN MAST [5359] (1940 – 1944) daughter of Harold and Evelyn (Morgan) Mast died after being struck by an auto in front of her home on Monroe St. in Millersburg. Charlene was coasting from the slope in the lawn out into the street when she was struck by an auto driven by Fred Jones, Nashville, who was on his way to visit Russell Donnelly, also of Monroe St. Mr. Jones and the girl's father, Harold K. Mast, rushed her to Pomerene Memorial hospital but she died enroute. Mr. Jones was absolved of any

---

[5357] The Review (OH) Dec 3, 2005 [5358] p. 2 - Alliance Review (OH) April 26, 1997, obtained by D. Sue Dible [5359] Coshocton Tribune (OH) Dec 26, 1944

blame by sheriff Harry Weiss and Coroner A. J. Earney, who returned a verdict of accidental death. **EVELYN MAXINE MAST** [5359A] (1930 – 2016) daughter of Harold and Evelyn (Morgan) Mast, married Donald Vogt. Maxine was employed at Gensemer's Clothing Store for five years and retired from Holmes-Wayne Electric following 42 years of service. She served on the Red Cross Board and was a Paint Township precinct worker for the Holmes County Board of elections for many years. She was an active member of the Holmes County Christian Women's and the Walnut Creek Fine Arts Club. She loved to travel and spend time with friends and family. She was a very kind and caring person with a generous soul, willing to help those in need.   **LINDA SUE MAST** Fifth great granddaughter of progenitor Nicholas Kegg.   **LYNZI CLARE MAST** Sixth great granddaughter of progenitor Nicholas Kegg.   **MARILYN KAYE MAST** [5360] (1946 – 2007) daughter of Harold and Evelyn (Morgan) Mast, married Lanny Lee Croskey with whom she was mother of (2). Marilyn worked as a hairdresser for 42 years. Marilyn was a member of the Presbyterian Church of Millersburg, where she sang in the choir.   **PHYLLIS MARJEAN MAST** Fifth great granddaughter of progenitor Nicholas Kegg.

MASTERS

DANIEL JOSEPH MASTERS Sixth great grandson of progenitor Nicholas Kegg.
DAVID WILLIAM MASTERS Sixth great grandson of progenitor Nicholas Kegg.
KELLY GALE MASTERS Sixth great granddaughter of progenitor Nicholas Kegg.

MATHER

JAY MATHER Sixth great grandson of progenitor Nicholas Kegg

MATHESON

ANGELA MATHESON Seventh great granddaughter of progenitor Nicholas Kegg.

MATHEWS

ANITA MATHEWS Sixth great granddaughter of progenitor Nicholas Kegg.   **HAIDEE MATHEWS** Sixth great granddaughter of progenitor Nicholas Kegg.   **MEGAN MATHEWS** Sixth great granddaughter of progenitor Nicholas Kegg.   **NICOLE MATHEWS** Sixth great granddaughter of progenitor Nicholas Kegg.   **RYAN MATHEWS** Sixth great grandson of progenitor Nicholas Kegg.   **STEPHANIE MATHEWS** Sixth great granddaughter of progenitor Nicholas Kegg.

MATHIS

AMY JO MATHIS Seventh great granddaughter of progenitor Nicholas Kegg.
AVERY MATHIS Seventh great granddaughter of progenitor Nicholas Kegg.
GRAYDON MATHIS Eighth great grandson of progenitor Nicholas Kegg.
OLIVIA MATHIS Eighth great granddaughter of progenitor Nicholas Kegg.

MATLOCK

CHERYL MATLOCK Seventh great granddaughter of progenitor Nicholas Kegg.
JAMES MATLOCK Seventh great grandson of progenitor Nicholas Kegg.
JERRY MATLOCK Seventh great grandson of progenitor Nicholas Kegg.
VICKIE RENEE MATLOCK (1971 – 1971) daughter of Gary and Roseanne (Chaney) Matlock.

[5359A] The Daily Record (OH) Jan 3, 2017   [5360] Daily Record (Wooster, OH) Apr 16, 2007

MATOVINA

KATHLEEN MATOVINA Sixth great granddaughter of progenitor Nicholas Kegg.
MICHAEL MATOVINA Sixth great grandson of progenitor Nicholas Kegg.
MITCHELL GRAY MATOVINA Sixth great grandson of progenitor Nicholas Kegg.

MATT

JAMES V. MATT Fifth great grandson of progenitor Nicholas Kegg.
PETER DOUGLAS MATT Fifth great grandson of progenitor Nicholas Kegg.

MATTERS

AMY MATTERS Seventh great granddaughter of progenitor Nicholas Kegg.

MATTEVI

DARCY S. MATTEVI Fifth great granddaughter of progenitor Nicholas Kegg.
DARLA R. MATTEVI Fifth great granddaughter of progenitor Nicholas Kegg.
DEBORAH K. MATTEVI Fifth great granddaughter of progenitor Nicholas Kegg.
DIANE M. MATTEVI Fifth great granddaughter of progenitor Nicholas Kegg.

MATTHAEI

AIDAN MATTHAEI Eighth great grandson of progenitor Nicholas Kegg.
JERILYN MATTHAEI Sixth great granddaughter of progenitor Nicholas Kegg.
JOANNA MATTHAEI Eighth great granddaughter of progenitor Nicholas Kegg.
MATTHEW J. MATTHAEI Seventh great grandson of progenitor Nicholas Kegg.
MICHAEL NOLAN MATTHAEI Seventh great grandson of progenitor Nicholas Kegg.
SOPHIE MATTHAEI Eighth great granddaughter of progenitor Nicholas Kegg.
STEVEN PALMER MATTHAEI [5361] (1953 – 2018) aka "Steve", son of Geraldine (Stuckey) Matthaei, married Linda Jacobson with whom he was father of (2). Steve enjoyed woodworking in earlier years. He also enjoyed golfing and fishing with his sons. Steve also played softball with his company's team for many years.

MATTHEWS

JASON MATTHEWS Seventh great grandson of progenitor Nicholas Kegg.
JENNIFER MATTHEWS Seventh great granddaughter of progenitor Nicholas Kegg.
ZACH MATTHEWS Seventh great grandson of progenitor Nicholas Kegg.

MATTHIES

ADDISON MATTHIES Seventh great granddaughter of progenitor Nicholas Kegg.
DYLAN MATTHIES Seventh great grandson of progenitor Nicholas Kegg.

MATTINGLY

JULIA DRUSILLA MATTINGLY Fourth great granddaughter of progenitor Nicholas Kegg.

[5361] Newcomer Funeral Home (Denver, CO)

MATTISON

SHARON SUE MATTISON Fifth great granddaughter of progenitor Nicholas Kegg.
RYAN A MATTSON Seventh great grandson of progenitor Nicholas Kegg.

MAUCLAIR

MATTHEW R. MAUCLAIR aka "Matt", Sixth great grandson of progenitor Nicholas Kegg.

MAUDLIN

CARRIE RACHELLE MAUDLIN Seventh great granddaughter of progenitor Nicholas Kegg. **JAY MAUDLIN** Seventh great grandson of progenitor Nicholas Kegg. **KEVIN J. MAUDLIN** Sixth great grandson of progenitor Nicholas Kegg. **MEGAN NOEL MAUDLIN** Seventh great granddaughter of progenitor Nicholas Kegg. **MELISSA ALEXIS MAUDLIN** Seventh great granddaughter of progenitor Nicholas Kegg. **MELODY GRACE MAUDLIN** Seventh great granddaughter of progenitor Nicholas Kegg. **MORGAN MAUDLIN** Seventh great granddaughter of progenitor Nicholas Kegg. **RICKY J. MAUDLIN** Sixth great grandson of progenitor Nicholas Kegg **RYAN JAY MAUDLIN** Seventh great grandson of progenitor Nicholas Kegg. **VICK MAUDLIN** Seventh great grandson of progenitor Nicholas Kegg.

MAUK

ELIZABETH SUSAN MAUK aka "Betsy", Sixth great granddaughter of progenitor Nicholas Kegg.
ROBERT HARTSAUK MAUK [5362] (1898 – 1931) son of Ward and Cora (Hartsauk) Mauk was employed as an auto body mechanic.

MAUST

ROBERT E. MAUST Eighth great grandson of progenitor Nicholas Kegg.
STEPHEN MAUST Eighth great grandson of progenitor Nicholas Kegg.
TANGY MAUST Eighth great granddaughter of progenitor Nicholas Kegg.

MAVRAEDIS

BRYAN ALAN MAVRAEDIS Sixth great grandson of progenitor Nicholas Kegg.
CHRIS JOHN MAVRAEDIS (1927 – 1987) son of John and Rube (Messinger) Mavraedis married Lorraine Freda Gerberding with whom he was father of (6). **CHRIS LOREN MAVRAEDIS** Sixth great grandson of progenitor Nicholas Kegg. **DYLAN MAVRAEDIS** Seventh great grandson of progenitor Nicholas Kegg. **FRANCIS DWAYNE MAVRAEDIS** [5363] (1930 – 1975) aka "Frank", son of John and Rube (Messinger) Mavraedis married twice; first to Luella Campbell with whom he was father of (1). Later, he married Patsy Jane Pendergraft with whom he was father of (2). Frank was a Sgt. In the Air Force. In 1954 he was stationed at Williams Air Force Base. **GREGORY ALAN MAVRAEDIS** Sixth great grandson of progenitor Nicholas Kegg. **KIMBERLY LUCILLE MAVRAEDIS** (1957 – 2003) daughter of Chris and Lorraine (Gerberding) Mavraedis, married Stephen E. Rigdon with whom she was mother of (2). **LANCE J. MAVRAEDIS** Seventh great grandson of progenitor Nicholas Kegg. **LISA KAYE MAVRARDIS** Sixth great granddaughter of progenitor Nicholas Kegg. **MICHAEL DAVID MAVRAEDIS** Sixth great grandson of progenitor Nicholas Kegg.

[5363] The Austin American Statesman (TX), Dec 27, 1975, obtained by D. Sue Dible

MONICA A. MAVRAEDIS Seventh great granddaughter of progenitor Nicholas Kegg.
PAMELA ANN MAVRAEDIS Sixth great granddaughter of progenitor Nicholas Kegg.
STEPHANIE THERESA MAVRAEDIS Seventh great granddaughter of progenitor Nicholas Kegg.

MAXWELL

BILLIE MAE MAXWELL Sixth great granddaughter of progenitor Nicholas Kegg. **FRANKLIN MAXWELL** Sixth great grandson of progenitor Nicholas Kegg. **GLEN C. MAXWELL** Sixth great grandson of progenitor Nicholas Kegg. **HARRISON MAXWELL** Seventh great grandson of progenitor Nicholas Kegg. **HARRY ANDREW MAXWELL** Sixth great grandson of progenitor Nicholas Kegg. **TRACI LYNN MAXWELL** Seventh great granddaughter of progenitor Nicholas Kegg.

MAY

ADA L. MAY (1859 – 1861) daughter of David and Helen (Bruner) May. **AMBROSE MAY** [5364] (1861 – 1926) son of John and Elizabeth (Kegg) May, married Alice A. Bushey. Ambrose was reared in Cumberland, Md. where his father was engaged for some time keeping a tavern. His education was secured in the school of that location. After moving to Ohio in 1881 he became a prominent farmer. **BETH MAY** Fifth great granddaughter of progenitor Nicholas Kegg. **BRITTANY MAY** Fifth great granddaughter of progenitor Nicholas Kegg. **CARL FREDERICK MAY** Sixth great grandson of progenitor Nicholas Kegg. **CHARLES ARDEN MAY** [5365] (1898 – 1966) son of Charles and Mary (Garthright) May, married Eleanor Vashtie McDonald with whom he was father of (1). Charles was a member of the Methodist Church. **CHARLES S. MAY** (1865 – 1931) son of David and Helen (Bruner) May, married Mary Elizabeth Garthright with whom he was father of (7). **CHESTER FRANKLIN MAY** [5366] (1887 – 1969) son of Henry and Mahala (Barnes) May, married Naomi Gladys Wishard with whom he was father of (4). **DAVID F. MAY** Fifth great grandson of progenitor Nicholas Kegg. **DAVID FRANK MAY** [5367] (1833 – 1901) son of John and Elizabeth (Kegg) May, married Helen Mae Bruner with whom he was father of (5). David had been a carpenter for many years. **DONALD W. MAY** Fifth great grandson of progenitor Nicholas Kegg. **DOROTHEA MAXINE MAY** [5368] (1912 – 1987) daughter of Harry and Minnie (Kolfflesh) May, married Albert Emil Tamm with whom she was mother of (4). **ELIZABETH ANN MAY** Sixth great granddaughter of progenitor Nicholas Kegg. **FLORA RUTH MAY** (1895 – 1993) daughter of Charles and Mary (Garthright) May married twice; first to Ernest Lee Jones with whom she was mother of (2). Later, she married Clarence Monroe Neathery. **FLORENCE GERTRUDE MAY** [5369] (1919 – 1996) aka "Trudy" daughter of Chester and Naomi (Wishard) May, married Guido Camillo D'Annunzio with whom she was mother of (4). Trudy was a certified substitute teacher for Hamilton School District, where she taught special and elementary education. Before retiring, she was a medical secretary at St. Francis Hospital, Trenton, N.J. Active in local affairs, she was a charter member of the Gouldsboro Senior Citizens Group. She was a member of Grace Lutheran Church, Gouldsboro, and served on the church council and was a member of the Elizabeth Circle W.E.L.C.A. of the church. In addition, she was a member of Order of Eastern Star, Trenton, where she was a past worthy matron and had recently received her 25-year pin. She was also a member of Grace E. Barthold Chapter 216, Order of Eastern Star, Olyphant **FREDERICK E. MAY** Fifth great grandson of progenitor Nicholas Kegg. **FREDERICK ELLSWORTH MAY** [5370] (1914 – 1952) aka "Fred", son of Harry and Minnie (Kolfflesh) May, married twice; first to Mary Elsie Edwards with whom he was father of (1). Later, he married Virginia Elaine Lockhart. Fred served in the Army four years overseas and 14 months in Korea. Fred was stationed at Fort Dix when he was found dead in his automobile parked on a deer trail leading off the Lakehurst Road. Fred was well known in Masonic circles.

[5364] p.11 - Mansfield News (OH) June 13, 1926 [5365] San Antonio Express (TX) Oct 3, 1966 [5366] The Baltimore Sun (MD) Aug 1, 1969 [5367] Cumberland Times (MD) Jan 25, 1901 [5368] p.2 - Morning Herald (Hagerstown, MD) July 26, 1930 [5369] The Times-Tribune (Scranton, PA) June 2, 1996 [5370] p4 Trenton Evening Times (NJ) Dec 4, 1952

GLENN MAY Sixth great grandson of progenitor Nicholas Kegg. **GLENN B. MAY** Fifth great grandson of progenitor Nicholas Kegg. **GLENN BALDWIN MAY** [5371] (1923 – 2007) son of Chester and Naomi (Wishard) May, married Virginia Talbott with whom he was father of (2). **HARRY FISK MAY** (1891 – 1969) son of Charles and Mary (Garthright) May, married Cora Rebecca Nicolson Wallace with whom he was father of (1). **HARRY S. MAY** [5372] (1885 – 1944) son of Henry and Mahala (Barnes) May married twice; first to Minnie S. Kolfflesh with whom he was father of (2). Later, he married Eva May Jones Lizer. Harry was a member of St. Mary's Catholic Church and Hagerstown B. P. O. Elks. **HENRY E. MAY** [5373] (1860 – 1928) son of David and Helen (Bruner) May, married Mahala Jane Barnes with whom he was father of (2). Henry was a member of St. Paul's Methodist Church and the Men's Bible Class. **HENRY R. MAY** (1846 – 1854) son of John and Elizabeth (Kegg) May. **JACOB DANIEL MAY** Seventh great grandson of progenitor Nicholas Kegg. **JOHN DAVID MAY** Fifth great grandson of progenitor Nicholas Kegg. **JOHN E. MAY** Sixth great grandson of progenitor Nicholas Kegg. **JOSEPH MAY** (1840 – 1915) aka "Joe", son of John and Elizabeth (Kegg) May married Jennie Armedia (Tilford) Nugent was a bridge carpenter and watchman. His death certificate states that Charles G. Rogers crushed his skull. **JOSEPH GARTHRIGHT MAY** [5374] (1909 – 1983) aka "Skip", son of Charles and Mary (Garthright) May, married Elizabeth Dawson. Skip was a retired lieutenant colonel in the United States Air Force and was also a former antigue dealer in Shreveport, La. He was a member of BPO Elks Lodge 2481 and Proctor-Kildow Post 71, American Legion. **KATHERINE LEON MAY** [5375] (1862 – 1934) aka "Kate", daughter of David and Helen (Bruner) May married Andrew J. Taylor Rouzer with whom she was mother of (7). **LOTTIE VIRGINIA MAY** [5376] (1854 – 1948) daughter of John and Elizabeth (Kegg) May, married Joseph White Smith with whom she was mother of (2). Lottie was a member of the Lutheran church she passed away on her 94th Birthday. **LUCRETIA EVE MAY** [5377] (1849 – 1926) daughter of John and Elizabeth (Kegg) May, married Jackson C. Harper with whom she was mother of (5). **MARY H. MAY** [5378] (1901 – 2002) daughter of Charles and Mary (Garthright) May married twice; first to Emory Decorsey Bolden with whom she was mother of (3). Later, she married Carleton Edward Helbig. Mary was a charter member of the Oakland Civic Club and the Loar Auxiliary and a lifetime member of the American Legion. She was also a member of the Maryland Federation of Republican Women, St. Mark's Lutheran Church, and the Garrett County Historical Society. **MARY JANE MAY** [5379] (1916 – 1982) daughter of Chester and Naomi (Wishard) May, married Harry Wesley Yeagy. **MARYANN MAY** [5380] (1835 – 1876) daughter of John and Elizabeth (Kegg) May, married Henry Wertz with whom she was mother of (6). **MONIQUE MAY** Sixth great granddaughter of progenitor Nicholas Kegg. **NATALIE MAY** Sixth great granddaughter of progenitor Nicholas Kegg. **NORA L. MAY** (1868 – 1928) daughter of David and Helen (Bruner) May married twice; first to Benjamin F. Heffner with whom she was mother of (8). Later, she married Carl Youngbluth. **PATRICIA ANN MAY** Fourth great granddaughter of progenitor Nicholas Kegg. **PHYLLIS MAY** Fifth great granddaughter of progenitor Nicholas Kegg. **ROXANNE V. MAY** Sixth great granddaughter of progenitor Nicholas Kegg. **RUTH MAY** Fifth great granddaughter of progenitor Nicholas Kegg. **SAMUEL MAY** (abt 1858 –?) son of John and Elizabeth (Kegg) May was employed as a hotel clerk. **STEVE MAY** Fifth great grandson of progenitor Nicholas Kegg. **TODD C. MAY** Sixth great grandson of progenitor Nicholas Kegg. **TRAVIS M. MAY** Seventh great grandson of progenitor Nicholas Kegg. **VERA HELEN MAY** [5381] (1894 – 1936) daughter of Charles and Mary (Garthright) May. **VERA MARJORIE MAY** (1919 – 1994) daughter of Charles and Eleanor (MCDonald) May, married three times. **WILBUR DEWEY MAY** [5382] (1899 – 1937) son of Charles and Mary (Garthright) May, married Gretchen J. Miller with whom he was father of (1). Wilbur was a former automobile salesman. **WILLIAM MAY** (abt 1841 – bef 1887) son of John and Elizabeth (Kegg) May.

[5371] Baltimore Sun (MD) Mar 13, 2007 [5372] p.2 - Daily Mail (MD) Dec 22, 1944 [5373] Daily Mail (MD) Mar 15, 1928 [5374] p.16 Cumberland Evening Times (MD) Oct 25, 1983 [5375] Everett Press (PA) Sept. 21, 1934 [5376] Daily Globe (OH) Feb 25, 1948, obtained by D. Sue Dible [5377] p.2 -The Mail (MD) Jan 29, 1909 [5378] Cumberland Times (MD) Jan 24, 2002 [5379] The Evening Sun (Baltimore, MD) July 27, 1982 [5380] Bedford County PA. Archives Vol. 6, Pg 37 obtained by Bob Rose [5381] rootsweb.com obituary transcribed by Pat Thompson [5382] p.9 Cumberland

WILLIAM FRANKLIN MAY [5383] (1921 – 1992) son of Chester and Naomi (Wishard) May, married Florence Mildred Harple with whom he was father of (3).

MAYDEN

MICHAEL MAYDEN, aka "M. J.", Seventh great grandson of progenitor Nicholas Kegg.

MAYER

CHARLES MAYER (1907 – 1922) aka "Chas", son of Peter and Jessie (Friend) Mayer.
GEORGIA JESSIE MAYER [5384] (1905 – 1976) daughter of Peter and Jessie (Friend) Mayer, married Russell T. Tolan with whom she was mother of (1).

MAZZAFERRO

CHRISTINE MARIE MAZZAFERRO Sixth great granddaughter of progenitor Nicholas Kegg.
MATTHEW THOMAS MAZZAFERRO Sixth great grandson of progenitor Nicholas Kegg.
MELANY L. MAZZAFERRO Fifth great granddaughter of progenitor Nicholas Kegg.
THOMAS MAZZAFERRO Fifth great grandson of progenitor Nicholas Kegg.
TODD M. MAZZAFERRO Sixth great grandson of progenitor Nicholas Kegg.

MAZZUCA

CHRISTAN L. MAZZUCA Sixth great granddaughter of progenitor Nicholas Kegg.

MC KIM

PRUDENCE M. MC KIM Fifth great granddaughter of progenitor Nicholas Kegg.

MCADAMS

CHRISTOPHER PATRICK MCADAMS Sixth great grandson of progenitor Nicholas Kegg.
KELLEY NICOLE MCADAMS Sixth great granddaughter of progenitor Nicholas Kegg.
PAUL MCADAMS Fifth great grandson of progenitor Nicholas Kegg.
STEVEN MCADAMS [5385] (1957 – 1987) son of William and Lucy (Kelley) McAdams, married Valerie Ann Fry. Steven was killed during the bicycle portion of the third annual Governor's Cup Triathlon in Boulder, Colo., when he fell in the path of a pickup truck.

MCALLISTER

REBECCA G. MCALLISTER Sixth great granddaughter of progenitor Nicholas Kegg.
VICKKI E. MCALLISTER Sixth great granddaughter of progenitor Nicholas Kegg.

MCARDLE

MICHAEL MCARDLE Seventh great grandson of progenitor Nicholas Kegg.

Evening Times (MD) Aug 16, 1937 [5383] The Baltimore Sun (MD) May 15, 1992 [5384] The Indianapolis Star (IN) Jan 15, 1976 [5385] p.22 Washington Times (DC) June 30, 1987

MCBRIDE

BRIAN D. MCBRIDE Sixth great grandson of progenitor Nicholas Kegg. **CARSEN MCBRIDE** Seventh great grandson of progenitor Nicholas Kegg. **CASEY L. MCBRIDE** Fifth great grandson of progenitor Nicholas Kegg. **CHELSEA MARIE MCBRIDE** Seventh great granddaughter of progenitor Nicholas Kegg. **CHRISTINE L. MCBRIDE** Fifth great granddaughter of progenitor Nicholas Kegg. **DENNIS LEE MCBRIDE** [5385A] (1938 – 2004) son of Martin and Myrtle (Erickson) McBride married twice, first to Diane Marie Parker with whom he was father of (2). Dennis enjoyed fishing, hunting, gardening, watching sports, and especially spending time with his grandchildren. **JAMES R. MCBRIDE** (1938 – 1948) aka "Jimmy", son of Joe and Ruth (Lang) McBride. **KYLE WILLIAM MCBRIDE** [5386] (1966 – 1986) son of Joe and Gay (Scroggs) McBride was a student at Florida Southern College and was employed by Bowen Supply Co. as a salesman. **MARTIN ALBERT MCBRIDE** (1912 – 1986) son of Albert and Edith (Knouf) McBride married twice. first to Myrtle Jeanette Erickson with whom he was father of (2). Later, he married Lois Haxby with whom he was father of (1). **MOLLY ANN MCBRIDE** Sixth great granddaughter of progenitor Nicholas Kegg.

MCBROOM

LYLE MCBROOM Fifth great grandson of progenitor Nicholas Kegg.
RITA MCBROOM Fifth great granddaughter of progenitor Nicholas Kegg.

MCCALL

BENJAMIN ENNIS MCCALL [5387] (1979 – 2009) son of Brad and Lori McCall, married Michelle Heaberlin. Ben was employed as a dive supervisor with Cal Dive Corp., a Houston, Texas, based company that provides underwater assistance and repair for the gas and oil industry in the Gulf of Mexico. Ben enjoyed golfing, boating, and home improvement projects. **LISA MCCALL** Sixth great granddaughter of progenitor Nicholas Kegg.

MCCALLISTER

CAMERON MCCALLISTER Seventh great grandson of progenitor Nicholas Kegg.
SHANE MCCALLISTER Seventh great grandson of progenitor Nicholas Kegg.

MCCANN

KELLYN MCCANN Seventh great granddaughter of progenitor Nicholas Kegg. **LAINE MCCANN** Seventh great grandson of progenitor Nicholas Kegg. **REID MCCANN** Seventh great grandson of progenitor Nicholas Kegg. **TONI MCCANN** Seventh great granddaughter of progenitor Nicholas Kegg. **TY MCCANN** Seventh great grandson of progenitor Nicholas Kegg.

MCCARL

CHARLES LEROY MCCARL (1940 – 1940) son of Roy and Marguerite (Childers) McCarl.
JUDY KAY MCCARL Sixth great granddaughter of progenitor Nicholas Kegg.

MCCARRAHER

COURTNEY MCCARRAHER Seventh great granddaughter of progenitor Nicholas Kegg.

[5385A] p.18 Des Moines Register (IA) Dec 26, 2004 [5386] The Courier (Waterloo, IA) Dec 10, 1986 [5387] Newton Daily News (IA) Sep 22, 2009

MCCARTER

MARCIE MCCARTER Fifth great granddaughter of progenitor Nicholas Kegg.
MICHELLE MCCARTER Fifth great granddaughter of progenitor Nicholas Kegg.

MCCARTNEY

DOUGLAS ALLEN MCCARTNEY Seventh great grandson of progenitor Nicholas Kegg.
HARRISON E. MCCARTNEY aka "Harry", Seventh great grandson of progenitor Nicholas Kegg.
HEATHER MARIE MCCARTNEY Seventh great granddaughter of progenitor Nicholas Kegg.
JOHN MCCARTNEY Eighth great grandson of progenitor Nicholas Kegg.
JUSTIN MCCARTNEY Eighth great grandson of progenitor Nicholas Kegg.
ROBIN KAY MCCARTNEY Seventh great granddaughter of progenitor Nicholas Kegg.

MCCAULEY

EDWARD MCCAULEY Sixth great grandson of progenitor Nicholas Kegg.
ELLA MCCAULEY Seventh great granddaughter of progenitor Nicholas Kegg.
PRESTON MCCAULEY Seventh great grandson of progenitor Nicholas Kegg.

MCCLAFLIN

TAMMY LOU MCCLAFLIN Sixth great granddaughter of progenitor Nicholas Kegg.

MCCLAIN

JONATHAN MCCLAIN Sixth great grandson of progenitor Nicholas Kegg.
JOSHUA MCCLAIN Sixth great grandson of progenitor Nicholas Kegg.

MCCLELLAN

CARL JACK SCHRECENGOST MCCLELLAN [5388] (1930 -2012) son of Jack and Helen (Both) Schrecengost McClellan was adopted by Vernon Harry McClellan. Carl was a graduate of Johnson University and Christian Theological Seminary. He pastored churches in Ohi at; Palestine, Zanesville, Obetz and most recently was named Pastor Emeritus of Fairfield Christian Church where he and Kathryn served twelve years as director of the Barnabas Ministry. During his seminary and clinical pastoral training he pastored Christian churches in; Brodhead, Kentucky, Keensburg, Illinois, Trafalgar, Indiana, and Topeka, Kansas. Carl was chaplain for the Ohio Youth Commission for 22 years at both Fairfield School for Boys and Training Center for Youth. **CHANTEE MARIE MCCLELLAN** Fifth great granddaughter of progenitor Nicholas Kegg. **DONALD L MCCLELLAN** Fifth great grandson of progenitor Nicholas Kegg. **EARL RAYMOND MCCLELLAN** (1920 – 1921) son of Howard and Maude (Ditch) McClellan. **HOWARD GEORGE MCCLELLAN** [5389] (1908 – 1987) aka "George" son of Howard and Maude (Ditch) McClellan married Gladys Vaugh with whom he was father of (5). Later, he married Vivian Patterson. George was employed as a state meat inspector in the Coshocton area. He was a member at Prairie Chapel Church, Moose Lodge and Disabled American Veterans of Coshocton. **KENNETH PAUL MCCLELLAN** (1923 – 1992) son of Howard and Maude (Ditch) McClellan, married Bernice Wanda Inherst. **KIMBERLY RENEE MCCLELLAN** Fifth great granddaughter of progenitor Nicholas Kegg. **MABEL M. MCCLELLAN** (1899 – 1971) daughter of Howard and Maude (Ditch) McClellan, married Clem C. Curry with whom she was mother of (4).

[5388] Lancaster Eagle Gazette (PA) December 29, 2012 [5389] Tribune (Coshocton, OH) Aug 4, 1987

MELISSA A. MCCLELLAN Fifth great granddaughter of progenitor Nicholas Kegg.
NANCY CAROL MCCLELLAN (1941 – 1943) daughter of Howard and Gladys (Seibert) McClellan.
ROBERT MCCLELLAN Fifth great grandson of progenitor Nicholas Kegg.
VERNON HARRY MCCLELLAN (1904 – 1990) son of Howard and Maude (Ditch) McClellan married three times; first to Helen Hilda Both with whom he was father of (4). He married Tressie Lavita Strance and later, married Zona Margaret Stott. **VERNON HARRY MCCLELLAN** (1940 – 1940) son of Vernon and Hilda (Both) McClellan. **VIOLA SARAHBELLE MCCLELLAN** (1914 – 2000) daughter of Howard and Maude (Ditch) McClellan married four times; first to Harold Jenkins, then to John Ezverniccanu, followed by Cletus Arelius Prechtel and later, she married Lucion C. Choate.
VIRGINIA CATHERINE MCCLELLAN [5390] (1907 – 1967) daughter of Howard and Maude (Ditch) McClellan, married John Cecil Blake.

MCCLINTIC

JAMES ANDREW MCCLINTIC [5391] (1907 – 1951) son of George and Grace (Morgart) McClintic, died of bums suffered when a fire destroyed his house trailer.
JOHN RAYMOND MCCLINTIC (1905 – 1989) son of George and Grace (Morgart) McClintic.
MARGARET E. MCCLINTIC [5392] (1908 – 1986) daughter of George and Grace (Morgart) McClintic, married Edwin G. Schaper with whom she was mother of (1).

MCCOMBS

GRAYSON MCCOMBS Eighth great grandson of progenitor Nicholas Kegg.

MCCORMICK

ANGELA RENAE MCCORMICK, aka "Angie", Sixth great granddaughter of progenitor Nicholas Kegg. **RACHELLE LEIGH MCCORMICK** Sixth great granddaughter of progenitor Nicholas Kegg. **RHONDA GAIL MCCORMICK** Sixth great granddaughter of progenitor Nicholas Kegg. **SUZANNE DEE MCCORMICK** Sixth great granddaughter of progenitor Nicholas Kegg.

MCCOY

BETTY LOU MCCOY (1919 – 1972) daughter of Hausmer and Della (Knouf) McCoy, married Mac John Randall with whom she was mother of (2). Betty Lou was a talented musician graduating from Drake University where she was a member of the Chi Onega sorority and other societies. Betty Lou was employed as a music teacher.

MCCRACKEN

MEGAN MARIE MCCRACKEN Sixth great granddaughter of progenitor Nicholas Kegg.
MOLLY M MCCRACKEN Sixth great granddaughter of progenitor Nicholas Kegg.

MCCREARY

HEATHER LYNN MCCREARY [5392A] (1988 – 1993) daughter of Michael and Heidi (Elder) McCreary.

[5390] Sacramento Bee (CA) Feb 11, 1967 [5391] Daily Banner (IN) Feb 1, 1951 [5392] p.3 - Bluffton News-Banner (IN) Feb 17, 1986, obtained by D. Sue Dible [5392A] p.B3- Lancaster Eagle-Gazette (OH) Dec 21, 1993, contributed by D. Sue Dible.

MCCULLY

MARTHA A. MCCULLY Fifth great granddaughter of progenitor Nicholas Kegg.
SHARON G. MCCULLY Fifth great granddaughter of progenitor Nicholas Kegg.

MCCURDY

AUDREY ELLEN MCCURDY [5392B] aka "LaLa" (1945 – 2010) daughter of Edward and Audrey (Roach) McCurdy married three times, first to Keith Kephart with whom she was mother of (1). She married Robert William Bodensteiner with whom she was mother of (1), later married Robert Wayne Steinberger. **CAROL A MCCURDY** Fifth great granddaughter of progenitor Nicholas Kegg.
DENNIS RAY MCCURDY Fifth great grandson of progenitor Nicholas Kegg.

MCDANIEL

ALLAN LEROY MCDANIEL [5392C] aka "Mac" (1939 – 2017) son of Merle and Ethel (Webb) McDaniel married twice; first to Reda J. Deal with whom he was father of (2). Later, he married Donna with whom he was father of (2). Allan was a social person who enjoyed golf, bowling, cards and time spent with his fur-babies, Belle and Beau. He was devoted to his Indigo Creek family and was always there to lend a hand to a neighbor who needed help. **ALLAN L. MCDANIEL** Fifth great grandson of progenitor Nicholas Kegg. **ALMA LOUISE MCDANIEL** [5393] (1923 – 1935) daughter of Roy and Katie (Kautebaugh) McDaniel. **ALMEDA MCDANIEL** aka "Meadie" Fourth great granddaughter of progenitor Nicholas Kegg. **ANN M. MCDANIEL** (1874 – 1878) daughter of William and Mariah (Wonders) McDaniel. **ANNIE HESTER MCDANIEL** [5394] (1926 – 2003) daughter of Lloyd andTrella (Jones) McDaniel, married George W. R. Carrico with whom she was mother of (3). Annie was a Watkins Home Products representative for 20 years. She was a foster parent of 28 children. **ARTHUR JAMES MCDANIEL** [5395] (1917 – 2007) son of William and Annie (Shull) McDaniel married twice; first to Evelyn Ruth Strayer with whom he was father of (4). Later, he married Adeline Gerhke. Arthur retired as a district sales manager from Bixby-Zimmer Engineering. He was a member of Friendship Community Church, Sunset Lodge 623 F&AM, Syria Shrine and Greater Washington Area Senior Citizens. He previously enjoyed playing in the Senior Citizens bowling league for 12 years, where he served as president and chaplain and was a former member of Greene County Country Club and past president of the golf league. He also enjoyed hunting, fishing and playing in the church dartball league. **BARRY MCDANIEL** Fifth great grandson of progenitor Nicholas Kegg. **BARRY EUGENE MCDANIEL** [5395A] (1941 – 1999) son of Irene May McDaniel, married Linda Faye Fowler with whom he was father of (1). Barry served with the United States Navy aboard the USS Roosevelt during VietNam. **BONNIE LOU MCDANIEL** Fourth great granddaughter of progenitor Nicholas Kegg. **CARL J. MCDANIEL** Fourth great grandson of progenitor Nicholas Kegg. **CAROL MCDANIEL** Fourth great granddaughter of progenitor Nicholas Kegg. **CAROL ANN MCDANIEL** Fourth great granddaughter of progenitor Nicholas Kegg. **CAROLYN MCDANIEL** Fourth great granddaughter of progenitor Nicholas Kegg. **CHARLOTTE LYNN MCDANIEL** Fifth great granddaughter of progenitor Nicholas Kegg. **CHRISTOPHER LEE MCDANIEL** Eighth great grandson of progenitor Nicholas Kegg. **CLYDE WESLEY MCDANIEL** [5396] (1911 – 1970) son of William and Annie (Shull) McDaniel, married Dorothy Elizabeth Wolford with whom he was father of (1). Clyde was a member of Tire Hill Church of the Brethren, Lodge 48, Loom, Johnstown; and Ideal Volunteer Fire Company.

[5392B] Des Moines Register (IA) May 25, 2010 [5392C] The Sun News (SC) July 19, 2017 [5393] Johnstown Tribune-Democrat (PA) Oct 12, 1935, obtained by D. Sue Dible [5394] Archives by Meyersdale Library Daily American (PA) Nov 22, 2003, transcribed by Kerry L. Miller [5395] Observer-Reporter (Washington, PA) Nov 22, 2007 [5395A] Florida Times Union (Jacksonville) Feb 25, 1999 [5396] Bedford County Historical Society Pioneer Library, book 116, p. 177 obtained by D. Sue Dible

CONNIE MCDANIEL Fourth great granddaughter of progenitor Nicholas Kegg. **DANIEL M. MCDANIEL** (1866 – 1874) son of William and Mariah (Wonders) McDaniel. **DAVID L. MCDANIEL** Fourth great grandson of progenitor Nicholas Kegg. **DAVID PATRICK MCDANIEL** Fifth great grandson of progenitor Nicholas Kegg. **DENISE MCDANIEL** Fourth great granddaughter of progenitor Nicholas Kegg. **DONNA FAITH MCDANIEL** (1939 – 1939) daughter of Arthur and Evelyn (Strayer) McDaniel. **EDITH M. MCDANIEL** (1901 – 1924) daughter of Joseph and Mary Jane (Gross) McDaniel, married Harry Eugene Huster with whom she was mother of (1). **ESTHER PEARL MCDANIEL** [5396A] (1903 – 1989) daughter of Joseph and Mary Jane (Gross) McDaniel, married Henry Wingard with whom she was mother of (2). **EUGENE JOEL MCDANIEL** [5397] (1955 – 1962) son of William and Edith (Dietz) McDaniel. **FOSTER OWEN MCDANIEL** [5398] (1909 – 1996) aka "Toss", son of William and Annie (Shull) McDaniel married twice; first to Alice Elizabeth Koontz. Later, he married Margaret Marie Marti with whom he was father of (2). **GARY MCDANIEL** Fifth great grandson of progenitor Nicholas Kegg. **GLADYS ALMEDA MCDANIEL** [5399] (1907 – 1983) daughter of William and Annie (Shull) McDaniel, married James Samuel Devine with whom she was mother of (4). **HARLEY MCDANIEL** Fifth great grandson of progenitor Nicholas Kegg. **HERBERT MCDANIEL** (1910 – 1910) son of Joseph and Mary Jane (Gross) McDaniel. **HOLLY RENEE MCDANIEL** Eighth great granddaughter of progenitor Nicholas Kegg. **IONA MAE MCDANIEL** [5400] aka "Nonia" (1942 – 1986) daughter of Roy and Emma (Sala) McDaniel. **IRENE MAY MCDANIEL** [5401] (1921 – 2008) daughter of William and Annie (Shull) McDaniel was mother of (1). Later, she married Lewis Wesley Crislip with whom she was mother of (2). Irene retired after about 30 years of service as a garment worker. Following retirement, she was employed by Green Thumb of Pennsylvania for several years. **JAMES MCDANIEL** Fourth great grandson of progenitor Nicholas Kegg. **JANE MCDANIEL** Fourth great granddaughter of progenitor Nicholas Kegg. **JOHN CHARLES MCDANIEL** (1914 – 1994) son of Joseph and Mary Jane (Gross) McDaniel. **JOSEPH EARL MCDANIEL** [5402] (1911 – 1933) aka "Earl", son of Joseph and Mary Jane (Gross) McDaniel was locally well known as an amateur Baseball pitcher. Earl was a member of the Flood City A.C. team of the Moxliam Baseball League last year and was also affiliated with the Croatian Fraternal Union team of the City League. He had played several years previously with various local independent teams. **JOSEPH FRANKLIN MCDANIEL** [5402A] aka "Joel" (1870 – 1955) son of William and Mariah (Wonders) McDaniel married Mary Jane Gross with whom he was father of (11). Joel had been employed by the Johnstown Traction Co. for 33 years. He was a member of Christ EUB church, Union Aerie 2092 of FOE, Royal Oak; Second Horizons Club, Royal Oak Public Library. **JUDITH MCDANIEL** Fourth great granddaughter of progenitor Nicholas Kegg. **JUDITH ANN MCDANIEL** aka "Judy", Fourth great granddaughter of progenitor Nicholas Kegg. **KELLY MCDANIEL** Sixth great granddaughter of progenitor Nicholas Kegg. **KEVIN MCDANIEL** Sixth great grandson of progenitor Nicholas Kegg. **KIMBERLY LYNN MCDANIEL** Eighth great granddaughter of progenitor Nicholas Kegg. **LEE FRANKLIN MCDANIEL** [5403] (1919 – 1981) son of William and Annie (Shull) McDaniel married twice; first to Doris Ruth Rager with whom he was father of (2). Later, he married Bertha Emily Courtly with whom he was father of (3). **LEE WILLIAM MCDANIEL** Fourth great grandson of progenitor Nicholas Kegg. **LESTER S. MCDANIEL** [5403A] aka "Mac" (1923 – 1982) son of William and Annie Catherine (Shull) McDaniel married Vetty Lou Heslop with whom he was father of (2). A member of Franklin Street United Methodist Church and Ferndale Volunteer Fire Company, Lester was a Veteran of World War II, former employee of Hoff Builder and Supply. **LESTER S. MCDANIEL** Fourth great grandson of progenitor Nicholas Kegg. **LINDA LEE MCDANIEL** Fourth great granddaughter of progenitor Nicholas Kegg. **LLOYD E. MCDANIEL** [5404] (1904 – 1973) son of William and

---

[5396A] Johnstown Tribune-Democrat (PA) Mar 31, 1989 contributed by Brian Cartwright [5397] Johnstown Tribune-Democrat (PA) Sep 10, 1962, obtained by D. Sue Dible [5398] p.14 Pittsburgh Post-Gazette (PA) Jan 12, 1996 [5399] Johnstown Tribune-Democrat (PA), Nov 5, 1983, obtained by D. Sue Dible [5400] Johnstown Tribune-Democrat (PA) Aug 7, 1986, obtained by D. Sue Dible [5401] Johnstown Tribune-Democrat (PA) June 28, 2008 [5402] Johnstown Tribune-Democrat (PA) Apr 4, 1933, obtained by D. Sue Dible [5402A] p.2 -Bedford Gazette (PA) Dec 9, 1955 [5403] p.16 Pittsburgh Post-Gazette (PA) June 26, 1981 [5403A] Johnstown Tribune-Democrat (PA) Oct 21, 1982, contributed by D. Sue Dible [5404] Johnstown Tribune-Democrat (PA) obtained by D. Sue Dible

Annie (Shull) McDaniel, married Trella Jones with whom he was father of (3). **LORENA MCDANIEL** (5404A) aka "Maggie" (1895 – 1963) daughter of Joel and Mary Jane (Gross) McDaniel, married Frederick William Riddinger with whom she was mother of (2). **MARGARET MARIA MCDANIEL** (5404B) (1905 – 1989) daughter of Joel and Mary Jane (Gross) McDaniel married five times, first to Ross Glen Seese with whom she was mother of (4). Later she married Fred Brown, Jack Brown, Charles Denver Schwardt and Henry John Boerkoel. Margaret was a member of the Memorial Baptist Church and the Salvation Army Golden Agers. **MARY ELLEN MCDANIEL** (5405) (1868 – 1929) aka "Maria", daughter of William and Mariah (Wonders) McDaniel, married Emanuel Troutman with whom she was mother of (4). **MARY ELLEN MCDANIEL** (1917 – 2004) daughter of Joseph and Mary Jane (Gross) McDaniel, married John Wesley Bracken. **MELVIN B. MCDANIEL** (1936 – 1966) son of Roy and Emma (Sala) McDaniel, married Jeaneatt Thompson Locklear. **MERLE E. MCDANIEL** Fourth great grandson of progenitor Nicholas Kegg. **MERLE W. MCDANIEL** (5406) (1913 – 1996) son of William and Annie Shull, married Ethel June Webb with whom he was father of (4). Merle retired from the Florence Mining Co. in New Florence. He was a charter member of Tire Hill Local 998, UMWA, and Jerome Volunteer Fire Dept. Also, member of Ferndale Sportsmen; New Florence Local 1257, UMWA; Jerome Nest 556, Polish Falcons of America, and Jerome Post 802, American Legion. **MICHAEL MCDANIEL** Fifth great grandson of progenitor Nicholas Kegg. **MONA KAY MCDANIEL** Fourth great granddaughter of progenitor Nicholas Kegg. **OLIVER MCDANIEL** Ninth great grandson of progenitor Nicholas Kegg. **PATRICIA LEE MCDANIEL** (1945 – 1945) daughter of Warren and Wanda (Hershiser) McDaniel. **PATRICIA MARIE MCDANIEL** (5407) (1956 – 2001) daughter of Robert and Marian (Urbassik) McDaniel, married Anthony R. Lopresti with whom she was mother of (2). **PAUL E. MCDANIEL** Fourth great grandson of progenitor Nicholas Kegg. **PAUL WILLIAM MCDANIEL** Fourth great grandson of progenitor Nicholas Kegg. **PERCY WILBUR MCDANIEL** (1899- ?) son of Joseph and Mary Jane (Gross) McDaniel. **RACHEL CATHERINE MCDANIEL** (1859 – 1935) daughter of William and Mariah (Wonders) McDaniel, married James C. Stickler. **RICHARD A. MCDANIEL** Fourth great grandson of progenitor Nicholas Kegg. **ROBERT EARL MCDANIEL** aka "Bob", Fourth great grandson of progenitor Nicholas Kegg. **ROBIN LYN MCDANIEL** Fifth great granddaughter of progenitor Nicholas Kegg. **ROGER CLYDE MCDANIEL** Fourth great grandson of progenitor Nicholas Kegg. **RONALD LEE MCDANIEL** Fifth great grandson of progenitor Nicholas Kegg. **ROY CHARLES MCDANIEL** (5408) (1902 – 1961) son of William and Annie (Shull) McDaniel married twice; first to Katie Malinda Kaultebaugh with whom he was father of (1). Later he married Emma Sala with whom he was father of (9). **ROY CONRAD MCDANIEL** (5409) (1932 – 1933) son of Roy and Emma (Sala) McDaniel died due to tubercular meningitis. This little one suffered intense pain during the short illness, and it seemed better to have God call him home than to see him suffer. **SALLY ANN MCDANIEL** Fourth great granddaughter of progenitor Nicholas Kegg. **SANDRA MCDANIEL** Fourth great granddaughter of progenitor Nicholas Kegg. **RUTH KATHERN MCDANIEL** (5409A) (1907 – 1999) daughter of Joel and Mary Jane (Gross) McDaniel married twice, first to Stanley Robert Wright with whom she was mother of (1). Later she married Cecil Scribner. Ruth was a retired cashier from Glosser Bros. Department Store and Gateway Truck Stop, Breezewood. **SCOTT ALAN MCDANIEL** Fifth great grandson of progenitor Nicholas Kegg. **SUSAN MCDANIEL** (1833 – 1887) daughter of Joseph and Rachel Myers Kegg was mother of (1). **SUSANNAH ELIZABETH MCDANIEL** (5410) (1872 – 1943) daughter of William and Mariah (Wonders) McDaniel married twice; first to George Washington Ressler with whom she was mother of (5). Later, she married Stanley White.

(5404A) Johnstown Tribune-Democrat (PA) Aug 3, 1963, contributed by D. Sue Dible (5404B) Petoskey News-Review (MI) serving Emmet Co., Emmet County Genealogical Society (5405) Altoona Mirror (PA) Dec 26, 1929 Find A Grave memorial# 125161981 Created by: Sky (5406) Daily American (PA) Dec 16, 1996 Archives by Meyersdale Library Transcribed and proofread by Martha Matsuda (5407) p.6 sec B The Plain Dealer (OH) Aug 26, 2001 obtained by D. Sue Dible (5408) Gospel Herald Volume LV, Number 3 Jan 16, 1962 (5409) Gospel Herald - Vol. XXVI, No. 16 July 20, 1933 (5409A) Johnstown Tribune-Democrat (PA) Nov 17, 1999 contributed by D. Sue Dible (5410)

VIOLA PEARL MCDANIEL (1926 – 1926) daughter of William and Annie (Shull) McDaniel. **VIOLET MCDANIEL** [5411] aka "Mickey" (1924 – 2016) daughter of Lloyd and Trella (Jones) McDaniel, married Charles A. Geise with whom she was mother of (1). Mickey was employed at the Lock Haven Chair Factory, Sylvania Electric Products of Lock Haven and Weis Market of Lock Haven before working for the B. Snowiss Fur Co. of Lock Haven for 45 years until her retirement. During WWII, Mickey worked at Holmstead Field, Middleton, Pa on bomber planes. Mickey and her husband also owned and operated the Four Seasons Tavern, Charleton, Pa. She was very active in the Lock Haven Moose Lodge, Chapter 215. **WANDA CHERYL MCDANIEL** Fourth great granddaughter of progenitor Nicholas Kegg. **WARREN HAROLD MCDANIEL** son of Warren and Wanda (Hershiser) McDaniel. **WILLIAM A. MCDANIEL** (1835 - 1910) son of Joseph and Rachel Myers (Kegg) McDaniel, married Mariah Wonders with whom he was father of (7). **WILLIAM CALVIN MCDANIEL** (1863 – 1883) son of Susan McDaniel. **WILLIAM F. MCDANIEL** [5412] (1918 – 1998) son of Joseph and Mary Jane (Gross) McDaniel married twice first to Viola Bell. Later, he married Edith Bernice Dietz with whom he was father of (5). William was a charter member of the Venice Moose Lodge. **WILLIAM HENRY MCDANIEL** [5413] (1927 – 1975) son of Roy and Emma (Sala) McDaniel had been an operating engineer for Burns and Roe Construction Co. and at Sharp Memorial Hospital. William was a retired senior Navy chief boilerman; he served in World War II and the Korean War. He was a member of Fleet Reserve Association Branch 61 in Chula Vista and a former member of the Operating Engineers Union Local 501. **WILLIAM STEPHEN MCDANIEL** [5414] (1877 – 1960) son of William and Mariah (Wonders) McDaniel, married Annie Catherine Shull with whom he was father of (11). William was a retired employee of the Bird Coal Co., Johnstown. He was a member of the Tire Hill Church of the Brethren and of the UMWA. **WILSON NATHANIEL MCDANIEL** (1844 – 1924) son of Joseph and Rachel Myers (Kegg) McDaniel, married Minerva Wolf.

MCDERMOTT

ELAINE MARIE MCDERMOTT Fifth great granddaughter of progenitor Nicholas Kegg. **ELEANOR CORNELIA MCDERMOTT** Fifth great granddaughter of progenitor Nicholas Kegg. **ELIZABETH JANICE MCDERMOTT** [5414A] (1928 – 2008) daughter of James and Maybell (Franz) McDermott married Merrill Drexell Sather with whom she was mother of (6). A degree in education, Elizabeth taught one year of Home Economics for a high school in Corvallis before starting her family. Later, Elizabeth supported herself and her children by opening up her doors and providing daycare. She touched and influenced many lives. Her door was always open and there was always plenty of food to go around. She was always trying to feed you. Her passion was for children. She was room mother, Campfire leader, Cub leader, PTA officer and seamstress for everything. One of her proudest accomplishments was to have all five of her sons earn Eagle Awards. She loved visiting with friends and watching sports, especially OSU and Gongaza basketball. She was loved by all who knew her. **JAMES COWAN MCDERMOTT** [5414B] (1945 – 2005) son of James and Elaine (Ort) McDermott. **JAMES ELLIS MCDERMOTT** [5414C] (1902 – 1962) son of James and Mattie (Dean) McDermott, married Maybell V. Franz with whom he was father of (1). James, assistant manager of the Greyhound Post House, formerly was purchasing agent for Portland International Airport. At one time he operated a cigar store in the Failing building and had also been employed by Gray and Co. and Lang and Co. **JOHN MICHAEL MCDERMOTT** Fifth great grandson of progenitor Nicholas Kegg. **MARY ANN MCDERMOTT** [5415] (1898 – 1971) daughter of James and Mattie (Dean) McDermott married twice; first to Robert Barney Veeder with whom she was mother of (1). Later, she married James Harold Haughy. Mary was a retired Tehama County school teacher, she was a member of St. Peter's Episcopal Church, Menzaleh Temple No. 16. Daughters of the Nile of Sacramento, Red Bluff Nile Club, 50-year member of Order of

p.2 Bedford Gazette (PA) Oct 23, 1943 [5411] Donald Walker Funeral Home (SC) [5412] Sarasota Herald-Tribune (FL) Jan 9, 1998 [5413] p.8 San Diego Union (CA) Sep 17, 1975 [5414] Bedford County Historical Society (PA), book 3 p.2305 obtained by D. Sue Dible [5414A] Spokesman-Review (Spokane, WA) Dec 6, 2008 [5414B] Baltimore Sun (MD) May 14, 2005 [5414C] p.42- Oregonian (OR) Sep 4, 1962 [5415] The Sacramento Bee (CA) Jan 26, 1971

Eastern Star, a member of Vesper Chapter OES of Red Bluff; past president of the Red Bluff Business and Professional Women's Club, and past adviser of Rainbow Girls.

MATTIE MEARLE MCDERMOTT (1890 – 1979) daughter of James and Mattie (Dean) McDermott, married Theodore Wheeler Lockwood.

MCDONALD

COLLEEN MCDONALD Fifth great granddaughter of progenitor Nicholas Kegg.
MICHAEL WYMAN MCDONALD Fifth great grandson of progenitor Nicholas Kegg.
PATRICK GAYLAND MCDONALD [5416] (1934 – 2000) son of Harry and Violet (Rice) McDonald married three times. He was father of (3). Patrick was employed as a truck driver.
WILLIAM J. MCDONALD aka "Bill", Fifth great grandson of progenitor Nicholas Kegg.

MCDONOUGH

PAUL MCDONOUGH Sixth great grandson of progenitor Nicholas Kegg.
STEFAN MCDONOUGH Sixth great grandson of progenitor Nicholas Kegg.

MCELHENY

CONNER MCELHENY Seventh great grandson of progenitor Nicholas Kegg.
KATE MCELHENY Seventh great granddaughter of progenitor Nicholas Kegg.

MCFALL

FRANK BENTON MCFALL [5416A] (1884 – 1958) son of Henry and Nellie (Snavely) McFall, married Gladys Essex Conroy with whom he was father of (4). Frank was a member of Garden City Lodge No. 141, F. & A.M. of Chicago, Ill., and San Francisco Islam Temple. **JEANNE ESSEX MCFALL** (1910 – 1977) daughter of Frank and Gladys (Conroy) McFall, married Victor Basil Lowry with whom she was mother of (1). **RALPH STERLING MCFALL** (1886 -?) son of Henry and Nellie (Snavely) McFall. **SHIRLEY ELLINGER MCFALL** (1915 – 1924) daughter of Frank and Gladys (Conroy) McFall.

MCFARLAND

CHRISTINA E. MCFARLAND Sixth great granddaughter of progenitor Nicholas Kegg.
WADE ROY MCFARLAND Sixth great grandson of progenitor Nicholas Kegg.

MCFARLANE

JAMEE M. MCFARLANE Sixth great granddaughter of progenitor Nicholas Kegg.

MCGAHUEY

CHERYL ELAINE MCGAHUEY Sixth great granddaughter of progenitor Nicholas Kegg.
ROGER ALAN MCGAHUEY Sixth great grandson of progenitor Nicholas Kegg.

MCGEE

SCOTT MCGEE Seventh great grandson of progenitor Nicholas Kegg.

[5416] Herald-Republican (Angola, IN) March 22, 2000, obtained by D. Sue Dible [5416A] The San Francisco Examiner (CA) Dec 22, 1958

STEVE MCGEE Seventh great grandson of progenitor Nicholas Kegg.
SUSAN MCGEE Seventh great granddaughter of progenitor Nicholas Kegg.

MCGILVRAY

ERIN R. MCGILVRAY Sixth great granddaughter of progenitor Nicholas Kegg.
JENNIFER L. MCGILVRAY aka "Jenna", Sixth great granddaughter of progenitor Nicholas Kegg.

MCGINNIS

PATRICIA ANN MCGINNIS Fifth great granddaughter of progenitor Nicholas Kegg.
WILLIAM CRAIG MCGINNIS Fifth great grandson of progenitor Nicholas Kegg.

MCGLAUN

JACOB MCGLAUN Seventh great grandson of progenitor Nicholas Kegg.
JOSEPH MCGLAUN aka "Joe", Seventh great grandson of progenitor Nicholas Kegg.

MCGREVY

PATRICK MCGREVY Fifth great grandson of progenitor Nicholas Kegg.

MCGUIRE

BARBARA ANN MCGUIRE Fifth great granddaughter of progenitor Nicholas Kegg.
CHRISTINE MCGUIRE Fifth great granddaughter of progenitor Nicholas Kegg.
DANIEL RAY MCGUIRE [5417] (1964 – 1998) son of Ralph and Charlene (Barnes) McGuire was father of (1). Daniel was employed by Peck's Services as a roofer. He was a member of the First Christian Church, and he served four years in the U. S. Marine Corps.
JAMES CARROLL MCGUIRE Fifth great grandson of progenitor Nicholas Kegg.
JASON LEE MCGUIRE Fifth great grandson of progenitor Nicholas Kegg.
JEFFREY CARL MCGUIRE Fifth great grandson of progenitor Nicholas Kegg.
JOHN K. MCGUIRE Fifth great grandson of progenitor Nicholas Kegg.
KATHY MCGUIRE 5th great granddaughter of progenitor Nicholas Kegg.
MARCY JO MCGUIRE Fifth great granddaughter of progenitor Nicholas Kegg.
MARGARET LYNNE MCGUIRE Fifth great granddaughter of progenitor Nicholas Kegg.
MARTIN J. MCGUIRE Fifth great grandson of progenitor Nicholas Kegg.
MICHAEL MCGUIRE [5418] (1959 – 1961) son of John and Norita (Barnes) McGuire.
REBECCA LOUISE MCGUIRE Fifth great granddaughter of progenitor Nicholas Kegg.
SEAN MCGUIRE Sixth great grandson of progenitor Nicholas Kegg.

MCHENRY

KHLOE MCHENRY Seventh great granddaughter of progenitor Nicholas Kegg.
KYNDALL RAE MCHENRY Seventh great granddaughter of progenitor Nicholas Kegg.

MCINERNEY

KERRIGAN DANAE MCINERNEY Ninth great granddaughter of progenitor Nicholas Kegg.

[5417] Salem News (OH) Jan 5,1998, obtained by D. Sue Dible [5418] p.8 - Salem News (OH) May 18, 1961, obtained by D. Sue Dible

MCILVAINE

DARREN E. MCILVAINE Seventh great grandson of progenitor Nicholas Kegg.
EDWARD J. MCILVAINE Sixth great grandson of progenitor Nicholas Kegg.
KAREN LYNN MCILVAINE Sixth great granddaughter of progenitor Nicholas Kegg.
LAUREN MCILVAINE Seventh great granddaughter of progenitor Nicholas Kegg.

MCINTYRE

AMBER ELAINE MCINTYRE Sixth great granddaughter of progenitor Nicholas Kegg.
DEE MCINTYRE Fifth great grandson of progenitor Nicholas Kegg.
JOHN FRANCIS MCINTYRE [5418A] (1941 – 2012) son of John and Fern (Gillilan) McIntyre will be remembered as a teacher and the former owner of Johnny Macs.
KLARK D. MCINTYRE Sixth great grandson of progenitor Nicholas Kegg.

MCKAY

MATTHEW MCKAY Sixth great grandson of progenitor Nicholas Kegg.
NICHOLAS MCKAY Sixth great grandson of progenitor Nicholas Kegg.

MCKEE

C. BRUCE MCKEE Seventh great grandson of progenitor Nicholas Kegg.
DEREK J. MCKEE Seventh great grandson of progenitor Nicholas Kegg.
JACQUELYN MICHELLE MCKEE Seventh great granddaughter of progenitor Nicholas Kegg.
JENNIFER CHRISTINE MCKEE Seventh great granddaughter of progenitor Nicholas Kegg.

MCKENZIE

ANDREW MCKENZIE Sixth great grandson of progenitor Nicholas Kegg. **BONNIE ANN MCKENZIE** Fifth great granddaughter of progenitor Nicholas Kegg. **COLLIN MCKENZIE** Seventh great grandson of progenitor Nicholas Kegg. **JENICA MCKENZIE** Sixth great granddaughter of progenitor Nicholas Kegg. **JOSEPH J. MCKENZIE** Fifth great grandson of progenitor Nicholas Kegg. **KEVIN M. MCKENZIE** Sixth great grandson of progenitor Nicholas Kegg. **MARY ANN MCKENZIE** [5419] (1941 – 2004) daughter of Byard and Winifred Ann Frost (Turner) McKenzie, married Elmer Minnick. Mary Ann was a member of St. Ann's Shrine and was a supply person for Flushing Shirt Factory, Grantsville. **MICHAEL MCKENZIE** Sixth great grandson of progenitor Nicholas Kegg. **REBECCA MCKENZIE** Sixth great granddaughter of progenitor Nicholas Kegg. **SARAH MCKENZIE** Seventh great granddaughter of progenitor Nicholas Kegg. **TIMOTHY T. MCKENZIE** Fifth great grandson of progenitor Nicholas Kegg. **WILLIAM P. MCKENZIE** Fifth great grandson of progenitor Nicholas Kegg.

MCKIM

AIDEN MCKIM Eighth great grandson of progenitor Nicholas Kegg. **BRENT MCKIM** Seventh great grandson of progenitor Nicholas Kegg. **CORY MCKIM** Seventh great grandson of progenitor Nicholas Kegg. **JOEL MCKIM** Seventh great grandson of progenitor Nicholas Kegg.
MARJORIE MCKIM Fifth great granddaughter of progenitor Nicholas Kegg.
PATRICIA MCKIM Fifth great granddaughter of progenitor Nicholas Kegg.

[5418A] The Arizona Republic (AZ) Jan. 24, 2012 [5419] Republican (Oakland, MD) April 23, 2004

MCKINNEY

BRYCE RAYMOND MCKINNEY Sixth great grandson of progenitor Nicholas Kegg. **CAMERON ALLEN MCKINNEY** Sixth great grandson of progenitor Nicholas Kegg. **LANA JUNE MCKINNEY** Sixth great granddaughter of progenitor Nicholas Kegg. **PHILIP GERALD MCKINNEY** Sixth great grandson of progenitor Nicholas Kegg.

MCKNIGHT

BRITTNY MCKNIGHT Seventh great granddaughter of progenitor Nicholas Kegg. **CONNIE LYNN MCKNIGHT** [5419A] (1963 – 2017) daughter of Walter and Mary Esther (Goldizen) McKnight married/divorced mother of (3). Connie worked as a local representative for Dr. Pepper Snapple out of Lawrence, Kansas for many years. Connie enjoyed gardening, arts and crafts, and music. **DANNY MCKNIGHT** (1956 – 1956) son of Leonard and Dorothy (Wyckoff) McKnight. **DARREN DALE MCKNIGHT** Sixth great grandson of progenitor Nicholas Kegg. **DAVID R. MCKNIGHT** [5419B] (1956 – 2012) son of Leonard and Dorothy (Wyckoff) McKnight, married Susan Hyder and was a stepfather to her children. David worked at Wire Rope Corp. for 34 years. He was an avid Chiefs Football fan and loved John Wayne. David enjoyed spending time with his family. **DORRIS ANN MCKNIGHT** Fifth great granddaughter of progenitor Nicholas Kegg. **EDITH ILENE MCKNIGHT** [5419C] (1943 – 2002) daughter of Leonard and Dorothy (Wyckoff) McKnight was married three times and was mother of (1). Edith had been a bartender for the former Green Valley Bar for numerous years. **JOHN STANLEY MCKNIGHT** [5420] (1942 – 2014) son of Leonard and Dorothy (Wyckoff) McKnight, married Joan Elsie Goldizen. **MARK ALLEN MCKNIGHT** Sixth great grandson of progenitor Nicholas Kegg. **MICHAEL MCKNIGHT** Fifth great grandson of progenitor Nicholas Kegg. **PENNY MCKNIGHT** Sixth great granddaughter of progenitor Nicholas Kegg. **RONALD BERT MCKNIGHT** [5420A] aka "Ronnie" (1944 – 2010) son of Leonard and Dorothy (Wyckoff) McKnight, married twice, he was father of (4) with his first wife Susan, later he married Judy Kissick. Ronald served in the US Army. He worked at Mead and Johnson Controls. He enjoyed playing cards, having cookouts with family and car rides with friends. **RONNIE MCKNIGHT** Sixth great grandson of progenitor Nicholas Kegg. **STARLA ANN MCKNIGHT** [5420B] (1968 – 2013) daughter of Ronald and Sharon McKnight was a mother of (3). Starla worked at Saxton Chateau Health Care Center for 15 years as a CNA. She loved to oil paint and ride motorcycles. **STEVEN MCKNIGHT** Sixth great grandson of progenitor Nicholas Kegg. **THOMAS EUGENE MCKNIGHT** [5420C] (1949 – 1965) aka "Tommy" son of Leonard and Dorothy Ilene (Wyckoff) McKnight. **WALTER CLYDE MCKNIGHT** Sixth great grandson of progenitor Nicholas Kegg. **WALTER CLYDE MCKNIGHT** [5421] (1939 – 2000) aka "Sonny", son of Leonard and Dorothy (Wyckoff) McKnight married twice; first to Mary Esther Goldizen with whom he was father of (4). Later, he married Shirley Jean Thompson. Sonny served in the Marine Corps. He had been employed by Leaverton Auto Supply for 23 years and retired from Dick's Auto Parts. **WAYNE WESLEY ALLEN MCKNIGHT** (1941 – 1973) son of Leonard and Dorothy (Wyckoff) McKnight.

MCLALLEN

DENNIS MCLALLEN Sixth great grandson of progenitor Nicholas Kegg.
LINDA MCLALLEN Sixth great granddaughter of progenitor Nicholas Kegg.

MCLAREN

HEATHER L. MCLAREN Fifth great granddaughter of progenitor Nicholas Kegg.

[5419A] Lindley Funeral Home (MO) [5419B] Newspress Now (MO) Nov 18, 2012 [5419C] Kansas City Star (MO) Aug 20, 2002, contributed by D. Sue Dible [5420] Kansas City Star (MO) Mar 25, 2014 [5420A] <funeralplan.com/obits/> [5420B] St. Joseph News-Press (MO) Feb 6, 2013 [5420C] The Palm Beach Post (FL) Sept. 30, 1965 [5421] St. Joseph News-Press (MO) Nov 20, 2000

IAN JOSEPH MCLAREN Fifth great grandson of progenitor Nicholas Kegg. **ROBERT STEWART MCLAREN** Fourth great grandson of progenitor Nicholas Kegg. **SEAN GRAHAM MCLAREN** Fifth great grandson of progenitor Nicholas Kegg. **SHARON LYN MCLAREN** Fourth great granddaughter of progenitor Nicholas Kegg. **TIMOTHY DANIE MCLAREN** Fourth great grandson of progenitor Nicholas Kegg. **HANNON L. MCLAREN** Fifth great granddaughter of progenitor Nicholas Kegg. **WENDY SUE MCLAREN** Fourth great granddaughter of progenitor Nicholas Kegg.

MCLAUGHLIN

JERRY W. MCLAUGHLIN Fifth great grandson of progenitor Nicholas Kegg.
LAURA JEAN MCLAUGHLIN Fifth great granddaughter of progenitor Nicholas Kegg.
RANCIE L. MCLAUGHLIN Fifth great grandson of progenitor Nicholas Kegg.
SCOTT MCLAUGHLIN Fifth great grandson of progenitor Nicholas Kegg.

MCMAHAN

ADRIAN ORPHEUS MCMAHAN [5421A] aka "Mac" (1918 – 2009) son of John and Lottie (Devore) McMahan married Bernice Hildegarde Powell. Mac served in the US Army during WW II. He and his wife moved to Albuquerque in 1953 from Fort Wayne where he had worked for Eckrich Meat Company. Mac worked for and retired from Excelsior Laundry in Albuquerque. **AIMEE SUE MCMAHAN** Sixth great granddaughter of progenitor Nicholas Kegg. **CARRIE A. MCMAHAN** Sixth great granddaughter of progenitor Nicholas Kegg. **CATHY LEE MCMAHAN** [5421B] (1955 – 1971) daughter of Robert and Joan (Sommers) McMahan was struck by a car and killed as she was walking along the Leo-Grabill Road. She suffered multiple internal injuries and was pronounced dead at the scene. Police said Cathy apparently was walking on the pavement in the westbound lane. The motorist apparently was traveling about 40 miles an hour and told police that she did not see the victim until after the impact. **CINDY LOU MCMAHAN** Fifth great granddaughter of progenitor Nicholas Kegg. **COURTLAND VIRGIL MCMAHAN** [5422] (1913 – 1980) son of John and Lottie (Devore) McMahan, married Norma A. Courter. Courtland was employed by Magnavox for 47 years. **DEBRA LOU MCMAHAN** Fifth great granddaughter of progenitor Nicholas Kegg. **EMILY MCMAHAN** Seventh great granddaughter of progenitor Nicholas Kegg. **JEANIE CHRISTINE MCMAHAN** Sixth great granddaughter of progenitor Nicholas Kegg. **JENNIFER LYNN MCMAHAN** Sixth great granddaughter of progenitor Nicholas Kegg. **JOHN EMANUEL MCMAHAN** [5423] (1886 – 1932) son of John and Alice (Kegg) McMahan, married Lottie Muriel Devore with whom he was father of (7). John was proprietor of the O.K. Barber Shop, 1618 South Calhoun Street. Mr. McMahan was a member of the Grace Reformed Church and a member of the Improved Order of Redmen. He was a Scottish Rite Mason, a member of the Sol D. Bayless Lodge No. 350, F. and A.M., the Cadesnia Grotto No. 50, and was secretary-treasurer of the Fort Wayne Barbers Union. **JOHN HARRISON MCMAHAN** Fifth great grandson of progenitor Nicholas Kegg. **JUDSON QUINN MCMAHAN** [5423A] (1889 – 1973) son of John and Alice Amelia (Kegg) McMahan married twice, first to Gladys Ethelyne Cloore and later to Virginia Izora Goodrich. A WWI US Army veteran, Judson retired from Jud's Emporium. **KATHRYN PATRICIA MCMAHAN** [5423B] (1926 – 1992) daughter of John and Lottie (Devore) McMahan married William Leo Lieberman with whom she was mother of (1). Kathryn was a registered nurse. **JULIE MARIE MCMAHAN** Sixth great granddaughter of progenitor Nicholas Kegg. **KENNETH MCMAHAN** Fifth great grandson of progenitor Nicholas Kegg. **KENNETH EDWARD MCMAHAN** [5423C] son of Richard and Ruth Ann (Bruns) McMahan married Cynthia Ann Wilkins with whom he was father of (4). Ken served his country in the United States Army from 1971 to 1974. He retired from Dana Corporation in Fort Wayne after

---

[5421A] ABQJournal (NM) Sept. 6, 2009 [5421B] Fort Wayne Journal Gazette (IN) June 15, 1971 contributed by D. Sue Dible [5422] Fort Wayne Journal Gazette (IN) July 3, 1980, obtained by D. Sue Dible [5423] p.8 - Fort Wayne News Sentinel (IN) Aug 1, 1932, obtained by D. Sue Dible [5423A] Fort Wayne Journal Gazette (IN) Oct 24, 1973 contributed by D. Sue Dible [5423B] Fort Wayne News Sentinel (IN) Nov 19, 1992 contributed by D. Sue Dible

many years of service. **KENNETH MICHAEL MCMAHAN** Sixth great grandson of progenitor Nicholas Kegg. **KYLE MCMAHAN** Sixth great grandson of progenitor Nicholas Kegg. **LINDSAY MCMAHAN** Fifth great granddaughter of progenitor Nicholas Kegg. **MARK ALAN MCMAHAN** Sixth great grandson of progenitor Nicholas Kegg. **MICHAEL B. MCMAHAN** Fifth great grandson of progenitor Nicholas Kegg. **OBERLIN AQUILLA MCMAHAN** [5423D] aka "Max" (1911 – 1963) son of John and Lottie (Devore) McMahan, married Marjorie DeLong with whom he was father of (3). Active in the Republican party, he was committeeman of precinct 202. Max was a member of the Crescent Avenue Evangelical United Brethren Church and was a veteran of World War II. He was also a neighborhood commissioner for the Boy Scouts of America. **RANDALL MCMAHAN** aka "Randy" Fifth great grandson of progenitor Nicholas Kegg. **RICHARD ZION MCMAHAN** [5423E] (1928 – 1996) son of John and Lottie (Devore) McMahan married twice, first to Ruth Ann Marie Bruns with whom he was father of (2), later he married Florence Marie Parlee. A Korean War Army veteran, Richard retired from Peter Eckrich & Sons after 37 years of service. **RICHARD MCMAHAN** aka "Ricky" 5th great grandson of progenitor Nicholas Kegg. **ROBERT EUGENE MCMAHAN** [5424] (1921 – 1990) aka "Rick", son of John and Lottie (Devore) McMahan, married Joan Lou Sommers with whom he was father of (4). Rick was a veteran of World War II. He retired from Conrail where he had been employed as a conductor. **SEAN P. MCMAHAN** Sixth great grandson of progenitor Nicholas Kegg. **SHANNON MARIE MCMAHAN** Sixth great granddaughter of progenitor Nicholas Kegg. **SKYLA MCMAHAN** Sixth great granddaughter of progenitor Nicholas Kegg. **VIVIAN PRISCILLA MCMAHAN** [5425] (1915 – 2006) aka "Pat", daughter of John and Lottie (Devore) McMahan, married twice; first to Donald Delos Harris and later, to Harry Edwin Davis. Pat retired from Associated Tires where she had been employed as a bookkeeper for 31 years. Pat was a volunteer of the First Baptist Church where she sewed Cancer pads. **WILLIAM ALLEN MCMAHAN** Fifth great grandson of progenitor Nicholas Kegg.

MCMAHON

CAROL DAWN MCMAHON Fifth great granddaughter of progenitor Nicholas Kegg. **DONALD MCMAHON** Fourth great grandson of progenitor Nicholas Kegg. **JAMES R. MCMAHON** [5425A] (1952 – 2005) son of Richard and Hilda (Diehl) McMahon married Colleen M. Harman with whom he was father of (3). James was known as a good family man. He was a member of the National Rifle Association and loved hunting. James was employed as a job superintendent with Stone Valley Construction. **JAMEY MCMAHON** Fifth great granddaughter of progenitor Nicholas Kegg. **JANEL MCMAHON** Fifth great granddaughter of progenitor Nicholas Kegg. **JANICE MCMAHON** Fifth great granddaughter of progenitor Nicholas Kegg. **JASON MCMAHON** Fifth great grandson of progenitor Nicholas Kegg. **JOANNE MCMAHON** Fourth great granddaughter of progenitor Nicholas Kegg. **JOSELYN MCMAHON** Sixth great granddaughter of progenitor Nicholas Kegg. **KAREN MCMAHON** Fourth great granddaughter of progenitor Nicholas Kegg. **KELLY MCMAHON** Fifth great granddaughter of progenitor Nicholas Kegg. **KIMBERLY MCMAHON** Fifth great granddaughter of progenitor Nicholas Kegg. **LISA MICHELLE MCMAHON** Fourth great granddaughter of progenitor Nicholas Kegg. **RICHARD MCMAHON** Fifth great grandson of progenitor Nicholas Kegg. **RICHARD ELIAS MCMAHON** Fourth great grandson of progenitor Nicholas Kegg. **RONALD MCMAHON** 4th great grandson of progenitor Nicholas Kegg. **WANDA JUSTINE MCMAHON** Fifth great granddaughter of progenitor Nicholas Kegg.

MCMASTER

BRIAN PATRICK MCMASTER Fifth great grandson of progenitor Nicholas Kegg.

[5423C] Fort Wayne Newspapers (IN) Jan 18, 2014 [5423D] Fort Wayne Journal Gazette (IN) Jan 20, 1963, contributed by D. Sue Dible [5423E] p.8A - News Sentinel (IN) Oct 22, 1996 [5424] p.13 - Fort Wayne News Sentinel Jan 31, 1990 [5425] Fort Wayne News Sentinel (IN) Feb 28, 2006 [5425A] Huntingdon Daily News Obituaries Contributed for use in USGenWeb Archives by Ken Boonie

COLLEEN VICTORIA MCMASTER Fifth great granddaughter of progenitor Nicholas Kegg.
MAUREEN L. MCMASTER Fifth great granddaughter of progenitor Nicholas Kegg.
MICHAEL DENNIS MCMASTER Fifth great grandson of progenitor Nicholas Kegg.
MICHAEL DENNIS MCMASTER JR. Sixth great grandson of progenitor Nicholas Kegg.
STEPHANIE PATRICIA MCMASTER Sixth great granddaughter of progenitor Nicholas Kegg.
WAYNE RYAN MCMASTER Sixth great grandson of progenitor Nicholas Kegg.

MCMULLEN

CHRISTOPHER GERALD MCMULLEN Sixth great grandson of progenitor Nicholas Kegg.
PATRICK MICHAEL MCMULLEN Sixth great grandson of progenitor Nicholas Kegg.
SCOTT THOMAS MCMULLEN Sixth great grandson of progenitor Nicholas Kegg.

MCNAMARA

ANGELA MCNAMARA Seventh great granddaughter of progenitor Nicholas Kegg.
EMILY MCNAMARA Seventh great granddaughter of progenitor Nicholas Kegg.
JACOB MCNAMARA Seventh great grandson of progenitor Nicholas Kegg.
MATTHEW MCNAMARA Seventh great grandson of progenitor Nicholas Kegg.
NICOLE MCNAMARA Seventh great granddaughter of progenitor Nicholas Kegg.
RICKY MCNAMARA Seventh great granddaughter of progenitor Nicholas Kegg.

MCNEAL

CAROLYN PALMER MCNEAL Seventh great granddaughter of progenitor Nicholas Kegg. **PALMER MCNEAL** Seventh great grandson of progenitor Nicholas Kegg. **ROB MCNEAL** Seventh great grandson of progenitor Nicholas Kegg. **RYAN MCNEAL** Seventh great grandson of progenitor Nicholas Kegg.

MCNUTT

BEA MCNUTT Sixth great granddaughter of progenitor Nicholas Kegg. **DONALD HAROLD MCNUTT** [5425B] (1941 – 1992) son of Loy and Lola (Wyckoff) McNutt, married Cheryl Ruth Marie (Lund) Grunlien with whom he was father of (1). Donald was a maintenance worker and custodian for the Maywood Baptist Church for three years. He served in the Army from 1960 to 1971, then was a helicopter mechanic in the Army Reserve in St. Paul until he left as a staff sergeant in 1982. Donald was a veteran of the Vietnam War. He was a member of the Black Powder Rifle Association. He formerly was a Mason. **LA VONNE MONIQUE MCNUTT** aka "Lolly" Seventh great granddaughter of progenitor Nicholas Kegg. **LEE MCNUTT** Sixth great grandson of progenitor Nicholas Kegg. **LORETTA MCNUTT** Sixth great granddaughter of progenitor Nicholas Kegg. **VICTORIA G. MCNUTT** aka "Vicki" Sixth great granddaughter of progenitor Nicholas Kegg.

MCPHEE

KEVIN MCPHEE Sixth great grandson of progenitor Nicholas Kegg. **PATRICK MCPHEE** aka "Rick" Sixth great grandson of progenitor Nicholas Kegg. **WILLIAM JOSEPH MCPHEE JR.** [5426] aka "Joe" (1955 – 2011) son of William and Nancy (Cowell) McPhee married Patricia Marie Simmons. Joe served for many years in the Restaurant Management field and shared his joy of golf, home projects, and cooking with friends and family.

[5425B] Kansas City Star (MO) Nov 20, 1992 [5426] Herald Tribune (FL) Nov. 9, 2011

MCPHERSON

ASHLYN MCPHERSON Seventh great granddaughter of progenitor Nicholas Kegg.
BRIANNON MCPHERSON Seventh great granddaughter of progenitor Nicholas Kegg.
CRAIG RANDALL MCPHERSON Fifth great grandson of progenitor Nicholas Kegg.
DALE M MCPHERSON Fifth great grandson of progenitor Nicholas Kegg.

DECLAN MCPHERSON Seventh great grandson of progenitor Nicholas Kegg.
ERIN MCPHERSON Seventh great granddaughter of progenitor Nicholas Kegg.
KEELIN MCPHERSON Seventh great grandson of progenitor Nicholas Kegg.
MORGAN MCPHERSON Seventh great granddaughter of progenitor Nicholas Kegg.

MCREYNOLDS

AVERY DURELLE MCREYNOLDS Sixth great grandson of progenitor Nicholas Kegg.
ZACHARY DAVID MCREYNOLDS Sixth great grandson of progenitor Nicholas Kegg.

MCVEIGH

ERNESTENE BEULAH MCVEIGH (1906 – 1989) daughter of Loeta (Goodlive) McVeigh, married James Kenneth Fast. Ernestine was employed as a Springfield school teacher.

MCVICKER

ROBERT LEE MCVICKER [5427] (1918 – 1971) son of Arthur and Anna (Hillegass) McVicker, married Jessie Virginia Ball. Robert was employed as a safety inspector in the Department of Labor and Industry, and then transferred to the Pennsylvania Turnpike Commission, where he was employed in various capacities. Prominent in Republican party circles, he was a Republican committeeman from Harrison Township for several years and served as a truant officer for Bedford area schools. He was a veteran of service in World War Two, and a member of both American Legion Post 113, and the Loyal Order of Moose No. 480. He was a member of the Milligans Cove Christian Church.

MCWILLIAMS

CAROL MCWILLIAMS [5427A] (1953 – 2018) daughter of Robert and Dorothy (Small) McWilliams married twice; first to David Joe Burke with whom she was mother of (1). Carol always had a big smile and an even bigger heart. **DALE RICHARD MCWILLIAMS** Sixth great grandson of progenitor Nicholas Kegg. **ROBERT MCWILLIAMS** Seventh great grandson of progenitor Nicholas Kegg.
SHARON MCWILLIAMS Sixth great granddaughter of progenitor Nicholas Kegg.
WILLIAM CLIFTON MCWILLIAMS [5427B] aka "Bill" (1959 – 2019) son of Robert and Dorothy (Small) McWilliams married Roberta Rose Menzies with whom he was father of (1). Bill loved his job of 19 years in the military funeral honors. He was medically retired from the United States Army and loved being a firefighter for DCFD "829". In his younger years, he loved to be outdoors, playing softball as well as umpiring, paintballing, bowling, hunting, golfing, fishing and camping.

MEAD

CARRIE JANE MEAD Seventh great granddaughter of progenitor Nicholas Kegg.
CHARLES FREDERICK MEAD Sixth great grandson of progenitor Nicholas Kegg.

[5427] Bedford Gazette (PA) Aug 23, 1971 [5427A] Family Funeral Care (Indianapolis, IN) [5427B] Null & Son (Rollo, MO)

HARLEIGH ROBYNE MEAD Seventh great granddaughter of progenitor Nicholas Kegg.
JANE A. MEAD Sixth great granddaughter of progenitor Nicholas Kegg.
SCOTT LEROY MEAD Sixth great grandson of progenitor Nicholas Kegg.

MEADOWS

CHRISTIE MEADOWS Sixth great granddaughter of progenitor Nicholas Kegg. **LOGAN MEADOWS** Seventh great grandson of progenitor Nicholas Kegg. **MARK C. MEADOWS** Sixth great grandson of progenitor Nicholas Kegg. **NICHOLAS MEADOWS** Seventh great grandson of progenitor Nicholas Kegg. **REBECCA MEADOWS** Seventh great granddaughter of progenitor Nicholas Kegg. **RYAN LELAND MEADOWS** Fifth great grandson of progenitor Nicholas Kegg. **TYLER MEADOWS** Sixth great grandson of progenitor Nicholas Kegg.

MEALY

NICHOLAS CHRISTIAN MEALY Fifth great grandson of progenitor Nicholas Kegg.

MEANS

DELL ARCHER MEANS [5428] (1922 – 1974) son of Clyde and Mida (Knouf) Means, married Elizabeth L. Jennings with whom he was father of (1). Dell had been a livestock buyer for Armour & Co. and later with the Dubuque Packing Co. He was a member of the St. Joseph Holy Name Society, the Elks Club of Creston, and the Knights of Columbus of Corning, Iowa. **MICHAEL D. MEANS** Fifth great grandson of progenitor Nicholas Kegg. **RUBY LUCILLE MEANS** [5428A] (1920 – 2005) daughter of Clyde and Mida (Knouf) Means married Gail Bakerink with whom she was mother of (4). Ruby retired from Laura Scudder. She was a member of St. Paul's Lutheran Church and the Christian Friendship Club and enjoyed playing bingo.

MEARKLE

ASHELYN JOY MEARKLE Sixth great granddaughter of progenitor Nicholas Kegg.
CHARLOTTE SUE MEARKLE Fifth great granddaughter of progenitor Nicholas Kegg.
HAYDN RAY MEARKLE Fifth great grandson of progenitor Nicholas Kegg. **STACY MEARKLE** Sixth great granddaughter of progenitor Nicholas Kegg. **TRACEY LEE MEARKLE** [5429] (1948 – 2020) son of T. Allen and Kathleen (Pennel) Mearkle. Tracy served in the United States Army during the Vietnam War as a SPC4. He worked as a mechanic for many years. Tracy loved traveling to Florida and spending time with his family and friends. He enjoyed hunting, fishing, racing and loved his vehicle.
ZACHARY VANCE MEARKLE (2009 – 2009) son of Hillary (Kegg) Mearkle.

MEEK

AMANDA MEEK Sixth great granddaughter of progenitor Nicholas Kegg. **JANETTE CAROL MEEK** [5430] (1958 – 2011) daughter of Charles and Patricia (Reed) Meek married Mark Lee Merriman first learned how to weave while attending Crescent Valley High School. Her loom was filled with projects of all kinds. She experimented with spinning and dying her own wool, and loved incorporating found objects into her work. Her work was displayed in several galleries in Southern Oregon. Janet was particularly proud of an honorable mention for an entry at the Firehouse Gallery in Grants Pass. She also had a showing at the River Gallery in Independence, and the Corvallis Art Center. When Janette wasn't

---

[5428] p.11 - Adams County Free Press (IA) Oct 31, 1974 [5428A] p.B4 - Modesto Bee (CA) Nov 23, 2005 [5429] Bedford Gazette (PA) July 7, 2020, obtained by Bob Rose [5430] Corvallis Gazette-Times (OR) Aug 15, 2011, obtained by D. Sue Dible

creating, she enjoyed being outdoors with her husband and faithful canine sidekick, exploring in the mountains or meandering along the coast. **LEXI MEEK** Sixth great granddaughter of progenitor Nicholas Kegg. **LORENE KAREN MEEK** Fifth great granddaughter of progenitor Nicholas Kegg. **LYNNE ELLEN MEEK** Fifth great granddaughter of progenitor Nicholas Kegg.

MEEKS

KATHRYN LYNN MEEKS Sixth great granddaughter of progenitor Nicholas Kegg.
PATRICIA LEE MEEKS Sixth great granddaughter of progenitor Nicholas Kegg.

MEGGS

ELISE MEGGS Seventh great granddaughter of progenitor Nicholas Kegg.
ETHAN BOYD MEGGS Seventh great grandson of progenitor Nicholas Kegg.

MEISSNER

BARBARA MEISSNER Fifth great granddaughter of progenitor Nicholas Kegg.
CHAD D. MEISSNER Sixth great grandson of progenitor Nicholas Kegg.
JACOB R. MEISSNER aka "Jake", Sixth great grandson of progenitor Nicholas Kegg.
TORRE LYNN MEISSNER Sixth great grandson of progenitor Nicholas Kegg.

MELLINGER

ANNA MARGARET MELLINGER [5431] (1915 – 1936) daughter of William and Herma (Myers) Mellinger. **GEORGE BARNETT MELLINGER** [5432] (1917 – 2005) son of William and Herma (Myers) Mellinger married twice; first to Margaret Eleanor Lyons. Later, he married Margaret Kellermann Agnew. Full of kindness, George had a unique personality. He was an active member of AA since 1948, enjoyed helping those with a drinking problem.

MELLOTT

ANGELA MELLOTT Seventh great granddaughter of progenitor Nicholas Kegg. **CHRISTOPHER M. MELLOTT** Eighth great grandson of progenitor Nicholas Kegg. **CINDY MELLOTT** Seventh great granddaughter of progenitor Nicholas Kegg. **CINDY L. MELLOTT** Seventh great granddaughter of progenitor Nicholas Kegg. **DARLENE R. MELLOTT** Sixth great granddaughter of progenitor Nicholas Kegg. **GLENN E. MELLOTT** [5433] (1911 – 1995) son of Russell and Olive (Bussard) Mellott, married Mary Alice Barton with whom he was father of (5). Glenn had farmed most of his life. **GREG MELLOTT** Seventh great grandson of progenitor Nicholas Kegg. **JENNIFER MELLOTT** Seventh great granddaughter of progenitor Nicholas Kegg. **KIRSTIN MELLOTT** Eighth great granddaughter of progenitor Nicholas Kegg. **LENA M. MELLOTT** Eighth great granddaughter of progenitor Nicholas Kegg. **LILA JANE MELLOTT** Sixth great granddaughter of progenitor Nicholas Kegg. **LINDA MELLOTT** Sixth great granddaughter of progenitor Nicholas Kegg. **LOIS J. MELLOTT** Eighth great granddaughter of progenitor Nicholas Kegg. **MABEL L. MELLOTT** [5434] (1910 – 1990) daughter of Russell and Olive (Bussard) Mellott, married Earl Leo Whipkey with whom she was mother of (2). Mabel earned her teacher's certification from Beckley College in West Virginia in 1929. She was a member of Mt. Lebanon Women's Club, Mt. Lebanon United Methodist Church and the church's All Twos Club.

[5431] p.7 - The Daily Courier (PA) March 16, 1936 [5432] Dayton Daily News (OH) May 26, 2005 [5433] Bedford Inquirer (PA) Sept 29,1995, obtained by Duke Clark [5434] Bedford County Genealogical Society obituary obtained by D. Sue Dible

MARCIA MELLOTT Sixth great granddaughter of progenitor Nicholas Kegg. **MARILYN MELLOTT** Sixth great granddaughter of progenitor Nicholas Kegg. **MARVIN C. MELLOTT** [5435] (1940 – 1947) son of Floyd and Dorothy (Smith) Mellott. **MICHELLE MELLOTT** Eighth great granddaughter of progenitor Nicholas Kegg. **MISTY MELLOTT** Eighth great granddaughter of progenitor Nicholas Kegg. **RICHARD E. MELLOTT** Seventh great grandson of progenitor Nicholas Kegg. **ROGER MELLOTT** Sixth great grandson of progenitor Nicholas Kegg. **TRENTEN MELLOTT** Eighth great grandson of progenitor Nicholas Kegg. **TROY A. MELLOTT** Seventh great grandson of progenitor Nicholas Kegg. **TYLAR MELLOTT** Eighth great grandson of progenitor Nicholas Kegg. **VERA LEONE MELLOTT** [5435A] (1915 – 1996) daughter of Russell and Olive May (Bussard) Mellott married Elmer Francis Diggs with whom she was mother of (1). Vera was an accomplished artist in many mediums. She taught reading in the Community College System in Maryland.

MELOY

PATRICK E. MELOY Seventh great grandson of progenitor Nicholas Kegg.

MELTON

ALYSSA MYCHELLE MELTON Seventh great granddaughter of progenitor Nicholas Kegg.

MELVIN

KAITLYN MELVIN aka "Kaity", Eighth great granddaughter of progenitor Nicholas Kegg.

MENDEZ

ARIANNA MICAELA MENDEZ Eighth great granddaughter of progenitor Nicholas Kegg.
LEAH MENDEZ Eighth great granddaughter of progenitor Nicholas Kegg.

MENTZ

HENRY MENTZ Eighth great grandson of progenitor Nicholas Kegg.
WALTER MENTZ Eighth great grandson of progenitor Nicholas Kegg.

MENTZER

EPHRAIM DANIEL MENTZER (1886 – 1951) son of David and Anna (Kegg) Mentzer. **HEYDEN FRANCIS MENTZER** (1899 -?) son of David and Anna (Kegg) Mentzer. **JOHN JOSEPH MENTZER** [5436] (1888 – 1961) son of David and Anna (Kegg) Mentzer, married Helen Edna Miller. John was employed by the Altoona Mirror where he was a lithotype printer. **MARY ELIZABETH MENTZER** [5437] (1885 – 1973) aka "Lizzie", daughter of David and Anna (Kegg) Mentzer, married Francis Philip Sanders with whom she was mother of (6). Mary was a retired employee of Mount Aloysius Junior College, Cresson. **WILLIAM LAWRENCE MENTZER** [5438] (1882 – 1926) son of David and Anna (Kegg) Mentzer. William was a member of St. Marks' Catholic church. He was also a member of Holy Name society.

[5435] Bedford County Historical Society (PA), Book 128 p.25 obtained by D. Sue Dible [5435A] Bedford Inquirer (PA) Nov 29, 1996, contributed by Duke Clark [5436] Altoona Mirror (PA) Dec 30, 1961 [5437] Altoona Mirror (PA) Apr 30, 1973

MEREDITH

ANDREA COLLEEN MEREDITH Sixth great granddaughter of progenitor Nicholas Kegg.
CHARLES A. MEREDITH aka "Froggy", Sixth great grandson of progenitor Nicholas Kegg.
HOPE KRISTI MEREDITH Sixth great granddaughter of progenitor Nicholas Kegg.
KAREN MEREDITH Sixth great granddaughter of progenitor Nicholas Kegg.
PATRICIA MEREDITH Sixth great granddaughter of progenitor Nicholas Kegg.
WILLIAM MEREDITH (1965 – 1965) aka "Billy", son of William and Sandra (Martin) Meredith.
WILLIAM ERNEST MEREDITH aka "Woody", Sixth great grandson of progenitor Nicholas Kegg.

MERRICK

ASHLEY MERRICK Seventh great granddaughter of progenitor Nicholas Kegg.
JUSTIN MERRICK Seventh great grandson of progenitor Nicholas Kegg.
ZACHARY MERRICK Seventh great grandson of progenitor Nicholas Kegg.

MERROW

CODY MERROW Seventh great grandson of progenitor Nicholas Kegg.

MERRYMAN

JOHN CHARLES MERRYMAN Fifth great grandson of progenitor Nicholas Kegg.
TIMOTHY ALLEN MERRYMAN Fifth great grandson of progenitor Nicholas Kegg.

MERSHON

CHRISTOPHER D. MERSHONE Seventh great grandson of progenitor Nicholas Kegg.
PAULA MARIE MERSHON [5439] (1953 – 2012) daughter of Charles and Phyllis (Kegg) Mershon was mother of (1). She married David Thomas Herr.

MESS

DOROTHY L. MESS Fifth great granddaughter of progenitor Nicholas Kegg. **EDITH MESS** [5440] (1914 – 2004) daughter of William and Lena (Rice) Mess, married Kenneth E. Fleming with whom she was mother of (2). Edith worked at the Cornhusker and Hilton hotels until she retired. **FRANK WILLIAM MESS** [5441] (1909 – 1985) son of William and Lena (Rice) Mess, married Isabelle May Carr with whom he was father of (4). **GLADYS MABEL MESS** [5442] (1912 – 2005) daughter of William and Lena (Rice) Mess, married James Tinsley. Gladys worked at her mother-in-law's chicken ranch. **HOMER CLAIR MESS** (1917 – 1988) son of William and Lena (Rice) Mess was a veteran of WWII, Korea serving in the U.S. Navy. **LEROY MESS** Fifth great grandson of progenitor Nicholas Kegg. **LESLIE W. MESS** Fifth great grandson of progenitor Nicholas Kegg. **LESLIE W. MESS** Sixth great grandson of progenitor Nicholas Kegg. **MARY C. MESS** (1907 – 2001) daughter of William and Lena (Rice) Mess. **ROY F. MESS** [5443] (1906 – 1972) son of William and Lena (Rice) Mess was employed by the city Sanitation Department until he retired. Roy was a member of the First Baptist Church. **SHIRLEY MESS** Fifth great granddaughter of progenitor Nicholas Kegg.

[5438] obituary clipping obtained by Franny Dodson shared by Mary Kelley Blendy [5439] The Indianapolis Star (IN) Nov. 20, 2012 [5440] Kearney Hub (NE) Oct 28, 2004 [5441] Kearney Hub (NE) July 7, 2006 [5442] Kearney Hub (NE) Sept 10, 2005 [5443] p.12 – Kearney Daily Hub (NE) Feb 22, 1972, obtained by D. Sue Dible

MESSENGER

M. J. MESSENGER Sixth great grandson of progenitor Nicholas Kegg.
SPENCER MESSENGER Sixth great grandson of progenitor Nicholas Kegg.

MESSINGER

DYLAN RUSSELL MESSINGER Eighth great grandson of progenitor Nicholas Kegg. **JAMES MESSINGER** Fifth great grandson of progenitor Nicholas Kegg. **JOHN JOSEPH MESSINGER** (1915 – 1993) son of Francis and Hazel (Dwigans) Messinger, married Nedra Eilene Crawford. **JOSEPH MESSINGER** Fifth great grandson of progenitor Nicholas Kegg. **KATHERINE FAYE MESSINGER** (1922 – 1982) daughter of Francis and Hazel (Dwigans) Messinger, married Charles Fremont Day, Jr. Katherine was employed as a clerical worker at the U.S. Air base. **KATIE MESSINGER** Sixth great granddaughter of progenitor Nicholas Kegg. **LOLA MARIE MESSINGER** (1918 – 1981) daughter of Francis and Hazel (Dwigans) Messinger, married Leonard P. Thommes. **MARY ELIZABETH MESSINGER** (1920 – 1992) daughter of Francis and Hazel (Dwigans) Messinger, married Cleo Earl Lay with whom she was mother of (2). Later, she married William Gilbert. **OWEN NICHOLAS MESSINGER** Eighth great grandson of progenitor Nicholas Kegg. **ROSS MESSINGER** Sixth great grandson of progenitor Nicholas Kegg. **RUBE LOUISE MESSINGER** [5444] (1911 – 1974) daughter of Francis and Hazel (Dwigans) Messinger married twice, first to John C. Mavraedis with whom she was mother of (2). Later, she married J. M. Burbridge. Rube was employed by Pacific Northwest Bell Telephone Co. **WILLIAM MESSINGER** Sixth great grandson of progenitor Nicholas Kegg. **WILLIAM DALE MESSINGER** [5445] (1912 – 1991) aka "Bill", son of Francis and Hazel (Dwigans) Messinger, married Marcena Kastanas with whom he was father of (2). Bill served in the U.S. Navy for 22 years, during which time he served on the U.S.S. Chicago. Bill was a longtime employee of Allied Chemicals.

METCALF

LAUREN METCALF Sixth great granddaughter of progenitor Nicholas Kegg.

METTS

ALLISON METTS Seventh great granddaughter of progenitor Nicholas Kegg.
DALTON JAMES METTS Seventh great grandson of progenitor Nicholas Kegg.

METZ

AMY G. METZ Sixth great granddaughter of progenitor Nicholas Kegg.
CAMERON METZ Seventh great grandson of progenitor Nicholas Kegg.
DIANA L. METZ Sixth great granddaughter of progenitor Nicholas Kegg.
KEVIN N. METZ Sixth great grandson of progenitor Nicholas Kegg.
KIRSTEN METZ Seventh great granddaughter of progenitor Nicholas Kegg.

MEYER

AARON JOHN MEYER Sixth great grandson of progenitor Nicholas Kegg.
WENDY MARIE MEYER Sixth great granddaughter of progenitor Nicholas Kegg.

[5444] Statesman Journal (Salem, OR) Oct 21, 1974 [5445] Glenwood Public Library obituary clipping obtained by D. Sue Dible

MEYERS

BARBARA MEYERS Fifth great granddaughter of progenitor Nicholas Kegg. **BEVERLY MEYERS** Fifth great granddaughter of progenitor Nicholas Kegg. **CAROL MEYERS** Fifth great granddaughter of progenitor Nicholas Kegg. **DARYLE EILEEN MEYERS** [5446] (1925 – 2009) aka "Peenie", daughter of Harvey and Cora (Hillegass) Meyers, married William E. Gnagey Jr. Peenie was a telephone operator and supervisor for GTE for many years. She was a member of New Hope United Church of Christ, Daughters of the American Revolution, Forbes Road Chapter, where she was a former regent. Peenie was a former member of the Salisbury Fire Co. and Ladies Auxiliary. She enjoyed genealogy and did all of her family tree. **HARRIET ARLINE MEYERS** [5447] (1919 – 1995) daughter of Harvey and Cora (Hillegass) Meyers, married Virgil Edward Vaughn with whom she was mother of (6). Harriet had been employed as an L.P.N. in the O.B. Department of Somerset Hospital. She sang in the church choir and was a member of Forbes Road Chapter of D.A.R., Trinity Chapter 138 O.E.S., Somerset; Berlin Mountaineer Homemakers, First Society of Farm Women and Pius Spring Woman's Club. Harriet volunteered for many years with the Red Cross bloodmobile and as a nurse for Cub Scout and Girl Scout Day camps. **HARVEY P. MEYERS** Fifth great grandson of progenitor Nicholas Kegg. **JOHN PHILLIP MEYERS** [5448] (1917 – 1995) son of Robert and Mary (Speicher) Meyers, married Hazel Weimer with whom he was father of (3). John was a Veteran of World War II, serving in the U.S. Navy. He was a retired grocer in Rockwood and New Lexington and Charlottesville, Va. **JUDY MEYERS** Fifth great granddaughter of progenitor Nicholas Kegg. **KATHERN LOUISE MEYERS** [5449] (1931 – 2002) aka "Louise", daughter of Harold and Kathern (Ansell) Meyers, married Glenn Calton Fountain with whom she was mother of (4). Louise was the former owner and proprietor of the Laurel Hill Restaurant in New Lexington and retired from General Electric Corp. in Cincinnati, Ohio, where she was awarded for her commitment and dedication. **KATHY MEYERS** Fifth great granddaughter of progenitor Nicholas Kegg. **KENNETH ERIG MEYERS** (1939 – 1940) son of William and Orvada (Meyers) Meyers. **MARJORIE CLARISSA MEYERS** [5450] (1913 – 2015) daughter of Harvey and Cora (Hillegass) Meyers, married Carl Allen Hay with whom she was mother of (2). Marjorie grew up attending the country schools of Kammerer and Wagaman as well as Meyersdale High School. She attended Catherman's Business School in Cumberland, Maryland. She had been an active member of the Berlin Area Historical Society, Forbes Road Chapter Daughters of the American Revolution, The First Society of Farm Women, and New Hope United Church of Christ. She was a homemaker and an old-fashioned farmer's wife who worked the fields and milked cows until she was 80 years old. She was always neatly dressed, her hair styled, and had a gracious, friendly, and pleasant disposition. She was always anxious to hear of the daily workings on the farm and had advice to give when necessary. She was up to date with current events and took great interest in the presidential elections and the royal family especially Princes William and Harry. **MARY WILHELMINA MEYERS** [5451] (1911 – 1996) aka "Wilhelmina", daughter of Robert and Mary (Speicher) Meyers, married Clarence George Reis with whom she was mother of (3). Wilhelmina was a homemaker. **ORVADA E. MEYERS** [5452] (1916 – 2011) daughter of Harvey and Cora (Hillegass) Meyers, married William Kenneth Meyers with whom she was mother of (3). Orvada was a lifetime farmer and homemaker and along with her husband received the Century Farm Award in 1984. She was a member of the Fifth Society of Farm Women for 50 years, a member of Forbes Road D.A.R., National and State Farmers Union and a member of Amity United Church of Christ, Meyersdale. **ROBERT LEE MEYERS** [5453] (1913 – 1990) son of Robert and Mary (Speicher) Meyers, married Evelyn Custer with whom he was father of (2). Retired, Robert had been the former owner and operator of the Amoco Gas Station, Brighton Road, Northside, Pittsburgh.

[5446] Daily American (PA) Mar 27, 2009 [5447] Daily American (PA) Feb 8, 1995, Meyersdale Library [5448] Daily American (PA) July 7, 1995 Myersdale Library transcribed by Marilyn Boula [5449] Daily American (PA) Dec 28, 2002, Meyersdale Library transcribed by Patty Millich/Alice James [5450] Daily American (PA) Sep 21, 2015 [5451] Central Brevard Library obituary clipping obtained by D. Sue Dible [5452] Daily American (PA) Oct 30, 2011 [5453] Daily American (PA) May 18, 1990 Meyersdale Library transcribed by Lynn Beatty

WILLIAM RICHARD MEYERS [5454] (1941 – 1995) son of William and Orvada (Meyers) Meyers was a technician for Somerset County Dairy Herd Improvement Assn. for 27 years. William was a veteran of the Vietnam era and a member of the Amity United Church of Christ, Meyersdale.

MICHAELS

EVAN CHRISTOPHER MICHAELS Seventh great grandson of progenitor Nicholas Kegg.
KEITH MICHAELS Seventh great grandson of progenitor Nicholas Kegg.
ROBERT RAY MICHAELS Sixth great grandson of progenitor Nicholas Kegg.
VANESSA MICHAELS Seventh great grandson of progenitor Nicholas Kegg.
WILLIAM ALLEN MICHAELS Sixth great grandson of progenitor Nicholas Kegg.

MICK

CAROLYN MICK Fifth great granddaughter of progenitor Nicholas Kegg.
GARY MICK Fifth great grandson of progenitor Nicholas Kegg.
JON MICK Sixth great grandson of progenitor Nicholas Kegg.
JOSHUA MICK Sixth great grandson of progenitor Nicholas Kegg.
ROB MICK Sixth great grandson of progenitor Nicholas Kegg.

MICKEM

JEFFREY LYNN MICKEM Sixth great grandson of progenitor Nicholas Kegg.
TIMOTHY LEE MICKEM Sixth great grandson of progenitor Nicholas Kegg.

MIDDLETON

ADAM MIDDLETON Seventh great grandson of progenitor Nicholas Kegg. **BRENT MIDDLETON** Seventh great grandson of progenitor Nicholas Kegg. **BRYLON MIDDLETON** Ninth great grandson of progenitor Nicholas Kegg. **CASSANDRA JANE MIDDLETON** Eighth great granddaughter of progenitor Nicholas Kegg. **DAVID MIDDLETON** Eighth great grandson of progenitor Nicholas Kegg. **DAVID ALLEN MIDDLETON** Seventh great grandson of progenitor Nicholas Kegg. **EMMA MIDDLETON** Ninth great granddaughter of progenitor Nicholas Kegg. **ERIC STEVE MIDDLETON** Seventh great grandson of progenitor Nicholas Kegg. **KRISTINE MIDDLETON** Sixth great granddaughter of progenitor Nicholas Kegg. **MICHAEL EDWARD MIDDLETON** Seventh great grandson of progenitor Nicholas Kegg. **NATASHA LEA MIDDLETON** Eighth great granddaughter of progenitor Nicholas Kegg. **NATHAN L. MIDDLETON** Seventh great grandson of progenitor Nicholas Kegg. **RYAN MIDDLETON** Seventh great grandson of progenitor Nicholas Kegg. **SCOTT ALAN MIDDLETON** Sixth great grandson of progenitor Nicholas Kegg. **SINDI ANN MIDDLETON** Sixth great granddaughter of progenitor Nicholas Kegg. **TODD ALLEN MIDDLETON** Seventh great grandson of progenitor Nicholas Kegg. **WILLIAM DAVID MIDDLETON** [5455] (1952 – 2010) aka "Bill", son of Edward and Katherine (Timmons) Middleton was co-founder of Blue Skies, a program to help young adults struggling with addiction to drugs and alcohol. **WILLIAM PAUL MIDDLETON** Seventh great grandson of progenitor Nicholas Kegg.

MIHALY

PAUL S. MIHALY Sixth great grandson of progenitor Nicholas Kegg.
PETER B. MIHALY Sixth great grandson of progenitor Nicholas Kegg.

[5454] Daily American (PA) Feb 13, 1995 Meyersdale Library transcribed by Pam McConkey [5455] Sandusky Register (OH) Feb 19, 2010

MIKA

TANNER MIKA Eighth great grandson of progenitor Nicholas Kegg.
TAYTUM MIKA Eighth great granddaughter of progenitor Nicholas Kegg.

MILBERT

BAILEY ELIZABETH MILBERT Eighth great granddaughter of progenitor Nicholas Kegg.
CAILYN MILBERT aka "Cay", Eighth great granddaughter of progenitor Nicholas Kegg.

MILBOURN

JOSHUA COLIN MILBOURN Eighth great grandson of progenitor Nicholas Kegg.
MAREN ELIZABETH MILBOURN Eighth great granddaughter of progenitor Nicholas Kegg.
WILL FRANKLIN MILBOURN Eighth great grandson of progenitor Nicholas Kegg.

MILES

BRAD MILES Seventh great grandson of progenitor Nicholas Kegg.
RUSHMORE ALEXANDER MILES Eighth great grandson of progenitor Nicholas Kegg.
SCOTT MILES Seventh great grandson of progenitor Nicholas Kegg.
SUNNI MILES Seventh great granddaughter of progenitor Nicholas Kegg.

MILEY

SAVANNAH LEIGH MILEY Seventh great granddaughter of progenitor Nicholas Kegg.

MILFORD

ROBERT L. MILFORD Fifth great grandson of progenitor Nicholas Kegg.
TRENITA L. MILFORD Fifth great granddaughter of progenitor Nicholas Kegg.
VIRGIL LINLEY MILFORD [5456] (1920 – 1981) aka "Pattie", son of Henry and Leona (Nelson) Milford, married Juanita Alice Kerby with whom he was father of (2). Pattie retired from Beech Aircraft Corp., where he had been employed as a technical writer.

MILLER

ALECIA ANN MILLER Sixth great granddaughter of progenitor Nicholas Kegg. **ALEX R. MILLER** Seventh great grandson of progenitor Nicholas Kegg. **ALICIA MILLER** Seventh great granddaughter of progenitor Nicholas Kegg. **ALVIN C. MILLER** Fifth great grandson of progenitor Nicholas Kegg. **ANDREW MILLER** Sixth great grandson of progenitor Nicholas Kegg. **ANDREW KEITH MILLER** (1991 – 1994) son of Brian and Christine (Fink) Miller. **ANNA MILLER** Eighth great granddaughter of progenitor Nicholas Kegg. **ANNETTE GAYLE MILLER** Fifth great granddaughter of progenitor Nicholas Kegg. **APOLLOS MILLER** Eighth great grandson of progenitor Nicholas Kegg. **AVA S. MILLER** Seventh great granddaughter of progenitor Nicholas Kegg. **BELLA MILLER** Eighth great granddaughter of progenitor Nicholas Kegg. **BENJAMIN A. MILLER** Sixth great grandson of progenitor Nicholas Kegg. **BENJAMIN RILEY MILLER** Seventh great grandson of progenitor Nicholas Kegg. **BETH ANN MILLER** Sixth great granddaughter of progenitor Nicholas Kegg. **BETTY J. MILLER** Fifth great granddaughter of progenitor Nicholas Kegg.

[5456] Wichita Eagle (KS) June 20, 1981, obtained by D. Sue Dible

BRAELYN MICHELLE MILLER Eighth great granddaughter of progenitor Nicholas Kegg. **BRANDON MILLER** Seventh great grandson of progenitor Nicholas Kegg. **BRIAN E. MILLER** Seventh great grandson of progenitor Nicholas Kegg. **BRITTANY MILLER** Seventh great granddaughter of progenitor Nicholas Kegg. **BRUCE MILLER** Fifth great grandson of progenitor Nicholas Kegg. **BUD MILLER** Fifth great grandson of progenitor Nicholas Kegg. **CADE ANDREW MILLER** Eighth great grandson of progenitor Nicholas Kegg. **CAROL SUE MILLER** Seventh great granddaughter of progenitor Nicholas Kegg. **CARRIE MILLER** Fifth great granddaughter of progenitor Nicholas Kegg. **CARTER MILLER** Ninth great grandson of progenitor Nicholas Kegg. **CHARLES MILLER** aka "Butch", Fifth great grandson of progenitor Nicholas Kegg. **CHARLES E. MILLER** Fifth great grandson of progenitor Nicholas Kegg. **CHARLES E. MILLER** [5457] (1927 – 2010) son of Clarence and Florence (Turner) Miller, married Henrietta Williams with whom he was father of (2). A U.S. Navy veteran with eight years of service, Charlie served on the CV37 Princeton and the Norton Sound Missile Launcher from 1945 to 1953. Charlie retired from Penn Machine Co. **CHERYL ANN MILLER** Seventh great granddaughter of progenitor Nicholas Kegg. **CHRISTIAN MILLER** Seventh great grandson of progenitor Nicholas Kegg. **CINDY MILLER** Fifth great granddaughter of progenitor Nicholas Kegg. **CLARENCE MILLER** Sixth great grandson of progenitor Nicholas Kegg. **CLIFFORD MILLER** Fifth great grandson of progenitor Nicholas Kegg. **COURTNEY LYN MILLER** Sixth great granddaughter of progenitor Nicholas Kegg. **DANIEL MILLER** aka "Boone", Seventh great grandson of progenitor Nicholas Kegg. **DANIELLE J. MILLER** Fifth great granddaughter of progenitor Nicholas Kegg. **DARA MILLER** Sixth great grandson of progenitor Nicholas Kegg. **DARRYL JOHN MILLER** Sixth great grandson of progenitor Nicholas Kegg. **DAVID MILLER** Sixth great grandson of progenitor Nicholas Kegg. **DEBORAH MILLER** Fifth great granddaughter of progenitor Nicholas Kegg. **DEBORAH J. MILLER** aka "Debbie", Fifth great granddaughter of progenitor Nicholas Kegg. **DEBRA KATHERINE MILLER** Sixth great granddaughter of progenitor Nicholas Kegg. **DENISE MILLER** Sixth great granddaughter of progenitor Nicholas Kegg. **DEWAYNE E. MILLER** Fifth great grandson of progenitor Nicholas Kegg. **DOMINIC CHRISTOPHER MILLER** Ninth great grandson of progenitor Nicholas Kegg. **DONALD R. MILLER** (1928 – 1933) son of Clyde and Geraldine (Rose) Miller. **DOROTHY R. MILLER** [5458] (1926 – 2009) daughter of Clyde and Geraldine (Rose) Miller married twice; first to Hubert P. Oster with whom she was mother of (2). Later, she married Paul Raymond Clark. Dorothy was a homemaker, worked for Austintown Schools, retiring in 1983, and had worked as a hostess at various restaurants in the area. Dorothy enjoyed spending time with family and friends, traveling and taking care of her home. **DOUGLAS MILLER** Sixth great grandson of progenitor Nicholas Kegg. **DRAYDEN JAY MILLER** Ninth great grandson of progenitor Nicholas Kegg. **ELIZABETH JEAN MILLER** Seventh great granddaughter of progenitor Nicholas Kegg. **ELIZABETH PAULINE MILLER** Sixth great granddaughter of progenitor Nicholas Kegg. **ELLIE MILLER** Eighth great granddaughter of progenitor Nicholas Kegg. **FLORA J. MILLER** Fifth great granddaughter of progenitor Nicholas Kegg. **FRED E. MILLER** Fifth great grandson of progenitor Nicholas Kegg. **GARY MILLER** Fifth great grandson of progenitor Nicholas Kegg. **GARY MILLER** Sixth great grandson of progenitor Nicholas Kegg. **GARY PAUL MILLER** [5459] (1944 – 2003) son of Paul and June (Cessna) Miller was father of (3). Gary worked in the computer industry for 40 years and was employed at IBM, Surbus and LDI in Westlake. In addition, he owned and operated Apex Computer Corp. Gary enjoyed riding his Harley Davidson motorcycle, auto racing and playing baseball, softball and racquetball. He also coached youth baseball, football and soccer. **GLENDA R. MILLER** Fifth great granddaughter of progenitor Nicholas Kegg. **GREG MILLER** Fifth great grandson of progenitor Nicholas Kegg. **HARRY P. MILLER** [5460] (1921 – 2000) son of Clarence and Florence (Turner) Miller, married Ruth Fay Whetstone with whom he was father of (1). Harry was a millwright for Bethlehem Steel Corporation

---

[5457] Tribune Democrat (PA) Sept 23, 2010 [5458] The Vindicator (OH) Oct 6, 2009 [5459] Elyria Chronicle Telegram (OH) July 31, 2003, obtained by D. Sue Dible [5460] p.3 - Bedford Inquirer (PA) July 14, 2000, obtained by Bob Rose

in Johnstown. He served in the U.S. Navy during World War II in the Asiatic Pacific campaign and the Philippine Liberation. **HAZEL J. MILLER** Fifth great granddaughter of progenitor Nicholas Kegg. **ISAAC MILLER** Fifth great grandson of progenitor Nicholas Kegg. **JACOB M. MILLER** Seventh great grandson of progenitor Nicholas Kegg. **JAMES MILLER** Eighth great grandson of progenitor Nicholas Kegg. **JAMES L. MILLER** Fifth great grandson of progenitor Nicholas Kegg. **JAMES PAUL MILLER** Sixth great grandson of progenitor Nicholas Kegg. **JAMES ROBERT MILLER** Seventh great grandson of progenitor Nicholas Kegg. **JANICE LEE MILLER** Seventh great granddaughter of progenitor Nicholas Kegg. **JASMINE MILLER** Seventh great granddaughter of progenitor Nicholas Kegg. **JASON MILLER** Sixth great grandson of progenitor Nicholas Kegg. **JAY MILLER** Sixth great grandson of progenitor Nicholas Kegg. **JEANETTE MARIE MILLER** Fifth great granddaughter of progenitor Nicholas Kegg. **JEFFREY L. MILLER** Fifth great grandson of progenitor Nicholas Kegg. **JO ELLEN MILLER** Fifth great granddaughter of progenitor Nicholas Kegg. **JOEY MILLER** Eighth great grandson of progenitor Nicholas Kegg. **JOHN MILLER** Fifth great grandson of progenitor Nicholas Kegg. **JOHN DAVID MILLER** [5461] (1955 – 2011) son of David and Mary Lou (Phenning) Miller married Janet Carol with whom he was father of (3). John was a U.S. Navy veteran. **JOHN E. MILLER** Fifth great grandson of progenitor Nicholas Kegg. **JOHN K. MILLER** Fifth great grandson of progenitor Nicholas Kegg. **JONATHAN MILLER** Eighth great grandson of progenitor Nicholas Kegg. **JONATHAN CLAYTON MILLER** Sixth great grandson of progenitor Nicholas Kegg. **JOSEPH HENRY MILLER** Sixth great grandson of progenitor Nicholas Kegg. **JUDITH ANN MILLER** [5462] (1950 – 1996) daughter of Robert and Betty Jane (Daley) Miller, married Walter Paul Drosjack with whom she was mother of (2). **KANDY MILLER** Seventh great granddaughter of progenitor Nicholas Kegg. **KAREN LOUISE MILLER** [5463] (1956 – 2019) daughter of Robert and Betty Jane (Daley) Miller, married Richard P. Boes with whom she was mother of (3). Karen was known for her generosity and gave to many charities. She enjoyed cooking, baking and oil painting and loved spending time with her children and grandchildren. She was a fan of Ellen DeGeneres and had the opportunity to attend the show. **KAREN SUE MILLER** Sixth great granddaughter of progenitor Nicholas Kegg. **KATE MILLER** Fifth great granddaughter of progenitor Nicholas Kegg. **KATHRYN MILLER** Third great granddaughter of progenitor Nicholas Kegg. **KAYCIE B. MILLER** Seventh great granddaughter of progenitor Nicholas Kegg. **KAYLA D. MILLER** Eighth great granddaughter of progenitor Nicholas Kegg. **KAYLA MARIE MILLER** Sixth great granddaughter of progenitor Nicholas Kegg. **KERRY ALAN MILLER** Fifth great grandson of progenitor Nicholas Kegg. **KIM MILLER** Eighth great granddaughter of progenitor Nicholas Kegg. **KIMBERLY S. MILLER** [5464] (1970 – 2021) daughter of Christine A. Beegle married Kenneth Harr, later she married Kenneth Williams. Kimberly was employed at ACE Hardware in Everett and Pepple's Construction, New Enterprise. She enjoyed collecting T-shirts, tanning and doing her nails. **KRISTINA LYNN MILLER** Sixth great granddaughter of progenitor Nicholas Kegg. **LEONARD G. MILLER** Fifth great grandson of progenitor Nicholas Kegg. **LEONARD G. MILLER** Sixth great grandson of progenitor Nicholas Kegg. **LEVI S. MILLER** Sixth great grandson of progenitor Nicholas Kegg. **LINCOLN DOUGLAS MILLER** Seventh great grandson of progenitor Nicholas Kegg. **LINDA MILLER** Fourth great granddaughter of progenitor Nicholas Kegg. **LINDA MILLER** Fifth great granddaughter of progenitor Nicholas Kegg. **LINDA DIANE MILLER** Fifth great granddaughter of progenitor Nicholas Kegg. **LINDA EILEEN MILLER** Fifth great granddaughter of progenitor Nicholas Kegg. **LORI E. MILLER** Fifth great granddaughter of progenitor Nicholas Kegg. **MARCUS PAUL MILLER** Sixth great grandson of progenitor Nicholas Kegg. **MARILYN J. MILLER** aka "Marnie" Fifth great granddaughter of progenitor Nicholas Kegg. **MARILYN KAY MILLER** (1936 – 1997) daughter of Vernard and Hazel (Bodle) Miller. **MARJORIE MILLER** Fifth great granddaughter of progenitor Nicholas Kegg. **MARY MILLER** Fifth great granddaughter of progenitor Nicholas Kegg. **MARY CAROL MILLER** Third great granddaughter of progenitor Nicholas Kegg.

[5461] The Tennessean (TN) Dec. 10, 2011 [5462] Johnstown Democrat-Tribune (PA) Apr 15, 1996, obtained by D. Sue Dible [5463] The Tube City Almanac (McKeesport and Mon-Yough Area, PA) July 2, 2019 [5464] Bedford Gazette (PA) Jan 16, 2021

MATT MILLER Seventh great grandson of progenitor Nicholas Kegg. **MATTHEW S. MILLER** Sixth great grandson of progenitor Nicholas Kegg. **MAURICE M. MILLER** Sixth great grandson of progenitor Nicholas Kegg. **MIA MILLER** Eighth great granddaughter of progenitor Nicholas Kegg. **MICAH JOEL MILLER** (1984 – 2006) son of William and Mildred Elaine (Kegg) Miller. **MICHAEL E. MILLER** (abt 1875 - ?) son of Jeremiah and Susanna (Kegg) Miller. **MICHAEL WILLIAM MILLER** Third great grandson of progenitor Nicholas Kegg. **MICHAEL WILLIAM MILLER** [5465] (1961 – 2015) aka "Bill", son of William and Ruth (Cessna) Miller, married Cheryl Griffiths with whom he was father of (1). Bill worked at Kennametal and was a member of the Bedford VFW. **MILDRED LOUISE MILLER** [5465A] (1909 – 1980) daughter of John and Amelia (Pritchard) Miller married Joseph Jackson Norton with whom she was mother of (3). Mildred was a graduate of the College of Idaho in Caldwell. She was a member of the Key Center Ward, Church of Jesus Christ of Latter-day Saints. **MYLES RICHARD MILLER** Sixth great grandson of progenitor Nicholas Kegg. **NANCY ELIZABETH MILLER** Third great granddaughter of progenitor Nicholas Kegg. **NATHAN MILLER** Fourth great grandson of progenitor Nicholas Kegg. **NICKY MILLER** Eighth great granddaughter of progenitor Nicholas Kegg. **NELLIE V. MILLER** [5466] (1913 – 1996) daughter of Clarence and Florence (Turner) Miller, married Eugene E. Scritchfield with whom she was mother of (1). **NOAH DOUGLAS MILLER** Seventh great grandson of progenitor Nicholas Kegg. **NORA MILLER** Sixth great granddaughter of progenitor Nicholas Kegg. **OLLIE J. MILLER** [5467] (1912 – 1985) son of Clarence and Florence (Turner) Miller, married Mabel Davis with whom he was father of (5). A World War II veteran, Ollie retired from former Franklin Division, Johnstown Plant, Bethlehem Steel Corp. **OLLIE J. MILLER** [5468] (1947 – 1991) son of Ollie and Mabel (Davis) Miller, married Delores Wachs with whom he was father of (2). A Navy veteran, Ollie was employed as assistant foreman for Mears Enterprises, Indiana County. **PATRICIA ANN MILLER** (1936 – 2016) daughter of Vernard and Hazel (Bodle) Miller, married Lowell Truman Shore. **PAUL MILLER** Sixth great grandson of progenitor Nicholas Kegg. **PAUL E. MILLER** Fifth great grandson of progenitor Nicholas Kegg. **PAUL VICTOR MILLER** [5468A] (1917 – 1996) son of John and Amelia (Pritchard) Miller, married Donna Marie Hester with whom he was father of (5). Paul served in the Army during World War II. He was an electrical contractor and owned his own business, M & M Electric, in Visalia for 30 years before retiring. He was a member of St. Mary's Catholic Church and the Knights of Columbus. **PAULA JO MILLER** Fifth great granddaughter of progenitor Nicholas Kegg. **PEARL MILLER** (1919 – 1919) daughter of Clarence and Florence (Turner) Miller. **PHOEBE E. MILLER** Seventh great granddaughter of progenitor Nicholas Kegg. **PRESTON D. MILLER** Sixth great grandson of progenitor Nicholas Kegg. **RALPH E. MILLER** [5469] (1954 – 2001) son of Charles and Henrietta (Williams) Miller, married Cindy Lehman with whom he was father of (3). Ralph was an independent newspaper carrier for the Tribune-Democrat for 11 years. Formerly employed by Penn Machine, Consolidated Coal Co., Central City and UPJ as a printer and in the maintenance department. **RANDAL LAMON MILLER** (1952 – 2006) aka "Randy" son of David and Mary Lou (Phenning) Miller. **RAY F. MILLER** (1883 – 1905) son of Jeremiah and Susanna (Kegg) Miller. **REBECCA J. MILLER** Sixth great granddaughter of progenitor Nicholas Kegg. **REESE MILLER** Eighth great grandson of progenitor Nicholas Kegg. **REX PETERSON MILLER** Sixth great grandson of progenitor Nicholas Kegg. **RICHARD P. MILLER** Third great grandson of progenitor Nicholas Kegg. **RICHARD P. MILLER JR.** Fourth great grandson of progenitor Nicholas Kegg. **RIAYN MILLER** Eighth great granddaughter of progenitor Nicholas Kegg. **ROBERT MILLER** Fifth great grandson of progenitor Nicholas Kegg. **ROBERT C. MILLER** [5469A] (1934 – 2006) son of Clarence and Florence (Turner) Miller married Dorothy Irene Kegg with whom he was father of (3). Robert retired from SCM Metals Products, Johnstown, after 34 years of service. **ROBERT R. MILLER** (1929 – 2001) son of Clyde and Geraldine (Rose) Miller **RODNEY MILLER** Sixth great grandson of

---

[5465] Timothy A Berkebile Funeral Home (PA) obtained by D. Sue Dible [5465A] p.D-14; Tacoma News Tribune Sep 12, 1980 contributed by D. Sue Dible [5466] p.3 - Bedford Inquirer (PA) Nov 29, 1996 [5467] Tribune Democrat (PA) Mar 10, 1985, obtained by Dorothy (Kegg) Miller [5468] Johnstown Tribune Democrat (PA) Aug 1991obtained by Dorothy (Kegg) Miller [5468A] Visalia Times-Delta (CA) Tulare County Library 1996 [5469] Daily American (PA) Dec 11, 2001, Meyersdale Library transcribed by Donna Thomas

progenitor Nicholas Kegg. **ROSE MILLER** Fifth great granddaughter of progenitor Nicholas Kegg. **ROXANA MILLER** Sixth great granddaughter of progenitor Nicholas Kegg. **RUSSELL ALLEN MILLER** Sixth great grandson of progenitor Nicholas Kegg. **RUTH MILLER** Fifth great granddaughter of progenitor Nicholas Kegg. **RUTH ANN MILLER** Fifth great granddaughter of progenitor Nicholas Kegg. **SAMANTHA MILLER** Fourth great granddaughter of progenitor Nicholas Kegg. **SAMUEL MILLER** Seventh great grandson of progenitor Nicholas Kegg. **SANDRA L. MILLER** Fifth great granddaughter of progenitor Nicholas Kegg. **SARA MILLER** Seventh great granddaughter of progenitor Nicholas Kegg. **SHAUN CHRISTOPHER MILLER** [5470] (1990 – 2019) son of Brian and Christine (Fink) Miller was a father of (2). Shaun loved the outdoors, tattoos, rock climbing and motorcycle riding. **SONIA MILLER** Fifth great granddaughter of progenitor Nicholas Kegg. **SONJOA L. MILLER** Fifth great granddaughter of progenitor Nicholas Kegg. **STEPHANIE ANN MILLER** Sixth great granddaughter of progenitor Nicholas Kegg. **STEVEN MILLER** Third great grandson of progenitor Nicholas Kegg. **STEPHEN L. MILLER** aka "Steve" Sixth great grandson of progenitor Nicholas Kegg. **STEPHEN MICHAEL MILLER** Sixth great grandson of progenitor Nicholas Kegg. **SUSAN MILLER** Fifth great granddaughter of progenitor Nicholas Kegg. **SYDNEY P. MILLER** Seventh great grandson of progenitor Nicholas Kegg. **TABITHA JOY MILLER** Sixth great granddaughter of progenitor Nicholas Kegg. **TAMARA SUE MILLER** aka "Tammy", Sixth great granddaughter of progenitor Nicholas Kegg. **TAMMY MILLER** Fifth great granddaughter of progenitor Nicholas Kegg. **TAMMY MARIE MILLER** Sixth great granddaughter of progenitor Nicholas Kegg. **TED THOMAS MILLER** Fifth great grandson of progenitor Nicholas Kegg. **TERRI L. MILLER** Fourth great granddaughter of progenitor Nicholas Kegg. **TIMOTHY DAVID MILLER** (1968 – 1968) son of James and Lillian (Diehl) Miller. **TRAVIS J. MILLER** Seventh great grandson of progenitor Nicholas Kegg. **TYLER DOUGLAS MILLER** Seventh great grandson of progenitor Nicholas Kegg. **VICKIE MILLER** Fifth great granddaughter of progenitor Nicholas Kegg. **VIVIAN VERA MILLER** [5070A] (1913 – 2005) daughter of John and Amelia (Pritchard) Miller married Willard Wood Shawhan with whom she was mother of (2). Vivian received her teaching credential from the College of Idaho. She served as an elementary school teacher with the Pierce County Public School System for more than 20 years. Vivian was a very active member of Tacoma's First United Methodist Church and United Methodist Women, and also served as volunteer with the Tacoma Chamber of Commerce. Vivian enjoyed gardening, sewing and reading. **WILMONT G. MILLER** aka "Bud", Fifth great grandson of progenitor Nicholas Kegg.

MILLIGAN

ERIN ELIZABETH MILLIGAN Sixth great granddaughter of progenitor Nicholas Kegg.
SHAWN MARIE MILLIGAN Sixth great granddaughter of progenitor Nicholas Kegg.

MILLIN

EMILY IRENE MILLIN [5471] (1899 – 1970) daughter of Albert and Carrie (Kegg) Millin, married Clayton Daniel Kauffman with whom she was mother of (1).
MABEL CARBARINS MILLIN (1907 – 1965) daughter of Albert and Carrie (Kegg) Millin, married Oliver Paul Young with whom she was mother of (1).
MILDRED PEARL MILLIN [5471A] (1897 – 1987) daughter of Albert and Carrie (Kegg) Millin married Harry Mohn Brenner with whom she was mother of (3).
SARA VIOLA MILLIN (1901 – 1989) daughter of Albert and Carrie (Kegg) Millin, married Howard S. Binkley with whom she was mother of (1).
STANLEY W. MILLIN (1905 – 1974) son of Albert and Carrie (Kegg) Millin.

[5469A] Tribune Democrat (PA) June 03, 2006 [5470] Bedford Gazette (PA) Oct 22, 2019 [5070A] Napa News (CA) Feb 5, 2005 [5471] p.7 - Morning Herald (PA) Sept. 21, 1938 [5471A] <http://archiver.rootsweb.ancestry.com/>

MILLS

ALVIN LEE MILLS [5472] (1937 – 2022) son of Alvin Webster and Mary (Margaret) Diehl married Gail Marcia Bear with whom he was father of (8). Later, he married Peggy (Lowery) Guy. Alvin joined the United States Air Force where he served as a Military Police Officer. Upon returning home from his service, Alvin worked as a self-employed truck driver for many years until his retirement. He enjoyed spending time outdoors by going fishing, hunting, and golfing. **ANDREW W. MILLS** Fifth great grandson of progenitor Nicholas Kegg. **BECKY SUE MILLS** Sixth great granddaughter of progenitor Nicholas Kegg. **BENJAMIN MILLS** Seventh great granddaughter of progenitor Nicholas Kegg. **BRIAN S. MILLS** Sixth great grandson of progenitor Nicholas Kegg. **GERALD WAYNE MILLS** Sixth great grandson of progenitor Nicholas Kegg. **JUDITH LYNNE MILLS** Fifth great granddaughter of progenitor Nicholas Kegg. **KENNETH P. MILLS** Sixth great grandson of progenitor Nicholas Kegg. **MARK ALLEN MILLS** Fifth great grandson of progenitor Nicholas Kegg. **MEAGAN RENEE MILLS** [5473] (1987 – 1987) daughter of Michael and Carol (Szarenski) Mills. **MELANIE A. MILLS** Sixth great granddaughter of progenitor Nicholas Kegg. **MICHAEL VANCE MILLS** Sixth great grandson of progenitor Nicholas Kegg. **PAUL EDWARD MILLS** Fifth great grandson of progenitor Nicholas Kegg. **POLLY A. MILLS** Sixth great granddaughter of progenitor Nicholas Kegg. **RICHARD CEDRIC MILLS** Fifth great grandson of progenitor Nicholas Kegg. **ROBIN ELIZABETH MILLS** [5474] (1965 – 1965) daughter of William and Nancy (Walkley) Mills. **RYAN MILLS** Seventh great grandson of progenitor Nicholas Kegg. **SCOTT D. MILLS** Sixth great grandson of progenitor Nicholas Kegg. **SHERYL LEE MILLS** Fifth great granddaughter of progenitor Nicholas Kegg. **STEPHEN WAYNE MILLS** [5475] (1949 – 1963) son of Alvin and Mary (Diehl) Mills was killed in a head-on auto accident on Route 522 south of McConnellsburg. **TRACEY J. MILLS** Sixth great granddaughter of progenitor Nicholas Kegg. **TROY L. MILLS** Sixth great grandson of progenitor Nicholas Kegg. **WILLIAM W. MILLS** Sixth great grandson of progenitor Nicholas Kegg.

MILNER

AUBREY MILNER Eighth great granddaughter of progenitor Nicholas Kegg.
BLAKE MILNER Eighth great grandson of progenitor Nicholas Kegg.
SAMANTHA MILNER Eighth great granddaughter of progenitor Nicholas Kegg.

MINAKER

ERIC MINAKER Sixth great grandson of progenitor Nicholas Kegg.

MINEAR

CHARLES FRANK MINEAR Fifth great grandson of progenitor Nicholas Kegg.
TRACY LYNN MINEAR Sixth great granddaughter of progenitor Nicholas Kegg.
VIRGINIA LEA MINEAR aka "Jinnie", Fifth great granddaughter of progenitor Nicholas Kegg.

MINEHART

CHAD WILLIAM MINEHART Fifth great grandson of progenitor Nicholas Kegg.
CHANDLER MINEHART Sixth great grandson of progenitor Nicholas Kegg.
CHARLEIGH REESE MINEHART Sixth great granddaughter of progenitor Nicholas Kegg.

[5472] Donelson Funeral Home Everett, PA [5273] Orlando Sentinel (FL) Sep 22, 1987 [5474] Cumberland Times (MD) Dec 20, 1965 [5475] Fulton County News (PA) May 1963

ROBIN LYNN MINEHART Fifth great granddaughter of progenitor Nicholas Kegg.
WENDY LOUISE MINEHART Fifth great granddaughter of progenitor Nicholas Kegg.

MINER

KAYLEE MINER Sixth great granddaughter of progenitor Nicholas Kegg.
ROBERT G. MINER Fifth great grandson of progenitor Nicholas Kegg.

MINIER

BETH ILENE MINIER Fifth great granddaughter of progenitor Nicholas Kegg. **BRADFORD MINIER** Sixth great grandson of progenitor Nicholas Kegg. **BRYAN CHRISTIAN MINIER** Fifth great grandson of progenitor Nicholas Kegg. **BRYAN E. MINIER** Sixth great grandson of progenitor Nicholas Kegg. **ELLA MAY MINIER** (born abt. 1878) daughter of Jesse and Eva (Greene) Minier. **ERICA MINIER** Sixth great granddaughter of progenitor Nicholas Kegg. **HOLLIS MINIER** Seventh great granddaughter of progenitor Nicholas Kegg. **JOHN MINIER** Fifth great grandson of progenitor Nicholas Kegg. **JOHN MINIER** Sixth great grandson of progenitor Nicholas Kegg. **LOYAL GREENE MINIER** [5476] (1888 – 1955) son of Jesse and Eva (Greene) Minier married twice; first to Gertrude Antonine Ohlsen with whom he was father of (6). Later, he married Anna D. Mast. Loyal received his master's degree from Indiana university in 1932 and then taught at Jefferson high school, Lafayette, Ind., for 27 years. He retired in 1950. He was a member of the Berrien Springs Lion club and was a Master Key member of the Lafayette Lions club. **MARY ELLEN MINIER** [5476A] (1929 – 1986) daughter of Loyal and Gertrude (Ohlsen) Minier married Jack Dassenko with whom she was mother of (2). As a music teacher she taught at Minneapolis Junior Academy (Minneapolis), Newbury Park (California), Instituto Adventista del Uruguay (South Africa), and Walla Walla College (Washington). Mary Ellen was a social worker, and one of the first women ordained as a local elder of the Walla Walla College church. **MASON MINIER** Seventh great grandson of progenitor Nicholas Kegg. **MAX MINIER** Seventh great grandson of progenitor Nicholas Kegg. **MICHAEL ALAN MINIER** Fifth great grandson of progenitor Nicholas Kegg. **MYLES KEITH MINIER** Seventh great grandson of progenitor Nicholas Kegg. **PAUL ANTON MINIER** (1930 – 1932) son of Loyal and Gertrude (Ohlsen) Minier. **RUTH JEAN MINIER** [5476B] aka "Jean" (1924 – 1994) daughter of Loyal and Gertrude (Ohlsen) Minier married John Leonard Scheldt with whom she was mother of (3). Jean was a cafeteria manager at Mirror Lake Junior High School, and later at Riviera Middle School. She also was a licensed practical nurse at local hospitals. **STEPHANI MINIER** Sixth great granddaughter of progenitor Nicholas Kegg.

MINNICH

GRACE REBECCA MINNICH [5477] (1912 – 2002) aka "Rebecca", daughter of John and Grace (Cessna) Minnich married twice; first to William Statler Taylor with whom she was mother of (4). Later, she married Edwin Alexander Hartley. Rebecca retired after 25 years as a senatorial secretary for the state of Pennsylvania and as a legal secretary for Koontz, Koontz & Crabtree. **JOHN A. MINNICH** [5477A] son of John and Grace (Cessna) Minnich married twice, first to Josephine B. Fidler and later to Katherine Mervine. John practiced law in Bedford County from 1934 until he retired in 1990. He also worked as a law clerk for Judge J. Colvin Wright for more than 10 years. He was a member of Bedford Lodge No. 320 F&AM, Altoona Consistory and the Jaffa Temple. He was also a member of Bedford Elks Lodge No. 1707, a member of the former Reed-Cessna Orchestra, the Antique Automobile Club of America [5476] including the Fort Bedford region and the Allegheny Mountain region of the club. He was also a member

Herald-Press (St. Joseph, MI) Jan 31, 1955 [5476A] p.30 (942) Adventist Review Archives Aug 28, 1986 [5476B] St. Petersburg Times (FL) Sept 15, 1994 [5477] Bedford Inquirer (PA) Sep 6, 2002, obtained by Nancy Agnew Peché transcribed by Bob Rose [5477A] p.3 - Bedford Inquirer (PA) Aug 2, 1991

of the Bedford County Amateur Radio Society.

MINTMIER

RUTH MARGARET MINTMIER [5478] (1920 – 2004) daughter of Frederick and Mabel (Kegg) Mintmier, married Raymond Lytle Snavely with whom she was mother of (1). Ruth was a former bookkeeper for Bantly Hardware. She was a member of Eastern Star and was a former Choraleer of Johnstown.

MINTZER

ELEANOR MINTZER [5479] (1901 – 1967) daughter of Adolph and Ida (Kegg) Mintzer, married James Bryson Cobaugh. **GERTRUDE R. MINTZER** [5480] (1899 – 1984) daughter of Adolph and Ida (Kegg) Mintzer, married Thomas Leo Cassidy with whom she was mother of (1).

MISLEH

JOSEPH RICHARD MISLEH Sixth great grandson of progenitor Nicholas Kegg.
MARK WILLIAM MISLEH Sixth great grandson of progenitor Nicholas Kegg.
TERESA MISLEH aka "Terri", Sixth great granddaughter of progenitor Nicholas Kegg.

MITCH

JUSTIN MITCH Seventh great grandson of progenitor Nicholas Kegg.
RYAN MITCH Seventh great grandson of progenitor Nicholas Kegg.

MITCHELL

CASSIE DEE MITCHELL Seventh great granddaughter of progenitor Nicholas Kegg.
CHRISTOPHER RYAN MITCHELL Seventh great grandson of progenitor Nicholas Kegg.
CLAYTON JAMES MITCHELL Sixth great grandson of progenitor Nicholas Kegg.
COLIN JEFFREY MITCHELL Seventh great grandson of progenitor Nicholas Kegg.
REESE HAMILTON MITCHELL Seventh great grandson of progenitor Nicholas Kegg.

MOATS

AMY LYNN MOATS Seventh great granddaughter of progenitor Nicholas Kegg.
LAURA MICHELLE MOATS Seventh great granddaughter of progenitor Nicholas Kegg.

MOBUS

JACQUELINE S. MOBUS aka "Jackie" Sixth great granddaughter of progenitor Nicholas Kegg.
JOHN B. MOBUS II Sixth great grandson of progenitor Nicholas Kegg.
KATHY JO MOBUS [5480A] (1961 – 2015) daughter of John and Patricia (Steach) Mobus married Leonard R. Malloy with whom she was mother of (1). Kathy was employed as a Sales Support Analyst with over 20 dedicated years with Highmark Blue Shield located in Camp Hill. She enjoyed reading, traveling to the beach and was very talented with her crafting abilities, but her favorite activity was spending time with her family and friends; to know her was to love her.

[5478] Tribune Democrat (PA) Oct 10, 2004 [5479] Tribune-Democrat (PA) Nov 9, 1967, obtained by D. Sue Dible [5480] Tribune-Democrat (PA) July 27, 1984 [5480A] Bedford Gazette (PA) Dec 26, 2015

SHARON L. MOBUS Sixth great granddaughter of progenitor Nicholas Kegg.
TERESA A. MOBUS aka "Terri", Sixth great granddaughter of progenitor Nicholas Kegg.

MOCK

CHRISTINE MOCK Sixth great granddaughter of progenitor Nicholas Kegg. **JENNIFER LEE MOCK** Sixth great granddaughter of progenitor Nicholas Kegg. **MAKAYLA MOCK** Seventh great granddaughter of progenitor Nicholas Kegg. **PAULETTE MARNO MOCK** [5481] (1947 – 2003) daughter of Paul and Bonnie (Thompson) Mock married four times; first to Ronald Dean Cogger with whom she was mother of (2). She married Mr. Kozlowski with whom she was mother of (1). Later, she married Dennis John Christenson followed by Marcel Dupree. Paulette was retired from Ocean Springs Cranberry where she worked in quality control. She was an avid gardener, and enjoyed landscaping, painting, animals and butterflies. **R. J. MOCK** Eighth great grandson of progenitor Nicholas Kegg. **RAYMOND LEROY MOCK** Seventh great grandson of progenitor Nicholas Kegg.

MOFFETT

BARRY WAYNE MOFFETT Fifth great grandson of progenitor Nicholas Kegg.
VIVIAN OLIVIA MOFFETT (1938 – 1993) daughter of Walter and Joene (Kegg) Moffett married twice, first to Thomas J. Fleming and later to James Harry Baggaley.

MOFFITT

JESSICA JADE MOFFITT Seventh great granddaughter of progenitor Nicholas Kegg.

MOHNEY

BRITTANY NICHOLE MOHNEY Seventh great grandson of progenitor Nicholas Kegg. **DAVID WILSON MOHNEY** Sixth great grandson of progenitor Nicholas Kegg. **JACOB ANTHONY MOHNEY** Seventh great grandson of progenitor Nicholas Kegg. **ROBERT STEPHEN MOHNEY** [5481A] (1967 – 1996) son of Robert and Jacklyn (Wilson) Mohney, married Angela R. Bowers. He backed his red Pontiac Firebird out of his Westerville driveway and disappeared on July 16, 1996, at the age of 29. Westerville police investigating Robert Mohney's disappearance told his wife years ago that they thought he had been killed. His Firebird was found near the Hoover Reservoir spillway, less than a mile from his home. Missing for 11 years, Angela had her husband declared legally dead in 2007. **SUSAN PATRICIA MOHNEY** [5481B] (1969 – 2016) daughter of Robert and Jacklyn (Wilson) Mohney, married Trenton Davis with whom she was mother of (2). Susan was a graduate of Tri-County Adult Career Center with a license in Cosmetology.

MOLLOY

LORILEE V. MOLLOY Seventh great granddaughter of progenitor Nicholas Kegg.
LUKE MOLLOY aka "Chip", Seventh great grandson of progenitor Nicholas Kegg.
MADDIE MOLLOY Eighth great granddaughter of progenitor Nicholas Kegg.

MONAHAN

CECELIA GAIL MONAHAN Fifth great granddaughter of progenitor Nicholas Kegg.
DAVID WILLIAM MONAHAN Fifth great grandson of progenitor Nicholas Kegg.

[5481] Daily Journal (MS) July 4, 2003 [5481A] Columbus Dispatch (OH) May 8, 2013 [5481B] Columbus Dispatch (OH) July 19, 2016

JEFFREY MONAHAN Sixth great grandson of progenitor Nicholas Kegg.

MONDARY

MAURICE ALVIN MONDARY Sixth great grandson of progenitor Nicholas Kegg.
MELISSA CATHERINE MONDARY (1966 – 1966) daughter of Maurice and Barbara (Storz) Mondary.

MONN

DONNA KAY MONN Fifth great granddaughter of progenitor Nicholas Kegg.
NANCY LEE MONN Fifth great granddaughter of progenitor Nicholas Kegg.
PATRICIA A. MONN Fifth great granddaughter of progenitor Nicholas Kegg.
TREVOR MONN Sixth great grandson of progenitor Nicholas Kegg.

MONROE

CARL MONROE Sixth great grandson of progenitor Nicholas Kegg. **CHARLES RONALD MONROE** Fifth great grandson of progenitor Nicholas Kegg. **CRYSTAL LOUISE MONROE** Sixth great granddaughter of progenitor Nicholas Kegg. **DEMETRA MONROE** Sixth great granddaughter of progenitor Nicholas Kegg. **JAMES A. MONROE** [5482] (1975 – 1999) son of Charles and Patricia (Slaven) Monroe, married Tamara J. Murray. James was fatally shot in the chest by a city officer as he lunged at the officer with a knife. The officers had been called by friends when he put a knife to his throat and told friends he intended to kill himself. Relatives staged public protests since the death of the 23-year-old and expressed frustration with the grand jury's decision clearing the Muncie officer. **JASON ALLEN MONROE** Sixth great grandson of progenitor Nicholas Kegg. **TERRY A. MONROE** Sixth great grandson of progenitor Nicholas Kegg. **TRACY OVIS MONROE** [5482A] (1936 – 2016) son of Ovis and Mabel (Houck) Monroe was father of (2) with Carolyn Louise Johnson, later he was father of (2) with Sandra Tishner. Tracy was a musician all of his life and an avid fisherman. He served in the US Navy from 1955 to 1958.

MONTAGUE

AMBER MONTAGUE Seventh great granddaughter of progenitor Nicholas Kegg.
HEATHER MARIE MONTAGUE Seventh great granddaughter of progenitor Nicholas Kegg.

MONTGOMERY

CARRIE MONTGOMERY Fourth great granddaughter of progenitor Nicholas Kegg.
EDWIN EARL MONTGOMERY (1955 – 1956) son of Edwin and Mary Louise (Morrow) Montgomery.
JASON MONTGOMERY Fourth great grandson of progenitor Nicholas Kegg.
JERRY RAY MONTGOMERY Sixth great grandson of progenitor Nicholas Kegg.

MOODY

CAMERON MOODY Seventh great grandson of progenitor Nicholas Kegg.
MACY MOODY Seventh great granddaughter of progenitor Nicholas Kegg.

[5482] p.A2 Star Press (Muncie, IN) Aug 4, 2015 [5482A] The Star Press (IN) Mar. 31, 2016

MOONEY

LEAH MOONEY Sixth great granddaughter of progenitor Nicholas Kegg.
MAX MOONEY Sixth great grandson of progenitor Nicholas Kegg.

MOORE

BETH MOORE Sixth great granddaughter of progenitor Nicholas Kegg. **BILL DUBBS MOORE** [5482B] aka "Dubby" (1927 – 2012) son of Carl and Lottie (Dubbs) Moore, married Patsy Lou Buschor with whom he was father of (2). Dubby retired as Van Wert City Chief of Police after 25 years of service. He had also worked at his father's movie theater - The Ohio Theater - until its closing in 1959. He was a member of St. Mary of the Assumption Catholic Church, Van Wert. He was an avid car enthusiast and a member of Van Wert F.O.P. Lodge 62, Van Wert Knights of Columbus Council 6034, Van Wert Elks Lodge 1197, and Van Wert Masonic Lodge 218. **CHARLES MOORE** Sixth great grandson of progenitor Nicholas Kegg. **CLIFTON MOORE** Seventh great grandson of progenitor Nicholas Kegg. **CRYSTAL MOORE** Sixth great granddaughter of progenitor Nicholas Kegg. **DREW MOORE** Seventh great grandson of progenitor Nicholas Kegg. **HARVEY EDWARD MOORE** (1929 – 1999) son of Boyd and Marie (Diehl) Moore. **HULDAH ANN MOORE** [5483] (1902 – 2000) daughter of William and Cora (Shaw) Moore married Mr. Johnson with whom she was mother of (2). Huldah was a theatre organist for silent movies, a concert organist performing in Lima, Bowling Green, Wooster, Akron, Jamestown, N.Y., Union City, Pa., and a pianist for several orchestras, organist for Findley churches and St. Luke's Methodist Church in Columbus. She graduated from the Findley Conservatory of Music, attended the Cincinnati Conservatory of Music and was a student of Lawrence Hughes at Ohio State University. A longtime resident of Upper Arlington, she was a 45-year member of First Community Church where she helped establish the Over Fifty Club, an area leader for Easter Seals for 15 years, a supporter of the Republican Party and a member of OSU Mother's Club, Group Y. **JAMES ALBERT MOORE** (1935 – 1936) son of Boyd and Marie (Diehl) Moore. **JENNIFER MOORE** Sixth great granddaughter of progenitor Nicholas Kegg. **LISA DAWN MARIE MOORE** Sixth great granddaughter of progenitor Nicholas Kegg. **LYNN MOORE** Seventh great granddaughter of progenitor Nicholas Kegg. **MICHAEL MOORE** [5484] (1926 – 2011) aka "Mikie", son of Boyd and Marie (Diehl) Moore married twice; first to Dorothy J. Zeller. Later, he married Doris Mae Beall with whom he was father of (6). Mikie was a member of Christ Lutheran Church for the Deaf for many years where he volunteered as a carpenter, also he and Dave Watts made the wood cross for the church and was also a deacon for a few years. Michael worked at precision Steel Company for 23 years, Sunroof Company for 10 years, Aetna Specialist for 10 years before retiring. **MICHAEL CHRISTOPHER MOORE** Sixth great grandson of progenitor Nicholas Kegg. **MICHAEL W. MOORE** Seventh great grandson of progenitor Nicholas Kegg. **MICHAELLA MOORE** Sixth great granddaughter of progenitor Nicholas Kegg. **MICHAELLE MOORE** Seventh great granddaughter of progenitor Nicholas Kegg. **MISTEE MOORE** Sixth great granddaughter of progenitor Nicholas Kegg. **MITCHELL L. MOORE** Sixth great grandson of progenitor Nicholas Kegg. **NICOLE MOORE** Seventh great granddaughter of progenitor Nicholas Kegg. **REBECCA MOORE** Sixth great granddaughter of progenitor Nicholas Kegg. **RONNIE MOORE** Sixth great grandson of progenitor Nicholas Kegg **SANDRA KAY MOORE** Sixth great granddaughter of progenitor Nicholas Kegg. **STEPHANIE JO MOORE** Sixth great granddaughter of progenitor Nicholas Kegg. **SUSAN MOORE** Sixth great granddaughter of progenitor Nicholas Kegg. **SUSIE M. MOORE** Sixth great granddaughter of progenitor Nicholas Kegg. **TIMOTHY CARL MOORE** Sixth great grandson of progenitor Nicholas Kegg. **WILLIAM C. MOORE** Sixth great grandson of progenitor Nicholas Kegg.

[5482B] Times Bulletin (OH) Oct 5, 2012 [5483] p.3B-Northwest Columbus News (OH) Aug 9, 2000 [5484] The Plain Dealer (Cleveland, OH) - June 10, 2011

MOOREHEAD

MEGAN MOOREHEAD Ninth great granddaughter of progenitor Nicholas Kegg.
TRENT MOOREHEAD Ninth great grandson of progenitor Nicholas Kegg.

MOOREHOUSE

DEANE LELAN ALLEN MOOREHOUSE (1920 – 2010) aka "Baba", son of Lee and Lula (Dean) Moorehouse, married Audrey Lucille Sirpless with whom he was father of (4); "Baba", was a nickname given to him by Charles Manson. **DEANE THOMAS MOOREHOUSE** Fifth great grandson of progenitor Nicholas Kegg. **JOAN CECILE MOOREHOUSE** (1925 – 1998) daughter of Lee and Lula (Dean) Moorehouse married twice; first to Mr. Larson and later, to William W. Rinehart with whom she was mother of (2). **KATHLEEN ADAIR MOOREHOUSE** Fifth great granddaughter of progenitor Nicholas Kegg. **MURIEL MAE MOOREHOUSE** (1912 – 1997) daughter of Lee and Lula (Dean) Moorehouse married four times; first to Isaac Lester McKim with whom she was mother of (3). She married Harry Francis Ward, Henry Tetlow and Mr. Miller. **RUTH FLORENCE MOOREHOUSE** (1923 – 1930) daughter of Lee and Lula (Dean) Moorehouse. **SHARON LEE MOOREHOUSE** Fifth great granddaughter of progenitor Nicholas Kegg. **TODD WILLIAM MOOREHOUSE** Sixth great grandson of progenitor Nicholas Kegg. **WILLIAM A. MOOREHOUSE** (1913 – 1995) son of Lee and Lula (Dean) Moorehouse married twice; first to Lillian Beatrice Lusian and later, to Annabelle Sirpless Fouts.

MORA

ELIANA JASMINE MORA Seventh great granddaughter of progenitor Nicholas Kegg.

MORALES

ASHLEY MORALES Sixth great granddaughter of progenitor Nicholas Kegg. **CARL DUANE MORALES** Sixth great grandson of progenitor Nicholas Kegg. **CHRISTOPHER KENT MORALES** Seventh great grandson of progenitor Nicholas Kegg. **DOUGLAS KENT MORALES** Sixth great grandson of progenitor Nicholas Kegg. **INDA MARIE MORALES** Sixth great granddaughter of progenitor Nicholas Kegg. **MADISON RAE MORALES** Ninth great granddaughter of progenitor Nicholas Kegg. **MIA MARIE MORALES** Seventh great granddaughter of progenitor Nicholas Kegg. **STUART MORALES** Sixth great grandson of progenitor Nicholas Kegg.

MORAN

ALEXANDER THOMAS MORAN Sixth great grandson of progenitor Nicholas Kegg.

MOREL

BRIEN MOREL Sixth great grandson of progenitor Nicholas Kegg.
KATE MOREL Sixth great granddaughter of progenitor Nicholas Kegg.
KEVIN MOREL Sixth great grandson of progenitor Nicholas Kegg.

MORELLO

MICHAEL EDWARD MORELLO Sixth great grandson of progenitor Nicholas Kegg.
PEGGY JO MORELLO Sixth great granddaughter of progenitor Nicholas Kegg.
STEVEN JOHN MORELLO Sixth great grandson of progenitor Nicholas Kegg.

SUZANNE MARIE MORELLO Sixth great granddaughter of progenitor Nicholas Kegg.
TIMOTHY CARL MORELLO (1957 – 1999) son of Bernard and Virginia (Morrow) Morello.

MORENO

ALEXANDRIA JOSEFA MORENO Eighth great granddaughter of progenitor Nicholas Kegg. **JACKSON DURHAM MORENO** Eighth great grandson of progenitor Nicholas Kegg. **MICHAEL MORENO** Sixth great grandson of progenitor Nicholas Kegg. **MICHAEL T. MORENO** Fifth great grandson of progenitor Nicholas Kegg.

MOREY

CLARISSA J. MOREY Sixth great granddaughter of progenitor Nicholas Kegg. **DEBRA MOREY** Sixth great granddaughter of progenitor Nicholas Kegg. **DIANE LYNN MOREY** Fifth great granddaughter of progenitor Nicholas Kegg. **GEORGE J. MOREY** Sixth great grandson of progenitor Nicholas Kegg. **LEONARD LAVERN MOREY** [5485] (1955 – 2015) aka "Lonnie", son of Leonard and Betty (Kegg) Morey. Lonnie was a caring and compassionate person. He had an awesome sense of humor and, because of this, was often the target of co-worker's practical jokes. He loved cooking and trying new recipes he learned watching cooking shows. Lonnie liked to ride motorcycles. He also raised pigs. We all face difficulties in life. Lonnie was no exception; he suffered a hip injury while he was still young. The injury was a source of lifelong pain, and he could have chosen to be disabled. Instead, he joined CETA and obtained a position at Tehama County Social Services. Through this program, he was hired as a permanent employee. He worked in the eligibility department of Social Services. He was highly respected for his knowledge of program rules and regulations and was called a walking regulations manual. He retired from Social Services in 2007. **TERRY R. MOREY** Fifth great granddaughter of progenitor Nicholas Kegg.

MORGAN

BONITA MARIE MORGAN [5486] (1931 – 2013) daughter of Vernon and Opal (Knouf) Morgan married three times; first to Pastor Eldon R. Schmidt with whom she was mother of (2). She married Henry Gordon Campbell and lastly, Darrell Laverne Small. **CHRISTOPHER ANDREW MORGAN** Seventh great grandson of progenitor Nicholas Kegg. **CLINT EDWARD MORGAN** Sixth great grandson of progenitor Nicholas Kegg. **DARRELL W. MORGAN** Seventh great grandson of progenitor Nicholas Kegg. **DAVID EDWARD MORGAN** Fifth great grandson of progenitor Nicholas Kegg. **DAWN ELAINE MORGAN** Fifth great granddaughter of progenitor Nicholas Kegg. **DIANNE EILEEN MORGAN** Fifth great granddaughter of progenitor Nicholas Kegg. **DONALD EARL MORGAN** [5486A] aka "Don" (1932 – 2018) son of Vernon and Opal (Knouf) Morgan married twice, first to Shirley Joan Highsmith with whom he was father of (3). Later, he married Gloria Moreno. Don graduated Salutatorian from Sedro Woolley High School in 1950 and joined the United States Air Force the following year. He enjoyed his retirement after 20 years of service. He had a love for the Bible and a love for Jehovah, symbolizing his dedication when he was baptized in February 1977. He became a minister for the next 41 years. In that time, he became well known in his community as someone always ready to lend a helping hand to any in need. His greatest joy was offering spiritual help and comfort from the Bible. **EVELYN GLADYS MORGAN** [5487] (1906 – 1976) daughter of William and Rosa (Biggs) Morgan, married Harold Korns Mast with whom she was mother of (6). **GARY LEE MORGAN** (1931 – 1931) son of Murrel and Norma (Knouf) Morgan. **JUNE ARLENE MORGAN** Fourth great granddaughter of progenitor Nicholas Kegg. **LORI G. MORGAN** Seventh great granddaughter of progenitor Nicholas Kegg. **RICHARD CLINT MORGAN** Seventh great grandson of progenitor Nicholas Kegg.

[5485] Hoyt-Cole Chapel of the Flowers Red Bluff, CA [5486] Lemley Chapel Funeral Directors, WA [5486A] Pennington Funeral Home (TX) [5487] p.2 Wooster Daily Record (OH) Mar 18, 1976, obtained by D. Sue Dible

MORGART

ALICE REBECCA MORGART [5488] (1917 – 2004) aka "Rebecca", daughter of Richard and Ruby (Harclerode) Morgart, married Frank R. Kasper. Rebecca was a retired employee of LeBow Sewing Factory. **BARBARA ANN MORGART** Fourth great granddaughter of progenitor Nicholas Kegg. **CHARLES RICHARD MORGART** [5489] (1915 – 1998) aka "Buss", son of Richard and Ruby (Harclerode) Morgart, married Vida Hilda Foor with whom he was father of (1). Buss was raised by his foster parents, the late John and Della Nave. Buss had worked as a heavy equipment operator. **DEBRA LYNE MORGART** Fifth great granddaughter of progenitor Nicholas Kegg. **GRACE VIRGINIA MORGART** [5490] (1882 – 1919) daughter of Charles and Mary (Shoemaker) Morgart, married George Hugh McClintic with whom she was mother of (4). Grace was a member of the Third Presbyterian church and of several Church societies. **HILDA JUNE MORGART** Sixth great granddaughter of progenitor Nicholas Kegg. **IONE PEARL MORGART** [5491] (1913 – 1993) daughter of Richard and Ruby (Harclerode) Morgart, married Joseph Edward Cook. Ione worked as a Red Cross volunteer graylady at Camp Leroy Johnson Hospital, New Orleans, during World War ll. She also was a ceramic craftsperson for many years. **JANET LAVERNE MORGART** [5491A] (1930 – 1950) daughter of Curtis and Margaret (Pennel) Morgart. **KYLEE L. MORGART** Sixth great granddaughter of progenitor Nicholas Kegg. **LUKE JASON MORGART** Sixth great grandson of progenitor Nicholas Kegg. **MARLA KAY MORGART** Fifth great granddaughter of progenitor Nicholas Kegg. **MARY JANE MORGART** (1927 – 1928) daughter of Curtis and Margaret (Pennel) Morgart. **MICHELLE LEANN MORGART** Fifth great granddaughter of progenitor Nicholas Kegg. **THOMAS L. MORGART** Fifth great grandson of progenitor Nicholas Kegg.

MORIARTY

CATHELINA MORIARTY (born abt. 1918) daughter of Patrick and Pauline (Diehl) Moriarty. **DENNIS BRUCE MORIARTY** Fifth great grandson of progenitor Nicholas Kegg. **HOWARD P. MORIARTY** Fifth great grandson of progenitor Nicholas Kegg. **HOWARD W. MORIARTY** [5491B] (1932 – 2007) son of Patrick and Pauline (Diehl) Moriarty, married Cora Belle Kunkle with whom he was father of (3). Prior to his retirement, Howard was a Baptist minister. He especially enjoyed conducting the Bible study group at Harmon House, Mt. Pleasant. He also worked in the maintenance department at Walworth and Westmoreland Manor. Howard loved to fish and read. He was a family man. **MARY LOUISE MORIARTY** (1937 – 2004) daughter of Patrick and Pauline (Diehl) Moriarty married three times; first to Mr. Kellerman, followed by Mr. Seanor and later, to Robert Henry Wagner. **SANDRA MORIARTY** Fifth great granddaughter of progenitor Nicholas Kegg.

MORLAND

ABBY MORLAND Seventh great granddaughter of progenitor Nicholas Kegg. **ANTHONY ALLEN MORLAND** (1966 – 1966) Eight-day old son of Leo and Sandra (Anderson) Morland died of Meningitis. **BRAD M. MORLAND** Sixth great grandson of progenitor Nicholas Kegg. **BRIAN TODD MORLAND** Sixth great grandson of progenitor Nicholas Kegg. **ELIZABETH A. MORLAND** Sixth great granddaughter of progenitor Nicholas Kegg. **JACK MORLAND** Seventh great grandson of progenitor Nicholas Kegg. **JASON THOMAS MORLAND** [5491C] (1976 – 2014) son of William and Sally (Fleckenstein) Morland, married Crystal Bunch with whom he was father of (2). Jason was a branch manager for Ferguson Enterprises. He loved to fish and be in the outdoors, coaching little league and watching NASCAR. **LEO H. MORLAND** Fifth great grandson of progenitor Nicolas Kegg.

[5488] obituary clipping obtained and transcribed by Harriet Clapper [5489] obituary clipping Obtained by Jim Boor Contributed by Bob Longbottom [5490] Bedford Gazette (PA) June 6, 1919, obtained by Bob Rose [5491] obituary clipping Obtained by Jim Boor Contributed by Bob Longbottom [5491A] Johnstown Tribune Newspaper (PA) Nov 17, 1950 [5491B] Tribune Review (Greensburg, PA) [5491C] Lafayette Journal & Courier (IN) Jan 14, 2014

MARK J. MORLAND Sixth great grandson of progenitor Nicholas Kegg. **MELANIE GAIL MORLAND** Sixth great granddaughter of progenitor Nicholas Kegg. **REBECCA JANE MORLAND** Sixth great granddaughter of progenitor Nicholas Kegg. **RUTH ELLEN MORLAND** Fifth great granddaughter of progenitor Nicholas Kegg. **WILLIAM CHARLES MORLAND** [5491D] (1949 – 2016) son of Leo and Betty Ruth (Kerr) Morland, married Sally Ann Fleckenstein with whom he was father of (3). William worked for Ferguson Enterprises and retired in 2008. He enjoyed fishing, restoring cars and going to car shows.

MORLOCK

MELLISSA ANNE MORLOCK Seventh great granddaughter of progenitor Nicholas Kegg.

MORONE

PAMELA SUE MORONE [5491E] (1950 – 2015) daughter of Philip and Jacqueline (Fisher) Morone married twice, first to Rick Wolcott and later to George L. Throm. Pam attended Russell Sage School of Nursing and earned her registered nursing degree. Pam owned and operated her own electrology business in Cranston, RI. Pam had a dynamite personality that could stir any pot and would laugh at the results. **PATRICE SHEREE MORONE** Fifth great granddaughter of progenitor Nicholas Kegg. **PATRICK STEVEN MORONE** Fifth great grandson of progenitor Nicholas Kegg. **PAULETTE SELENE MORONE** Fifth great granddaughter of progenitor Nicholas Kegg. **PHILIP SCOTT MORONE** Fifth great grandson of progenitor Nicholas Kegg. **PRESTON SETH MORONE** Fifth great grandson of progenitor Nicholas Kegg. **PRISCILLA SHAWN MORONE** Fifth great granddaughter of progenitor Nicholas Kegg.

MOROZEK

ETHAN MOROZEK Seventh great grandson of progenitor Nicholas Kegg.

MORRAL

ARLIE WILLIAM MORRAL Eighth great grandson of progenitor Nicholas Kegg. **KAMERON LANCE MORRAL** Seventh great grandson of progenitor Nicholas Kegg. **KORTNEY BLAIR MORRAL** Seventh great granddaughter of progenitor Nicholas Kegg. **PATSY ANN MORRAL** Sixth great granddaughter of progenitor Nicholas Kegg.

MORRIS

ANGELA MORRIS Seventh great granddaughter of progenitor Nicholas Kegg. **BETTY JANE MORRIS** Fifth great granddaughter of progenitor Nicholas Kegg. **CHRISTINE SUSAN MORRIS** Sixth great granddaughter of progenitor Nicholas Kegg. **DANIEL MORRIS** Seventh great grandson of progenitor Nicholas Kegg. **HAZEL MARGARET MORRIS** [5492] (1925 – 2005) daughter of Israel and Estella (Knootz) Morris, married Ralph Donald Smith with whom she was mother of (2). Hazel was a homemaker and a secretary for several different farm implement dealers. She was a lifetime member of Friends Cove United Church of Christ, and a member of the Order of Eastern Star, Bedford Springs Chapter No. 41. **JAMES E. MORRIS** Fifth great grandson of progenitor Nicholas Kegg. **JAY LEE MORRIS** [5493] (1935 – 2002) son of Claude and Alice (Kennedy) Morris, married Judith Johnson with whom he was father of (2). Jay obtained his private pilot's license while in high school, working at

---

[5491D] Journal & Courier (IN) May 22, 2016 [5491E] Glick Family Funeral Home (Boca Raton, FL) contributed by D. Sue Dible [5492] p.3 - Bedford Inquirer (PA) June 3, 2005, obtained by Bob Rose [5493] The Idaho Statesman (ID) Mar 17, 2002

the airport in Ardmore to pay for his lessons. His passion for flying began early in life; he was an air scout as a teenager. In his early twenties, Jay served as specialist third class in the U.S. Army at Fort Lewis, Wash., and as a ski instructor with the Army in Alaska. Jay worked for Rex Lanham Co. as a company pilot and power line construction supervisor. Later, he became vice president for Adco West Manufacturing; a company that built sawmill machinery. Jay died in a plane crash. **JENNIFER MORRIS** Sixth great granddaughter of progenitor Nicholas Kegg. **JOHN EARL MORRIS** [5494] (1893 – 1972) son of Samuel and Elizabeth (Kegg) Morris, married Ruth Alice Weicht with whom he was father of (1). John was a retired farmer. **JOHN PATRICK MORRIS** aka "Pat", Fifth great grandson of progenitor Nicholas Kegg. **KENNETH M. MORRIS** Fifth great grandson of progenitor Nicholas Kegg. **LOIS ANN MORRIS** Fifth great granddaughter of progenitor Nicholas Kegg. **MARGARET LEE MORRIS**, aka "Peggy", Fifth great granddaughter of progenitor Nicholas Kegg. **MAUREEN A. MORRIS** Fifth great granddaughter of progenitor Nicholas Kegg. **MICHAEL MORRIS** Fifth great grandson of progenitor Nicholas Kegg. **MICHELLE M. MORRIS** Fifth great granddaughter of progenitor Nicholas Kegg. **NOELLE MORRIS** Seventh great granddaughter of progenitor Nicholas Kegg. **PATRICIA EILEENE MORRIS** Fifth great granddaughter of progenitor Nicholas Kegg. **ROBERT SHANNON MORRIS** Fifth great grandson of progenitor Nicholas Kegg. **SEAN P. MORRIS** Eighth great grandson of progenitor Nicholas Kegg. **SUSAN ANNE MORRIS** Fifth great granddaughter of progenitor Nicholas Kegg. **SUSANNA MORRIS** [5495] (1891 – 1981) daughter of Samuel and Elizabeth (Kegg) Morris, married Harrison H. Hoover with whom she was mother of (7). A homemaker, Susannah was a member of Everett Zion Lutheran Church. **TIMOTHY MORRIS** Seventh great grandson of progenitor Nicholas Kegg. **VIRGINIA LEE MORRIS** Fifth great granddaughter of progenitor Nicholas Kegg.

MORROW

BETTY MARIE MORROW (1920 – 1986) daughter of Sanny and Madge (Chaney) Morrow, married and divorced Donald Bert Cranbourne.
BEVERLY ANN MORROW Fifth great granddaughter of progenitor Nicholas Kegg.
GARY CLAY MORROW Sixth great grandson of progenitor Nicholas Kegg.
KEVIN LEE MORROW [5496] (1964 – 2015) son of Ronald and Mary Louise (Kegg) Morrow. Kevin worked many years for Yellow Freight Company.
LOUIS JOHN MORROW Seventh great grandson of progenitor Nicholas Kegg. **MARGIE JAYNE MORROW** (1927 – 1985) daughter of Sanny and Madge (Chaney) Morrow, married Clinton Garvin with whom she was mother of (1). **MARY LOUISE MORROW** [5497] (1928 – 2019) daughter of Leonard and Mae Valier (Johnson) Morrow married Kenneth Clark with whom she was mother of (2). Later, she married Edwin Earl Montgomery with whom she was mother of (2). Mary Lou was retired from Southview High School as a secretary. **MICHAEL JAMES MORROW** Seventh great grandson of progenitor Nicholas Kegg. **SANNY GENE MORROW** [5498] (1922 – 2006) aka "Pete", son of Sanny and Madge (Chaney) Morrow, married Wanda LaVonne (Wall) with whom he was father of (3). Pete retired from the Long Beach Naval Shipyard after many years of service.
SEAN RICHARD MORROW Seventh great grandson of progenitor Nicholas Kegg.
SHARON ARLENE MORROW Fifth great granddaughter of progenitor Nicholas Kegg.
STEVEN E. MORROW Sixth great grandson of progenitor Nicholas Kegg.
TAMMY LYNN MORROW Seventh great granddaughter of progenitor Nicholas Kegg.
TOMMIE JEAN MORROW Sixth great granddaughter of progenitor Nicholas Kegg.
VIRGINIA MAYE MORROW (1930 – 2017) daughter of Leonard and Mae (Johnson) Morrow, married Bernard Carl Morello with whom she was mother of (5).

[5494] Bedford County, PA clipping-Duke Clark Obituary collection p.2996 [5495] Bedford County, PA clipping-Duke Clark Obituary collection p.2116 [5496] Pittsburgh Post-Gazette (PA) Oct 2, 2015

MORSE

ALANNAH MORSE Seventh great granddaughter of progenitor Nicholas Kegg. **ASHLEY MORSE** Seventh great granddaughter of progenitor Nicholas Kegg. **BRADLEY DAVID MORSE** Seventh great grandson of progenitor Nicholas Kegg. **BRANDON SCOTT MORSE** Seventh great grandson of progenitor Nicholas Kegg. **CATHY M. MORSE** Fifth great granddaughter of progenitor Nicholas Kegg. **CONSTANCE SUE MORSE** aka "Connie", Fifth great granddaughter of progenitor Nicholas Kegg. **DANICA MORSE** Eighth great granddaughter of progenitor Nicholas Kegg. **DONOVAN SPENCER MORSE** Seventh great grandson of progenitor Nicholas Kegg. **DRAIDYN MORSE** Ninth great granddaughter of progenitor Nicholas Kegg. **GARY WILMONT MORSE** [5499] (1941 – 2008) son of Elvin and Helen (Shaw) Morse, married Melvina Marie Barton with whom he was father of (4). Gary was employed with New Enterprise Stone and Lime Company for over 30 years, where he worked in the concrete paving division until his retirement. He enjoyed deer hunting and helping friends and neighbors with their farming tasks throughout the Crystal Spring area and was a devoted owner and operator of his Farmall Series H Tractor. **GREGORY JAMES MORSE** Sixth great grandson of progenitor Nicholas Kegg. **HARRISON MORSE** Seventh great grandson of progenitor Nicholas Kegg. **IAN MORSE** Eighth great grandson of progenitor Nicholas Kegg. **JACEY MORSE** Ninth great grandchild of progenitor Nicholas Kegg. **JAMES WALTER MORSE** Sixth great grandson of progenitor Nicholas Kegg. **JOHN ROBERT MORSE** Sixth great grandson of progenitor Nicholas Kegg. **JOSHUA MORSE** Sixth great grandson of progenitor Nicholas Kegg. **JULIE MARIE MORSE** Sixth great granddaughter of progenitor Nicholas Kegg. **KEITH MORSE** Seventh great grandson of progenitor Nicholas Kegg. **KENDALL MORSE** Ninth great granddaughter of progenitor Nicholas Kegg. **KEVIN MORSE** Sixth great grandson of progenitor Nicholas Kegg. **KRYSTAL MORSE** Seventh great granddaughter of progenitor Nicholas Kegg. **KYLE RICHARD MORSE** [5500] (2010 – 2010) son of Andrew and Lena (Mellott) Morse. **MAYLA JOAN MORSE** Seventh great granddaughter of progenitor Nicholas Kegg. **MICHELLE L. MORSE** Sixth great granddaughter of progenitor Nicholas Kegg. **RAY E. MORSE** Fifth great grandson of progenitor Nicholas Kegg. **RONALD KEITH MORSE** Sixth great grandson of progenitor Nicholas Kegg. **SAMAREH AKILAH MORSE** Seventh great granddaughter of progenitor Nicholas Kegg. **SHANE A. MORSE** Sixth great grandson of progenitor Nicholas Kegg. **SHONDA RENEE MORSE** Sixth great granddaughter of progenitor Nicholas Kegg. **STEPHEN MORSE** Sixth great grandson of progenitor Nicholas Kegg. **THOMAS MORSE** Sixth great grandson of progenitor Nicholas Kegg. **TRINITY MAY MORSE** Ninth great granddaughter of progenitor Nicholas Kegg. **TROY SAMUEL MORSE** Sixth great grandson of progenitor Nicholas Kegg. **WANDA SUE MORSE** [5501] (1949 – 1955) daughter of Elvin and Helen (Shaw) Morse was stricken suddenly ill Sunday afternoon after being at Sunday School that morning. Wanda died at approximately 3 o'clock Monday morning. Dr. J. W. Nycum the attendant physician said that he believed the disease was caused by a pneumococcus virus and might have come from a latent infection. The type is not considered as infectious to others as other forms of meningitis. Nevertheless, it was thought advisable to quarantine the family for a period of from seven to ten days and take other precautions. Local doctors stated that this was the first case of meningitis in the county in the last eight to ten years.

[5497] Fayetteville Observer (NC) Sep 5, 2019, obtained by D. Sue Dible [5498] Long Beach Press-Telegram (CA) Aug. 2, 2006 [5499] Fulton County News (PA) Apr.25, 2008 [5500] Bedford Gazette (PA) Feb 1, 2010, obtained by D. Sue Dible [5501] pgs. 1 & 3-Bedford Gazette (PA) Feb15, 1955

MORT

DEBORAH N. MORT Sixth great granddaughter of progenitor Nicholas Kegg. **ELAINE S. MORT** Sixth great granddaughter of progenitor Nicholas Kegg. **HERBERT LLOYD MORT** Fifth great grandson of progenitor Nicholas Kegg. **JEANNE A. MORT** Sixth great granddaughter of progenitor Nicholas Kegg. **JUDITH MAY MORT** Fifth great granddaughter of progenitor Nicholas Kegg. **KENNETH L. MORT** Sixth great grandson of progenitor Nicholas Kegg. **MONTE MENLO MORT** [5502] (1944 – 2010) son of Harold and Thelma (Williams) Mort, married Shirley with whom he was father of (3). Monte was a heavy equipment operator. He loved hunting and fishing. **TANA MORT** Sixth great granddaughter of progenitor Nicholas Kegg. **TIA LEIGH MORT** Sixth great granddaughter of progenitor Nicholas Kegg. **TROY MORT** Sixth great grandson of progenitor Nicholas Kegg.

MORTIMORE

DEBORAH KAY MORTIMORE Sixth great granddaughter of progenitor Nicholas Kegg.
HARRY WILLIAM MORTIMORE Sixth great grandson of progenitor Nicholas Kegg.
JESSE JAMES MORTIMORE Seventh great grandson of progenitor Nicholas Kegg.
SHELBY MARIE MORTIMORE Seventh great granddaughter of progenitor Nicholas Kegg.

MORTON

DONNA MORTON Fifth great granddaughter of progenitor Nicholas Kegg. **ELLA MORTON** Seventh great granddaughter of progenitor Nicholas Kegg. **FREDERICK JAY MORTON** [5503] (1923 – 1987) son of Peter and Mary (Fisher) Morton, married Helen M. Reese with whom he was father of (2). Frederick was a retired serviceman for Texas-Eastern Gas Transmissions and a member of Wesley United Methodist Church, West Melbourne. **JACE MORTON** Seventh great grandson of progenitor Nicholas Kegg. **JUSTIN P MORTON** Sixth great grandson of progenitor Nicholas Kegg.
RUTH MARGARET MORTON Fourth great granddaughter of progenitor Nicholas Kegg.
SARA ELLEN MORTON Fourth great granddaughter of progenitor Nicholas Kegg.
SUNNY MICHELLE MORTON Sixth great granddaughter of progenitor Nicholas Kegg.

MOSES

DAMIAN MOSES Seventh great grandson of progenitor Nicholas Kegg.
MARK MOSES Seventh great grandson of progenitor Nicholas Kegg.
NICKI MOSES Seventh great granddaughter of progenitor Nicholas Kegg.

MOSHER

ABBIE MOSHER Eighth great granddaughter of progenitor Nicholas Kegg.
BEN MOSHER Eighth great grandson of progenitor Nicholas Kegg.
SAM MOSHER Eighth great grandson of progenitor Nicholas Kegg.

MOSIER

AMY MOSIER Sixth great granddaughter of progenitor Nicholas Kegg. **CHRISTOPHER R. MOSIER** Sixth great grandson of progenitor Nicholas Kegg. **EDWARD STEVEN MOSIER** Sixth great grandson of progenitor Nicholas Kegg. **JONATHAN ISAAC MOSIER** Sixth great grandson of progenitor Nicholas Kegg. **MICHAEL MOSIER** Sixth great grandson of progenitor Nicholas Kegg.

[5502] Siskiyou Daily News (Yreka, CA) Dec 8, 2010 [5503] p.B4 - Orlando Sentinel (FL) Apr 7, 1987

SUSAN CHRISTINE MOSIER Sixth great granddaughter of progenitor Nicholas Kegg. **TERRY REX MOSIER** Sixth great grandson of progenitor Nicholas Kegg. **TIMOTHY RONALD MOSIER** Sixth great grandson of progenitor Nicholas Kegg. **VALERIE KAY MOSIER** (1960 – 1960) daughter of Clifford and Lavone (Sickels) Mosier.

MOSKO

ELIJAH MOSKO Seventh great grandson of progenitor Nicholas Kegg. **EMMA MOSKO** Seventh great granddaughter of progenitor Nicholas Kegg. **GRADE MOSKO** Seventh great grandson of progenitor Nicholas Kegg. **JORDAN MOSKO** Seventh great grandson of progenitor Nicholas Kegg. **LEVI JAMES MOSKO** Seventh great grandson of progenitor Nicholas Kegg. **RYAN MOSKO** Seventh great grandson of progenitor Nicholas Kegg. **TARA MOSKO** Seventh great granddaughter of progenitor Nicholas Kegg.

MOTTIN

GAVIN MOTTIN Seventh great grandson of progenitor Nicholas Kegg.

MOUNCE

TIMMY LEE MOUNCE, aka "T. J.", Sixth great grandson of progenitor Nicholas Kegg.

MOUNTS

CHRISTIAN ALLAN MOUNTS [5504] (1980 – 2009) son of Allen and Cheryl (Sharrock) Mounts.

MOUSER

DEBBIE E. MOUSER Sixth great granddaughter of progenitor Nicholas Kegg.
MATTHEW MOUSER Seventh great grandson of progenitor Nicholas Kegg.
SCOTT D MOUSER Seventh great grandson of progenitor Nicholas Kegg.

MOUSTAFA

SHEREEF MOUSTAFA Fifth great grandson of progenitor Nicholas Kegg.
TAMIR M. MOUSTAFA Fifth great grandson of progenitor Nicholas Kegg.

MOWER

ABBY MOWER Seventh great granddaughter of progenitor Nicholas Kegg.
BAILEY MOWER Seventh great granddaughter of progenitor Nicholas Kegg.

MOWRY

ALFRED EUGENE MOWRY [5505] (1943 – 1946) son of Quentin and Sylvia (Fochtman) Mowry. **ARIENE ELIZABETH MOWRY** [5506] (1922 – 2004) daughter of Howard and Mary (Kegg) Mowry, married Clarence Lee Smith with whom she was mother of (4). Ariene was a homemaker and previously was employed by Goodyear during WWII. **ARLO CARSON MOWRY** [5507] (1906 – 1967) son of Charles and Margaret (Corley) Mowry, married Bertha Golden Harrison with whom he was father of (1).

[5504] Springfield News-Sun (OH) Nov. 11, 2009 [5505] p.5 Bedford Gazette (PA) Jan 9, 1947 [5506] p.7 – Altoona Mirror (PA) July 5, 2004

Arlo was an instructor in the Chestnut Ridge School System, teaching at the Schellsburg Elementary School. He had been a schoolteacher for 33 years. **AUSTIN HOMER MOWRY** [5508] (1881 – 1941) son of William and Amanda (Kerr) Mowry. **CHARLES BYARD MOWRY** [5509] (1876 – 1964) son of William and Amanda (Kerr) Mowry, married Margaret B. Corley with whom he was father of (2). Charles was a retired farmer, and a lifelong member of St. Mark's United Church of Christ, New Buena Vista. **ELAINE MOWRY** Sixth great granddaughter of progenitor Nicholas Kegg. **INFANT MOWRY** (1955 – 1955) son of William and Ruth (Biddle) Mowry. **JAMES Q. MOWRY** aka "Jimmy", Fifth great grandson of progenitor Nicholas Kegg. **JOY ANNE MOWRY** Fifth great granddaughter of progenitor Nicholas Kegg. **KATHIE MOWRY** Sixth great granddaughter of progenitor Nicholas Kegg. **MARY ANNA ELIZABETH MOWRY** [5510] (1910 – 1935) daughter of Charles and Margaret (Corley) Mowry had been a teacher in the Juniata Township schools. She was also a teacher of the Sunday school class of St John's Reformed Church at Buena Vista and was also an active member of the church. **PATRICK J. MOWRY** Fifth great grandson of progenitor Nicholas Kegg. **QUENTIN CARPENTER MOWRY** [5511] (1921 – 1969) son of Warren and Fanny (Carpenter) Mowry, married Sylvia Fochtman with whom he was father of (3). **W. MARTIN MOWRY** [5512] (1911 – 1978) son of Warren and Fanny (Carpenter) Mowry, married Dorothy A. Miller with whom he was father of (3). W. Martin was a retired employee of Kelly Springfield Tire Company in Cumberland, MD. He was also a retired farmer and a member of the Milligans Cove Christian Church of Buffalo Mills RD. **WARREN KERR MOWRY** [5513] (1878 – 1947) son of William and Amanda (Kerr) Mowry, married Fanny Mary Carpenter with whom he was father of (2). **WILLIAM F. MOWRY** Fifth great grandson of progenitor Nicholas Kegg. **WILLIAM OSCAR MOWRY** [5513A] aka "Bill" (1940 – 2018) son of W. Martin and Dorothy (Miller) Mowry married Janet I. Hillegass with whom he was father of (2) Bill worked at Kennametal for 43 years. Along with his wife, he was well known as the co-owner of Mowry's Produce along Route 31. Bill raised sweet corn and strawberries for many years and sold Christmas trees. He enjoyed walking through the woods and fields with his faithful German Shepherd, Kawligah, and his blind cat, Bingo. Bill spent time gardening, reading his Bible, watching Fox News and Christian programs and visiting with family and friends. **WILLIS P. MOWRY** [5514] (1884 – 1913) son of William and Amanda (Kerr) Mowry was a bright young man and a student. He had been in ill health for some years, causing him to become very melancholy and he feared that he might injure some member of his family. In a temporary fit of insanity after reading the paper, went into his room and secured a revolver which had been loaded possibly ten years before; standing before the mirror in his room he fired a bullet into his right eye, death being instantaneous.

MOYER

ADDY L. MOYER Seventh great granddaughter of progenitor Nicholas Kegg.
LEELAND MOYER Seventh great grandson of progenitor Nicholas Kegg.
MIKE MOYER Sixth great grandson of progenitor Nicholas Kegg.
PAIZLEE NICOLE MOYER Seventh great granddaughter of progenitor Nicholas Kegg.

MROCZEK

AURORA ROSE MROCZEK Eighth great granddaughter of progenitor Nicholas Kegg.

MUELLER

AUSTIN MUELLER Eighth great grandson of progenitor Nicholas Kegg.
KRISTEN NANCY MUELLER Eighth great granddaughter of progenitor Nicholas Kegg.

[5507] p.5 - Bedford Inquirer (PA) Feb 9, 1967 [5508, 5509, 5510, 5511, 5512] Bedford County Genealogical Society obituary clipping obtained by D. Sue Dible [5513] Bedford Gazette (PA) Dec 23, 1947 [5513A] Bedford Gazette (PA) Feb 19, 2018, contributed by Bob Rose [5514] Bedford Gazette (PA) Aug 29, 1913

MUILENBURG

GABE MUILENBURG Seventh great grandson of progenitor Nicholas Kegg.
KRAGER MUILENBURG Seventh great grandson of progenitor Nicholas Kegg.
LANE MUILENBURG Seventh great grandson of progenitor Nicholas Kegg.

MULDOON

JAMES THOMAS MULDOON Sixth great grandson of progenitor Nicholas Kegg.
LINDA S. MULDOON Sixth great granddaughter of progenitor Nicholas Kegg.
SHARON JANE MULDOON Sixth great granddaughter of progenitor Nicholas Kegg.

MULL

CHAD W. MULL Sixth great grandson of progenitor Nicholas Kegg.
JORDON TYLER MULL Eighth great grandson of progenitor Nicholas Kegg.
RAELYN PATRICIA MULL Eighth great granddaughter of progenitor Nicholas Kegg.
ROBERT HARRY MULL Seventh great grandson of progenitor Nicholas Kegg.
STANLEY R. MULL Sixth great grandson of progenitor Nicholas Kegg.

MULLAN

CHRISTOPHER JAMES MULLAN Seventh great grandson of progenitor Nicholas Kegg.
HEATHER DIANE MULLAN Seventh great granddaughter of progenitor Nicholas Kegg.
KIMBERLY LYNN MULLAN Seventh great granddaughter of progenitor Nicholas Kegg.

MULLANEY

PATRICK MULLANEY Seventh great grandson of progenitor Nicholas Kegg.
TARA MULLANEY Seventh great granddaughter of progenitor Nicholas Kegg.

MULLER

ELIZABETH MUELLER Seventh great granddaughter of progenitor Nicholas Kegg.
GEORGE MULLER Seventh great grandson of progenitor Nicholas Kegg.

MULLIN

FRANCIS ISAAC MULLIN Sixth great grandson of progenitor Nicholas Kegg.
GREGORY MORGAN MULLIN Seventh great grandson of progenitor Nicholas Kegg.

MULLINS

MICHELLE MULLINS Sixth great granddaughter of progenitor Nicholas Kegg.
THOMAS LEO MULLINS Sixth great grandson of progenitor Nicholas Kegg.

MUNCH

TIMOTHY ALLEN MUNCH Seventh great grandson of progenitor Nicholas Kegg.

MUNCY

BEATRICE ANN MUNCY (1930 – 1931) daughter of Ralph and Anna (Van Tuyl) Muncy.
GAIL SEYMOUR MUNCY (1907 – 1908) son of John and Maud (Ackley) Muncy.

MUNDOK

GREGORY A. MUNDOK Sixth great grandson of progenitor Nicholas Kegg.
JAMES F. MUNDOK Sixth great grandson of progenitor Nicholas Kegg.

MUNN

ANDREW JOHN MUNN Sixth great grandson of progenitor Nicholas Kegg. **CHARLES CHRISTOPHER MUNN** Sixth great grandson of progenitor Nicholas Kegg. **DARLENE MARGUERITTE MUNN** (1935 – 1998) daughter of Roy and Elsie (Schmidt) Munn, married Edward Arthur Fitzgerald with whom she was mother of (2). **GLEASON MUNN** [5515] (1918 – 2011) son of Royal and Gleason (Stuckey) Munn, married Rayna Bernee Schram with whom he was father of (1). **JAMES ERIC MUNN** Fifth great grandson of progenitor Nicholas Kegg. **MICHAEL JAMES MUNN** Sixth great grandson of progenitor Nicholas Kegg. **PAUL WILLIAM MUNN** Sixth great grandson of progenitor Nicholas Kegg. **ROY LEMUAL MUNN** (1915 – 1993) son of Royal and Gleason (Stuckey) Munn, married Elsie Schmidt with whom he was father of (1). **STACY RAMAE MUNN** Sixth great granddaughter of progenitor Nicholas Kegg.

MUNOZ

GRACE MUNOZ Sixth great granddaughter of progenitor Nicholas Kegg.
MADDY ROSE MUNOZ Sixth great granddaughter of progenitor Nicholas Kegg.

MUNYON

BRANDON SCOTT MUNYON Eighth great grandson of progenitor Nicholas Kegg.
WILLIAM JARED MUNYON Eighth great grandson of progenitor Nicholas Kegg.

MURAR

BRANDY MURAR Seventh great granddaughter of progenitor Nicholas Kegg. **BRITTANY MURAR** Seventh great granddaughter of progenitor Nicholas Kegg. **MARK JOSEPH MARAR JR.** [5516] (1994 – 2017) son of Mark and Vicki (Deeds) Murar worked for Cardinal Aggregate, Inc. Mark loved the outdoors, whether it was hunting, fishing, farming, riding dirt bikes or shooting guns, he loved everything about it.

MURATORI

MEADOW ANNE MURATORI Seventh great granddaughter of progenitor Nicholas Kegg.

MURCH

COURTNEY MARIE MURCH Sixth great granddaughter of progenitor Nicholas Kegg.
MICHAEL S. MURCH Sixth great grandson of progenitor Nicholas Kegg.

[5515] Chico Enterprise Record (CA) Aug 24, 2011 [5516] The Blade (OH) Oct. 13, 2017

MURPHY

ALEAH MURPHY Eighth great granddaughter of progenitor Nicholas Kegg. **CRAIG N. MURPHY** Seventh great grandson of progenitor Nicholas Kegg. **ETHAN MURPHY** Eighth great grandson of progenitor Nicholas Kegg. **ISAIAH MURPHY** Eighth great grandson of progenitor Nicholas Kegg. **JACEY RENEE MURPHY** Seventh great granddaughter of progenitor Nicholas Kegg. **JOSHUA C. MURPHY** Seventh great grandson of progenitor Nicholas Kegg. **KATHERINE MURPHY** Seventh great granddaughter of progenitor Nicholas Kegg. **EVI C. MURPHY** Seventh great grandson of progenitor Nicholas Kegg. **MARK MURPHY** [5517] (1967 – 2005) son of Douglas and Karen (Chalfant) Murphy. **SARAH EILEEN MURPHY** (1983 – 1988) daughter of Larry and Terry (James) Murphy. **SHERRY MURPHY** Seventh great granddaughter of progenitor Nicholas Kegg. **SHONNEY LYNN MURPHY** Seventh great granddaughter of progenitor Nicholas Kegg.

MURRAY

JACOB MURRAY Eighth great grandson of progenitor Nicholas Kegg. **JIM MURRAY** Fifth great grandson of progenitor Nicholas Kegg. **L. E. MURRAY** Fifth great grandson of progenitor Nicholas Kegg. **LINDA MURRAY** Fifth great granddaughter of progenitor Nicholas Kegg. **MICHAEL JAMES MURRAY** Eighth great grandson of progenitor Nicholas Kegg. **MICHELLE L. MURRAY** Eighth great granddaughter of progenitor Nicholas Kegg. **ROB MURRAY** Fifth great grandson of progenitor Nicholas Kegg.

MURRIETTA

NICO MURRIETTA Sixth great grandson of progenitor Nicholas Kegg.
TALIA MURRIETTA Sixth great granddaughter of progenitor Nicholas Kegg.

MUSKEVITSCH

JAMES EARL MUSKEVITSCH Fifth great grandson of progenitor Nicholas Kegg.
JAMIE SUE MUSKEVITSCH Fifth great granddaughter of progenitor Nicholas Kegg.

MUSSELMAN

BRETT MUSSELMAN Seventh great grandson of progenitor Nicholas Kegg.
CENA ANN MUSSELMAN Sixth great granddaughter of progenitor Nicholas Kegg.
CRYSTAL JANE MUSSELMAN Sixth great granddaughter of progenitor Nicholas Kegg.
KARA MUSSELMAN Seventh great granddaughter of progenitor Nicholas Kegg.

MUSSER

ELIZABETH MUSSER (1925 – 2007) aka "Betty", daughter of Lewis and Ruth (Trimble) Musser, married Wayne Joslen with whom she was mother of (1). **GARRETT MUSSER** Sixth great grandson of progenitor Nicholas Kegg. **GAVIN MUSSER** Sixth great grandson of progenitor Nicholas Kegg. **GLENN ALLEN MUSSER** Fifth great grandson of progenitor Nicholas Kegg. **HENRY HARBAUGH MUSSER** [5518] (1897 – 1948) son of Joseph and Minerva (Turner) Musser. **MARCE MAY MUSSER** [5519] (1900 – 1987) daughter of Joseph and Minerva (Turner) Musser, married Carroll John Reber with whom she was mother of (2). **MARY ELIZABETH MUSSER** (1908 – 1959)

[5517] Bodnar-Mahoney Funeral Home Cleveland, Ohio obtained by D. Sue Dible [5518] p.19 Pittsburgh Post-Gazette (PA) May 22, 1948, obtained by D. Sue Dible [5519] p.4 Pittsburgh Post-Gazette Sep 30, 1922/Philadelphia Daily News (PA) Jan 26, 1987

daughter of Joseph and Minerva (Turner) Musser, married Royce Wilbert Kennedy with whom she was mother of (2).   **MICHAEL LEWIS MUSSER** Fifth great grandson of progenitor Nicholas Kegg.
MORGAN LEA MUSSER Sixth great granddaughter of progenitor Nicholas Kegg.
NETTIE BRUBAKER MUSSER (1890 – 1901) daughter of Joseph and Minerva (Turner) Musser.
ROSE ANN MUSSER (1905 – 1909) daughter of Joseph and Minerva (Turner) Musser.

MYERS

ALINE MYERS (1911 – 1980) daughter of Harley and Retha (Cagg) Myers, married Lawrence Fabian Wempe.   **BLAKE HAMILTON MYERS** Sixth great grandson of progenitor Nicholas Kegg. **BRITTANY MYERS** Seventh great granddaughter of progenitor Nicholas Kegg.   **BRYAN P. MYERS** Sixth great grandson of progenitor Nicholas Kegg.   **CHARLOTTE SUE MYERS** Fifth great granddaughter of progenitor Nicholas Kegg.   **CONSTANCE LYNN MYERS** aka "Connie", Fifth great granddaughter of progenitor Nicholas Kegg.   **CYNTHIA LOU MYERS** [5520] (1958 – 2013) daughter of William and Ada (Kegg) Myers married twice; first to Eric Clapper, later to Norman Sollenberger with whom she was mother of (3). Cindy worked in the lab at UPMC Bedford Memorial Hospital as a microbiologist for 15 years. She then worked at DelGrosso's in Tipton and later, was a purchasing manager at the Omni Bedford Springs Resort and Spa. Cindy enjoyed gardening, raising goats on the family farm, "Wil-La-Be" and making homemade soaps and jellies. She took great pride in attending her children's sporting events and was a loyal Pittsburgh Pirates and Steelers' fan.   **ERIC MYERS** Sixth great grandson of progenitor Nicholas Kegg.   **EVAN THOMAS MYERS** Sixth great grandson of progenitor Nicholas Kegg.   **FARIDA EUGENIA MYERS** Fourth great granddaughter of progenitor Nicholas Kegg.   **FRANK MYERS** (1895 – 1896) son of Burdine and Anna (Kerr) Myers. **GEORGE RICHARD MYERS** Fifth great grandson of progenitor Nicholas Kegg.   **GEORGE RYAN MYERS** Sixth great grandson of progenitor Nicholas Kegg.   **JAMES F. MYERS** (1934 – 2014) aka "Freddie", son of Meril and Mary (Leveling) Myers, married Marilyn Frances Goodman with whom he was father of (4).   **JAMES FREDERICK MYERS** [5521] (1952 – 2009) aka "Guitar Jim", son of James and Marilyn (Goodman) Myers married twice; first to Marilyn Sue Brown with whom he was father of (1). Later, he married Kimberly. Guitar Jim enjoyed playing the guitar, writing songs and playing music with his friends.   **JAMES ROSS MYERS** Sixth great grandson of progenitor Nicholas Kegg.   **JENE TEX MYERS** (1919 – 1946) son of Harley and Retha (Cagg) Myers.   **JENNIFER MYERS** Sixth great granddaughter of progenitor Nicholas Kegg.   **JERAL REX MYERS** (1918 – 1990) son of Harley and Retha (Cagg) Myers married twice; first to Rosemary Gastineau and later, to Percy Jones Witt. **JEREMY MYERS** Seventh great grandson of progenitor Nicholas Kegg.   **JOHN H. MYERS** (1895 – 1897) son of Burdine and Anna (Kerr) Myers.   **KAYLA MYERS** Seventh great granddaughter of progenitor Nicholas Kegg.   **KRISTA LEIGH MYERS** Sixth great granddaughter of progenitor Nicholas Kegg.   **KYLE RAY MYERS** Sixth great grandson of progenitor Nicholas Kegg.   **LAUREN ELIZABETH MYERS** Sixth great granddaughter of progenitor Nicholas Kegg.   **LINDA PATRICIA MYERS** Fifth great granddaughter of progenitor Nicholas Kegg.   **LLOYD J. MYERS** (1908 – 1951) son of Harley and Retha (Cagg) Myers.   **MADELINE THELMA MYERS**, (1914 – 1989) daughter of Harley and Retha (Cagg) Myers, married Lawrence Neil Harden with whom she was mother of (6). **MERIL A. MYERS** [5522] (1903 – 1959) son of Harley and Retha (Cagg) Myers, married Mary Elizabeth Leveling with whom he was father of (3).   **PAULA J. MYERS** Sixth great granddaughter of progenitor Nicholas Kegg.   **RACHEL LYNN MYERS** Sixth great granddaughter of progenitor Nicholas Kegg. **ROBERT A. MYERS**, aka "Robbie", Fifth great grandson of progenitor Nicholas Kegg.   **ROGER A. MYERS** Fourth great grandson of progenitor Nicholas Kegg.   **SCOTT THOMAS MYERS** Fifth great grandson of progenitor Nicholas Kegg.   **TERRI MYERS** Fifth great granddaughter of progenitor Nicholas Kegg.   **TREY AUSTIN MYERS** Sixth great grandson of

---

[5520] Bedford Gazette (PA) May 17, 2013, obtained by Bob Rose [5521] Muskogee Phoenix (OK) Mar 25, 2009 [5522] Independent Star-News (CA) Oct 4, 1959

progenitor Nicholas Kegg.   **VAUGHN WILLIAM MYERS** Fifth great grandson of progenitor Nicholas Kegg.   **VICKIE IRENE MYERS** Fifth great granddaughter of progenitor Nicholas Kegg.   **ZACHARY AARON MYERS** Seventh great grandson of progenitor Nicholas Kegg.

MYERSON

CAROL B. MYERSON Sixth great granddaughter of progenitor Nicholas Kegg.
DANA L. MYERSON Sixth great granddaughter of progenitor Nicholas Kegg.

MYLIUS

JANET GAYLE MYLIUS Fourth great granddaughter of progenitor Nicholas Kegg.
KATHRYN LYNN MYLIUS Fourth great granddaughter of progenitor Nicholas Kegg.
PATRICIA JEAN MYLIUS Fourth great granddaughter of progenitor Nicholas Kegg.

NACHTRIEB

BRADY NACHTRIEB Seventh great grandson of progenitor Nicholas Kegg.
DANNYE NACHTRIEB Seventh great grandson of progenitor Nicholas Kegg.
KINSLEE VYE NACHTRIEB Eighth great granddaughter of progenitor Nicholas Kegg.
PERRY NACHTRIEB Seventh great grandson of progenitor Nicholas Kegg.

NADWODNY

JUSTIN NADWODNY Sixth great grandson of progenitor Nicholas Kegg.
MARINA NADWODNY Sixth great granddaughter of progenitor Nicholas Kegg.

NAGAYAMA

KEILY NAGAYAMA Seventh great granddaughter of progenitor Nicholas Kegg.
KRISANDA NAGAYAMA Seventh great granddaughter of progenitor Nicholas Kegg.

NANNA

AGNES OPAL NANNA (1903 – 1986) daughter of Irvin and Ellen (Cagg) Nanna, married Thomas Vaughn Withers with whom she was mother of (4).   **CALVIN DAVID NANNA** [5523] (1926 – 2014) son of Harmon and Dora (Miller) Nanna, married Helen Frances Sailley with whom he was father of (2).   **DAVID S. NANNA** Fifth great grandson of progenitor Nicholas Kegg.   **DEBORAH GALE NANNA** Fifth great granddaughter of progenitor Nicholas Kegg.   **ELCIE EILEEN NANNA** (1890 – 1968) daughter of Irvin and Ellen (Cagg) Nanna married twice; first to Herbert Swingle and later, to Harry Alflen.   **ELISA A. NANNA** (1889 -?) daughter of Irvin and Ellen (Cagg) Nanna.   **GLADYS NAOMI NANNA** (1901 – 1956) daughter of Irvin and Ellen (Cagg) Nanna.   **HARMON VERMONT NANNA** [5524] (1884 – 1953) aka "Mont", son of Irvin and Ellen (Cagg) Nanna, married Dora Elizabeth Miller with whom he was father of (5).   **HAROLD HENRY NANNA** [5525] (1899 – 1994) son of Irvin and Ellen (Cagg) Nanna married twice; first to Vacie V. Herdman and later, to Garnett A. Thornton.   **LARRY ROSS NANNA** Fourth great grandson of progenitor Nicholas Kegg.   **LORI ANNETTE NANNA** Fifth great granddaughter of progenitor Nicholas Kegg.   **MARGARET A. NANNA** [5526] (1885 – 1971) aka "Maggie", daughter of Irvin and Ellen (Cagg) Nanna married twice; first to Frederick Meeker and later, to Alvin W. Fleck.

[5523] Sun-Sentinel (FL) June 2, 2011 [5524] p.26 Pittsburgh Press (PA) July 19, 1968 [5525] Athens Messenger (OH) Jul 8, 1994, obtained by D. Sue Dible [5526] p.28 Pittsburgh Post-Gazette (PA) Apr 13, 1971

MAY ICEL NANNA (1893 – 1939) daughter of Irvin and Ellen (Cagg) Nanna married and divorced Mr. Churchill. **PAUL IRWIN NANNA** [5527] (1928 – 2011) son of Harmon and Dora (Miller) Nanna, married Elma Sanderson. **ROSS ANDREW NANNA** [5528] (1895 – 1979) son of Irvin and Ellen (Cagg) Nanna, married Myrtle Louise Mathena. **SCOTT LARRY NANNA** Fifth great grandson of progenitor Nicholas Kegg.

NAST

ANGELA ANNETTE NAST Seventh great granddaughter of progenitor Nicholas Kegg.
EDWARD W. NAST [5529] (1979 – 1999) son of Edward and Bonny (Beaty) Nast was employed as a construction laborer. Edward enjoyed hunting and the outdoors.

NATHANS

EDWARD RICHARD NATHANS [5530] (1917 – 1944) son of Gordon and Pauline (Graham) Nathans, married Caroline G. Jozwick was reported missing in action in Europe on August 18, 1944. He was staff sergeant of the 130th infantry, anti-tank corps. His family anxiously awaited word of him for four months before his death had been verified in France. Staff Sgt. Edward Richard Nathans was awarded the Purple Heart.

NAUGLE

ANNA REBECCA NAUGLE [5531] (1882 – 1972) daughter of Samuel and Mary (Beegle) Naugle married twice; first to Ira Furry Berkheimer with whom she was mother of (1). Later, she married William F. Mowery. Anna was a member of the Duncansville Lutheran Church and Camp 134, P.O. of A.
EMANUEL B. NAUGLE [5532] (1885 – 1935) son of Samuel and Mary (Beegle) Naugle, married Amanda Ada aka, "Alice" Diehl with whom he was father of (4). Emanuel was a widely respected truck driver returning to Bedford with a truck load of produce. He had been in the habit of getting off of the truck at Pine Hill Mountain grade and walking up the hill to keep from getting sleepy. As the vehicle was crawling up the steep grade it is believed that Naugle slipped and fell under the dual wheel of the truck. His chest had been crushed. The accident occurred on Pine Hill Mountain four miles south of Breezewood. Emanuel was a member of the Lutheran church and of P.O.S. of A and, the P.O. of A.;
LINNIE MAE NAUGLE [5533] (1893 – 1967) daughter of Samuel and Mary (Beegle) Naugle, married William Victor Kidd with whom she was mother of (7). **ORPHA SARAH NAUGLE** [5534] (1889 – 1906) aka "Sarah", daughter of Samuel and Mary (Beegle) Naugle, married William Roy Waltman with whom she was mother of (1). Sarah was of a quiet, amiable disposition and was esteemed by all who knew her. **ROBERT E. NAUGLE** [5535] (1915 – 1954) son of Emanuel and Amanda (Diehl) Naugle, married Ethel Steel with whom he was father of (2). Robert was an employee of the Sinclair Refining Co. He was a member of the Wolfsburg Methodist Church. **VIVIAN D. NAUGLE** [5536] (1912 – 1998) daughter of Emanuel and Amanda (Diehl) Naugle was a retired schoolteacher after 38 years, primarily at Colerain Elementary School. She was also a member of the Ladies Auxiliary of Homewood Retirement Center, Martinsburg; a life member of the Bedford County Retired Public School State Employee Association and the Pennsylvania State Retired Teachers Association; a member of the P.O. of A.; and a member of the Bedford Senior Citizens.

NAVE

CASSADIE NAVE Sixth great granddaughter of progenitor Nicholas Kegg.

[5527] Florida Times-Union (FL) Aug. 14, 2011 [5528] The Marion Star (OH) Sep 12, 1996 [5529] p.9 Fort Wayne News Sentinel (IN) Nov 15, 1999, obtained by D. Sue Dible [5530] Chicago Tribune (IL) Dec 15, 1944 [5531] Altoona Mirror (PA) Apr 17, 1972 [5532] p.3 -The Daily News (Huntingdon, PA) June 22, 1935 [5533] Bedford Gazette (PA) Jan 19, 1967 [5534] Bedford Gazette (PA) March 2, 1906 [5535, 5536] Bedford County Historical Society b/9 p3323 obtained by D. Sue Dible

CODY M. NAVE Sixth great grandson of progenitor Nicholas Kegg.   **JACOB GLEN NAVE** Sixth great grandson of progenitor Nicholas Kegg.   **JOLENE D. NAVE**, aka "Jojo", Sixth great granddaughter of progenitor Nicholas Kegg.   **RHETT NAVE** Seventh great grandson of progenitor Nicholas Kegg.

NAVIN

ALEX P NAVIN (2004 – 2004) son of Todd and Christine (Patterson) Navin.
JOSEPH ALLEN NAVIN Seventh great grandson of progenitor Nicholas Kegg.

NEAL

ADDISON NEAL Seventh great granddaughter of progenitor Nicholas Kegg.   **CALEB NEAL** Seventh great grandson of progenitor Nicholas Kegg.   **COLTON NEAL** Seventh great grandson of progenitor Nicholas Kegg.   **JADA MARIE NEAL** Eighth great granddaughter of progenitor Nicholas Kegg.   **JEREMY ERNEST NEAL** Eighth great grandson of progenitor Nicholas Kegg.   **MIRANDA NEAL** Seventh great granddaughter of progenitor Nicholas Kegg.   **SYDNEY NEAL** Seventh great granddaughter of progenitor Nicholas Kegg.

NEALIS

TRACY L. NEALIS Sixth great granddaughter of progenitor Nicholas Kegg.

NEE

JOSEPH MARTIN NEE (1935 – 1935) aka "Joey", son of Russell and Phyllis (Rose) Nee.
JUSTINE NEE, Sixth great granddaughter of progenitor Nicholas Kegg.

NEEB

ANDREW NEEB Seventh great grandson of progenitor Nicholas Kegg.
ZACHARY NEEB Seventh great grandson of progenitor Nicholas Kegg.

NEELY

DIANA LUCILLE NEELY (1948 – 1949) daughter of Vernon and Betty (Waggerman) Neely.
MEGGAEN CYLE NEELY Sixth great granddaughter of progenitor Nicholas Kegg.
MIKE NEELY Fifth great grandson of progenitor Nicholas Kegg.
VERNON ROY NEELY Fifth great grandson of progenitor Nicholas Kegg.

NEICE

DEVIN NEICE Seventh great grandson of progenitor Nicholas Kegg.
RYKER NEICE Eighth great grandson of progenitor Nicholas Kegg.

NEILSON

MATTHEW NEILSON Sixth great grandson of progenitor Nicholas Kegg.

NELSEN

BEATHA C. NELSEN Sixth great granddaughter of progenitor Nicholas Kegg.
PATSY LYNN NELSEN Sixth great granddaughter of progenitor Nicholas Kegg.

NELSON

ANGELA JOY NELSON Sixth great granddaughter of progenitor Nicholas Kegg. **ARIANA NELSON** Seventh great granddaughter of progenitor Nicholas Kegg. **DAVID M. NELSON** Fifth great grandson of progenitor Nicholas Kegg. **DERRICK NELSON** Sixth great grandson of progenitor Nicholas Kegg. **ELDORA MAE NELSON** [5537] (1923 – 2007) daughter of Melvin and Irene (Lowe) Nelson married twice; first to James Elbert Wilson with whom she was mother of (3). Later, she married Eugene Andrew Dragg with whom she was mother of (2). Eldora was a homemaker. **ERIC NELSON** Fifth great grandson of progenitor Nicholas Kegg. **ETHEL ROSE NELSON** [5538] (1887 – 1977) daughter of Joseph and Elizabeth (Bodle) Nelson, married Samuel Daniel Yoder with whom she was mother of (6). Ethel was a member of the Church of Christ, Blackwell's Eastern Star chapter and the Relief Corps. **GRADY NELSON** Fifth great grandson of progenitor Nicholas Kegg. **GRADY LYLE NELSON** Sixth great grandson of progenitor Nicholas Kegg. **ISABELL MARGARET NELSON** (abt 1904 –?) daughter of Joseph and Elizabeth (Bodle) Nelson, married Herschel Oliver Shirley with whom she was mother of (2). **JARAH NELSON** Seventh great grandson of progenitor Nicholas Kegg. **JARED NELSON** Sixth great grandson of progenitor Nicholas Kegg. **JOHNNIE JO NELSON** Fourth great granddaughter of progenitor Nicholas Kegg. **JUDITH NELSON** Fifth great granddaughter of progenitor Nicholas Kegg. **KATHLEEN NELSON** Fifth great granddaughter of progenitor Nicholas Kegg. **KENNETH ORVILLE NELSON** (1910 – 1999) son of Joseph and Elizabeth (Bodle) Nelson, married Mary Leota Weaver with whom he was father of (1). **KIRK NELSON** Fifth great grandson of progenitor Nicholas Kegg. **KRISTY NELSON** Sixth great granddaughter of progenitor Nicholas Kegg. **LEONA MARY NELSON** [5539, 5540] (1889 – 1955) daughter of Joseph and Elizabeth (Bodle) Nelson, married Henry Otas Milford with whom she was mother of (1). **LUCEILL ELIZABETH NELSON** [5541] (1907 – 1990) daughter of Joseph and Elizabeth (Bodle) Nelson, married Raymond Leslie Waggerman with whom she was mother of (3); Luceill was a member of the First United Methodist Church of Bay City. **LYNNE NELSON** Fifth great granddaughter of progenitor Nicholas Kegg. **MAVIE MATILDA NELSON** [5542] (1900 – 1986) daughter of Joseph and Elizabeth (Bodle) Nelson, married Carl Christ Fredrick with whom she was mother of (4). **MELVIN LYLE NELSON** [5543] (1893 – 1943) son of Joseph and Elizabeth (Bodle) Nelson, married Irene Virginia Lowe with whom he was father of (5). Melvin was a veteran of the first World war and a member of the Christian church at Deer Creek. Melvin had been employed as a mechanic. He also belonged to the American Legion and D.A. V. groups in Enid. **MELVIN LYLE NELSON** [5544] (1925 – 1974) son of Melvin and Irene (Lowe) Nelson, married Mary with whom he was father of (6). Melvin was an employee of Trans-Con Trucking Co. He was found dead in the sleeping compartment of his semi-trailer rig. Police said Melvin went to sleep in a special compartment of the truck cab while he and his partner were driving in New Mexico. The partner, Jerry Balser of Oklahoma City, told officers he drove the truck into Hereford and pulled up to a truck stop so the two could eat. Balser said he attempted to wake Nelson but found him dead. Authorities said an autopsy was performed Sunday at Amarillo, but those results were not yet available. A police department spokesman said carbon monoxide poisoning was not likely because Balser was not ill. Melvin served in the U.S. Navy during WWII. **NANCY NELSON** Fifth great granddaughter of progenitor Nicholas Kegg. **NATHAN LEONARD NELSON** aka "Nasty Nate" (1947 – 2006) son of Melvin and Mary Nelson married Sonia S. Pike. Nate served aboard the guided missile frigate USS Gridley. The Senior Chief Petty officer obtained the following U.S. Navy certificates. Cold War, Decommissioning and Order of the Golden Dragon. **NEMALIE NELSON** aka "Lee" Fourth great granddaughter of progenitor Nicholas Kegg. **OLIVE NELSON** Seventh great granddaughter of progenitor Nicholas Kegg.

[5537] Jersey Journal (NJ) Oct 15, 2007 [5538] Blackwell Journal-Tribune (OK) Apr 4, 1977, obtained by D. Sue Dible [5539] The Medford Patriot-Star (OK) May 22, 1913 [5540] Blackwell Journal Tribune (OK) Apr 19, 1971 [5541] Daily Tribune (TX) Dec 1990 [5542] p.6B - Wichita Eagle (KS) April 27, 1986 [5543] Public Library of Enid and Garfield County obituary clipping obtained by D. Sue Dible [5544] pg. 27 – The Oklahoman (OK) Jan 14, 1974, obtained by D. Sue Dible

REBECCA J. NELSON [5544A] (1942 – 2012) daughter of Merle and Imogene (Beegle) Nelson married twice, first to Robert R. Carley with whom she was mother of (2), later to Richard Lee Murray. Rebecca had worked as a clerk at the Salvation Army. She was a member of the Foursquare Gospel Church and had belonged to a sewing club. **ROBERT ADRIAN NELSON** [5545] (1974 – 1974) son of Grady Nelson. **ROSCOE JAMES NELSON** [5546] (1895 – 1961) son of Joseph and Elizabeth (Bodle) Nelson, married Marian Edna Roberts who had been his childhood romance of more than 20 years. Roscoe served in France with the 111th engineers of the 36th division a unit with one of the longest records of service at the front of any of the American forces. He is a graduate of the University Preparatory school at Tonkawa and took accounting at the Hills Business college at Oklahoma City. Roscoe became a successful farmer. **STANLEY JOSEPH NELSON** (1938 – 1938) son of Merle and Imogene (Beegle) Nelson. **SUSAN NELSON** Fifth great granddaughter of progenitor Nicholas Kegg. **THANE NELSON** [5546A] (1931 – 2003) son of Melvin and Irene (Lowe) Nelson married Sylvia Sampson with whom he was father of (2). Thane was a veteran of the Korean War. **WILLIE NELSON** Sixth great grandson of progenitor Nicholas Kegg.

NESS

MICHELLE NESS Seventh great granddaughter of progenitor Nicholas Kegg.
STEPHANIE NESS Seventh great granddaughter of progenitor Nicholas Kegg.

NESTLE

GWENDOLYN NESTLE Seventh great granddaughter of progenitor Nicholas Kegg.
MARTIN NESTLE Seventh great grandson of progenitor Nicholas Kegg.
MIRIAM NESTLE Seventh great granddaughter of progenitor Nicholas Kegg.

NEUDER

CHAYNE NEUDER Eighth great grandson of progenitor Nicholas Kegg. **DARLA NEUDER** Sixth great granddaughter of progenitor Nicholas Kegg. **JASON JAMISON NEUDER** Seventh great grandson of progenitor Nicholas Kegg. **JESSICA JUNE NEUDER** Seventh great granddaughter of progenitor Nicholas Kegg. **JUDITH DIANE NEUDER** Sixth great granddaughter of progenitor Nicholas Kegg. **KAREN NEUDER** Sixth great granddaughter of progenitor Nicholas Kegg. **MAGGIE ELIZABETH NEUDER** Seventh great granddaughter of progenitor Nicholas Kegg. **THOMAS ELDON NEUDER** [5546B] (1947 – 2017) son of Eldon and Verna June (Everetts) Neuder married Jill Rae Jamenson with whom he was father of (3). Tom proudly served his country in the US Air Force during the Vietnam Era. He worked as a broker/realtor for Tri-County Property Realty and was later employed by Jason Langley Realty. Tom was a member of the St. Colman of Cloyne Catholic Church, the Fayette County Board of Realtors, and the American Legion. He was an avid golfer and also had a love for sports cars but more importantly, he loved being a husband, father, and grandfather.

NEUDORF

NIKOLAUS NEUDORF Seventh great grandson of progenitor Nicholas Kegg.

NEVERMAN

CHRISTOPHER D. NEVERMAN Eighth great grandson of progenitor Nicholas Kegg.
JACOB NEVERMAN aka "Jake", Eighth great grandson of progenitor Nicholas Kegg.

[5544A] Hinchliff-Pearson-West Galesburg Chapel [5545] p.52 – The Oklahoman (OK) Apr 25, 1974, obtained by D. Sue Dible [5546] Springfield Leader and Press (MO) Aug 9, 1961 [5546A] p.11A - Daily Oklahoman (OK) May 20, 2003 [5546B] Record Herald (OH) July 15, 2017

KATHRYN G. NEVERMAN aka "Katie", Eighth great granddaughter of progenitor Nicholas Kegg.
NICK NEVERMAN Eighth great grandson of progenitor Nicholas Kegg.

NEVILLE

TRAVIS NEVILLE Seventh great grandson of progenitor Nicholas Kegg.

NEVIS

CHRISTOPHER J. NEVIS Sixth great grandson of progenitor Nicholas Kegg. **DAVID LEON NEVIS** Fifth great grandson of progenitor Nicholas Kegg. **JAMES WILFRED NEVIS** Fifth great grandson of progenitor Nicholas Kegg. **KYLEIGH NICOLE NEVIS** Sixth great granddaughter of progenitor Nicholas Kegg. **TAYLOUR D. NEVIS** Sixth great grandson of progenitor Nicholas Kegg.

NEW

LARRY E. NEW Sixth great grandson of progenitor Nicholas Kegg. **SARAH NEW** Sixth great granddaughter of progenitor Nicholas Kegg. **SHANNON NEW** Sixth great granddaughter of progenitor Nicholas Kegg. **STEPHEN NEW** Sixth great grandson of progenitor Nicholas Kegg. **SUSAN NEW** Sixth great granddaughter of progenitor Nicholas Kegg.

NEWMAN

AMBER NEWMAN Eighth great granddaughter of progenitor Nicholas Kegg.
RODNEY I. NEWMAN Fifth great grandson of progenitor Nicholas Kegg.

NEWSWANGER

CHRISTINE NEWSWANGER Sixth great granddaughter of progenitor Nicholas Kegg.
DAVID NEWSWANGER Sixth great grandson of progenitor Nicholas Kegg.
JOHN R. NEWSWANGER Sixth great grandson of progenitor Nicholas Kegg.

NICCUM

ANTHONY WAYNE NICCUM Seventh great grandson of progenitor Nicholas Kegg. **LILY NICCUM** Eighth great granddaughter of progenitor Nicholas Kegg. **LISA MARIE NICCUM** (1988 – 1989) daughter of Dennis and Barbara (Baird) Niccum. **TENEKA NICCUM** [5546C] (1981 – 2017) daughter of Dennis and Barbara (Baird) Niccum married David Lee Osborne with whom she was mother of (3). Teneka was a cashier and prepped food for McDonalds. Teneka enjoyed watching movies, playing computer games, and doing family-oriented activities.

NICKELS

GOLDIE A. NICKELS (1895 – 1928) daughter of Sherman and Anna (Cagg) Nickels. **IONEA G. NICKELS** [5547] (1898 – 1988) daughter of Sherman and Anna (Cagg) Nickels, married William W. Wallace. Ionea was employed as a clerk for the Dugan Drugstore and the Alkire Grocery Store. **KAI JAMES NICKELS** Sixth great grandson of progenitor Nicholas Kegg. **ROBERT D. NICKELS** Fourth great grandson of progenitor Nicholas Kegg. **SHERMAN CURTISS NICKELS** [5548] (1908 – 1974) aka "Curtis", son of Sherman and Anna (Cagg) Nickels, married Ida with whom he was father of

---

[5546C] LaGrange Standard & News (IN) April 7, 2017, contributed by D. Sue Dible [5547] St. Joseph Gazette (MO) April 18, 1988 [5548] St. Joseph News-Press (MO) Feb 25, 1974

(1) Curtis was a farmer and a welder.   **WARREN NICKELS** (1910 – 1910) son of Sherman and Anna (Cagg) Nickels.

NICKLOW

JAMIE DAWN NICKLOW Sixth great granddaughter of progenitor Nicholas Kegg.

NICOL

AVA NICOL Eighth great granddaughter of progenitor Nicholas Kegg.   **ELLA NICOL** Eighth great granddaughter of progenitor Nicholas Kegg.   **IAN NICOL** Eighth great grandson of progenitor Nicholas Kegg.   **ISAAC NICOL** Eighth great grandson of progenitor Nicholas Kegg.   **MEGAN ELIZABETH NICOL** Eighth great granddaughter of progenitor Nicholas Kegg.   **RACHEL NICOL** Eighth great granddaughter of progenitor Nicholas Kegg.   **TANYA NICOL** Seventh great granddaughter of progenitor Nicholas Kegg.   **TRENT C. NICOL** Seventh great grandson of progenitor Nicholas Kegg.   **TROY K. NICOL** Seventh great grandson of progenitor Nicholas Kegg.

NICOLS

JOANN MARIE NICOLS Sixth great granddaughter of progenitor Nicholas Kegg.
MARCY MAE NICOLS Sixth great granddaughter of progenitor Nicholas Kegg.
TIMOTHY NICOLS Sixth great grandson of progenitor Nicholas Kegg.

NIXON

CHRISTOPHER STEVEN NIXON Sixth great grandson of progenitor Nicholas Kegg.
HARRY A. NIXON Fifth great grandson of progenitor Nicholas Kegg.
LEE ANN NIXON Fifth great granddaughter of progenitor Nicholas Kegg.
STEVEN WAYNE NIXON Fifth great grandson of progenitor Nicholas Kegg.

NOBILE

LUCAS M. NOBILE Sixth great grandson of progenitor Nicholas Kegg.

NODICH

CHRISTOPHER PETER NODICH Fifth great grandson of progenitor Nicholas Kegg.
ELIZABETH MARIA NODICH Fifth great granddaughter of progenitor Nicholas Kegg.
GREGORY CHARLES NODICH Fifth great grandson of progenitor Nicholas Kegg.
PATRICIA DIANE NODICH Fifth great granddaughter of progenitor Nicholas Kegg.

NOFFERT

GAIL NOFFERT Fifth great granddaughter of progenitor Nicholas Kegg.
LORIE NOFFERT Fifth great granddaughter of progenitor Nicholas Kegg.
NANCY NOFFERT Fifth great granddaughter of progenitor Nicholas Kegg.

NOLAN

DAYVA NOLAN Eighth great granddaughter of progenitor Nicholas Kegg.

NORBERG

BRANDON BLAKE NORBERG aka "Blake", Sixth great grandson of progenitor Nicholas Kegg.
CHARLES DEAN NORBERG Fifth great grandson of progenitor Nicholas Kegg.
ELIZABETH SIEREN NORBERG Sixth great granddaughter of progenitor Nicholas Kegg.

NORMAN

CHRISTINA LEA NORMAN Sixth great granddaughter of progenitor Nicholas Kegg. **GENEVIEVE CATHERINE NORMAN** (1919 – 2006) daughter of John and Anita (Wyckoff) Norman, married George S. Warren. **HELEN LOUISE NORMAN** (1909 – 1943) daughter of John and Anita (Wyckoff) Norman, married Everett Melvin Arrants with whom she was mother of (6). **JAMES ALBERT NORMAN** (1917 – 1989) aka "Jim", son of John and Anita (Wyckoff) Norman. **JESSE OWEN NORMAN** (1929 – 2015) son of John and Anita (Wyckoff) Norman married Patricia E. Crozier with whom she was mother of (3). **JOHN NORMAN JR.** (1925 – 1946) son of John and Anita (Wyckoff) Norman was a veteran of WWI, having served in the U. S. Navy. **LOUIS WILLIAM NORMAN** (1912 – 1971) son of John and Anita (Wyckoff) Norman. **MARY H. NORMAN** (1923 – 1941) daughter of John and Anita (Wyckoff) Norman. **STACEI R. NORMAN** Sixth great granddaughter of progenitor Nicholas Kegg. **TAMMI G. NORMAN** Sixth great granddaughter of progenitor Nicholas Kegg. **VICTORIA NORMAN** (1921 – 2004) daughter of John and Anita (Wyckoff) Norman, married Raymond H. Clark with whom she was mother of (2). **WANDA RUTH NORMAN** [5549] (1915 – 1962) daughter of John and Anita (Wyckoff) Norman married twice; first to John Milton Carlson with whom she was mother of (1). Later, she married Lawrence Wesley Sheck with whom she was mother of (2). Wanda was a principal and teacher of the kindergarten at Prince of Peace Lutheran Church Azalea Park for three years, a member of the Veterans of Foreign Wars Auxiliary Post 881, Wellington, Kan., honorary member of the N. C. O. Wives club, McCoy AFB, and a member of the L.W.M.I., the missionary Society.

NORMENT

ALDEN NORMENT Eighth great grandson of progenitor Nicholas Kegg.
AYRABELLA RAYNE NORMENT Eighth great granddaughter of progenitor Nicholas Kegg.
GWENDOLYN NORMENT Eighth great granddaughter of progenitor Nicholas Kegg.

NORRIS

DARLENE JOYCE NORRIS Fifth great granddaughter of progenitor Nicholas Kegg.
DEBORAH A. NORRIS Seventh great granddaughter of progenitor Nicholas Kegg.
GARY LEE NORRIS Fifth great grandson of progenitor Nicholas Kegg.
GENEVA GRACE NORRIS Seventh great granddaughter of progenitor Nicholas Kegg.
GERALD WILLIAM NORRIS Fifth great grandson of progenitor Nicholas Kegg.
JEREMY DAVID NORRIS Seventh great grandson of progenitor Nicholas Kegg.
KAREN L. NORRIS Seventh great granddaughter of progenitor Nicholas Kegg.
LISA MARIE NORRIS Sixth great granddaughter of progenitor Nicholas Kegg.
MAKOTA Z. NORRIS [5550] (1999 – 2005) aka "Cletus", son of Mike and Laurie (Keister) Norris.
MARION JEAN NORRIS Fifth great granddaughter of progenitor Nicholas Kegg.
MICHELE DONETTE NORRIS Sixth great granddaughter of progenitor Nicholas Kegg.
NATHAN EMANUEL NORRIS Sixth great grandson of progenitor Nicholas Kegg.
PAMELA J. NORRIS Seventh great granddaughter of progenitor Nicholas Kegg.

[5549] p.6B-Orlando Evening Star (FL) June 16, 1962 [5550] Brazzell Funeral Homes, IN

ROBERT WARREN NORRIS Sixth great grandson of progenitor Nicholas Kegg. **SAMUEL ALEX NORRIS** Sixth great grandson of progenitor Nicholas Kegg. **SHERIDAN LEE NORRIS** Sixth great grandson of progenitor Nicholas Kegg. **SYLVIA JANE NORRIS** Fifth great granddaughter of progenitor Nicholas Kegg. **WILLIAM TODD NORRIS** Sixth great grandson of progenitor Nicholas Kegg.

NORTHROP

ANDREW NORTHROP Sixth great grandson of progenitor Nicholas Kegg. **BRADFORD NORTHROP** aka "Brad", Fifth great grandson of progenitor Nicholas Kegg. **DAVID NORTHROP** Sixth great grandson of progenitor Nicholas Kegg. **DAVID STANLEY NORTHROP** Fifth great grandson of progenitor Nicholas Kegg. **MICHAEL PATRICK NORTHROP** [5551] (1977 – 1994) son of David and Alice (Hines) Northrop was a junior at Lakeland High School and employed at Kroger grocery store, Sturgis. **STUART C. NORTHROP** Fifth great grandson of progenitor Nicholas Kegg. **TED NORTHROP** Sixth great grandson of progenitor Nicholas Kegg.

NORTHRUP

CHRISTOPHER ALLAN NORTHRUP [5552] (1971 – 2022) son of Arthur and Deborah (Norris) Northrup. Although Chris focused more on his social life than his studies during his time at North Central High School, he discovered a love for academics in college, having attended both IUPUI and Indiana State University. He aspired to be a high school history teacher and relied on libraries to keep him supplied with sci-fi movies and nonfiction books. Chris liked to exercise, especially outside. As a kid, he roamed around Williams Creek. He loved riding for miles on his bike as a teen. PT was one of his favorite parts of his stint in the Marines. Chris also liked to go out to eat. He always was open to trying a new place and encouraged generous tipping, having spent many years as a server himself. He liked to laugh at stand-up comedy and sing karaoke, with song choices ranging from Frank Sinatra to Avril Lavigne, depending on the crowd. **HEATHER NORTHRUP** Seventh great granddaughter of progenitor Nicholas Kegg. **HOLLY M. NORTHRUP** Seventh great granddaughter of progenitor Nicholas Kegg.

NORTON

JAMES NORTON Sixth great grandson of progenitor Nicholas Kegg. **JOHN NORTON** Sixth great grandson of progenitor Nicholas Kegg. **RICHARD LEE NORTON** (1937 – 1991) son of Joseph and Mildred (Miller) Norton married three times; first to Linda Lee Mitchell, then to Darlene Campas. Later, he married Barbara Hansen. **STEPHANIE NORTON** Fourth great granddaughter of progenitor Nicholas Kegg. **THOMAS LEE NORTON** Fifth great grandson of progenitor Nicholas Kegg. **WILLIAM CHARLES NORTON** aka "Bill" [5553] (1936 – 2018) son of James and Dorothy (Price) Norton married Donna with whom he was father of (2). Bill's happiest days were working for the Fire Dept. where he served the Buchanan City Fire Dept. for 37 years or riding one of his John Deere tractors. Bill retired from Clark Equipment after 37 years. He then retired from Cook Nuclear after 17 years and worked 4 years at Four Winds, Dowagiac. Bill also served the Buchanan City Police Reserve; was a director of SMCAS; served Buchanan City Commission; Buchanan Area Senior Center Board of Directors and Michiana Two-Cylinder VP.

NORWOOD

DEBRA LYNN NORWOOD Sixth great granddaughter of progenitor Nicholas Kegg.
EDWARD LANDON NORWOOD [5554] (1960 – 2016) son of Edward and Marilyn (Smith) Norwood,

---

[5551] Michigan Obituaries/Familysearch.org Film Number 007596631 [5552] Neptune Society, IN [5553] Hoven Funeral Home, MI [5554] Toledo Blade (OH) Mar 13, 2016

FRANK NYIRI Sixth great grandson of progenitor Nicholas Kegg. **FRED NYIRI** Sixth great grandson of progenitor Nicholas Kegg. **IRMA JEAN NYIRI** Sixth great granddaughter of progenitor Nicholas Kegg. **JOHN IMLER NYIRI** Sixth great grandson of progenitor Nicholas Kegg. **KYLE NYIRI** Seventh great grandson of progenitor Nicholas Kegg. **RICK NYIRI** Sixth great grandson of progenitor Nicholas Kegg.

O'BRIEN

ANDY O'BRIEN Fifth great grandson of progenitor Nicholas Kegg. **IAN MICHAEL O'BRIEN** Fifth great grandson of progenitor Nicholas Kegg. **TIMOTHY B. O'BRIEN** Fifth great grandson of progenitor Nicholas Kegg. **BERNADETTE O'BRIEN** Sixth great granddaughter of progenitor Nicholas Kegg. **CATHERINE O'BRIEN** Sixth great granddaughter of progenitor Nicholas Kegg. **DAVID O'BRIEN** Sixth great grandson of progenitor Nicholas Kegg. **FRANK O'BRIEN** Sixth great grandson of progenitor Nicholas Kegg. **ISABEL ROSE O'BRIEN** Sixth great granddaughter of progenitor Nicholas Kegg. **JACKIE O'BRIEN** Sixth great granddaughter of progenitor Nicholas Kegg. **JEFFREY H. O'BRIEN** Sixth great grandson of progenitor Nicholas Kegg. **JENNIFER O'BRIEN** Sixth great granddaughter of progenitor Nicholas Kegg. **KELLEY O'BRIEN** Sixth great granddaughter of progenitor Nicholas Kegg. **KRISTEN M. O'BRIEN** Sixth great granddaughter of progenitor Nicholas Kegg. **LAWRENCE O'BRIEN** Sixth great grandson of progenitor Nicholas Kegg. **LIBBY O'BRIEN** Sixth great granddaughter of progenitor Nicholas Kegg. **MIKE O'BRIEN** Sixth great grandson of progenitor Nicholas Kegg. **STEPHANIE O'BRIEN** Sixth great granddaughter of progenitor Nicholas Kegg.

O'CONNELL

COLLIN MCCALL O'CONNELL Seventh great grandson of progenitor Nicholas Kegg.
JOSEPH MCCALL O'CONNELL, aka "Joe", Sixth great grandson of progenitor Nicholas Kegg.

O'DELLICK

ALBERT L. O'DELLICK Sixth great grandson of progenitor Nicholas Kegg.
BRENDAN O'DELLICK Seventh great grandson of progenitor Nicholas Kegg.
KIERSTEN O'DELLICK Seventh great granddaughter of progenitor Nicholas Kegg.
NICHOLAS O'DELLICK Seventh great grandson of progenitor Nicholas Kegg.

O'DIER

ASHLEY NICOLE O'DIER Sixth great granddaughter of progenitor Nicholas Kegg. **HARLEIGH BETH O'DIER** Sixth great granddaughter of progenitor Nicholas Kegg. **JACQUELINE CELENE O'DIER** Fifth great granddaughter of progenitor Nicholas Kegg. **ROBERT ARTHUR O'DIER** Fifth great grandson of progenitor Nicholas Kegg. **TERESA S. O'DIER** Fifth great granddaughter of progenitor Nicholas Kegg.

O'HARA

NATALIE LYNN O'HARA Seventh great granddaughter of progenitor Nicholas Kegg.
NATHAN O'HARA Seventh great grandson of progenitor Nicholas Kegg.

O'NEAL

CYNTHIA D. O'NEAL Sixth great granddaughter of progenitor Nicholas Kegg. **COREY A. O'NEAL** Seventh great grandson of progenitor Nicholas Kegg. **GLENN A. O'NEAL** Sixth great grandson of progenitor Nicholas Kegg. **HARLEY EUGENE O'NEAL** Sixth great grandson of progenitor

Nicholas Kegg. **KATHY MARIE O'NEAL** [5560A] (1953 – 2010) daughter of Glenn and Vera (Donaldson) O'Neal married twice; first to Phil Christopher with whom she was mother of (3). Later, she married Wayne Bush Jr. Kathy was a member of the Labelle Womens Club and a member of the Community Emergency Response Team for Hendry Co. in Florida. **LINDA KAY O'NEAL** Fifth great granddaughter of progenitor Nicholas Kegg. **LORETTA ELLEN O'NEAL** [5560B] daughter of Ralph and Edna (Calhoun) O'Neal married Raymond E. Craig with whom she was mother of (4). Loretta was a loving and caring homemaker who enjoyed cooking so much that she also worked as a cook at the Travelers Rest, the Gateway Restaurant, and the Wildwood Inn. Loretta loved to read, in particular books about flower gardening and plants, helping her to grow beautiful gardens around her home. She also enjoyed swimming and fishing, and she and her husband Ray were like "two peas in a pod," together always and forever. **MONTY G. O'NEAL** Seventh great grandson of progenitor Nicholas Kegg. **NANCY O'NEAL** Sixth great granddaughter of progenitor Nicholas Kegg. **TORI O'NEAL** Eighth great granddaughter of progenitor Nicholas Kegg.

O'NEILL

HELEN MYRTLE O'NEILL [5561] (1892 – 1975) daughter of Thomas and Mary Evalena (Cagg) O'Neill married twice; first to Horton Lucas Bing with whom she was mother of (2). Later, she married Corwin F. Fierce. **JENNIFER O'NEILL** Seventh great granddaughter of progenitor Nicholas Kegg. **JOSHUA O'NEILL** Seventh great grandson of progenitor Nicholas Kegg. **LAWRENCE GARDNER O'NEILL** (1916 – 1981) son of Walter and Bessie (Gardner) O'Neill. **MEGHAN O'NEILL** Seventh great granddaughter of progenitor Nicholas Kegg. **NANCY VIRGINIA O'NEILL** Fifth great granddaughter of progenitor Nicholas Kegg. **WALTER EARL O'NEILL** [5562] (1890 – 1940) son of Thomas and Mary Evalena (Cagg) O'Neill, married Bessie Gardner with whom he was father of (2).

O'SHEA

NORA JEAN O'SHEA Eighth great granddaughter of progenitor Nicholas Kegg.

OBERG

CHRISTOPHER DANA OBERG Sixth great grandson of progenitor Nicholas Kegg.

OBERLECHNER

SHANNON LUCILLE OBERLECHNER Sixth great granddaughter of progenitor Nicholas Kegg.
SONIA JOY OBERLECHNER Sixth great granddaughter of progenitor Nicholas Kegg.

ODDO

LILY ODDO Seventh great granddaughter of progenitor Nicholas Kegg.

ODELL

BRADY LEE ODELL [5563] (1980 – 2008) son OF Norman and Janene (Scherbarth) Odell was father of (1). Brady entered the U.S. Marine Corp. Following an injury, he was honorably discharged. He then went to WyoTech School in Laramie, Wyoming studying Hot Rod and Auto Body repair. Brady was employed as a conductor for BNSF Railroad. He enjoyed fishing and hunting and was devoted to his son.

[5560A] NewsZap (FL) Jun 23, 2010 [5560B] Dalla Valle Funeral Home (PA) [5561] p.6 Columbus Dispatch (OH) Mar 30, 1942 [5562] p.7 Logan Daily News (OH) June 20, 1940 [5563] Star-Herald (NE) Mar 18, 2008

DRAKE ODELL Eighth great grandson of progenitor Nicholas Kegg. **MEGAN ODELL** Seventh great granddaughter of progenitor Nicholas Kegg. **MICHAEL ODELL** Seventh great grandson of progenitor Nicholas Kegg.

ODEND'HAL

ASHLEY N. ODEND'HAL Seventh great granddaughter of progenitor Nicholas Kegg. **DANIELLE LEIGH ODEND'HAL** Seventh great granddaughter of progenitor Nicholas Kegg. **FARRELL COFFMAN ODEND'HAL** Sixth great grandson of progenitor Nicholas Kegg. **FORREST PORTER ODEND'HAL** Sixth great grandson of progenitor Nicholas Kegg. **FORTUNE ODEND'HAL VI** Seventh great grandson of progenitor Nicholas Kegg. **FORTUNE ODEND'HAL V** Sixth great grandson of progenitor Nicholas Kegg. **FRANCIS ODEND'HAL** Sixth great granddaughter of progenitor Nicholas Kegg. **LAUREN ODEND'HAL** Seventh great granddaughter of progenitor Nicholas Kegg. **TAYLOR ODEND'HAL** Seventh great granddaughter of progenitor Nicholas Kegg.

OEY

CAROLINE ROSE OEY Sixth great granddaughter of progenitor Nicholas Kegg.
CHRISTOPHER JAMES OEY Sixth great grandson of progenitor Nicholas Kegg.
MARISSA OEY aka "Misha", Sixth great granddaughter of progenitor Nicholas Kegg.

OGIER

CONNIE SUE OGIER [5564] (1951 – 2007) daughter of Ralph and Louise (Laird) Ogier, married Alfred Smith. Connie was always cheerful, optimistic, and enthusiastic. She worked for five years at Coover Chevrolet in Nevada as a receptionist and bookkeeper. Connie was a member of the Community of Christ church, in which she was ordained as a priest in 1987. Although she was never blessed with children of her own, she loved working with children in Sunday school classes, church camps, and the Coralville Young Peacemakers Club. Some of the happiest times of her life revolved around her puppet ministry. For many years, Connie and Fred wrote and performed puppet plays and taught puppetry classes for both children and adults. Throughout her life, Connie was an inspiration to everyone who knew her.
RALPH JAMES OGIER aka "Jim", Sixth great grandson of progenitor Nicholas Kegg.

OHLER

JONATHAN PETER OHLER Seventh great grandson of progenitor Nicholas Kegg.

OKIMOTO

KEVIN OKIMOTO Fourth great grandson of progenitor Nicholas Kegg.
SAYA OKIMOTO Fourth great granddaughter of progenitor Nicholas Kegg.

OLER

GEORGE EDGAR OLER [5565] (1877 – 1945) son of William and Louisa (Kegg) Oler worked as a mail boy at a very early age in the Pennsylvania Railroad Company mail room. Later, he went to Pittsburgh to enter the coal business where he was employed as an auditor for the East Liberty Coke and Coal Company and Rca Mines.

[5564] Gay & Ciha Funeral and Cremation Service of Iowa City [5565] Bedford Gazette (PA) Aug 24, 1945

OLEWILER

BRAIDEN OLEWILER Seventh great grandson of progenitor Nicholas Kegg.
HAILEIGH OLEWILER Seventh great granddaughter of progenitor Nicholas Kegg.

OLIVEIRA

ANTHONY E. OLIVEIRA Sixth great grandson of progenitor Nicholas Kegg.

DANIEL JORGE OLIVEIRA [5566] (1986 – 1988) son of Fernando and Denise (Whetstone) Oliveira.
KARINA W. OLIVEIRA Sixth great granddaughter of progenitor Nicholas Kegg.
NATHAN E. OLIVEIRA Sixth great grandson of progenitor Nicholas Kegg.

OLIVER

EMILY JEAN OLIVER Sixth great granddaughter of progenitor Nicholas Kegg.
KAILEY OLIVER Seventh great granddaughter of progenitor Nicholas Kegg.
TRAVIS HUGH OLIVER Sixth great grandson of progenitor Nicholas Kegg.
WESLEY OLIVER Seventh great grandson of progenitor Nicholas Kegg.

OLIVIERI

ANTHONY OLIVIERI Sixth great grandson of progenitor Nicholas Kegg.
ASHLEY FRYE OLIVIERI Sixth great granddaughter of progenitor Nicholas Kegg.
NICOLE OLIVIERI Sixth great granddaughter of progenitor Nicholas Kegg.

OLMSTEAD

BONNIE LEE OLMSTEAD [5567] (1916 – 1991) daughter of Fred and Emma (Hoffmire) Olmstead married twice; first to Robert Stephen Nelson with whom she was mother of (1). Later, she married John Phillip Williams with whom she was mother of (1). Before retiring, Bonnie was a service representative for Southwestern Bell for 20 years. She was a member of St. Philip's Episcopal Church, the Joplin Woman's Club and Daughters of the American Revolution. Bonnie did volunteer work at the genealogy department at the Joplin Public Library and Oak Hill gift shop. **CAROL A. OLMSTEAD** Sixth great granddaughter of progenitor Nicholas Kegg. **WILLIAM D. OLMSTEAD** Sixth great grandson of progenitor Nicholas Kegg.

OLSON

HEATHER MARIE OLSON Seventh great granddaughter of progenitor Nicholas Kegg.

OLTMANNS

BRIAN OLTMANNS Sixth great grandson of progenitor Nicholas Kegg.
JEFF OLTMANNS Sixth great grandson of progenitor Nicholas Kegg.

OMAN

AVERY JAMES OMAN Seventh great grandson of progenitor Nicholas Kegg.
RILYN GRACE OMAN Seventh great granddaughter of progenitor Nicholas Kegg.

[5566] Patriot-News (PA) Feb 28, 1988 [5567] The Joplin Globe (MO) Jan 13, 1991, obtained by D. Sue Dible

OMPS

CHRISTINE DIANE OMPS aka "Chris", Seventh great granddaughter of progenitor Nicholas Kegg.
ELIZABETH OMPS aka "Beth", Seventh great granddaughter of progenitor Nicholas Kegg.
ROBIN L. OMPS Seventh great granddaughter of progenitor Nicholas Kegg.

OPRA

DANIEL OPRA Seventh great grandson of progenitor Nicholas Kegg.
MIRALLA OPRA Seventh great granddaughter of progenitor Nicholas Kegg.

ORLANDO

BRENDON ORLANDO Seventh great grandson of progenitor Nicholas Kegg.
TIMOTHY RICHARD ORLANDO Sixth great grandson of progenitor Nicholas Kegg.

ORR

GINGER SUE ORR Seventh great granddaughter of progenitor Nicholas Kegg.

ORT

ANNA MARYLAND ORT [5568, 5569] (1915 – 1992) daughter of Clarence and Margaret (McFarland) Ort, married Richard Frederick Schumann with whom she was mother of (2). **ANNA M. ORT** [5570] (1887 – 1957) daughter of Lewis and Caroline (Turner) Ort, married Oscar Marelius Sorensen. **JOHN LEWIS ORT** [5571] (1881 – 1959) son of Lewis and Caroline (Turner) Ort, married Marie Smith with whom he was father of (2). John engaged in catering service and operated confectionary stores in Lonaconing and Cumberland with his brother Clarence. In 1902 the two brothers opened a bakery in Midland, operating it until 1945. In 1936 they bought the Cumberland Bakery and operated it in conjunction with the Midland plant until 1945, when the two bakeries were combined and named the Ort Brothers Bakery. **JOHN LEWIS ORT** [5572] (1924 – 1971) son of John and Marie (Smith) Ort, married Lydia Lorraine Campbell with whom he was father of (3). John was employed as inspector for the State Roads Commission and was a member of Centre Street United Methodist Church. **KAREN LOU ORT** Fifth great granddaughter of progenitor Nicholas Kegg. **KELLY ANN ORT** Sixth great granddaughter of progenitor Nicholas Kegg. **LARRY GILBERT ORT** Fifth great grandson of progenitor Nicholas Kegg. **LEWIS J. ORT** [5572A] (1918 – 2001) son of Clarence and Margaret (McFarland) Ort married Pearl Mae Fleetwood with whom he was father of (4). A baker turned philanthropist; Lewis began his career in a family-owned bakery. He devised a way of using fiber from soybean hulls to bake what was hailed as this country's first diet white bread *and* marketed the bread's recipe nationally under the name Less. He also owned Karib Inc., a company that blended vitamins into a mix that was sold to bakeries in Central and South America for use in enriched-flour bread. He won baking industry awards for his designs for baking pans. He was frequently referred to as Mr. Western Maryland for his humanitarian service, which included raising millions of dollars for hospitals, burn centers, churches and orphanages. He led a building drive for Frostburg State University's library, named in his honor. Mr. Ort was a major donor to Johns Hopkins Hospital's Wilmer Eye Institute, where he and other family members endowed the Lewis J. Ort Chair of Ophthalmology. He was robust, enthusiastic, positive, happy and vigorous -- a

---

[5568] p.8 Cumberland Times (MD) Oct 13, 1992 [5569] Cumberland Times News (MD) Dec 10, 1992 [5570] p.14 - Cumberland Evening Times May 24, 1957 [5571] Cumberland Evening Times (MD) Dec. 9, 1959 [5572] p.4 - Cumberland News (MD) July 31, 1971 [5572A] p.4B - The Sun (Baltimore, MD) - Sept 29, 2001.

larger-than-life figure, a huge man with a huge commitment to philanthropy. He was stunningly generous throughout the world and supported any religious group he could think of without any restrictions. He was a great example of American generosity with no quid pro quo   **MARLEE LEE ORT** Fifth great granddaughter of progenitor Nicholas Kegg. **TANA KIM ORT** Fifth great granddaughter of progenitor Nicholas Kegg. **THOMAS P. ORT** Fifth great grandson of progenitor Nicholas Kegg. **VIRGINIA MCFARLAND ORT** [5572B] (1910 – 1980) daughter of Clarence and Margaret (McFarland) Ort married and divorced Joseph William Linton Jr. **WALTER CLAYTON ORT** (born abt. 1883) son of Lewis and Caroline (Turner) Ort, married Emma Lucretia Beachy with whom he was father of (1).

ORTALE

SOPHIA ORTALE Sixth great granddaughter of progenitor Nicholas Kegg.

ORTEGA

EDUARDO AREK ALEXANDER ORTEGA Eighth great grandson of progenitor Nicholas Kegg.
SHANTEL ALEXIA SOPHIA ORTEGA Eighth great granddaughter of progenitor Nicholas Kegg.

ORTIZ

ADRIANA MIA ORTIZ Sixth great granddaughter of progenitor Nicholas Kegg. **BRENNA L. ORTIZ** Seventh great granddaughter of progenitor Nicholas Kegg. **ELIZABETH NICOLE ORTIZ** Seventh great granddaughter of progenitor Nicholas Kegg. **EMILY ORTIZ** Seventh great granddaughter of progenitor Nicholas Kegg. **JUAN ORTIZ** Sixth great grandson of progenitor Nicholas Kegg. **KELLY MARIE ORTIZ** Seventh great granddaughter of progenitor Nicholas Kegg. **KIARA ORTIZ** Seventh great granddaughter of progenitor Nicholas Kegg.

OSBORN

CLIFTON EVERETT OSBORN Fifth great grandson of progenitor Nicholas Kegg.
CLIFTON EVERETT OSBORN Sixth great grandson of progenitor Nicholas Kegg.
JEANETTE M. OSBORN Sixth great granddaughter of progenitor Nicholas Kegg.
MARGARET ELLEN OSBORN Fifth great granddaughter of progenitor Nicholas Kegg.
WAYNE ANDREW OSBORN Sixth great grandson of progenitor Nicholas Kegg.

OSBOURN

DAWN OSBOURN Sixth great granddaughter of progenitor Nicholas Kegg.
KIMBERLY OSBOURN Sixth great granddaughter of progenitor Nicholas Kegg.

OSBOURNE

DANIEL OSBOURNE Eighth great grandson of progenitor Nicholas Kegg.
KAITLYN OSBOURNE Eighth great granddaughter of progenitor Nicholas Kegg.
KAYLA OSBOURNE Eighth great granddaughter of progenitor Nicholas Kegg.

OSBURN

GARRETT OSBURN Seventh great grandson of progenitor Nicholas Kegg.

[5572B] p.10C- Plain Dealer (OH) Dec 10, 1976

LAUREN OSBURN Seventh great granddaughter of progenitor Nicholas Kegg.

OSOLING

CHRISTINA ANNE OSOLING Sixth great granddaughter of progenitor Nicholas Kegg.
JOHN PATRICK OSOLING (1936 – 1993) son of John and Ada (Calhoun) Osoling married Mary Louise Barkley with whom he was father of (1). A graduate of Benjamin Franklin School of Accounting, John began his career employed by the Frank Levy accounting firm as a junior accountant.
ROBERT LEE OSOLING [5573] (1940 – 1944) son of John and Ada (Calhoun) Osoling.

OSTER

DEBRA L. OSTER Sixth great granddaughter of progenitor Nicholas Kegg. **VICKI DAWN OSTER** [5573A] (1945 – 1999) daughter of Hubert and Dorothy (Miller) Oster married John H. Gomochak with whom she was mother of (1). Vicki was a homemaker.

OSTERHOUT

AVA OSTERHOUT Seventh great granddaughter of progenitor Nicholas Kegg. **MELISSA OSTERHOUT** Sixth great granddaughter of progenitor Nicholas Kegg. **ROBERT EDWARD OSTERHOUT** Sixth great grandson of progenitor Nicholas Kegg. **ROBERT EDWARD OSTERHOUT** [5573B] (2013 – 2014) son of Robert and Jill (Bodge) Osterhout. Robert brought a special joy to his entire family with his wonderfully sweet and cheerful nature. His smile was contagious as he played throughout the day. **SARA OSTERHOUT** Seventh great granddaughter of progenitor Nicholas Kegg.

OSTMANN

KATIE OSTMANN Seventh great granddaughter of progenitor Nicholas Kegg.
SEAN OSTMANN Seventh great grandson of progenitor Nicholas Kegg.

OSTRANDER

BROOKE ANN OSTRANDER Seventh great granddaughter of progenitor Nicholas Kegg.
LAUREN TAYLOR OSTRANDER Seventh great granddaughter of progenitor Nicholas Kegg.

OSTROWSKI

LAUREN OSTROWSKI Sixth great granddaughter of progenitor Nicholas Kegg.
MATTHEW OSTROWSKI Sixth great grandson of progenitor Nicholas Kegg.
ZACHARY OSTROWSKI Sixth great grandson of progenitor Nicholas Kegg.

OSWALD

BRIAN OSWALD Sixth great grandson of progenitor Nicholas Kegg. **JASON OSWALD** Sixth great grandson of progenitor Nicholas Kegg. **JIMMY OSWALD** Sixth great grandson of progenitor Nicholas Kegg. **JOSEPH ROBERT OSWALD** aka "Joe", Sixth great grandson of progenitor Nicholas Kegg. **KITTY OSWALD** Sixth great granddaughter of progenitor Nicholas Kegg. **RICHARD OSWALD** aka "Rich", Sixth great grandson of progenitor Nicholas Kegg.

[5573] Bedford County Historical Society (PA), book 127, p 83 obtained by D. Sue Dible [5573A] p.B6 - Vindicator (OH) May 16, 1999, contributed by D. Sue Dible [5573B] Bucks County Courier Times (PA) Apr 14, 2014

OSWALT

CLINT OSWALT Sixth great grandson of progenitor Nicholas Kegg.

OTT

AVA OTT Eighth great granddaughter of progenitor Nicholas Kegg. **DALE PATRICK OTT** Sixth great grandson of progenitor Nicholas Kegg. **DENNIS TYLER OTT** [5573C] (1990 – 2018) son of Dennis and Kimberly (Bowser) Ott was father of (1). Tyler was employed in the warehouse industry, working for LKQ Penn–Mar, Inc., and Southern Enterprises LLC. When in school, Tyler participated in wrestling and baseball programs. He enjoyed playing baseball, softball, riding motorcycles, and was a fan of the Philadelphia Eagles. Tyler was a kindhearted soul who enjoyed helping others. **DIRK EDWARD OTT** Sixth great grandson of progenitor Nicholas Kegg. **JONATHAN KIRBEN OTT** Seventh great grandson of progenitor Nicholas Kegg. **KATHERINE OTT** Sixth great granddaughter of progenitor Nicholas Kegg. **MARGARET E. OTT** [5574] (1903 – 1985) daughter of John and Rhoda (Smith) Ott, married Carl Clifford James with whom she was mother of (6). **MIRIAM VIRGINIA OTT** [5575] (1915 – 1980) daughter of John and Rhoda (Smith) Ott, had been employed as a cook at the county jail. **NOEL KIRBEN OTT** Sixth great grandson of progenitor Nicholas Kegg. **TAMMY OTT** Sixth great granddaughter of progenitor Nicholas Kegg. **TYLER OTT** Seventh great grandson of progenitor Nicholas Kegg. **TYLER JACOB OTT** Seventh great grandson of progenitor Nicholas Kegg.

OVERLY

RACHEAL A. OVERLY Seventh great granddaughter of progenitor Nicholas Kegg.

OVERSTREET

MARY FRANCIS OVERSTREET [5575A] (1914 – 2008) daughter of William and Audna (Kerr) Overstreet married Corbett Benjamin Davis. Mary retired as Secretary to the Chaplain of Carilion Roanoke Memorial Hospital and then worked as a "Pink Lady" at the hospital volunteering over 9000 hours.

OVERTON

CHUCK OVERTON Sixth great grandson of progenitor Nicholas Kegg.
VICKY ANN OVERTON [5575B] (1956 – 2017) daughter of Charles and Charlotte (Davis) Overton married Mr. Knutson with whom she was mother of (3). Vicky was employed at Parkview Medical Center. She enjoyed reading, brain games and Andy Griffith.

OWEN

SARAH ELIZABETH OWEN Sixth great granddaughter of progenitor Nicholas Kegg.

OWENS

AUDREY JANE OWENS Fourth great granddaughter of progenitor Nicholas Kegg. **BETTY LOUISE OWENS** (1923 – 2003) daughter of Herbert and Helen (Howard) Owens married three times; first to Robert King with whom she was mother of (1). Later she married Fred D. Moore and Mr. Mangum.

[5573C] Fogelsanger-Bricker Funeral Home & Crematorium, Inc., Shippensburg [5574] Bedford Gazette (PA) Aug 14, 1985 [5575] Bedford Gazette (PA) April 1, 1980 [5575A] p.B6 - Roanoke Times (VA) April 30, 2008 [5575B] Des Moines Register (IA) Nov. 29, 2017

CHRISTINA OWENS Seventh great granddaughter of progenitor Nicholas Kegg. **CHRISTOPHER BRIAN OWENS** Seventh great grandson of progenitor Nicholas Kegg. **DAVID PATRICK OWENS** Fourth great grandson of progenitor Nicholas Kegg. **DIANA LYNN OWENS** Sixth great granddaughter of progenitor Nicholas Kegg. **DYLAN OWENS** Seventh great grandson of progenitor Nicholas Kegg. **EDWARD BRENT OWENS** Seventh great grandson of progenitor Nicholas Kegg. **ELIZABETH K. OWENS** (abt 1900 -?) daughter of Harry and Mary (Kegg) Owens. **ELSIE MILDRED OWENS** [5576] (1911 – 1931) daughter of Harry and Mary (Kegg) Owens, married Albert Edward Felton with whom she was mother of (1). **HARRY OWENS** Fourth great grandson of progenitor Nicholas Kegg. **HERBERT CHARLES OWENS** [5577] (1905 – 1954) son of Harry and Mary (Kegg) Owens married twice; first to Helen Ruth Howard with whom he was father of (3). Later, he married Lillian C. Murray with whom he was father of (2). Herbert was employed by the Salvation Army of which he was a member. **HERBERT DAVID OWENS** (1926 – 1926) son of Herbert and Helen (Howard) Owens. **IVY J. OWENS** Sixth great granddaughter of progenitor Nicholas Kegg. **JACK MCCLELLAN OWENS** [5578, 5579] (1934 – 2018) son of James and Maude (Burkett) Owens, married Shirley Ann Stevenson with whom he was father of (2). **JAMES BRADLEY OWENS** Seventh great grandson of progenitor Nicholas Kegg. **JAMES WILLIAM OWENS** Fourth great grandson of progenitor Nicholas Kegg. **JOYCE ELAINE OWENS** [5580] (1941 – 2008) daughter of Clarence and Wilma (Wehrle) Owens, married Gary Albert Brown with whom she was mother of (4). Joyce held employment in various careers throughout her life including in-home health care and manufacturing; she always held the job of mother and grandmother as her highest priority. Joyce was known for her deep devotion to family, her incredible generous spirit, sharp wit and a backbone of pure steel. Throughout her life, she loved the outdoors. An avid gardener, her lawn proudly displayed years of hard work. Nothing thrilled her more than her multiplying hostas, a new peony bush or her strawberry patch being bountiful. She hunted and fished alongside her husband and children, handling a rifle or shotgun like a pro, rarely missing a shot. A devoted animal lover, she has a special fondness for dogs, especially her constant companion, a Chihuahua named Lucy. She was actively involved with her children's and grandchildren's activities. Joyce took great joy in all the accomplishments and successes of her family. **LYELL GARY OWENS** Fifth great grandson of progenitor Nicholas Kegg. **MARK OWENS** Sixth great grandson of progenitor Nicholas Kegg. **MARY AGNES OWENS** [5581] (1909 – 1987) daughter of Harry and Mary (Kegg) Owens, married Frank Joseph Udotch with whom she was mother of (3). Mary was a member of St. Michael's Catholic Church, Cary, where she was a member of the Young at Heart. She was also a member of the Cary VFW Auxiliary. **MARY MARGUERITE OWENS** Fourth great granddaughter of progenitor Nicholas Kegg. **PATRICIA OWENS** Fourth great granddaughter of progenitor Nicholas Kegg. **PAUL J. OWENS** Fifth great grandson of progenitor Nicholas Kegg. **PHYLLIS JEAN OWENS** [5581A] aka "Jeannie" (1927 – 2014) daughter of Donald and Fannie (Hoyman) Owens married twice, she was mother of (1) to her first spouse. Later, she married Harold J. Hochstein with whom she was mother of (1). **RICHARD BRYCE OWENS** Seventh great grandson of progenitor Nicholas Kegg. **ROBERT CHRIS OWENS** (1943 – 1943) son of Clarence and Wilma (Wehrle) Owens. **STEPHANIE OWENS** Seventh great granddaughter of progenitor Nicholas Kegg. **VICTORIA MARIE OWENS** [5582] (1947 – 2008) daughter of James and Victoria (Robak) Owens married Richard L. London with whom she was mother of (5).

OWENSBY

ALEX OWENSBY Seventh great grandson of progenitor Nicholas Kegg.

[5576] Johnstown Tribune Democrat (PA) Nov 12, 1931 obtained by D. Sue Dible [5577] Tribune-Democrat (PA) July 14, 1954 [5578] p.2 - Bedford Gazette (PA) Nov 1, 1955 [5579] Cumberland Times-News (MD) Aug 4, 2018 [5580] Leon Journal-Reporter (IA) Jan 9, 2008, transcribed by Sharon R. Becker [5581] Altoona Mirror (PA) Oct 23, 1987 [5581A] Tribune Democrat (PA) Dec 24, 2014 [5582] Tillman Funeral Home & Crematory (FL)

OYLER

BONNIE L. OYLER Fifth great granddaughter of progenitor Nicholas Kegg. **DONNA L OYLER** Fifth great granddaughter of progenitor Nicholas Kegg. **MEGAN ANN OYLER** Seventh great granddaughter of progenitor Nicholas Kegg. **NIKKI SUE ANN OYLER** (5582A) (1983 – 2002) daughter of Anthony and Patricia (Belcher) Oyler married William Frieszell with whom she was mother of (1). **PAUL EDWARD OYLER** aka "Pete" Fifth great grandson of progenitor Nicholas Kegg. **THOMAS H OYLER** Fifth great grandson of progenitor Nicholas Kegg. **TODD EDWARD OYLER** Sixth great grandson of progenitor Nicholas Kegg.

PACE

GREGORY LAWSON PACE Eighth great grandson of progenitor Nicholas Kegg.
ISAAC SAMUEL PACE Eighth great grandson of progenitor Nicholas Kegg.

PACKE

JARED PACKE Seventh great grandson of progenitor Nicholas Kegg.
TROY PACKE Seventh great grandson of progenitor Nicholas Kegg.

PAE

JESSICA PAE Sixth great granddaughter of progenitor Nicholas Kegg.
REBECCA L. PAE Sixth great granddaughter of progenitor Nicholas Kegg.

PAGALING

BOBBY PAGALING aka "Little Hawk", Seventh great grandson of progenitor Nicholas Kegg. **JOHN PAGALING** aka "Swift Horse", Seventh great grandson of progenitor Nicholas Kegg. **SAMPSON PAGALING** aka "Standing Bear", Seventh great grandson of progenitor Nicholas Kegg.

PAGE

CAMERON PAGE Seventh great grandson of progenitor Nicholas Kegg. **CHARLES H. PAGE** Fifth great grandson of progenitor Nicholas Kegg. **CLIFFORD NEWTON PAGE** aka "Butch", Sixth great grandson of progenitor Nicholas Kegg. **ELISABETH PAGE** Fifth great granddaughter of progenitor Nicholas Kegg. **JEREMIAH PAGE** Seventh great grandson of progenitor Nicholas Kegg **SHAWN AMY PAGE** (5582B) (1960 – 2016) daughter of John and Sandra (Stuckey) Page married twice, first to John Wesley Carter with whom she was mother of (1). Later, to David Leimer with whom she was mother of (2). Shawn was a homemaker and a union laborer working various jobs. She loved fishing, deer hunting (i.e. shooting squirrels), play pool and riding Harley's. Shawn loved spending time with her grandchildren and cooking for the entire family. She always told everyone, "You know you're my favorite." **SHAWNA MARIE PAGE** Seventh great granddaughter of progenitor Nicholas Kegg.

PAIGE

CATRINA MARIA PAIGE (5582C) (1979 – 2007) daughter of James and Cindy (Edwards) Paige was mother of (2). Her death was the result of a gunshot wound. **CURTIS LEE PAIGE** Seventh great grandson of progenitor Nicholas Kegg.

(5582A) p.1A - Chronicle-Tribune (IN) Jan 21, 2002 (5582B) Quad City Times (IA) Jan 27, 2016 (5582C) Fort Wayne Newspapers (IN) Aug. 29, 2007

JACQUELINE PAIGE Sixth great granddaughter of progenitor Nicholas Kegg. **JAMES PAIGE** Seventh great grandson of progenitor Nicholas Kegg. **JEREMIAH JOSEPH PAIGE** Eighth great grandson of progenitor Nicholas Kegg. **MICHAEL DEWIGHT PAIGE** Seventh great grandson of progenitor Nicholas Kegg. **PEARL JAMES PAIGE** Seventh great granddaughter of progenitor Nicholas Kegg. **SHAWN PAIGE** Seventh great grandson of progenitor Nicholas Kegg. **STEPHEN PAIGE** Seventh great grandson of progenitor Nicholas Kegg.

PAIRAN

GINA MARIE PAIRAN (5582D) (1963 – 2015) daughter of Donald and Julia (Boose) Pairan married Roger Masters with whom she was mother of (3). Gina was named Parent of the Year for 2014-2015 at Eureka College. Among other career positions, Gina was the director of the Henry Early Learning Center. She was a member and past president of the Henry American Legion Auxiliary and a member of the Henry Rotary Club and St. Peter's Lutheran Church in East Peoria. Gina enjoyed scrapbooking, reading, dancing and always wishing to help with any event for children. Her children were a large part of her life. **JOHN DOUGLAS PAIRAN** Fifth great grandson of progenitor Nicholas Kegg.

PAJEWSKI

BRANDON THOMAS PAJEWSKI Eighth great grandson of progenitor Nicholas Kegg.
DERRICK RYAN PAJEWSKI Eighth great grandson of progenitor Nicholas Kegg.
HAILEY PAJEWSKI Eighth great granddaughter of progenitor Nicholas Kegg.

PALERMO

DREW STEPHEN PALERMO Seventh great grandson of progenitor Nicholas Kegg.

PALMER

AUSTIN S. PALMER Seventh great grandson of progenitor Nicholas Kegg. **CHRISTINE LOUISE PALMER** Sixth great granddaughter of progenitor Nicholas Kegg. **FRANK RONALD PALMER** Fifth great grandson of progenitor Nicholas Kegg. **KALEB C. PALMER** Seventh great grandson of progenitor Nicholas Kegg. **LOGAN PALMER** Fifth great grandson of progenitor Nicholas Kegg. **LOGAN STEPHEN PALMER** (5583) (1994 – 2017) son of Sidney and Theresa (Karcher) Palmer truly lived a life that mattered and made an impact on everyone he met. Logan enlisted in the Navy in April 2016, completed Basic Training and received further training in US Navy Class C School in San Diego, finishing 3rd in his class. His first assignment was to the USS John S McCain (DDG-56). Petty Officer 2nd Class Palmer was one of 10 sailors lost on the warship USS John McCain after a collision with a tanker near Singapore. Palmer died a true hero, surviving the initial collision but staying in harm's way to try and help his fellow shipmates. **MADISON PALMER** Seventh great granddaughter of progenitor Nicholas Kegg. **ROBERT BRIAN PALMER** Sixth great grandson of progenitor Nicholas Kegg. **SARI PALMER** Seventh great granddaughter of progenitor Nicholas Kegg. **SIDNEY L. PALMER** Sixth great grandson of progenitor Nicholas Kegg. **TRESCIA LEA PALMER** Sixth great granddaughter of progenitor Nicholas Kegg. **WILLIAM ROBERT PALMER** (5584) (1949 – 2014) aka "Billy", son of Francis and Betty (Sturtz) Palmer, married Deborah Jean Meekins. William was a retired electrician for the Elizabeth River Tunnel Commission.

(5582D) Peoria Journal Star (IL) Nov. 13, 2015, contributed by D. Sue Dible (5583) Herald & Review (IL) Sep 10, 2017, obtained by D. Sue Dible

PALMISANO

ALICE KERR PALMISANO Fifth great granddaughter of progenitor Nicholas Kegg.
ANNA CARMELA PALMISANO Fifth great granddaughter of progenitor Nicholas Kegg.

PANCHAL

MARIE LEANDRA LOUISE PANCHAL [5585] (1993 – 1993) daughter of Rajendra and Marie (Kegg) Panchal.

PANKA

GUS PANKA Sixth great grandson of progenitor Nicholas Kegg.
JOSLYN PANKA Sixth great granddaughter of progenitor Nicholas Kegg.
ROSE PANKA Sixth great granddaughter of progenitor Nicholas Kegg.

PARENT

ADA MARGARET PARENT [5586] (1874 – 1955) daughter of Hiram and Emeline (Kegg) Parent married twice; first to Louis A. Boissenet with whom she was mother of (4). Later, she married William Loranzo Dinius. **ELWOOD W. PARENT** [5587] (1913 – 2000) son of Hiram and Christine (Balzke) Parent was a Navy veteran of World War II, serving as a corpsman. Elwood had been employed as a postal clerk. He was a member of the Southland Masonic Lodge No. 256 F. & A.M., the Lakeland York Rite Bodies, where he was past commander and past high priest. In addition, he was a member of the Scottish Rite and Egypt Shrine Temple, Tampa, and the Order of Easter Star and the Amaranth. **EMMA PARENT** [5588, 5589] (1866 – 1954) daughter of Hiram and Emeline (Kegg) Parent married three times; first to Alvin Etheridge Baer with whom she was mother of (4). She married Frederick Eugene Dyer and later, married Martin D. Stroyer. **GRACE EDITH PARENT** [5590] (1879 – 1963) daughter of William and Edna (Firestine) Parent, married Frederick Henry Fell. Grace was a member of Lakeside Aid Society. **HELEN M. PARENT** [5591] (1914 – 2000) daughter of Hiram and Christine (Balzke) Parent, married Richard E. Ryder with whom she was mother of (3). Helen was a homemaker and a member of Star of the East Chapter 514 Order of Eastern Star. **HIRAM PARENT** [5592] (1881 – 1964) son of William and Edna (Firestine) Parent, married Christine H. Balzke with whom he was father of (2). Hiram was a retired meat cutter and a member of St. John's United Church of Christ; **KITTIE GRACE PARENT** [5593] (1863 – 1941) daughter of Hiram and Emeline (Kegg) Parent, married Alfred Lawson Garver with whom she was mother of (3). Kitty was a member of West Creighton Avenue Christian church. **MARY J. PARENT** [5594] (1859 – 1910) daughter of Hiram and Emeline (Kegg) Parent, married Johnson Steele with whom she was mother of (6). Mary was a member of the Methodist Episcopal Church and of Ben Hur court No. 15. **WILLIAM PARENT** [5595] (1857 – 1907) son of Hiram and Emeline (Kegg) Parent, married Edna Firestine with whom he was father of (2). William was a veteran of the Spanish-American war and was in the employ of the Moellering Construction Company. He was also a member of the Maccabees tent No 54.

PARISH

MATTHEW OSYRUS PARISH Ninth great grandson of progenitor Nicholas Kegg.

[5584] Sturtevant Funeral Home & Crematory, VA [5585] Modesto Bee (CA) June 2, 1993 [5586] The Fort Wayne Journal Gazette (IN) Aug 25, 1909 [5587] p.B4 - Ledger (FL) March 8, 2000 [5588] p.10 - Fort Wayne Journal Gazette July 19, 1911 [5589] p.10 - Fort Wayne News (IN) Nov. 26, 1914 [5590] Fort Wayne Journal Gazette (IN) June 26, 1963, obtained by D. Sue Dible [5591] p.6B - News-Sentinel (IN) June 29, 2000 [5592] Fort Wayne Journal Gazette (IN) May 14, 1964, obtained by D. Sue Dible [5593] p.6 - Journal Gazette, (IN) Oct 7, 1941 [5594] p.3 - Fort Wayne Journal Gazette Feb 20,1910 obtained by D. Sue Dible [5595] p.5 - Fort Wayne Journal Gazette Sept 7, 1907

PARKER

EMILY NICHOLE PARKER Sixth great granddaughter of progenitor Nicholas Kegg. **LINDSEY PARKER** Seventh great granddaughter of progenitor Nicholas Kegg. **MARIAH LOUE PARKER** Sixth great granddaughter of progenitor Nicholas Kegg. **TANNER PARKER** Seventh great grandson of progenitor Nicholas Kegg. **TYLER PARKER** Seventh great grandson of progenitor Nicholas Kegg.

PARKERSON

DANIELLE PARKERSON Seventh great granddaughter of progenitor Nicholas Kegg.
DANNY JAY PARKERSON Seventh great grandson of progenitor Nicholas Kegg.

PARKS

ARTHUR GEORGE PARKS [5596] (1923 – 2012) son of Arthur and Hazel (Kegg) Parks, married Robbie J. Cluck with whom he was father of (1). Later, he married Linda Carole Mueller. Arthur tried his hand in two service-oriented careers. He provided our country his devoted service of protection in the United States Air Force for over 13 years, nearly 3 of which were served in a foreign country. Arthur also served as a law enforcement official with the United States Capital Police, in Washington D.C. His choice in careers proves to be evidence of the strong moral character he possessed to serve others. **BILLIE JO PARKS** [5597] (1969 – 2016) daughter of progenitor Robert and Margie (Rusk) Parks was the mother of (3). Raised in Louisiana, she found herself in Idaho and this is where her story really began. She met a wonderful man who had a beautiful daughter and together they became a great family. Billie Jo made great friends while in Idaho. **BRYCE PARKS** Seventh great grandson of progenitor Nicholas Kegg. **DEBRA PARKS** [5598] (1963 – 2019) aka "Debbie" daughter of Robert and Margie (Rusk) Parks was mother of (1) loved nature in all its forms and spent her time camping, tending to her plants, and watching the hummingbirds on her porch with her roommate and best friend Linda. She made sure to have 'grandma night' once a week with her grandchildren and enjoyed visiting with friends and planning trips with her family. Debra was an advocate for children in need and worked as a cafeteria manager at Round Rock Independent School District. **JAMES DARYL PARKS** Fifth great grandson of progenitor Nicholas Kegg. **JUSTIN TYLER PARKS** Sixth great grandson of progenitor Nicholas Kegg. **MARJORIE ALICE PARKS** (1928 – 1932) daughter of Arthur and Hazel (Kegg) Parks. **RIKKI PARKS** (1995 – 1995) son of Rikki and Traci (Wolford) Parks. **RIKKI ALAN PARKS** Fifth great grandson of progenitor Nicholas Kegg. **ROBERT ARTHUR PARKS** aka "Bob" (1944 – 2013) son of Arthur and Robbie (Cluck) Parks married Janet Marie Abent with whom he was father of (1). Later, he married Margie Ann Rusk with whom he was father of (4). Just like his father Bob provided our country his devoted service of protection in the United States Air Force. **ROBERT EMORY PARKS** [5598A] (1935 – 1993) son of Arthur and Hazel (Kegg) Parks married twice; first to Anna Belle Earp with whom he was father of (6). Robert joined what became the U.S. Postal Service as a mail carrier in Silver Spring. Later, he carried mail out of the Brookeville station, then returned to Silver Spring as a mechanic in the district's motor vehicle maintenance office, where he worked until retiring. **ROBERT RYAN PARKS** Fifth great grandson of progenitor Nicholas Kegg. **ROBIN PARKS** Sixth great granddaughter of progenitor Nicholas Kegg. **SHARON PARKS** Fifth great granddaughter of progenitor Nicholas Kegg. **TARAH PARKS** Seventh great granddaughter of progenitor Nicholas Kegg. **TERESA LYNNE PARKS** Sixth great granddaughter of progenitor Nicholas Kegg. **TIFFANY PARKS** Seventh great granddaughter of progenitor Nicholas Kegg. **TIMOTHY PARKS** [5598B] (1960 – 2019) son of Robert and Anna (Earp) Parks married twice; first to Tammy S. Stotelmyer with whom he was father of (1).

[5596] Ramsey Funeral Home, Georgetown, TX [5597] Flahiff Funeral Home & Crematory (ID) obtained by D. Sue Dible [5598] Beck Funeral and Cremations (TX) [5598A] Washington Post (DC) Dec 28, 1993 [5598B] Herald Mail (Hagerstown, MD) Feb 2, 2019

Later, he married Tawnie Sue Socks. Tim was a born-again Christian. He loved Harley-Davidson and being around family. He had been employed as a director from a number of logistic services. He was well versed on a number of topics making him a wonderful conversationalist. Tim always had a way to make people feel comfortable and made them laugh. He never met a stranger. His outgoing personality and sense of humor helped make him one of a kind.

TIMOTHY PARKS Sixth great grandson of progenitor Nicholas Kegg.
TIMOTHY PARKS Seventh great grandson of progenitor Nicholas Kegg.
TROY PARKS Sixth great grandson of progenitor Nicholas Kegg.
WILLIAM ARTHUR PARKS Fifth great grandson of progenitor Nicholas Kegg.

PARRISH

CHARLENE LORAINE PARRISH Fifth great granddaughter of progenitor Nicholas Kegg.
MARLANA PARRISH Seventh great granddaughter of progenitor Nicholas Kegg.
MICHAEL PARRISH Seventh great grandson of progenitor Nicholas Kegg.
ROBERT R. PARRISH Fifth great grandson of progenitor Nicholas Kegg.

PARSLEY

HOLLY JEANNE PARSLEY Seventh great granddaughter of progenitor Nicholas Kegg.
KAYO SCOTT PARSLEY Seventh great grandson of progenitor Nicholas Kegg.

PARSONS

DAVID W. PARSONS Seventh great grandson of progenitor Nicholas Kegg.
LACIE PARSONS Sixth great granddaughter of progenitor Nicholas Kegg.
WHITNIE PARSONS Sixth great granddaughter of progenitor Nicholas Kegg.

PASCUZZI

GINA NICOLE PASCUZZI Eighth great granddaughter of progenitor Nicholas Kegg.
ISABEL ROSE PASCUZZI Ninth great granddaughter of progenitor Nicholas Kegg.
TONY PASCUZZI Eighth great grandson of progenitor Nicholas Kegg.
VINCENT ANTHONY PASCUZZI Ninth great granddaughter of progenitor Nicholas Kegg.

PATE

LANDON PATE Seventh great grandson of progenitor Nicholas Kegg.
PRESTON PATE Seventh great grandson of progenitor Nicholas Kegg.

PATTERSON

CHRISTINE JOANNE PATTERSON aka "Christi" Sixth great granddaughter of progenitor Nicholas Kegg.
JAMES CAGG PATTERSON Fifth great grandson of progenitor Nicholas Kegg.
GRANT PATTERSON Seventh great grandson of progenitor Nicholas Kegg.
MARCUS PATTERSON Seventh great grandson of progenitor Nicholas Kegg.
MARK ALLAN PATTERSON Sixth great grandson of progenitor Nicholas Kegg.
RONALD VERNON PATTERSON Fifth great grandson of progenitor Nicholas Kegg.
SCOTT ANDREW PATTERSON Sixth great grandson of progenitor Nicholas Kegg.

PATTON

ADRIEN DWAYNE PATTON Seventh great grandson of progenitor Nicholas Kegg.
CARMEN LOUISE PATTON Seventh great granddaughter of progenitor Nicholas Kegg.
FELECIA ANN PATTON Seventh great granddaughter of progenitor Nicholas Kegg.
GABRIELLE KAYLENE PATTON Eighth great granddaughter of progenitor Nicholas Kegg.
JAMAINE DEWIGHT PATTON Seventh great grandson of progenitor Nicholas Kegg.
KE'ANNA ASHA-ROLINE PATTON Eighth great granddaughter of progenitor Nicholas Kegg.
LOUIS OT PATTON Seventh great grandson of progenitor Nicholas Kegg.
LYDIA RAYNE PATTON Seventh great granddaughter of progenitor Nicholas Kegg.
MICHELLE LEE PATTON Seventh great granddaughter of progenitor Nicholas Kegg.

PAVELKA

ADAM PAVELKA Sixth great grandson of progenitor Nicholas Kegg. **MARY PAVELKA** Fifth great granddaughter of progenitor Nicholas Kegg. **MICHELLE PAVELKA** Sixth great granddaughter of progenitor Nicholas Kegg. **ROSALYN PAVELKA** Fifth great granddaughter of progenitor Nicholas Kegg. **SARA CHRISTINE PAVELKA** Sixth great granddaughter of progenitor Nicholas Kegg. **STANLEY PAVELKA** Fifth great grandson of progenitor Nicholas Kegg. **SYLVIA FRANCIS PAVELKA** Fifth great granddaughter of progenitor Nicholas Kegg.

PAVLICK

CONNIE PAVLICK Fifth great granddaughter of progenitor Nicholas Kegg.
GEORGE HITE PAVLICK Fifth great grandson of progenitor Nicholas Kegg.
KERRI S. PAVLICK Sixth great granddaughter of progenitor Nicholas Kegg.
KIMBERLY C. PAVLICK Sixth great granddaughter of progenitor Nicholas Kegg.
LUKE PAVLICK Seventh great grandson of progenitor Nicholas Kegg.
REGAN PAVLICK Seventh great granddaughter of progenitor Nicholas Kegg.

PAWLAK

KASSIE DAYE PAWLAK Sixth great granddaughter of progenitor Nicholas Kegg.
KATELY BETH PAWLAK Sixth great granddaughter of progenitor Nicholas Kegg.
MICHAH EDWIN PAWLAK Sixth great grandson of progenitor Nicholas Kegg.
THOMAS ANDREW PAWLAK Sixth great grandson of progenitor Nicholas Kegg.

PEACOCK

ABIGAIL L. PEACOCK Eighth great granddaughter of progenitor Nicholas Kegg.
AMY E. PEACOCK Eighth great granddaughter of progenitor Nicholas Kegg.
MICHAEL EVAN PEACOCK Eighth great grandson of progenitor Nicholas Kegg.

PEARCE

MATTHEW AARON PEARCE Sixth great grandson of progenitor Nicholas Kegg.

PEARSON

CHRISTINA MARIE PEARSON aka "Christie", Sixth great granddaughter of progenitor Nicholas Kegg. **JOHN ERIC PEARSON** Sixth great grandson of progenitor Nicholas Kegg.

PEASE

JASON DAVID PEASE Sixth great grandson of progenitor Nicholas Kegg.

PEDERSEN

CHRISTIAN PEDERSEN Seventh great grandson of progenitor Nicholas Kegg.
ERIKA PEDERSEN Seventh great granddaughter of progenitor Nicholas Kegg.

PEDLEY

BARBARA PEDLEY Fifth great granddaughter of progenitor Nicholas Kegg.
BENJAMIN WILLIAM PEDLEY Sixth great grandson of progenitor Nicholas Kegg.
BRETT MEREDITH PEDLEY Sixth great grandson of progenitor Nicholas Kegg.
CRAIG MICHAEL PEDLEY Fifth great grandson of progenitor Nicholas Kegg.
DEBRA ANN PEDLEY Fifth great granddaughter of progenitor Nicholas Kegg.
DEVEREUX WILLIAM PEDLEY (1923 – 1989) son of Lionel and Rela (Kegg) Pedley married Patricia Pettey with whom he was father of (3).
DIANE BLAISE PEDLEY Fifth great granddaughter of progenitor Nicholas Kegg.
DOUGLAS ANTHONY PEDLEY Fifth great grandson of progenitor Nicholas Kegg.
GLENN P. PEDLEY Fifth great grandson of progenitor Nicholas Kegg.
HOLLY A. PEDLEY (1963 – 1967) daughter of Philip and Dixie (Morgan) Pedley.
MARK R. PEDLEY Fifth great grandson of progenitor Nicholas Kegg.
MARTIN BEDFORD PEDLEY Fifth great grandson of progenitor Nicholas Kegg.
MATTHEW B. PEDLEY Sixth great grandson of progenitor Nicholas Kegg.
PAULA PEDLEY (1956 – 1960) Fifth great granddaughter of progenitor Nicholas Kegg.
PHILIP BARLOWMASSICKS PEDLEY (1917 – 2011) son of Lionel and Rela (Kegg) Pedley, married Dixie Lee Morgan with whom he was father of (5). Philip was a WWII Veteran. He owned and operated Pedley Manufacturing of Safety-Fall protection Nets.
STANHOPE ELLSWORTH PEDLEY (1921 – 2000) son of Lionel and Rela (Kegg) Pedley, married Mary D. Ennes with whom he was father of (3).
VICTORIA ANN PEDLEY Fifth great granddaughter of progenitor Nicholas Kegg.

PEE

DANETTE GWEN PEE aka "Peewee" Sixth great granddaughter of progenitor Nicholas Kegg.
DEANA GWYNEE PEE Sixth great granddaughter of progenitor Nicholas Kegg.
DEBRA A. PEE Sixth great granddaughter of progenitor Nicholas Kegg.
DENISE L. PEE Sixth great granddaughter of progenitor Nicholas Kegg.
SANDRA YVONNE PEE Sixth great granddaughter of progenitor Nicholas Kegg.

PEIL

LORI ANN PEIL Sixth great granddaughter of progenitor Nicholas Kegg.
SUSANNE GAIL PEIL Sixth great granddaughter of progenitor Nicholas Kegg.

PENA

BETHANY MARIE PENA Fourth great granddaughter of progenitor Nicholas Kegg.
JOSHUA C. PENA Fourth great grandson of progenitor Nicholas Kegg.

PENDLETON

JUSTIN BRADY PENDLETON Seventh great grandson of progenitor Nicholas Kegg.

PENMAN

CAITLIN PENMAN Seventh great granddaughter of progenitor Nicholas Kegg. **CHELSEA LYNN PENMAN** Seventh great granddaughter of progenitor Nicholas Kegg. **HEATHER PENMAN**, aka "Mindy", Seventh great granddaughter of progenitor Nicholas Kegg. **HUNTER PENMAN** Eighth great grandson of progenitor Nicholas Kegg. **JAMES S. PENMAN** aka "Jimmy", Sixth great grandson of progenitor Nicholas Kegg. **JONATHAN PENMAN** Seventh great grandson of progenitor Nicholas Kegg. **JONATHAN R. PENMAN** Sixth great grandson of progenitor Nicholas Kegg. **LARRY ALLEN PENMAN** Sixth great grandson of progenitor Nicholas Kegg. **MEGAN PENMAN** Seventh great granddaughter of progenitor Nicholas Kegg. **MICHAEL JOSEPH PENMAN** Sixth great grandson of progenitor Nicholas Kegg. **ROBERT E. PENMAN** Sixth great grandson of progenitor Nicholas Kegg. **ROBERT PENMAN III** Seventh great grandson of progenitor Nicholas Kegg. **ROBERT PENMAN IV** Eighth great grandson of progenitor Nicholas Kegg. **TARA PENMAN** Seventh great granddaughter of progenitor Nicholas Kegg.

PENNEL

ARCHIE JACKSON PENNEL [5599] (1906 – 2002) aka "Jack", son of Simon and Bertha (Weaverling) Pennel, married Mildred Rawlings with whom he was father of (4). Jack was a farmer, school bus driver and former manager of the Rainsburg General Store. **CHARLENE L. PENNEL** Fifth great granddaughter of progenitor Nicholas Kegg. **DELORES PENNEL** [5599A] (1931 – 2022) daughter of Archie and Mildred (Rawlings) Pennel married Archie J. Shoemaker. Delores served as Past Matron of the Saxton Chapter No. 161 Order of the Eastern Star. She enjoyed crafting. **DUANE F. PENNEL** aka "Butch" Fifth great grandson of progenitor Nicholas Kegg. **FRANCIS PENNEL** [5600] (1930 – 1954) son of Archie and Mildred (Rawlings) Pennel. **HELEN VIRGINIA PENNEL** [5601] (1918 – 1982) daughter of Simon and Bertha (Weaverling) Pennel, married Carl E. Williams with whom she was mother of (5). Helen was a member of the Rainsburg Methodist Church, and the P. O. of A. of Charlesville. **JAMES WILLIAM PENNEL** [5602] (1928 – 2009) aka "Jim", son of Archie and Mildred (Rawlings) Pennel, married Nancy A. Seigh with whom she was mother of (4). Jim served in the United States Navy during the Korean Conflict. He drove truck for most of his life working for Kelly Springfield until his retirement. He enjoyed working search word puzzles, feeding and watching the birds and squirrels around his home and loved the nature around him. He also enjoyed snow blowing and mowing his lawn. Jim enjoyed outdoor chores. **JAMIE LYNN PENNEL** [5603] (1978 – 1979) daughter of Duane and Karen (Mock) Pennel. **KAREN M. PENNEL** Fifth great granddaughter of progenitor Nicholas Kegg. **KATHLEEN MAE PENNEL** [5603A] (1927 – 2019) daughter of Archie and Mildred (Rawlings) Pennel married T. Allen Mearkle with whom she was mother of (3). Kathleen enjoyed bowling and pinochle. **LAVERNE PENNEL** [5604] (1904 – 1997) daughter of Simon and Bertha (Weaverling) Pennel, married John Elvin Perdew with whom she was mother of (4). **LILLIAN BELL PENNEL** [5605] (1870 – 1928) daughter of Andrew and Sophia (Stuckey) Pennell. **MARGARET LOUISE PENNEL** [5606] (1908 – 1981) daughter of Simon and Bertha (Weaverling) Pennel, married Curtis Riley Morgart with whom she was mother of (3). Margaret was a member of the Yeager Lutheran Church Women, and the P.O. of A. of Friends Cove. **MILDRED LENORE PENNEL** [5607] (1900 – 1940) daughter of Simon and Bertha

---

[5599] Bedford Inquirer (PA) Feb 8, 2002, obtained by Bob Rose [5599A] Bedford Gazette (PA) Oct 18, 2022 [5600] Bedford Gazette (PA) Sept 13, 1954 [5601] Bedford County Genealogical Society obituary clipping obtained by D. Sue Dible [5602] Akers Funeral Home Bedford County, PA [5603] Bedford County Genealogical Society obituary clipping obtained by D. Sue Dible [5603A] Bedford Gazette (PA) May 7, 2019 contributed by Bob Rose [5604] Bedford Gazette (PA) Mar 15, 1997 [5605] Bedford Gazette (PA) April 20, 1928 [5606] PA newspaper obituary clipping obtained by Jim Boor transcribed by Bob Longbottom [5607] Bedford County, PA newspaper obituary clipping obtained and transcribed by Bob Rose

(Weaverling) Pennel, married Walter Franklin Koontz with whom she was mother of (9). Mildred was a member of the Reformed church and took an active interest in church and community affairs. **SHELLEY A. PENNEL** Fifth great granddaughter of progenitor Nicholas Kegg. **SIMON GRANT PENNEL** [5608] (1868 – 1960) son of Andrew and Sophia (Stuckey) Pennell, married Bertha May Weaverling with whom he was father of (6). **WILLIAM STANLEY PENNEL** [5609] (1901 – 1994) son of Simon and Bertha (Weaverling) Pennel, married Sophia Lucille Koontz with whom he was father of (2). William retired as an electrician at the Glenn L. Martin Co., Baltimore. He was a member of Yeagur Lutheran Church, Rainsburg, and at the time of his death the oldest resident of Friends Cove.

PENNELL

ANDREW MICHAEL PENNELL Seventh great grandson of progenitor Nicholas Kegg.
ANDREW WILGER PENNELL [5610] (1917 – 1996) son of Andrew and Mary (Wilger) Pennell, married Hazel Georgia Reed with whom he was father of (3). Andrew was an aircraft and sheet metal worker for the Civil Service. He was an Army veteran of World War II.
ANDREW WILGER PENNELL aka "Andy" 6th great grandson of progenitor Nicholas Kegg.
CLARA B. PENNELL [5611] (1867 – 1933) daughter of Andrew and Sophia (Stuckey) Pennell, married William F. James. Clara was a member of the Methodist Church and had been organist for ten years.
CLYDE WILLIAM PENNEL [5612] (1924 – 2013) son of William and Sophia (Koontz) Pennell, married Ruth T. Satterfield with whom he was father of (2). **EVELYN PENNELL** [5613] (1920 – 1991) daughter of Andrew and Mary (Wilger) Pennell, married Lester E. Arnold with whom she was mother of (2). **HOWARD REED PENNELL** (1946 – 2000) son of Andrew and Hazel (Reed) Pennell.
IDA MARY PENNELL [5614] (1866 – 1940) daughter of Andrew and Sophia (Stuckey) Pennell, married Samuel Shaffer with whom she was mother of (2). Ida was an active member of the Rainsburg Lutheran Church and of the Patriotic Order of America. **JANINE H. PENNELL** Sixth great granddaughter of progenitor Nicholas Kegg. **JESSIE JOANN PENNELL** Sixth great granddaughter of progenitor Nicholas Kegg. **JOYCE L. PENNELL** Sixth great granddaughter of progenitor Nicholas Kegg. **MARGARET VIOLA PENNELL** (1918 – 1995) daughter of Andrew and Mary (Wilger) Pennell, married William Alexander Ballantine with whom she was mother of (4). **PAMELA PENNELL** Sixth great granddaughter of progenitor Nicholas Kegg. **ROBERT NORMAN PENNELL** [5615] (1927 – 1972) son of William and Sophia (Koontz) Pennel, married Velma Ann Martin with whom he was father of (3). Robert served with the Air Force on Guam in the Pacific Theatre during World War Two. He was a fire fighter in the city of Baltimore. **SHARON L. PENNELL** Sixth great granddaughter of progenitor Nicholas Kegg. **SHERRIE MARIE PENNELL** Seventh great granddaughter of progenitor Nicholas Kegg. **THOMAS ROBERT PENNELL** Sixth great grandson of progenitor Nicholas Kegg.

PEPPLE

ASHLEY LOUISE PEPPLE Sixth great granddaughter of progenitor Nicholas Kegg. **BRENDA PEPPLE** Seventh great granddaughter of progenitor Nicholas Kegg. **BRIAN D. PEPPLE** Seventh great grandson of progenitor Nicholas Kegg. **BRITTANI NICOLE PEPPLE** Sixth great granddaughter of progenitor Nicholas Kegg. **CAROLYN L. PEPPLE** Fifth great granddaughter of progenitor Nicholas Kegg. **CHARLOTTE M. PEPPLE** Fifth great granddaughter of progenitor Nicholas Kegg. **DALE R. PEPPLE** Sixth great grandson of progenitor Nicholas Kegg. **DARRELL E. PEPPLE** [5615A] (1941 – 2014) son of S. Dale and Lena (Smith) Pepple married Janice Ickes with whom he was father of (2). Darrell retired from Bedford Valley Petroleum after putting in 26 years. He

---

[5608] Bedford County Genealogical Society obituary clipping obtained by D. Sue Dible [5609] Bedford Gazette (PA) Sep 12, 1994 [5610] Orlando Sentinel (FL) Jan 15, 1996 [5611] Bedford County Genealogical Society obituary clipping obtained by D. Sue Dible [5612] Baltimore Sun (MD) Oct. 29, 2013 [5613] The Evening Sun (Baltimore, MD) Jan 2, 1992 [5614] Altoona Mirror (PA) Aug 26, 1940 [5615] Bedford County Genealogical Society obituary clipping obtained by D. Sue Dible [5615A] Bedford Gazette (PA) Jan 16, 2014, contributed by Bob Rose

was a member of the Loyal Order of Moose, Lodge 480. Darrell loved spending time with his daughters and grandchildren, especially attending any events or sports his grandchildren were involved in. He enjoyed watching Penn State football, Pittsburgh Steeler football, NASCAR, Fox News, and politics. Darrell loved to joke and tease with everyone he knew. He had a huge heart and enjoyed doing things for others. **DONALD P. PEPPLE** [5615B] (1933 – 2019) son of S. Dale and Lena (Smith) Pepple, married Delores A. Henderson with whom he was father of (1). Don served in the United States Army as a corporal during the Korean War. Don spent his entire life working hard and was an excellent mechanic in his younger years. He owned and operated the Atlantic/Arco service station at the Bedford Interchange and along with his wife owned and operated the Western Auto Store in Bedford. Don was a man of his word, proudly served his country, and had strong convictions in life. He was a member of the Everett Masonic Lodge F &A.M. No. 524 and the Everett American Legion Post No. 8. **GLENN OTIS PEPPLE** Fifth great grandson of progenitor Nicholas Kegg. **JEANNETTE PEPPLE** Seventh great granddaughter of progenitor Nicholas Kegg. **JENNIFER PEPPLE** Seventh great granddaughter of progenitor Nicholas Kegg. **JOANN PEPPLE** [5616] (1935 – 2021) daughter of S. Dale and Lena (Smith) Pepple married Richard F. Mellott with whom she was mother of (3). Joann was an avid Pittsburgh Steelers fan who enjoyed caring for her home, gardening, flower gardening, going out to eat and going on vacation. **JOHN WILLIAM PEPPLE** [5616A] aka "Bill" (1939 – 2022) son of S. Dale and Lena (Smith) Pepple married Joyce Means with whom he was father of (2). Bill served in the 2nd Armor Division in the United States Army. He was employed as a foreman/supervisor in the receiving department at Hedstrom for over thirty years. Bill enjoyed every aspect of spending time with his family. He enjoyed being in the outdoors, hunting in Snake Spring Valley. Bill took great care of and pride in his home, vehicles and lawn. He assisted in the annual marking of Veteran's graves in the Ritchey and Hershberger cemeteries. **JOSHUA J. PEPPLE** Sixth great grandson of progenitor Nicholas Kegg. **L. MARCINE PEPPLE** [5617] (1931 – 2010) aka "Marcie", daughter of S. Dale and Lena (Smith) Pepple, married Melvin Dwight Norris with whom she was mother of (3). Marcie was a strong, independent woman who was cherished by her family. For over thirty-five years, she was an employee of Hedstrom Manufacturing where she displayed an unrivaled work ethic and dedication to her career. In her spare time, Marcine enjoyed shopping, decorating her home, working in her yard and playing with her black Pomeranian, "Ziggy." Marcie had a direct type of personality with an honest approach to life. She had a quick wit, was open and always had a listening ear. **LAVANDA PEPPLE** [5618] (1910 – 1998) daughter of David and Ida (Diehl) Pepple, married Henry J. Muller. Lavanda was a retired copy editor for a publishing company and a member of Faith United Methodist Church in Hudson. **LEWIS S. PEPPLE** Fifth great grandson of progenitor Nicholas Kegg. **LINDA PEPPLE** Sixth great granddaughter of progenitor Nicholas Kegg. **MELINDA S. PEPPLE** Fifth great granddaughter of progenitor Nicholas Kegg. **MICHELE PEPPLE** Seventh great granddaughter of progenitor Nicholas Kegg. **PAUL W. PEPPLE** Fifth great grandson of progenitor Nicholas Kegg. **RANDY F. PEPPLE** Sixth great grandson of progenitor Nicholas Kegg. **ROBERT DEAN PEPPLE** [5619] (1937 – 2009) aka "Dean", son of S. Dale and Lena (Smith) Pepple, married Betty L. McCune with whom he was father of (4). Dean served in the U.S. Army as a Private during the Korean Conflict. He retired from the PA Turnpike, prior to that, Dean and Betty owned and operated the Western Auto Store in Everett from 1971-1981 and previously he was employed at Standard Register as a carbon process operator. Dean was a member of Everett F&AM Lodge #524, Harrisburg Consistory, Shawnee Forest #167 and the American Legion Post #8. Dean enjoyed the outdoors and was an avid hunter; he was especially passionate about turkey hunting. **SHARON L. PEPPLE** Seventh great granddaughter of progenitor Nicholas Kegg. **SHELVY PEPPLE** Sixth great granddaughter of progenitor Nicholas Kegg. **TAMMIE A. PEPPLE** Seventh great granddaughter of progenitor Nicholas Kegg. **TERESA R. PEPPLE** Seventh great granddaughter of progenitor Nicholas Kegg. **THOMAS L. PEPPLE** Seventh great grandson of progenitor Nicholas Kegg

[5615B] Bedford Gazette (PA) March 28, 2019, contributed by Bob Rose [5616] Bedford Gazette (PA) Aug 4, 2021 [5616A] Bedford Gazette (PA) Dec 21, 2022 [5617] Akers Funeral Home (Bedford County, PA) [5618] Tampa Tribune (FL) May 6, 1998 [5619] Bedford County obituary/pa-roots.org/obtained and posted by Bob McKinley.

TODD A. PEPPLE (5619A) (1971 – 1993) son of Dale and Nancy (Cogan) Pepple was a helicopter dispatcher with the 247th Medical Detachment of the United States Army, stationed at Fort Irwin, CA and had received the Army Service Ribbon, the National Defense Service Medal and the M 16 Expert Badge. Todd was an Eagle Scout from Troop 53 in Salladasburg, a 1989 graduate of Jersey Shore High School and had attended Bloomsburg University. **TRACY L. PEPPLE** Seventh great grandson of progenitor Nicholas Kegg. **WILLIAM PEPPLE** Sixth great grandson of progenitor Nicholas Kegg.

PERDEW

ALAN CARR PERDEW (5619B) (1947 – 1995) son of Paul and Elma (Carr) Perdew married Janet Walters with whom he was father of (2). Alan was an employee of Zeigler Inc., Hagerstown, as a chief mechanical engineer. A veteran of the U.S. Army. **BRADLEY JOHN PERDEW** Eighth great grandson of progenitor Nicholas Kegg. **CINDY PERDEW** Seventh great granddaughter of progenitor Nicholas Kegg. **DONALD PENNELL PERDEW** (5619C) (1933 – 2000) son of John and Laverne (Pennell) Perdew, married Patricia McCahan with whom he was father of (2). Donald was a US. Army veteran who had served in Korea. He was a former member of Bedford American Legion Post 113 and Bedford VFW Post 1527. He retired from Kennametal Inc. **ELEANOR L. PERDEW** Sixth great granddaughter of progenitor Nicholas Kegg. **EUGENE MELTON PERDEW** (5619D) (1926 – 1997) son of Jacob and Mary Nina (James) Perdew married Doris Jean Adams with whom he was father of (1). Eugene served in the Navy on the Battleship Bon Homme Richard during WW II. For 37 years, he owned and operated East End Tractor Sales. **HAROLD THEODORE PERDEW** (5620) (1929- 2006) aka "Dutz", son of John and Laverne (Pennell) Perdew, married Joan E. Bowie with whom he was father of (2). Dutz worked in aerial mapping until he retired. He served in the U.S. Air Force during the Korean War. **JOHN F. PERDEW** (5621) (1907 – 1969) son of John and Nellie (Cessna) Perdew. **JOHN JAMES PERDEW** Seventh great grandson of progenitor Nicholas Kegg. **JOHN JAMES PERDEW** (5622) (1925 – 1982) son of John and Laverne (Pennell) Perdew, married Olive Jean Foor with whom he was father of (2). John was a truck driver for Continental Transportation Co. He was a U.S. Army veteran of World War II. **JOHN P. PERDEW** Fifth great grandson of progenitor Nicholas Kegg. **KAREN LYNN PERDEW** Seventh great granddaughter of progenitor Nicholas Kegg. **KATHLEEN ANN PERDEW** Eighth, great granddaughter of progenitor Nicholas Kegg. **LORI PERDEW** Seventh great granddaughter of progenitor Nicholas Kegg. **MICHELLE ASHLEY PERDEW** Sixth great granddaughter of progenitor Nicholas Kegg. **MICHELLE LEE PERDEW** Eighth great granddaughter of progenitor Nicholas Kegg. **ROBERT J. PERDEW** Seventh great grandson of progenitor Nicholas Kegg. **SANDRA L. PERDEW** Seventh great granddaughter of progenitor Nicholas Kegg. **SANDRA LYNNE PERDEW** (5623) (1959 – 1986) daughter of Donald and Patricia (McMahan) Perdew married Mr. Price with whom she was the mother of (3). Sandra was employed as a clerk at Mr. Donut. **SARA K. PERDEW** (5623A) (1916 – 1990) daughter of Jacob and Mary Nina (James) Perdew married Richard Lee Swartzwelder with whom she was mother of (2). **THOMAS AUSTIN PERDEW** (5624) (1908 – 1954) son of John and Nellie (Cessna) Perdew, married Anne Laverne Conway. Thomas was the owner and manager of the Ideal Office Supply Company. He was active in civic affairs and had served as an air raid warden during World War II. **TOM ARCHIE PERDEW** (5625, 5626) (1928 – 1989) son of James and Beatrice (Shoemaker) Perdew married Jane Louise James. Chief Master Sergeant of the United States Air Force, Tom served in WWII, Korea and Vietnam. **WILLIAM CARL PERDEW** Seventh great grandson of progenitor Nicholas Kegg.

(5619A) Bedford County Historical Society (PA) b/ 77 p. 102 obtained and contributed by D. Sue Dible (5619B) p3C-Cumberland Times News (MD) Nov 10, 1995 (5619C) p.3 - Bedford Inquirer (PA) Nov 10, 2000, contributed by Bob Rose (5619D) p.10 – Bedford Gazette (PA) Jan 8, 1997 (5620) p.B-5 The San Diego Union-Tribune (CA) Jan 24, 2006 (5621) Cumberland Evening Times Jan 23, 1969 (5622) Bedford Inquirer (PA) Dec 31, 1982 (5623) Book 69, p.97, Bedford County Historical Society obtained by D. Sue Dible (5623A) p.3 – Bedford Inquirer (PA) June 29, 1990 (5624) Cumberland Evening Times (MD) Nov 26, 1954 (5625) Bedford Gazette (PA) Dec 22, 1948 (5626) Ledger (FL) Aug. 25, 2005

PERDUE

DEBRA ROBIN PERDUE Fourth great granddaughter of progenitor Nicholas Kegg.

PERKINS

JOLEENE BERNIECE PERKINS Seventh great granddaughter of progenitor Nicholas Kegg.
KAYCEE LEI PERKINS Seventh great granddaughter of progenitor Nicholas Kegg.
SAYDEE LYNN PERKINS Seventh great granddaughter of progenitor Nicholas Kegg.

PERRIN

ABIGAIL PERRIN Eighth great granddaughter of progenitor Nicholas Kegg.
DEBRA SUSAN PERRIN Sixth great granddaughter of progenitor Nicholas Kegg.
DENISE E. PERRIN Sixth great granddaughter of progenitor Nicholas Kegg.
DIANA LYNN PERRIN Sixth great granddaughter of progenitor Nicholas Kegg.
DWIGHT WAYNE PERRIN Sixth great grandson of progenitor Nicholas Kegg.
JOSHUA DWIGHT PERRIN Seventh great grandson of progenitor Nicholas Kegg.
ROBERT WAYNE PERRIN Seventh great grandson of progenitor Nicholas Kegg.

PERRY

CAMIE PERRY Sixth great granddaughter of progenitor Nicholas Kegg. **CARLA JEAN PERRY** Seventh great granddaughter of progenitor Nicholas Kegg. **CINDY PERRY** Sixth great granddaughter of progenitor Nicholas Kegg. **CLAY PERRY** Sixth great grandson of progenitor Nicholas Kegg. **DARLA SUE PERRY** (1959 – 1963) daughter of John and Patricia (Karns) Perry. **EVAN PERRY** Seventh great grandson of progenitor Nicholas Kegg. **MACKENZIE BLAKE PERRY** Seventh great granddaughter of progenitor Nicholas Kegg. **PATRICIA LYNN PERRY**, aka "Tricia", Seventh great granddaughter of progenitor Nicholas Kegg. **PAULA RENEE PERRY** Seventh great granddaughter of progenitor Nicholas Kegg. **RYAN LEE PERRY** Seventh great grandson of progenitor Nicholas Kegg.

PETERS

ANDREW C. PETERS Seventh great grandson of progenitor Nicholas Kegg. **ARIANNA ELIZABETH PETERS** Seventh great granddaughter of progenitor Nicholas Kegg. **CAROL FAYE PETERS** Sixth great granddaughter of progenitor Nicholas Kegg. **CHARLENE YVONNE PETERS** Sixth great granddaughter of progenitor Nicholas Kegg. **CINDY SUE PETERS** Fifth great granddaughter of progenitor Nicholas Kegg. **DANIEL W. PETERS** Seventh great grandson of progenitor Nicholas Kegg. **DAVID PETERS** Sixth great grandson of progenitor Nicholas Kegg. **JACK PETERS** Seventh great grandson of progenitor Nicholas Kegg. **JEAN LOUISE PETERS** Fifth great granddaughter of progenitor Nicholas Kegg. **JENNA PETERS** Seventh great granddaughter of progenitor Nicholas Kegg. **JOANN E. PETERS** [5626A] (1924 – 2017) daughter of William and Clara (Wise) Peters married twice, first to John Orion Evans with whom she was mother of (4). Later, she married James F. Porter Jr., Joanne had a successful career in real estate. She was a talented woman with many interests. She loved gardening; played tennis but excelled at bowling and golf; was a good cook, passionate bridge player, seamstress, and an "attention to detail" hostess of wonderful parties for her many friends and family. She and her husband, Jim, traveled the world, and loved sailing "Winsome" on Long Island Sound. **JOHN PETERS** Sixth great grandson of progenitor Nicholas Kegg.

[5626A] Toledo Blade (OH) Apr. 23, 2017

KADEN PETERS Eighth great grandson of progenitor Nicholas Kegg. **KIMBERLEE PETERS** Sixth great granddaughter of progenitor Nicholas Kegg. **LIAM PETERS** Eighth great grandson of progenitor Nicholas Kegg. **LINDA ARLENE PETERS** Fifth great granddaughter of progenitor Nicholas Kegg. **MARJORIE BELLE PETERS** [5626B] (1915 – 1996) daughter of William and Clara (Wise) Peters, married Francis Wilson Sayre with whom she was mother of (5). Marjorie was a volunteer at Toledo Hospital, the American Red Cross and Flower Hospital, a member of Dendarah Court Ladies Shrine, all in Toledo, and the Wally Byam Caravan Club International. **MARK DANIEL PETERS** Sixth great grandson of progenitor Nicholas Kegg. **MATTHEW PETERS** Seventh great grandson of progenitor Nicholas Kegg. **MATTHEW THOMAS PETERS** aka "Matt", Sixth great grandson of progenitor Nicholas Kegg. **ROBERTA JEAN PETERS** [5627] (1944 – 2015) daughter of Charles and Dorothy (Scheller) Peters. **RON CHRIS PETERS** Fifth great grandson of progenitor Nicholas Kegg. **SANDRA ELAINE PETERS** Fifth great granddaughter of progenitor Nicholas Kegg. **STANLEY RICHARD PETERS** Fifth great grandson of progenitor Nicholas Kegg. **STEPHEN THOMAS PETERS**, aka "Steve", Sixth great grandson of progenitor Nicholas Kegg. **SUSAN PETERS** Sixth great granddaughter of progenitor Nicholas Kegg.

PETERSON

CHRISTY PETERSON Sixth great granddaughter of progenitor Nicholas Kegg. **GREGORY PETERSON** Sixth great grandson of progenitor Nicholas Kegg. **JENNIFER PETERSON** Sixth great granddaughter of progenitor Nicholas Kegg. **KENSLEY PETERSON** Eighth great granddaughter of progenitor Nicholas Kegg. **LORI PETERSON** Sixth great granddaughter of progenitor Nicholas Kegg. **MELISSA PETERSON** Sixth great granddaughter of progenitor Nicholas Kegg. **STEPHANIE PETERSON** aka "Nikki", Seventh great granddaughter of progenitor Nicholas Kegg. **TAMMI JANE PETERSON** Fifth great granddaughter of progenitor Nicholas Kegg. **TERRYL ROBERT PETERSON** (1958 – 1996) son of Earl and Patricia (Major) Peterson. **THOMAS CHRISTIAN PETERSON** Seventh great grandson of progenitor Nicholas Kegg. **SHANE PETERSON** Sixth great grandson of progenitor Nicholas Kegg.

PETTENGER

ZACHARY ADAM PETTENGER Sixth great grandson of progenitor Nicholas Kegg.

PETTIETTE

AARON L. PETTIETTE Sixth great grandson of progenitor Nicholas Kegg.

PETTIT

BENJAMIN FRANKLIN PETTIT Fifth great grandson of progenitor Nicholas Kegg.
PATRICK DOUGLAS PETTIT [5628] aka "Pat" (1942 – 2012) son of Benjamin and Addie (Smith) Pettit married Juanita Maxine Daniels Millard. Patrick was a Vietnam veteran having served in the Air Force.

PFAUS

ANDREW MARK PFAUS Fifth great grandson of progenitor Nicholas Kegg.
CATHERINE ANN PFAUS Fifth great granddaughter of progenitor Nicholas Kegg.
GREGORY ANDREW PFAUS Fifth great grandson of progenitor Nicholas Kegg.

[5626B] p.4 - The Tampa Tribune (FL) Feb 27, 1996 [5627] Honolulu Star-Advertiser June 16, 2015 [5628] Sun Herald (Biloxi, MS) Sep 20, 2012

MARK PFAUS Sixth great grandson of progenitor Nicholas Kegg.
SAMUEL PFAUS Sixth great grandson of progenitor Nicholas Kegg.

PFENNING

ALBERT DEWEY PFENNING [5658] (1920 – 1995) son of Clarence and Lucy (Smith) Pfenning, married Geraldine Abbie Blick with whom he was father of (2). Albert was an avid woodworker and enjoyed auctions. **ALBERTA NANCY PFENNING** Fifth great granddaughter of progenitor Nicholas Kegg. **ALFRED A. PFENNING** Fifth great grandson of progenitor Nicholas Kegg. **ANDREW GRANT PFENNING** [5659] (1989 – 1989) son of Mark and Sheila (Gibson) Pfenning. **CAROLYN PFENNING** Fifth great granddaughter of progenitor Nicholas Kegg. **CASEY L. PFENNING** Sixth great grandson of progenitor Nicholas Kegg. **CHARLES ANSON PFENNING** [5660] (1918 – 1997) son of Clarence and Lucy (Smith) Pfenning married twice; first to Mary O. Confer with whom he was father of (1). Later, he married Mary Lou (Swihart) Mireley. Charles retired from Kirsch Co.; he was a veteran of WWII. **CHRISTOPHER PFENNING** Sixth great grandson of progenitor Nicholas Kegg. **CLARENCE F. PFENNING** [5661] (1916 – 1973) son of Clarence and Lucy (Smith) Pfenning, married Juliet M. Patnaude with whom he was father of (2). Clarence owned and operated the Pfenning Dairy Bar in Howe for many years. He then bought and operated the Pfenning Standard Gasoline Station. He alsowas employed by the Montgomery Ward Furniture Department, Sturgis. **CYNTHIA PFENNING** Sixth great granddaughter of progenitor Nicholas Kegg. **DANIEL LEE PFENNING** aka "Danny", Fifth great grandson of progenitor Nicholas Kegg. **GIDEON LEE PHENNING** Seventh great grandson of progenitor Nicholas Kegg. **GREGORY LEE PFENNING** Fifth great grandson of progenitor Nicholas Kegg. **HANNAH ELIZABETH PFENNING** Sixth great granddaughter of progenitor Nicholas Kegg. **JONATHAN PFENNING** Sixth great grandson of progenitor Nicholas Kegg. **JOSIAH DANIEL PFENNING** Sixth great grandson of progenitor Nicholas Kegg. **LINDA PFENNING** Fifth great granddaughter of progenitor Nicholas Kegg. **MARGARET ANN PFENNING** [5661A] (1932 – 2015) daughter of Clarence and Lucy (Smith) Pfenning married three times; first to Ernest Norwood Draime with whom she was mother of (3). She married Sherman B. Wise with whom she was mother of (1). Later, she married Herman Seibert Freet. **MARGERY RUTH PFENNING** [5662] (1925 – 2012) daughter of Clarence and Lucy (Smith) Pfenning, married Paul F. Juday with whom she was mother of (9). **MARIAN PFENNING** [5662A] (1941 – 2005) daughter of Clarence and Lucy (Smith) Pfenning married twice, first to Gerald V. McLaughlin with whom she was mother of (3). Later, she married Robert P. Woodbury with whom she was mother of (1). Marian was a homemaker. **MARK ALLEN PFENNING** Fifth great grandson of progenitor Nicholas Kegg. **MARY LOU PFENNING** [5663] (1930 – 2008) daughter of Clarence and Lucy (Smith) Pfenning, married David Miller with whom she was mother of (5). **PAUL ARNOLD PFENNING** [5664] (1936 – 2020) son of Clarence and Lucy (Smith) Pfenning married Annette R. Lassus with whom he was father of (3). Paul served his country honorably in the United States Navy. He was a hardworking man, and a devoted civil servant. Paul owned and operated The Toggery Cleaners in Ligonier with his wife, Annette for nearly 40 years, was a police officer for ten years, and retired from the Ligonier Fire Department as Fire Chief. Paul attended Brighton Chapel for over 30 years, enjoyed fishing, and more than anything, he enjoyed his grandchildren and great-grandchildren. **RICHARD C. PFENNING** [5665] (1923 – 2003) aka "Dick", son of Clarence and Lucy (Smith) Pfenning, married Florence M. Ledyard with whom he was father of (3). Dick was a U.S. Army veteran of World War II. He was an employee of Sturgis Iron & Metal for 17 years before his retirement. **RONALD CAMERON PFENNING** Fifth great grandson of progenitor Nicholas Kegg. **SCARLETT JEAN PFENNING** Seventh great grand - daughter of progenitor Nicholas Kegg. **STEVEN CARL PFENNING** Fifth great grandson of progenitor Nicholas Kegg.

[5658] p.2B - Ocala Star-Banner (FL) April 3, 1995 [5659] gen.nobleco.lib.in.us/Obituaries [5660] p.4A - The News-Sentinel (Fort Wayne, IN) July 15, 1997 [5661] p.27 Elkhart Truth (IN) May 31, 1973, obtained by D. Sue Dible [5661A] Stemm-Lawson-Peterson Funeral Home (IN) [5662] Citrus County Chronicle (FL) May 10, 2012 [5662A] p.A6 - The Elkhart Truth (IN) Sept 28, 2005 [5663] The Tennessean (TN) Mar. 27, 2008 [5664] Yeager Funeral Home (Ligonier, IN)

TERESA MARIE PFENNING Fifth great granddaughter of progenitor Nicholas Kegg.
TIMOTHY ARRINGTON PFENNING Fifth great grandson of progenitor Nicholas Kegg.

PFLEIDERER

CAROLE ELIZABETH PFLEIDERER Fifth great granddaughter of progenitor Nicholas Kegg.
GARY LEE PFLEIDERER [5666] (1942 – 2001) son of Carl and Margaret (Hershiser) Pfleiderer married Beverly Donovan.

PFUND

GABY PFUND Seventh great granddaughter of progenitor Nicholas Kegg.
ZACHARY PFUND Seventh great grandson of progenitor Nicholas Kegg.

PHALEN

LISA A. PHALEN [5666A] (1963 – 2003) daughter of Richard and Suzanne (Riggs) Phalen married twice; first to Bruce B. Berkebile with whom she was mother of (2). Later, she married James V. Lannen with whom she was mother of (1). Lisa served in the U.S. Army. **PATRICK J. PHALEN** Sixth great grandson of progenitor Nicholas Kegg. **SHELLY PHALEN** Sixth great granddaughter of progenitor Nicholas Kegg. **TRISHA PHALEN** Sixth great granddaughter of progenitor Nicholas Kegg.

PHENICIE

BRUCE PHENICIE Seventh great grandson of progenitor Nicholas Kegg. **ELLA PHENICIE** Ninth great granddaughter of progenitor Nicholas Kegg. **JAMES PHENICIE** Seventh great grandson of progenitor Nicholas Kegg. **MICHAEL PHENICIE** Seventh great grandson of progenitor Nicholas Kegg. **NATHAN CHRISTOPHER PHENICIE** Eighth great grandson of progenitor Nicholas Kegg. **OWEN PHENICIE** Ninth great grandson of progenitor Nicholas Kegg. **STEPHEN CHRISTOPHER PHENICIE** Eighth great grandson of progenitor Nicholas Kegg. **YVONNE MARIE PHENICIE** Seventh great granddaughter of progenitor Nicholas Kegg.

PHILLIP

SCOTT C. PHILLIP Sixth great grandson of progenitor Nicholas Kegg. **THOMAS L. PHILLIP** Sixth great grandson of progenitor Nicholas Kegg. **WENDY NICOLE PHILLIP** Seventh great granddaughter of progenitor Nicholas Kegg. **WILLIAM MICHAEL PHILLIP** Sixth great grandson of progenitor Nicholas Kegg.

PHILLIPPO

KELLY L. PHILLIPPO Fifth great granddaughter of progenitor Nicholas Kegg.

PHILLIPS

CASSANDRA PHILLIPS Sixth great granddaughter of progenitor Nicholas Kegg. **CHRISTOPHER LEE PHILLIPS** Sixth great grandson of progenitor Nicholas Kegg. **DIANNA PHILLIPS** Sixth great granddaughter of progenitor Nicholas Kegg. **LACEY RAE PHILLIPS** Seventh great granddaughter of progenitor Nicholas Kegg. **MARIA PHILLIPS** Seventh great granddaughter of progenitor Nicholas Kegg.

[5665] Hackman Family Funeral Homes (Sturgis, MI) [5666] p.4B The Miami Herald (FL) Sept 3, 2001 [5666A] La Salle County Genealogy Guild obituary collection

MATTHEW PHILLIPS Seventh great grandson of progenitor Nicholas Kegg.
MELISSA PHILLIPS Seventh great granddaughter of progenitor Nicholas Kegg.
NATHAN PHILLIPS Seventh great grandson of progenitor Nicholas Kegg.
TARA RAE PHILLIPS Seventh great granddaughter of progenitor Nicholas Kegg.

PHIPPS

JOHN LOUIS PHIPPS Seventh great grandson of progenitor Nicholas Kegg.
JONI LYNELLE PHIPPS Sixth great granddaughter of progenitor Nicholas Kegg.
OBED PAUL PHIPPS Sixth great grandson of progenitor Nicholas Kegg.

PIATT

BRENT A. PIATT Seventh great grandson of progenitor Nicholas Kegg.
BROOKE PIAT Seventh great granddaughter of progenitor Nicholas Kegg.

PICANO

MATTHEW P. PICANO Sixth great grandson of progenitor Nicholas Kegg.

PICCO

JADEN P. PICCO Ninth great granddaughter of progenitor Nicholas Kegg.
LILIANA E. PICCO Ninth great granddaughter of progenitor Nicholas Kegg.
MACIE LEANN PICCO (2008 – 2009) daughter of Shawn and Larissa (Ward) Picco.

PICK

JANE PICK Fifth great granddaughter of progenitor Nicholas Kegg.
MILLARD E. PICK Fifth great grandson of progenitor Nicholas Kegg.

PICKENS

AMBER NICOLE PICKENS Sixth great granddaughter of progenitor Nicholas Kegg.
CAITLIN MORNINGSTAR PICKENS Fifth great granddaughter of progenitor Nicholas Kegg.
CONNER PICKENS Sixth great grandson of progenitor Nicholas Kegg.
KARIEL LYANN PICKENS Fifth great granddaughter of progenitor Nicholas Kegg.
MAXWELL DANE PICKENS Fifth great grandson of progenitor Nicholas Kegg.
ZACHARY COLE PICKENS Fifth great grandson of progenitor Nicholas Kegg.

PIEL

DANIEL NATHAN PIEL Sixth great grandson of progenitor Nicholas Kegg.
SETH ADAM PIEL Sixth great grandson of progenitor Nicholas Kegg.

PIGGOTT

COURTNEY MICHELLE PIGGOTT Seventh great granddaughter of progenitor Nicholas Kegg.
THOMAS SHAUN PIGGOTT Seventh great grandson of progenitor Nicholas Kegg.

PILGRIM

BROOKLYN GRACE PILGRIM Seventh great granddaughter of progenitor Nicholas Kegg.

PILKINGTON

BLAIRE RACHEL PILKINGTON Eighth great granddaughter of progenitor Nicholas Kegg
CAITLIN MACEY PILKINGTON Eighth great granddaughter of progenitor Nicholas Kegg
JAY BANKS KURTZ PILKINGTON Seventh great grandson of progenitor Nicholas Kegg.
SCOTT AARON PILKINGTON Seventh great grandson of progenitor Nicholas Kegg.

PILLEY

DESMOND PILLEY Eighth great grandson of progenitor Nicholas Kegg. **JEREMY PILLEY** Seventh great grandson of progenitor Nicholas Kegg. **SKYLIN PILLEY** Eighth great granddaughter of progenitor Nicholas Kegg. **TRAVIS PILLEY** Seventh great grandson of progenitor Nicholas Kegg.

PINE

GRANITE PINE Eighth great grandson of progenitor Nicholas Kegg. **JASON LEE PINE** Seventh great grandson of progenitor Nicholas Kegg. **JAXON PINE** Eighth great grandson of progenitor Nicholas Kegg. **JENNIFER LORRAINE PINE** [5666B] (1981 – 1999) daughter of George and Pamela (Leese) Pine. Jennifer was a member of the chorus and FHA. She was planning to enter the U.S. Air Force after graduation. She was a part-time employee of White Tail Ski Resort. **LOGAN PINE** Eighth great grandson of progenitor Nicholas Kegg.

PION

AVERY PION Eighth great granddaughter of progenitor Nicholas Kegg.
MAGGIE PION Eighth great granddaughter of progenitor Nicholas Kegg.

PIRIE

ARLENE BERNICE PIRIE [5667] (1907 – 2003) daughter of William and Maude (Knouf) Pirie, married Carsten Taylor Johnsten with whom she was mother of (2). Arlene graduated with an Elementary Education degree from the University of Northern Iowa, Cedar Falls, Iowa. She taught school at Radcliffe, Iowa. **CHRISTINE ELIZABETH PIRIE** Fourth great granddaughter of progenitor Nicholas Kegg. **GRACE FLORENCE PIRIE** [5668] (1903 – 1990) daughter of William and Maude (Knouf) Pirie, married Forrest L. Allen. Grace graduated from Coe College in 1923, with a B.A. degree. She was a music teacher for seven years. **JAMES WILLIAM PIRIE** (1912 – 1988) son of William and Maude (Knouf) Pirie, married Frances Jessina with whom he was father of (3). **LESTA JEAN PIRIE** (1909 – 1977) daughter of William and Maude (Knouf) Pirie, married C. Gerald Darsee. **MARSHA ANN PIRIE** 4th great granddaughter of progenitor Nicholas Kegg. **WILLIAM J. PIRIE** Fourth great grandson of progenitor Nicholas Kegg.

PISCIOTTA

ASHLEI DIANNE PISCIOTTA Eighth great granddaughter of progenitor Nicholas Kegg.
FALLON PISCIOTTA Ninth great granddaughter of progenitor Nicholas Kegg.

[5666B] genealogybuff.com, obtained by D. Sue Dible [5667] Mitchell County Press-News (Iowa) Oct 22, 2003/iagenweb.org [5668] p.2B Cedar Rapids Gazette (IA) Sep 27, 1990

PITTMAN

ANDREW RICHARD PITTMAN Eighth great grandson of progenitor Nicholas Kegg. **DAKOTA PITTMAN** Seventh great grandson of progenitor Nicholas Kegg. **DULENE LOUISE PITTMAN** Sixth great granddaughter of progenitor Nicholas Kegg. **ELLEN PITTMAN** Sixth great granddaughter of progenitor Nicholas Kegg. **EMMA LOU PITTMAN** Seventh great granddaughter of progenitor Nicholas Kegg. **JAMES PITTMAN** Eighth great grandson of progenitor Nicholas Kegg. **SUMMER PITTMAN** Eighth great granddaughter of progenitor Nicholas Kegg.

PIZIO

ALYSSA N. PIZIO Seventh great granddaughter of progenitor Nicholas Kegg.
JUSTIN D. PIZIO Seventh great grandson of progenitor Nicholas Kegg.

PLASKER

DONNA PLASKER Sixth great granddaughter of progenitor Nicholas Kegg.
JENNIFER PLASKER Sixth great granddaughter of progenitor Nicholas Kegg.

PLATT

APRIL PLATT Sixth great granddaughter of progenitor Nicholas Kegg.
JAMES PLATT Sixth great grandson of progenitor Nicholas Kegg.

PLEBAN

LINDSEY SUZANNE PLEBAN Sixth great granddaughter of progenitor Nicholas Kegg.
ROSS ADAM PLEBAN Sixth great grandson of progenitor Nicholas Kegg.

PLEISS

HEIDI LYNN PLEISS Sixth great granddaughter of progenitor Nicholas Kegg.

PLUTA

BILL M. PLUTA Sixth great grandson of progenitor Nicholas Kegg.

POFFENBERGER

CHRISTOPHER D. POFFENBERGER Sixth great grandson of progenitor Nicholas Kegg. **DALICE L. POFFENBERGER** [5669,5670] (1905 – 1973) daughter of Clyde and Lydia (Knouf) Poffenberger, married Frank Valentine Malinowsky. **GEORGE PAUL POFFENBERGER** (1940 – 1970) son of George and Eleanor (Mort) Poffenberger. **GEORGE PAUL POFFENBERGER** [5671] (1909 – 1986) son of Clyde and Lydia (Knouf) Poffenberger married twice; first to Eleanor Mort with whom he was father of (1). Later, he married Anna Gettman Flohr. George was a retired Union Pacific Railroad employee. **JOSEPH W. POFFENBERGER** (1907 – 1970) son of Clyde and Lydia (Knouf) Poffenberger, married Lorraine Ellen Needham with whom he was father of (2).
KAREN LYN POFFENBERGER Sixth great granddaughter of progenitor Nicholas Kegg.

[5669] Western Kansas World (KS) Feb 23, 1950 [5670] p.7 The Salina Journal (KS) Mar 15, 1996

POLETTI

AUSTIN CHRISTOPHER POLETTI Eighth great grandson of progenitor Nicholas Kegg.
BRANDON CHRISTOPHER POLETTI Eighth great grandson of progenitor Nicholas Kegg.

POLING

VIOLET MARIE POLING (1918 – 2003) daughter of Hugh and Etta (Streight) Poling married four times; first to Mr. Cox, then to Henry Edward Pierce. Later, she married Mr. Jacob followed by Mr. Vita with whom she was mother of (1).

POLUMBO

TINA MARIE POLUMBO Seventh great granddaughter of progenitor Nicholas Kegg.

PONDER

KIMBERLY M. PONDER Sixth great granddaughter of progenitor Nicholas Kegg.

PONTIUS

DORIAN K. PONTIUS Sixth great grandson of progenitor Nicholas Kegg.
JARROD B. PONTIUS Sixth great grandson of progenitor Nicholas Kegg.

POOLE

JACQUELINE LEE POOLE aka "Jackie", Sixth great granddaughter of progenitor Nicholas Kegg.

POPA

ADAM POPA Sixth great grandson of progenitor Nicholas Kegg. **HANNAH POPA** Seventh great granddaughter of progenitor Nicholas Kegg. **JIM POPA** Sixth great grandson of progenitor Nicholas Kegg. **MATTHEW POPA** Seventh great grandson of progenitor Nicholas Kegg.
SHAUNA ROSE POPA (1993 – 1997) daughter of Adam and Saundra (Pierson) Popa.

POPE

MARLEY POPE Sixth great granddaughter of progenitor Nicholas Kegg.

POPLO

BRENDA S. POPLO Eighth great granddaughter of progenitor Nicholas Kegg.
CHARLES ANTHONY POPLO Eighth great grandson of progenitor Nicholas Kegg.
HEIDI N. POPLO Eighth great granddaughter of progenitor Nicholas Kegg.
STACY L. POPLO Eighth great granddaughter of progenitor Nicholas Kegg.

POPOVICH

CELIA MAIE POPOVICH [5672] (1951 – 1997) daughter of Frank and Marjorie (Bushnell) Popovich. Celia was a volunteer worker at James Cancer Clinic.

[5669] Western Kansas World (KS) Feb 23, 1950 [5670] p.7 The Salina Journal (KS) Mar 15, 1996 [5671] Denver Post (CO) Nov 27, 1986

CYNTHIA ANN POPOVICH Fourth great granddaughter of progenitor Nicholas Kegg.
FRANK A. POPOVICH Fourth great grandson of progenitor Nicholas Kegg.
MARSHA MAIE POPOVICH Fourth great granddaughter of progenitor Nicholas Kegg.

PORTENIER

JASON PORTENIER Seventh great grandson of progenitor Nicholas Kegg.

PORTER

ANDREW WILLIAM PORTER aka "Andy" Sixth great grandson of progenitor Nicholas Kegg.
ASHLEY NICOLE PORTER Seventh great granddaughter of progenitor Nicholas Kegg.
AUGUST PERKINS PORTER (born abt. 1869) son of H. Virgil and Sarah (Kegg) Porter.
BESSIE BROWN PORTER [5672A] (1918 – 2016) daughter of H. Norton and Bessie (Rossiter)Porter married Joseph L. Woods with whom she was mother of (4). A former office worker of the old Stewart's department store on York Road later was employed at the Maryland National Bank became Realtor. Bessie later had a cameo appearance in a 1974 John Waters film. The couple lived on Wickford Road in Roland Park, and later on Goodale Road in Homeland, where Mr. Waters, the Baltimore filmmaker, filmed a scene in their living room for his 1974 cult classic "Female Trouble." Some of the cast included Divine, Pat Moran, Edith Massey, Mink Stole and David Lochary. Mrs. Woods had a cameo role playing Divine's mother. Bessie was a Baltimore Orioles fan and enjoyed photography, travel, raising Siamese cats and collecting antique furniture. **BLAIR PORTER** Seventh great granddaughter of progenitor Nicholas Kegg. **BURGOYNE HOLLY PORTER** [5673] (1906 – 1992) adopted son of H. Norton and Bessie (Rossiter) Porter, married and was father of (6). **CATHRYN KEGG PORTER** [5674] (1913 – 1984) daughter of H. Norton and Bessie (Rossiter) Porter, married Charles Hyland Page with whom she was mother of (2). Cathryn's first job was as a secretary to the purchasing agent for Pan American World Airways. Later, she spent 15 years working for the tax assessment office Cathryn was also a superintendent of the Sunday School at St. John's in Mount Washington. **CHARLES W. PORTER** [5675] (1891 – 1909) son of Charles and Jessie (Jones) Porter stepped on a rusty nail which enter his foot. One-week later tetanus developed and after a hard struggle succumbed to dreaded malady. **DAVID N. PORTER** Sixth great grandson of progenitor Nicholas Kegg. **EDITH KATHERINE PORTER** [5676] (1884 – 1951) daughter of H. Virgil and Sarah (Kegg) Porter, married Elmer Schreiner with whom she was mother of (5). Edith was an Episcopalian and a member ofthe Civitan Club. **EVA PORTER** Fifth great granddaughter of progenitor Nicholas Kegg. **FRANK PORTER** (born abt. 1876) son of H. Virgil and Sarah (Kegg) Porter. **GINGER PORTER** Sixth great granddaughter of progenitor Nicholas Kegg. **GLORIA LEE PORTER** Fifth great granddaughter of progenitor Nicholas Kegg. **H. NORTON PORTER** [5677] (1882 – 1918) son H. Virgil and Sarah (Kegg) Porter, married Bessie Rossiter with whom he was father of (5). H. Norton was a dentist. He was responsible for organizing a branch of the National Rifle Assoc. in 1915. **H. NORTON PORTER** [5678] (1917 – 1992) son of H. Norton and Bessie (Rossiter) Porter, married Ellen Pope with whom he was father of (2). Horace was employed by the Winchester and Woods Co. in Baltimore in 1927. He later assumed ownership of the company and served as president until it closed in 1990. Horace was a member of the Beaver Club in Baltimore **HORACE NORTON PORTER** Fifth great grandson of progenitor Nicholas Kegg. **HORACE NORTON PORTER** aka "Chip", Fifth great grandson of progenitor Nicholas Kegg. **HORACE VIRGIL PORTER** [5678A] (1939 – 2013) son of Horace and Edythe (Mercury) Porter, married Patricia Ann Walther with whom he was father of (2). Horace served with the United States Marine Corps Reserves. He had worked as a meat cutter with A & P Grocery Stores and then retired, after 40 years, as co-owner and

---

[5672] Columbus Dispatch (OH) May 10, 1997 [5672A] Baltimore Sun (MD) March 23, 2016 [5673] The Evening Sun (Baltimore, MD) Jan 3, 1992 [5674] The Baltimore Sun (MD) July 22, 1984 [5675] p.9 - Evening Times (MD) March 18.1909 [5676] Akron-Summit County Public Library obituary clipping obtained by D. Sue Dible [5677] Baltimore Sun (MD) Oct. 6, 1918 [5678] The Star-Democrat (Easton, MD) Aug 4, 1992 [5678A] Helsley-Johnson Funeral Home & Cremation Center (WVA) [5679] The Baltimore Sun, Baltimore (MD) March 29, 1964

operator of the Food Rite Groceteria in Mt. Airy, MD. He was a member of the Junior Order of United American Mechanics Council #117 in Berkeley Springs, Deer Cinch Rod & Gun Club in Crappo, MD, the Amalgamated Meat Cutters Union in Baltimore, West Virginia Farm Association, the Morgan County Farm Bureau and was a lifetime member of the NRA. Virgil enjoyed hunting, fishing, target shooting, land stewardship and landscaping his farm. **HORACE V. PORTER** [5679] (1910 – 1964) son of H. Norton and Bessie (Rossiter) Porter, married Edythe Delores Mercury with whom he was father of (3). **J. MERRITT PORTER** Fifth great grandson of progenitor Nicholas Kegg. **JAMES PORTER** Seventh great grandson of progenitor Nicholas Kegg. **JAMES S. PORTER** Fifth great grandson of progenitor Nicholas Kegg. **JENNIFER PORTER** Sixth great granddaughter of progenitor Nicholas Kegg. **JESSICA L. PORTER** Seventh great granddaughter of progenitor Nicholas Kegg. **JULIE LYNN PORTER** Sixth great granddaughter of progenitor Nicholas Kegg. **KENNETH WALTER PORTER** Fifth great grandson of progenitor Nicholas Kegg. **LEVI PORTER** Seventh great grandson of progenitor Nicholas Kegg. **LISA MICHELLE PORTER** [5680] (1968 – 2005) daughter of Horace and Martha (Reuwer) Porter, married Jeffrey Michael Dzbynski with whom she was mother of (1). **MARTHA PORTER** [5681] (1904 – 1993) daughter of Frank and Rena (Brilhart) Porter, married Thomas Fred O'Brien with whom she was mother of (2). Martha was a member of Visitation Catholic Church. She graduated from Lindenwood College, St. Louis. **NANCY LEE PORTER** Fifth great granddaughter of progenitor Nicholas Kegg. **NANCY S. PORTER** Fourth great granddaughter of progenitor Nicholas Kegg. **SARA VIRGINIA PORTER** [5682] (1911 – 1975) daughter of H. Norton and Bessie (Rossiter) Porter, married Joseph G. Finnerty with whom she was mother of (3). **SHIRLEY PORTER** [5683] (1929 – 2007) daughter of George and Bernice (Dwigans) Porter, married Robert Richard Jontz with whom she was mother of (2). Shirley and Bob operated the Bob Jontz Insurance Agency in Stuart until retiring. She was a member of the Clinton United Methodist Church, Stephen Ministries and PEO Chapter EN. Shirley was active in several bridge clubs, was involved in many church activities and served on various boards and committees over the years. She enjoyed dancing, playing bridge, trips to Branson, MO, and simply spending time with her husband Bob. **TODD ANTHONY PORTER** Sixth great grandson of progenitor Nicholas Kegg. **TRACEY ANN PORTER** Sixth great granddaughter of progenitor Nicholas Kegg. **VERNER PORTER** (born abt.1879) son of H. Virgil and Sarah (Kegg) Porter.

POTIKER

HALEY MICHELE POTIKER Sixth great granddaughter of progenitor Nicholas Kegg.
SPENCER LOUIS POTIKER Sixth great grandson of progenitor Nicholas Kegg.

POTTENGER

LEWIS P. POTTENGER (born abt. 1870) son of Richard and Drewzillia (Kegg) Pottenger.

POTTS

AMY POTTS Seventh great granddaughter of progenitor Nicholas Kegg. **EDNA LUCILE POTTS** [5684] (1887 – 1935) daughter of Cyrus and Rebecca (Beaver) Potts, married Ralph Emerson Bell. Edna possessed a keen mind and was an executive of well-known ability. She was called upon to give much of her time to various activities of the community. For several years, she was superintendent of the primary department of the Llyswen Presbyterian Sunday school, and she was active is social, civic and political life of the county. She was interested in sports and was a well-known golfer, winning the cup offered by the Blairmont Women's Golf Association for three seasons, entitling her to permanent possession of the trophy. She was chairman of the Blairmont Women's Golf association for several years and was active in

[5680] Baltimore Sun (MD) March 23, 2005 [5681] Kansas City Star (MO) July 6, 1993 [5682] The Evening Sun (Baltimore, MD) July 24, 1975 [5683] Des Moines Register (IA) Jan 1, 2008 [5684] Altoona Mirror (PA) April 1, 1935

the affairs of the American Legion auxiliary here. Active in civic and political affairs, Edna formerly served as president of the Blair County Council of Republican Women. She possessed a pleasing personality and had a host of friends in all walks of life. **MEGAN POTTS** Eighth great granddaughter of progenitor Nicholas Kegg. **RICHARD DAVID POTTS** [5684A] aka "Rick" (1976 – 2015) son of David and Janice (Machan) Potts was father of (1). Employed in the maintenance department at Michigan Tool Works in Sturgis, Rick also worked as a volunteer fireman and EMT with the Centreville Fire Department, Parker's Ambulance Service in Sturgis and Gentz Farms in Colon. He was an Eagle Scout and enjoyed hunting, fishing, watching NASCAR his favorite driver being Kevin Harvick. Rick always put others needs before his own, always willing to give a lending hand when he could. **STELLA VIRGINIA POTTS** [5685] (1883 – 1976) daughter of Cyrus and Rebecca (Beaver) Potts, married Maurice Garwood Irvine.

POULTER

LORI POULTER Sixth great granddaughter of progenitor Nicholas Kegg.
TIM POULTER Sixth great grandson of progenitor Nicholas Kegg.

POWELL

AARON CLINTON POWELL Sixth great grandson of progenitor Nicholas Kegg. **ANDREA POWELL** [5685A] (1977 – 2013) daughter of Charles and Luanne (Stalling) Powell. Andrea graduated from ITT with an associate degree in graphic design. **ASHLYN POWELL** Seventh great granddaughter of progenitor Nicholas Kegg. **CARTER EVAN POWELL** Seventh great grandson of progenitor Nicholas Kegg. **CHAD POWELL** Ninth great grandson of progenitor Nicholas Kegg. **CHARLES MICHAEL POWELL** [5686] (1957 – 2013) aka "Michael", son of Charles and Betty (Hill) Powell, married Luanne Stalling with whom he was father of (2). Michael was a Master Craftsman and Outdoorsmen who enjoyed making furniture, camping, fishing, tooling around the yard, and a good joke. **CHARLES WILLIAM POWELL** (1895 – 1952) son of James and Mary (Cagg) Powell, married Mary Rebecca Kohler with whom he was father of (6). **CHARLES WILLIAM POWELL** [5687] (1932 – 1997) aka "Buddy", son of Charles and Mary (Kohler) Powell, married Betty Lou Hill with whom he was father of (1). **CHAROLET JEAN POWELL** [5688] (1930 – 1993) daughter of Charles and Mary (Kohler) Powell married twice; first to Elbert Junior Henderson with whom she was mother of (2). Later, she married Robert Bertram Ringhiser. **EDNA JOANNE POWELL** [2001] (1927 – 2010) daughter of Charles and Mary (Kohler) Powell married twice; first to Donald Keith Carroll with whom she was mother of (6). **ETHAN POWELL** Seventh great grandson of progenitor Nicholas Kegg. **FOSTER JAMES POWELL** [5689] (1904 – 1952) son of James and Mary (Cagg) Powell, married Margaret E. Showalter. Forster was employed as a glassworker for Lancaster Lens. **HAELEY POWELL** Seventh great granddaughter of progenitor Nicholas Kegg. **HANNAH CAT POWELL** Sixth great granddaughter of progenitor Nicholas Kegg. **HEATHER POWELL** Eighth great granddaughter of progenitor Nicholas Kegg. **IAN POWELL** Eighth great grandson of progenitor Nicholas Kegg. **JAMES FOSTER POWELL** [5690] (1921 – 2002) son of Pearl and Rena (Decker) Powell married twice; first to Charlene Virginia Craft and later, to Joan Avean (Adkins) Roberts. **JEFFRY WILLIAM POWELL** Seventh great grandson of progenitor Nicholas Kegg. **KELLY DIANE POWELL** Sixth great granddaughter of progenitor Nicholas Kegg. **KELLI S. POWELL** Seventh great granddaughter of progenitor Nicholas Kegg. **KRIS POWELL** Seventh great grandson of progenitor Nicholas Kegg. **KRISTI J. POWELL** 7th great granddaughter of progenitor Nicholas Kegg. **MARY MAE POWELL** [5691] (1897 – 1971) daughter of James and Mary (Cagg) Powell, married Claude Samuel Eads with whom

---

[5684A] Hackman Family Funeral Home (MI) contributed by D. Sue Dible [5685] Altoona Mirror (PA) Oct 7, 1976 [5685A] Denton Record-Chronicle (TX) Oct 7, 2013 [5686] Mulkey- Mason Funeral Home Denton, Texas [5687] Lancaster Eagle-Gazette (OH) Aug 10, 1997 [5688] Lancaster Eagle-Gazette (OH) June 17, 1993 [5689] Lancaster Eagle-Gazette (OH) Feb 26, 1952 [5690] Logan Daily News (OH) Nov 1, 2002 [5691] p.16 The Advocate (OH) May 13, 1971

she was mother of (1). Mary was a member of the Thornville United Methodist Church. **MARY MARGARET POWELL** [5692] (1929 – 1991) daughter of Charles and Mary (Kohler) Powell, married Charles Hedrick Hamilton with whom she was mother of (2). Mary was Co-founder, secretary and treasurer, Charles H. Hamilton Construction Co. **MELISSA CLAIRE POWELL** Fifth great granddaughter of progenitor Nicholas Kegg. **MICHAEL DON POWELL** (1943 – 1975) son of William and Doris (Schoepflin) Powell, married Judith Cox. **PEARL JOEL POWELL** [5693] (1899 – 1968) son of James and Mary (Cagg) Powell, married Rena Evelyn Decker with whom he was father of (2). Pearl was a retired coal miner. **PETER JON POWELL** Seventh great grandson of progenitor Nicholas Kegg. **RAE JEAN POWELL** Sixth great granddaughter of progenitor Nicholas Kegg. **RAYMOND POWELL** [5693A] (1936 – 2011) son of Charles and Mary (Kohler) Powell, married Virginia Joyce Gross with whom he was father of (3). A veteran of the U.S. army, Raymond was a member of The Church of Jesus Christ of Latter-Day Saints where he served as a Bishop for nine years and other various callings. He was a former member of the Classic Cruisers and had a love for old Fords. **RONALD CLINTON POWELL** [5694] (1947 – 2013) son of Charles and Mary (Rohler) Powell married twice; first to Judy C. Jones later, he married Sharon K (Pugh) Mowery with whom he was father of (3). **ROSELLA JUNE POWELL** [5695] (1922 – 2005) aka "Rosie", daughter of Pearl and Rena (Decker) Powell married twice; first to Clyde Cromwell Snyder with whom she was mother of (1). Later, she married Ralph Lester McDonald with whom she was mother of (2). **SHANNON COY POWELL** (1965 – 1988) son of Keith (birth name Kegg), (adopted surname Powell) and Linda (Mostert) Powell. **SHANNON MARIE POWELL** Sixth great granddaughter of progenitor Nicholas Kegg. **SOPHIE POWELL** Seventh great granddaughter of progenitor Nicholas Kegg. **STACIE POWELL** Sixth great granddaughter of progenitor Nicholas Kegg. **SUE POWELL** Sixth great granddaughter of progenitor Nicholas Kegg.

POWERS

AMANDA POWERS Sixth great granddaughter of progenitor Nicholas Kegg.
BRIAN J. POWERS Sixth great grandson of progenitor Nicholas Kegg.
CRAIG J. POWERS Sixth great grandson of progenitor Nicholas Kegg.

PRACHT

DARRELL PRACHT Seventh great grandson of progenitor Nicholas Kegg.
MICHELLE PRACHT Sixth great granddaughter of progenitor Nicholas Kegg.
MITCHELL PRACHT Sixth great grandson of progenitor Nicholas Kegg.

PRATT

ALEXIS GRACE PRATT aka "Lexy," Seventh great granddaughter of progenitor Nicholas Kegg. **CHARLES FLETCHER PRATT** Seventh great grandson of progenitor Nicholas Kegg. **CHARLES WALLACE PRATT** (1937 – 2003) son of Fletcher and Alice (Evans) Pratt married Joan Lucille Grabbe with whom he was father of (3). **CONNIE JO PRATT** Fifth great granddaughter of progenitor Nicholas Kegg. **DAVID WALLACE PRATT** Fifth great grandson of progenitor Nicholas Kegg. **HILARY PRATT** (1949 – 2001) daughter of Wallace and Florence (Woodfin) Pratt. **JENNIFER PRATT** Fifth great granddaughter of progenitor Nicholas Kegg. **JOSEPH BROOKS PRATT** Sixth great grandson of progenitor Nicholas Kegg. **JOSEPH HENRY PRATT** [5696] aka "Jody" (1973 – 2019) son of Peter and Anne (Winterbotham) Pratt. Jody was athletic, handsome, popular, and intelligent beyond belief. Jody graduated from The Plan II Honors Program at the University of Texas in 1996,

---

[5692] p.9 Cincinnati Enquirer (OH) Oct 7, 1991. [5693] p.2 Logan Daily News (OH) March 28, 1968 [5693A] Lancaster Eagle-Gazette (OH) Oct 29, 2011 [5694] Lancaster Eagle-Gazette (OH) Sept. 26, 2013 [5695] Logan Daily News (OH) Apr 4, 2005 [5696] Houston Chronicle (TX) Feb. 26, 2019, obtained by D. Sue Dible

where he was a Silver Spur and a member of the SAE Fraternity following in his dad's footsteps. He went on to earn a degree from the South Texas School of Law. Jody was loved and admired by all who knew him. **KAREN ANN PRATT** Fifth great granddaughter of progenitor Nicholas Kegg. **KIMBERLY ANNE PRATT** [5696A] (1961 – 2015) daughter of Peter and Anne (Winterbotham) Pratt, married James Edward Bashaw with whom she was mother of (2). Kim received a Bachelor of Arts in Sociology from Southern Methodist University in 1984, where she was a member of Phi Mu sorority. Kim taught at the Awty International School and the Oaks at Briargrove. Kim was a member of the Houston Country Club, the Coronado Club, and a Sustaining Member of the Junior League of Houston. The happiest times of her life were entertaining in her home or at "the Club". Her stated goal as she made loudly clear to her husband and children was to shriek "I'm trying to have a nice party!" **LEXY PRATT** Seventh great granddaughter of progenitor Nicholas Kegg. **MELINDA BETH PRATT** Sixth great granddaughter of progenitor Nicholas Kegg. **NANCY JANE PRATT** (1918 – 1980) daughter of Wallace and Pearl (Stuckey) Pratt married twice; first to W. M. Reid with whom she was mother of (2). Later, she married Augustine John Tucker with whom she was mother of (4). **PAMELA PRATT** [5696B] (1951 – 2005) daughter of Wallace and Florence (Woodfin) Pratt, married Scott R. Powell with whom she was mother of (1). **PETER EVANS PRATT** [5696C] (1938 – 2007) son of Fletcher and Alice (Evans) Pratt, married Anne Winterbotham with whom he was father of (4). Peter enjoyed a lifelong career in the financial services industry and was widely admired by his peers and enjoyed many friendships among his colleagues at Rotan Mosle, Kidder, Peabody and Paine Webber from where he retired. Peter was an avid sportsman who enjoyed tennis, hunting, and fishing. He was also a wonderful competitor who ran in four marathons including running the New York City marathon twice. **PETER EVANS PRATT** [5697] aka "Pito" (1963 – 2018) son of Peter and Anne (Winterbotham) Pratt married Catherine Anne Hale with whom he was father of (3). Pito was a member of Phi Delta Theta Fraternity. From UT he went on to earn a degree from St. Mary's University School of Law with a JD. Pito loved being an attorney, and several of his happiest times were had while working towards his many professional achievements. He worked diligently and painstakingly to build a practice that made his children proud of him. He had enjoyed spending time in Cloudcroft, New Mexico and looked forward to having his children join him when time allowed. Pito was a great conversationalist and counsel for all his children. His comforting nature will be one of his most missed traits. Always the loudest voice in the room, he was passionate about many things, especially his comic book collection. **SCOTT RENFERT PRATT** [5697A] (1964 – 2011) son of Peter and Anne (Winterbotham) Pratt. Scott graduated from the University of Texas, where he enjoyed being a member of the Phi Delta Theta Fraternity and the company of his fraternity brothers. After graduation from the University of Texas School of law, Scott was employed as a Deputy Agent for Legal Affairs of the U.S. Comptroller of the Currency in Washington, D.C. Scott was at his happiest when he later became employed as a Vice President of James E. Bashaw & Co., a nationally recognized broker firm. While working for JebCo, as it is known, Scott lovingly referred to his boss and brother-in-law, Jeb, as Jesse Bananasaw, a moniker which gave Jeb no end of delight and laughter to this day. Scott was a long-time member of the Kiwanis Club of Houston and served as a board member of the Periwinkle Foundation and the Houston Council on Drugs and Alcohol. **SHREVE STEWART PRATT** Seventh great grandson of progenitor Nicholas Kegg. **SUSAN HEATHER PRATT** Sixth great granddaughter of progenitor Nicholas Kegg. **SUSANNA R. PRATT**, aka "Susy", Sixth great granddaughter of progenitor Nicholas Kegg. **ST CLARE PRATT** Fifth great granddaughter of progenitor Nicholas Kegg. **WALLACE HOUSTON PRATT** [5697B] (1921 – 1975) son of Wallace and Pearl (Stuckey) Pratt, married Florence Sonia Woodfin with whom he was father of (4).

PREG

JESSICA JOAN PREG Sixth great granddaughter of progenitor Nicholas Kegg.
TIMOTHY DAVID PREG Sixth great grandson of progenitor Nicholas Kegg.

[5696A] Houston Chronicle (TX) Apr 6, 2015 [5696B] Newsday (NM) Jan. 5, 2006 [5696C] Houston Chronicle (TX) Feb 17, 2007 [5697] Houston Chronicle (TX) Feb. 6, 2018, obtained by D. Sue Dible [5697A] Houston Chronicle (TX) Sep 8, 2011 [5697B] p.17 Bridgeport Post (CT) Jan 25, 1975

PREGONY

ANDREW PREGONY Seventh great grandson of progenitor Nicholas Kegg.

PRENTICE

CECIL WILLIAM PRENTICE [5698] (1888 – 1950) son of Orpheus and Mary (Kegg) Prentice, married Clelly Garney with whom he was father of (1). Cecil was a farmer. **EDITH MARIE PRENTICE** [5699] (1897 – 1989) daughter of Orpheus and Mary (Kegg) Prentice, married Robert Charles Lewis with whom she was mother of (3). **ELIZABETH PAGE PRENTICE** Fifth great granddaughter of progenitor Nicholas Kegg. **GEORGE DENNISON PRENTICE** [5700] (1889 – 1954) son of Orpheus and Mary (Kegg) Prentice, married Etta Adelia Collins with whom he was father of (1). Dr. Prentice was pastor of the Homer Presbyterian church for seven years until he left to take a pastorate in Whiteland. **JAMES MCDONALD PRENTICE** Fourth great grandson of progenitor Nicholas Kegg. **JOANNE ELIZABETH PRENTICE** Fourth great granddaughter of progenitor Nicholas Kegg. **JOHN LAURENCE PRENTICE** [5701] (1892 – 1962) son of Orpheus and Mary (Kegg) Prentice, married Helen Binnie with whom he was father of (2). John was former pastor of Presbyterian Churches in Indianapolis, Bedford, Paoli and Seymour. The Rev. John Prentice graduated from Wabash College in 1915 and from McCormick Seminary in Chicago in 1918. He received his Doctor of Divinity degree from Wabash in 1943. The Rev. was responsible for organizing the Prentice Presbyterian Church in 1929. He was past president of the Seymour Rotary Club, president of the Jackson County Red Cross Chapter during World War II, a member of the U. S. Trotting and Horse Breeders Associations, a Mason and a Shriner. **JOHN WILLIAM PRENTICE** Fourth great grandson of progenitor Nicholas Kegg. **KATHERINE ANN PRENTICE** Fifth great granddaughter of progenitor Nicholas Kegg. **LAURA MARGUERITE PRENTICE** [5702] (1902 – 1975) daughter of Orpheus and Mary (Kegg) Prentice, married William Albert Clabaugh. Laura attended Wooster College in Ohio and Hanover College. She was a member of the Franklin United Presbyterian Church. **MARGARET ELIZABETH PRENTICE** [5703] (1919 – 1931) daughter of Rev. John and Helen (Binnie) Prentice. **MARGARET LOUISE PRENTICE** Fourth great granddaughter of progenitor Nicholas Kegg. **MARY ELIZABETH PRENTICE** Fifth great granddaughter of progenitor Nicholas Kegg. **OLA MARIE PRENTICE** [5703A] (1917 – 1996) daughter of Cecil and Clelly (Garney) Prentice, married John Lee Barkley with whom she was mother of (2). Ola assisted her husband in operation of Barkley Painting, had been secretary at St. Elizabeth Hospital Medical Center, worked at Green Giant for a number of years, taught at Faith Christian Academy in Crawfordsville and tutored students in her home. Mrs. Barkley was a member of Battle Ground Bible Church and choir. She enjoyed her grandchildren, bird watching, flower gardening and her cats. **RICHARD SCOTT PRENTICE** [5703B] aka "Dick" (1946 – 2012) son of Robert and Marjorie (Wiley) Prentice married Elizabeth Ann Sterrett with whom he was father of (3). Dick was a Eagle Scout with 2 palms. He worked on staff as a merit badge counselor for several years at Camp Tonkawa outside Buffalo Gap, TX. He attended the 1960 Jamboree at Colorado Springs, CO and took a picture of President Dwight Eisenhower who later autographed it. After graduating with a BA in Chemistry from Austin College in Sherman, TX. Dick joined the army with specialized training in the chemical corps before landing at Ft. Benning, GA in a smoke generator company marking drop zones for parachute jumpers. Dick was accepted into Officer Candidate School. He was commissioned as a Second Lieutenant and went to Ft. Gordon, GA for Signal School training. Finally, he was assigned to the 121st Signal Bn, 1st Infantry Division, Ft. Riley, KS where he served as Company XO and CO. One of the missions for the 1st Infantry Division at that time was to deploy to West Germany for a month to show America's resolve to defend

---

[5698] Journal and Courier (Lafayette, Indiana) Nov 24, 1950 [5699] Springfield News-Sun (OH) May 1, 1989, obtained by D. Sue Dible [5700] Library obituary clipping dated 4/2/1954, obtained by D. Sue Dible [5701] p.4 Flora Hoosier Democrat (IN) Sep 20, 1962 [5702] p.16 - Daily Journal (IN) July 30, 1975, obtained by D. Sue Dible [5703] The Indianapolis Star (IN) Sep 17, 1931 [5703A] Library obituary clipping contributed by D. Sue Dible [5703B] Nalley-Pickle & Welch Funeral Home & Crematory of Midland, TX contributed by D. Sue Dible [5703C] Midland Reporter-Telegram (TX) Dec 19, 2010

against Russian threats in exercises called Reforger. Dick participated in two Reforger deployments. On the second deployment, Dick experienced his first encounter with corporate restructuring. The armymandated 6-month early outs in late 1971 for almost everyone as demobilization from the Vietnam War began. His colonel requested he participate in the fall Reforger, which extended his deployment. After leaving the army, Dick registered at Texas Tech University as a graduate student in the Chemical Engineering Department on the GI bill. Among other positions, he worked for ARCO in Midland and Odessa on a variety of water floods and other assets. **ROBERT GEORGE PRENTICE** [5703C] aka "Bob" (1920 – 2010) son of George and Etta (Collins) Prentice married Marjorie Randall Wiley with whom he was father of (3) Bob graduated from Wooster with a degree in Geology in one hand and a draft notice in the other. After basic training, he went to Officers Candidate School at Fort Belvoir, Virginia where he was commissioned a 2nd Lieutenant. Bob served four years in the Corps of Engineers, US Army and attained the rank of Captain. Bob took advantage of the GI Bill and went to the University of Pittsburgh and obtained a degree in Petroleum Engineering. He was a senior research engineer with Stanolind Oil and Gas. He spent three years developing and operating the first miscible fluid flood attempted in the United States. Bob started his own consulting business and, in the seventies, founded Prentice Petroleum, Inc. **ROBERT WILEY PRENTICE** Fifth great grandson of progenitor Nicholas Kegg. **SUSAN LANE PRENTICE** Fourth great granddaughter of progenitor Nicholas Kegg. **WILLIAM HAROLD PRENTICE** [5703D] aka "Bill" (1921 – 2000) son of Rev. John and Helen (Binne) Prentice married twice, first to Margery Jean Macdonal with whom he was father of (3), later to Elizabeth Ann Crawford. Bill founded Prentice Real Estate as principal broker in 1964, established the Pub & Jugg Shoppe in Brownstown, and was active in horse racing as co-owner. He was a World War II Army veteran and served aboard the battleship USS Missouri. At age 64, he was one of the oldest active owner/drivers of Formula V race cars in the Ohio Region and was a member of the Sports Car Club of America, earning the honor of driving instructor.

PRIBULA

MICHELLE LYNN PRIBULA aka "Shelly" Sixth great granddaughter of progenitor Nicholas Kegg.

PRICE

ALAYJAH PRICE Seventh great granddaughter of progenitor Nicholas Kegg. **ALEXANDER PRICE** Eighth great grandson of progenitor Nicholas Kegg. **ALLISON PRICE** Seventh great granddaughter of progenitor Nicholas Kegg. **ALYSSA PRICE** Eighth great granddaughter of progenitor Nicholas Kegg. **ANDREW PRICE** Sixth great grandson of progenitor Nicholas Kegg. **ANNE M. PRICE** Seventh great granddaughter of progenitor Nicholas Kegg. **BARRY PRICE** Fifth great grandson of progenitor Nicholas Kegg. **BRANDON PRICE** Fifth great grandson of progenitor Nicholas Kegg. **BRENDA JOYCE PRICE** Fifth great granddaughter of progenitor Nicholas Kegg. **CARA PRICE** Eighth great granddaughter of progenitor Nicholas Kegg. **CAROLYN RUTH PRICE** (1953 – 1954) daughter of Omer and Doris (Miller) Price. **COURTNEY PRICE** Eighth great granddaughter of progenitor Nicholas Kegg. **DAVID PRICE** Seventh great grandson of progenitor Nicholas Kegg. **DEACON MICHAEL PRICE** Sixth great grandson of progenitor Nicholas Kegg. **DEBORAH PRICE** Seventh great granddaughter of progenitor Nicholas Kegg. **DEBORAH PRICE** Seventh great granddaughter of progenitor Nicholas Kegg. **DEBRA PRICE** Seventh great granddaughter of progenitor Nicholas Kegg. **DONALD RAYMOND PRICE** [5704] (1935 – 2022) son of Melvin and Ethel Mae (Calhoun) Price married Marcia Joy Vos with whom he was father of (3). Don lived in 15 different states because of his father's occupation. The state of Washington was one of his favorites, where his father helped build the Grand Coulee Dam. While attending high school there, he was asked to play a trumpet-solo intro to "Hail to the Chief" for Harry Truman, who was dedicating the

---

[5703D] Times-Mail (IN) Jun 16, 2000 [5704] The Timberjay (MN) June 3, 2022

completed dam. One of his first jobs was being a soda jerk and he started young finding assorted jobs to help finance his love for "toys" and to buy gas for "cruising". Don had a passion for flying that started at a young age by building model airplanes and he constantly had an airplane, large or small, being rebuilt or constructed from a kit in his shops. He began flight instruction in his teens to become a pilot and continued flying a floatplane all his life. He also enjoyed modifying cars and took pride in keeping all vehicles - new and classic - in top shape. Don spent hours kicking tires at classic car events such as Back to the Fifties in St. Paul, where he recently showed his latest classic car, a 1957 Chevy. Don forever stayed busy doing projects for himself, family and friends. He belonged to organizations such as car clubs, helped organize the Cook St. Louis County Rescue Squad, and was a member and officer for lake and resort associations. Committed to the churches where he lived, Don reminisced about how he braved climbing the church tower when first installing the bell. Although not always active, he was also proud to be a lifetime Masonic member. **DORIS PRICE** Fifth great granddaughter of progenitor Nicholas Kegg. **EDWARD M. PRICE JR** Seventh great grandson of progenitor Nicholas Kegg. **ELIAS PRICE** Seventh great grandson of progenitor Nicholas Kegg. **ERIN PRICE** Eighth great granddaughter of progenitor Nicholas Kegg. **GAIL PRICE** Fifth great granddaughter of progenitor Nicholas Kegg. **H. LONNIE PRICE** Fifth great grandson of progenitor Nicholas Kegg. **HAZEL PAULINE PRICE** [5704A] (1927 – 2019) daughter of Franklin and Minnie (Morris) Price married Joseph Henry Miller with whom she was mother of (4). Hazel was a lifetime member of The North Fort Myers First Baptist Church. **JACOB LUCAS CARL PRICE** Seventh great grandson of progenitor Nicholas Kegg. **JENNIFER PRICE** Sixth great granddaughter of progenitor Nicholas Kegg. **JERRY LYNN PRICE** Sixth great grandson of progenitor Nicholas Kegg. **JOHN FRANKLIN PRICE** Fifth great grandson of progenitor Nicholas Kegg. **JULIE PRICE** Sixth great granddaughter of progenitor Nicholas Kegg. **KAITLYN PRICE** Eighth great granddaughter of progenitor Nicholas Kegg. **KATHRYN E. PRICE** [5705] (1915 – 2000) daughter of George and Ada (Beegle) Price, married Alvin Gordon Hyman with whom she was mother of (1). Kathryn was employed as a secretary. **KEN W. PRICE** Fifth great grandson of progenitor Nicholas Kegg. **KENNETH PRICE** Seventh great grandson of progenitor Nicholas Kegg. **KENNETH B. PRICE** [5705A] aka "Ken" (1915 – 2006) son of George and Ada (Beegle) Price married twice, first to Marjorie Haywood and later to Adel Rosenberg with whom he was father of (4). Ken served with the Coast Guard, the Coast Guard Reserve before retiring as a chief petty officer. Ken had been employed as a lineman for Ohio Bell and transferred to Pacific Telephone and Telegraph. Ken enjoyed telling stories about buildings he wired for phones -- including Olympic Memorial Hospital. He also enjoyed fishing. **KRISTEN PRICE** Eighth great granddaughter of progenitor Nicholas Kegg. **MARK PRICE** Fifth great grandson of progenitor Nicholas Kegg. **MARK PRICE** Sixth great grandson of progenitor Nicholas Kegg. **MELISSA PRICE** Sixth great granddaughter of progenitor Nicholas Kegg. **NICHOLAS PRICE** Seventh great grandson of progenitor Nicholas Kegg. **OWEN JAMES PRICE** Sixth great grandson of progenitor Nicholas Kegg. **RICHARD W. PRICE** (1930 – 1930) son of Franklin and Minnie (Morris) Price. **ROBERT F. PRICE** (1916 – 1916) son of Franklin and Minnie (Morris) Price. **SETH PRICE** Eighth great grandson of progenitor Nicholas Kegg. **TERRY LEE PRICE** Sixth great grandson of progenitor Nicholas Kegg. **TRENT PRICE** Seventh great grandson of progenitor Nicholas Kegg. **VELTA MARIE PRICE** Fifth great granddaughter of progenitor Nicholas Kegg. **VIRGINIA PRICE** Fifth great granddaughter of progenitor Nicholas Kegg. **ZACHARY PRICE** Seventh great grandson of progenitor Nicholas Kegg. **ZACHARY PRICE** Seventh great grandchild of progenitor Nicholas Kegg.

PRIEST

DAVID RAY PRIEST [5706] (1964 – 1967) son of Vincent and Dorothy (Whetstone) Priest.

[5704A] Bedford Gazette (PA) July 17, 2019, contributed by Bob Rose [5705] p.4 Gazette (Colorado Springs, CO) June 12, 2000 [5705A] Drennan V Ford Funeral Home (WA) [5606] Walla Walla Union Bulletin (WA) April 13, 1967

PRINCE

PAIGE NOELLE PRINCE Eighth great granddaughter of progenitor Nicholas Kegg.

PRITCHARD

BRIANNA NICOLE PRITCHARD Eighth great granddaughter of progenitor Nicholas Kegg.
CHELSEA JEAN PRITCHARD Eighth great granddaughter of progenitor Nicholas Kegg.
DAWSON RILEY PRITCHARD Eighth great grandson of progenitor Nicholas Kegg.
MARK THOMAS PRITCHARD (2002 – 2002) son of Mark and Carla (Perry) Pritchard.

PRITTS

DAVID PRITTS Fifth great grandson of progenitor Nicholas Kegg.
JACLYN DAWN PRITTS Sixth great granddaughter of progenitor Nicholas Kegg.
MICHAEL BRIAN PRITTS Sixth great grandson of progenitor Nicholas Kegg.

PRY

EMILY PRY Sixth great granddaughter of progenitor Nicholas Kegg.
PHIL PRY Sixth great grandson of progenitor Nicholas Kegg.

PRYFOGLE

KIM PRYFOGLE Fifth great granddaughter of progenitor Nicholas Kegg. **LAWRENCE LEE PRYFOGLE** [5706A] aka "Larry" (1937 – 2011) son of Kenneth and Harriet (Bowers) Pryfogle married Ann Elizabeth Cherry with whom he was father of (1). Larry was known for his wide-ranging interests, knowledge and dry wit. Larry was a veteran of the Army and Marines. He retired from Columbus Public Schools after 30 years. He spent his retirement through community involvement, serving as a Columbus Zoo Docent, member of the Westerville Lion's Club, Hanby House Docent, graduate of the Westerville Citizens' Police Academy, and pursuing his interests in Tai Chi, swimming, history, music, old time movies and reading. **MAYA CATHERINE PRYFOGLE** Seventh great granddaughter of progenitor Nicholas Kegg. **SCOTT KENNETH PRYFOGLE** Sixth great grandson of progenitor Nicholas Kegg. **ZACHARY PRYFOGLE** Seventh great grandson of progenitor Nicholas Kegg.

PSENICSKA

BRYCE RICHARD STERLING PSENICSKA Seventh great grandson of progenitor Nicholas Kegg.
CAYLEE PSENICSKA Seventh great granddaughter of progenitor Nicholas Kegg.

PUCKETT

JUDY LYNN PUCKETT Fifth great granddaughter of progenitor Nicholas Kegg.
KAREN SUE PUCKETT Fifth great granddaughter of progenitor Nicholas Kegg.
RONALD ERVIN PUCKETT Fifth great grandson of progenitor Nicholas Kegg.

PUGH

AEDAN KENNETH PUGH Eighth great grandson of progenitor Nicholas Kegg.
AMAYA ROSE PUGH Eighth great granddaughter of progenitor Nicholas Kegg.

[5706A] Columbus Dispatch (OH) Feb. 13, 2011

EILEEN M. PUGH [5707] (1969 – 2018) daughter of Charles and Virginia (Cagg) Pugh married Michael A. Banks with whom she was mother of (1). Later she married Eric Bruneau. Eileen worked as a nurse's aide for many years. She enjoyed taking car trips, attending concerts, horror movies and loved the Pittsburgh Steelers. Her passion was spending time with her family. **INFANT PUGH** (1954 – 1954) daughter of Charles and Virginia (Cagg) Pugh. **RICHARD PUGH** Fifth great grandson of progenitor Nicholas Kegg. **RICHARD PUGH JR.** Sixth great grandson of progenitor Nicholas Kegg. **TERESA LOUISE PUGH** Sixth great granddaughter of progenitor Nicholas Kegg.

PURCELL

EARL LEE PURCELL Sixth great grandson of progenitor Nicholas Kegg.

PURPIGLIO

GEORGE PURPIGLIO Sixth great grandson of progenitor Nicholas Kegg.

QUEEN

HENRY CURTIS QUEEN [5708] (1983 – 1983) son of Curtis and Robin (Whetstone) Queen.
JUSTIN CURTIS QUEEN Fifth great grandson of progenitor Nicholas Kegg.
SAMANTHA QUEEN Fifth great granddaughter of progenitor Nicholas Kegg.

QUERRY

JOSHUA BRIAN QUERRY Sixth great grandson of progenitor Nicholas Kegg.

QUINBY

BENTLEY QUINBY Eighth great grandson of progenitor Nicholas Kegg. **DEBORAH ANNE QUINBY** Fifth great granddaughter of progenitor Nicholas Kegg. **EMILY CATHERINE QUINBY** Sixth great granddaughter of progenitor Nicholas Kegg. **LISA QUINBY** Fifth great granddaughter of progenitor Nicholas Kegg. **MICHAEL SEAN QUINBY** Fifth great grandson of progenitor Nicholas Kegg. **NANCY LYNNE QUINBY** Fifth great granddaughter of progenitor Nicholas Kegg. **SANDRA LOUISE QUINBY** Fifth great granddaughter of progenitor Nicholas Kegg. **STEPHANIE ANN QUINBY** Fifth great granddaughter of progenitor Nicholas Kegg.

QUINN

NATASHA QUINN Seventh great granddaughter of progenitor Nicholas Kegg.
NAYETTE QUINN Seventh great granddaughter of progenitor Nicholas Kegg.

RABAI

AMANI RABAI Seventh great grandson of progenitor Nicholas Kegg. **ANDRE RABAI** Seventh great grandson of progenitor Nicholas Kegg. **HADI RABAI** Seventh great granddaughter of progenitor Nicholas Kegg. **JACOB RABAI** Seventh great grandson of progenitor Nicholas Kegg. **JEAN LUC RABAI** Seventh great grandson of progenitor Nicholas Kegg. **JEFFREY STEDWILL RABAI** [5710] (1991 – 2015) son of Bilal and Mary (Stedwill) Rabai was an exceptional musician and a person of extreme generosity and kindness. As a parting gift, he chose to be an organ and tissue donor.

[5707] Shea Funeral Homes (VT) [5708] p.4 - Altoona Mirror (PA) June 6, 1983 [5709] Sturgis Daily Journal (MI) transcribed by Carole Lynn (MOHNEY) CARR [5710] Toledo Blade (OH) May 31, 2015

NOUR RABAI Seventh great granddaughter of progenitor Nicholas Kegg.
STEPHEN RABAI Seventh great grandson of progenitor Nicholas Kegg.

RADER

KELLY L. RADER Sixth great granddaughter of progenitor Nicholas Kegg.
RICK D. RADER Sixth great grandson of progenitor Nicholas Kegg

RAFFERTY

DANIEL L. RAFFERTY [5711] (1954 – 1954) son of Daniel and Helen (Turner) Rafferty.
JAMES W. RAFFERTY Fifth great grandson of progenitor Nicholas Kegg.
LARRY DAVID RAFFERTY Fifth great grandson of progenitor Nicholas Kegg.
ROBIN RAFFERTY Fifth great granddaughter of progenitor Nicholas Kegg.

RAGER

ADAM RAGER Sixth great grandson of progenitor Nicholas Kegg. **BELLE RAGER** Seventh great granddaughter of progenitor Nicholas Kegg. **BRADY RAGER** Seventh great grandson of progenitor Nicholas Kegg. **CAMREN M. RAGER** [5712] (2000 – 2006) son of Randy and Tammy (Orosz) Rager was a shy, energetic little boy who loved playing ball, loved animals, swimming, SpongeBob SquarePants and was happy go lucky. He belonged to Little Steps Day Care, and Small Steps Day Care. He would have been a first grader. **CURTIS RAGER** Sixth great grandson of progenitor Nicholas Kegg. **DAMEN RAGER** [5713] (2003 – 2006) son of Randy and Tammy (Orosz) Rager was a very strong-willed boy who loved playing ball, trucks, Game Boy and loved animals and SpongeBob SquarePants. He belonged to the Little Steps Day Care. **DANA MARK RAGER** Fifth great grandson of progenitor Nicholas Kegg. **GARY G. RAGER** Fifth great grandson of progenitor Nicholas Kegg. **GEORGE DENNING RAGER** Fifth great grandson of progenitor Nicholas Kegg. **JACOB RAGER** Seventh great grandson of progenitor Nicholas Kegg. **JENNIFER RAGER** aka "Jenn", Sixth great granddaughter of progenitor Nicholas Kegg. **JOANNA RAGER** Sixth great granddaughter of progenitor Nicholas Kegg. **JOE RAGER** Sixth great grandson of progenitor Nicholas Kegg. **KAILYN RAGER** Seventh great granddaughter of progenitor Nicholas Kegg. **KEMP ALLEN RAGER** Seventh great grandson of progenitor Nicholas Kegg. **KEMP ALLEN RAGER** Sixth great grandson of progenitor Nicholas Kegg. **RANDY EUGENE RAGER** Sixth great grandson of progenitor Nicholas Kegg. **SARA RAGER** Seventh great granddaughter of progenitor Nicholas Kegg. **SETH WILLIAM RAGER** Seventh great grandson of progenitor Nicholas Kegg. **TRACY RAGER** Sixth great granddaughter of progenitor Nicholas Kegg.

RAINE

PAUL MCNIGHT RAINE [5714] (1931 – 2015) son of Austin and Lucille (Johnson) Raine married twice; first to Carolyn Mary Flowers with whom he was father of (1). Later, he married Geneen L. Richmond. Paul was the owner of numerous grocery stores throughout Central Ohio.
SHIRLEY DAUNE RAINE [5715] (1930 – 2013) daughter of Austin and Lucille (Johnson) Raine married twice; first to James Edward Boggs. Later, she married Lisle M. Clark with whom she was mother of (1).
STEVEN PAUL RAINE (1952 – 1993) son of Paul and Carolyn (Flowers) Raine married and divorced Dottie G. White. Steven was a veteran.

[5711] Evening Times (MD) Dec 7, 1954 [5712, 5713)] Tribune Democrat (PA) Aug 3, 2006 [5714] Columbus Dispatch (OH) July 17, 2015 [5715] The Columbus Dispatch (OH) Apr. 28, 2013

RAINES

CHARLES EDWARD RAINES aka "Chuck" Sixth great grandson of progenitor Nicholas Kegg. **MELISSA SUE RAINES** Sixth great granddaughter of progenitor Nicholas Kegg.

RAINS

JULIANNE ELIZABETH RAINS Seventh great granddaughter of progenitor Nicholas Kegg.

RAMBO

TYLER RAMBO Eighth great grandson of progenitor Nicholas Kegg.

RAMER

DORIS RAMER Fifth great granddaughter of progenitor Nicholas Kegg. **JAMES RAMER** Fifth great grandson of progenitor Nicholas Kegg. **JANET RAMER** Fifth great granddaughter of progenitor Nicholas Kegg. **MICHAEL RAMER** Fifth great grandson of progenitor Nicholas Kegg. **MONTE L RAMER** Fourth great grandson of progenitor Nicholas Kegg. **NICHOLAS AARON RAMER** Fifth great grandson of progenitor Nicholas Kegg.

RAMSEY

AUTUMN B. RAMSEY Seventh great granddaughter of progenitor Nicholas Kegg. **BEVERLY RAMSEY** Sixth great granddaughter of progenitor Nicholas Kegg. **CHLOE ELIZABETH RAMSEY** [5716] (2004 – 2004) daughter of Steven and Jenna (Jay) Ramsey. **DONNIE RAMSEY** Sixth great grandson of progenitor Nicholas Kegg. **GAIGE WILLIAM RAMSEY** Seventh great grandson of progenitor Nicholas Kegg. **JADYN ASHLEE RAMSEY** Seventh great granddaughter of progenitor Nicholas Kegg. **JOEY RAMSEY** Sixth great grandson of progenitor Nicholas Kegg. **LIAH PAIGE RAMSEY** Seventh great granddaughter of progenitor Nicholas Kegg. **RONALD LEE RAMSEY** aka "Ronnie", Sixth great grandson of progenitor Nicholas Kegg. **STEVEN RAMSEY** Seventh great grandson of progenitor Nicholas Kegg. **STEVEN E. RAMSEY** Sixth great grandson of progenitor Nicholas Kegg. **WAYNE RAMSEY** Sixth great grandson of progenitor Nicholas Kegg.

RANDALL

JANE ANN RANDALL Fifth great granddaughter of progenitor Nicholas Kegg.
JOHN MAC RANDALL Fifth great grandson of progenitor Nicholas Kegg.

RANDELL

JOELLEN RANDELL Sixth great granddaughter of progenitor Nicholas Kegg.

RANDOLPH

RICHARD STEVEN RANDOLPH Fourth great grandson of progenitor Nicholas Kegg.
ROBERT EARL RANDOLPH Fourth great grandson of progenitor Nicholas Kegg.

RANKER

DANETTE LAVERNE RANKER Fifth great granddaughter of progenitor Nicholas Kegg.

[5716] Bedford Inquirer (PA) Sep 24, 2004, obtained by Bob Rose

DANIEL LEE RANKER Fifth great grandson of progenitor Nicholas Kegg. **DARLA LORRAINE RANKER** Fifth great granddaughter of progenitor Nicholas Kegg. **DARRYL LYNN RANKER** Fifth great grandson of progenitor Nicholas Kegg. **DIANE LOUISE RANKER** Fifth great granddaughter of progenitor Nicholas Kegg.

RANSDELL

DWIGHT DEAN RANSDELL Sixth great grandson of progenitor Nicholas Kegg. **ELIZABETH ROBB RANSDELL** Seventh great granddaughter of progenitor Nicholas Kegg. **EMILY RANSDELL** Sixth great granddaughter of progenitor Nicholas Kegg. **JOEL WARD RANSDELL** aka "Joey", Seventh great grandson of progenitor Nicholas Kegg. **MATTHEW SALY RANSDELL** Seventh great grandson of progenitor Nicholas Kegg. **WARD RICHARDS RANSDELL** Sixth great grandson of progenitor Nicholas Kegg.

RAPSKY

FRANK RAPSKY Sixth great grandson of progenitor Nicholas Kegg.

RASMUSSEN

JORDAN RAY RASMUSSEN Seventh great grandson of progenitor Nicholas Kegg.

RATHBUN

MONTGOMERY RATHBUN Seventh great grandson of progenitor Nicholas Kegg. **MORGAN RATHBUN** Seventh great granddaughter of progenitor Nicholas Kegg.

RAY

ANGELS RAY Sixth great grandson of progenitor Nicholas Kegg. **BRENT RAY** Fifth great grandson of progenitor Nicholas Kegg. **DENNY RAY** Fifth great grandson of progenitor Nicholas Kegg. **DEWARD EDWARD RAY** Sixth great grandson of progenitor Nicholas Kegg. **GRIER RAY** Seventh great grandson of progenitor Nicholas Kegg. **HARRIET ROSE RAY** (1921 – 2001) daughter of William and Margaret (Kegg) Ray married twice; first to Leo Joseph Seitz. Later, she married Samuel Dandrea with whom she was mother of (4). **HEATHER ELAINE RAY** Sixth great granddaughter of progenitor Nicholas Kegg. **HOLLY ELAINE RAY** Sixth great granddaughter of progenitor Nicholas Kegg. **JESSE RAY** Seventh great grandson of progenitor Nicholas Kegg. **JOHN T. RAY** Fifth great grandson of progenitor Nicholas Kegg. **JOHN WESLEY RAY** Sixth great grandson of progenitor Nicholas Kegg. **JOSEPH RAY** Sixth great grandson of progenitor Nicholas Kegg. **JOY RAY** Fifth great granddaughter of progenitor Nicholas Kegg. **KAYLA RAY** Seventh great granddaughter of progenitor Nicholas Kegg. **MARSHA RAY** Fifth great granddaughter of progenitor Nicholas Kegg. **RAYMOND ROBERT RAY** (1926 – 1976) son of William and Margaret (Kegg) Ray, married Maxine (Kranwinkle) Alexander with whom he was father of (5). **RICHARD VANCE RAY** Fifth great grandson of progenitor Nicholas Kegg. **SHELLEY RAY** Fifth great granddaughter of progenitor Nicholas Kegg. **STEVE RAY** Fifth great grandson of progenitor Nicholas Kegg. **THOMAS LANE RAY** Sixth great grandson of progenitor Nicholas Kegg. **WILLIAM CHARLES RAY** [5717] (1924 – 2003) son of William and Margaret (Kegg) Ray, was father of (3). He married Velma Ann Cole.

[5717] Press-Telegram (CA) Feb 14, 2003/FindAGrave memorial# 104777304

RAYMOND

BRUCE D. RAYMOND Sixth great grandson of progenitor Nicholas Kegg. **DEE ANN RAYMOND** Sixth great granddaughter of progenitor Nicholas Kegg. **GLEA RAYMOND** Fifth great granddaughter of progenitor Nicholas Kegg. **HOWARD R. RAYMOND** Fifth great grandson of progenitor Nicholas Kegg. **MARILYN KAY RAYMOND** (5717A) (1937 – 2011) daughter of Harland and Maxine (Munn) Raymond married twice, first to Eldan Crone with whom she was mother of (3), later to Gary Gray. Marilyn was a telephone switchboard operator for Northwestern Bell and a secretary at the Methodist Church, both in Broken Bow. She also worked on a potato harvest crew outside of Malta, Idaho and later was an Office Manager for a mental health facility in Scottsbluff NE, before retiring from the Aging Office there. **MARY ELLEN RAYMOND** Fifth great granddaughter of progenitor Nicholas Kegg. **MATTHEW DOUGLAS RAYMOND** Seventh great grandson of progenitor Nicholas Kegg. **ROBERT RAYMOND** Sixth great grandson of progenitor Nicholas Kegg. **SCOTT RAYMOND** Sixth great grandson of progenitor Nicholas Kegg. **SHIRLEE FAYE RAYMOND** Fifth great granddaughter of progenitor Nicholas Kegg. **THOMAS FREDRICK RAYMOND** Fifth great grandson of progenitor Nicholas Kegg.

REAGEN

COLLEEN REAGEN Sixth great granddaughter of progenitor Nicholas Kegg.
DENNIS REAGEN Sixth great grandson of progenitor Nicholas Kegg.

REAMER

AARICKA MARIE REAMER Sixth great granddaughter of progenitor Nicholas Kegg.
AARON MATTHEW REAMER Sixth great grandson of progenitor Nicholas Kegg.
JEREMY ROBERT REAMER Sixth great grandson of progenitor Nicholas Kegg.

REBER

ALEX REBER Sixth great grandson of progenitor Nicholas Kegg. **ALEXANDER WARREN REBER** Sixth great grandson of progenitor Nicholas Kegg. **ASHLEY REBER** Sixth great granddaughter of progenitor Nicholas Kegg. **CARROLL JOHN REBER** (5718) (1923 – 2014) aka "Jack", son of Carroll and Marcee (Musser) Reber, married Nana Yocum with whom he was father of (2). Jack served with the army in the European theatre during World War II. **GEORGE YOCUM REBER** Fifth great grandson of progenitor Nicholas Kegg. **JOHN REBER** Fifth great grandson of progenitor Nicholas Kegg. **PAUL CROWL REBER** (5718A) (1959 – 2015) son of Richard and Joanne (Crowl) Reber, married Shannon Dee Warren with whom he was father of (1). Paul served as executive director of Stratford Hall, the ancestral home and birthplace of Gen. Robert E. Lee and oversaw a massive restoration of the historic Virginia plantation. Dr. Reber devoted his career to historic preservation in the Washington area and raised millions of dollars for conservation efforts. Before arriving at Stratford Hall, he held executive roles with the White House Endowment Fund, George Washington's Mount Vernon estate and the historic Decatur House Museum in Northwest Washington. Paul was a former adjunct history professor at the University of North Carolina at Greensboro and a historian-in-residence at American University. He was a board member of the nonprofit Association for the Preservation of Historic Congressional Cemetery, vice chairman of the Virginia Tourism Corp. and a member of the Metropolitan Club. **RICHARD MUSSER REBER** (5718B) aka "Dick" (1931 – 2017) son of Carroll and Marcee (Musser) Reber, married Joanne Crowl with whom he was father of (1). Dick joined the U.S. Army, serving just

---

(5717A) Heer-Dahl Mortuary (Fort Morgan, CO) (5718) Miami Herald (FL) Jan 5, 1984 (5718A) Washington Post (DC) Sep 2, 2015 (5718B) LancasterOnline (PA) Jan 4, 2018

prior to the end of the Korean War. Dick embarked on a long and successful engineering career. He began working for Piasecki Helicoper, where he helped design the Polaris Missile Launching System, and later joined Boeing Vertol as a Senior Flight Test Engineer. At Boeing, he conducted tests on the Sea King Helicopter, one of the most versatile and enduring helicopter designs of the century. He was subsequently employed by Westinghouse, which sent him around the globe to set up nuclear power plants and to design steam turbines. He ended his career working as a Logistics Engineer for the General Electric Corporation in Valley Forge, PA. Dick's abiding interest, apart from his family and engineering, was Freemasonry. Notwithstanding Dick's achievements in engineering and years of dedicated service in Freemasonry, these pursuits were of secondary importance compared to the love and affection he felt for his family.

REBOVICH

DAVID J. REBOVICH Eighth great grandson of progenitor Nicholas Kegg.
MICHAEL W. REBOVICH Eighth great grandson of progenitor Nicholas Kegg.
STEPHEN MICHAEL REBOVICH [5718C] (1971 – 1994) son of David and Debra (Diehl) Rebovich. Stephen graduated with honors from Kenmore High School.

REDDECLIFF

ANDREW REDDECLIFF Sixth great grandson of progenitor Nicholas Kegg. **CARLA LYN REDDECLIFF** Sixth great granddaughter of progenitor Nicholas Kegg. **CURTIS PAUL REDDECLIFF** Sixth great grandson of progenitor Nicholas Kegg. **AVID LYNN REDDECLIFF** Fifth great grandson of progenitor Nicholas Kegg. **FAYE IRENE REDDECLIFF** Fifth great granddaughter of progenitor Nicholas Kegg. **HANNAH REDDECLIFF** Sixth great granddaughter of progenitor Nicholas Kegg. **HEIDI JO REDDECLIFF** Fifth great granddaughter of progenitor Nicholas Kegg **JAMES LYNN REDDECLIFF** Fifth great grandson of progenitor Nicholas Kegg. **JANICE LEE REDDECLIFF** Sixth great granddaughter of progenitor Nicholas Kegg. **JARED REDDECLIFF** Seventh great grandson of progenitor Nicholas Kegg. **JERE MEAD REDDECLIFF** (1936 – 2011) son of Curtis and Iva (Bussard) Reddefliff, married Kathryn Harris with whom he was father of (2). **LUANN REDDECLIFF** Fifth great granddaughter of progenitor Nicholas Kegg. **MAGGIE REDDECLIFF** Sixth great granddaughter of progenitor Nicholas Kegg. **PATRICIA ANN REDDECLIFF** Sixth great granddaughter of progenitor Nicholas Kegg. **SCOTT REDDECLIFF** Sixth great grandson of progenitor Nicholas Kegg. **SUSAN CAROL REDDECLIFF** Sixth great granddaughter of progenitor Nicholas Kegg. **WILLIAM SCOTT REDDECLIFF** Fifth great grandson of progenitor Nicholas Kegg. **ZOE REDDECLIFF** Seventh great granddaughter of progenitor Nicholas Kegg.

REDINGER

ALLEN REDINGER Sixth great grandson of progenitor Nicholas Kegg.
LORI ANN REDINGER Sixth great granddaughter of progenitor Nicholas Kegg.
REGINA REDINGER Seventh great granddaughter of progenitor Nicholas Kegg.
SAMANTHA REDINGER Seventh great granddaughter of progenitor Nicholas Kegg.
TROY L. REDINGER Sixth great grandson of progenitor Nicholas Kegg.

REDNER

SARAH JEANNETTE REDNER Sixth great granddaughter of progenitor Nicholas Kegg.

[5718C] Akron Beacon Journal (OH) March 23, 1994, contributed by D. Sue Dible

REED

ADAM REED Sixth great grandson of progenitor Nicholas Kegg. **ASHLEY D. REED** Sixth great granddaughter of progenitor Nicholas Kegg. **BOB REED** Fifth great grandson of progenitor Nicholas Kegg. **CARL ALBERT REED** (5718D) (1919 – 2009) son of Ross and Sally (Harclerode) Reed, married Mary Glee McDaniel with whom he was father of (1). Carl served in the United States Army during World War II as a Technician Fifth Grade with the 122nd Field Artillery Battalion in the Philippines, receiving the Good Conduct Medal, the Army Occupation Medal (Japan), the Asiatic Pacific Theater Ribbon, and the World War II Victory Medal. He was employed as a trackman for the Pennsylvania Railroad and Conrail for over 32 years. Carl had also worked as a laborer at New Enterprise Stone and Lime. Carl was a member of Bedford Moose Lodge No. 480 and of the Everett Sportsmen's Club. **CAROL DIANE REED** Sixth great granddaughter of progenitor Nicholas Kegg. **CHRISTIE REED** Fifth great granddaughter of progenitor Nicholas Kegg. **DANIEL REED** Seventh great grandson of progenitor Nicholas Kegg. **DANIEL ALLEN REED** Sixth great grandson of progenitor Nicholas Kegg. **DORTHA IDA REED** (1906 – 1994) daughter of James and Effie (Kegg) Reed married four times; first to Lewis Hodges, then Mr. Hager. She married Mr. King and Mr. Crawford. **ELIZABETH L. REED** (5718E) aka "Betty" (1927 – 2015) daughter of Chester and Ethel (Kegg) Reed, married Milton J. Bergstein with whom she was mother of (2). Betty graduated from Penn State University with a BS in Clinical Psychology. She was a member of the PARC board and was a volunteer at Schlow Library for 13 years. **ERIK JAMES REED** Sixth great grandson of progenitor Nicholas Kegg. **ERIN REED** Sixth great granddaughter of progenitor Nicholas Kegg. **GREG ALAN REED** Eighth great grandson of progenitor Nicholas Kegg. **HANNAH REED** Seventh great granddaughter of progenitor Nicholas Kegg. **HELEN M. REED** (1908 - ?) daughter of James and Effie (Kegg) Reed had been married twice; first to James Gannon and later to William Charles Pell. **JENNIFER REED** Eighth great granddaughter of progenitor Nicholas Kegg. **JENNIFER LEIGH REED** Seventh great granddaughter of progenitor Nicholas Kegg. **JESSE MELVIN REED** (5719) (1924 – 1984) son of Ross and Sally (Harcherode) Reed married twice; first to Lena Phyllis Burkett with whom he was father of (1). Later, Jesse married Joan Ruth Steele with whom he was father of (1). He served in the U.S. Army during World War II, retired in May of 1984, after 20 years in the Pennsylvania National Guard, was employed by New Enterprise Stone & Lime Company, Blacktop Division, member of VFW Post #2088, American Legion Post #8, and Improved Order of Redmen Wambic Tribe #507. **KAREN REED** Seventh great granddaughter of progenitor Nicholas Kegg. **JESSE MELVIN REED** (5719A) aka "Robin" (1959 – 2011) son of Jesse and Joan (Steele) Reed. Robin first worked as a Chef at the Maritime Institute in Baltimore, and after moving back to Bedford County, owned and operated his own landscaping and transportation company. He enjoyed taking care of his antique shop at Founders Crossing in Bedford, and with a good eye for detail, enjoyed buying antiques to restore for sale. He was a caring man who was always willing to help others. **KENNETH PHILIP REED** (5719B) (1950 – 1988) son of Ross and Cora (Pepple) Reed, married Debra Harclerode with whom he was father of (2). Ken was employed by New Enterprise Stone and Lime Co. at Ashcom as a foreman in the pulverizing plant. He had been employed by New Enterprise for 18 years. He was president of the Everett Sportsmen's Club, and a member of Teamsters Local 453 of Cumberland, Md., and of the National Rifle Association. **LILLIAN REED** Ninth great granddaughter of progenitor Nicholas Kegg. **LORA JEAN REED** (1936 – 1987) daughter of Roy and Jeanne (Kennedy) Reed, married William Franklin Bowman with whom she was mother of (2). **MARIA REED** Eighth great granddaughter of progenitor Nicholas Kegg. **MARY ELIZABETH REED** (5719C) (1944 – 2001) daughter of Melvin and Josephine (Bowlus) Reed, married John Kimber with whom she was mother of (2). Manager of H & R Block at Long Leaf Mall in Wilmington, Mary was also Treasurer of Kimber Investments, Inc., in Columbia, S. C. She had worked as a tutor for the Cape Fear Literacy Council and was an avid indoor gardener and especially loved her orchids. Mary had a sense of

---

(5718D) p.3 - Bedford Inquirer (PA) Nov 6, 2009, contributed by Bob Rose (5718E) Koch Funeral Home (PA) (5719) Bedford County Genealogical Society obituary obtained by D. Sue Dible (5719A) Dallavalle Funeral Home (PA) (5719B) Bedford County Genealogical Society obituary obtained and contributed by D. Sue Dible (5719C) p.6B - Sunday Star-News (NC) July 22, 2001

humor and contagious smile. **MEREDITH REED** Eighth great granddaughter of progenitor Nicholas Kegg. **PATRICIA ANN REED** [5719D] (1931 – 2019) daughter of Chester and Ethel (Kegg) Reed married Vernon Blades Derrickson with whom she was mother of (4). Later she married Dana Collins Belser. Pat was an accomplished artist, hosting many shows in the D.C. and Delaware areas. She was an avid lover of the beach, with her favorite past time being spending time with family and friends. She also enjoyed playing golf, painting, bird watching and traveling. Pat was an active member of Rehoboth Art League, Rehoboth Beach Country Club and Columbia Country Club in Chevy Chase, Md.
PETER REED Fifth great grandson of progenitor Nicholas Kegg. **RICHARD REED** Fifth great grandson of progenitor Nicholas Kegg. **ROBERT DEAN REED** aka "Bobby", Sixth great grandson of progenitor Nicholas Kegg. **ROSEMARY REED** (died 1949) daughter of Roy and Jeanne (Kennedy) Reed. **ROSS KENNETH REED** [5719E] (1916 – 2008) son of Ross and Sally (Harclerode) Reed, married Cora Fanny Pepple with whom he was father of (2). Ross served in the United States Army during World War II with the 3188th Ordnance Ammunition Company at the Black Hills Depot in Igloo, S.D., where he was a Private First Class, working as a clerk, earning his Marksman Rifle and Expert Bayonet qualifications and receiving the Good Conduct Medal. After service to his country, Ken began his lifelong work as a truck driver for New Enterprise Stone and Lime Company at the Ashcom plant, having a perfect driving record when he retired. In his early years, he enjoyed playing baseball with the teams around Everett, and throughout his life, enjoyed working on his HO scale train layout at his Lincoln Highway home, having built the layout himself, making houses and other buildings out of matchsticks. Ken was also an eager gardener, keeping up wild black raspberry shrubs and was well known for the many berries grown that he shared with so many people. He also liked to hunt with his family and friends at their Clearfield County camp, especially hunting deer, and truly enjoyed traveling with his wife Cora all around the states and was a kind and helpful man.
THOMAS PATRICK REED Seventh great grandson of progenitor Nicholas Kegg.
THOMAS SHELDON REED [5719F] (1922 – 1999) son of Ross and Sally (Harclerode) Reed, married Alice Roxine McClure with whom he was father of (1). An honorable discharge from the U.S. Army after World War II, Thomas retired from the Norfolk NAS jet engine rework facility.
THOMAS SHELDON REED Sixth great grandson of progenitor Nicholas Kegg.

REES

DAVID THOMAS REES Fifth great grandson of progenitor Nicholas Kegg.
DEANA JO REES Fifth great granddaughter of progenitor Nicholas Kegg.
KORIN JOAN REES Sixth great granddaughter of progenitor Nicholas Kegg.
MILDRED JANE REES Fifth great granddaughter of progenitor Nicholas Kegg.

REFFNER

CAMDEN B. REFFNER Eighth great grandson of progenitor Nicholas Kegg.
ELIZA J. REFFNER Eighth great granddaughter of progenitor Nicholas Kegg.
IAN C. REFFNER Eighth great grandson of progenitor Nicholas Kegg.

REFSLAND

ANGELA RAE REFSLAND Sixth great granddaughter of progenitor Nicholas Kegg.
DANIELLE RAE LYNN REFSLAND Sixth great granddaughter of progenitor Nicholas Kegg.
JASON DANIEL REFSLAND Sixth great grandson of progenitor Nicholas Kegg.

[5719D] Cape Gazette (DE) May 21, 2019, obtained and contributed by D. Sue Dible [5719E] Bedford Inquirer (PA) Dec 19, 2008, contributed by Bob Rose [5719F] p. B6 - The Virginian-Pilot (Norfolk, VA) July 19, 1999

REGNER

JAMES LEE REGNER [5720] (1944 – 1976) son of Hermuth and Mildred (Hollenbeck) Regner married Janet Cunningham. James was employed as a lineman for Fruit Belt Electric company, was electrocuted near Keeler, the result of the snowstorm which swept parts of southwestern Michigan **KIRK REGNER** Sixth great grandson of progenitor Nicholas Kegg. **MICHELLE LYNN REGNER** [5721] (1970 – 1993) daughter of Robert and Nancy (Harris) Regner. **ROBERT KAY REGNER** Fifth great grandson of progenitor Nicholas Kegg. **SCOTT REGNER** Sixth great grandson of progenitor Nicholas Kegg.

STEVEN JOEL REGNER Sixth great grandson of progenitor Nicholas Kegg.
WAYNE L. REGNER Fifth great grandson of progenitor Nicholas Kegg.

REGULA

CARRIE LYNN REGULA Sixth great granddaughter of progenitor Nicholas Kegg.
KEITH WILLIAM REGULA Sixth great grandson of progenitor Nicholas Kegg.

REICH

CRYSTAL REICH Seventh great granddaughter of progenitor Nicholas Kegg.
D. J. REICH Seventh great grandson of progenitor Nicholas Kegg.

REICHARD

ALAN RAY REICHARD Fifth great grandson of progenitor Nicholas Kegg. **ALLYSSA RAE REICHARD** Seventh great granddaughter of progenitor Nicholas Kegg. **BETH REICHARD** Sixth great granddaughter of progenitor Nicholas Kegg. **CHARLES WAYNE REICHARD** Fifth great grandson of progenitor Nicholas Kegg. **CYNTHIA REICHARD** Sixth great granddaughter of progenitor Nicholas Kegg. **DAVID P. REICHARD** Sixth great grandson of progenitor Nicholas Kegg. **EMILY NICOLE REICHARD** Seventh great granddaughter of progenitor Nicholas Kegg. **FRANCIS EDWARD REICHARD** Sixth great grandson of progenitor Nicholas Kegg. **JANET SUE REICHARD** Fifth great granddaughter of progenitor Nicholas Kegg. **JASON ALAN REICHARD** Sixth great grandson of progenitor Nicholas Kegg. **LOGAN MARIE REICHARD** Seventh great granddaughter of progenitor Nicholas Kegg. **LORI KRISTI REICHARD** Sixth great granddaughter of progenitor Nicholas Kegg. **MARGARET EVELYN REICHARD** Fifth great granddaughter of progenitor Nicholas Kegg. **PHILLIP JAY REICHARD** [5722] (1931 – 2018) son of Ellis and Anna (Shafer) Reichard married twice; first to Marguerite Ellen Hoban with whom he was father of (9). Later, he married Connie Louise Chapman. Phillip joined the U.S. Navy, where he served for 20 years. He was a veteran of the Korean War and was wounded in the Vietnam War. After he retired from the Navy, Phillip served 10 years in the civil service, and then joined Merchant Marines for 10 years. **PHILLIP JAY REICHARD** Sixth great grandson of progenitor Nicholas Kegg. **RACHELL REICHARD** Seventh great granddaughter of progenitor Nicholas Kegg. **RICHARD ALAN REICHARD** Sixth great grandson of progenitor Nicholas Kegg. **SEAN MICHAEL REICHARD** Sixth great grandson of progenitor Nicholas Kegg.

REICHERT

ASHLYNN REICHERT Sixth great granddaughter of progenitor Nicholas Kegg.
CARLY KAY REICHERT Seventh great granddaughter of progenitor Nicholas Kegg.

[5720] The Herald-Palladium (Saint Joseph, Michigan) Nov 6, 1976 [5721] The South Bend Tribune (IN) Dec 15, 1993 [5722] Sturgis Journal (MI) Sept. 19, 2018

ERIC REICHERT Sixth great grandson of progenitor Nicholas Kegg. **HARVEY DAVID REICHERT** (5723) (1953 – 2004) son of David and Betty (Stuckey) Reichert married and was father of (2). Harvey farmed near Minatare and began working for Trinidad Bean in 1994. Harvey attended Salem Congregational Church in Scottsbluff. **JAMES REICHERT** Sixth great grandson of progenitor Nicholas Kegg. **JASE ETHAN REICHERT** Seventh great grandson of progenitor Nicholas Kegg. **JEREMY REICHERT** Sixth great grandson of progenitor Nicholas Kegg. **JERRY RAY REICHERT** (5723A) (1955 – 2018) son of David and Betty (Stuckey) Reichert married Kimberly with whom he was father of (1). Jerry was a self-employed farmer. **KATIE REICHERT** Sixth great granddaughter of progenitor Nicholas Kegg. **ROBERT MARK REICHERT** Fifth great grandson of progenitor Nicholas Kegg. **RYAN REICHERT** Sixth great grandson of progenitor Nicholas Kegg. **SHIRAH MAE REICHERT** Seventh great granddaughter of progenitor Nicholas Kegg.

REICHLEY

BENJAMIN REICHLEY Sixth great grandson of progenitor Nicholas Kegg. **JACQUELINE REICHLEY** Sixth great granddaughter of progenitor Nicholas Kegg. **JOHN REICHLEY** Sixth great grandson of progenitor Nicholas Kegg. **ROBERT REICHLEY** Sixth great grandson of progenitor Nicholas Kegg.

REID

EDWARED BROWN REID (5724) (1943 - 2019) aka "Ed", son of W.M. & Nancy Jane (Pratt) Reid married Constance Lynn Spector with whom he was father of (1). Later, he married Connie Jean Goldston and Ellen (Wilder) Bradbury. After Ed received his PHD in organic chemistry at Rice University he taught chemistry at the University of Houston, then worked in the international petrochemical industry. He moved to Santa Fe and became the Development Director of Western States Arts Foundation. He later sold real estate, first with Santa Fe Properties and then for Barker Realty. Ed served his community as President of the Board of Big Brothers, Big Sisters of Santa Fe Throughout his childhood, Ed spent summers with his grandfather, Wallace Everett Pratt, a distinguished petroleum geologist who owned a 6,000-acre ranch in west Texas that he later donated to create the Guadalupe Mountains National Park. At the ranch, Ed fell in love with nature, wildlife and adventure. He learned to drive a Jeep at nine, he lived on his own as a teenager in a remote cabin, hunted for lost treasure in caves, and explored the high mountains. Ed returned to the Guadalupe's throughout his entire life, sharing his stories and his love for the landscape, Ed fully appreciated his life. He was never happier than when he was climbing a ruin in the Yucatan with a camera slung around his neck, or photographing rare birds, or working on a project at their cabin in Holy Ghost Canyon, or singing and playing his guitar, or cooking up a pot of jambalaya, or taking advantage of the history, art and culture of Santa Fe and Merida. His kindness and good humor captured everyone he ever met. **JENNIFER REID** Sixth great granddaughter of progenitor Nicholas Kegg. **LAUREN CYD REID** Sixth great granddaughter of progenitor Nicholas Kegg. **MCKENNA REID** Seventh great granddaughter of progenitor Nicholas Kegg. **WALLACE PRATT REID** aka "Wally" Sixth great grandson of progenitor Nicholas Kegg. **WILLIAM MCCORMICK REID JR**. (5725) (1941 - 1999) aka "Will", son of W.M. & Nancy Jane (Pratt) Reid married Alice Broomell Haldeman with whom he was father of (2). William received his Ph.D. in geology at the University of Texas. Throughout his career Will worked for the Environmental Protection Agency, Earth Satellite Corporation and Condon, Reid and Associates. Some of Will's many endeavors included committees such as Save Our Springs in Austin, Texas and the Hill Country Citizens Alliance in Crested Butte, Colorado, Will's enthusiasm for the outdoors was shared with family and friends throughout his life.

(5723) Scottsbluff Star Herald (NE) Feb 14, 2004, obtained by Henry L. Schmick (5723A) Star Herald (NB) Mar 23, 2018 (5724) Santa Fe New Mexican Oct. 12, 2019 (5725) Austin American-Statesman (TX) Nov. 5, 1999

REIFSTECK

CHRISTOPHER BRUCE REIFSTECK Seventh great grandson of progenitor Nicholas Kegg.
JEFFREY VAUGHN REIFSTECK Seventh great grandson of progenitor Nicholas Kegg.
JULIE LIN REIFSTECK Seventh great granddaughter of progenitor Nicholas Kegg.

REIGHARD

AVIS CAROLINE REIGHARD [5726] (1900 – 1920) daughter of Joseph and Maude (Biddle) Reighard. Avis had been ill with tuberculosis for more than three years and spent one year in the Cresson sanitorium with the hope of regaining her health. **CLEO JOANN REIGHARD** [5726A] aka Joann" (1933 – 2016) daughter of John and Goldie (Inglis) Reighard married George John Bowers with whom she was mother of (5). Joann was employed as a cafeteria worker for the Lancaster City School District. She enjoyed knitting, making Afghan's and doll making. **JOHN F. REIGHARD** [5727] (1910 – 1983) son of Joseph and Maude (Biddle) Reighard married twice; first to Goldie Mae Inglis with whom he was father of (2). Later, he married Evelyn Mary Wharton. John retired from Sun Pipeline Company after 33 years of service. **JOHN F. REIGHARD** Fifth great grandson of progenitor Nicholas Kegg. **MARY E. REIGHARD** (1908 – 1908) of Joseph and Maude (Biddle) Reighard.

REILEY

DONALD CRESS REILEY [5727A] aka "Pat" (1939 – 2016) son of Donald and Mary (Shoemaker) Reiley. Don earned joint degrees in Metallurgical Engineering and Physics from Carnegie Mellon University and Franklin & Marshall College (F&M). At F&M, he was recently inducted into their prestigious William A. Schnader Society for all his contribution to their college. Later, Don became a licensed Professional Engineer (PE) and earned a law degree from the Washington School of Law of the American University. After law school and passing the bar, he became a member of the Bedford County Bar Association. Don initially worked for NASA in New Orleans and Huntsville, Ala., but a major part of his career was spent working as a Patent Examiner and Classifier at the US Patent & Trademark Office in Washington, D.C (Patent Office). He worked at the Patent Office for about 40 years before retiring. After his government career, Don became a founding member of the Patent Counsel Group L.L.P. With his friends and co-counsel John Gladstone Mills III and Robert C. Highley, Don co-authored an eight-volume treatise entitled Patent Law Fundamentals on intellectual property law. This comprehensive set provides a detailed source covering all the bases of current patent law. It provides help for research on any patent issue and assists in the formulation of strategies for applying for a new patent or litigating an existing patent. It also illustrates how to prepare a patent application with additional emphasis on claim drafting. Additionally, this treatise presents a step-by-step approach to dealing with patent prosecution before the Patent Office. The impact of this study cannot be underestimated in light of this detailed treatment. Attorney Reiley left an indelible mark on the development of patent law, both nationally and internationally. Don enjoyed many activities including traveling, playing chess and attending numismatic shows and auctions. He was an active member of St. John's United Church of Christ and the Chessnut Club. Don especially enjoyed playing chess and socializing with his friends about local and American history. He also was an avid follower of baseball, football and high school wrestling. **ERIN REILEY** Fifth great granddaughter of progenitor Nicholas Kegg. **IAN REILEY** Fifth great grandson of progenitor Nicholas Kegg. **MARY ROSALIND REILEY** [5727B] aka "Rosy" (1940 – 1982) daughter of Donald and Mary (Shoemaker) Reiley, married Robert Harold Leppert with whom she was mother of (3). Rosy was a graduate of Johnstown Vo-Tech as a licensed practical nurse. **MATTHEW REILEY** Fifth great grandson of progenitor Nicholas Kegg. **R. MARTIN REILEY** [5727C] (1941 – 2011) son of

---

[5726] Bedford County Historical Society obituary clipping obtained by D. Sue Dible [5726A] Groffs Family Funeral & Cremation Services, Inc (PA) Aug 7, 2016 [5727] p.16 News-Press (Fort Myers, FL) Aug 10, 1983 [5727A] Bedford Gazette (PA) Aug 2, 2016, contributed by Bob Rose [5727B] p.11 Bedford Gazette (PA) June 11, 1982 [5727C] Timothy A. Berkebile Funeral Home

Don and Mary (Shoemaker) Reiley, married Karen Elizabeth Andre with whom he was father of (3). After graduating from W & J College and the University of Pennsylvania Law School, Martin joined the family law practice, Reiley & Reiley. He practiced law ever since. Martin was an avid reader, traveler, nature enthusiast, volunteer, and conversationalist. **ROBERT THOMAS REILEY** Fourth great grandson of progenitor Nicholas Kegg.

REILLY

KATHLEEN REILLY Sixth great granddaughter of progenitor Nicholas Kegg.
LIAM REILLY Sixth great grandson of progenitor Nicholas Kegg.
MAEVE REILLY Sixth great granddaughter of progenitor Nicholas Kegg.

REINSEL

KRISTINE LEE REINSEL Sixth great granddaughter of progenitor Nicholas Kegg.
STEVEN MATTHEW REINSEL Sixth great grandson of progenitor Nicholas Kegg.

REIS

DENNIS ROBERT REIS Fifth great grandson of progenitor Nicholas Kegg.
MARGARET ANN REIS Fifth great granddaughter of progenitor Nicholas Kegg.
NANCY JEAN REIS Fifth great granddaughter of progenitor Nicholas Kegg.
ROBERT C. REIS Sixth great grandson of progenitor Nicholas Kegg.

REMER

CHRISTOPHER B. REMER Seventh great grandson of progenitor Nicholas Kegg.
JEFFREY BRYAN REMER Seventh great grandson of progenitor Nicholas Kegg.

RENDA

ANTHONY RENDA Seventh great grandson of progenitor Nicholas Kegg.
CAROL ANN RENDA Sixth great granddaughter of progenitor Nicholas Kegg.
FRANKLIN ANTHONY RENDA aka "Frank" Sixth great grandson of progenitor Nicholas Kegg.
SUZANNE RENDA Sixth great granddaughter of progenitor Nicholas Kegg.
NICKOLAS RENDA Seventh great grandson of progenitor Nicholas Kegg.

RENNA

ALLIE RENNA Seventh great granddaughter of progenitor Nicholas Kegg.
NICHOLAS RENNA Seventh great grandson of progenitor Nicholas Kegg.

RENNER

MICHELLE MARIE RENNER Fifth great granddaughter of progenitor Nicholas Kegg.

RENO

DAVID E. RENO Fifth great grandson of progenitor Nicholas Kegg.   **DAVID EDWARD RENO** [5727D] (1917 – 1998) son of David and Margaret (Heffner) Reno, married Helen V. Koman with whom he was father of (2).   **JONATHAN RENO** Sixth great grandson of progenitor Nicholas Kegg.

[5727D] p.B6 Pittsburgh Post-Gazette (PA) Oct 13, 1998

ROBERTA RENO aka "Bobbie" Fifth great granddaughter of progenitor Nicholas Kegg.
SAMANTHA RENO Sixth great granddaughter of progenitor Nicholas Kegg.

REPP

EILEEN GOLDIE REPP [5727E] (1911 – 1962) daughter of Willard and Nannie Belle (Cramer) Repp, married Charles Dean Youse. Eileen was employed as a beautician.   **MARY EVELYN REPP** (1916 – 1990) daughter of Willard and Nannie Belle (Cramer) Repp, married Thomas George Bleakney with whom she was mother of (2).   **PATRICIA L. REPP** [5727F] aka "Pat" (1936 – 2013) daughter of Perry and Emma (Austin) Repp married Paul J. Vining with whom she was mother of (5). Pat was a bookkeeper for Vining Slaughter Haus. She was a member of the Legion Auxilary and St. Joseph Catholic Church. She enjoyed playing bingo and facebook on her computer.   **PERRY DAVID REPP** (1913 – 1957) son of Willard and Nannie Belle (Cramer) Repp, married Emma Austin with whom he was father of (1). A two-car collision resulted in a fractured skull that took his life.

RESSLER

BARRY LAYNE RESSLER Fifth great grandson of progenitor Nicholas Kegg.   **BONNIE RAE RESSLER** Fifth great granddaughter of progenitor Nicholas Kegg.   **CLEVA ALVERNA RESSLER** [5728] (1916 – 2003) daughter of Frank and Ima (Amick) Ressler, married Blair Ivan Cornell with whom she was mother of (6). A homemaker, Cleva was affiliated with the former Rainsburg Methodist Church. **CLYDE AUSTIN RESSLER** [5728A] (1932 – 2016) son of Frank and Ima Pearl (Amick) Ressler married Betty Jean Mowry with whom he was father of (4). Clyde opened the ESSO Station at the Bedford Interchange and then he purchased the ESSO Station at Railroad Street, which later became known as Ressler's Exxon. Over the years, the station won many awards. Clyde retired as owner, selling the station to his son. He then continued working for his son, Clyde is a life member of the Bedford Volunteer Fire Company No. 1 Inc. and held the rank of Assistant Chief for many years. He was elected fire chief in 1976 and was a founding member of the Bedford Ambulance Service and held the title of director emeritus. He was a life member of the Bedford Elks and was presented with the Elks Lodge Distinguished Citizenship Award for Meritorious Service to Humanity. Clyde attended Friendship Missional Church in Friendship Village, where he was a member of the Benevolent Fund Committee. Clyde was an avid hunter and in 1989, bagged a 12-point buck. He enjoyed golfing and spending the winters in Sebring, Fla. **DEBORA KAY RESSLER** Fifth great granddaughter of progenitor Nicholas Kegg.   **DOROTHY MARETA RESSLER** [5728B] (1924 – 2009) daughter of Frank and Ima Pearl (Amick) Ressler married John Leroy Greenawalt with whom she was mother of (2). Dorothy had worked at Snyder's Gateway in Breezewood for 25 years. In the early 1950's she was presented with an award as the first "Foster Mother of the Year" from the Bedford County Child Welfare Services. She loved playing bingo with the senior citizens at the Fort Bedford Inn and reading her Bible.   **ELENOR LEVERNE RESSLER** (1936 – 1936) daughter of Frank and Ima (Amick) Ressler.   **ELLIS GEORGE RESSLER** (1919 – 1924) son of Frank and Ima (Amick) Ressler.   **EMILY RESSLER** (1890 – 1894) daughter of George and Susannah (McDaniel) Ressler. **FRANK EDWARD RESSLER** [5728C] (1892 – 1965) son of George and Susannah (McDaniel) Ressler married Ima Pearl Amick with whom he was father of (13). Frank was constable in the Rainsburg Borough for many years. **INFANT RESSLER** (1898 – 1898) child of George and Susannah (McDaniel) Ressler.   **INFANT RESSLER** (1938 – 1938) son of Frank and Ima (Amick) Ressler.   **JAMES DALE RESSLER** [5729] (1921 – 1944) son of Frank and Ima (Amick) Ressler was a casualty of WWII. Pvt. Ressler had entered the armed forces three years prior to his death and, had been overseas for almost a year before he was killed in Action in Italy.   **JAMES PAUL RESSLER** Fifth great grandson of progenitor Nicholas Kegg.   **JEREMY LYNN RESSLER** Sixth great grandson of

---

[5727E] The Palladium-Item and Sun-Telegram (Richmond, IN) June 8, 1962 [5727F] The Huntington County TAB (IN) Dec 17, 2013 [5728] Bedford Inquirer (PA) June 27, 2003, obtained by Bob Rose [5728A] Bedford Gazette (PA) Nov 11, 2016, contributed by Bob Rose [5728B] Berkebile Funeral Home (PA) [5728C] Bedford Gazette (PA) Jan 18, 1965, obtained by Connie Detar contributed by Bob Rose [5729] Bedford Gazette (PA) Aug 4, 1944

progenitor Nicholas Kegg. **JOSEPH RESSLER** (1922 – 1922) son of Frank and Ima (Amick) Ressler. **KAREN JEAN RESSLER** Fifth great granddaughter of progenitor Nicholas Kegg. **LOIS RESSLER** (1930 – 1930) daughter of Frank and Ima (Amick) Ressler. **MAE RUTH RESSLER** [5730] (1929 – 1989) aka "Ruth", daughter of Frank and Ima (Amick) Ressler married four times; first to Charles Joseph Sill. She married John A. Townsend with whom she was mother of (2). She married John Robert Wicker and Robert W. Dennis with whom she was mother of (2). Ruth was employed by the Bedford Spring Hotel before moving to Naples. In Naples she was employed by the Collier County Sheriff's Department for nine years under Sheriff Doug E. Hendry. She also retired from Public Markets, after 15 years of service. She moved to Punta Gorda in 1967 where she had been employed by the Charlotte County Sheriff's Department in Punta Gorda for seven years. Ruth was a member of the Fraternal Order of Policewomen's Auxiliary. **PAUL LUTHER RESSLER** [5730A] (1934 – 2013) son of Frank and Ima (Amick) Ressler married Ethel Miller with whom he was father of (5). Paul retired from Eastern Trucking Company and Ressler's Exxon and Towing. Throughout his life he enjoyed woodworking and made furniture for family and friends. Even after retiring from Ressler's Towing, he enjoyed going to the garage several days a week to hang out with his friends and help when needed. **PAULINE E. RESSLER** (1931 – 1931) daughter of Frank and Ima (Amick) Ressler. **ROBERT LYNN RESSLER** Fifth great grandson of progenitor Nicholas Kegg. **RHODA M. RESSLER** (1894 -1894) daughter of George and Susannah (McDaniel) Ressler. **SARAH IRENE RESSLER** (1896 – 1932) daughter of George and Susannah (McDaniel) Ressler. **SCOTT RESSLER** Fifth great grandson of progenitor Nicholas Kegg. **TAMERA FAY RESSLER** aka "Tammy", Fifth great granddaughter of progenitor Nicholas Kegg. **TERRY J. RESSLER** Fifth great grandson of progenitor Nicholas Kegg. **WILLIAM LAWRENCE SHIMER RESSLER** [5731] (1926 – 1996) son of Frank and Ima (Amick) Ressler, married Bertha Jane Sivits with whom he was father of (1). William was a WWII Army veteran; he had served on the Pacific Theater and had served with the Merchant Marines. Mr. Ressler had worked at the Bedford Springs Hotel for 38 years. He was a member of the Bedford American Legion Post 113, the Fort Bedford Honor Guard and a life member of the Bedford VFW Post 7527 and was of the Protestant Faith.

RESTLY

LYNDSEY RESTLY Fifth great granddaughter of progenitor Nicholas Kegg.

RETTIG

CHARLES OMAR RETTIG [5731A] aka "Bulldog" (1925 – 1990) son of Adam and Marie (Houck) Rettig married Ruth Marie Grubaugh with whom he was father of (3). Charles retired after 22 years at Ford Motor Co. in Lima and was a member of its Ford Retirees Club. He was a World War II Navy veteran. He also was a member of the Church of Christ Disciples; Liberty Conservation Club and VFW post, all in Ada. **DANIEL MARTIN RETTIG** Seventh great grandson of progenitor Nicholas Kegg. **DAVID MICHAEL RETTIG** Seventh great grandson of progenitor Nicholas Kegg. **MICHAEL DAVID RETTIG** [5732] aka Mike" (1947 – 2016) son of Charles and Ruth (Grubaugh) Rettig married Imogene Archer with whom he was father of (1). He married Pelma Arlene Snyder with whom he was father of (2). Later, he married Shirley Coburn Phillips. Mike worked as a pin grinder at Ford Motor Company of Lima for 41 years, where he was known as "Bull Pup". He was a Vietnam Veteran who served in the U.S. Army. **PAMELA L. RETTIG** Sixth great granddaughter of progenitor Nicholas Kegg. **PATRICIA ANN RETTIG** [5733] (1948 – 2014) daughter of Charles and Ruth (Grubaugh) Rettig married Larry Leroy Lawrence with whom she was mother of (2). Patricia was a homemaker. She was a member of the Alger Assembly of God Church. **ROBERT HEROLD RETTIG** (1923 – 1989) son of Adam and Marie (Houck) Rettig married and divorced Jean with whom he was father of (8) Robert

---

[5730] Fort Myers News-Press (FL) May 10, 1989, obtained by D. Sue Dible [5730A] Berkebile Funeral Home (PA) [5731] Bedford County Historical Society Pioneer Library (PA), book 79, p. 154 obtained by D. Sue Dible [5731A] Library obituary contributed by D. Sue Dible [5732] The Lima News (OH) Jun. 18, 2016 [5733] Hanson-Neely Funeral Home (Ada, OH)

was a veteran of WWII. **SHERI LOU RETTIG** Seventh great granddaughter of progenitor Nicholas Kegg.

REXWINKLE

AMBER REXWINKLE Eighth great granddaughter of progenitor Nicholas Kegg. **CHEROKEE LYNN REXWINKLE** [5733A, 5733B] (1994 – 2012) son of Rodney and Susy Michelle (Barreiro) Rexwinkle. Cherokee was a crew member of Redd Iron Inc. of Brighton, Colorado pursuing his dream of being a welder and eventually moving to Alaska to weld on the pipeline. Cherokee was a member of National Honor Society and received First Place in Skills USA District Welding Competitions for 2011 and 2012, as well as placing 2nd in the 2012 state welding competition. Cherokee had a passion for the outdoors and loved to hunt and fish. **DEVON REXWINKLE** Eighth great grandson of progenitor Nicholas Kegg. **RODNEY LEE REXWINKLE** Seventh great grandson of progenitor Nicholas Kegg.

REYES

CAMDEN REYES Seventh great grandson of progenitor Nicholas Kegg.
CECELIA REYES Seventh great granddaughter of progenitor Nicholas Kegg.

REYFF

CHERIE LEE REYFF Fifth great granddaughter of progenitor Nicholas Kegg. **DIANNE LORAINE REYFF** Fifth great granddaughter of progenitor Nicholas Kegg. **FREDERICK A. REYFF** [5734] (1899 – 1969) son of August and Myrtle (Kline) Reyff, married Wilma E. Snyder with whom he was father of (1). Frederick retired from C.G. Conn Ltd., where he had been employed as a tool designer. After he retired, Fred worked at both Key Machine and Star Machine, Inc

REYNOLDS

CHRISTINE REYNOLDS Seventh great granddaughter of progenitor Nicholas Kegg. **CHRISTOPHER EMILIO REYNOLDS** Seventh great grandson of progenitor Nicholas Kegg. **DAVID SOL REYNOLDS** Sixth great grandson of progenitor Nicholas Kegg. **DIANE REYNOLDS** Seventh great granddaughter of progenitor Nicholas Kegg. **DIANE T. REYNOLDS** [5735] (1945 – 1945) daughter of Dean and Anna (Diehl) Reynolds. **LEA ROSE REYNOLDS** Seventh great granddaughter of progenitor Nicholas Kegg. **MEGAN ELIZABETH REYNOLDS** Seventh great granddaughter of progenitor Nicholas Kegg. **MICHAEL ALAN HERSHISER REYNOLDS** Fifth great grandson of progenitor Nicholas Kegg. **NANCY C. SUSAN HERSHISER REYNOLDS** Fifth great granddaughter of progenitor Nicholas Kegg. **TAMARA SHARON REYNOLDS** Sixth great granddaughter of progenitor Nicholas Kegg.

RHEA

MATT RHEA Sixth great grandson of progenitor Nicholas Kegg.
MEREDITH RHEA Sixth great granddaughter of progenitor Nicholas Kegg.

RHODES

ANGELA RHODES Seventh great granddaughter of progenitor Nicholas Kegg. **DEACH RHODES** Seventh great grandson of progenitor Nicholas Kegg. **HALEY G. RHODES** Seventh great granddaughter of progenitor Nicholas Kegg. **HANNAH JEAN RHODES** Eighth great granddaughter

---

[5733A] Denver Post (CO) June 15, 2012 [5733B] Tabor-Rice Funeral Home (CO) [5734] p.22 - The Elkhart Truth (IN) Jan 9, 1969 [5735] p.12 - Huntingdon Daily News (PA) Oct 18, 1945

of progenitor Nicholas Kegg. **JENNIFER RHODES** Sixth great granddaughter of progenitor Nicholas Kegg. **JESSICA RHODES** Sixth great granddaughter of progenitor Nicholas Kegg.
KATIE SUE RHODES Eighth great granddaughter of progenitor Nicholas Kegg.

RICE

ALAN D. RICE Fifth great grandson of progenitor Nicholas Kegg. **ASHLEY RICE** Sixth great granddaughter of progenitor Nicholas Kegg. **ATTLEY RICE** (1915 – 1915) son of Charles and Cora (Inks) Rice. **AVIS MARIE RICE** [5736] (1940 – 2009) daughter of Ernest and Althea (Parsons) Rice, married Dale Howard Lindstrom with whom she was mother of (4). **BARRY CHARLES RICE** Fifth great grandson of progenitor Nicholas Kegg. **BETTY JEANETTE RICE** [5737] (1921 – 2006) daughter of Charles and Cora (Inks) Rice married twice; first to Myron D. Wiley with whom she was mother of (2). Later, she married Lavoid H. Lehman with whom she was mother of (2). **BRADLEY D. RICE** Fifth great grandson of progenitor Nicholas Kegg. **BRIAN L. RICE** Fifth great grandson of progenitor Nicholas Kegg. **BRIANA RICE** Sixth great granddaughter of progenitor Nicholas Kegg. **CHARLEEN RICE** [5738] (1947 – 2003) daughter of Donald and Alice (Wiser) Rice married Robert James Roth with whom she was mother of (1). Charleen was a beautician and business owner. **CHARLES RICE** Fifth great grandson of progenitor Nicholas Kegg. **CHELSIE DAWN RICE** Sixth great granddaughter of progenitor Nicholas Kegg. **CHESTER RICE** (1886 – 1936) son of Winfield and Sarah (Mawhorter) Rice. **CHRISTINE REBECCA RICE** Seventh great granddaughter of progenitor Nicholas Kegg. **CHRISTOPHER RONALD RICE** Seventh great grandson of progenitor Nicholas Kegg. **CHUCK RICE** Fifth great grandson of progenitor Nicholas Kegg. **CLARENCE RICE** [5739] (1891 – 1965) son of Winfield and Sarah (Mawhorter) Rice, married Edith Marie McDonald with whom he was father of (3). **CLEO RICE** (1901 – 1901) daughter of Charles and Cora (Inks) Rice. **COLTIN RICE** Ninth great grandson of progenitor Nicholas Kegg. **CORA B. RICE** [5740] (1884 – 1962) daughter of Emanuel and Hattie (Huff) Rice, married William Sherman Price with whom she was mother of (1). **CYNTHIA KATHRYN RICE**, aka "Cindy", Fifth great granddaughter of progenitor Nicholas Kegg. **DALE RICE** Sixth great grandson of progenitor Nicholas Kegg. **DANIEL A. RICE** (1862 – 1944) son of Israel and Susannah (Kegg) Rice married three times; first to Mary Jane Besset with whom he was father of (1). He married Gertrude Elizabeth Wenner and Anna L. (Johnson) Dome. **DANIEL JENNINGS RICE** aka "Danny", Sixth great grandson of progenitor Nicholas Kegg. **DARLENE RICE** Fifth great granddaughter of progenitor Nicholas Kegg. **DARLENE K. RICE** Fifth great granddaughter of progenitor Nicholas Kegg. **DEAN RICE** Sixth great grandson of progenitor Nicholas Kegg. **DELBERT L. RICE** Fifth great grandson of progenitor Nicholas Kegg. **DONALD GENE RICE** [5741] (1924 – 1984) son of Floyd and Ada (Jeffreys) Rice, married Alice Elaine Wiser with whom he was father of (5). Donald served in the U.S. Navy Seebees during WWII and after his discharge he lived at Clarks where he farmed. Donald owned Quality Market for four years and managed Palmer Co-op Station. He had been head custodian at Palmer Public School. Donald was a member of the American Legion. **DORIS HELENE RICE** (1919 – 1995) daughter of Floyd and Ada (Jeffreys) Rice, married Roland Dale Gibson with whom she was mother of (3). **ELSIE M. RICE** [5742] (1919 – 2009) daughter of Leon and Molly (Hofmeister) Rice married twice; first to Eugene P. Wager with whom she was mother of (1). He was killed in action in the Philippines during World War II. Later, she married Vaughn Franklin Wessell with whom she was mother of (2). **EMANUEL C. RICE** [5743] (1863 – 1937) son of Israel and Susannah (Kegg) Rice, married Hattie Evelyn Huff with whom he was father of (2); Emanuel died from injuries received when he was struck by a car while riding his bicycle at the intersection of North Front and Prairie Ronde streets. **EMILY RICE** Sixth great granddaughter of progenitor Nicholas Kegg. **ERNEST RICE** [5744] (1932 – 1973) son of Ernest and Lucile (Heckaman) Rice was a member of the Topeka Mennonite Church.

[5736] Omaha World-Herald (NE) Feb 16, 2009 [5737] p.25 - The Mennonite (Vol. 10, No. 3.) Feb 6, 2007 [5738] Grand Island Independent (NE) Sep 7, 2003, obtained by D. Sue Dible [5739] Ligonier Leader (IN) Oct 20, 1965, obtained by D. Sue Dible [5740] p.20 The News-Palladium (MI) Sep 13, 1962 [5741] Palmer Journal (NE) transcribed by Linda Berney [5742] Elkhart Truth (IN) Sep 19, 2009

ERNEST L. RICE [5745] (1903 – 1984) son of Charles and Cora (Inks) Rice, married Lucile Evelyn Heckaman with whom he was father of (1). Ernest was a farmer. **ERVIN D. RICE** (1906 – 1908) son of Charles and Cora (Inks) Rice. **ETHYL IRENE RICE** [5746] (1895 – 1987) daughter of Emanuel and Hattie (Huff) Rice, married J. Clinton Harden with whom she was mother of (1). Ethel was a retired schoolteacher. **FLOYD FRANKLIN RICE** [5747] (1891 – 1966) son of Eugene and Mary (Dorr) Rice, married Ada Estella Jeffreys with whom he was father of (4). **GARY RICE** Fifth great grandson of progenitor Nicholas Kegg. **GARY GENE RICE** Fifth great grandson of progenitor Nicholas Kegg. **GERALD LEE RICE** (1947 – 1947) son of Reginald and Helen (Nielsen) Rice. **GERALDINE E. RICE** [5748] (1918 – 1994) aka "Jerry", daughter of Ralph and Edna (Mader) Rice, married Lawrence W. Jones with whom she was mother of (2). Geraldine and her husband owned Jones Motor Company in Aurora for more than 30 years. "Jerry" was a member of the Aurora United Methodist Church, was active in the Women's Society and a morning circle. She was also a member of the Aurora Order of the Eastern Star Chapter #93, and had served as past matron, she also belonged to the Merry Janes Extension Club. **HAROLD FRANCIS RICE** (1943 – 1943) son of Albert and Frances (Mustard) Rice. **IONA W. RICE** [5749] (1918 – 1965) daughter of Floyd and Ada (Jeffreys) Rice, married Edward A. Booth with whom she was mother of (7). **IVAN GERALD RICE** [5750] (1908 – 1991) son of Charles and Cora (Inks) Rice, married Mabel Halterman with whom he was father of (4). **JACE RICE** Seventh great grandson of progenitor Nicholas Kegg. **JAMI JO RICE** Sixth great granddaughter of progenitor Nicholas Kegg. **JASPER EUGENE RICE** [5751] (1910 – 1984) son of Guy and Edith (Betsworth) Price, married Lola Melissa Corcilius with whom he was father of (2). **JEFFREY TODD RICE** Sixth great granddson of progenitor Nicholas Kegg. **JERRY RICE** Sixth great granddson of progenitor Nicholas Kegg. **JORDAN RICE** Sixth great grandson of progenitor Nicholas Kegg. **JORDAN ELIZABETH RICE** Sixth great granddaughter of progenitor Nicholas Kegg. **JOSLYN RICE** Seventh great granddaughter of progenitor Nicholas Kegg. **JUDY RICE** Fifth great granddaughter of progenitor Nicholas Kegg. **KARL EDSEL RICE** [5752] (1919 – 1979) son of Clarence and Edith McDonald) Rice, married Betty Lung with whom he was father of (2). Karl was a farmer and a veteran of WW II, a member of Cromwell United Methodist Church and American Legion. **KENSEY RICE** Sixth great granddaughter of progenitor Nicholas Kegg. **KIELAN RICE** Seventh great grandson of progenitor Nicholas Kegg. **KURT RICE** Sixth great grandson of progenitor Nicholas Kegg. **LAURIE ANN RICE** Fifth great granddaughter of progenitor Nicholas Kegg. **LEILA GLADYS RICE** [5753] (1902 – 1964) daughter of Charles and Cora (Inks) Rice, married Albert W. Sheley with whom she was mother of (3). **LENA BELL RICE** [5754] (1880 – 1968) daughter of Eugene and Mary (Dorr) Rice, married William David Mess with whom she was mother of (7). **LEON WALDORF RICE** [5755] (1888 – 1975) aka "Lee", son of Daniel and Mary (Basset) Rice, married Molly R. Hofmeister with whom he was father of (5). Lee was a prominent Penn Township farmer. Lee was a former member of the Pleasant Hill school board and a member of the Newton Community Club. **LESLIE HERCHEL RICE** [5756] (1899 – 1988) son of Charles and Cora (Inks) Rice, married Lonetta Mishler with whom he was father of (2). Leslie worked at Coppes Kitchen in Nappanee for 40 years and was a member of Nappanee Church of the Brethren. **LUCILLE EVELYN RICE** [5757] (1910 – 2000) daughter of Charles and Cora (Inks) Rice married twice; first to Robert D. Anders with whom she was mother of (2). Later, she married Edward Julius Wagner. Lucille retired after working for International Harvester (Navistar), Ft. Wayne, Ind., for 28 years. **LYLE RICE** (1897 – 1897) son of Charles and Cora (Inks) Rice. **MARGARET J. RICE** [5758] (1921 – 1995) daughter of Clarence and Edith (McDonald) Rice. **MARIANNE LYNNE RICE** Seventh great granddaughter of progenitor Nicholas Kegg. **MARY FLORENCE RICE** [5759] (1893 – 1965) daughter of Eugene and Mary (Dorr) Rice, married James Orval

---

[5743] The South Bend Tribune (IN) Oct 19, 1937 [5744, 5745] Noble County Library obituary obtained by D. Sue Dible [5746] The Tampa Tribune (FL) Sep 16, 1987 [5747] The Palmer Journal, Oct 27, 1966, transcribed by Linda Berney [5748] Higby-McQuiston Mortuary, NE [5749] The Columbus Telegram (NE) Dec 12, 1996 [5750] Noble County Library obituary obtained by D. Sue Dible [5751] Grand Island Independent (NE) March 11, 2000 [5752] Noble County Library obituary obtained by D. Sue Dible [5753] p.6 The South Bend Tribune (IN) Aug 27, 1964 [5754] Kearney Daily Hub (NE) May 17, 1968, obtained by D. Sue Dible [5755, 5756] Library obituary obtained by D. Sue Dible [5757] p.4 - Grand Forks Herald (ND) Aug 8, 2000 [5758] p.8A - News-Sentinel (IN) March 4, 1995 [5759] Sunday Orgonian (OR) July 4, 1965

Betsworth with whom she was mother of (3). Mary was killed when a car driven by her husband crashed into a concrete abutment on Barrett Road. Hood River County sheriff's deputies reported that the sun had temporarily blinded her husband and that he did not see the roadside structure. **MAYGAN RICE** Ninth great granddaughter of progenitor Nicholas Kegg. **MEGAN LYNNE RICE** Seventh great granddaughter of progenitor Nicholas Kegg. **MELEASE D. RICE** [5760] (1916 – 1987) daughter of Clarence and Edith (McDonald) Rice, married Henry C. Chaffee with whom she was mother of (4). **MESHEAL RICE** Sixth great granddaughter of progenitor Nicholas Kegg. **MICHAEL RICE** Sixth great grandson of progenitor Nicholas Kegg. **MOLLY ANN RICE** Sixth great granddaughter of progenitor Nicholas Kegg. **MORGAN RICE** Sixth great granddaughter of progenitor Nicholas Kegg. **NANCY A. RICE** (1852 – 1916) aka "Nannie", daughter of Israel and Susannah (Kegg) Rice, married Samuel A. Bray with whom she was mother of (3). **ORLEN FLOYD RICE** [5761] (1926 – 2006) son of Ralph and Edna (Mader) Rice, married Caroline Wilhelmina Pader with whom he was father of (1). **OWEN RICE** Sixth great grandson of progenitor Nicholas Kegg. **PAMELA E. RICE** Fifth great granddaughter of progenitor Nicholas Kegg. **PATRICIA MARIE RICE** Sixth great granddaughter of progenitor Nicholas Kegg. **PAULA J. RICE** Fifth great granddaughter of progenitor Nicholas Kegg. **RAELYN RICE** Ninth great granddaughter of progenitor Nicholas Kegg. **RALPH VERNON RICE** [5762] (1896 – 1979) aka "Vernon", son of Eugene and Mary (Dorr) Rice, married Edna Loretta Mader with whom he was father of (3). Ralph worked with several banks before becoming associated with Commercial National Bank in 1929. By the time he retired in 1967 he had attained the positions of senior vice president and cashier. After retirement he was associated with SCORE, a volunteer program operated by the Small Business Administration. Vernon had been active in the affairs of Trinity United Methodist Church, serving on the church board, the finance board and teaching Sunday school for several years. He also was past president of the Grand Island Kiwanis Club and past district governor for the Nebraska-Iowa district. He was past master of Ashlar Lodge No. 33, A.F.& A.M., past worthy patron of Andrew Chapter No. 41, Order of Eastern Star, and was a member of the Tehama Shrine. He had been active in Scouting, receiving the Boy Scouts Silver Beaver Award, and he also served on the St. Francis Hospital Board. He presently was serving on the Salvation Army board, of which he had been a member for 50 years, and he was on the Goodwill Industries board; **RANDY RICE** Eighth great grandson of progenitor Nicholas Kegg. **REGINALD CALVIN RICE** [5763] (1917 – 2008) aka "Reggie", son of Roy and Jeanette (Kiser) Rice, married Helen Vibian Nielsen with whom he was father of (3). Reggie was a retired CEO of Prawl Engineering Corp., Past Post Commander of American Legion Post 112, Member of VFW Post 2503 and Voiture Locale 206, 40 & 8. **RICHARD DALE RICE** Fifth great grandson of progenitor Nicholas Kegg. **RICK RICE** Fifth great grandson of progenitor Nicholas Kegg. **RODNEY ALAN RICE** Fifth great grandson of progenitor Nicholas Kegg. **ROY EUGENE RICE** [5764] (1888 – 1980) son of Eugene and Mary (Dorr) Rice, married Jeanette Kiser with whom he was father of (1). Roy was engaged in defense work at the Cornhusker Army Ammunition Plant and at the Grand Island Air Base during World War II. After the war he worked as an accountant on Grand Island. Later, Roy worked for a time in the Chapman Bank and at the First National Bank of Grand Island. He became part-owner of the St. Libory Bank and then full owner of the bank in Maxwell. **RUSSELL RICE** Fifth great grandson of progenitor Nicholas Kegg. **SAVANNA ASHLEY RICE** Seventh great granddaughter of progenitor Nicholas Kegg. **STANLEY D. RICE** [5765] (1918 – 2006) son of Leon and Molly (Hofmeister) Rice. **STEPHANIE LYNN RICE** Sixth great granddaughter of progenitor Nicholas Kegg. **TAYLOR RICE** Sixth great grandson of progenitor Nicholas Kegg. **TENA ELIZABETH RICE** Fifth great granddaughter of progenitor Nicholas Kegg. **VIOLET KATHRYN RICE** [5766] (1914 – 1988) aka "Kay", daughter of Charles and Cora (Inks) Rice married twice; first to Harry Lyman McDonald with whom she was mother of (3). Later, she married Lester Harold Smith with whom she was mother of (2). Kay was employed at Essex Wire, Ligonier, for more than 25 years. She was a member of Ligonier

---

[5760] Sturgis Daily Journal (MI) transcribed by Carole Lynn (Mohney) Carr [5761] Grand Island Independent (NE) March 31, 2006 [5762] Find A Grave Memorial# 134918739 Created by: diaNEB [5763] Grand Island Independent (NE) Feb13, 2008 [5764] Find A Grave Memorial# 145731439 Created by: diaNEB [5765] South Bend Tribune (MI) Feb 21, 2006 [5766, 5767] Noble County (IN) Library obituary.

United Methodist Church, Good Samaritans and Perry Twp Homemakers' Club. **WILLIAM RICE** Fifth great grandson of progenitor Nicholas Kegg. **WINFIELD SCOTT RICE** [5767] (1854 – 1931) son of Israel and Suzannah (Kegg) Rice, married Sarah Mawhorter with whom he was father of (2).

RICH

HAROLD DEAN RICH (1937 – 1998) son of Harold and Alberta (Clark) Rich.
SHIRLEY J. RICH Fifth great granddaughter of progenitor Nicholas Kegg.

RICHARDS

AMY EILEEN RICHARDS (1915 – 1987) daughter of Edward and Naomi (Dwigans) Richards, married George Perry Baker. **DAVID ERNEST RICHARDS** Sixth great grandson of progenitor Nicholas Kegg. **DON FREDERICK RICHARDS** [5768] (1921 – 1976) son of Miles and Pearl (Gillian) Richards, married Dorothy Eloise Smith with whom he was father of (2). Don was owner of the Richards-Knupp Insurance Agency here. A World War II veteran, Mr. Richards was a member of the American Legion, the Knights of Columbus, and Kiwanis. **DONALD F. RICHARDS** Fifth great grandson of progenitor Nicholas Kegg. **DONNY RICHARDS** Sixth great grandson of progenitor Nicholas Kegg. **ERIKA RICHARDS** Sixth great granddaughter of progenitor Nicholas Kegg. **JENNIFER RICHARDS** Sixth great granddaughter of progenitor Nicholas Kegg. **JERRY W. RICHARDS** Fifth great grandson of progenitor Nicholas Kegg. **KANDICE RICHARDS**, aka "Kandi", Sixth great granddaughter of progenitor Nicholas Kegg. **KENNETH E. RICHARDS** Fifth great grandson of progenitor Nicholas Kegg. **KENNETH EDWARD RICHARDS** (1917 – 1985) son of Edward and Naomi (Dwigans) Richards, married George Etta Mae Dickey with whom he was father of (2). **LARRY D. RICHARDS** [5769] (1939 – 2008) son of Wesley and Louise (Peterson) Richards, married Donna with whom he was father of (2). Larry served in the U.S. Marine Corps from 1959 to 1990, spending 13 months in Vietnam between 1966-1967. In June 1990 he became a project manager for Computer Sciences Corporation and retired from CSC. Larry was an avid golfer. This past year he served as President of Cary Senior Golfer's Association. **LARRY D. RICHARDS** Sixth great grandson of progenitor Nicholas Kegg. **OPAL RUBY RICHARDS** (1903 – 1992) daughter of Miles and Pearl (Gillian, married Lysle Lane Crosson with whom she was mother of (5). **RICHARD RICHARDS** Fifth great grandson of progenitor Nicholas Kegg. **RUSS RICHARDS** Fifth great grandson of progenitor Nicholas Kegg. **VICTORIA JANE RICHARDS** Fifth great granddaughter of progenitor Nicholas Kegg. **WESLEY DEAN RICHARDS** [5770] (1919 – 1991) son of Edward and Naomi (Dwigans) Richards, married Louise R. Peterson with whom he was father of (3).

RICHARDSON

BLAKE TYLER RICHARDSON Seventh great grandson of progenitor Nicholas Kegg.
KATIE RICHARDSON Seventh great granddaughter of progenitor Nicholas Kegg.
KEVIN WADE RICHARDSON Sixth great grandson of progenitor Nicholas Kegg.

RICHMOND

HELEN LUCILLE RICHMOND (1914 – 1992) daughter of Oliver and Edith (Knouf) Richmond, married Albert Russell Kingery with whom she was mother of (3). **MILDRED IRENE RICHMOND** [5771] (1916 – 2010) daughter of Oliver and Edith (Knouf) Richmond married three times; first to Theodore Gordon with whom she was mother of (1). She later married Mr. Johnson and Alfred T. Sehabiague. Mildred was a homemaker. **RALPH HOWARD RICHMOND** (1919 – 1992) son of Oliver and Edith (Knouf) Richmond.

[5768] p.2 - Cedar Rapids Gazette (IA)Feb 2, 1976 [5769] yellowfootprints.com (NC) obtained by D. Sue Dible [5770] Iowa Library Obituary obtained by D. Sue Dible [5771] Lodi News-Sentinel (CA) Oct 30, 2010

RICK

ELLEN FRANCES RICK Sixth great granddaughter of progenitor Nicholas Kegg.
MARGARET KATHLEEN RICK Sixth great granddaughter of progenitor Nicholas Kegg.

RIDDINGER

CONNIE JEAN RIDDINGER Fifth great granddaughter of progenitor Nicholas Kegg.
FREDERICK W. RIDDINGER [5772] (1921 – 1973) son of Frederick and Lorena (McDaniel) Riddinger, married Mary Jane Lehman with whom he was father of (1). Frederick was a veteran of World War II. He was supervisor at Johnstown Plant, Bethlehem Steel Corp. Member of Westmont United Methodist Church and the Bethleham Supervisors Club. **ISABELL ERMA RIDDINGER** [5273] (1917 – 1998) daughter of Frederick and Lorena (McDaniel) Riddinger, married Ralph P. Kimmel with whom she was mother of (1). Isabell was a member of Moxham Colonial Church of the Brethren and, past member of Sunnehanna Country Club; Rotary Anns and Elks.

RIDDLE

JEFFREY DELL RIDDLE Sixth great grandson of progenitor Nicholas Kegg.

RIDLER

BRIAN RIDLER Sixth great grandson of progenitor Nicholas Kegg.
DIANE RIDLER Sixth great granddaughter of progenitor Nicholas Kegg.
JACOB RIDLER Seventh great grandson of progenitor Nicholas Kegg.
LAURA RIDLER Sixth great granddaughter of progenitor Nicholas Kegg.
MARGARET E. RIDLER Fifth great granddaughter of progenitor Nicholas Kegg.
MONTE RIDLER Sixth great grandson of progenitor Nicholas Kegg.
NICHOLAS RIDLER Seventh great grandson of progenitor Nicholas Kegg.
PAMELA RIDLER Sixth great granddaughter of progenitor Nicholas Kegg.
PERRY RIDLER Sixth great grandson of progenitor Nicholas Kegg.

RIEGLE

AARON DAVID RIEGLE Seventh great grandson of progenitor Nicholas Kegg.
ADAM CHRISTOPHER RIEGLE Seventh great grandson of progenitor Nicholas Kegg.
BABY TWINS RIEGLE (1934 – 1934) children of Hallie and Ethel (Kidd) Riegle. **CADE RIEGLE** Seventh great grandson of progenitor Nicholas Kegg. **DENISE RIEGLE** Sixth great granddaughter of progenitor Nicholas Kegg. **ELI RIEGLE** Seventh great grandson of progenitor Nicholas Kegg. **GRANT RIEGLE** Seventh great grandson of progenitor Nicholas Kegg. **ISABELLE RIEGLE** Seventh great granddaughter of progenitor Nicholas Kegg. **KURT RIEGLE** Sixth great grandson of progenitor Nicholas Kegg. **JOSHUA RIEGLE** Seventh great grandson of progenitor Nicholas Kegg. **LANE RIEGLE** Seventh great grandson of progenitor Nicholas Kegg. **MARK EDWARD RIEGLE** Sixth great grandson of progenitor Nicholas Kegg. **NANCY A. RIEGLE** Sixth great granddaughter of progenitor Nicholas Kegg. **OLIVE PAULINE RIEGLE** (1933 – 1933) daughter of Hallie and Ethel (Kidd) Riegle. **RONALD RIEGLE** Sixth great grandson of progenitor Nicholas Kegg. **SARAH DEANNE RIEGLE** Seventh great granddaughter of progenitor Nicholas Kegg. **SETH RIEGLE** Seventh great grandson of progenitor Nicholas Kegg.

[5772] Johnstown Tribune-Democrat (PA) Nov 27, 1973 [5773] Johnstown Tribune-Democrat (PA) Nov 13, 1998, obtained by D. Sue Dible

RIFFLE

LOGAN RIFFLE Eighth great grandson of progenitor Nicholas Kegg.
SYDNEY RIFFLE Eighth great granddaughter of progenitor Nicholas Kegg.

RIGDON

COULTER J. RIGDON Seventh great grandson of progenitor Nicholas Kegg.

RIGGEN

JO LYNN RIGGEN Sixth great granddaughter of progenitor Nicholas Kegg.

RIGGS

SUZANNE LEE RIGGS Fifth great granddaughter of progenitor Nicholas Kegg.

RIGHTNOUR

AUSTIN RIGHTNOUR Eighth great grandson of progenitor Nicholas Kegg. **CHARLES ALLEN RIGHTNOUR** [5773A] (1976 – 2023) son of Charles and Deborah Kay (Mortimore) Rightnour worked as an over-the-road truck driver. He was father of (2). **JUSTIN RIGHTNOUR** Eighth great grandson of progenitor Nicholas Kegg. **MICHAEL LEE RIGHTNOUR** Seventh great grandson of progenitor Nicholas Kegg.

RILEY

CAROLYN RILEY Seventh great granddaughter of progenitor Nicholas Kegg. **DAVID E. RILEY** Seventh great grandson of progenitor Nicholas Kegg. **JOHN EDWARD RILEY** Seventh great grandson of progenitor Nicholas Kegg. **MARY ELIZABETH RILEY** Seventh great granddaughter of progenitor Nicholas Kegg. **RICHARD RILEY** Seventh great grandson of progenitor Nicholas Kegg. **RICHARD RILEY** Eighth great grandson of progenitor Nicholas Kegg.

RINARD

TREVOR RINARD Seventh great grandson of progenitor Nicholas Kegg.

RINEHART

AMY KRISTEN RINEHART Sixth great granddaughter of progenitor Nicholas Kegg. **CHRISTINE MARIE RINEHART** Sixth great granddaughter of progenitor Nicholas Kegg. **JERI WILLIAM RINEHART** Fifth great grandson of progenitor Nicholas Kegg. **RACHEL ELIZABETH RINEHART** [5774] (1970 – 2019) daughter of James and Mariann (Berkebile) Rinehart married Joe Warhime with whom she was mother of (1). Rachel was a graduate of Malone University, with a major in social science and loved the study of cultures. She was a true Anglophile. Rachel loved many things, especially history and fine foods, baking, beautiful flowers, cheese, and chocolate. She had a discriminating taste and impeccable manners, with a witty but always kind, sense of humor. **STEPHEN JAMES RINEHART** Sixth great grandson of progenitor Nicholas Kegg.

[5773A] Bedford Gazette (PA) Feb 7, 2023, obtained by Bob Rose [5774] The Repository (OH) Sept 1, 2019, obtained by D. Sue Dible

RIOS

ANABELLE RIOS Seventh great granddaughter of progenitor Nicholas Kegg.
FERNANDO RIOS Seventh great grandson of progenitor Nicholas Kegg.
LILIANA RIOS Seventh great granddaughter of progenitor Nicholas Kegg.

RISLEY

EMILY KATHLEEN RISLEY Sixth great granddaughter of progenitor Nicholas Kegg.
MEGAN FRANCES RISLEY Sixth great granddaughter of progenitor Nicholas Kegg.

RISTEY

KARA RISTEY Seventh great granddaughter of progenitor Nicholas Kegg.
SEAN MITCHELL RISTEY Seventh great grandson of progenitor Nicholas Kegg.

RITAN

ANDREW RITAN Sixth great grandson of progenitor Nicholas Kegg. **ELIZABETH RITAN** Sixth great granddaughter of progenitor Nicholas Kegg. **JOHN LEIF RITAN** [5774A] (1933 – 2010) son of Andrew and Mary (Laird) Ritan married Virginia with whom he was father of (3). After completing his Radiology residency at University Hospital in Tulsa, Oklahoma, he joined the U.S. Air Force and was posted at the USAF Maxwell Hospital in Montgomery, Alabama. Later, he became an associate with the Middletown Ohio Hospital Radiology Department where he became a director. John was active in many civic organizations throughout his adult life. Among those in which he was most involved included All Souls Unitarian Church, the founding of Hope Unitarian Church, discussion leader and president of Great Books Reading Program, all in Tulsa Oklahoma. In Ohio he served as president of the Butler County Medical Society, president of Butler County Planned Parenthood, and a member of the Greater Cincinnati Planned Parenthood Board. He was president of the Middletown Symphony and guest conductor two years. John was also a member and chair of numerous hospital committees as well as on the Middletown Hospital Foundation Board. **MARIA TAYLOR VAUGHAN RITAN** Sixth great granddaughter of progenitor Nicholas Kegg. **MARY ELLEN RITAN** Fifth great granddaughter of progenitor Nicholas Kegg.

RITCHEY

BRANT D. RITCHEY Eighth great grandson of progenitor Nicholas Kegg. **JACOB ETHAN RITCHEY** Seventh great grandson of progenitor Nicholas Kegg. **JARED RITCHEY** [5774B] (1981 – 2014) son of Daniel and Marcia (Mellott) Ritchey married LeAnn Guyer with whom he was father of (1). Jared graduated with a degree in business from Pennsylvania State University. He was employed by Guyer Brothers Inc. in New Enterprise for several years. Jared enjoyed hunting and spending time with his family and friends. He could be found in his free time on the farm; he loved farming. **JORDON RITCHEY** Seventh great grandson of progenitor Nicholas Kegg. **LISA ANN RITCHEY** Seventh great granddaughter of progenitor Nicholas Kegg. **LYNN RITCHEY** Seventh great grandson of progenitor Nicholas Kegg.

RITCHIE

BRYCEN RITCHIE Seventh great grandson of progenitor Nicholas Kegg.

[5774A] Journal-News (OH) Dec. 28, 2010 [5774B] Bedford Gazette (PA) May 7, 2014, contributed by Bob Rose

CYNTHIA MARIE RITCHIE Eighth great granddaughter of progenitor Nicholas Kegg. **LEE ROBERT RITCHIE** aka "Bob", Fifth great grandson of progenitor Nicholas Kegg. **INFANT RITCHIE** (1924 – 1924) child of William and Margaret (Nycum) Ritchie. **WILLIAM A. RITCHIE** [5775] (1926 – 2003) aka "Billy", son of William and Margaret (Nycum) Ritchie, professor emeritus of political science was well published in professional journals, he was a contributing author of the book "The New Europe and the World," published by WMU's New Issues Press. Ritchie spoke frequently on campus and elsewhere on all manner of European history and politics. Before joining the WMU faculty, he served as an instructor and assistant professor at the University of Delaware.

RITTER

BRAD RITTER Fifth great grandson of progenitor Nicholas Kegg. **CHRISTINA RITTER** Fifth great granddaughter of progenitor Nicholas Kegg. **KRISTINA RITTER** Seventh great granddaughter of progenitor Nicholas Kegg. **MICHAEL W. RITTER** Sixth great grandson of progenitor Nicholas Kegg. **TELKA ROSE RITTER** Fifth great granddaughter of progenitor Nicholas Kegg.

RITZ

LUANNE MARGARET RITZ Sixth great granddaughter of progenitor Nicholas Kegg.

RIVERA

CARLOS RIVERA Seventh great grandson of progenitor Nicholas Kegg.
SAMUEL RIVERA Seventh great grandson of progenitor Nicholas Kegg.

RIZZI

BLAKE RIZZI Seventh great grandson of progenitor Nicholas Kegg.
MARRIAH RIZZI Seventh great granddaughter of progenitor Nicholas Kegg.

ROACH

AUDREY PEARL ROACH [5775A] (1926 – 1991) daughter of John and Mary (Knouf) Roach married twice, first to Edward Lee McCurdy with whom she was mother of (3), later to Cleo Robert Beveridge with whom she was mother of (2). Audrey retired from Communications Data Services and previously worked for Look magazine. **BRIAN LEE ROACH** Sixth great grandson of progenitor Nicholas Kegg. **DANIEL ROACH** aka "Danny" Fifth great grandson of progenitor Nicholas Kegg. **DAVID ROACH** aka "Dave" Fifth great grandson of progenitor Nicholas Kegg. **DENISE ROACH** Sixth great granddaughter of progenitor Nicholas Kegg. **JACK ROACH** Sixth great grandson of progenitor Nicholas Kegg. **JENNIFER ROACH** Sixth great granddaughter of progenitor Nicholas Kegg. **JOHN ALVIN ROACH** [5775B] (1921 – 2014) son of John and Mary (Knouf) Roach, married Florence Irene Michael with whom he was father of (5). John served internationally as an aircraft mechanic for 7 years in the United States Navy during and after WWII. Later, he became a diesel mechanic working for Rock Island Trucking and Briggs Motor Freight in addition to farming. **JOHN ROACH** Fifth great grandson of progenitor Nicholas Kegg. **MARY ROACH** Sixth great granddaughter of progenitor Nicholas Kegg. **MARY ELLEN ROACH** [5775C] (1932 – 2002) daughter of John and Mary (Knouf) Roach married Clyde Leroy Jagerson with whom she was mother of (1). Mary Ellen was a homemaker and had worked at Mass Mutual Insurance Co., and for Visiting Nurse Association. She was a member of the Faithful Chapter of Eastern Star and of the Unity Church of Des Moines. She enjoyed spending time with friends and family, reading and genealogy.

[5775] WMU News (MI) March 13, 2003 [5775A] p.13A- Des Moines Register (IA) May 28, 1991 [5775B] Peterson Funeral Home (Carlisle, IA)

MEGGIE ROACH Sixth great granddaughter of progenitor Nicholas Kegg. **PHILLIP ROACH** aka "Phil" Fifth great grandson of progenitor Nicholas Kegg. **THAYER WILLARD ROACH** [5776] (1919 – 1933) son of John and Mary (Knouf) Roach would have completed his eighth-grade examinations and was planning on entering high school. At an early age he was deeply interested in Sunday school and church work and was converted two years ago and at that time was baptized in the Christian faith and became affiliated with the Cumming community church. Thayer was always thoughtful and kind. **THOMAS LEE ROACH** [5777] aka "Tom" (1942 – 2020) son of John and Florence (Michael) Roach married Mary with whom he was father of (5). Tom grew up on a farm, where he developed his strong work ethic. He was tasked with helping his mother kill and dress chickens—a chore he did begrudgingly and that resulted in his lifelong refusal to eat chicken. Tom followed in his father's footsteps by joining the Navy. He was stationed primarily in Puerto Rico, where his work as an aviation mechanic guided his future career. Tom was proud of his service, and in later years was rarely seen without his Naval aviation hat. Later, Tom worked at Armstrong Rubber Co. for 30 years, and retired from Firestone as an electrician. Tom had many hobbies over his lifetime: boating, skiing, woodworking, biking (both bicycles and motorcycles), target shooting, reading and gardening. He loved sharing the abundance of pumpkins from his patch with neighbors, friends and family. He was also known to wow his grandkids with an occasional experiment, such as launching plastic soda bottles high in the air and working together to make toy cars from scrap lumber. Tom fulfilled his lifelong dream of building a house on family land. **THOMAS ROACH** aka "Tom", Sixth great grandson of progenitor Nicholas Kegg. **TIM ROACH** Sixth great grandson of progenitor Nicholas Kegg.

ROAN

JAMIE ROAN Eighth great granddaughter of progenitor Nicholas Kegg.
JOSHUA ROAN Eighth great grandson of progenitor Nicholas Kegg.

ROBBINS

AMY NICOLE ROBBINS aka "Nikki", Seventh great granddaughter of progenitor Nicholas Kegg. **DAVID MERLE ROBBINS** 6th great grandson of progenitor Nicholas Kegg. **FORD MERLE ROBBINS** [5778] (1900 – 1943) son of Samuel and Millie (Colledge) Robbins, married Mary Elnora Loughry with whom he was father of (2). **JAMES ROBBINS** Sixth great grandson of progenitor Nicholas Kegg. **JAMES M. ROBBINS** [5778A] (1924 – 2011) son of Ford and Mary (Loughry) Robbins, married Virginia Lee Grim with whom he was father of (2). James was a graduate of Thiel College and the Lutheran Seminary at Gettysburg. During his years at the Seminary, he was a member of the Seminary Choir and was an accomplished organist. Rev. Robbins was ordained in July 1952 at his church, St. John's German Lutheran Church in Connellsville. After James retired, he served as supply pastor and interim pastor at various parishes for ten years. James was a delegate for the LCA National Convention in Chicago. He was a member of the Charleroi Kiwanis Club and the Charleroi Ministerial Organization where he held offices in both organizations. **JERRY TIMOTHY ROBBINS** [5779] (1984 – 2000) son of Timothy and Connie (Beegle) Robbins was a student at Southeast Bulloch High School, Brooklet, where he was a member of the football and baseball teams. He was a member of Statesboro A's Baseball Team, Sinkhole Hunting Club and Trinity Baptist Church. **MARENE E. ROBBINS** Sixth great granddaughter of progenitor Nicholas Kegg. **MELINDA J. ROBBINS** Sixth great granddaughter of progenitor Nicholas Kegg. **ROY S. ROBBINS** [5779A] (1926 – 2003) son of Ford and Mary (Loughry) Robbins married Josephine Elizabeth Fleischer with whom he was father of (2). Roy considered the seminary and served his church for many years as organist, but his calling was to teach. Roy taught at

---

[5775C] The Tribune (IA) March 21, 2002 [5776] Winterset Madisonian (IA) May 18, 1933, transcribed by Treva Patterson [5777] Bertrand Funeral Homes (IA) obtained by D. Sue Dible [5778] The Pittsburgh Post-Gazette (PA) Feb 12, 1943 [5778A] Schrock-Hogan Funeral Home & Cremation Services, Inc. (PA) [5779] p.B09 - The Augusta Chronicle (GA) Dec. 27, 2000 [5778] The Pittsburgh Post-Gazette (PA) Feb 12, 1943 [5778A] Schrock-Hogan Funeral Home & Cremation Services, Inc. (PA) [5779] p.B09 - The Augusta Chronicle (GA) Dec. 27, 2000 [5779A] Albuquerque Journal (NM) Aug 22, 2003

Ernie Pyle and History at Rio Grande HS. He also taught evenings at TVI. Roy was a kind, gentle soul who loved his students, his animals, and going out to eat. He never met a buffet he didn't like!
TYLER ROBBINS Seventh great grandson of progenitor Nicholas Kegg.

ROBERTS

ANGELA ROBERTS Sixth great granddaughter of progenitor Nicholas Kegg. **BEVERLY ANN ROBERTS** [5780] (1930 – 2012) daughter of Francis and Arlene (Woodson) Roberts, married Robert Donald Briese with whom she was mother of (3). Beverly was employed by the Newton Public Library. **BRANDI RACHELE ROBERTS** Sixth great granddaughter of progenitor Nicholas Kegg. **BRETT ROBERTS** Seventh great grandson of progenitor Nicholas Kegg. **CAROLE ROBERTS** Sixth great granddaughter of progenitor Nicholas Kegg. **CHAD JOSEPH ROBERTS** Sixth great grandson of progenitor Nicholas Kegg. **CYNTHIA RAE ROBERTS** aka "Cindy" Sixth great granddaughter of progenitor Nicholas Kegg. **DANIELLE MARIE ROBERTS** Sixth great granddaughter of progenitor Nicholas Kegg. **DAVID ROBERTS** Fifth great grandson of progenitor Nicholas Kegg. **DEBORAH ROBERTS** Sixth great granddaughter of progenitor Nicholas Kegg. **DENNIS CARTER ROBERTS** [5780A] aka "Denny" (1945 – 2012) son of Woodrow and Mildred (Haverfield) Roberts married three times, first to Alice Stamper with whom he was father of (1). Dennis later married Kandy Hart with whom he was father of (1). Last, he married Sharon Lewis. Denny served in the U.S. Navy during the Vietnam Conflict. He had been employed at Sutter's Home Decorating, Roberts Brothers Painting, and Mid-Ohio Glass before starting his own business. An avid reader, Denny enjoyed Bible studies and reading the Bible. He also enjoyed bowling, golf, racquetball, and fishing. **DIANE JANE ROBERTS** [5781] (1954 – 2005) daughter of William and Mary Jane (Milne) Roberts, married Stanley Kukla with whom she was mother of (2). **DOREEN L. ROBERTS** [5782] (1939 – 2013) daughter of William and Mary Jane (Milne) Roberts, married Edwin W. Frye with whom she was mother of (3). Doreen retired from the Franklin Area School District where she worked as an aide and secretary. Her hobbies included needlework, knitting, spending time with her family, card club and golf. She loved attending concerts, especially those of family members and The Franklin Silver Coronet Band. **DREW ROBERTS** Sixth great grandson of progenitor Nicholas Kegg. **DUANE CARL ROBERTS** Fifth great grandson of progenitor Nicholas Kegg. **EMILY ROBERTS** Seventh great granddaughter of progenitor Nicholas Kegg. **GERALDINE LEE ROBERTS** aka "Gerry" Sixth great granddaughter of progenitor Nicholas Kegg. **HAYLEE ROBERTS** Seventh great granddaughter of progenitor Nicholas Kegg. **JACK DUANE ROBERTS** [5782A] (1936 – 2019) son of Francis and Arline (Woodson) Roberts married Darlene Ann Negan with whom he was father of (5). Jack spent four years in active service in the United States Navy, being deployed each year to the Mediterranean Sea. He was an avid Hawkeye fan and John Wayne, The Duke, fan. Jack was employed as a junior high social studies teacher. He enjoyed coaching Girls High school Softball and Track. He was known to his fellow students as Mr. Roberts, aka Iron Shorts and Capt. Jack. Jack was a devoted Christian, and his heart was a lifeline of love for the Cornerstone Church of Christ south of Zearing, Iowa, known as "THE CHURCH IN THE CORNFIELD." He was of one of the Founding Fathers who started that church in 2003. **JAIME MARIE ROBERTS** Sixth great granddaughter of progenitor Nicholas Kegg. **JAMES E. ROBERTS** Fifth great grandson of progenitor Nicholas Kegg. **JARED DUANE ROBERTS** Sixth great grandson of progenitor Nicholas Kegg. **JASEY NOELLE ROBERTS** Seventh great granddaughter of progenitor Nicholas Kegg. **JASON ALLEN ROBERTS** Sixth great grandson of progenitor Nicholas Kegg. **JIM DARREL ROBERTS** aka "Jimmie" 5th great grandson of progenitor Nicholas Kegg. **JOHNNY RAY ROBERTS** Sixth great grandson of progenitor Nicholas Kegg. **JOYCE ROBERTS** Sixth great granddaughter of progenitor Nicholas Kegg. **KENNETH DEAN ROBERTS** (1938 – 2002) son of Daniel and Nina (Bergeman) Roberts. **LIBBY ROBERTS** Seventh great granddaughter of progenitor Nicholas Kegg. **LINDSEY JOY ROBERTS** Seventh great granddaughter of progenitor Nicholas Kegg.

[5780] Newton Daily News (IA) June 4, 2012 [5780A] News Journal (OH) Apr. 10, 2012 [5781] Shirley Funeral Home (PA) [5782] explorevenango.com [5782A] Fredregill Funeral and Cremation Care

MICHAEL ROBERTS Seventh great grandson of progenitor Nicholas Kegg. **NATHAN J. ROBERTS** aka "Nate", Sixth great grandson of progenitor Nicholas Kegg. **RODNEY ALAN ROBERTS** aka "Rod", Sixth great grandson of progenitor Nicholas Kegg. **TERRY DUANE ROBERTS** Sixth great grandson of progenitor Nicholas Kegg. **TREVOR SCOTT ROBERTS** [5782B] aka "Trev" (1986 – 2006) son of Ricky and Michele (Sontag) Roberts was a pre-delivery inspector for Keystone Corp. and a student at Ivy Tech. Trev was killed instantly after being ejected from the Jeep convertible that he was driving. **TYLER ROBERTS** Seventh great grandson of progenitor Nicholas Kegg. **VIOLET ROBERTS** Eighth great granddaughter of progenitor Nicholas Kegg. **WILLIAM FRANK ROBERTS** [5783] (1916 – 2006) son of Joseph and Ethel (Heffner) Roberts married Mary Jane Milne with whom he was father of (3). William was a retired plant engineer for Westinghouse Air Brake Co., Wilmerding, and was also a member of St. John's United Church of Christ, Larimer, where he served on the church consistory and was a former Sunday school superintendent. He was a member of Oak Hollow YMCA and the L.O.O.M., Lodge No. 236, Irwin.

ROBERTSON

HEIDI ROBERTSON Sixth great granddaughter of progenitor Nicholas Kegg.
KEVIN ROBERTSON Sixth great grandson of progenitor Nicholas Kegg.

ROBINETTE

CHARISSE ROBINETTE Sixth great granddaughter of progenitor Nicholas Kegg.
SOMER RENEE ROBINETTE Seventh great granddaughter of progenitor Nicholas Kegg.
STACY SHANE ROBINETTE Sixth great granddaughter of progenitor Nicholas Kegg.

ROBINSON

CHARITY T. ROBINSON Seventh great granddaughter of progenitor Nicholas Kegg. **CHARLEY ROBINSON** Sixth great grandson of progenitor Nicholas Kegg. **JACK ROBINSON** Eighth great grandson of progenitor Nicholas Kegg. **JANA ROBINSON** Seventh great granddaughter of progenitor Nicholas Kegg. **JOHN S. ROBINSON** Seventh great grandson of progenitor Nicholas Kegg. **KELLI M. ROBINSON** Sixth great granddaughter of progenitor Nicholas Kegg. **MARTY L. ROBINSON** Seventh great grandson of progenitor Nicholas Kegg. **ROBERT DAVID ROBINSON** (1937 – 1998) son of Phillip and Eva (Stuckey) Robinson. **TYRA CATHERINE ROBINSON** Sixth great granddaughter of progenitor Nicholas Kegg.

ROBISON

BOBBY JO ROBISON Sixth great granddaughter of progenitor Nicholas Kegg.
HOLLY FAYE ROBISON Sixth great granddaughter of progenitor Nicholas Kegg.
TONYA ROBISON Sixth great granddaughter of progenitor Nicholas Kegg.

ROCK

ANNA ROCK [5784] (1909 – 1963) daughter of Thomas and Effie (Beaver) Rock, married Thomas John Quinn. Anna was an employee of the United States National Bank, Westmont Branch. Anna was a member of Quota Club and a past president of the Mercy Hospital Guild. **DOROTHY ROCK** [5784A] (1913 – 1987) daughter of Thomas and Effie (Beaver) Rock married three times, first to Robert Samuel Cummings with whom she was mother of (2), then to Edward J. McIlvaine with whom she was mother

---

[5782B] gen.nobleco.lib.in. [5783] Tribune Review (PA) April 27, 2006, obtained by D. Sue Dible

of (1), last marriage to O. Stewart Penman. **KENDRA ROCK** Sixth great granddaughter of progenitor Nicholas Kegg. **KEVIN JAE ROCK** (1962 – 1962) son of Bernard and Nancy (Beegle) Rock. **MAE R. ROCK** (1911 – 1977) daughter of Thomas and Effie (Beaver) Rock. **NERISSA ROCK** Sixth great granddaughter of progenitor Nicholas Kegg.

ROCKS

CAM ROCKS Seventh great granddaughter of progenitor Nicholas Kegg.
ETHAN ROCKS Seventh great grandson of progenitor Nicholas Kegg.

ROCKWOOD

JOHN F. J. ROCKWOOD Sixth great grandson of progenitor Nicholas Kegg.
TERRI LYNN ROCKWOOD Sixth great granddaughter of progenitor Nicholas Kegg.

RODABAUGH

AARON ADAM RODABAUGH Fifth great grandson of progenitor Nicholas Kegg. **ANGEL RODABAUGH** Fifth great granddaughter of progenitor Nicholas Kegg. **BRANDY L. RODABAUGH** Sixth great granddaughter of progenitor Nicholas Kegg. **DALE EDWARD RODABAUGH** [5784B] (1937 – 2016) son of Lewis and Alma (Kegg) Rodabaugh married more than once. He was the father of (4). Dale was last married to Leanna (Russell) McKenney. Dale served in the US Army during the Korean Conflict. He was employed with RMI in Ashtabula for over 30 years and then over the road trucker until his retirement. He was a member of the Fraternal Order of Eagles and had been a past president of the Ashtabula High School Athletic Boosters. He was active as a Union Rep and was a Hearing Officer with Workers Comp while employed with RMI. He enjoyed hunting, fishing, traveling and had a lifelong Love of Classic Cars. **DALE EDWARD RODABAUGH JR.** [5784C] aka "Sonny" (1959 – 2010) son of Dale and Kathari (Wilbert) Rodabaugh. **DAVID W. RODABAUGH** Fifth great grandson of progenitor Nicholas Kegg. **CHRISTOPHER RODABAUGH** Sixth great grandson of progenitor Nicholas Kegg. **EVELINA A. RODABAUGH** [5784D] aka "Evy" (1939 – 2013) daughter of Lewis and Alma (Kegg) Rodabaugh. Evy had worked for the Ashtabula Star Beacon for over 35 years. She enjoyed doing puzzles; cats of all kinds, cooking and baking cookies, but most of all she loved spending time with her family. **LEONA RODABAUGH** Sixth great granddaughter of progenitor Nicholas Kegg.

RODOCKER

JACK E. RODOCKER Sixth great grandson of progenitor Nicholas Kegg.

RODRIGUEZ

ANTONIO WELLS RODRIGUEZ Seventh great grandson of progenitor Nicholas Kegg.
JOSELYN ROSE RODRIGUEZ Seventh great granddaughter of progenitor Nicholas Kegg.
JOSHUA RODRIGUEZ Seventh great grandson of progenitor Nicholas Kegg.

ROEB

BRIANNA ROEB Seventh great granddaughter of progenitor Nicholas Kegg.

[5784] Bedford Gazette (PA) Nov 6, 1963 [5784A] Bedford Inquirer (PA) Dec 18, 1987 [5784B] Fleming & Billman Funeral Directors and Crematory [5784C] The Star Beacon (Ashtabula, Ohio) March 28, 2010 [5784D] Star Beacon (OH) Dec 26, 2013

ROESNER

DEREK HALE ROESNER Sixth great grandson of progenitor Nicholas Kegg.
JOEL BEN ROESNER Sixth great grandson of progenitor Nicholas Kegg.
JORDON ROESNER Sixth great grandson of progenitor Nicholas Kegg.

ROESSLER

MARY ALICE ROESSLER aka "Puddy", Sixth great granddaughter of progenitor Nicholas Kegg.

ROETCISOENDER

JAMES HENRY ROETCISOENDER aka "Jamey", Seventh great grandson of progenitor Nicholas Kegg. **JASON MICHAEL ROETCISOENDER** Seventh great grandson of progenitor Nicholas Kegg.

ROGERS

BRIAN DOUGLAS ROGERS Seventh great grandson of progenitor Nicholas Kegg.

ROHM

PATRICIA LOUISE ROHM [5784E] aka "Pat" (1931 – 2001) daughter of Patrick and Harriet (Gump) Rohm married Orville Johnson with whom she was mother of (2). Patricia was a volunteer at Donahoe Manor Nursing Home.

ROHRER

BARBARA MARIE ROHRER Fifth great granddaughter of progenitor Nicholas Kegg.
ERIC JONATHAN ROHRER Fifth great grandson of progenitor Nicholas Kegg.
JANE ANNE ROHRER (1954 – 1954) daughter of Robert and Anne (Kern) Rohrer.
ROBERTA L. ROHRER Fifth great granddaughter of progenitor Nicholas Kegg.
SAMANTHA JANE ROHRER Sixth great granddaughter of progenitor Nicholas Kegg.

ROLAND

BRYAN MICHAEL ROLAND Seventh great grandson of progenitor Nicholas Kegg.
JEFFREY ROLAND Seventh great grandson of progenitor Nicholas Kegg.

ROMELLI

DOMINIC A. ROMELLI Seventh great grandson of progenitor Nicholas Kegg.

RONDO

ALICIA RONDO Eighth great granddaughter of progenitor Nicholas Kegg. **ISABEL RONDO** Eighth great granddaughter of progenitor Nicholas Kegg. **JEFFREY ALAN RONDO** [5785] (1969 – 2000) son of Thomas and Paullette Kay (Friemoth) Rondo married Tonda Jean Hindbaugh with whom he was father of (3). **JUSTIN RONDO** Eighth great granddaughter of progenitor Nicholas Kegg.

[5784E] p.3 - Bedford Inquirer (PA) March 9, 2001 [5785] The Daily Telegram (MI) March 11, 2000

KEISHA RANAE RONDO Eighth great granddaughter of progenitor Nicholas Kegg. **LEIGHTON RONDO** Ninth great grandson of progenitor Nicholas Kegg. **NATHAN RONDO** Eighth great grandson of progenitor Nicholas Kegg. **THOMAS RONDO** Seventh great grandson of progenitor Nicholas Kegg. **ZACHERY THOMAS RONDO** Eighth great grandson of progenitor Nicholas Kegg.

RONK

ALEX RONK Seventh great grandson of progenitor Nicholas Kegg. **BECCA RONK** Seventh great granddaughter of progenitor Nicholas Kegg. **JACKIE RONK** Seventh great granddaughter of progenitor Nicholas Kegg. **JOHN RAYMOND RONK** Sixth great grandson of progenitor Nicholas Kegg. **VICKIE LEE RONK** Sixth great granddaughter of progenitor Nicholas Kegg. **WILLIAM LEROY RONK** Sixth great grandson of progenitor Nicholas Kegg.

ROOS

JOEL ROOS Sixth great grandson of progenitor Nicholas Kegg. **JON ROOS** Sixth great grandson of progenitor Nicholas Kegg. **JOSH ROOS** Sixth great grandson of progenitor Nicholas Kegg. **JOY ROOS** Sixth great granddaughter of progenitor Nicholas Kegg.

ROSAGE

MEGAN ROSAGE Seventh great granddaughter of progenitor Nicholas Kegg.
STEVEN EDWARD ROSAGE [5785A] (1957 – 1990) son of James and Hazel (James) Rosage married Carolyn C. Wess with whom he was father of (1). Steven was a therapeutic activity aide for the Bedford County Sheltered Workshop and was a member of the Bedford American Legion Post No. 113.

ROSE

AMY BETH ROSE Sixth great granddaughter of progenitor Nicholas Kegg. **ARVILLA VESTA ROSE** [5785B] (1887 – 1954) daughter of Emanuel and Laura (Wertz) Rose married Cromwell C. Boor with whom she was mother of (2). Arvilla was a Cumberland Valley school teacher. **BREANN NICOLE ROSE** Eighth great granddaughter of progenitor Nicholas Kegg. **CLINTON ROSE** Seventh great grandson of progenitor Nicholas Kegg. **CROMWELL EMANUEL ROSE** [5786] (1907 – 1959) aka "Crum", son of Henry and Elsie (Hite) Rose married twice; first to Myrtle E. Miller with whom he was father of (1). Later, he married Helen C. Krueger with whom he was father of (2). **DANIEL LEE ROSE** aka "Dan", Eighth great grandson of progenitor Nicholas Kegg. **GERALD ROSE** Fifth great grandson of progenitor Nicholas Kegg. **GERALDINE HELEN ROSE** [5786A] (1905 – 1986) daughter of H. Reese and Elsie (Hite) Rose married Clyde E. Miller with whom she was mother of (6). **HAROLD L. ROSE** [5787] (1927 – 1995) aka "Jim", son of Cromwell and Myrtle (Miller) Rose, married Mary Lois Elliott with whom he was father of (2). Harold was a retired truck driver for the Celanese Corp., He was an Army veteran of World War II and Korea. Harold was a life member of the Cumberland Masonic Lodge 320. **HENRY REESE ROSE** [5788] (1881 – 1950) son of Emanuel and Laura (Wertz) Rose, married Elsie Laura Hite with whom he was father of (4). Henry was a member of the Bedford Valley Methodist Church and the Independent Order of Odd Fellows. **JANE LOUISE ROSE** Fourth great granddaughter of progenitor Nicholas Kegg. **JOSEPH ALLEN ROSE** Sixth great grandson of progenitor Nicholas Kegg. **JUNE C. ROSE** Fifth great granddaughter of progenitor Nicholas Kegg. **KENNETH MELVIN ROSE** Fourth great grandson of progenitor Nicholas Kegg. **LINDA MARY ROSE** Fourth great granddaughter of progenitor Nicholas Kegg.

[5785A] Bedford County Historical Society (PA), book 72, page 160 contributed by D. Sue Dible [5785B] p.3- Cumberland News (MD) Apr 6, 1954 [5786] p.6 Detroit Times (MI) Apr 5, 1959 [5786A] p.22 - Cumberland Evening Times (MD) Aug 15, 1986 [5787] Bedford Inquirer (PA) Aug 11, 1995, obtained by Bob Rose

MATTHEW ROSE aka "Matt", Seventh great grandson of progenitor Nicholas Kegg. **PHYLLIS LAVERNE ROSE** [5788A] (1913 – 1993) daughter of H. Reese and Elsie (Hite) Rose married Russell Martin Nee with whom she was mother of (3). Phyllis was a former co-owner/operator with her husband of the Cumberland Motel, Baltimore Pike; and Rose's Camp, Centreville. **RICHARD DALE ROSE** Eighth great grandson of progenitor Nicholas Kegg. **STILLBORN ROSE** (1928 – 1928) daughter of Henry and Elise (Hite) Rose. **TAMMY RENE ROSE** (1957 – 1957) daughter of Harold and Mary (Elliott) Rose. **TERRI LEA ROSE** Sixth great granddaughter of progenitor Nicholas Kegg. **TYLER BLAKE ROSE** Seventh great grandson of progenitor Nicholas Kegg. **ZELLA ROSE** [5789] (1880 – 1963) daughter of Emanuel and Laura (Wertz) Rose, married Howard H. Deaner with whom she was mother of (2). Zella was a member of the First United Church of Christ, the For-Get-Me-Not Rebecca Lodge of Hyndman and the WCTU of Hyndman.

ROSENBERGER

DANIEL TILTON ROSENBERGER Seventh great grandson of progenitor Nicholas Kegg.
JOHN DIEHL ROSENBERGER Seventh great grandson of progenitor Nicholas Kegg.

ROSS

ALEXANDER ROSS Sixth great grandson of progenitor Nicholas Kegg. **BARBARA ROSS** Fifth great granddaughter of progenitor Nicholas Kegg. **MARGARET SUE ROSS** aka "Peggy" Fifth great granddaughter of progenitor Nicholas Kegg. **ROY C. ROSS** Fifth great grandson of progenitor Nicholas Kegg. **ROY C. ROSS** Sixth great grandson of progenitor Nicholas Kegg. **WILLIAM ROSS** aka "Bill", Fifth great grandson of progenitor Nicholas Kegg.

ROSSER

SHAY WILLIAM ROSSER Eighth great grandson of progenitor Nicholas Kegg.
ZANE ROSSER Eighth great grandson of progenitor Nicholas Kegg.

ROTH

DEBBIE ROTH Sixth great granddaughter of progenitor Nicholas Kegg.
PATRICK MICHAEL ROTH (1979 – 2001) son of Cheryldellee Beegle.

ROTHMILLER

LEO EDWIN ROTHMILLER (1926 – 1950) son of Extra and Pearl (Betzler) Rothmiller.
LUCILLE MAXINE ROTHMILLER Fourth great granddaughter of progenitor Nicholas Kegg.

ROTZ

JESSICA LYNN ROTZ Sixth great granddaughter of progenitor Nicholas Kegg.
NICHOLAS ROTZ Sixth great grandson of progenitor Nicholas Kegg.

ROUDABUSH

ADALYN ROUDABUSH Eighth great granddaughter of progenitor Nicholas Kegg.
KADEN ROUDABUSH Eighth great granddaughter of progenitor Nicholas Kegg.
PAISLEY ROUDABUSH Eighth great granddaughter of progenitor Nicholas Kegg.

[5788] BU Data Book obtained by Bob Rose [5788A] p.8C - Cumberland Times News (MD) Feb 28, 1993 [5789] Rootsweb Archiver obituary transcribes by June M. Napora

ROUILLIER

MATTHEW ROUILLIER Seventh great grandson of progenitor Nicholas Kegg.
SAMANTHA ROUILLIER Seventh great granddaughter of progenitor Nicholas Kegg.

ROUTSONG

ALMA LOUISE ROUTSONG [5789A 5789B] (1924 – 1996) daughter of Carl and Esther (Miller) Routsong married Bruce Orr Brodie with whom she was mother of (2). Alma was a WAVE stationed in Kentucky during WWII. She became a novelist, best known for her lesbian fiction, which she published under the pen name Isabel Miller. Her pen name, Isabel Miller, is the combination of an anagram for "Lesbia" and her mother's birth name **ALVIN BENJAMIN ROUTSONG** [5790] (1891 – 1977) son of Frank and Louisa (Bryant) Routsong, married Mary Alleen Cramer. Alvin was an electrician in the Kalamazoo area for 50 years.   **ANGIE NORA ROUTSONG** [5790A] (1868 – 1933) daughter of David and Anna (Kegg) Routsong, married Frederick Augustus Scharmen with whom she was mother of (11).   **ANTHONY SYLVESTER ROUTSONG** [5791] (1863 – 1949) son of David and Anna (Kegg) Routsong, married Amanda M. Lavery Powlison.   **CARL JOHN ROUTSONG** [5792] (1897 – 1970) son of Warren and Amelia (Birmley) Routsong, married Esther L. Miller with whom he was father of (4). Carl was employed by Bell Telephone Company for several years, served as a city policeman for 10 years and as a guard foreman at Parts Mfg. Co., later was an employee of The Concrete Service, and was First Congregational church custodian. Carl was a member of Traverse City Eagles Club and a past president of the local Fraternal Order of Police. He served in the U. S. Army in World War I.   **CARLA JAN ROUTSONG** [5793] aka "C.J." (1954 – 2021) daughter of Gary and Betty Allene (Eikey) Routsong married Richard Keller Conder with whom she was mother of (1). CJ was known for her friendliness, sense of humor, and artistic talent. She was a graduate of Kendall College of Art and Design and worked as an Art Restoration Specialist. Her happiest times were when she got together with loved ones for lakeside bonfires, Trivial Pursuit, good music, and cold beer.   **CHARLES D. ROUTSONG** [5794] (1887 – 1947) son of Frank and Louisa (Bryant) Routsong was a veteran of the first World War, serving overseas in France. A sportsman, Mr. Routsong was an active hunter and fisherman for many years. He was a member of the Moose and Eagle lodges and the Traverse Region Dog and Sportsman's Club. **CHRISTY LEE ROUTSONG** [5795] (1947 – 2017) daughter of Richard and Jeanne (Straub) Routsong married five times; Christy was full of life and had a great sense of humor.   **DANIEL ROUTSONG** [5796] (1861 – 1946) son of David and Anna (Kegg) Routsong, married Ada Viola Smith. Daniel was an employee of Traverse City for 40 years.   **FRANK ROUTSONG** [5797] (1857 – 1945) son of David and Anna (Kegg) Routsong, married Louisa M. Bryant with whom he was father of (5).   **GARY MILLER ROUTSONG** [5797A] aka "pops" (1929 – 1991) son of Carl and Esther (Miller) Routsong, married Betty Eikey with whom he was father of (2). Gary was a sales representative for numerous years and was employed by the state of Michigan as manager of the Secretary of State's office in Escanaba, Newberry, St. Clair Shores, and Holland. He was a member of the Holland Amateur Ham Radio Club, licensed as an Extra Class, of the Holland Elks Lodge 1513, and of the Cherryland Amateur Radio Club in Traverse City.   **GEORGE A. ROUTSONG** [5798] (1888 – 1956) son of Frank and Louisa (Bryant) Routsong in addition to being a farmer was a carpenter by trade. He was a veteran of World War I, and a member of the local VFW.   **GLADYS M. ROUTSONG** [5799] (1894 – 1974) daughter of Warren and Amelia (Birmley) Routsong, married James Randolph Yenish with whom she was mother of (1).   **HARRY FRANKLIN ROUTSONG** [5800] (1885 – 1963) son of Frank and Louisa (Bryant) Routsong, married

---

[5789A] Traverse For Women published Jan 20, 2010 [5789B] p.6 - Record-Eagle (Traverse City, MI) June 20, 1947 [5790] p.12 - Traverse City Record Eagle (MI) March 02, 1977 [5790A] p.2 - Traverse City Record Eagle (MI) Feb 9, 1948 [5791] p.14 - Record-Eagle (MI) Dec 14, 1949 [5792] p.9 - Traverse City Record Eagle (MI) Feb 14, 1970 [5793] Grand Rapids Press (MI) Mar 28, 2021, obtained by D. Sue Dible [5794] p.2 - Record-Eagle (MI) Sept. 19, 1947 [5795] Ott-Laughlin Funeral Home (Winter Haven, FL) obtained by D. Sue Dible [5796] p.7 - Record-Eagle (MI) May 31, 1946 [5797] p.2 - Traverse City Record Eagle (MI) Aug 28, 1945 [5797A] familyseach.org obituary-Film Number: 007597936 ,Image Number: 01217 [5798] p.19 - Record-Eagle (MI) Feb 27, 1956 [5799] p.25 - Traverse City Record Eagle (MI) June 17, 1974 [5800] p. 17 Record-Eagle (MI) April 21, 1958

Helena Bickler.   **INFANT ROUTSONG** (1923 – 1923) son of Carl and Esther (Miller) Routsong.
JESSIE L. ROUTSONG [5801] (1892 – 1947) daughter of Frank and Louisa (Bryant) Routsong married twice; first to Frank William Burd with whom she was mother of (2). Later, she married John Herbert Heaslip.   **JOHN WARREN ROUTSONG** [5801A] (1960 – 2018) son of Gary and Betty (Eikey) Routsong married and was father of (2). John is remembered for his big heart. He always put others needs before his own. He loved to fish and spend time on the water.   **KATHRYN ROUTSONG** Sixth great granddaughter of progenitor Nicholas Kegg.   **MARILYNN ANNE ROUTSONG** [5802] (1923 – 2003) daughter of Jessie Routsong was raised by her Uncle Alvin and Aunt Mary Routsong. Marilynn married Glenn Bennett Vanderlaan with whom she was mother of (2). Marilynn was an RN for Borgess and Bronson Hospital.   **MIKAL JEANNE ROUTSONG** Fifth great granddaughter of progenitor Nicholas Kegg.   **NATHANIEL ROUTSONG** Seventh great grandson of progenitor Nicholas Kegg.   **PAULA ANN ROUTSONG** [5803] (1959 – 2021) daughter of Gary and Betty Allene (Eikey) Routsong married William Joseph Egan. Paula was a vegan and a member of the Chicago Alliance for Animals, where she played an integral part in the passage of the Chicago horse-drawn carriage ban.   **RICHARD WARREN ROUTSONG** [5803A] (1920 – 2008) son of Carl and Esther (Miller) Routsong married his high school sweetheart, Jeanne Marie Straub with whom he was father of (2). Richard received his pilot's wings and commission in the Army Air Forces at Kelly Field. He was a retired optometrist.   **SEBASTIAN ROUTSONG** [5804] (1859 – 1937) son of David and Anna (Kegg) Routsong.   **WARREN THOMAS ROUTSONG** [5805] (1865 – 1956) son of David and Anna (Kegg) Routsong, married twice first to Amelia Birmley with whom he was father of (2). After her death, he married her sister Louise E. Birmley.
WILLIAM ROUTSONG Sixth great grandson of progenitor Nicholas Kegg.

ROUZER

BENJAMIN FRANKLIN ROUZER [5806] (1889 – 1955) son of Andrew and Catherine (May) Rouzer.
FAMIE LEONE ROUZER [5807] (1901 – 1986) daughter of Andrew and Catherine (May) Rouzer, married Charles Henry Koerner with whom she was mother of (1).   **GENEVIEVE T. ROUZER** [5808] (1899 – 1938) daughter of Andrew and Catherine (May) Rouzer, married William P. Leahy.   **HARRY H. ROUZER** (1896 – 1918) son of Andrew and Catherine (May) Rouzer.   **JESSSIE HAMLIN ROUZER** [5809] (1886 – 1947) daughter of Andrew and Catherine (May) Rouzer married twice, first to Albert George Lehman with whom she was mother of (1). Later, she married Albert Sturtz with whom she was mother of (1).   **NINA PEARL ROUZER** [5810] (1891 – 1972) daughter of Andrew and Catherine (May) Rouzer, married Gilbert Haven Myers.   **OLIVE IRENE ROUZER** (1893 – 1923) daughter of Andrew and Catherine (May) Rouzer, married John Berlin Rodgers.

ROWE

KENNETH G. ROWE [5811] (1908 – 1980) son of Perry and Bertha (Steele) Rowe married twice; first to Emily Hattie Knoche Wilson and later, to Bertha Rumpit. Kenneth had been employed at the Tokheim Corp.   **LINDA ANN ROWE** Sixth great granddaughter of progenitor Nicholas Kegg.   **MARCIA GAIL ROWE** [5811A] (1944 – 2014) daughter of William and Mary (Kelley) Rowe married twice, first to Dwight E.C. Vollrath with whom she was mother of (2). Later, she married Donald L. Mitchell. Marcia formerly worked at Memorial Hospital of Union County, worked in the Paint Department at Honda for 17 years and owned and operated Hiway Bait and Tackle for 20 years in Marblehead with her husband Don and was always first and foremost a homemaker. Marcia loved fishing, riding motorcycles with Don, traveling, especially the trips with her grandchildren and spending time with her family.

[5801] p.5 - Traverse City Record Eagle (MI) Jan 21, 1947 [5801A] Reynolds Jonkhoff Funeral Home (MI) obituary contributed by D. Sue Dible [5802] Kalamazoo Gazette (MI) May 11, 2003 [5803] The Record-Eagle (MI) Apr 17, 2021, obtained by D. Sue Dible [5803A] St. Petersburg Times (FLA) June 15, 2002 [5804] Traverse City Record-Eagle (MI) March 11, 1937, obtained by D. Sue Dible [5805] p.8 Record-Eagle (MI) Jan 2, 1953 [5806] Bedford Gazette (PA) Sep 12, 1955 [5807] p.C8 Pittsburgh Press (PA) Aug 26, 1986 [5808] p.58 Pittsburgh Press (PA) Dec 16, 1938 [5809] p.28 Pittsburgh Press (PA) Jan 24, 1947 [5810] p.19 - Evening Standard (PA) March 17, 1972 [5811] Fort Wayne Journal Gazette (IN) Nov 1980, obtained by D. Sue Dible [5811A] News Herald (OH) Sept. 9, 2014

NORMA ELLEN ROWE [5811B] (1942 – 2017) daughter of William and Mary (Kelley)Rowe married twice, first to Donald Lee Martin with whom she was mother of (2). Later, she married Willard Frederick Hart with whom she was mother of (1). Norma enjoyed anything related to crafts and baking, musicals, watching the Indianapolis Colts football team and the Butler Bulldogs men's basketball team. And, of course, she relished her time with family. Moreover, if Norma was defined by any one key characteristic, it's that she was a teacher to the core. From the time that the desire to be a teacher took hold of her at the age of twelve, she taught as a mother, as a schoolteacher in private and public schools for over twenty years, as a cake decorating instructor, and as a top salesperson in a variety of retail industries. If there was one subject, she loved to teach most of all, it was poetry. Her sixth-grade students will never forget the passion with which she approached their annual project of writing a large notebook of poems on the five senses. **PAUL W. ROWE** [5811C] (1897 – 1962) son of Perry and Bertha (Steele) Rowe married Frieda G. Marquardt with whom he was father of (2). Paul was associated with the Mantee Lumber Co. in Oneco. Paul was a member of Sol D. Bayless Lodge 359, F & AM. **RALPH KNODE ROWE** [5812] (1901 – 1967) son of Perry and Bertha (Steele) Rowe married Lola Belle Shew. Ralph retired from International Harvester Co. with 30 years' service. **SAMUEL ROWE** Fifth great grandson of progenitor Nicholas Kegg. **SHERRI PATRICIA ROWE** Sixth great granddaughter of progenitor Nicholas Kegg. **SUSAN ROWE** Fifth great granddaughter of progenitor Nicholas Kegg. **SUSAN KATHERINE ROWE** Sixth great granddaughter of progenitor Nicholas Kegg.

ROWLAND

ADRIANNE ROWLAND Seventh great granddaughter of progenitor Nicholas Kegg.
JEREMY BENJAMIN ROWLAND Seventh great grandson of progenitor Nicholas Kegg.
STEPHANIE LEIGH ROWLAND Seventh great granddaughter of progenitor Nicholas Kegg.

ROYE

JENNIFER E. ROYE Fifth great granddaughter of progenitor Nicholas Kegg.

RUBIN

MACKENZIE ROSE RUBIN Seventh great granddaughter of progenitor Nicholas Kegg.

RUBY

DANNY EDWARD RUBY Seventh great grandson of progenitor Nicholas Kegg. **SAMUEL JAMES RUBY** Seventh great grandson of progenitor Nicholas Kegg. **TAMMY L. RUBY** Seventh great granddaughter of progenitor Nicholas Kegg. **TONYA L. RUBY** Seventh great granddaughter of progenitor Nicholas Kegg.

RUCH

KARL D. RUCH Sixth great grandson of progenitor Nicholas Kegg.

RUDE

JESSIE RUDE Sixth great granddaughter of progenitor Nicholas Kegg.

[5811B] Randall Roberts Funeral Home (IN) [5811C] Fort Wayne Journal Gazette (IN) Nov 15, 1962, contributed by D. Sue Dible [5812] Fort Wayne Journal Gazette (IN) Apr 14, 1967, obtained by D. Sue Dible

RUE

CALEB RUE Eighth great grandson of progenitor Nicholas Kegg.
REBEKAH ANN RUE Eighth great granddaughter of progenitor Nicholas Kegg.

RUGH

BECKY RUGH Seventh great granddaughter of progenitor Nicholas Kegg.
SUSAN RUGH Seventh great granddaughter of progenitor Nicholas Kegg.

RUHR

ASHLEY JO RUHR Eighth great granddaughter of progenitor Nicholas Kegg.
BRITTANY GENE RUHR Eighth great granddaughter of progenitor Nicholas Kegg.
HARLEY JOHN RUHR [5813] (1974 – 2000) son of Paul and Janet (Kelly) Ruhr was a construction worker and had also been employed with Pizza Hut.

RUNNION

CHELSEA RUNNION Eighth great granddaughter of progenitor Nicholas Kegg.
LELAH CATHERINE RUNNION Eighth great granddaughter of progenitor Nicholas Kegg.

RUPP

DAVID RUPP Eighth great grandson of progenitor Nicholas Kegg. **RICK RUPP** Seventh great grandson of progenitor Nicholas Kegg. **TERRY RUPP** Seventh great grandson of progenitor Nicholas Kegg. **TONY RUPP** Seventh great grandson of progenitor Nicholas Kegg.

RUSH

ANGELINA RUSH Sixth great granddaughter of progenitor Nicholas Kegg. **ELLIS JAMES RUSH** Sixth great grandson of progenitor Nicholas Kegg. **MICHAEL D. RUSH** Sixth great grandson of progenitor Nicholas Kegg. **TISA LYNNE RUSH** Sixth great granddaughter of progenitor Nicholas Kegg.

RUSSELL

CHLOE RUSSELL Sixth great granddaughter of progenitor Nicholas Kegg. **CLARA E. RUSSELL** (1885 – 1972) daughter of Julius and Mary Ellen (Kegg) Russell, married Harrison Gorton Cottrell. **CLAUDIA ROXANNE RUSSELL** aka "Roxie" Fifth great granddaughter of progenitor Nicholas Kegg. **DONALD JULIUS RUSSELL** (1924 – 1996) son of Jesse and Jessie (Bridwell) Russell married Beryl June Grant with whom he was father of (1). **JESSE JULIUS RUSSELL** [5814] (1889 – 1967) son of Julius and Mary Ellen (Kegg) Russell, married Jessie Ellen Bridwell with whom he was father of (3). **JESSIE EVELYN RUSSELL** (1917 – 1917) daughter of Jesse and Jessie (Bridwell) Russell. **MOLLIE L. RUSSELL** [5815] (1882 – 1976) daughter of Julius and Mary Ellen (Kegg) Russell married twice, first to Frederick Shannon Armstrong with whom she was mother of (1). Later, she married Edward Livingston Coonrod. **PAULA ANN RUSSELL** Sixth great granddaughter of progenitor Nicholas Kegg. **SEAN RUSSELL** Sixth great grandson of progenitor Nicholas Kegg. **SETH RUSSELL** Sixth great grandson of progenitor Nicholas Kegg.

[5813] Atlantic Public Library (IA) Mov 13, 2000, obtained by D. Sue Dible [5814] Record Searchlight (Redding CA) Feb 10, 1972 [5815] p.45-46; The Siskiyou Pioneer" 1957 Contributed by Joanne (Kegg) McReynolds

RUST

TRAVIS RUST Seventh great grandson of progenitor Nicholas Kegg.

RUTKOWSKI

KRISTINA ELIZABETH RUTKOWSKI Seventh great granddaughter of progenitor Nicholas Kegg.
MEGAN AMY RUTKOWSKI Seventh great granddaughter of progenitor Nicholas Kegg.
NATALIE QUINN RUTKOWSKI Seventh great granddaughter of progenitor Nicholas Kegg.
NICHOLAS EDWARD RUTKOWSKI Seventh great grandson of progenitor Nicholas Kegg.
SYDNEY LYNN RUTKOWSKI Seventh great granddaughter of progenitor Nicholas Kegg.

RUTLEDGE

BEVY JANE RUTLEDGE Fifth great granddaughter of progenitor Nicholas Kegg.

RYAN

BARBARA ANN RYAN (1934 – 1992) daughter of Wiley and Ivalue (Huddy) Ryan, married Mr. Lotz. **JACK RICHARD RYAN** (1932 – 1996) son of Wiley and Ivalue (Huddy) Ryan. **JAMES LINDLEY RYAN** Fifth great grandson of progenitor Nicholas Kegg. **SHIRLEY NADINE RYAN** [5816] (1927 – 2000) daughter of Wiley and Ivalue (Huddy) Ryan, married James Henry Johnson with whom she was mother of (1). **WILEY THOMAS RYAN** Fifth great grandson of progenitor Nicholas Kegg.

RYBERG

AMY LYNN RYBERG Sixth great granddaughter of progenitor Nicholas Kegg.

RYDER

GREGORY THOMAS RYDER Sixth great grandson of progenitor Nicholas Kegg. **JEAN LYNN RYDER** Fifth great granddaughter of progenitor Nicholas Kegg. **KEITH MICHAEL RYDER** Sixth great grandson of progenitor Nicholas Kegg. **MARILYN RYDER** Sixth great granddaughter of progenitor Nicholas Kegg. **ROBERT EDWARD RYDER** Fifth great grandson of progenitor Nicholas Kegg. **SCOTT EDWARD RYDER** Sixth great grandson of progenitor Nicholas Kegg. **STELLA ROSE RYDER** Seventh great granddaughter of progenitor Nicholas Kegg.

RYDZESKI

DENNIS JOHN RYDZESKI [5816A] (1957 – 2014) son of Norman and Marie (Diefenderfer) Rydzeski. Dennis was employed at American Seating Company for many years. He was a quiet man, but well liked and an avid chatter. **LEONARD BRUCE RYDZESKI** Sixth great grandson of progenitor Nicholas Kegg. **SHEILA A. RYDZESKI** Sixth great granddaughter of progenitor Nicholas Kegg. **SUSAN MARIE RYDZESKI** Sixth great granddaughter of progenitor Nicholas Kegg.

RYMERS

SEAN T. RYMERS Seventh great grandson of progenitor Nicholas Kegg.
SHELBY C. RYMERS Seventh great granddaughter of progenitor Nicholas Kegg.

[5816] Columbus Dispatch (OH) June 27, 2014 [5816A] Grand Rapids Press (MI) July 27, 2014

SACKMANN

NATALIE SACKMAN Seventh great granddaughter of progenitor Nicholas Kegg.

SAGE

BRE RAE SAGE Seventh great granddaughter of progenitor Nicholas Kegg. **LEANN SAGE** Seventh great granddaughter of progenitor Nicholas Kegg. **RONALD SAGE** Sixth great grandson of progenitor Nicholas Kegg. **SCOTT ALLEN SAGE** Sixth great grandson of progenitor Nicholas Kegg.

SAGER

RICHARD THOMAS SAGER Sixth great grandson of progenitor Nicholas Kegg. **ROBERT EUGENE SAGER** Sixth great grandson of progenitor Nicholas Kegg. **SUSAN LOUISE SAGER** Sixth great granddaughter of progenitor Nicholas Kegg.

SAKAMOTO

KRISTY JEAN SAKAMOTO Sixth great granddaughter of progenitor Nicholas Kegg.

SALAS

CRYSTAL SALAS Eighth great granddaughter of progenitor Nicholas Kegg.
JASON SALAS Eighth great grandson of progenitor Nicholas Kegg.
MICHAEL SILAS Eighth great grandson of progenitor Nicholas Kegg.

SALSTROM

ANDREW JAY SALSTROM Seventh great grandson of progenitor Nicholas Kegg.

SALTZMAN

KENNETH T. SALTZMAN (1924 – 1924) son of Lloyd and Vera (Turner) Saltzman. **KRIS SALTZMAN** Seventh great granddaughter of progenitor Nicholas Kegg. **LEONA GERTRUDE SALTZMAN** (1896 – 1970) daughter of Emery and Mabel (Laird) Saltzman, married William Harley Been with whom she was mother of (10). **LEROY LOREN SALTZMAN** [5817] (1901 – 1982) son of Emery and Mabel (Laird) Saltzman, married Caryl J. Williams. **LLOYD EMERY SALTZMAN** [5818] (1898 – 1988) son of Emery and Mabel (Laird) Saltzman married twice; first to Vera Turner with whom he was father of (4). Later, he married Georgietta M. Kelley with whom he was father of (1). Lloyd worked as a meat cutter until his retirement. **LLOYCE SALTZMAN** Sixth great grandson of progenitor Nicholas Kegg. **LLOYD JUNIOR SALTZMAN** [5819] (1920 – 1998) son of Lloyd and Vera (Turner) Saltzman, married Ruth Wilhelmine Marie Schulze with whom he was father of (2). Lloyd entered the United States Army Air Corps and was stationed in England. Later, Lloyd was employed as a truck driver until he retired. **PATRICIA A. SALTZMAN** Fifth great granddaughter of progenitor Nicholas Kegg. **SHERYL SALTZMAN** Sixth great granddaughter of progenitor Nicholas Kegg.

SAMBORN

CASEY SAMBORN Sixth great granddaughter of progenitor Nicholas Kegg.

[5817] Mount Ayr Record-News (IA) Nov 11, 1982, transcribed by Sharon R. Becker. [5818] Mount Ayr Record-News (IA) transcribed by Sharon R. Becker. [5819] State Center Enterprise (IA) Jan 15, 1998

CIARA LYNN SAMBORN Sixth great granddaughter of progenitor Nicholas Kegg.
PRICE SAMBORN Sixth great grandson of progenitor Nicholas Kegg.

SAMON

AISHA IVETTE SAMON Eighth great granddaughter of progenitor Nicholas Kegg.
CORYNA MARIE SAMON Eighth great granddaughter of progenitor Nicholas Kegg.
EMITT PHILLIP SAMON Seventh great grandson of progenitor Nicholas Kegg.

SAMPLE

LEE SAMPLE Sixth great grandson of progenitor Nicholas Kegg.

SAMPLEY

DESTINY SAMPLEY Eighth great granddaughter of progenitor Nicholas Kegg.
FAITH SAMPLEY Eighth great granddaughter of progenitor Nicholas Kegg.

SAMRA

ALEXZANDRA SAMRA aka "Ally", Eighth great granddaughter of progenitor Nicholas Kegg.

SAMS

AARON PAUL SAMS Sixth great grandson of progenitor Nicholas Kegg. **A.J. SAMS** Seventh great grandson of progenitor Nicholas Kegg. **AMY SAMS** Sixth great granddaughter of progenitor Nicholas Kegg. **COURTNEY J. SAMS** Sixth great granddaughter of progenitor Nicholas Kegg. **GARY SAMS** Fifth great grandson of progenitor Nicholas Kegg. **JACK SAMS** Seventh great grandson of progenitor Nicholas Kegg. **SHARON L. SAMS** Fifth great granddaughter of progenitor Nicholas Kegg. **TRAVIS A. SAMS** Sixth great grandson of progenitor Nicholas Kegg. **WHITNEY LYN SAMS** Sixth great granddaughter of progenitor Nicholas Kegg.

SAMUELS

ERIC SAMUELS Seventh great grandson of progenitor Nicholas Kegg.

SANDERS

AGNES DELLA SANDERS [5820] (1915 – 1989) daughter of Francis and Mary Elizabeth (Mentzer) Sanders, married Douglas Raymond Maccausland with whom she was mother of (1). **ANNA M. SANDERS** (1910 - 1958) daughter of Francis and Mary Elizabeth (Mentzer) Sanders, married George Lang McGinnis with whom she was mother of (1). **BETH ELAINE SANDERS** Sixth great granddaughter of progenitor Nicholas Kegg. **CARTER SANDERS** Eighth great grandson of progenitor Nicholas Kegg. **CLAIRE SANDERS** Eighth great granddaughter of progenitor Nicholas Kegg. **DOROTHY MARGARET SANDERS** [5821] (1918 – 2012) daughter of Francis and Mary Elizabeth (Mentzer) Sanders married twice; first to Alloysius Sherman Skelly with whom she was mother of (3). Later, she married Charles Norman Kidwell with whom she was mother of (2). Dorothy had been employed as a cook and was a member of Our Lady of Fatima, Maryland. **DYLAN SANDERS** Eighth great grandson of progenitor Nicholas Kegg. **EDNA MARIE SANDERS** [5822] (1911 – 1994) daughter

---

[5820] p.16 Pittsburgh Post-Gazette (PA) Aug 7, 1989 [5821] Tribune Democrat (PA) July 27, 2012 [5822] p. B3- Altoona Mirror (PA) Dec 14, 1994

of Francis and Mary Elizabeth (Mentzer) Sanders, married Edgar Cooney Conrad with whom she was mother of (2). Edna retired as head cook from Mount Aloysius College, Cresson. **EMMA GLAYS SANDERS** [5823] (1904 – 1960) daughter of John and Emma (Kegg) Sanders married three times; first to Dolph Bevens with whom she was mother of (1). She married Gene Coates with whom she was mother of (1). Later, she married William H. Lawrence. **JAMES F. SANDERS** (1907 – 1913) son of Francis and Mary Elizabeth (Mentzer) Sanders. **JOHN NELSON SANDERS** Sixth great grandson of progenitor Nicholas Kegg. **KIMBERLY ANN SANDERS** Sixth great granddaughter of progenitor Nicholas Kegg. **LANI SANDERS** Eighth great granddaughter of progenitor Nicholas Kegg. **LAYLA SANDERS** Eighth great granddaughter of progenitor Nicholas Kegg. **LILA IRENE SANDERS** [5824] (1903 – 1987) daughter of John and Emma (Kegg) Sanders, married Theodore F. Bevens with whom she was mother of (1). Lila was a homemaker. **LILLES F. SANDERS**, (1899 -?) daughter of John and Emma (Kegg) Sanders. **MICHAEL RODNEY SANDERS** Sixth great grandson of progenitor Nicholas Kegg. **SUSAN SANDERS** [5825] (1921 – 2000) daughter of Francis and Mary Elizabeth (Mentzer) Sanders, married Ture Swanson. Susan was a member of Our Lady of Lourdes Catholic Church, Enola, and a former member of Sacred Heart Catholic Church and the Ladies Auxiliary of the Moose, both in New Smyrna Beach.

SANDERSON

BILLIE SANDERSON Sixth great grandson of progenitor Nicholas Kegg.
CHAD SANDERSON Seventh great grandson of progenitor Nicholas Kegg.
CHARLES EVERETT SANDERSON Fifth great grandson of progenitor Nicholas Kegg.
DOROTHY SANDERSON Fifth great granddaughter of progenitor Nicholas Kegg.
JUDITH NELLE SANDERSON [5825A] aka "Judie" (1941 – 2019) daughter of Frank and Leona (Shafer) Sanderson married Clifford Atrle Lewis with whom she was mother of (6). Judie enjoyed crocheting, gardening, canning and flowers.
KELLY MARIE SANDERSON Sixth great granddaughter of progenitor Nicholas Kegg.
MITCHELL JAY SANDERSON Sixth great grandson of progenitor Nicholas Kegg.
NICHOLAS JAY SANDERSON Sixth great grandson of progenitor Nicholas Kegg.
RYAN SANDERSON Seventh great grandson of progenitor Nicholas Kegg.
SANDRA SUE SANDERSON Fifth great granddaughter of progenitor Nicholas Kegg.
SHELLY SANDERSON Sixth great granddaughter of progenitor Nicholas Kegg.
TIM SANDERSON Sixth great grandson of progenitor Nicholas Kegg

SANDLE

ALISON MARY SANDLE Sixth great granddaughter of progenitor Nicholas Kegg.
JAMES ANTHONY SANDLE Sixth great grandson of progenitor Nicholas Kegg.

SANDLIN

MARLON SANDLIN Fifth great grandson of progenitor Nicholas Kegg.
TERRILL LEE SANDLIN Fifth great grandson of progenitor Nicholas Kegg.

SANDOVAL

JAXON SANDOVAL aka "Jax", Ninth great grandson of progenitor Nicholas Kegg.
SCARLETT ROSE SANDOVAL Ninth great granddaughter of progenitor Nicholas Kegg.

[5823] p.13 Medford Mail Tribune (OR) April 29, 1960 [5824] p.66 Orgonian (OR) Feb 6, 1987 [5825] cumberlink.com/obituaries [5825A] KPCNews (IN) Apr. 19, 2019

SANFORD

KADEN SANFORD Seventh great grandson of progenitor Nicholas Kegg.
KIELLA SANFORD Seventh great granddaughter of progenitor Nicholas Kegg.
KYZIE JO SANFORD Seventh great granddaughter of progenitor Nicholas Kegg.

SANNER

MICHAEL SCOTT SANNER Fifth great grandson of progenitor Nicholas Kegg.
TAMMY SUE SANNER Fifth great granddaughter of progenitor Nicholas Kegg.

SAPPINGTON

CALEB J. SAPPINGTON Eighth great grandson of progenitor Nicholas Kegg.

SARDER

ADEN SARDER Eighth great grandson of progenitor Nicholas Kegg.
ADRIAN SARDER Eighth great granddaughter of progenitor Nicholas Kegg.
EVE SARDER Eighth great granddaughter of progenitor Nicholas Kegg.

SARGENT

CARRIE ANN SARGENT Seventh great granddaughter of progenitor Nicholas Kegg.
LARRY JAMES SARGENT [5826] (1972 – 2004) son of Larry and Carol (Spisak) Sargent, married Kelly J. Bartlo.

SARVER

ERICA SARVER Seventh great granddaughter of progenitor Nicholas Kegg.

SATHER

DEREK SATHER Sixth great grandson of progenitor Nicholas Kegg. **ERIC K. SATHER** Fifth great grandson of progenitor Nicholas Kegg. **LAURA MAYBELL SATHER** Fifth great granddaughter of progenitor Nicholas Kegg. **NICHOLAS MCDERMOTT SATHER** aka "Nick", Sixth great grandson of progenitor Nicholas Kegg. **RICHARD GEORGE SATHER** Fifth great grandson of progenitor Nicholas Kegg. **STEVEN J. SATHER** Fifth great grandson of progenitor Nicholas Kegg. **THOMAS M. SATHER** aka "Tom", Fifth great grandson of progenitor Nicholas Kegg.

SAVAGE

ASHLEY SAVAGE Seventh great granddaughter of progenitor Nicholas Kegg. **CAROL JEAN SAVAGE** Fifth great granddaughter of progenitor Nicholas Kegg. **CLARENCE BAYLEY SAVAGE** (1899 – 1979) son of Clarence and Lenora (Kegg) Savage married twice; first to Elsie (nee unknown). Later, he married Viola Gertrude Poole with whom he was father of (1).

SAVILLE

ASHLEY SAVILLE Seventh great granddaughter of progenitor Nicholas Kegg. **BEN SAVILLE** Seventh great grandson of progenitor Nicholas Kegg. **HANNAH MAE SAVILLE** Seventh great

---

[5826] Davis-Becker Funeral Home, OH

granddaughter of progenitor Nicholas Kegg. **JOE SAVILLE** Seventh great grandson of progenitor Nicholas Kegg.

SAWYER

ANN SAWYER Fifth great granddaughter of progenitor Nicholas Kegg. **DARREL SAWYER** Fifth great grandson of progenitor Nicholas Kegg. **DAWN SAWYER** Fifth great granddaughter of progenitor Nicholas Kegg. **DEAN ALFRED SAWYER** [5827] (1915 – 2001) son of William Chauncey and Mary Jane (Dean) Sawyer married Gwendolyn Eva White with whom he was father of (2). He married Ruth M. Shake, lastly, he married Enid Florance (Tinkum) Byer. Dean was supervisor of frozen foods at Milwaukee Foods. In his free time Dean enjoyed camping, fishing and traveling. **DONALD PHILLIP SAWYER** [5828] (1926 – 2015) son of William Chauncey and Mary Jane (Dean) Sawyer married Leone Joyce Sims with whom he was father of (3). Donald and Joyce farmed for many years just outside of Melrose, Wis. Donald enjoyed deer hunting, playing cards, and traveling. He and his wife traveled throughout most of the United States and Canada. **DOROTHY PHYLLIS SAWYER** [5829] (1926 – 2005) daughter of William Chauncey and Mary Jane (Dean) Sawyer married Gerald Gotthelf Wenzel with whom she was mother of (3). **EMILY SAWYER** Sixth great granddaughter of progenitor Nicholas Kegg. **EVANS DWAYNE SAWYER** aka "Bill", [5830] (1924 – 1998) son of William Chauncey and Mary Jane (Dean) Sawyer married Elaine Norgaard with whom he was father of (3). Bill served in the U.S. Navy during WWII. He farmed in the Melrose area and later was employed by Mathy Construction. He also owned the Champlin Service Station and Auto Body Shop. Prior to his retirement he was a rural mail carrier for the U.S. Postal Service. Bill was a member of the Melrose Volunteer Fire Department for 42 years during which time he served five years as fire chief. He was a lifetime member of the Melrose United Methodist Church. Bill was a 53-year member of the Neil S. Lewison American Legion Post 439 of Melrose, of which he served two terms as Commander. **HAROLD ELMER SAWYER** aka "Harry" [5831] (1918 – 2008) son of William Chauncey and Mary Jane (Dean) Sawyer married M. Lorraine Anderson with whom he was father of (4). Harry farmed for most of his life in Westpoint Township, where he served as the township assessor for 46 years. He was very proud to have earned his Eagle Scout in his youth but was most proud of his family and always had an open door to family and friends. Harry was a member of St. John's Lutheran Church. **JACOB THOMAS SAWYER** aka "The King," [5832] (1987 – 2017) son of Timothy and Anne (Tracey) Sawyer received a degree in mechanical design from Western Technical College (WTC) in 2007. He was top of his class at WTC which earned him an internship at Trane Company and later a full-time position as a mechanical draftsman. Jacob's early experience on the family dairy farm nurtured his passion for the outdoors. He cherished spending time at family gatherings and the Sawyer family cabin. He took pleasure in riding his ATV, relaxing on the sandbar, fishing and telling stories. He especially enjoyed camping on the river. His card playing success at deer camp earned him the nickname "The King." **JEFFREY THOMAS SAWYER** Sixth great grandson of progenitor Nicholas Kegg. **JENNIFER SAWYER** Fifth great granddaughter of progenitor Nicholas Kegg. **LARRY GENE SAWYER** Fifth great grandson of progenitor Nicholas Kegg. **MARIE SAWYER** Fifth great granddaughter of progenitor Nicholas Kegg. **MARY JANE SAWYER** Fifth great granddaughter of progenitor Nicholas Kegg. **MEREDITH SAWYER** Fifth great granddaughter of progenitor Nicholas Kegg. **MICHAEL SAWYER** Fifth great grandson of progenitor Nicholas Kegg. **MIKHAIL DONALD SAWYER** [5833] (1989 – 2010) son of Timothy and Anne (Tracey) Sawyer received his associate degree in architectural design from Western Technical College in 2010. In Mikhail's early years, he enjoyed spending time on the family farm in rural Melrose. His love for the outdoors continued throughout his life as he and his family spent most weekends at their cabin. At the cabin Mikhail loved riding four-wheeler, fishing, hunting, campfires, playing cards, and especially deer camp, where he and his dad would plan and cook the meals for all the

---

[5827] Rocky Mountain News (CO) Nov 13, 2001 [5828] Lacrosse Tribune (WI) Dec. 31, 2015 [5829] Lacrosse Tribune (WI) July 7, 2005 [5830] obitcentral.com Miscellaneous La Crosse County, WI [5831] Wisconsin State Journal (Madison, WI) May 25, 2008 [5832] The La Crosse Tribune (WI) April 13, 2017 [5833] The La Crosse Tribune (WI) Oct 7, 2010

hunters. He was also known for playing practical jokes, making pickles with his siblings, and could tell you anything you wanted to know about most sports teams. As a teenager Mikhail was also involved in a study through the University of North Carolina, Chapel Hill, to help the FDA approve a drug to assist others who also have Hunter's Syndrome. Mikhail flew to St. Louis, Mo., weekly for four years as a part of the study. Thanks to Mikhail and the other participants, the drug has been approved and is now available to help others with this rare genetic disorder. Mikhail's witty and exuberant personality will be greatly missed by all who knew him. **ROBERT GERALD SAWYER** (1920 – 1989) son of William Chauncey and Mary Jane (Dean) Sawyer married Patricia Barrett with whom he was father of (3). Later he married Harriet Elverna Amundson. **RUSSELL ALAN SAWYER** (1947 – 1954) son of Donald and Leone Joyce (Sims) Sawyer. **RYAN SAWYER** Sixth great grandson of progenitor Nicholas Kegg. **SANDRA SAWYER** Fifth great granddaughter of progenitor Nicholas Kegg. **STEFFANI SAWYER** Sixth great granddaughter of progenitor Nicholas Kegg. **STEVEN SAWYER** Sixth great grandson of progenitor Nicholas Kegg. **TERESA SAWYER** Fifth great granddaughter of progenitor Nicholas Kegg. **TIMOTHY DONALD SAWYER** Fifth great grandson of progenitor Nicholas Kegg. **TODD ROBERT SAWYER** Fifth great grandson of progenitor Nicholas Kegg. **THOMAS HAROLD SAWYER** Fifth great grandson of progenitor Nicholas Kegg. **TRACEY SAWYER** Fifth great granddaughter of progenitor Nicholas Kegg. **WILLIAM LESTER SAWYER** [5834] (1913 – 1992) son of William Chauncey and Mary Jane (Dean) Sawyer married Ruth Novella Clark with whom he was father of (1). William was a rural letter carrier for the U.S. Post Office until retiring Jan. 17, 1977. He was a member of the Decora F. and A.M. Lodge 177 in Galesville, the Valley of Eau Claire Scottish Rite and Zor A.A.O.N.M.S. in Madison.

SAXTON

CHRISTINA IRENE SAXTON Seventh great granddaughter of progenitor Nicholas Kegg. **LOGAN SAXTON** Eighth great grandson of progenitor Nicholas Kegg. **MITCHELL VERN SAXTON** Seventh great grandson of progenitor Nicholas Kegg. **RYAN CHARLES SAXTON** Eighth great grandson of progenitor Nicholas Kegg. **SCOTT CHARLES SAXTON** Seventh great grandson of progenitor Nicholas Kegg. **SHANNON MARIE SAXTON** Eighth great granddaughter of progenitor Nicholas Kegg. **STEPHANIE JEANNE SAXTON** Seventh great granddaughter of progenitor Nicholas Kegg.

SAYERS

CALEB ANDREW SAYERS Eighth great grandson of progenitor Nicholas Kegg.
TABITHA LYNN SAYERS Eighth great granddaughter of progenitor Nicholas Kegg.

SAYLOR

CAROLYN ANN SAYLOR Fifth great granddaughter of progenitor Nicholas Kegg. **DANN HOWARD SAYLOR** [5834A] son of Howard and Frances (Carradine) Saylor married Thelma Richardson Coffindaffe. Dann attended Garritt Evangelical Theological Seminary and became a member of United Methodist West Ohio Conference. The Reverend was an Evangelist for 15 years, pastored First Brethren Church in Columbus, Middle Creek and Mt. Zion U.M. Churches in Grover Hill, Bascom U.M. Church in Bascom, Calvary U.M. Church at Benton Ridge and Mercer and Mt. Zion U.M. Churches in Celina, Oh. Dann was also a former school bus driver for Columbus Public Schools and a veteran of U.S. Army. **DARL EDNA SAYLOR** [5834B] (1914 – 1995) daughter of Lloyd and Laura (Speicher) Saylor married three times; first to Andrew Miller Neilsen, then Riley B. Shafor. Later, she married Jerome Edward Thomas with whom she was mother of (1). **DOROTHY JEAN SAYLOR** Fifth great granddaughter of progenitor Nicholas Kegg. **HAROLD R. SAYLOR** Fifth great grandson of progenitor Nicholas Kegg

---

[5834] The Lacrosse Tribune (WI) April 7, 1992 [5834A] p. F7 - The Columbus Dispatch (OH) June 25, 1997. [5834B] The Akron Beacon Journal (OH) May 4, 1995, obtained by D. Sue Dible

HOWARD FRANKLIN SAYLOR [(5835)] (1909 – 1981) son of Lloyd and Laura (Speicher) Saylor married twice; first to Frances Carradine with whom he was father of (1). Later, he married Thea M. (Dronebarger) Webster. Howard had been employed at Akron Standard Molds for 33 years, where he worked as an inspection foreman. He was a member of National Lodge No. 568 F & AM, Ancient Accepted Scottish Rite Valley of Akron 32nd Degree, and Barberton Moose Lodge No. 759. **JANET NAOMI SAYLOR** Fifth great granddaughter of progenitor Nicholas Kegg. **JOHN SPEICHER SAYLOR** [(5836)] (1911 – 1992) son of Lloyd and Laura (Speicher) Saylor married three times; first to Rachel N. Dixon with whom he was father of (2). He married Suzanne Dorothy (Wezey) Stafford and later, married Mary Evelyn (Shasteen) Jones. John retired from B.F. Goodrich after 44 years' service. He was past president of Goodrich Local 5 and was a 32nd Degree Mason of Canal Fulton Lodge 514. He was also a member of the Scottish Rite, Akron Chapter. **KATHRYN BERNICE SAYLOR** [(5837)] (1916 – 2011) aka "Peg", daughter of Lloyd and Laura (Speicher) Saylor married twice; first to Howard Jacob Thomas with whom she was mother of (1). Later, she married Carl Monroe Zeis. **MABEL MARGARETTA SAYLOR** [(5838)] (1905 – 1979) daughter of Lloyd and Laura (Speicher) Saylor, married William Thomas Wilder with whom she was mother of (3). **PRUDENCE VIOLA SAYLOR** [(5839)] (1906 – 1993) daughter of Lloyd and Laura (Speicher) Saylor married twice; first to Charles Edwin Colegrove with whom she was mother of (1). Later, she married Robert P. Hamilton. Prudence had worked at the Goodyear Tire & Rubber Co. and was a licensed beautician. She was a member of the Randolph United Methodist Church, Order of the Eastern Star Chapter 46, of Ravenna and the Daughters of the American Revolution. **ROSS HAROLD SAYLOR** [(5840)] (1908 – 1987) son of Lloyd and Laura (Speicher) Saylor, married Anna May Neiderhouse with whom he was father of (3). Ross was employed with the Akron Board of Education for 42 years. He was active with a Retired School Employee's Organization. He was a member of Akron Masonic Lodge No. 83 F&AM, and the Yusef Khan Grotto. **SHIRLEY JEAN SAYLOR** aka "Jeanie", Fifth great granddaughter of progenitor Nicholas Kegg.

SAYRE

AMY CATHERINE SAYRE Seventh great granddaughter of progenitor Nicholas Kegg. **BRIAN CRAIG SAYRE** Seventh great grandson of progenitor Nicholas Kegg. **CAROLE MAE SAYRE** Seventh great granddaughter of progenitor Nicholas Kegg. **CAROLYN SAYRE** Sixth great granddaughter of progenitor Nicholas Kegg. **CARY L. SAYRE** Sixth great grandson of progenitor Nicholas Kegg. **CHRISTINE MARIE SAYRE** [(5841)] (1963 – 2006) daughter of Richard and Ronna (Turner) Sayre married twice; first to Carey Allen Ehrman with whom she was mother of (2). Later, she married Jon Douglas Ingalls with whom she was mother of (1). Christine loved to sing and play the guitar. She was employed at Guardian Industries in Milbury, Ohio. Christine was involved with Jesus and Teen Challenge Ministries in Avon Park, Florida. She had also volunteered her time with Habitat for Humanity in Ottawa County. **DAVID MICHAEL SAYRE** [(5842)] (1939 – 2005) son of Harry and Louise (Schmalzreid) Sayre, married Carolyn Sue (England) Sumner with whom he was father of (1). David was a veteran of the U.S. Army and served in Germany. He was employed for 39 years as a freight conductor with the New York Central Railroad and Conrail. David was an avid auto enthusiast, belonging to the National Camaro and Corvair clubs in the 1960s and '70s, and was a renowned drag racer in this area, winning a National Crown in 1965. **DIANNE SAYRE** Seventh great granddaughter of progenitor Nicholas Kegg. **JENNY SAYRE** Seventh great granddaughter of progenitor Nicholas Kegg. **JOEL SAYRE** Seventh great grandson of progenitor Nicholas Kegg. **LAWRENCE EDWARD SAYRE** Sixth great grandson of progenitor Nicholas Kegg. **MADISON SAYRE** Seventh great granddaughter of progenitor Nicholas Kegg. **NATHAN SAYRE** Seventh great grandson of progenitor Nicholas Kegg.

[(5835)] Akron, OH Library obituary obtained by D. Sue Dible [(5836)] p.B6 - Akron Beacon Journal (OH) Oct 8, 1992 [(5837)] Sarasota Herald-Tribune (FL) Apr 15, 2011 [(5838)] p.7 Akron Beacon Journal (OH) Feb 8, 1979, obtained by D. Sue Dible [(5839)] p.B6 - Akron Beacon Journal (OH) Dec16, 1993 [(5840)] p.D9 - Akron Beacon Journal (OH) Oct 8, 1987 [(5841)] Crosser Funeral Home, OH obtained by D. Sue Dible [(5842)] Elkhart Truth (IN) Nov 32, 2005

RICHARD WILLIAM SAYRE [5842A] (1936 – 2007) son of Francis and Marjorie (Peters) Sayre married Ronna Lee Turner with whom he was father of (3). Richard was a retired Tool & Die Maker and loved to tinker with tools. **STEVEN KING SAYRE** [5843] (1942 – 1966) son of Harry and Louise (Schmalzreid) Sayre married Janet Sue LeCount with whom he was father of (2). Steven suffered fatal injuries when his motorcycle collided with a car on Ind. 19 north of Elkhart. **STEVEN P. SAYRE** Sixth great grandson of progenitor Nicholas Kegg. **SUZANNE FAYE SAYRE** [5843A] (1939 – 2003) daughter of Francis and Marjorie (Peters) Sayre married Thomas Allen Robbins. Suzanne was a retired registered nurse. **TERESA LEE SAYRE** Sixth great granddaughter of progenitor Nicholas Kegg. **TRUMAN SAYRE** Seventh great grandson of progenitor Nicholas Kegg. **WILLIAM C. SAYRE** aka "Bill" Sixth great grandson of progenitor Nicholas Kegg.

SBISA

AMBER SBISA Eighth great granddaughter of progenitor Nicholas Kegg. **EDWIN B. SBISA** Seventh great grandson of progenitor Nicholas Kegg. **EDWIN H. SBISA** Sixth great grandson of progenitor Nicholas Kegg. **EMILY FAITH SBISA** Eighth great granddaughter of progenitor Nicholas Kegg. **JOSEPH P. SBISA** Sixth great grandson of progenitor Nicholas Kegg. **VICTORIA A. SBISA** Sixth great granddaughter of progenitor Nicholas Kegg.

SCANGA

CARRIE A. SCANGA Fifth great granddaughter of progenitor Nicholas Kegg.
SARA E. SCANGA Fifth great granddaughter of progenitor Nicholas Kegg.

SCHABERG

AMANDA RENEE SCHABERG Seventh great granddaughter of progenitor Nicholas Kegg.
AUSTIN EDWARD SCHABERG Seventh great grandson of progenitor Nicholas Kegg.

SCHAEFER

NATALIE SCHAEFER Eighth great granddaughter of progenitor Nicholas Kegg.
TATE SCHAEFER Eighth great grandson of progenitor Nicholas Kegg.

SCHAEFFER

JESSICA LYN SCHAEFFER Seventh great granddaughter of progenitor Nicholas Kegg.
KEVIN SCHAEFFER Sixth great grandson of progenitor Nicholas Kegg.
LOREN WILLIAM SCHAEFFER Seventh great grandson of progenitor Nicholas Kegg.
RYAN SCHAEFFER Sixth great grandson of progenitor Nicholas Kegg.
SHAWN SCHAEFFER Sixth great grandson of progenitor Nicholas Kegg.

SCHAEN

PATRICIA ANN SCHAEN [5843B] aka "Paty" (1942 – 2015) daughter of Ernest and Margaret (Turner) Schaen married twice, first to Melvin Joseph Fischer with whom she was mother of (3), later she married Larry Hanson. Paty enjoyed hunting, fishing, camping and hiking. She especially loved working on cars.

SCHAMBRON

ALFRED W. SCHAMBRON Fifth great grandson of progenitor Nicholas Kegg.

[5842A] Library obituary clipping obtained and contributed by D. Sue Dible [5843] Kokomo Tribune (IN) Aug 29, 1966 [5843A] St. Petersburg Times (FL) Feb 1, 2003 [5843B] Yamhill Valley NewsRegister (OR) June 30, 2015, contributed by D. Sue Dible

ALFRED SCHAMBRON Sixth great grandson of progenitor Nicholas Kegg.
DEBORAH SUE SCHAMBRON Sixth great granddaughter of progenitor Nicholas Kegg.
JUSTIN WILEY SCHAMBRON Sixth great grandson of progenitor Nicholas Kegg.

SCHAPER

ELLEN LOU SCHAPER Fifth great granddaughter of progenitor Nicholas Kegg.

SCHARMEN

ADRIA CRISTINA SCHARMEN Sixth great granddaughter of progenitor Nicholas Kegg. **AMMIE A. SCHARMEN** [5843C] (1930 – 2013) daughter of Oscar and Geraldine (Konruff) Scharmen married Herbert Arthur Sloppy with whom she was mother of (2). Ammie graduated from Edward W. Sparrow hospital school of nursing and had been employed at the Maybury sanitarium, and the state hospital. **AMY ELINOR SCHARMEN** [5843D] (1892 – 1973) daughter of Frederick and Angie (Routsong) Scharmen married twice, first to John Wesley Kirkpatrick with whom she was mother of (8). Later, she married Hugh Butler. Amy was a homemaker and a member of the Garnet Community Baptist Church. **AMY ELIZABETH SCHARMEN** Sixth great granddaughter of progenitor Nicholas Kegg. **AMY M. SCHARMEN** Fifth great granddaughter of progenitor Nicholas Kegg. **ARNOLD WILLIAM SCHARMEN** [5843E] (1893 – 1984) son of Frederick and Angie (Routsong) Scharmen. Arnold was a laborer in many fields working in Michigan and Iowa before 1923 when he moved to Germany. About 1935 he went to work in Denmark and returned to America during the war. Arnold returned to Europe and lived in Switzerland until 1948 when a way was open for him to return to Düsseldorf, Germany where he remained. **BEATRICE BERNADETTE SCHARMEN** Fifth great granddaughter of progenitor Nicholas Kegg. **BERNICE MARGARET SCHARMEN** (1916 – 2004) daughter of Edwin and Margaret (McGregor) Scharmen, married Leonard William Noffert with whom she was mother of (3). **BRANDY SCHARMEN** Fifth great granddaughter of progenitor Nicholas Kegg. **CARL AUGUSTUS SCHARMEN** (1897 – 1987) son of Frederick and Angie (Routsong) Scharmen married Annie Laurie McGregor with whom he was father of (3). **CARTER FRASE SCHARMEN** Sixth great grandson of progenitor Nicholas Kegg. **CASSANDRA LEE SCHARMEN** Fifth great granddaughter of progenitor Nicholas Kegg. **CHARLES FREDERICK SCHARMEN**, aka "Chuck", Fourth great grandson of progenitor Nicholas Kegg. **CHRISTINE RUTH SCHARMEN** Fifth great granddaughter of progenitor Nicholas Kegg. **CHRISTOPHER D. SCHARMEN** aka "Chris", Fifth great grandson of progenitor Nicholas Kegg. **CORY CLAY SCHARMEN** Fifth great grandson of progenitor Nicholas Kegg. **DAVID ALLEN SCHARMEN** (1948 – 2013) son of Stewart and Stephanie (Pacocha) Scharmen was father of (2). **DEBORAH JOYCE SCHARMEN** Fifth great granddaughter of progenitor Nicholas Kegg. **DEBRA SUE SCHARMEN** (1961 – 1961) daughter of Gary and Karen (Hicks) Scharmen. **DONALD WILLIAM SCHARMEN** Fourth great grandson of progenitor Nicholas Kegg. **DUSTIN SCHARMEN** Sixth great grandson of progenitor Nicholas Kegg. **EDWIN ARTHUR SCHARMEN** [5844] (1889 – 1977) son of Frederick and Angie (Routsong) Scharmen married twice; first to Margaret Mae McGregor with whom he was father of (4). Later, he married Elizabeth R. (Petticrew) Bopry. Edwin retired from the city of Detroit in 1950. **GARY STEWART SCHARMEN** Fifth great grandson of progenitor Nicholas Kegg. **GARY STEWART SCHARMEN JR.** [5844A] (1975 – 2016) son of Gary and Nancy (Craig) Stewart. **GARY WAYNE SCHARMEN** [5844B] (1942 – 2003) son of Loy and Adria (Doremire) Scharmen, married Karen Sue Hicks with whom he was father of (1). **GARY REX SCHARMEN** Fifth great grandson of progenitor Nicholas Kegg. **GEORGE ALLEN SCHARMEN** [5844C] (1926 – 1999) son of Randall and Sue (Sheppard) Scharmen married three times; first to Donna Marie Bateson with whom he was father of (4). He married June O. Quinn with whom he was father of

---

[5843C] Star Tribune (MN) Oct 24, 2013 [5843D] p.7 - The Evening News (Sault Sainte Marie, MI) Jan 13, 1972 [5843E] http://www.tellingthetruth.info/history_pioneering/germany.php [5844] p.27 - Traverse City Record Eagle (MI) Sept 8, 1977 [5844A] Mandziuk Funeral Home (MI) [5844B] Traverse City Record-Eagle (MI) Jan 4, 2004

(1). Later, he married Mary Rackowitz. George enlisted in the U.S. Navy. He was a radioman on an LST (Landing Ship, Tank) in beach assaults under Japanese fire. After returning to his ship's homeport in San Diego, George was left behind in a hospital for treatment of an illness. Two weeks later, his ship sunk in the Pacific and most of the crew was lost. After the war he had a long successful Media career. He was anchorman of "12 Star Final" during the era when KONO-TV (now KSAT) introduced the vivid and graphic format to local television news. George helped establish in San Antonio what later became a stereotype of local TV news: leading with stories providing maximum visual impact - such as fires and car wrecks, as well as shootings, robberies and other crime. "It was unlike anything that appeared in San Antonio before that time. After retiring from the news business, he operated the SWC Club on East Elmira Street. **GEORGE ALLEN SCHARMEN** Fifth great grandson of progenitor Nicholas Kegg. **GERALDINE ROSALIE SCHARMEN** [5845] (1934 – 2013) aka "Rose", daughter of Oscar and Geraldine (Konruff) Scharmen, married James Burton Hansen with whom she was mother of (2). Rose earned her undergraduate degree from Western Michigan University and her master's degree in early childhood development from Central Michigan University. She started in occupational therapy and art education but then spent most of her teaching career in special education with the Traverse Bay Area Intermediate School District. She worked with the homebound, in the classroom, in administration, and most often with the youngest handicapped children. Rose enjoyed painting, reading and writing poetry and reading extensively about history, sociology, religion and psychology. **GUY PATRICK SCHARMEN** Fifth great grandson of progenitor Nicholas Kegg. **JAMES EDWARD SCHARMEN** [5845A] aka "Jim" (1948 – 2007) son of Leon and Clara (Tyler) Scharmen married Rosemarie Salai. Jim was a commercial artist and he made snow statues. He was a member of the Grand Traverse Ice Yacht Club, he loved music and played the steel guitar, banjo, piano and the saw. Jim enjoyed fishing, boating, windsurfing, cross country skiing, iceboating, playing horseshoes, and driving his classic MG. Jim loved to cook and was known for his BBQ ribs. He was an avid Tiger fan and was looking forward to taking his pontoon boat out and listening to the ball game on his XM radio. Jim managed Scheck Sign Systems and was an owner of the Cloth Envelope Company. Jim was a veteran of the US Navy. **JEAN LOIS SCHARMEN** (1926 – 1992) daughter of Carl and Annie (McGregor) Scharmen married George Ura Coon with whom she was mother of (1). Jean was a veteran of WWII having served as a Nursing Corps cadet. **JENNY SCHARMEN** Sixth great granddaughter of progenitor Nicholas Kegg. **JILL SCHARMEN** Fifth great granddaughter of progenitor Nicholas Kegg. **JOHANNA SCHARMEN** Fourth great granddaughter of progenitor Nicholas Kegg. **JOHN PAUL SCHARMEN** [5845B] aka "J.P." (1966 – 2009) son of Paul and Sharon (Chapin) Scharmen married Melody Lynne Steel. JP worked as a tow-truck driver for AAA. **JOSHUA SCHARMEN** aka Josh", Sixth great grandson of progenitor Nicholas Kegg. **JOY MANE SCHARMEN** Sixth great granddaughter of progenitor Nicholas Kegg. **KIM EDWARD SCHARMEN** Fifth great grandson of progenitor Nicholas Kegg. **LARRY LOY SCHARMEN** (1949 – 2016) son of Loy and Adria (Doremire) Scharmen married Barbara Will with whom he was father of (2). **LAURA AGNES SCHARMEN** [5845C] (1899 – 1992) daughter of Frederick and Angie (Routsong) Scharmen, married George Frederick Snell with whom she was mother of (7). Laura had a keen interest in local and world news and politics. **LAURA M. SCHARMEN** (1914 – 2003) daughter of Edwin and Margaret (McGregor) Scharmen married Martin Charles Blank with whom she was mother of (3). **LENORE SCHARMEN** Fifth great granddaughter of progenitor Nicholas Kegg. **LEON THEODORE SCHARMEN** [5846] (1903 – 1996) son of Frederick and Angie (Routsong) Scharmen, married Clara Tyler with whom he was father of (3). **LEONA JUNE SCHARMEN** [5846A] aka "June" (1935 – 2011) daughter of Oscar and Geraldine (Konruff) Scharmen married Richard Ritter with whom she was mother of (3). June was a warm and loving person. She practiced cosmetology before obtaining a two-year degree at Northwestern Michigan College. Later, she obtained a Bachelor of Arts degree from Michigan State University. June was employed as a Social Worker for the State of Michigan in Grand Rapids and Hastings. **LORALEE SCHARMEN** Fifth great granddaughter of progenitor

---

[5845] Record-Eagle Traverse City (MI) July 22, 2013 [5845A] Canton Observer (Plymouth, MI) Mar15, 2007 [5845B] Las Vegas Sun (NV) May 27, 2009 [5845C] p.6 – Benzie County Record – Patriot (MI) Nov 25, 1992 [5846] Vermeulen Funeral Home. Plymouth, MI [5846A] Record-Eagle (MI) April 11, 2011

Nicholas Kegg. **LOREN ERNEST SCHARMEN** (5847) (1933 – 2013) son of Wilmer and Virginia (Triplett) Scharmen married five times; first to Tomilee Hoofman, then to Nela J. Roike, Ina Milburn (Hall) Stubbs. Later, he married Sandra Jo (Gerasco) Jones and Emily Ann (Montague) Forrest. **LOY ARTHUR SCHARMEN** (5848) (1921 – 2006) son of Edwin and Margaret (McGregor) Scharmen, married Adria Pearl Doremire with whom he was father of (4). A veteran of World War II, Loy retired from the Ford Motor Company in 1978. Loy enjoyed being in the woods and visiting with family and friends. **MARGARET A. SCHARMEN** Fifth great granddaughter of progenitor Nicholas Kegg. **MERRILL EDWARD SCHARMEN** (5848A) (1924 – 2016) son of Edwin and Margaret (McGregor) Scharmen married Audrey Yvonne Frost with whom he was father of (4). A WW II veteran with a distinguished 32-year career in the United States Air Force. Merrill was just 20 years old when he and his crew flew an assembly-line-new B-24 from Topeka, KS, to Wharton Field, England. The trip took 60 hours in 11 days with 6 stops via Florida, Trinidad, Brazil, Senegal and Morocco. On June 17, 1944, 10 days after D-Day, he embarked on the first of 35 missions as pilot of B-17s and B-24s in the 8th Air Force, European Theatre of Operations. He wrote in his combat diary of his bomber crew #BJ103: "The enlisted men are my pride and joy, best bunch of boys out". Through 1945, he continued flying special missions and VIP transport with the Air Transport Command 6th Ferrying Group. Later, while serving as a police officer in his hometown of Detroit, Merrill was recalled to active duty Assigned to the Strategic Air Command 15th Air Force SAC, he flew B-36 and B-52 bombers out of Carswell AFB, Texas, Walker AFB, New Mexico and March AFB, California. In 1968, Merrill went once again to war as the Chief of Bomber Division for the Strategic Air Command in South Vietnam. The last years of his career were served at the Pentagon, as Deputy Director for Support and Services with the Defense Intelligence Agency. He continued to fly up until his retirement. Merrill volunteered with the Coast Guard Auxiliary, teaching navigation and boating safety classes and conducting weekend rescue patrols around Chesapeake Bay. He was also an active member of the Drum Point Club during its formative years. Despite the demands of his military career, Merrill always made time for his family and friends, devoting his talent, love and support to the community around him. With the patience of a saint, his temperament was always gracious, kind, humble and witty right up to his last days on earth. There is no doubt that 'the Colonel' was an outstanding member of 'The Greatest Generation'. **MICHAEL ALAN SCHARMEN** Fifth great grandson of progenitor Nicholas Kegg. **MICHAEL WAYNE SCHARMEN** (1946 – 1989) son of Stewart and Stephanie (Pacocha) Scharmen. **MICHELLE VELVET SCHARMEN** Sixth great granddaughter of progenitor Nicholas Kegg. **NORA LEE SCHARMEN** (5849) (1929 – 1946) daughter of Carl and Annie (McGregor) Scharmen. **OSCAR OREN SCHARMEN** (1907 – 1982) son of Frederick and Angie (Routsong) Scharmen married Geraldine Opal Konruff with whom he was father of (5). **PABLO SCHARMEN** Sixth great grandson of progenitor Nicholas Kegg. **PAUL RICHARD SCHARMEN** (5849A) (1937 – 2016) son of Wilmer and Virginia (Triplett) Scharmen married Sharon Chapin with whom he was father of (3). A man of God who exhibited complete integrity and gentleness, Paul was a veteran of the U.S. Navy. He retired from NASA, Ames Research Center, where he won several awards for excellence for his skills in modelmaking. Paul loved running, participated in marathons, regularly competed in races throughout the area for several years and joined a men's soccer team for a few years. A member of Hillside Evangelical Free Church, a Sunday school teacher for many years. **RANDALL BLAIR SCHARMEN** (1922 – 1987) son of Randall and Sue (Sheppard) Scharmen married twice; first to Lula Beatrice Young with whom he was father of (3). Later, he married Myrle Stanford with whom he was father of (3). **RANDALL ROSCOE SCHARMEN** (5850) (1895 – 1975) son of Frederick and Angie (Routsong) Scharmen, married Sue Sheppard with whom he was father of (2). Randall was a life member of the United Craft Masonic Lodge No. 534 in Detroit. **ROGER ARNOLD SCHARMEN** (1941 – 2002) son of Walter and Alveeda (Hamlett) Scharmen married and was father of (1). Roger was a Vietnam veteran having served in the U.S. Navy. **ROGER BLAIR SCHARMEN** Fifth great grandson of progenitor Nicholas Kegg. **RONALD LEWIS SCHARMEN** Fourth great grandson of progenitor

(5847) Island Cremations & Funeral Home (Merritt Island, FL) (5848) Record-Eagle (MI) March 8, 2006 (5848A) The Calvert Recorder (MD) Sep 1, 2016 (5849) p.25 Detroit News (MI) May 20, 1946 (5849A) San Jose Mercury News/San Mateo County Times Jan. 16, 2017 (5850) p.6 – Playground Daily News (FL) Oct 28, 1975

Nicholas Kegg. **SHAWNNA SCHARMEN** Sixth great granddaughter of progenitor Nicholas Kegg. **SHERYL JEAN SCHARMEN** Fifth great granddaughter of progenitor Nicholas Kegg. **STEWART ARNOLD SCHARMEN** (1921 – 2003) son of Carl and Annie (McGregor) Scharmen married twice, first to Stephanie Pacocha with whom he was father of (3). Later he married Ann Barbara Supranowicz. Stewart was a veteran of WWII having served in the U.S. Airforce. **SUSAN GABRIELLE SCHARMEN** Fifth great granddaughter of progenitor Nicholas Kegg. **THOMAS N. SCHARMEN** [5851] (1950 – 2020) son of Merrill and Audrey (Frost) Scharmen married Maria Veronica Fuentes with whom he was father of (2). Tom was employed for over 20 years in the NM Dept. of Health. He was a public health advocate, a visionary, a mentor and a hero to many. Tom developed the NM Community Data Collaborative to bring data to communities who could use it in policy change. Before NM Tom lived in Mexico, where his passion for public health started in the village of Urique and through the Copper Canyon region where he worked as a health promoter. He built a homestead in Urique, Entre Amigos is still open to guests and his long-lasting paradise. Before Mexico Tom was a dedicated student of philosophy, literature and art, wrote poetry and played the guitar. **TRACY L. SCHARMEN** Fifth great granddaughter of progenitor Nicholas Kegg. **VIRGINIA LEE SCHARMEN** aka "Ginny" Fourth great granddaughter of progenitor Nicholas Kegg. **VIRGINIA LUCILLE SCHARMEN** [5851A] (1932 – 2007) daughter of Oscar and Geraldine (Konruff) Scharmen, married Marvin Howard Evans with whom she was mother of (5). Virginia was a homemaker who didn't care much for cooking, but always made sure her children had a hot meal before school. She made sure that they were raised with a strong work ethic and desire to learn new things. Virginia began her days early, about 5:30 a.m., and spent them reading, doing crossword puzzles, playing solitaire, and watching select television programming such as M.A.S.H. and E.R. She also loved to watch golf, even though she never played the game herself. Spending time with her grandchildren and watching the birds at her bird feeder were her other great loves. **WALTER LEWIS SCHARMEN** [5852] (1911 – 1995) son of Frederick and Angie (Routsong) Scharmen, married Alveeda Mary Hamlett with whom he was father of (2). **WALTER LEWIS SCHARMEN** Fifth great grandson of progenitor Nicholas Kegg. **WESLEY EDWARD SCHARMEN** Sixth great grandson of progenitor Nicholas Kegg. **WILMER ERNEST SCHARMEN** [5852A] (1904 – 1988) son of Frederick and Angie (Routsong) Scharmen married twice, first to Virginia Elizabeth Triplett with whom he was father of (3), later he married Jeanette Cobots Moschella. Wilmer was a retired administrator for the Social Security Administration and was a member of the Unitarian Universalist Fellowship. He was a member of Theosophical Society.

SCHEETZ

ALLISON SCHEETZ Sixth great granddaughter of progenitor Nicholas Kegg.

SCHEITLER

DOUGLAS EUGENE SCHEITLER Sixth great grandson of progenitor Nicholas Kegg.
LORI A. SCHEITLER Sixth great granddaughter of progenitor Nicholas Kegg.
RANDALL L. SCHEITLER Sixth great grandson of progenitor Nicholas Kegg.
RICHARD ANDREW SCHEITLER Sixth great grandson of progenitor Nicholas Kegg.

SCHELDT

APRIL LYNN SCHELDT Fifth great granddaughter of progenitor Nicholas Kegg.
JOHN SCHELDT Fifth great grandson of progenitor Nicholas Kegg.
SANDRA JEAN SCHELDT Fifth great granddaughter of progenitor Nicholas Kegg.

[5851] Albuquerque Journal (NM) Jan 17, 2021, obtained by D. Sue Dible [5851A] Legacy.com originally published in the Record-Eagle [5852] Lansing State Journal (MI) Feb 20, 1995 [5852A] p.B6 - Orlando Sentinel (FL) March 20, 1988

SCHELLENBERG

ANNE SCHELLENBERG Fifth great granddaughter of progenitor Nicholas Kegg.
BILL SCHELLENBERG Fifth great grandson of progenitor Nicholas Kegg.
BOB SCHELLENBERG Fifth great grandson of progenitor Nicholas Kegg.
CHRISTINE MARIE SCHELLENBERG Fifth great granddaughter of progenitor Nicholas Kegg.
EVIE SCHELLENBERG Sixth great granddaughter of progenitor Nicholas Kegg.
JIM SCHELLENBERG Fifth great grandson of progenitor Nicholas Kegg.
JOANN MARIE SCHELLENBERG Fifth great granddaughter of progenitor Nicholas Kegg.
KELLEY SCHELLENBERG Fifth great granddaughter of progenitor Nicholas Kegg.
MARY PATRICIA SCHELLENBERG Fifth great granddaughter of progenitor Nicholas Kegg
MATT SCHELLENBERG Fifth great grandson of progenitor Nicholas Kegg.
RIK SCHELLENBERG Fifth great grandson of progenitor Nicholas Kegg.
T.D. SCHELLENBERG Sixth great grandson of progenitor Nicholas Kegg.
TOM SCHELLENBERG Fifth great grandson of progenitor Nicholas Kegg.

SCHELLER

BETTE ROSE SCHELLER aka "Betty" [5853] (1936 – 2020) daughter of Wilbur and Rose (Walz) Scheller married Gary Jess Brown with whom she was mother of (2). **CHLODINE HELEN SCHELLER** [5854] (1921 – 1996) daughter of Everett and Twila (Catt) Scheller married twice; first to Warren Andrew Bracelin with whom she was mother of (3). Later, she married Alfred Galen Mather with whom she was mother of (1). Chlodine was a homemaker and once a saleswoman for Shaklee vitamin products. **CLEO NAN SCHELLER** [5854A] aka "Nan" (1928 – 2005) daughter of Everett and Twila (Catt) Scheller married Ivan Emil Bernards with whom she was mother of (3). Nan worked as a Secretary at Columbus Grade School in the late 1940's. She loved taking care of people and was instrumental in setting up PCIC (Pregnancy Counseling and Information Center). She raised greyhound dogs, loved gardening and cooking. She was a member of the St. James Catholic Church and Catholic Daughters. She started the Right To Life in Yamhill County in the early 1980's. The family said "Nan made the world a better place with her unselfishness, love and dedication to everyone that knew her. She had so many wonderful qualities that we all strive for in our lives. **DAKOTA RAY SCHELLER** Seventh great grandson of progenitor Nicholas Kegg. **DIXIE L. SCHELLER** Sixth great granddaughter of progenitor Nicholas Kegg. **DONNA RAYE SCHELLER** [5854B] (1925 – 1986) daughter of Everett and Twila (Catt) Scheller married Rex Otto Bracelin with whom she was mother of (2). Donna had been co-owner, with her husband of Carlton cleaners. **DOROTHY MAXINE SCHELLER** [5854C] (1923 – 2002) daughter of Everett and Twila (Catt) Scheller married Lt. Col. Charles M. Peters with whom she was mother of (7). A military wife, Dorothy shared with her family many times "I had 7 wonderful children. I was married for 57 years. I had a wonderful life, and I will never complain". **ELLA PAULINE SCHELLER** [5855] (1919 – 2005) daughter of Harold and Lillian (Gurss) Scheller married William Bonnicksen with whom she was mother of (1). Pauline was employed at Weld County General Hospital. She enjoyed dancing and watching and attending sporting events. Pauline was a member of First Christian Church, Evans Senior Center, Amico Club and Veterans of Foreign Wars Post 2121. **ERNEST NEILL SCHELLER** [5856] (1925 – 2019) aka "Ernie" son of Harold and Lillian (Gurss) Scheller married Bernice Pearl Baker with whom he was father of (3). Ernest joined the Navy after high school and served with the Seabees during World War II in the Aleutian Islands. Ernie spent his adult life raising and caring for Herford cows. He enjoyed hunting, fishing, working on the farm and being in the garden with Bernice. He most of all enjoyed time with his family.

[5853] Northwest Adventists Jan. 13, 2021obtained by D. Sue Dible [5854] The Oregonian (OR) Aug 8, 1996, obtained by D. Sue Dible [5854A] Macy and Son Funeral Home (OR) obituary contributed by D. Sue Dible [5854B] obituary contributed by Karen Wiley [5854C] News-Register (OR) July 24, 2002 [5855] Greeley Tribune (CO) Oct 1, 2005 [5856] The Journal (CO) Apr. 11, 2019, Ertel Funeral Home (Cortez, CO)

EVERETT LEWIS SCHELLER (1903 – 1959) son of Lewis and Eva (Wyckoff) Scheller married Twila Fae Catt with whom he was father of (5). **FRANCIS FORD SCHELLER** [5857] (1912 – 1992) son of Lewis and Eva (Wyckoff) Scheller, married Ruth Arlene Joy with whom he was father of (1). **HAROLD CHRISTIAN SCHELLER** (1901 – 1947) son of Lewis and Eva (Wyckoff) Scheller, married Lillian Gurss with whom he was father of (2). **KRIS SCHELLER** Sixth great granddaughter of progenitor Nicholas Kegg. **MARY LOU SCHELLER** Fifth great granddaughter of progenitor Nicholas Kegg. **NANCY SCHELLER** Sixth great granddaughter of progenitor Nicholas Kegg. **RUTH ADELIA SCHELLER** [5857] (1906 – 1991) daughter of Lewis and Eva (Wyckoff) Scheller married Walter Edmond Wiley with whom she was mother of (1). Ruth fulfilled her childhood dream of becoming a schoolteacher. She taught at West Guerney and at Rosencran schools immediately after high school and later taught at the Browning School east of Hale, Colorado. **SAMUEL LEWIS SCHELLER** [5857A] aka "Sam" (1925 – 2012) son of Wilbur and Rose (Walz) Scheller married Ruby Pierson with whom he was father of (4). Sam had an auctioneering talent and a passion for cattle trading. The Greeley Christian School called upon Sam for the annual Benefit Pie Sale. His auctioneering talent merited "outrageous" prices for a standard pie to the delight of the school. His love for the livestock sale barn started early while helping his father manage the family-owned sale barn in Steamboat Springs, Colorado. From there, they owned and operated Sunset Sale Barn in Greeley, Colo. The staff at Brush Livestock became his second family as Sam attended the monthly dairy sale for 65 years. Eventually, Wheat farming north of Pierce, Colorado became Sam's livelihood for 59 years even though it was cattle trading that continued to be his passion. Sam was an active member of the Greeley Seventh-Day Adventist Church for 63 years. **SANDRA MAE SCHELLER**, aka "Sandy" Sixth great granddaughter of progenitor Nicholas Kegg. **SHARON ROSE SCHELLER** Sixth great granddaughter of progenitor Nicholas Kegg. **SHERYL ANN SCHELLER** Sixth great granddaughter of progenitor Nicholas Kegg. **SHIRLEY DELORES SCHELLER** [5857B] (1926 – 2018) daughter of Wilbur and Rose (Walz) Scheller, married Adolfo James Achabal with whom she was mother of (1). Shirley spent her first 12 years growing up on the family farm in Saint Frances, Kansas. In 1935 the family farm and most of the livestock was lost in the Republican River Flood. This occurred in the middle of the great depression when there were no government services or financial assistance. The family was without a home. Neighbors, friends and family pitched in to help. A local farmer had an old sod house on his property called a "soddy" and he offered this to the family. Having nowhere else to go, they moved into the sod house where they lived for 3 years. Her mother put sheeting over the ceiling to keep dirt off the table. In 1938 the family moved to Longmont Colorado where Shirley graduated from high school. In 1952 the family moved to Greeley, Colorado. Shortly after the family moved to Colorado, Shirley moved to Boise Idaho, where she worked at the old Idaho Seventh Day Adventist Conference office on Cassia Street. She also was the treasurer for the Boise Central Seventh Day Adventist church for 16 years. Later Shirley worked by AJ's side as the bookkeeper for their business, Boise-Winnemucca Stages until she retired. Shirley loved exercising, eating healthy and staying fit. **SHIRLEY LINNEA SCHELLER** Sixth great granddaughter of progenitor Nicholas Kegg. **STEPHEN R. SCHELLER** aka "Steve" Sixth great grandson of progenitor Nicholas Kegg. **STEVE SCHELLER** Fifth great grandson of progenitor Nicholas Kegg. **WILBUR JOSEPH SCHELLER** [5857C] (1899 – 1990) son of Lewis and Eva (Wyckoff) Scheller, married Rose Marie Walz with whom he was father of (4). Wilbur was involved in the agriculture and livestock business. **WILLIAM J. SCHELLER** aka "Bill", Fifth great grandson of progenitor Nicholas Kegg.

SCHERBARTH

ANGELA SCHERBARTH Seventh great granddaughter of progenitor Nicholas Kegg.
BRIAN SCHERBARTH Sixth great grandson of progenitor Nicholas Kegg.
BRIDGET SCHERBARTH Seventh great granddaughter of progenitor Nicholas Kegg.

[5857] Find A Grave Memorial# 72188138 Created by: Karen Wiley [5857A] Basin Republican-Rustler (WY) Aug 16, 2012 [5857B] Cloverdale Funeral Home (WA) [5857C] Greeley Tribune (CO) June 19, 1990

CRAIG SCHERBARTH Sixth great grandson of progenitor Nicholas Kegg.
JANENE A. SCHERBARTH Sixth great granddaughter of progenitor Nicholas Kegg.
KURT SCHERBARTH Seventh great grandson of progenitor Nicholas Kegg.
KYLE SCHERBARTH Seventh great grandson of progenitor Nicholas Kegg.
ROBERT W. SCHERBARTH Sixth great grandson of progenitor Nicholas Kegg.
SHEILA SCHERBARTH Seventh great granddaughter of progenitor Nicholas Kegg.
STEPHEN L. SCHERBARTH Sixth great grandson of progenitor Nicholas Kegg.
SUZAN E. SCHERBARTH Sixth great granddaughter of progenitor Nicholas Kegg.

SCHIEFER

BRENDA SCHIEFER Seventh great granddaughter of progenitor Nicholas Kegg.
CRAIG SCHIEFER Seventh great grandson of progenitor Nicholas Kegg.
GARY SCHIEFER Seventh great grandson of progenitor Nicholas Kegg.

SCHIFF

AUGUSTUS KELLEY SCHIFF Sixth great grandson of progenitor Nicholas Kegg.
RUBY SCHIFF Sixth great granddaughter of progenitor Nicholas Kegg.

SCHLEICHER

RHEAN SCHLEICHER Seventh great grandchild of progenitor Nicholas Kegg.
KELSEY SCHLEMMER Sixth great granddaughter of progenitor Nicholas Kegg.
TYLER SCHLEMMER Sixth great grandson of progenitor Nicholas Kegg.

SCHMALZRIED

BETTY ANN SCHMALZRIED [5858] (1920 – 2004) aka "Tilly", daughter of Jean and Jennette (Kegg) Schmalzried, married Hilbert H. Andrews. Tilly was a homemaker. She was a member of the Welcome Wagon of Fort Pierce, past President of the Bridge Club of Fort Pierce, and a longtime patron of Archie's Seabreeze of Fort Pierce Beach. **KATHRYN NELL SCHMALZRIED** [5858A] (1921 – 1995) daughter of Jean and Jennette (Kegg) Schmalzried, married Richard Eugene Cooper with whom she was mother of (1). Kathryn was a homemaker and member of the Church of Christ Scientist and the Ladies of the Moose. **LOUISE ETHEL SCHMALZRIED** [5859] (1918 – 1985) daughter of Jean and Jennette (Kegg) Schmalzried married twice; first to Harry Deloss Sayre with whom she was mother of (2). Later, she married Donald Leslie Pocock. Louise retired from the Elkhart Truth as a proofreader and TV section editor.

SCHMIDT

ANDREW CHRISTIAN SCHMIDT Fifth great grandson of progenitor Nicholas Kegg. **DAMON DOUGLAS SCHMIDT** Fifth great grandson of progenitor Nicholas Kegg. **DARRELL D. SCHMIDT** Fifth great grandson of progenitor Nicholas Kegg. **EMMA ROSE SCHMIDT** Seventh great granddaughter of progenitor Nicholas Kegg. **GASTON DALE SCHMIDT** Eighth great grandson of progenitor Nicholas Kegg. **KRISTIN SCHMIDT** Sixth great granddaughter of progenitor Nicholas Kegg. **MATTHEW SCHMIDT** Sixth great grandson of progenitor Nicholas Kegg. **POLLY ANN SCHMIDT** [5860] (1963 – 2006) daughter of Richard and Jaime (Stuckey) Schmidt, married Mr. Stevens.

[5858] Find A Grave Memorial# 9788627 Created by: Millennium Memorials [5858A] Elkhart Truth (IN) Jun 22, 1995, contributed by D. Sue Dible
[5859] The South Bend Tribune (IN) Jan 3, 1985 [5860] Chicago Suburban Daily Herald (IL) Aug 15, 2006

SUZY SCHMIDT Fifth great granddaughter of progenitor Nicholas Kegg.
COLE SCHMIT Seventh great grandson of progenitor Nicholas Kegg.
CONNER SCHMIT Seventh great grandson of progenitor Nicholas Kegg.
KAYLA SCHMIT Seventh great granddaughter of progenitor Nicholas Kegg.

SCHMITT

TERRI JO SCHMITT Sixth great granddaughter of progenitor Nicholas Kegg.
TONYA SCHMITT Sixth great granddaughter of progenitor Nicholas Kegg.

SCHNEIDER

LOUIS NEAL SCHNEIDER Seventh great grandson of progenitor Nicholas Kegg.
RHIANNON NOELLE SCHNEIDER Seventh great granddaughter of progenitor Nicholas Kegg.

SCHNEITER

HEATHER D. SCHNEITER Sixth great granddaughter of progenitor Nicholas Kegg.

SCHNITZLER

BRIAN SCHNITZLER Sixth great grandson of progenitor Nicholas Kegg.
ERIC SCHNITZLER Sixth great grandson of progenitor Nicholas Kegg.

SCHNITZSPAHN

JACK THOMAS SCHNITZSPAHN Seventh great grandson of progenitor Nicholas Kegg.
NICHOLAS RYAN SCHNITZSPAHN Seventh great grandson of progenitor Nicholas Kegg.

SCHOEPFLIN

BETTY SCHOEPFLIN Seventh great granddaughter of progenitor Nicholas Kegg. **BEVERLY SCHOEPFLIN** Seventh great granddaughter of progenitor Nicholas Kegg. **BILL SCHOEPFLIN** Seventh great grandson of progenitor Nicholas Kegg. **BOB SCHOEPFLIN** Seventh great grandson of progenitor Nicholas Kegg. **CHARLES DONALD SCHOEPFLIN** aka "Charlie", Seventh great grandson of progenitor Nicholas Kegg. **DORIS ELYNOR SCHOEPFLIN** [5860A] aka "Dode" (1922 – 2007) daughter of Eldo and Lona (Guertin) Schoepflin, married William S. Powell with whom she was mother of (5). Dode worked as a proofreader at the McMinnville News-Register. She later worked in the insurance industry for 52 years and was an owner and agent of Powell Insurance in Springfield. **ELDO EARL SCHOEPFLIN** [5860B] aka "Bud" (1931 – 2008) son of Eldo H. and Ruth (McCracken) Schoepflin, married Beverly Bastar with whom he was father of (7). Bud was very proud of his military service in the Marines. He retired from Public Service Co. of Colorado after 41 years of service. Bud was a Little League coach in football and officiated high school football for many years in the Denver area. Bud was an avid weightlifter for most of his life. His real passion however was baseball, which he pursued from age 8 on the sand lots of west Denver until his 75th year, both as a player, and later, as an umpire. He umpired 16 Junior College World Series. He assigned umpires for the Western Athletic Conference for many years. **ELDO HENRY SCHOEPFLIN** [5861] (1904 – 1954) son of Alonzo and Florence (Thompson) Schoepflin married four times; first to Lona Minerva Guertin with whom he was

[5860A] Register-Guard, The (Eugene, OR) Nov 6, 2007 [5860B] Denver Post (CO) June 29, 2008 [5861] Denver Post (CO) June 29, 2008

father of (1). He married Ruth McCracken with whom he was father of (1). He married Virginia Isabella Pickens with whom he was father of (1). Later, he married Grace Millard. **FLORENCE BELLE SCHOEPFLIN** (1925 – 1986) aka "Jeannie", daughter of Eldo and Virginia (Pickens) Schoepflin married twice; first to Angelo A. Berolo with whom she was mother of (2). Later, she married Lee R. Britt with whom she was mother of (2). **JAMES SCHOEPFLIN** aka "Jim", Seventh great grandson of progenitor Nicholas Kegg. **JOHN A. SCHOEPFLIN** Seventh great grandson of progenitor Nicholas Kegg.

SCHOETTLER

DONALD ROY SCHOETTLER Sixth great grandson of progenitor Nicholas Kegg. **ELNORA MARETTE SCHOETTLER** (1921 – 2001) daughter of Leroy and Alta (Pharrher) Schoettler married Marvin Alvie Damron. **GEORGIA MAY SCHOETTLER** (1902 – 1947) daughter of Walter and Della Mae (Smith) Schoettler married Claude Raymond Treece. Later she married Roscoe H. Bower. **LEROY ALEXANDER SCHOETTLER** (1896 – 1931) aka "Roy", son of Walter and Della Mae (Smith) Schoettler married Alta Pharrher with whom he was father of (3). **MABEL SCHOETTLER** (1898 – 1979) daughter of Walter and Della Mae (Smith) Schoettler married Ira Edward King with whom she was mother of (1). Later, she married Carl Antone Von Kendell with whom she was mother of (3). Last, she married Ralph L. Thayer. **MARY LOUISE SCHOETTLER** (1927 – 2013) daughter of Leroy and Alta (Pharrher) Schoettler married John Dean Armstrong with whom she was mother of (5). **ROBERT GLEN SCHOETTLER** Sixth great grandson of progenitor Nicholas Kegg. **ROBERT LEROY SCHOETTLER** (1922 – 1994) son of Leroy and Alta (Pharrher) Schoettler, married Marian Belle Rood with whom he was father of (3). **RUTH SCHOETTLER** [5862] (1900 – 1960) daughter of Walter and Della Mae (Smith) Schoettler married Burton Gustave Laibe, later she married Bernard Jerome Cassidy. Ruth was the owner of the Sixth Street Liquor store at 105 East Sixth street, Auburn. **SUSAN EILENE SCHOETTLER** Sixth great granddaughter of progenitor Nicholas Kegg.

SCHOFIELD

GEORGE WILLIAM SCHOFIELD (1925 – 1993) son of George and Bessie (Beaver) Schofield married Margaret Jane Vestrand with whom he was father of (2). **KEVIN G. SCHOFIELD** Fifth great grandson of progenitor Nicholas Kegg. **MARIAN JEAN SCHOFIELD** (1927 – 1943) daughter OF George and Bessie (Beaver) Schofield. **SHIRLEY J SCHOFIELD** Fifth great granddaughter of progenitor Nicholas Kegg.

SCHOLLE

AUBREY SCHOLLE Eighth great granddaughter of progenitor Nicholas Kegg. **CONNER SCHOLLE** Eighth great grandson of progenitor Nicholas Kegg. **LIAM SCHOLLE** Eighth great grandson of progenitor Nicholas Kegg. **NATHAN ALEXANDER SCHOLLE** Eighth great grandson of progenitor Nicholas Kegg.

SCHOLLENBERGER

JASON A. SCHOLLENBERGER Sixth great grandson of progenitor Nicholas Kegg.
JULIE A. SCHOLLENBERGER Sixth great granddaughter of progenitor Nicholas Kegg.

SCHORY

CHRISTOPHER ANDREW SCHORY Sixth great grandson of progenitor Nicholas Kegg.

[5862] Garrett Clipper (IN) Sep 29, 1960

JOSHUA ROBERT SCHORY Sixth great grandson of progenitor Nicholas Kegg.

SCHOTT

CLAY GARRETT SCHOTT Seventh great grandson of progenitor Nicholas Kegg. **EVELYN SCHOTT** Eighth great granddaughter of progenitor Nicholas Kegg. **JACOB SCHOTT** Seventh great grandson of progenitor Nicholas Kegg. **SETH GARNER SCHOTT** Seventh great grandson of progenitor Nicholas Kegg. **SIENA SCHOTT** Eighth great granddaughter of progenitor Nicholas Kegg. **TESSA SCHOTT** Eighth great granddaughter of progenitor Nicholas Kegg. **TYLER B. SCHOTT** aka "Ty", Seventh great grandson of progenitor Nicholas Kegg. **ZOE SCHOTT** Seventh great granddaughter of progenitor Nicholas Kegg.

SCHRACK

CARMEN SCHRACK Sixth great granddaughter of progenitor Nicholas Kegg. **JOSEPH EARL SCHRACK** [5863] (1890 – 1973) son of Joseph and Minnie (Graham) Shrock, married Fanny Elizabeth Stahly with whom he was father of (1). Earl was a painter, who after attending several art schools as a young man, traveled and studied in Europe, and taught art classes for many years. He followed the esoteric Christian tradition as an active member of the Rosicrucian Fellowship. He also taught art at the Nicholas Roerich Museum in New York. For several years, Earl published an esoteric journal called Toward the Highest. **WESTLEY SCHRACK** Sixth great grandson of progenitor Nicholas Kegg.

SCHREIBER

HEATHER SCHREIBER Seventh great granddaughter of progenitor Nicholas Kegg.
JERRY SCHREIBER Seventh great grandson of progenitor Nicholas Kegg.
LUCAS SCHREIBER Seventh great grandson of progenitor Nicholas Kegg.

SCHREINER

EDITH PORTER SCHREINER [5864] (1911 – 1912) daughter of Elmer and Edith (Porter) Schreiner; **ELIZABETH MILTON SCHREINER** [5865] (1908 – 1912) daughter of Elmer and Edith (Porter) Schreiner. **ETHEL PENELOPE SCHREINER** [5865A] aka "Nizza" (1920 – 2014) daughter of Elmer and Edith (Porter) Schreiner, married Charles Lee Mangus with whom she was mother of (1). Nizza was an Art teacher, founder of the Mercer County Spinners and Weavers Guild.
SARAH CATHERINE SCHREINER [5866] (1907 – 1978) daughter of Elmer and Edith (Porter) Schreiner, married Carl A. Aschman with whom she was mother of (2).
VIRGINIA NORTON SCHREINER (1913 – 1992) daughter of Elmer and Edith (Porter) Schreiner, married Donald Raphael Cleveland with whom she was mother of (1).

SCHRENGOHST

CATHERINE SCHRENGOHST (1920 – 2006) aka "Cathy," daughter of Harvey and Netia (Gillilan) Schrengohst married James B. Pace. Later, she married Richard Ira Weaver. **ESTHER MAE SCHRENGOHST** (1917 – 2005) daughter of Harvey and Netia (Gillilan) Schrengohst married James Willard Dake with whom she was mother of (2). **MILDRED DORIS SCHRENGOHST** [5867] (1914 – 1956) daughter of Harvey and Netia (Gillilan) Schrengohst married Mitchell Azparren. Mildred was formerly chief telephone operator at Minden. Active in community affairs, Mildred was a member of the auxilliary of the Veterans of Foreign Wars at Minden and was past president of that organization.

[5863] Rootsweb Archiver contributed by Bonnie Schrack [5864] p.8 - Bedford Gazette (PA) May 17, 1912 [5865] The Bedford Gazette (PA) Feb 16, 1912 [5865A] The Herald (PA) Feb 13, 2014 [5866] The Valley Independent (PA) Nov 30, 1978

RUTH SCHRENGOHST [5868] (1911 – 1996) daughter of Harvey and Netia (Gillilan) Schrengohst married Martin Azparren with whom she was mother of (1). Ruth was a former secretary of Reno's Sports Car Club. She was a past president of South Reno's Homemaker's Club and the Carson Valley United Methodist Church and a volunteer for the Reno chapter of the American Cancer Society.

SCHROER

MICHELLE SCHROER Sixth great granddaughter of progenitor Nicholas Kegg.

SCHRUM

AVERY SCHRUM Seventh great grandson of progenitor Nicholas Kegg.
CHLOE SCHRUM Seventh great granddaughter of progenitor Nicholas Kegg.

SCHUERMAN

ELIZABETH LEANN SCHUERMAN aka "Liz", Seventh great granddaughter of progenitor Nicholas Kegg.   **JACOB SETH SCHUERMAN** Seventh great grandson of progenitor Nicholas Kegg.
SYDNEY MARIE SCHUERMAN Seventh great granddaughter of progenitor Nicholas Kegg.

SCHUETTE

ASTA VIONE SCHUETTE Sixth great granddaughter of progenitor Nicholas Kegg.
MAX R. SCHUETTE Sixth great grandson of progenitor Nicholas Kegg.

SCHUITEMAN

CHAISE SCHUITEMAN Seventh great grandson of progenitor Nicholas Kegg.
PAIGE ELLEN SCHUITEMAN [5869] (1993 – 2003) daughter of Todd and Cheryl (Lenderink) Schuiteman, was riding her bike as she anxiously awaited her church group to arrive at her house. Tragically, she was struck by a car and sustained very serious head injuries. In the spirit of Paige's true generosity and Christian character, she was able to give the gift of life through multiple organ donations. God was able to use Paige's death to breathe life into five critically ill children, who may have otherwise died. Paige was a conscientious, hilarious, smart-as-a-whip child with a huge heart and a special love and passion for young children and babies. She excelled at gymnastics, loving her family, and giving of herself.   **TREY SCHUITEMAN** Seventh great grandson of progenitor Nicholas Kegg.

SCHULER

CAROLYN LOUISE SCHULER Fifth great granddaughter of progenitor Nicholas Kegg.
CRAIG SCHULER Fifth great grandson of progenitor Nicholas Kegg.   **DAVID SCHULER** Fifth great grandson of progenitor Nicholas Kegg.   **EMILY SCHULER** Seventh great granddaughter of progenitor Nicholas Kegg.   **LINDA ANN SCHULER** Fifth great granddaughter of progenitor Nicholas Kegg.   **PATTY SCHULER** Seventh great granddaughter of progenitor Nicholas Kegg.
SUSAN ELAYNE SCHULER Fifth great granddaughter of progenitor Nicholas Kegg

SCHULTZ

AMY SCHULTZ Seventh great granddaughter of progenitor Nicholas Kegg.
BROOKE ELIZABETH SCHULTZ Seventh great granddaughter of progenitor Nicholas Kegg

[5867] Reno Gazette-Journal (NV) Jan 26, 1956 [5868] Reno Gazette-Journal (NV) Dec 17, 1996 [5869] Grand Rapids Press (MI) Oct 23, 2003, obtained by D. Sue Dible

ELLEN KAY SCHULTZ Sixth great granddaughter of progenitor Nicholas Kegg. **KIRA SCHULTZ** Seventh great granddaughter of progenitor Nicholas Kegg. **TRENT SCHULTZ** Sixth great grandson of progenitor Nicholas Kegg. **WILLIAM J. SCHULTZ** Fifth great grandson of progenitor Nicholas Kegg.

SCHULZ

ALEX SCHULZ Eighth great granddaughter of progenitor Nicholas Kegg. **BEAU SCHULZ** Seventh great grandson of progenitor Nicholas Kegg. **BROCK SCHULZ** Eighth great grandson of progenitor Nicholas Kegg. **DODIE SCHULZ** Seventh great granddaughter of progenitor Nicholas Kegg. **FREDRICK SCHULZ** [5869A] aka "Fred" (1946 – 2011) son of Lawrence and Marrabell (Been) Schulz married Constance Masic with whom he was father of (2). **JOY LYNN SCHULZ** Sixth great granddaughter of progenitor Nicholas Kegg. **MELISSA SUE SCHULZ** Sixth great granddaughter of progenitor Nicholas Kegg. **MELODY SCHULZ** Sixth great granddaughter of progenitor Nicholas Kegg. **SANDRA SCHULZ** Sixth great granddaughter of progenitor Nicholas Kegg.

SCHUMANN

HARRY ROBERT SCHUMANN [5870] (1946 – 1947) son of Richard and Anna (Ort) Schumann. **LEWIS RICHARD SCHUMANN** Fifth great grandson of progenitor Nicholas Kegg. **SCOTT LEWIS SCHUMANN** Sixth great grandson of progenitor Nicholas Kegg.

SCHWAB

GWENDOLYN SCHWAB Sixth great granddaughter of progenitor Nicholas Kegg. **JULIE ANN SCHWAB** Sixth great granddaughter of progenitor Nicholas Kegg.

SCHWALBAUCH

CARL DEREK SCHWALBAUCH Sixth great grandson of progenitor Nicholas Kegg.

SCHWARZ

ABIGAIL SCHWARZ aka "Abby", Sixth great granddaughter of progenitor Nicholas Kegg. **EMMA SCHWARZ** Sixth great granddaughter of progenitor Nicholas Kegg. **EVAN SCHWARZ** Sixth great grandson of progenitor Nicholas Kegg.

SCHWENGER

PAUL CLAYCOMB SCHWENGER Seventh great grandson of progenitor Nicholas Kegg. **WALTER JOHN SCHWENGER** Seventh great grandson of progenitor Nicholas Kegg.

SCHWERY

TELA SCHWERY Sixth great granddaughter of progenitor Nicholas Kegg.

SCHWIEBERT

HEIDI L. SCHWIEBERT Fourth great granddaughter of progenitor Nicholas Kegg. **KATHY SCHWIEBERT** Fourth great granddaughter of progenitor Nicholas Kegg.

[5869A] Lebanon Express (OR) Nov 29, 2011, contributed by D. Sue Dible [5870] p.14 Cumberland Evening Times (MD) Jan 24, 1947, obtained by D. Sue Dible

SCHWIRIAN

HARVEY FREDERICK SCHWIRIAN Sixth great grandson of progenitor Nicholas Kegg.
THOMAS ARTHUR SCHWIRIAN Sixth great grandson of progenitor Nicholas Kegg.
ZELLA MELINDA SCHWIRIAN Sixth great granddaughter of progenitor Nicholas Kegg.

SCOTT

CRAIG SCOTT Sixth great grandson of progenitor Nicholas Kegg. **DAVID NORRIS SCOTT** [5870A] (1964 – 1991) son of David and Barbara (Norris) Scott married Diana Rose Richardson. A graduate of Wabash College and Purdue University, David was an account manager for Air Products and Chemical Corp., Allentown, Pa. **DOUGLAS SCOTT** Sixth great grandson of progenitor Nicholas Kegg. **EFFIE LEOTA SCOTT** (1910 – 1966) daughter of Charles Andrew and Sadie (Sidders) Scott. Twin sister of Eva Leora Scott, married Henry Lee Bishop with whom she was mother of (5). **EMMA WINONA SCOTT** (1910 – 1966) daughter of Glenn and Ruth (Wyckoff) Scott, married Victor Ivan Stafford. **EVA LEORA SCOTT** [5871] (1893 – 1952) daughter of Charles Andrew and Sadie (Sidders) Scott. Twin sister of Effie Leota Scott, married Ernest F. Hamilton with whom she was mother of (3). **JAMES H. SCOTT** Sixth great grandson of progenitor Nicholas Kegg. **JILL SCOTT** Sixth great granddaughter of progenitor Nicholas Kegg. **JOSEPH ALAN SCOTT** Sixth great grandson of progenitor Nicholas Kegg. **KEITH SCOTT** Sixth great grandson of progenitor Nicholas Kegg. **KIMBERLY ANN SCOTT** Seventh great granddaughter of progenitor Nicholas Kegg. **MERLYN DWIGHT SCOTT** (1939 – 1939) son of Ralph and Grace (Evans) Scott. **MICHELLE SCOTT** Sixth great granddaughter of progenitor Nicholas Kegg. **MICHELLE EILEEN SCOTT** Sixth great granddaughter of progenitor Nicholas Kegg. **RALPH JOHN SCOTT** [5872] (1913 – 1991) son of Glenn and Ruth (Wyckoff) Scott, married Grace E. Evans with whom he was father of (3). **ROB R. SCOTT** Sixth great grandson of progenitor Nicholas Kegg. **ROBERT HAMILTON SCOTT** (1925 – 2008) son of Ewig and Mauree (Sneer) Scott married Rosemary Eileen Frailey with whom he was father of (2).

SCRITCHFIELD

NATHANIEL E. SCRITCHFIELD Sixth great grandson of progenitor Nicholas Kegg.
RHIANNON N. SCRITCHFIELD Sixth great granddaughter of progenitor Nicholas Kegg.
SHIRLEY MAY SCRITCHFIELD Fifth great granddaughter of progenitor Nicholas Kegg.

SEABROOK

GAY SEABROOK Fifth great granddaughter of progenitor Nicholas Kegg.

SEAGER

ELISHE SEAGER Sixth great granddaughter of progenitor Nicholas Kegg.
JOSHUA SEAGER Sixth great grandson of progenitor Nicholas Kegg.

SEAVEY

IAN KONALA SEAVEY Seventh great grandson of progenitor Nicholas Kegg.
JOHN CARL SEAVEY (1942 – 1999) aka "Jon", son of Cecil and Helen (Audley) Seavey, married JoAnn Charvet with whom he was father of (2).
SARA F. SEAVEY Seventh great granddaughter of progenitor Nicholas Kegg.

[5870A] p.35 Indianapolis Star (IN) Feb 10, 1991 [5871] Ravenna News (NE) Sep 18, 1952 [5872] Heer Mortuary (CO) Nov 2007

SECKEL

BOBBIE JO SECKEL Seventh great granddaughter of progenitor Nicholas Kegg.
NICOLE MARIE SECKEL Seventh great granddaughter of progenitor Nicholas Kegg.
ROBIN LYNN SECKEL Seventh great granddaughter of progenitor Nicholas Kegg.

SEEL

BILLY SEEL Eighth great grandson of progenitor Nicholas Kegg. **BOBBIE JEAN SEEL** Seventh great granddaughter of progenitor Nicholas Kegg. **DARL LEE SEEL** Seventh great grandson of progenitor Nicholas Kegg. **HERBERT SEEL** aka "Herbie", Seventh great grandson of progenitor Nicholas Kegg. **JOSIE SEEL** Eighth great granddaughter of progenitor Nicholas Kegg. **KATHERINE SEEL** Seventh great granddaughter of progenitor Nicholas Kegg. **MICHAEL JAMES SEEL** Eighth great grandson of progenitor Nicholas Kegg. **SOLOMON SEEL** Seventh great grandson of progenitor Nicholas Kegg.

SEELEY

JANINE MARIE SEELEY [5873] (1969 – 1969) daughter of Everett and Carolyn (Burd) Seeley. **RANDY J. SEELEY** Sixth great grandson of progenitor Nicholas Kegg. **ROBERT E. SEELEY** Sixth great grandson of progenitor Nicholas Kegg. **THOMAS E. SEELEY** Seventh great grandson of progenitor Nicholas Kegg.

SEEMANN

CASSIE SEEMANN Seventh great granddaughter of progenitor Nicholas Kegg.
WILLIAM SEEMANN Seventh great grandson of progenitor Nicholas Kegg.

SEESE

ALBERT A. SEESE Fifth great grandson of progenitor Nicholas Kegg. **BARBARA A. SEESE** Fifth great granddaughter of progenitor Nicholas Kegg. **BENITA L. SEESE** Fifth great granddaughter of progenitor Nicholas Kegg. **BRIAN SEESE** Seventh great grandson of progenitor Nicholas Kegg. **DANIEL SEESE** Seventh great grandson of progenitor Nicholas Kegg. **DONALD C. SEESE** [5873A] (1928 – 2014) son of Ross and Margaret (McDaniel) Seese married Mae Louise Robinson with whom he was father of (4). A World War II Veteran of the U.S. Army, Don served in the Military Police at Los Alamos, N.M. Don was a life member of American Legion Post 268, Muncy, 40 et 8 Voiture 382, Williamsport, and Highland Lake Manor, Hughesville. He was also a member of the Young Men's Democratic Club of Williamsport, and a charter lifetime member of the "Good Sam" Club. Don owned and operated the former D&L Sunoco Service in Newberry. He also retired as a driver for STEP Inc. and the Pattern Makers Association of Detroit. Don enjoyed watching NASCAR, the Game Show Network, Detroit Tigers baseball and western movies. A "Mopar Junkie," he owned more than 50 Chrysler product vehicles since buying his first car in 1945. **DONNA J. SEESE** Fifth great granddaughter of progenitor Nicholas Kegg. **GREGORY LEE SEESE** Fifth great grandson of progenitor Nicholas Kegg. **LINDA J. SEESE** Fifth great granddaughter of progenitor Nicholas Kegg. **NELLIE JANE SEESE** [5874] (1923 – 2019) aka "Jane", daughter of Ross and Margaret (McDaniel) Seese, married John C. Lucus with whom she was mother of (4). Jane worked at the former Sylvania Electric for 29 years on Westminster Drive before retirement. She belonged to the Special Treasures of Cedar Chest Red Hat Society, the Hepburn

---

[5873] p.26 Record-Eagle, (Traverse City, MI) June 19, 1969 [5873A] Sun Gazette (PA) Dec 1, 2014 [5874] Knight-Confer Funeral Home, Inc (Williamsport, PA)

Lycoming County Senior Citizens club and went to the Senior Center exercise class in South Williamsport. She enjoyed playing games, puzzles, gardening, cross stitching and computer games. Jane especially enjoyed watching Penn State football, Philadelphia Phillies games and the Game Show Channel. She was an avid traveler who enjoyed bus trips and cruises. **PATRICIA J. SEESE** Fifth great granddaughter of progenitor Nicholas Kegg. **ROBETTA LOUISE SEESE** [5874A] aka "Betty" (1925 - 2009) daughter of Ross and Margaret (McDaniel) Seese married John Frederick Lucas with whom she was mother of (5). Betty was a member of Memorial Baptist Church, the Monroe Lape Sunday School Class, was a deaconess, choir member, financial secretary and helped in the craft room during Vacation Bible School. Betty was also a member of the Hepburn-Lycoming Senior Citizens and loved to walk the bike path and work in her flower beds. **WILLIAM GLEN SEESE** [5875] (1922 – 1996) son of Ross and Margaret (McDaniel) Seese, married Elizabeth Blanche Shores with whom he was father of (3). William was a veteran of WWII.

SEIDEL

RENE SEIDEL Seventh great granddaughter of progenitor Nicholas Kegg.

SEIFERT

BONNIE RAE SEIFERT Sixth great granddaughter of progenitor Nicholas Kegg.
CHERYL DARLENE SEIFERT Fifth great granddaughter of progenitor Nicholas Kegg.
DONALD GEORGE SEIFERT Sixth great grandson of progenitor Nicholas Kegg.
PATRICIA ANN SEIFERT Sixth great granddaughter of progenitor Nicholas Kegg.

SELLERS

AMY SELLERS Fifth great granddaughter of progenitor Nicholas Kegg. **AUBREY JOY SELLERS** Seventh great granddaughter of progenitor Nicholas Kegg. **CHARLES WILLIAM RANDALL SELLERS** [5876] (1909 – 1983) son of Charles and Daisy (Beaver) Sellers married twice; first to Georgia West Solomon. Later, he married Julia Tirko with whom he was father of (2). **DORIS L. SELLERS** [5877] (1937 – 2009) daughter of Travers and Irene (Smith) Sellers, married Steve Hook with whom she was mother of (1). Doris was a homemaker and devoted herself to her family. In her free time, she enjoyed playing bingo. **JACALYN LOU SELLERS** aka "Jackie", Fourth great granddaughter of progenitor Nicholas Kegg. **JANEY MARIE SELLERS** Seventh great granddaughter of progenitor Nicholas Kegg. **JENNIFER SELLERS** Fifth great granddaughter of progenitor Nicholas Kegg. **JONATHAN SELLERS** Fifth great grandson of progenitor Nicholas Kegg. **LOIS ANNALEE SELLERS** Fifth great granddaughter of progenitor Nicholas Kegg. **KATHY SELLERS** Fifth great granddaughter of progenitor Nicholas Kegg. **MARION FLORENCE SELLERS** (1912 – 1990) daughter of Charles and Daisy (Beaver) Sellers, married Robert F. George Thomson. **TRAVERS N. SELLERS** [5878] (1907 – 2001) son of Charles and Daisy (Beaver) Sellers, married Irene Dora Smith with whom he was father of (2). Travers was a member of the UMWA, retiring from Reitz Coal Company's #4 Mine. **WILLIAM SELLERS** aka "Bill", Fifth great grandson of progenitor Nicholas Kegg.

SEMANEK

ALLAN EDWARD SEMANEK Sixth great grandson of progenitor Nicholas Kegg.
KAREN NANETTE SEMANEK Sixth great granddaughter of progenitor Nicholas Kegg.

[5874A] Knight-Confer Funeral Home, Inc. [5875] Petroskey News-Review (MI) Jan 24, 2007 [5876] Daily American (PA) May 28, 2012 [5877] Johnstown Tribune Democrat (PA) Mar 19, 2009 [5878] p.D7 Tribune Democrat (PA) May 17, 2001

SENPIE

SAMANTHA SENPIE aka "Samm", Seventh great granddaughter of progenitor Nicholas Kegg.

SENSOR

KATE NICOLE SENSOR Seventh great granddaughter of progenitor Nicholas Kegg.
SARAH ANN SENSOR Seventh great granddaughter of progenitor Nicholas Kegg.

SEREIKA

DELANEY SEREIKA Seventh great granddaughter of progenitor Nicholas Kegg.
TIERNEY SEREIKA Seventh great granddaughter of progenitor Nicholas Kegg.

SEVER

ELLERY SEVER Seventh great granddaughter of progenitor Nicholas Kegg.
OLIVIA SEVER Seventh great granddaughter of progenitor Nicholas Kegg.
RORY SEVER Seventh great grandson of progenitor Nicholas Kegg.

SEVILLE

CAMERON SEVILLE Seventh great grandson of progenitor Nicholas Kegg.

SEYMOUR

BONNIE SEYMOUR Seventh great granddaughter of progenitor Nicholas Kegg.

SHAFER

AARON SHAFER Seventh great grandson of progenitor Nicholas Kegg. **ANNA K. SHAFER** [5878A] (1905 – 2006) daughter of Jacob and Martha (Smith) Shafer married Ellis Ray Reichard with whom she was mother of (5). Anna was a homemaker. **ARNOLD FRANK SHAFER** Fifth great grandson of progenitor Nicholas Kegg. **ASHLEY SHAFER** Seventh great granddaughter of progenitor Nicholas Kegg. **BRANDON SHAFER** Seventh great grandson of progenitor Nicholas Kegg. **BRET MICHAEL SHAFER** [5878B] (1965 – 2018) son of Roland and Carol (Watkins) Shafer was father of (2). Bret was employed for many years at Monarch Industries. Later, he drove delivery trucks, a job he enjoyed traveling and got to see so much of the country. Bret enjoyed playing the guitar and was an avid KISS fan. He loved to watch NASCAR and the Detroit Lions. **CRYSTAL MARIE SHAFER** Seventh great granddaughter of progenitor Nicholas Kegg. **DALE EARL SHAFER** [5879] (1923 – 2011) son of Lloyd and Mabel (Bedford) Shafer was a self-employed Mechanic all his life. **DEAN SHAFER** Sixth great grandson of progenitor Nicholas Kegg. **DIANA LYN SHAFER** [5879A] (1950 – 2018) daughter of Arnold and Bonnie (Jennings) Shafer loved animals (all kinds) and her family. Diana was mother of (2). **DON L. SHAFER** Sixth great grandson of progenitor Nicholas Kegg. **DON MICHELE SHAFER** Sixth great grandson of progenitor Nicholas Kegg. **EDDIE E. SHAFER** (1929 – 1929) son of Glen and Pearl (Keller) Shafer. **ELIJAH LLOYD SHAFER**, aka "Eli", Seventh great grandson of progenitor Nicholas Kegg. **ERICK WAYNE SHAFER** Seventh great grandson of progenitor Nicholas Kegg. **GLEN SHAFER** Sixth great grandson of progenitor Nicholas Kegg.

[5878A] Elkhart Truth (IN) March 24, 2006 [5878B] The Elkhart Truth (IN) May 25, 2018, contributed by D. Sue Dible [5879] Carney-Frost Funeral Home (LaGrange, IN) [5879A] Samaritan Funeral Home (AZ) obtained by D. Sue Dible

GLEN JACOB SHAFER (5880) (1907 – 1976) son of Jacob and Martha (Smith) Shafer, married Pearl Alice Keller with whom he was father of (5). **GLENNA S. SHAFER** Sixth great granddaughter of progenitor Nicholas Kegg. **HOLLY SHAFER** Eighth great granddaughter of progenitor Nicholas Kegg. **ISAAC SHAFER** Seventh great grandson of progenitor Nicholas Kegg. **JACQUELINE SHAFER** Sixth great granddaughter of progenitor Nicholas Kegg. **JAMES LEE SHAFER** (5880A) (1935 – 1960) son of Glen and Pearl (Keller) Shafer was a Lagrange Rt. 2 truck driver who fell asleep before his truck left the road. State police said the trailer section of the outfit smashed into the cab, shearing off the top portion of the cab and demolishing it. The truck was carrying propane gas for a Kendallville firm. **JOHN HENRY SHAFER** (1925 – 1940) son of Jacob and Martha (Smith) Shafer. **JONAH SHAFER** Seventh great grandson of progenitor Nicholas Kegg. **JUSTICE SHAFER** Seventh great granddaughter of progenitor Nicholas Kegg. **KASH RHEA SHAFER** (5880B) (1903 – 1989) son of Jacob and Martha (Smith) Shafer married Helen Lucille Keller with whom he was father of (4). Kash retired from the Lagrange County Highway Dept. **KEITH SHAFER** Sixth great grandson of progenitor Nicholas Kegg. **KEITH WAYNE SHAFER** Fifth great grandson of progenitor Nicholas Kegg. **LARRY L. SHAFER** (5880C) (1941 – 2012) son of Glen and Pearl (Keller) Shafer married Margaret Sams with whom he was father of (2). Larry spent 38 years working for Boeing and retired from the Long Beach, California plant. He was a United States Air Force Veteran. Larry enjoyed fishing, camping and traveling. **LEONA FERN SHAFER** (5881) (1915 – 1991) daughter of Jacob and Martha (Smith) Shafer, married Frank Gardner Sanderson with whom she was mother of (6). **LINDA LOU SHAFER** (5882) (1940 – 2020) daughter of Kash and Helen (Keller) Shafer married three times. Linda was mother of (6). Linda loved to read, was an avid dog lover. **LLOYD HURLAN SHAFER** (5883) (1925 – 2012) son of Lloyd and Mabel (Bedford) Shafer, married Mary Sue Burnau with whom he was father of (4). **LLOYD HURLAN SHAFER** (5884) (1900 – 1979) son of Jacob and Martha (Smith) Shafer, married Mabel Lucile Bedford with whom he was father of (6). **LYNETTE L. SHAFER** Sixth great granddaughter of progenitor Nicholas Kegg. **MARJORIE NELL SHAFER** (5885) (1929 – 1998) aka "Margie", daughter of Lloyd and Mabel (Bedford) Shafer married twice; first to Wilbur Wayne Baird with whom she was mother of (6). Later, she married Arthur Ray Field. **MARTHA SHAFER** (5885A) (1930 – 2012) daughter of Lloyd and Mabel (Bedford) Shafer married Titus J. Speicher with whom she was mother of (5). Martha was a homemaker who enjoyed cooking, crocheting, embroidery, reading and most of all, her children and grandchildren. **MARY SHAFER** Sixth great granddaughter of progenitor Nicholas Kegg. **MARY LOU SHAFER** Fifth great granddaughter of progenitor Nicholas Kegg. **MATTHEW SHAFER** Seventh great grandson of progenitor Nicholas Kegg. **NORMA P. SHAFER** (5885B) aka "Stormy" (1931 – 2013) daughter of Glen and Pearl (Keller) Shafer married Howard Allen Beaty with whom she was mother of (5). Stormy retired from Aero (Modern-Air) in Angola, IN. Stormy was a member of Orland American Legion Auxiliary. **NORRIS LEE SHAFER** (5886) (1919 – 2002) aka "Bub", son of Jacob and Martha (Smith) Shafer, married Sylvia M. Campbell. Bub retired as a driver for Saidla Trucking Co. **PAMELA SHAFER** Sixth great granddaughter of progenitor Nicholas Kegg. **PAULA JEAN SHAFER** Sixth great granddaughter of progenitor Nicholas Kegg. **RICK SHAFER** Sixth great grandson of progenitor Nicholas Kegg. **RICK LEE SHAFER** (5886A) (1963 – 2016) son of Arnold and Lucy (Bishop) Shafer married Anna Barbara Vanderschuur with whom he was father of (6). **RICKY SHAFER** Seventh great grandson of progenitor Nicholas Kegg. **ROLAND KASH SHAFER** (5885B) aka "Ronnie" (1945 – 2018) son of Kash and Helen (Keller) Shafer married twice; first to Carol Watkins with whom he was father of (2). Later, he married Regenia (Schutz) Howell. Ronnie was a locksmith who turned a hobby into a business and was self-employed when he started Ron's Lock and

---

(5880) p.22 Elkhart Truth (IN) Apr 19, 1976, obtained by D. Sue Dible (5880A) p.2- Elkhart Truth (IN) March 10, 1960, contributed by D. Sue Dible (5880B) obituary newsclipping contributed by Paula Shafer-Aulbach (5880C) Frurip-May Funeral Home (IN) (5881) p.6A - The News-Sentinel (Fort Wayne, IN) Dec 11, 1991 (5882) Jackson Citizen Patriot (MI) Jan. 30, 2020 (5883) Elkhart Truth (IN) March 26, 2012 (5884) p.30 Elkhart Truth (IN) Sep 26, 1979, obtained by D. Sue Dible (5885) p.D10 - South Bend Tribune (IN) Dec 20, 1998 (5885A) Carney-Frost Funeral Home (LaGrange, IN) (5885B) Frurip-May Funeral Home (IN) (5886) Elkhart Truth (IN) Sep 22, 2002 (5886A) Sturgis Journal (MI) Apr. 30, 2016, obtained by D. Sue Dible

Key in LaGrange, IN. For many years he was the lead guitarist of "The Falcons". Ronnie was a member of the LaGrange American Legion Post #215 and the former LaGrange Eagles. He was a United States Army veteran. **ROXIE ROSE SHAFER** [5886B] (1908 – 2002) daughter of Jacob and Martha (Smith) Shafer married Clarence Albert Keller with whom she was mother of (6). Roxie retired from Kirsch Co. of Sturgis, Michigan. **SAMUEL SHAFER** Seventh great grandson of progenitor Nicholas Kegg. **TERRY SHAFER** Sixth great grandson of progenitor Nicholas Kegg. **TIMOTHY GLEN SHAFER** Sixth great grandson of progenitor Nicholas Kegg. **VICTORIA L. SHAFER** Sixth great granddaughter of progenitor Nicholas Kegg. **VIVA MAE SHAFER** [5886C] (1928 – 2022) daughter of Kash and Helen Lucille (Keller) Shafer married Fred R. Kaufman with whom she was mother of (3). Later she married Daniel E. Yoder. Viva was employed at Goodwill for eight years and retired from Publix Supermarket after 16 years in the deli department. **VIVIAN LOUISE SHAFER** [5887] (1924 – 2001) daughter of Lloyd and Mabel (Bedford) Shafer, married Ralph Wendell Machan with whom she was mother of (2). Vivian had worked at Weaver's Meat Locker and the W.R. Thomas Store while living in LaGrange. She loved working in her yard, playing Yahtzee, reading, and her Garfield collection. Vivian was especially noted for her generosity. She was always running errands and doing favors for her friends who couldn't drive. **WILLIAM D. SHAFER** aka "Bill", Sixth great grandson of progenitor Nicholas Kegg. **ZAKARIAS SHAFER** Seventh great grandson of progenitor Nicholas Kegg.

SHAFFER

ADAM SHAFFER Sixth great grandson of progenitor Nicholas Kegg. **ALAN D. SHAFFER** Fifth great grandson of progenitor Nicholas Kegg. **ALISA SHAFFER** Sixth great granddaughter of progenitor Nicholas Kegg. **ANN MARIE SHAFFER** aka "Annie", Seventh great granddaughter of progenitor Nicholas Kegg. **ANNABELLE LOUISE SHAFFER** [5887A] (1927 – 2019) daughter of Walter and Elsie (Shoemaker) Shaffer married John Martin Wakefield with whom she was mother of (3). Annabelle owned and operated the family dairy farm with her husband. She was a member and church leader of the friendship circle at the Friends Cove United Church of Christ. She was a member of the Bedford Hospital Auxillary and 50-plus year member of the Eastern Star and the Charlesville grange, state level grange and national level grange. **BRUCE SHAFFER** Eighth great grandson of progenitor Nicholas Kegg. **ELIZABETH ANN SHAFFER** Sixth great granddaughter of progenitor Nicholas Kegg. **GERALDINE M SHAFFER** Fifth great granddaughter of progenitor Nicholas Kegg. **GRACE ELENA SHAFFER** [5888] (1886 – 1977) daughter of Samuel and Ida (Pennell) Shaffer, married Harvey Elmer England with whom she was mother of (3). Grace was a member of St. John's United Church of Christ of Bedford and the Women's Guild of the church. **JAMES SHAFFER** Seventh great grandson of progenitor Nicholas Kegg. **JENNIFER ANN SHAFFER** Sixth great granddaughter of progenitor Nicholas Kegg. **JOHN WILLIAM SHAFFER** [5889] (1922 – 2006) son of Walter and Elsie (Shoemaker) Shaffer, married Dorothy Adeline Diest with whom he was father of (2). John retired as owner/operator, along with his wife, from Deist Cleaners of Bedford, which is one of Bedford's oldest continuously family-owned businesses since 1926. John was a member of the Bedford Presbyterian Church, the Bedford American Legion Post No. 113, Flickers Club, Bedford Elks Club, Bedford Masonic Lodge No. 320 F&AM, and a former member of the Bedford Lions Club. John served in the U.S. Army Air Force as a sergeant in WW II. **JOHN WILLIAM SHAFFER** Fifth great grandson of progenitor Nicholas Kegg. **JUDY FAYE SHAFFER** Fifth great granddaughter of progenitor Nicholas Kegg. **KRISTINA SHAFFER** Seventh great granddaughter of progenitor Nicholas Kegg. **LISA G. SHAFFER** Fifth great granddaughter of progenitor Nicholas Kegg. **LORI ANN SHAFFER** [5890] (1967 – 2022) daughter of Cecil and Faye (Eshelman) Shaffer married Shannon J. Young. Lori was owner/operator of LA Young Bookkeeping and previously worked for Gary Hollis Accounting. Lori was a loving, caring

---

[5886B] p.10A - The News-Sentinel (Fort Wayne, IN) Sept 21, 2002 [5886C] KPCNews (IN) Jun. 24, 2022, obtained by D. Sue Dible [5887] Sturgis Daily Journal (MI) Nov 2001 transcribed by Carole Lynn (MOHNEY) CARR [5887A] Bedford Gazette (PA) Sep 5, 2019 [5888] Bedford County Genealogical Society obituary obtained by D. Sue Dible [5889] p.3 - Bedford Inquirer (PA) Feb 24, 2006 [5890] Bedford Gazette (PA) July 30, 2022, obtained by Bob Rose

lady who loved all animals, especially her cats. **MALINDA LUCILLE SHAFFER** aka "Mindy", Seventh great granddaughter of progenitor Nicholas Kegg. **MARY SHAFFER** Seventh great granddaughter of progenitor Nicholas Kegg. **MCKENZIE NICOLE SHAFFER** Eighth great granddaughter of progenitor Nicholas Kegg. **NANCY SHAFFER** Fifth great granddaughter of progenitor Nicholas Kegg. **NORA EDITH SHAFFER** [5891] (1890 – 1983) daughter of Samuel and Ida (Pennell) Shaffer, married Simon Ellis England. Nora served as pianist, teacher, and as youth leader of Yeager Lutheran Church in Rainsburg. Nora was also a member of the PO of A. **PATRICIA LOU SHAFFER** Fifth great granddaughter of progenitor Nicholas Kegg. **RANDALL W. SHAFFER** [5891A] (1977 – 2002) son of Wayne and Sandra (Kerr) Shaffer was an operator at Wal-Mart Distribution Center. **ODNEY WAYNE SHAFFER** Fifth great grandson of progenitor Nicholas Kegg. **ROXANNE ELIZABETH SHAFFER** Fifth great granddaughter of progenitor Nicholas Kegg. **RUTH MARTHA SHAFFER** Sixth great granddaughter of progenitor Nicholas Kegg. **SHANNON ALAN SHAFFER** Seventh great grandson of progenitor Nicholas Kegg. **SUSAN ANNETTE SHAFFER** Fifth great granddaughter of progenitor Nicholas Kegg.

SHALOM

EDWARD SHALOM Seventh great grandson of progenitor Nicholas Kegg.
MERIT SHALOM Seventh great granddaughter of progenitor Nicholas Kegg.
NATHANIEL SHALOM Seventh great grandson of progenitor Nicholas Kegg.

SHANAHAN

BRANDON TERRANCE SHANAHAN Seventh great grandson of progenitor Nicholas Kegg.
DELANEY SHANAHAN Eighth great granddaughter of progenitor Nicholas Kegg.
JUSTIN ARNOLD SHANAHAN Seventh great grandson of progenitor Nicholas Kegg.
MARGOT SHANAHAN Eighth great granddaughter of progenitor Nicholas Kegg.

SHANK

AMANDA GRACE SHANK Seventh great granddaughter of progenitor Nicholas Kegg.
KATIE E. SHANK Seventh great granddaughter of progenitor Nicholas Kegg.

SHANKLE

CAROLINE LYN SHANKLE Fifth great granddaughter of progenitor Nicholas Kegg.
GINGER SHANKLE Fifth great granddaughter of progenitor Nicholas Kegg.
GLORIA J. SHANKLE Fifth great granddaughter of progenitor Nicholas Kegg

SHANNON

DENVER HITE SHANNON Fifth great grandson of progenitor Nicholas Kegg.
JACKSON ANDREW HARTMAN SHANNON (1909 – 1985) aka "Jack" son of Charles and Phebe (Hartman) Shannon married Marvel Mitchell.
KAREN SHANNON Fifth great granddaughter of progenitor Nicholas Kegg.
OLIVIA SHANNON Eighth great granddaughter of progenitor Nicholas Kegg.
SADIE SHANNON Eighth great granddaughter of progenitor Nicholas Kegg.

[5891] p.3 - Bedford Inquirer (PA) April 29, 1983 [5891A] Bedford Inquirer (PA) Aug 2, 2002, contributed by Bob Rose

SHARP

COLIN SHARP Seventh great grandson of progenitor Nicholas Kegg.
JANE A. SHARP Sixth great granddaughter of progenitor Nicholas Kegg.
JASON SHARP Sixth great grandson of progenitor Nicholas Kegg.
JEFFREY LEE SHARP Sixth great grandson of progenitor Nicholas Kegg.
JEREMY ALAN SHARP Sixth great grandson of progenitor Nicholas Kegg.
JEREMY THOMPSON SHARP Seventh great grandson of progenitor Nicholas Kegg.
JOELLEN SHARP Sixth great granddaughter of progenitor Nicholas Kegg.
SARAH ALANA SHARP Seventh great granddaughter of progenitor Nicholas Kegg.

SHARROCK

BRITTNEY LEANN SHARROCK Eighth great granddaughter of progenitor Nicholas Kegg. **CLARENCE EDGAR SHARROCK** [5892] (1914 – 1968) son of Stephen and Rose (Lowe) Sharrock, married Flora Agnes Hamilton with whom he was father of (3). **CHERYL SHARROCK** [5892A] (1960 – 2014) daughter of Richard and Judith (Sesslar) Sharrock married twice, first to Allen Mounts with whom she was mother of (1). Later, married Jerry Lee Daniels with whom she was mother of (5). **CHRISTOPHER BLAINE SHARROCK** aka "Chris" Sixth great grandson of progenitor Nicholas Kegg. **CODY EMERY SHARROCK** Eighth great grandson of progenitor Nicholas Kegg. **DARRELL CLEVE SHARROCK** Sixth great grandson of progenitor Nicholas Kegg. **DONALD LEE SHARROCK** Fifth great grandson of progenitor Nicholas Kegg. **FRANCINE MARIE SHARROCK** [5892B] (1933 – 2016) daughter of Paul and Zoe (McClure) Sharrock married Earl Duane Corbett with whom she was mother of (3). A sassy personality, Francine was a devout Christian who acted as her family's spiritual compass and her compassion and faith lead her to volunteer for numerous charities. She was immensely creative and had a lifelong passion for painting and crafting. Next to her devotion to God, she loved her family fiercely and enjoyed many wonderful adventures with them. **GARY BRIAN SHARROCK** Fifth great grandson of progenitor Nicholas Kegg. **HENRY CLEVELAND SHARROCK** (1885 – 1906) son of Stephen and Almeda (Withers) Sharrock, married Bertha Mable Bubb with whom he was father of (1). **JANE ELVIRA SHARROCK** [5893] (1887 – 1970) aka Jennie", daughter of Stephen and Almeda (Withers) Sharrock, married Fayette Hyman Carsner with whom she was mother of (2). **JEFFREY W. SHARROCK** [5892C] (1962 – 2015) son of Richard and Catherine (Heck) Sharrock married Shelly A. Smith with whom he was father of (2). **JEFFREY W. SHARROCK** Seventh great grandson of progenitor Nicholas Kegg. **JEFFREY W. SHARROCK** Eighth great grandson of progenitor Nicholas Kegg. **KERRY K. SHARROCK** Seventh great grandson of progenitor Nicholas Kegg. **PAUL SYDNEY SHARROCK** [5894] (1905 – 1996) son of Henry and Bertha (Bubb) Sharrock, married Zoe Elaine McClure with whom he was father of (3). Paul retired from Bunting Brass and Bronze, Toledo, Ohio. **RICHARD EDWARD SHARROCK** [5895] (1937 – 1969) aka "Dick" son of Clarence and Flora (Hamilton) Sharrock married twice; first to Judith Rae Sesslar with whom he was father of (1). Later he married Catherine Adelia Heck with whom he was father of (2). Dick was an employee of Cascade Corp. and veteran of the Korean conflict. **STEPHEN HENRY SHARROCK** (1862 – 1942) son of Henry and Elvira (Cagg) Sharrock married twice; first to Almeda Withers with whom he was father of (2). Later, he married Rose B. Lowe with whom he was father of (1).

SHAUB

ANDREW SHAUB Seventh great grandson of progenitor Nicholas Kegg.
HAYLEY SHAUB Seventh great granddaughter of progenitor Nicholas Kegg.

[5892] p.7 Bellefontaine Examiner (OH) Mar 9, 1981, obtained by D. Sue Dible [5892A] Springfield News-Sun (OH) May 2, 2014 [5892B] Toledo Blade (OH) Feb 2, 2016 [5892C] Springfield News-Sun (OH) Dec. 4, 2015 [5893] Toledo Blade (OH) Nov 22, 1970 [5894] Orlando Sentinel (FL) June 12, 1996 [5895] Springfield Daily News (OH) Oct 9, 1969

SHAVER

MATTHEW RICHARD SHAVER Sixth great grandson of progenitor Nicholas Kegg.
MICHAEL C. SHAVER Sixth great grandson of progenitor Nicholas Kegg.

SHAW

RANDY SHAW Seventh great grandson of progenitor Nicholas Kegg.
SUSAN SHAW Seventh great granddaughter of progenitor Nicholas Kegg.

SHAWVER

MARTIN BLAINE SHAWVER Seventh great grandson of progenitor Nicholas Kegg.
SALLY SHAWVER Seventh great granddaughter of progenitor Nicholas Kegg.

SHEA

MALLORY SHEA Seventh great granddaughter of progenitor Nicholas Kegg.

SHECK

JO ANN WESLIE SHECK Sixth great granddaughter of progenitor Nicholas Kegg.
VICKI SHECK Sixth great granddaughter of progenitor Nicholas Kegg.

SHEEDER

JARROD MATTHEW SHEEDER Seventh great grandson of progenitor Nicholas Kegg.
JASON MICHAEL SHEEDER Seventh great grandson of progenitor Nicholas Kegg.
JEFFREY TYLER SHEEDER Seventh great grandson of progenitor Nicholas Kegg.
JOSHUA TODD SHEEDER Seventh great grandson of progenitor Nicholas Kegg.
PAYTON SHEEDER Eighth great granddaughter of progenitor Nicholas Kegg.

SHEETZ

JENNIFER M. SHEETZ aka "Jenny", Seventh great granddaughter of progenitor Nicholas Kegg.
MARY ANN SHEETZ [5896] (1957 – 2015) daughter of Charles and Margaret (Baum) Sheetz, married Homer Houston Garrison with whom she was mother of (2).

SHEFFEL

AMANDA SHEFFEL Eighth great granddaughter of progenitor Nicholas Kegg.

SHEFFIELD

ETHAN SHEFFIELD Seventh great grandson of progenitor Nicholas Kegg.

SHELEY

CHARLES SHELEY Fifth great grandson of progenitor Nicholas Kegg.
DELBERT LEROY SHELEY [5897] (1923 – 1992) son of Albert and Leila (Rice) Sheley, married Eleanor M. Smith with whom he was father of (3). Delbert was a veteran of World War II.

[5896] Collins Funeral Home, MD obtained by D. Sue Dible [5897] p.79 The Palm Beach Post (FL) May 13, 1992

DEWAYNE LOUIS SHELEY [5898] (1926 – 2004) son of Albert and Leila (Rice) Sheley married three times; first to Bonnie M. Miller with whom he was father of (2). He married Karen Diane Bender with whom he was father of (1). Later, he married Patricia Ann VanDuyl. Dewayne served in the U.S. Army in the Pacific Theater during WW II. He was a dispatcher at the Ligonier State Police Post and was employed with Farm Bureau Insurance Co. in the Fort Wayne area and retired after many years as a claims adjuster. **JEAN ANN SHELEY** Fifth great granddaughter of progenitor Nicholas Kegg. **JON SHELEY** Fifth great grandson of progenitor Nicholas Kegg. **KAREN DELAYNE SHELEY** Fifth great granddaughter of progenitor Nicholas Kegg. **MATTHEW DEWAYNE SHELEY** Fifth great grandson of progenitor Nicholas Kegg. **MELVERE DELYLE SHELEY** [5898A] aka "Mel" (1932 – 2017) son of Albert and Leila (Rice) Sheley married Carolyn Rose Caskey with whom he was father of (4). Mel retired after 42 years with B & O Railroad. He was an active member of the Bremen Methodist Church as many leaders. Mel cooked pancakes for C.R.O.P. and went on mission trips, including one trip to Ecuador. He was a "jack of all trades" for his church, family and friends. He enjoyed and donated much to the Bremen Historical Society and was instrumental in getting the depot moved and finished. Mel was a good husband, dad, and grandpa. He was usually teaching and playing with the grandchildren, and it usually had something to do with trains. He took them on many trips and train rides. His favorite food was a rare steak and butterscotch pie, but don't dare serve him potato soup! Instead give him chocolate, bologna or cheese. **SANDRA LOU SHELEY** Fifth great granddaughter of progenitor Nicholas Kegg. **SHEILA SHELEY** Fifth great granddaughter of progenitor Nicholas Kegg. **SUZANNE SHELEY** Fifth great granddaughter of progenitor Nicholas Kegg. **WILLIAM D. SHELEY** Fifth great grandson of progenitor Nicholas Kegg.

SHELHAMER

MISTY SHELHAMER Seventh great granddaughter of progenitor Nicholas Kegg.

SHELTON

BENJAMIN SHELTON Sixth great grandson of progenitor Nicholas Kegg.
JENNIFER SUE SHELTON aka "Jenny" Sixth great granddaughter of progenitor Nicholas Kegg.
JOHN SHELTON Sixth great grandson of progenitor Nicholas Kegg.

SHENEMAN

QUINN SHENEMAN Eighth great granddaughter of progenitor Nicholas Kegg.

SHEPHERD

MICHAEL SHEPHERD Sixth great grandson of progenitor Nicholas Kegg.

SHEPPARD

SAMUEL SHEPPARD Seventh great grandson of progenitor Nicholas Kegg.
XAVIER SHEPPARD Seventh great grandson of progenitor Nicholas Kegg.

SHERRARD

LYNN LAVAUGH SHERRARD Fifth great granddaughter of progenitor Nicholas Kegg.
NANCY LEE SHERRARD Fifth great granddaughter of progenitor Nicholas Kegg.

[5898] The Advanced Leader May 27, 2004 [5898A] The Pilot News (IN) Nov. 27, 2017

SHERRERD

AMY SHERRERD Sixth great granddaughter of progenitor Nicholas Kegg.
ANDREW SHERRERD Sixth great grandson of progenitor Nicholas Kegg.
CREW SHERRERD Sixth great grandson of progenitor Nicholas Kegg.
DREW SHERRERD Seventh great grandson of progenitor Nicholas Kegg.
JOSEPH SHERRERD Seventh great grandson of progenitor Nicholas Kegg.
MAX SHERRERD Seventh great grandson of progenitor Nicholas Kegg.

SHERWOOD

CONNER SHERWOOD Seventh great grandson of progenitor Nicholas Kegg.
GARRETT JAMES SHERWOOD Seventh great grandson of progenitor Nicholas Kegg.
GREGG HOWARD SHERWOOD Sixth great grandson of progenitor Nicholas Kegg.
JORDAN SHERWOOD Seventh great grandson of progenitor Nicholas Kegg.
MEGAN JO SHERWOOD Sixth great granddaughter of progenitor Nicholas Kegg.
WHITNEY SHERWOOD Seventh great granddaughter of progenitor Nicholas Kegg.

SHILLING

TAMBRIA KAYE SHILLING Seventh great granddaughter of progenitor Nicholas Kegg.
TIMOTHY ALLEN SHILLING Seventh great grandson of progenitor Nicholas Kegg.
TRACY FAY SHILLING Seventh great granddaughter of progenitor Nicholas Kegg.

SHIMER

BARBARA LOUISE SHIMER [5898B] (1948 – 2013) daughter of Gus and Rowena (Wyckoff) Shimer married Wayland Wesley Rupp with whom she was mother of (2). Barbara loved nature and had a very kind heart for all living things. She worked at various jobs but took most pride in being a mom and housewife for her family. Barb enjoyed music and played the piano very well. She also was the first chair saxophone player in the Bedford Dance Band. **BETTY MARDELLA SHIMER** Sixth great granddaughter of progenitor Nicholas Kegg. **JACLYN SHIMER** Seventh great granddaughter of progenitor Nicholas Kegg. **MICHAEL EDWIN SHIMER** Sixth great grandson of progenitor Nicholas Kegg. **NEIL SHIMER** Seventh great grandson of progenitor Nicholas Kegg.

SHINDLEDECK

LYNNETTE M. SHINDLEDECK Sixth great granddaughter of progenitor Nicholas Kegg.
TODD D. SHINDLEDECK Sixth great grandson of progenitor Nicholas Kegg.

SHIPLEY

TANYA MICHELLE SHIPLEY (1968 – 1968) daughter of Gary and Susan (Straub) Shipley.

SHIPPEY

JEFF SHIPPEY Sixth great grandson of progenitor Nicholas Kegg.
MARSHA SHIPPEY Seventh great granddaughter of progenitor Nicholas Kegg.
SUSAN SHIPPEY Sixth great granddaughter of progenitor Nicholas Kegg.

[5898B] Clarinda Herald-Journal (IA) Apr 4, 2013

SHIRK

AMBER SHIRK Sixth great granddaughter of progenitor Nicholas Kegg. **BRITTANY SHIRK** Sixth great granddaughter of progenitor Nicholas Kegg. **CINDY L. SHIRK** Fifth great granddaughter of progenitor Nicholas Kegg. **JAY SHIRK** Fifth great grandson of progenitor Nicholas Kegg. **KIMBERLY SHIRK** Fifth great granddaughter of progenitor Nicholas Kegg. **MARANDA SHIRK** Sixth great granddaughter of progenitor Nicholas Kegg. **PAMELA SHIRK** Fifth great granddaughter of progenitor Nicholas Kegg. **RONALD SHIRK** Fifth great grandson of progenitor Nicholas Kegg. **RONALD JAMES SHIRK** Sixth great grandson of progenitor Nicholas Kegg. **WAYNE EUGENE SHIRK** [5898C] (1964 – 2008) son of Wayne and Joan (Hipp) Shirk, married Carrie Lynn Reibel with whom he was father of (2). Wayne worked as a welder for Hydra-Fab and A-1 Fabrication. He enjoyed fishing, hunting and waterskiing.

SHIRLEY

LYLE WAYNE SHIRLEY (1927 – 1993) son of Herschel and Isabell (Nelson) Shirley.

SHOAF

MAKENNA GAIL SHOAF Eighth great granddaughter of progenitor Nicholas Kegg.
MEGAN SHOAF Eighth great granddaughter of progenitor Nicholas Kegg.

SHOCKLEE

JONATHAN SHOCKLEE Sixth great grandson of progenitor Nicholas Kegg.

SHOCKLEY

KATIE LYNETTE SHOCKLEY [5898D] (1998 – 2009) daughter of Lance and Dana (Huster) Shockley. Katie loved to hunt, fish and just be outdoors. She was loved by everyone who knew her.
KRISTA MARIE SHOCKLEY Seventh great granddaughter of progenitor Nicholas Kegg.

SHOEMAKER

ADA MARY SHOEMAKER [5899] (1887 – 1959) daughter of Henry and Margaret (Sollenberger) Shoemaker was mother of (2). She married twice, first to William Warfield Brant. Later, she married Howard Warren Simmons. Ada worked for several years as a practical nurse. **ALBERT RONALD SHOEMAKER** [5900] (1940 – 1979) son of Josiah and Grace (Reichwine) Shoemaker, married Paricia Ann (Burkey) Friend with whom he was father of (4). Albert was a 20-year veteran of the U.S. Air Force and served in Vietnam. **AMANDA LEISE SHOEMAKER** Fifth great granddaughter of progenitor Nicholas Kegg. **BARBARA ELLEN SHOEMAKER** [5901] (1914 – 1989) daughter of Job and Flora (Crissey) Shoemaker, married Harry A. Feather with whom she was mother of (2). Barbara was a former teller at the Schellsburg Bank and attended business colleges in both Cumberland and Harrisburg and the Pennsylvania School of Art in Philadelphia. Mrs. Feather was a retired federal government career secretary in Washington, D.C. She had been a member of the Sarasota Art Association and Garden Club and was a very active member of the First United Methodist Church in Sarasota. **BEATRICE S. SHOEMAKER** [5902] (1909 – 1995) daughter of John and Louise (Koontz) Shoemaker married James W. Perdew with whom she was mother of (3). Beatrice was a homemaker. She was formerly the owner and operator of Anchor Bar, Winter Haven.

[5898C] p.7A- Macomb Daily (MI) Aug 26, 2008, contributed by D. Sue Dible [5898D] Shreveport Times (LA) June 7, 2009 [5899] Bedford County Genealogical Society obituary obtained by D. Sue Dible [5900] Akron-Summit County Public Library obituary obtained by D. Sue Dible [5901] Bedford Inquirer (PA) April 7, 1989, obtained by D. Sue Dible [5902] Lakeland Ledger (FL) July 14, 1995

BENJAMIN CALVIN SHOEMAKER [5903] (1903 – 1966) son of John and Louise (Koontz) Shoemaker, married Jessie Beatrice Doyle. Benjamin was a retired truck driver for the Eastern Trucking Co. **BENJAMIN FRANKLIN SHOEMAKER** (1917 – 1990) son of Ada Mary Shoemaker married Sarah A. (Miller) Moore. **BETTY JANE SHOEMAKER** [5904] (1925 – 1927) two-year-old daughter of Carl and Edna (Growden) Shoemaker died the result of whooping cough. **BETTY JEAN SHOEMAKER** (1946 – 1946) daughter of Tom and Elizabeth (Isett) Shoemaker. **CALVIN SHOEMAKER** Fifth great grandson of progenitor Nicholas Kegg. **CARL MELVIN SHOEMAKER** [5905] (1895 – 1986) son of John and Louise (Koontz) Shoemaker married twice; first to Edna Sarah Growden with whom he was father of (3). Later, he married Bertha Fisher. Carl was a retired farmer in Friends Cove. **CAROLE SHOEMAKER** aka "Sally" Fourth great granddaughter of progenitor Nicholas Kegg. **CAROLYN LOUISE SHOEMAKER** [5905A] (1928 – 2017) daughter of Frederick and Laura (Shoemaker) Shoemaker married Donald William Browne with whom she was mother of (2). **CHARLES FLETCHER SHOEMAKER** (1910 – 1913) son of Simon and Sara Belle (Fletcher) Shoemaker. **CHARLES HOWARD SHOEMAKER** [5906] (1868 – 1904) son of Josiah and Barbara (Stuckey) Shoemaker was a member of the Independent Order of Odd Fellows and the Reformed church, Rainsburg. **CHARLES JAMES SHOEMAKER** Fourth great grandson of progenitor Nicholas Kegg. **CHARLOTTE VIRGINIA SHOEMAKER** (1858 – 1889) aka "Jennie", daughter of Josiah and Barbara (Stuckey) Shoemaker. **CHRISTOPHER SHOEMAKER** Fifth great grandson of progenitor Nicholas Kegg. **CLARENCE CHARLES SHOEMAKER** [5907] (1891 – 1944) son of William and Sarah (England) Shoemaker, married Ella Britton. Dr. C.C. Shoemaker was a well-known Johnstown optometrist and civic leader. He served 18 months overseas in World War I, later becoming an active member of the American Legion. During 1942 he headed the Cambria County Voiture No. 43 of the Forty and Eight as its chef de gar. He was also identified with the Johnstown Lions Club and the Bedford Masonic Lodge and was a member of St. John's Evangelical and Reformed Church. **CLYDE CALVIN SHOEMAKER** Fourth great grandson of progenitor Nicholas Kegg. **DALE E. SHOEMAKER** Fifth great grandson of progenitor Nicholas Kegg. **DAVID S. SHOEMAKER** Fourth great grandson of progenitor Nicholas Kegg. **DOROTHY LORRAINE SHOEMAKER** [5908] (1927 – 2016) daughter of Frederick and Anna (Hillegass) Shoemaker, married George Mark Fisher with whom she was mother of (2). Dorothy had a loving smile and great sense of humor. She was an accomplished pianist, loved gospel music, and regularly played and sang in church choirs. Dorothy had a long career in banking and retired from Frederick County National Bank in Frederick. As an Army wife she enjoyed travel and with her husband visited 49 states and many countries in Europe. **EDWARD PAUL SHOEMAKER** [5908A] (1952 – 1993) son of William and Pearl (Holler) Shoemaker received a degree in agricultural science from Penn State University. He was employed as a high school teacher. Edward served as staff sergeant with Army in Vietnam and had belonged to National Guard for 15 years. **ELSIE MAE SHOEMAKER** [5909] (1897 – 1994) daughter of John and Louise (Koontz) Shoemaker, married Walter Clyde Shaffer with whom she was mother of (2). Elsie was a former schoolteacher, having taught from 1915 to 1918 in several one room schools in Colerain Township. She was an active member of the Friends Cove United Church of Christ and the church's oldest member. She was a Sunday school teacher and a member of the Friendship Circle Class and Homewood Home Auxiliary in Martinsburg. She was a charter member of the Colerain Unit of the Memorial Hospital of Bedford County Auxiliary and worked as a snack bar volunteer for many years. She was an active member of Charlesville Grange 698, a Bedford County Grange member and a Seventh-Degree member. She was a member of the Bedford Springs Chapter of the Order of Eastern Star, a member of the Colerain Township School Board and was instrumental in the decision to build the Colerain Township Elementary School building. **EMELINE LOU SHOEMAKER** (1929 -?) daughter of Harold and Bernice (Hummel) Shoemaker.

[5903] Bedford Inquirer (PA) July 21, 1966, obtained by D. Sue Dible [5904] Bedford Gazette (PA) Feb 4, 1927, obtained by Connie Detar, contributed by Bob Rose [5905] Bedford Gazette (PA) June 19, 1986 [5905A] McCammon Ammons Click Funeral Home (TN) [5906] Bedford Gazette (PA) March 4, 1904 [5907] Bedford Gazette (PA) Dec 15, 1944, obtained by Connie Detar contributed by Bob Rose [5908] Bedford Gazette (PA) Aug 8, 2016, obtained by Bob Rose [5908A] Daily American (PA) March 8, 1993 [5909] Bedford Gazette (PA) Aug 22, 1994

EMILY ELLEN SHOEMAKER [5910] (1915 – 2005) daughter of Simon and Sara (Fletcher) Shoemaker, married Henry Peter Brandau with whom she was mother of (3). **FAYE SHOEMAKER** Fourth great granddaughter of progenitor Nicholas Kegg. **FLORA BELLE SHOEMAKER** [5911] (1900 – 1990) daughter of John and Louise (Koontz) Shoemaker, married G. Randolph Burkett with whom she was mother of (2). Flora was the bookkeeper for Burkett Motors, prior to 1952 she was a teacher in the Colerain Township Elementary School. **FLORENCE ELLEN SHOEMAKER** [5912] (1882 – 1926) daughter of Henry and Margaret (Sollenberger) Shoemaker, married Michael Ephraim Diehl with whom she was mother of (1). Florence was a member of the brick Reformed church. **FREDERICK ELLIS SHOEMAKER** [5913] (1894 – 1978) son of Henry and Margaret (Sollenberger) Shoemaker, married Laura M. Shoemaker with whom he was father of (2). Frederick formerly operated a drug store in Everett and was a retired construction worker. **GAIL SHOEMAKER** Fifth great granddaughter of progenitor Nicholas Kegg. **GEORGE ROY SHOEMAKER** [5914] (1878 – 1950) son of Henry and Margaret (Sollenberger) Shoemaker, married Estella T. Diehl with whom he was father of (2). George held membership in Friends Cove Zion Reformed church. **GRACE M. SHOEMAKER** [5915] (1906 – 1972) daughter of George and Estella (Diehl) Shoemaker was a member of the Protestant faith. **HAROLD JOSIAH SHOEMAKER** [5916] (1937 – 2010) aka "Buzz", son of Josiah and Grace (Reichwine) Shoemaker, married Mary Ann Giesey with whom he was father of (4). Buzz was an Army veteran and retired from Latrobe Steel with 37 years of service. Buzz was an avid golfer and member of Cooperstown Club and the American Legion. **HAROLD TAYLOR SHOEMAKER** [5917] (1902 – 1964) son of Josiah and Laura (Diehl) Shoemaker, married Mary Jane Martin with whom he was father of (2). Harold was employed as a driver by Continental Transportation Co. He was a member of the Moose Lodge, Latrobe, Bedford Post 113, and the American Legion. **HELEN EVELYN SHOEMAKER** [5918] (1928 – 2017) daughter of Kenneth and Marian (Beegle) Shoemaker married twice; first to William Walter Porter with whom she was mother of (1). Later, she married William Koontz. **HELEN L. SHOEMAKER** [5919] (1905 – 1993) daughter of John and Louise (Koontz) Shoemaker, was a registered nurse and attended St. John's United Methodist Church. **HENRY FRANKLIN SHOEMAKER** [5920, 5921] (1855 – 1922) son of Josiah and Barbara (Stuckey) Shoemaker, married Margaret Sollenberger with whom he was father of (7). Henry lived all his life on the farm on which he died. Henry was a good citizen, good neighbor, up-to-date farmer and a good businessman, served as Secretary of the School Board in Colerain Township, for many years. He was a member of the Reformed Church, a member of the P. O. S. of A. and also a member of the Sons of the American Revolution. **INFANT SHOEMAKER** (1906 – 1906) son of Josiah and Laura (Diehl) Shoemaker. **JACK F. SHOEMAKER** Fourth great grandson of progenitor Nicholas Kegg. **JAMES ELMER SHOEMAKER** [5922] (1905 – 1930) son of Simon and Sara (Fletcher) Shoemaker. **JAMES H. SHOEMAKER** Fifth great grandson of progenitor Nicholas Kegg. **JAMES ROBERT SHOEMAKER** [5923] (1916 – 1987) aka "Bob", son of Job and Flora (Crissey) Shoemaker, married Shirley L. Wicklund with whom he was father of (3). James was a World War II veteran, serving as a Sea Bee. While in Iwo Jima he was wounded and received the Purple Heart. As a heavy machine operator, he worked on road construction for several years in several states and also Cuba and Jamaica. Bob was employed at LTV Steel Corporation for 20 years before retiring. **JENNA SHOEMAKER** Fifth great granddaughter of progenitor Nicholas Kegg. **JENNIFER SHOEMAKER** Fifth great granddaughter of progenitor Nicholas Kegg. **JILL SHOEMAKER** Fifth great granddaughter of progenitor Nicholas Kegg. **JOB MILTON SHOEMAKER** [5924] (1872 – 1917) son of Josiah and Barbara (Stuckey) Shoemaker, married Flora V. Crissey with whom he was father of (4). Job was the Railway Postal clerk running between Altoona and Cumberland **JOHN CALVIN SHOEMAKER** [5925] (1865 – 1926) son of Josiah and Barbara (Stuckey) Shoemaker married Louise Jane

---

[5910] Pittsburgh Post-Gazette (PA) Feb 13, 2005 [5911] Bedford Inquirer (PA) Aug 17, 1990 [5912] Bedford County Historical Society obituary (PA) obtained by D. Sue Dible [5913] Altoona Genealogical Society obituary obtained by D. Sue Dible [5914] The Bedford Gazette (PA) July 14,1950 [5915] Bedford County Historical Society obituary (PA) obtained by D. Sue Dible [5916] Tribune Review (PA) Feb 19, 2010 [5917] Bedford County Genealogical Society obituary (PA) obtained by D. Sue Dible [5918] Bedford Gazette (PA) April 10, 2017, obtained by Bob Rose [5919] p.2 -Tampa Tribune (FL) March 30, 1993 [5920] Biographical Review Vol. XXXII Containing Life Sketches of Leading Citizens of Bedford and Somerset Counties Pennsylvania [5921] Bedford Gazette (PA) Jan 5, 1923 [5922] Bedford Gazette (PA) Sept 19, 1930 [5923] p.3 – Bedford Inquirer (PA) May 29, 1987 [5924] Bedford Gazette (PA) Aug 3, 1917 [5925] Bedford County Genealogical Society obituary (PA) obtained by D. Sue Dible

Koontz with whom he was father of (7). John was a prominent farmer of Friend's Cove. He was a member of Rainsburg Lodge I.O.O.F. **JOHN EUGENE SHOEMAKER** [5925A] aka "Gene" (1929 – 2017) son of Kenneth and Marian (Beegle) Shoemaker married Mary Elizabeth Boor with whom he was father of (1). Gene was a school bus driver for 55 years and during that time he became a school bus contractor for the Bedford Area School District. He enjoyed hunting and fishing. **JOHN HENRY SHOEMAKER** [5925B] (1948 – 2011) son of Tom and Elizabeth (Isett) Shoemaker married Cindy C. Shelton with whom he was father of (1). John graduated from the University of Miami, FL with a bachelor's degree in biology and chemistry. John earned his master's degree from East Texas State University. He worked as a science teacher for Beckville I.S.D. for many years. **JOHN MILTON SHOEMAKER** (1918 – 1918) son of Job and Flora (Crissey) Shoemaker. **JOHN W. SHOEMAKER** aka "Jack", Fourth great grandson of progenitor Nicholas Kegg. **JOSEPH CALVIN SHOEMAKER** [5926] (1928 – 1976) son of Samuel and Hattie (Diehl) Shoemaker, married Joyce Leighty with whom he was father of (2). Joseph worked as a painter at Mt. Summit Inn, in Uniontown. **JOSIAH ALBERT SHOEMAKER** [5927] (1907 – 1955) son of Josiah and Laura (Diehl) Shoemaker, married Grace Margaret Reichwine with whom he was father of (7). **JOSIAH PHILIP SHOEMAKER** [5928] (1874 – 1920) son of Josiah and Barbara (Stuckey) Shoemaker, married Laura Blanche Diehl with whom he was father of (3). **KENNETH SHOEMAKER** [5929] (1906 – 1985) aka "Jim", son of John and Louise (Koontz) Shoemaker, married Marian O. Beegle with whom he was father of (3). Jim was a retired farmer and had operated a school bus service for 40 years. He was a member of the Bedford Elks, Moose, American Legion and Bedford County Sportsman's Club. **KENNETH EARL SHOEMAKER** Fourth great grandson of progenitor Nicholas Kegg. **LAURA JEAN SHOEMAKER** Fourth great granddaughter of progenitor Nicholas Kegg. **LAURA MINNIE SHOEMAKER** [5930] (1864 – 1937) daughter of Josiah and Barbara (Stuckey) Shoemaker, married Judge William John Diehl with whom she was mother of (6). **LINDA SHOEMAKER** Fifth great granddaughter of progenitor Nicholas Kegg. **MARGARET A. SHOEMAKER** [5931] (1862 – 1929) aka "Maggie", daughter of Josiah and Barbara (Stuckey) Shoemaker, married John C. Koontz with whom she was mother of (3). **MARGARET DEAN SHOEMAKER** [5930A] aka "Peggy" (1922 – 2001) daughter of Ross and Martha (Huff) Shoemaker married Mr. Zuk, no children were born to this union. **MARTHA SHOEMAKER** [5932] (1936 – 2009) aka "Marty", daughter of Frederick and Anna (Hillegass) Shoemaker, married Elwin Eugene Biggins with whom she was mother of (3). Marty was a stay-at-home and day-care mom who liked to knit, crochet and travel in her RV. **MARY ALICE SHOEMAKER** [5933] (1856 – 1920) daughter of Josiah and Barbara (Stuckey) Shoemaker, married Charles Howard Morgart with whom she was mother of (1). Mary was born on the Old Shoemaker homestead now owned by her brothers and died from blood poison caused by infection from a small scratch just one week previous. Mary was from girlhood a member of the Reformed Church of Rainsburg but transferred her membership to the Presbyterian Church at Fort Wayne. **MARY VALERIA SHOEMAKER** [5934] (1913 – 2004) daughter of Job and Flora (Crissey) Shoemaker, married Donald Cress Reiley with whom she was mother of (4). Mary was a member of Daughters of the American Revolution. **MICHELLE SHOEMAKER** Fifth great granddaughter of progenitor Nicholas Kegg. **NELLIE BLANCHE SHOEMAKER** (1879 – 1916) daughter of Henry and Margaret Sollenberger) Shoemaker, married Joseph Grant Diehl with whom she was mother of (1). **NORMAN FREDERICK SHOEMAKER** [5935] (1924 – 2009) son of Frederick and Laura (Shoemaker) Shoemaker married twice, first to June E. Dodds. Later, he married Jacqueline Fick with whom he was father of (1). Norman worked for CSX Railroad and served proudly in the United States Navy. **PAUL F. SHOEMAKER** Fourth great grandson of progenitor Nicholas Kegg. **PHYLLIS LEONE SHOEMAKER** aka "Penny", Fourth great granddaughter of progenitor Nicholas Kegg.

[5925A] Bedford Gazette (PA) Nov 3, 2017 contributed by Bob Rose [5925B] Jimerson-Lipsey Funeral Home (TX) [5926] Altoona Genealogical Society (PA) obituary obtained by D. Sue Dible [5927] Bedford Gazette (PA) Sept 19, 1955 [5928] Bedford Gazette (PA) Feb 27, 1920 [5929] Bedford County Genealogical Society obituary (PA) obtained by D. Sue Dible [5930] Bedford Gazette (PA) Feb 23, 1912 [5930A] Bedford County Historical Society (PA), book 92, page 132 contributed by D. Sue Dible [5931] p.3 - Bedford Gazette (PA) March 11,1955 [5932] p.3 - Bedford Inquirer (PA) Jan 1, 2010, obtained by Bob Rose [5933] Bedford Gazette (PA) May 7, 1920, obtained by Bob Rose [5934] Bedford Inquirer (PA) Jul 2, 2004, obtained by Bob Rose [5935] Florida Times-Union (FL) Oct 4, 2009

ROBERT SHOEMAKER Sixth great grandson of progenitor Nicholas Kegg. **ROBERT CRISSEY SHOEMAKER** Fourth great grandson of progenitor Nicholas Kegg. **ROBERTA SHOEMAKER** Fifth great granddaughter of progenitor Nicholas Kegg. **ROBIN SUSAN SHOEMAKER** Fifth great granddaughter of progenitor Nicholas Kegg. **ROSS FRANKLIN SHOEMAKER** [5936] (1890 – 1976) son of Henry and Margaret (Sollenberger) Shoemaker, married Martha Blanche Huff with whom he was father of (2). Ross was a veteran of World War I. He was a pharmacist and had operated the Shoemaker Pharmacy in Bedford for 20 years. He was last employed by the Whelan Drug Company in Washington, D.C. **ROY EDWARD SHOEMAKER** Fourth great grandson of progenitor Nicholas Kegg. **RUTH REBECCA SHOEMAKER** [5937] (1902 – 1981) daughter of George and Estella (Diehl) Shoemaker, married Glenn Morris with whom she was mother of (1). Ruth was a retired waitress having worked at the Fort Bedford Inn in Bedford. **SAMUEL SHOEMAKER** Fifth great grandson of progenitor Nicholas Kegg. **SAMUEL VIRGIL SHOEMAKER** [5938] (1884 – 1977) son of Henry and Margaret (Sollenberger) Shoemaker married three times; first to Grace Ada Reighard. He then married Hattie May Diehl with whom he was father of (2). Later, he married Nora Edith (Shaffer) England. Samuel was a retired farmer. He was a member of St. John's United Church of Christ, Bedford Lodge F & AM, and the Harrisburg Consistory. **SCOTT SHOEMAKER** Fifth great grandson of progenitor Nicholas Kegg. **SIMON E. SHOEMAKER** [5939] (1870 – 1953) son of Josiah and Barbara (Stuckey) Shoemaker, married Sara Belle Fletcher with whom he was father of (4). **SUSAN G. SHOEMAKER** Fourth great granddaughter of progenitor Nicholas Kegg. **THOMAS REEDER SHOEMAKER** Fourth great grandson of progenitor Nicholas Kegg. **TOM LEROY SHOEMAKER** [5940] (1912 – 1990) son of Simon and Sara (Fletcher) Shoemaker, married Elizabeth Isett with whom he was father of (3). Tom was a retired chemist for U.S. Steel Corp. He also was a consultant for the Mellon Institute. Tom was a member of the Edgewood Club, the Swissvale Senior Center and the American Chemical Society. **TOM LEROY SHOEMAKER** [5941] (1944 – 1964) son of Tom and Elizabeth (Isett) Shoemaker. **WILLARD JAMES SHOEMAKER** [5942] (1912 – 1996) later, spelled as Shumaker aka "Pete", son of Ada Mary Shoemaker married twice, first to Mary Lou Weaver with whom he was father of (1). Later, he married Jewel Cort Lucas. Pete was a U.S. Army veteran of World War II. Owner of S & A Chevrolet of Somerset; partner of the former Downtowner Motor Hotel of Johnstown; director of GTE for 26 years and a member and past president of Somerset Country Club. **WILLIAM SHOEMAKER** aka "Tommy", Seventh great grandchild of progenitor Nicholas Kegg. **WILLIAM A. SHOEMAKER** [5942A] aka "Bill" (1924 – 2014) son of Frederick and Anna (Hillegass) Shoemaker married Pearl Holler with whom he was father of (4). As an owner of Maple Cove Farms, Bill was a lifelong dairy farmer and maple syrup producer. He was very proud of being a third generation Bedford County maple syrup producer and continuing this family tradition to the fourth generation. He was a lifelong member of the Milligan's Cove Christian Church and served on the Church's Cemetery Association for many years. He served 40 years as a board director with Bedford County Farm Bureau and was a long-standing member of the Pennsylvania Farm Bureau Association. **WILLIAM E. SHOEMAKER** Fifth great grandson of progenitor Nicholas Kegg. **WILLIAM E. SHOEMAKER** [5943] (1860 – 1944) son of Josiah and Barbara (Stuckey) Shoemaker, married Sarah Elizabeth England with whom he was father of (2). William was engaged in farming and owned a general store in Rainsburg for many years. Later he moved to Bedford and formed a business partnership, which was known as the Guyer & Shoemaker Clothing Company. After retiring from business William served for a time as clerk for the Pennsylvania and Washington Hotels in Maryland. **WILLIAM HUMMEL SHOEMAKER** (1939 – 2001) son of Harold and Bernice (Hummel) Shoemaker.

[5936] Altoona Genealogical Society (PA) obituary obtained by D. Sue Dible [5937] p.3 - Bedford Inquirer (PA) July 10, 1981 [5938] Altoona Genealogical Society (PA) obituary obtained by D. Sue Dible [5939] p.2 - Bedford Gazette (PA) Feb 12, 1953 [5940] p.D24 -Pittsburgh Post-Gazette (PA) July 15, 1990 [5941] p.24 Pittsburgh Press (PA) June 19, 1964 [5942] Meyersdale Library obituary contributed by Richard Boyer [5942A] Bedford Gazette (PA) July 22, 2014, contributed by Bob Rose [5943] p.16 - Cumberland Evening Times (MD) Jan 21, 1944

SHOENTHAL

BARBARA LYNNE SHOENTHAL Fourth great granddaughter of progenitor Nicholas Kegg.
CATHERINE HELENA SHOENTHAL (1949 – 2009) daughter of Henry and Helena (Potts) Shoenthal. **DANIEL P. SHOENTHAL** Fifth great grandson of progenitor Nicholas Kegg.
DAVID W. SHOENTHAL Fifth great grandson of progenitor Nicholas Kegg. **DORIS LUCILLE SHOENTHAL** [5944] (1922 – 1996) daughter of William and Maud (Blackburn) Shoenthal, married Albert Wayne Wingard. Doris was a member of the New Paris United Methodist Church and the Colonial Dames, Bedford Manor Chapter. **HENRY WILLIAM SHOENTHAL** [5945] (1911 – 1996) son of William and Maud (Blackburn) Shoenthal, married Helena Catherine Potts with whom he was father of (2). Henry was a graduate of Juniata College and a former member of the Chestnut Ridge Area School Board. He owned and operated Shoenthal's Store in New Paris for more than 60 years.
HENRY WILLIAM SHOENTHAL Fourth great grandson of progenitor Nicholas Kegg.
LORRAINE ELEANOR SHOENTHAL [5946] (1947 – 2005) daughter of William and Emma (Schilling) Shoenthal, married Dr. Robert P. Beeman with whom she was mother of (2). Lorraine retired from Three Mile Island Nuclear Station as a Nuclear Chemist. She was a member of the Bedford United Methodist Church, the United Methodist Women, a life member of BMW Motorcycle Owners of America, BMW Riders Assoc., Vintage BMW Motorcycle Owners, life member of the National RifleAssociation, the Daughters of the American Revolution, and was a holder of a long distance award for 130,000 miles operating a BMW motorcycle. **RENNE L. SHOENTHAL** Fifth great granddaughter of progenitor Nicholas Kegg. **WILLIAM JAMES SHOENTHAL** [5946A] (1914 – 2001) son of William and Maud (Blackburn) Shoenthal married twice, first to Emma Barbara Schilling with whom he was father of (3), later to Marlene Joyce Pyatt. William was a family physician in New Hope for 35 years before retiring. Previously, he was a general practitioner in New Paris, Bedford County for six years.
WILLIAM JAMES SHOENTHAL aka "Jimmy" Fourth great grandson of progenitor Nicholas Kegg

SHOLL

CAMILLE SHOLL Seventh great granddaughter of progenitor Nicholas Kegg. **FLORENCE DORINE SHOLL** [5946B] (1911 – 1990) daughter of Joseph and Clarinda (Wise) Sholl married Raymond Edward Tuttle with whom she was mother of (2). Florence was a teacher at Hicksville Elementary School and worked as Librarian at Hicksville Public Library for many years. **GERALD JOSEPH SHOLL** [5946C] aka "Gary" (1939 – 2023) son of Joseph and Opal C. (Shull) Sholl married Ellen Jeanette Conley with whom he was father of (2). A high school running back star for the Aces, Gary broke many school records. He earned player of the week on multiple occasions. After graduation, Gary had an opportunity to continue playing football at Defiance College on scholarship but decided to enter the workforce. While pursuing the construction industry, Gary was able to continue his athletic career by playing a few seasons for the Fort Wayne Tigers semi-pro football team. Gary started Sholl Construction and successfully ran the business for 21 years, building over 200 structures in the tri-county area, with notable projects including Sholl Terrace, Brown Funeral Home, and private residences. While running his construction business, Gary owned and operated the Hicksville Lumber Yard for five years. Gary was a 35-year member of the Carpenters Union Local 232, and a 30-year member of the Hicksville Eagles Aerie #2556. In addition to his love of football and construction, Gary enjoyed the time spent at their family cottage.
GWENDOLYN JOYCE SHOLL Sixth great granddaughter of progenitor Nicholas Kegg. **JEANNE A. SHOLL** Sixth great granddaughter of progenitor Nicholas Kegg. **JOSEPH D. SHOLL** [5946D] (1969 – 2012) son of Gary and Ellen (Conley) Sholl was father of (2). Joseph was employed by ISI at Steel Dynamics in Butler, Indiana. He was a member of the Toledo Boilermakers Union. He loved yard work, gardening spending time with his children and caring for his four German shepherd dogs.

[5944] Duke Clark Bedford County (PA) obituary collection [5945] p.3 - Bedford Inquirer (PA) Dec 27, 1996 [5946] p.8 – Bedford Inquirer (PA) Sept 16, 2005 [5946A] Morning Call (PA) Aug 4, 2001 [5946B] p.5 - Defiance Crescent News (OH) Aug 25, 1990, contributed by D. Sue Dible [5946C] The Bryan Times (OH) Jan 24, 2023 [5946D] Defiance Crescent News (OH) Feb 28, 2012

JOSEPH GERALD SHOLL (5946E) (1912 – 1994) son of Joseph and Clarinda (Wise) Sholl married Opal C. Shull with whom he was father of (2). Joseph was a farmer, in the restaurant business, a carpenter, cabinet maker and a building contractor. A U.S. Navy veteran of World War II. He was a member of the VFW, American Legion and Hicksville Eagles   **JOSIE ELLEN SHOLL** Seventh great granddaughter of progenitor Nicholas Kegg.   **KARL WILHELM SHOLL** (5946F) (1896 – 1962) son of Joseph and Clarinda (Wise) Sholl. Karl entered the U.S. Navy in 1917 at Yorktown, Va, and served as a musician until his discharge in 1919. He was a barber in Hicksville until retiring.   **LORI SHOLL** Sixth great granddaughter of progenitor Nicholas Kegg.   **MARGARET E. SHOLL** Sixth great granddaughter of progenitor Nicholas Kegg   **MAURICE CLAIR SHOLL** (5946G) (1926 – 2006) son of Maurice and Freda (Maxwell) Sholl married Betty Laura Jackson with whom he was father of (4). Maurice served his country in the Army Air Corps and was honorably discharged Nov. 27, 1945. He began a long and Successful career centered around his love of nature by working as a game warden for the State of Ohio. Later, he worked for the US. Forest Service as a Ranger and Wildlife Biologist. Maurice actively pursued his interests in golfing, fishing, hunting gardening, and bird watching. An avid woodworker, he built countless pieces of furniture and home décor for family and friends.   **MICHAEL LOVEJOY SHOLL** Seventh great grandson of progenitor Nicholas Kegg.   **NORMAN LEE SHOLL** (5946H) (1927 – 1997) son of Maurice and Freda (Maxwell) Sholl worked as an electronic salesman for Lakeland Electronic Supply. He enjoyed traveling, especially air travel, and his daily stop at the Lone Pine Restaurant. **RORY SHOLL** Seventh great grandson of progenitor Nicholas Kegg.   **RYAN SINCLAIR SHOLL** (5947) (1977 – 2001) son of Daniel and Anne (Manion) Sholl, worked at Albertson's and Godfather's Pizza.

SHOLTIS

ASHLEY NICOLE SHOLTIS Seventh great granddaughter of progenitor Nicholas Kegg.
EVAN B. SHOLTIS Seventh great grandson of progenitor Nicholas Kegg.

SHONTERE

BRANDON SHONTERE (5948) (1987 – 2020) son of Duane and Valerie Jean (Lofland) Shontere loved fishing and spending time outdoors. Brandon loved drawing, animals and enjoyed listening to music.
MINDY S. SHONTERE Seventh great granddaughter of progenitor Nicholas Kegg.

SHOOK

CANDACE MAE SHOOK Seventh great granddaughter of progenitor Nicholas Kegg.   **H. RUDOLF SHOOK** (5949) (1912 – 1979) son of James and Nellie (Kerr) Shook was employed as a clerk by the Pennsylvania Department of Assistance for 30 years before retiring.   **HARLYN CHRISTOPER SHOOK** Seventh great grandson of progenitor Nicholas Kegg. **JAMES AMBROSE SHOOK** (5950) (1915 – 1983) son of James and Nellie (Kerr) Shook married Joan Lenore Eisenberg.
JUSTUS ALEXANDER SHOOK Seventh great grandson of progenitor Nicholas Kegg.
KRESSA MARIE SHOOK Seventh great granddaughter of progenitor Nicholas Kegg.
S. ELIZABETH SHOOK (5951) (1918 – 1993) daughter of James and Nellie (Kerr) Shook, married Rocco Richard Palmisano with whom she was mother of (2).

SHORT

WILLIAM THEODORE SHORT Sixth great grandson of progenitor Nicholas Kegg.

(5947) Portland Oregonian (OR) Apr 27, 2001 (5948) The News Star (LA) July 23, 2020 (5949) Reading Eagle (PA) Apr 9, 1979 (5950) The Philadelphia Inquirer (PA) Oct 28, 1953 (5951) p.14 - Cape Gazette (DE) July 9, 1993

SHOTT

JOANNA D. SHOTT Sixth great granddaughter of progenitor Nicholas Kegg.
JULIE D. SHOTT Sixth great granddaughter of progenitor Nicholas Kegg.

SHOWALTER

BRYCE D. SHOWALTER Eighth great grandson of progenitor Nicholas Kegg.
EVAN J. SHOWALTER Eighth great grandson of progenitor Nicholas Kegg.
SHANNON RICHARD SHOWALTER Seventh great grandson of progenitor Nicholas Kegg.

SHRADER

DAVID ALAN SHRADER Fifth great grandson of progenitor Nicholas Kegg. **KAIYA SHRADER** Sixth great granddaughter of progenitor Nicholas Kegg. **LORA ELIZABETH SHRADER** Fifth great granddaughter of progenitor Nicholas Kegg. **TES SHRADER** Sixth great granddaughter of progenitor Nicholas Kegg. **WALTER JOHN SHRADER** Fifth great grandson of progenitor Nicholas Kegg.

SHRINER

DARL LYNN SHRINER Fifth great grandson of progenitor Nicholas Kegg.
DAWN MARIE SHRINER (1983 – 1988) daughter of Daryl and Diana (Kumrow) Shriner.
DEREK MATTHEW SHRINER Sixth great grandson of progenitor Nicholas Kegg.
DUSTIN MICHAEL SHRINER Sixth great grandson of progenitor Nicholas Kegg.
REBECCA ANN SHRINER Fifth great granddaughter of progenitor Nicholas Kegg.

SHRIVASTAVA

LILA SHRIVASTAVA Seventh great granddaughter of progenitor Nicholas Kegg.
SADIE SHRIVASTAVA Seventh great granddaughter of progenitor Nicholas Kegg.

SHRIVER

CAMREN SHRIVER Seventh great grandson of progenitor Nicholas Kegg. **GRACIE SHRIVER** Seventh great granddaughter of progenitor Nicholas Kegg. **JANET MARIE SHRIVER** Fifth great granddaughter of progenitor Nicholas Kegg. **MARYN SHRIVER** Seventh great granddaughter of progenitor Nicholas Kegg. **NOAH SHRIVER** Seventh great grandson of progenitor Nicholas Kegg.
LIVIA ELIZABETH SHRIVER aka "Liv", Seventh great granddaughter of progenitor Nicholas Kegg.
PATRICIA YVONNE SHRIVER Fifth great granddaughter of progenitor Nicholas Kegg.
ROBERT WILLIAM SHRIVER aka Bobby", Fifth great grandson of progenitor Nicholas Kegg.
ROBERT WILLIAM SHRIVER aka Robby", Sixth great grandson of progenitor Nicholas Kegg.
TIMOTHY SCOTT SHRIVER aka Timmy", Sixth great grandson of progenitor Nicholas Kegg.

SHROCK

ALBERT LYNN SHROCK Fifth great grandson of progenitor Nicholas Kegg. **CALVIN DEAN SHROCK** Fifth great grandson of progenitor Nicholas Kegg. **CECELIA SHROCK** [5952] (1949 – 2011) aka "Mary", daughter of Cecil and Mary (Metcalf) Shrock married James Woods with whom she was mother of (4). Cecelia had been employed as an activity's director for Quail Ridge Nursing Home, West Siloam Springs, Oklahoma. **CECIL CLEDITH SHROCK** (1917 – 2011) son of James and

[5952] Westside Eagle Observer (AR) Jan 19, 2011

Agnes (Smith) Shrock, married Mary Alice (Metcalf) Chapman with whom he was father of (3). **DENVER WILLIAM SHROCK** Sixth great grandson of progenitor Nicholas Kegg. **ETHEL BEULAH SHROCK** [5953] (1888 – 1974) daughter of Samuel and Ida (Kegg) Shrock was employed in the payroll department of Glen Alden Coal Co. prior to retirement and was a member of the Seventh Day Adventist Church. **GENEVA M. SHROCK** [5954] (1882 – 1974) daughter of Samuel and Ida (Kegg) Shrock was employed as an instructor at the International Correspondence Schools for 54 years, before retiring. She was a member of the Seventh Day Adventist Church. **HAZEL EDITH SHROCK** [5955] (1891 – 1983) daughter of Samuel and Ida (Kegg) Shrock, married Elmer Wilson Johnson with whom she was mother of (2). Hazel was a member of the Prospect Street Presbyterian Church, Trenton. **HOPE GLENNA SHROCK** [5956] (1883 – 1913) daughter of Joseph and Mina (Graham) Shrock, married William Jesse Fairchild with whom she was mother of (2). When fourteen years of age Hope was baptized and united with the Seventh-day Adventist church at Ligonier. Hope was an active Christian worker from the days of her childhood. **JAMES HARVEY SHROCK** [5957] (1879 – 1966) son of Joseph and Mina (Graham) Shrock, married Agnes Smith with whom he was father of (4). Over 30 years of his life were spent in teaching, and many former students will remember him as the one who led them to Christ. **LOREITTA MARIE SHROCK** Fifth great granddaughter of progenitor Nicholas Kegg. **LORETA MAY SHROCK** (1923 – 1923) daughter of James and Agnes (Smith) Shrock. **THELMA DELORES SHROCK** (1915 – 1952) daughter of James and Agnes (Smith) Shrock. **WAYNE SHROCK** Fifth great grandson of progenitor Nicholas Kegg. **WAYNE CEDRICK SHROCK** [5958] (1924 – 1979) son of James and Agnes (Smith) Shrock married twice; first to Marjorie Lucille Metzker with whom he was father of (3). Later, he married Phyllis. **WILLIAM HARVEY SHROCK** [5959] (1945 – 2010) son of Cecil and Mary (Metcalf) Shrock was father of (1).

SHROYER

RACHEL SHROYER Eighth great granddaughter of progenitor Nicholas Kegg.
RANDALL SHROYER Eighth great grandson of progenitor Nicholas Kegg.

SHUFFIELD

KRISTIN LEIGH SHUFFIELD Seventh great granddaughter of progenitor Nicholas Kegg.

SHUSS

BETSY M. SHUSS Sixth great granddaughter of progenitor Nicholas Kegg. **DAN SHUSS** Seventh great grandson of progenitor Nicholas Kegg. **DANIEL R. SHUSS** Sixth great grandson of progenitor Nicholas Kegg. **DANIELLE SHUSS** Seventh great granddaughter of progenitor Nicholas Kegg. **MARK EDWARD SHUSS** Sixth great grandson of progenitor Nicholas Kegg. **SAMUEL J. SHUSS** Sixth great grandson of progenitor Nicholas Kegg. **STEVEN A. SHUSS** Sixth great grandson of progenitor Nicholas Kegg.

SHUMAKER

VICKI LU SHUMAKER (1950 – 1950) daughter of William and Mary Lou (Weaver) Shumaker.

SICKELS

CHRISTI LAVON SICKELS Sixth great granddaughter of progenitor Nicholas Kegg.
CYNTHIA SUSAN SICKELS, aka "Cindy", Sixth great granddaughter of progenitor Nicholas Kegg.

[5953] p.5 The Tribune (Scranton, PA) Aug 22, 1974 [5954] p.5 The Tribune (Scranton, PA) Feb 20, 1974 [5955] p.C3 Trenton Evening Times (NJ) Apr 19, 1983 [5956] p.6 - Lake Union Herald (MI) April 9, 1913 [5957] p.13 - Southern Tidings (GA) Sept 30, 1966 [5958] p. 15 - Lake Union Herald March 20, 1979 [5959] p.37 - Southwestern Union Record March 2010

DEBRA KAY SICKELS Sixth great granddaughter of progenitor Nicholas Kegg. **DIANE SICKELS** Sixth great granddaughter of progenitor Nicholas Kegg. **DOROTHY REXINE SICKELS** [5960] (1924 – 1987) daughter of Sherman and Fern Mildred (Wehrle) Sickels, married Richard E. Mosier with whom she was mother of (3). Dorothy worked during the war years at Buckley Airfield in Denver, then at the First National Bank in Denver. Later, Dorothy ran a day care center for over 20 years. **JEFFREY J. SICKELS** Sixth great grandson of progenitor Nicholas Kegg. **JOHN KEITH SICKELS** [5961] (1926 – 2016) son of Rex and Mildred (Wehrle) Sickels married twice, first to Norma Lee Bailey with whom he was father of (6) later to Juanita Beth Hacker. John spent his whole life on the farm raising crops, hogs, and cattle. He also had his own bulldozing business, Sickels Dozing, that he operated while farming. John loved working the soil, whether it be farming or doing dozer work. **LANA SICKELS** Sixth great granddaughter of progenitor Nicholas Kegg. **LAVONE KAY SICKELS** Fifth great granddaughter of progenitor Nicholas Kegg. **LELAND REX SICKELS** [5961A] (1932 – 2011) son of Sherman and Fern Mildred (Wehrle) Sickels, married Merylin Paist with whom he was father of (1). Leland served in the United States Army and was stationed in Germany in 1953. He loved farming, the mountains, and heavy machinery. **LESA SICKELS** Sixth great granddaughter of progenitor Nicholas Kegg. **LORA SICKELS** Sixth great granddaughter of progenitor Nicholas Kegg. **MARTHA LEA SICKELS** Fifth great granddaughter of progenitor Nicholas Kegg. **SAMUEL CHRIS SICKELS** [5961B] aka "Sam" (1928 – 2012) son of Rex and Mildred (Wehrle) Sickels married Evelyn Brown with whom he was father of (3). Sam was a gentle, kind, understanding and honest man. He served his country during the Korean Conflict in the United States Army. He was stationed at Kempo Airfield in South Korea as a radio operator. Sam chose farming as his occupation. He loved nature and God's world. Great pride was put into his farming. He thoroughly enjoyed his livestock, clean farm fields and high yields of crops. Sam wanted to leave the land he farmed better than when he started. He had a strong belief that man was just a steward of the land. **SHELLY SUZANNE SICKELS** Sixth great granddaughter of progenitor Nicholas Kegg. **SHIRLEY SUE SICKELS** [5161C] (1936 – 2014) daughter of Rex and Mildred (Wehrle) Sickels married twice, first to Bill Roberts with whom she was mother of (2). Later, she married Corwin Karr with whom she was mother of (3). Shirley was a homemaker until the children started school. She got a job at the Cap Factory. Then later in life she did mending and sewing in her home. **VICKI LYNN SICKELS** Sixth great granddaughter of progenitor Nicholas Kegg. **ZANE SICKELS** Seventh great grandson of progenitor Nicholas Kegg.

SICKLES

DYLAN SICKLES Seventh great grandson of progenitor Nicholas Kegg.
MADDISYN BAILLEY SICKLES aka "Maddy" Seventh great granddaughter of progenitor Nicholas Kegg.

SIDDERS

ASHELYN SIDDERS Eighth great granddaughter of progenitor Nicholas Kegg. **AUDREY ELIZABETH SIDDERS** Seventh great granddaughter of progenitor Nicholas Kegg. **AUSTIN WESLEY SIDDERS** Seventh great grandson of progenitor Nicholas Kegg. **BARBARA FAYE SIDDERS** (1910 – 1979) daughter of Samuel Martin and Edna (Sheldon) Sidders, married James Robert Barkley with whom she was mother of (7). Later she married Mr. Britton. **BENJAMIN DAVID SIDDERS** Seventh great grandson of progenitor Nicholas Kegg. **BEULAH FRANCIS SIDDERS** (1892 – 1949) daughter of Harry and Amelia (Piercy) Sidders, married Carl Philip Granere with whom she was mother of (1). **BEVERLY KAY SIDDERS** Fifth great granddaughter of progenitor Nicholas Kegg. **BLANCHE SIDDERS** (1892 – 1949) daughter of Harry and Amelia (Piercy) Sidders, married Faye Harley McCay with whom she was mother of (1). Later, she married Ray Calvin Amick.

[5960] Mount Ayr Record-News transcription by Sharon R. Becker IAGENWEB [5961] Mount Ayr Record News (IA) Aug 3, 2016 [5961A] News Press Now (IA) May 22, 2011 [5961B] Mount Ayr Record News (IA) Aug 8, 2012 [5961C] Mount Ayr Record News (IA) May 7, 2014

BRIAN ROBERT SIDDERS Seventh great grandson of progenitor Nicholas Kegg. **BRYANNA MECHEL SIDDERS** Seventh great granddaughter of progenitor Nicholas Kegg. **CARL SIDDERS** Fourth great grandson of progenitor Nicholas Kegg. **CARL BERDETT SIDDERS** (1908 – 1973) son of Samuel Martin and Edna (Sheldon) Sidders, married Agnes Leona Zirger with whom he was father of (1). **CHARLETTA MAYE SIDDERS** [5962] (1878 – 1959) aka "Charity' or "Chat" daughter of Joseph and Blanche (Laird) Sidders, married Noah Marion Warnstaff with whom she was mother of (3). **CORDELIA SIDDERS** Fifth great granddaughter of progenitor Nicholas Kegg. **DALE VERNON SIDDERS** Sixth great grandson of progenitor Nicholas Kegg. **DALLAS NEAL SIDDERS** Fifth great grandson of progenitor Nicholas Kegg. **DANIEL LYNDEL SIDDERS** Sixth great grandson of progenitor Nicholas Kegg. **DANIELLE ELIZABTH SIDDERS** Seventh great granddaughter of progenitor Nicholas Kegg. **DANNY RAY SIDDERS** Sixth great grandson of progenitor Nicholas Kegg. **DANNY RAY SIDDERS JR.** [5963] (1969 – 2022) son of Danny and Elaine (Galik) Sidders married Robyn N. Jones was a disgraced former police officer from Florida with a history of domestic violence was shot and killed in the home of his former girlfriend after he defied two protective orders filed against him. **DAVID RAY SIDDERS** Seventh great grandson of progenitor Nicholas Kegg. **DAVID WATSON SIDDERS** Sixth great grandson of progenitor Nicholas Kegg. **DEAN ARDEN SIDDERS** Fifth great grandson of progenitor Nicholas Kegg. **DEANNA SIDDERS** Sixth great granddaughter of progenitor Nicholas Kegg. **DEJUAN SIDDERS** Sixth great grandson of progenitor Nicholas Kegg. **DELFORD HAROLD SIDDERS** aka "Del" (1916 – 2004) son of Samuel and Edna Arabelle (Sheldon) Sidders married Lena Mae Griffin with whom he was father of (3). **DUANE NEAL SIDDERS** Sixth great grandson of progenitor Nicholas Kegg. **EARL EVERITT SIDDERS** (1908 - 1910) son of William and Carrie Edith (Poland) Sidders. **EMILY ANN SIDDERS** Seventh great granddaughter of progenitor Nicholas Kegg. **ERLINE W SIDDERS** Third great grandson of progenitor Nicholas Kegg. **FRANCES ETHEL SIDDERS** (1898 – 1969) daughter of Samuel Martin and Edna (Sheldon) Sidders, married Luther Curtis weeks with whom she was mother of (3). Later, she married Henry Heyen. **FRANK JAMES SIDDERS** [5964] (1883 – 1954) son of Joseph and Blanche (Laird) Sidders married Nellie Roseberry. Later he married Flossie Ann Babb. **FRED MELVIN SIDDERS** (1921 – 1995) son of Samuel Martin and Edna (Sheldon) Sidders married Dorris J. Magill. **GAIL M SIDDERS** Fifth great granddaughter of progenitor Nicholas Kegg. **GARY LEE SIDDERS** Sixth great grandson of progenitor Nicholas Kegg. **GARY LEE SIDDERS JR.** [5965] (1971 – 2020) son of Gary and Eileen (Mahoney) Sidders married Amy Marie Stevens with whom he was father of (2). Gary's personality was a unique one with his smart aleck comments and dad jokes. He was loved by everyone. The love for his wife was unmatched, and he never let her forget it. Gary strived for the happiness of his family and did it selflessly. He was the man who would take it as a challenge to get his daughter to Broadway just because she said she would never see Harry Potter and the Cursed Child. He was the man who would nod his head and pretend he knew about science to bond with his eldest daughter. Gary constantly taught his daughters how to rule the world and work hard for their futures. **GLADYS AGNES SIDDERS** [5966] (1894 – 1955) daughter of Samuel Martin and Edna (Sheldon) Sidders, married Virgil Everett Speicher with whom she was mother of (3). **GREGORY DEAN SIDDERS** Sixth great grandson of progenitor Nicholas Kegg. **HARRY ELLSWORTH SIDDERS** [5967] (1865 – 1948) son of Joseph and Blanche (Laird) Sidders, married Amelia Frances Piercy with whom he was father of (3). **HEATHER SIDDERS** Sixth great granddaughter of progenitor Nicholas Kegg. **HELEN LOUISE SIDDERS** [5968] (1913 – 2000) daughter of Laird and Ina Belle (Fitzgerald) Sidders, married Roy Miles Bishop with whom she was mother of (4). **HERBERT C SIDDERS** (1880 -1880) son of Joseph and Blanche (Laird) Sidders. **IVA JEAN SIDDERS** Sixth great granddaughter of progenitor Nicholas Kegg. **JACQUELYN MARIE SIDDERS** Seventh great granddaughter of progenitor Nicholas Kegg. **JENIFER KAY SIDDERS** Sixth great granddaughter of progenitor Nicholas Kegg. **JERRY RAY SIDDERS** Sixth great grandson of progenitor Nicholas Kegg. **JO ANN SIDDERS** (1935 – 1984)

[5962] La Grande Observer (OR) Oct 22, 1959 [5963] Washington Examiner (DC) March 2, 2022 [5964] Nance County Journal (NE) March 18, 1954 [5965] Baldwin Fairchild Funeral Home (Altamonte Springs, FL) [5966] Northwest Oklahoman and Ellis County News (OK) Jan 28, 1955 [5967] The Nance County Journal (NE) Feb 12, 1948 [5968] Grand Island Independent (NE) Oct 29, 2000

boxer Tommy Morrison along with participating in Men's League Hockey while living in the Tulsa, OK area. **VIRGIL LEWIS SIDDERS** (1914 – 1984) son of Samuel Martin and Edna (Sheldon) Sidders married Ila Faye Bodenheimer with whom he was father of (3). **WILLA DEL SIDDERS** [5984] (1934 – 2019) daughter of Vernon William and Iva (Waggoner) Sidders married Robert Charles Freelend with whom she was mother of (4). Willa taught school in rural Merrick County District. During the summer, she traveled to Washington D.C. to work for the FBI. Willa loved teaching but took some time off to focus on her children. It wasn't long before she returned to work part time in an insurance office and eventually leading to real estate in 1968 freeing her to be on call and allowing her to work at home and in the greenhouses. She joined Central Farm Development Co., became a partner, and eventually bought it out and it became Central Realty and Insurance. Willa went on to manage Central City Housing Authority. Willa volunteered as a 4-H Leader for years, taught Red Cross Swimming from 1956 until the late 60's, Red Cross Director, Jr. Women's Club, instrumental in creating Lone Tree Park, Litzenberg Hospital Pink Lady, Sunday School teacher, Organist, Layreader, School Board, Industrial Steering Committee, Educational Advisory Committee, Chamber Vice President, Chamber President, Merrick County Ag and Industrial President, Housing Coordinator, Fitness Center Board Member for 10 years, Fine Arts Center proponent, Merrick County Entertainment Group, Central Nebraska Housing Authority Board, City Council, PEO Chapter AB, and a Teammates Member. **WILLIAM LEWIS SIDDERS** [5985] (1873 – 1948) son of Joseph and Blanche (Laird) Sidders married Carrie Edith Poland with whom he was father of (5). William spent most of his life engaged in farming. **YVONNE LENORA SIDDERS** Fifth great granddaughter of progenitor Nicholas Kegg.

SIEMENS

BRACSTON SIEMENS aka "Brax" Seventh great grandson of progenitor Nicholas Kegg.

SIEVERT

JACOB SIEVERT aka Jake" Seventh great grandson of progenitor Nicholas Kegg.
KACEY SIEVERT Seventh great granddaughter of progenitor Nicholas Kegg.

SIGAL

STACEY JO SIGAL Sixth great granddaughter of progenitor Nicholas Kegg.

SILBAUGH

DONLEY RAY SILBAUGH Fifth great grandson of progenitor Nicholas Kegg.

SILLER

ALLEN GEORGE SILLER Sixth great grandson of progenitor Nicholas Kegg.
DARYL MARTIN SILLER Sixth great grandson of progenitor Nicholas Kegg.
JONATHAN LAYTON SILLER Sixth great grandson of progenitor Nicholas Kegg.
JULIE ANN SILLER Sixth great granddaughter of progenitor Nicholas Kegg.
JOYCE NORENE SILLER Sixth great granddaughter of progenitor Nicholas Kegg.

SILVASY

LISA ANN SILVASY Fifth great granddaughter of progenitor Nicholas Kegg.

[5984] The Republican-Nonpareil (NE) May 15, 2019 [5985] The Nance County Journal (NE) June 24, 1948

SIMCOX

BABY SIMCOX (1905 – 1905) daughter of William and Clara (Haight) Simcox.
CHARLES EVERETT SIMCOX, (1909 – 1925) son of William and Clara (Haight) Simcox.
HOWARD DOW SIMCOX [5986] (1908 – 1982) son of William and Clara (Haight) Simcox, married Barbara Marion Sullivan. Howard was a retired fireman for the Kimberly-Clark Corp. in Mount Shasta, member of the Oddfellows Lodge No. 370, Mount Shasta; American Legion Craft Post No. 157; Veterans of Foreign Wars and Siskiyou Senior Citizens. Howard was a veteran of World War II.
THEODORE HAIGHT SIMCOX (1906 – 1980) aka "Teddy", son of William and Clara (Haight) Simcox. **WILLIAM DOW SIMCOX** [5986A] (1878 – 1957) son of Joel and Cecelia (Kegg) Simcox married Clara Alice Simcox with whom he was father of (5).

SIMES

BRYCE SIMES Seventh great grandson of progenitor Nicholas Kegg. **CLIFTON C. SIMES** Seventh great grandson of progenitor Nicholas Kegg. **DAVID WILLIAM SIMES** Sixth great grandson of progenitor Nicholas Kegg. **MARJORIE ANN SIMES** Sixth great granddaughter of progenitor Nicholas Kegg. **DIXIE SIMMS** Sixth great granddaughter of progenitor Nicholas Kegg.
JILL SIMMS Sixth great granddaughter of progenitor Nicholas Kegg.
WENDY SIMMS Sixth great granddaughter of progenitor Nicholas Kegg.

SIMMONS

JENNA J. SIMMONS Seventh great granddaughter of progenitor Nicholas Kegg.
KAITLYN A. SIMMONS Seventh great granddaughter of progenitor Nicholas Kegg.
MICHELLE RENEE SIMMONS Sixth great granddaughter of progenitor Nicholas Kegg.
NATHAN RANDALL SIMMONS Seventh great grandson of progenitor Nicholas Kegg.
NICOLLE R. SIMMONS Sixth great granddaughter of progenitor Nicholas Kegg.
TODD MITCHELL SIMMONS Seventh great grandson of progenitor Nicholas Kegg.

SIMMS

LAURA DIANE SIMMS aka "Di", Sixth great granddaughter of progenitor Nicholas Kegg.
LESLIE RAYMOND SIMMS [5987] aka "Les" (1948 – 1999) son of James and Laura (Cannon) Simms married Janet Marguerite Pursell with whom he was father of (1). Les was a Navy veteran of the Vietnam War and was employed as a nursing assistant for the Ohio Veterans Administration Hospital. Les was a member of the Bass Anglers Sportsmen Society.
LYNN SUZANNE SIMMS Sixth great granddaughter of progenitor Nicholas Kegg.
MIKEL ANNE SIMMS Seventh great granddaughter of progenitor Nicholas Kegg

SIMPSON

KRYSTAL LEANN SIMPSON Fifth great granddaughter of progenitor Nicholas Kegg.
MONTANA SIMPSON Seventh great granddaughter of progenitor Nicholas Kegg.

SIPE

JESSICA SIPE Seventh great granddaughter of progenitor Nicholas Kegg.

[5986] Siskiyou Daily News (CA) Nov 4, 1982, Genealogical Society Siskiyou County pulled by Jennifer Bryan [5986A] p.39- Sacramento Bee (CA) Aug 1, 1957 [5987] p.14-The Orlando Sentinel (FL) Dec 18, 1999

SIPERLY

DOUGLAS SIPERLY aka "Doug", Sixth great grandson of progenitor Nicholas Kegg.
NICHOLAS CHRISTOPHER SIPERLY aka "Nick", Sixth great grandson of progenitor Nicholas Kegg. **TORI SIPERLY** Seventh great granddaughter of progenitor Nicholas Kegg.

SISK

HANNAH ELIZABETH SISK Seventh great granddaughter of progenitor Nicholas Kegg.

SISTLER

SAMUEL DARIUS SISTLER [5988] (1971 – 2006) son of Byron and Barbara (Walling) Sistler, carried on his father's genealogical publishing business.

SIVERTSEN

BENJAMIN ODIN SIVERTSEN Sixth great grandson of progenitor Nicholas Kegg.
KARRIE L. SIVERTSEN Sixth great granddaughter of progenitor Nicholas Kegg.
MICHELLE AMY SIVERTSEN Sixth great granddaughter of progenitor Nicholas Kegg.

SJOLSVOLD

DANIEL ROY SJOLSVOLD [5989] (1957 – 2017) aka "Diesel Dan", son of Peter and Jean (Eide) Sjolsvold married Diane Fay Heiberg with whom he was father of (1). Later, he married Sally Barbara Moe. Dan was a former gravel truck driver for Schermer Construction driving a gravel truck constructing logging roads in the area for 23 years. Dan was also known around the community as 'Diesel Dan' or 'Big 10'. A graduate of Grand Forks College, Dan joined the U.S. Army in 1978 and was Honorably Discharged in 1981. Dan loved fishing and went to Alaska a couple of years ago where he caught a huge King Salmon.   **LAURIE JEAN SJOLSVOLD** [5990] (1959 – 2022) aka "Lu", daughter of Peter and Jean (Eide) Sjolsvold married Donald Henry Udovich with whom she was mother of (1). Jean had a few jobs including working as a housekeeper for the country star, Dave Dudley, at a resort he owned in Wisconsin. She worked for Grays Harbor County as a flagger and for General Electric during mill shutdowns in Alaska as a "gopher". She ended up working at the Blue Beacon in Aberdeen, where she worked for 30 years. She would jokingly say "I worked every shift and job there except for a cook." ending up in the bar. She was very proud of her job and loved all her customers and friends she created on the job. Most of her friends called her Lu, LuLu, Lorski, or Laurie Bitch, but the one who melted her heart was Grandma Lu. Lu liked Lifetime movies, crossword puzzles, baking, sewing, and vodka. She was especially fond of butterflies and hummingbirds. She was working on a quilt made from Crown Royal bags. Her brothers-in-law said that she could fry chicken better than their mom.
PETER SJOLSVOLD Seventh great grandson of progenitor Nicholas Kegg.
THELMA MARIE SJOLSVOLD Sixth great granddaughter of progenitor Nicholas Kegg

SKELLY

JOSEPH ALEXANDER SKELLY (1945 – 1945) son of Alloysius and Dorothy (Sanders) Skelly.
MARY MARGARET SKELLY [5991] (1938 – 2018) daughter of Alloysius and Dorothy (Sanders) Skelly, married Oscar Anderson Ashby with whom she was mother of (1). Mary enjoyed arts and crafts and was a cat lover.   **SUSAN SKELLY** Fifth great granddaughter of progenitor Nicholas Kegg.

[5988] www.ajlambert.com/history/obt_ss.pdf [5989] The Daily World (WA) June 24, 2017 [5990] Harrison Family Mortuary, WA [5991] The Winchester Star (VA) May 11, 2019

SKILLERN

ISABELLE SKILLERN Eighth great granddaughter of progenitor Nicholas Kegg.

SKUFCA

CONNER VAUGHN SKUFCA Eighth great grandson of progenitor Nicholas Kegg.

SLAGLE

CARTER SLAGLE Seventh great grandson of progenitor Nicholas Kegg. **DAMON SLAGLE** Sixth great grandson of progenitor Nicholas Kegg. **DEREK SLAGLE** Sixth great grandson of progenitor Nicholas Kegg. **ETHAN RYAN SLAGLE** Sixth great grandson of progenitor Nicholas Kegg. **HELEN CHRISTINE SLAGLE** [5992] (1917 – 1974) daughter of George and Bonnie (Bragg) Vonslagle, married Harold Elwyn Feather with whom she was mother of (2). Helen was employed as the office manager for Haney Associates, Inc., of Chicago, a professional fund-raising agency. **IAN M. SLAGLE** Sixth great grandson of progenitor Nicholas Kegg. **JUSTIN SLAGLE** Sixth great grandson of progenitor Nicholas Kegg. **MICHAEL LOUIS SLAGLE** Fifth great grandson of progenitor Nicholas Kegg. **ORVIS EUGENE SLAGLE** [5992A] aka "Gene" (1921 – 1983) son of George and Bonnie (Bragg) VonSlagle married Estelle A. Leppert with whom he was father of (3). Gene was a barber's manufacturing sales manager in Anderson and a member of St. Mary's Catholic Church, Anderson. He was a lifetime member of the Kendallville V.F.W.; a member of the Kendallville Elks Lodge; and charter president of the Kendallville Kiwanis. He was a World War II veteran and a member of the Moose Lodge 150, Anderson. **PAMELA SUE SLAGLE** Fifth great granddaughter of progenitor Nicholas Kegg. **THOMAS EUGENE SLAGLE** Fifth great grandson of progenitor Nicholas Kegg.

SLAIN

MARY LEE SLAIN Fifth great granddaughter of progenitor Nicholas Kegg.
MICHAEL JOHN SLAIN [5992B] son of Victor and Marian (Armstrong) Slain married twice, first to Michele McGann with whom he was father of (1). Later he married Martha Kay Opliger. Michael worked for Evans Garment Restoration in sales. **MICHAEL JOHN SLAIN** Sixth great grandson of progenitor Nicholas Kegg. **VICKI DIANE SLAIN** Fifth great granddaughter of progenitor Nicholas Kegg.

SLATER

EVIE MARIE SLATER Seventh great granddaughter of progenitor Nicholas Kegg.
SAM M. SLATER Sixth great grandson of progenitor Nicholas Kegg.

SLAUGHTER

HOLLEE SLAUGHTER Eighth great granddaughter of progenitor Nicholas Kegg.

SLEIGHTER

ALEX L. SLEIGHTER Seventh great granddaughter of progenitor Nicholas Kegg.

[5992] The South Bend Tribune (IN) March 26, 1974 [5992A] Kendallville News-Sun (IN) July 11, 1983, contributed by D. Sue Dible [5992B] News-Sentinel (Fort Wayne, IN) Nov 17, 2011

SLOPPY

CANDACE LOUISE SLOPPY Fifth great granddaughter of progenitor Nicholas Kegg.
THOMAS SLOPPY Fifth great grandson of progenitor Nicholas Kegg.

SLOSMAN

HALEY SLOSMAN Seventh great granddaughter of progenitor Nicholas Kegg.

SMALL

CHESTER MARVIN SMALL (1915 – 1915) son of Clyde and Effie (Laird) Small.
CLEO MAXINE SMALL [5993] (1917 – 1970) daughter of Clyde and Effie (Laird) Small, married Walter New with whom she was mother of (1). Cleo was employed for 20 years as a clerk for the downtown Indianapolis store of L. S. Ayres & Co. **DORIS MARIE SMALL** (1924 – 1924) daughter of Clyde and Effie (Laird) Small. **DOROTHY JEAN SMALL** [5994] (1930 – 2013) daughter of Clyde and Effie (Laird) Small married twice; first to Robert Milton McWilliams with whom she was mother of (4). Later she married Max Charles Glenn. Dorothy enjoyed bowling, car racing and shopping.
MARY AGNES SMALL [5995] (1922 – 2007) daughter of Clyde and Effie (Laird) Small, married Robert J. Stinson with whom she was mother of (4). Mary had worked various jobs throughout her life. She had been active in Jackson County Habitat for Humanity. She also loved to just "get out and go".
MEREDITH GERALD SMALL [5996] (1920 – 1983) aka "Bus", son of Clyde and Effie (Laird) Small, married Wanetta June Keever. Bus retired from WABCO after 30 years of service.
MERVIL EUGENE SMALL (1928 – 1928) son of Clyde and Effie (Laird) Small.

SMEAD

SARAH SMEAD aka Sally" Fifth great granddaughter of progenitor Nicholas Kegg.

SMALLWOOD

CLAUDIA GRACE SMALLWOOD Sixth great granddaughter of progenitor Nicholas Kegg.
KEVIN LELAND SMALLWOOD Sixth great grandson of progenitor Nicholas Kegg.

SMITH

AARON PAUL SMITH Seventh great grandson of progenitor Nicholas Kegg. **ADDIE BELLE SMITH** [5997] (1922 – 2006) daughter of Iris and Dehlia (Yoder) Smith, married Benjamin Franklin Pettit with whom she was mother of (2). Addie was a retired seamstress and had worked out of her home. **ALLEN KEITH SMITH** aka "Keith" Sixth great grandson of progenitor Nicholas Kegg. **ALEXANDER SMITH** Eighth great grandson of progenitor Nicholas Kegg. **ALEXIS ANN SMITH** Sixth great granddaughter of progenitor Nicholas Kegg. **ALISHA SMITH** Sixth great granddaughter of progenitor Nicholas Kegg. **AMELIA ELIZABETH SMITH** [5998] (1880 – 1958) aka "Millie", daughter of Henry and Elizabeth (Kegg) Smith, married Daniel Snyder Grimes with whom she was mother of (2). Millie died of a head injury about an hour after a door of a parked automobile blew shut and knocked her down as she waited by the vehicle for a child to enter. **AMY SMITH** Sixth great granddaughter of progenitor Nicholas Kegg. **AMY KATHLEEN SMITH** Sixth great granddaughter of progenitor Nicholas Kegg. **ANDREW K. SMITH** Sixth great grandson of progenitor Nicholas Kegg. **ANDREW SMITH** Seventh great grandson of progenitor Nicholas Kegg.

[5993] The Indianapolis News (IN) March 19, 1970 [5994] Rollo Daily News (MO) May 6, 2013 [5995] Tribune (Seymour, Ind) April 19, 2007 [5996] Indianapolis Star (IN) Dec 22, 1983 [5997] p.A5 - The Truth (IN) Jan 17, 2006 [5998] p.4 - The Daily Courier (PA) June 16, 1958

ANNA LENA SMITH [5998A] (1918 – 2016) daughter of Harrison and Mary (Simon) Smith married Harry Lloyd Grubb with whom she was mother of (4). Anna was an accomplished seamstress and enjoyed shopping, cooking and eating out with friends. She was a kind, soft spoken and gentle woman. Anna started working at age 16 as a housekeeper for Mr. and Mrs. B.F. Whetstone in Everett. After her marriage, she was a housewife until her husband passed away. She then worked in the gift shop at Snyder's Gateway for 24 years. She later worked at Travelers Rest Restaurant for eight years. **ANNA RAE SMITH** Seventh great granddaughter of progenitor Nicholas Kegg. **ANTHONY SMITH** aka "Tony" Sixth great grandson of progenitor Nicholas Kegg. **ANTHONY KENT SMITH** [5998B] aka "Smitty" (1933 – 2016) son of Noel and Mildred (Johnson) Smith married Georgia O'Conner with whom he was father of (5). After graduating high school, Smitty joined the U.S. Marine Corps. Smitty was a Teamster for many years, driving for the Anaconda Mine in Yerington and Ringsby, Systems 99 and Yellow Freight in Reno. He was one of the first to be certified to haul triples in Nevada. Smitty and Georgia instilled solid family values in their children. He loved the outdoors whether it was hunting, fishing or camping and he passed that passion on to several generations. **APRIL MARIE SMITH** Sixth great granddaughter of progenitor Nicholas Kegg. **APRIL MARIE MAE SMITH** Sixth great granddaughter of progenitor Nicholas Kegg. **ARLO HUCKELBERRY SMITH** Eighth great grandson of progenitor Nicholas Kegg. **ARTHUR SMITH** Fifth great grandson of progenitor Nicholas Kegg. **BAILEY SMITH** Seventh great grandson of progenitor Nicholas Kegg. **BARBARA LOUISE SMITH** [5999] (1954 – 2018) daughter of Harold and Ethel (Hayes) Smith married Claude Darwin Helfrich with whom she was mother of (1), she married Billie Samuel Sullivan with whom she was mother of (2), she married Mr. Mills with whom she was mother of (1). And last she married Purl Robert Silk. Barbara was a member of Faith United Methodist Church and enjoyed doing needlepoint. **BETTIE SMITH** Sixth great granddaughter of progenitor Nicholas Kegg. **BETTY A. SMITH** Sixth great granddaughter of progenitor Nicholas Kegg. **BETTY JANE SMITH** aka "Jane", Fourth great granddaughter of progenitor Nicholas Kegg. **BEVERLY LOU SMITH** (1928 – 2010) daughter of Noel and Mildred (Johnson) Smith, married Mr. Collier. **BLAIR SMITH** Seventh great granddaughter of progenitor Nicholas Kegg. **BONITA ANNABELLE SMITH** [5999A] aka "Bonnie" (1938 – 2004) daughter of Noel and Mildred (Johnson) Smith, married Jay V. Williams with whom she was mother of (1). **BRANDEN TODD SMITH** Sixth great grandson of progenitor Nicholas Kegg. **BRANDON JAMES SMITH** Sixth great grandson of progenitor Nicholas Kegg. **BRENDA SMITH** Fifth great granddaughter of progenitor Nicholas Kegg. **BROCK SMITH** Sixth great grandson of progenitor Nicholas Kegg. **BUCK E. SMITH** Fifth great grandson of progenitor Nicholas Kegg. **CADEN SMITH** Seventh great grandson of progenitor Nicholas Kegg. **CAITLYN SMITH** Eighth great granddaughter of progenitor Nicholas Kegg. **CAMERON SMITH** Seventh great grandson of progenitor Nicholas Kegg. **CAROL ANN SMITH** Fifth great granddaughter of progenitor Nicholas Kegg. **CAROLYN ANN SMITH** Sixth great granddaughter of progenitor Nicholas Kegg. **CASEY SMITH** Seventh great granddaughter of progenitor Nicholas Kegg. **CATHERINE ELIZABETH SMITH** aka "Katie", Eighth great granddaughter of progenitor Nicholas Kegg. **CECELIA MAE SMITH** Seventh great granddaughter of progenitor Nicholas Kegg. **CHARLES ALBERT SMITH** [5999B] (1916 – 1988) son of Scott and Daily (Yoder) Smith married Elizabeth Martha Overly with whom he was father of (1). Charles was a long-distance truck driver. **CHARLES HENRY SMITH** aka "Hank," (1988 – 2013) son of David and Deborah (Scharmen) Smith. **CHASE SMITH** Eighth great grandson of progenitor Nicholas Kegg. **CHERYL SMITH** Sixth great granddaughter of progenitor Nicholas Kegg. **CHRISTIE SMITH** Sixth great granddaughter of progenitor Nicholas Kegg. **CHRISTIE MARIE SMITH** Sixth great granddaughter of progenitor Nicholas Kegg. **CHRISTINA DAWN SMITH** Seventh great granddaughter of progenitor Nicholas Kegg. **CHRISTOPHER SMITH** Sixth great grandson of progenitor Nicholas Kegg.

[5998A] Bedford Gazette (PA) Feb 12, 2016, contributed by Bob Rose [5998B] Reno Gazette-Journal (NV) Jan 15, 2016, contributed by D. Sue Dible [5999] Walley-Mills-Zimmerman Funeral Home (IN) obtained by D. Sue Dible [5999A] Spartanburg Herald Journal (SC) Aug 19, 2007 [5999B] p.B4-Elkhart Truth (IN) Dec 1, 1988, contributed by D. Sue Dible

CINDI SMITH Fifth great granddaughter of progenitor Nicholas Kegg. **CINDY LOU SMITH** Sixth great granddaughter of progenitor Nicholas Kegg. **CLAUDETTE MARIE SMITH** Sixth great granddaughter of progenitor Nicholas Kegg. **CLAUDIA E. SMITH** Fifth great granddaughter of progenitor Nicholas Kegg. **CLAUDIA PEARL SMITH** [5999C] (1932 – 2019) daughter of Harrison and Mary (Simon) Smith married Charles E. Miller with whom she was mother of (14). Throughout the years, Claudia worked as a cook and waitress at Howard Johnsons, Robert P. Smith School in Yellow Creek and Kountry Kettle Restaurant. She was a very active lady who enjoyed caring for her home and family. She also enjoyed going shopping for clothes with her daughter Kate, and getting her hair done every week then going to Kelly's Restaurant or Hoss's for lunch. She spent a lot of time on the back porch feeding her chipmunks and getting to pet them. She loved watching game shows Jeopardy, Wheel of Fortune, Price Is Right, and rooting for her sports teams, the Pirates, Pens, Penn State and the Cowboys. Claudia was famous for her cooking and baking. **CLINTON SMITH** Seventh great grandson of progenitor Nicholas Kegg. **COLIN SMITH** Seventh great grandson of progenitor Nicholas Kegg. **CONSTANCE LOUISE SMITH** [6000] (1939 – 2012) daughter of Mile and Helen Louise (Kerr) Smith. **COURTNEY MARIE SMITH** Eighth great granddaughter of progenitor Nicholas Kegg. **DAKOTA SMITH** Seventh great grandson of progenitor Nicholas Kegg. **DALE EMMETT SMITH** Fourth great grandson of progenitor Nicholas Kegg. **DALE ROBERT SMITH** (1951 – 2006) son of Robert and Charlotte (Kennel) Smith, married Dorina Isabelle West with whom he was father of (1). **DANA SMITH** Sixth great granddaughter of progenitor Nicholas Kegg. **DANIEL CHRISTOPHER SMITH** Seventh great grandson of progenitor Nicholas Kegg. **DANIEL F. SMITH** [6000A] (1949 – 2010) son of Harold and Ethel (Hayes) Smith, married Ada M. Whitman with whom he was father of (3). Dan was employed for 12 years as a buffer at Faries-McMeekan in Elkhart. He enjoyed bowling, playing cards with his friends and watching baseball games. **DANIEL F. SMITH** Sixth great grandson of progenitor Nicholas Kegg. **DARLENE G. SMITH** Fifth great granddaughter of progenitor Nicholas Kegg. **DAVID SMITH** Sixth great grandson of progenitor Nicholas Kegg. **DAVID SMITH** Fifth great grandson of progenitor Nicholas Kegg. **DAVID EUGENE SMITH** [6000B] (1952 – 2011) son of Michael and Shirley (Holderman) Smith married and divorced Nancy Lynn Hertsel. David enjoyed watching sporting events and was a US veteran. **DAVID FRANK SMITH** [6001] (1890 – 1968) son of Joseph and Lottie (May) Smith, was a retired timekeeper for the New York Central Railroad. **DAVID WILLIAM SMITH** Sixth great grandson of progenitor Nicholas Kegg. **DEAN L. SMITH** Fourth great grandson of progenitor Nicholas Kegg. **DELLA MAE SMITH** (1879 – 1915) daughter of Thomas and Sarah (Bodle) Smith, married Walter Alexander Schoettler with whom she was mother of (4). **D. J. SMITH** Seventh great grandson of progenitor Nicholas Kegg. **DONALD EUGENE SMITH** [6002] (1927 – 2004) aka "Jody", son of Harrison and Mary (Simon) Smith, married Dolores Rabahy. Jody was a veteran of World War II serving in the U.S. Army and a landscaper at Breezy Acres Park in Fairless Hills. He was an avid reader and loved to shoot pool. **DONNA SMITH** Sixth great granddaughter of progenitor Nicholas Kegg. **DONRITA SMITH** Fifth great granddaughter of progenitor Nicholas Kegg. **DOROTHY MAY SMITH** [6002A] (1917 – 2006) daughter of John and Jessie (Bussard) Smith married twice, first to Floyd N. Mellott with whom she was mother of (3) later, to Clarence J. Pepple with whom she was mother of (1). Dorothy worked on the family dairy farm, then later working various waitressing jobs in the local area. She then retired from Bedford Hospital in the dietary department. She enjoyed cooking for and spending time with her family. She also enjoyed gardening. **DWIGHT SMITH** Fifth great grandson of progenitor Nicholas Kegg. **EDWARD K. SMITH** Fourth great grandson of progenitor Nicholas Kegg. **EDWARD KEGG SMITH** [6003] (1876 – 1957) son of Henry and Elizabeth (Kegg) Smith, married Grace Whalley with whom he was father of (3). Edward served as secretary of the Y.M.C.A. He was a member of the Massillon area Boy Scout council, the Brewster Lion's club and the Masonic lodge. He was also director of the Brewster Building and Loan Co. **ELIZABETH SMITH** Sixth great granddaughter of progenitor Nicholas Kegg.

[5999C] Bedford Gazette (PA) Sep 7, 2019 [6000] Roanoke Times (VA) July 22, 2012 [6000A] Walley Mills Zimmerman Funeral Home (IN) [6000B] Elkhart Cremation Services [6001] p.14 - News Journal (OH) July 27, 1968 [6002] Bucks County Courier Times (Levittown, PA) July 18, 2004 [6002A] The Fulton County News (McConnellsburg, Pa.) June 29, 2006 [6003] Evening Independent (OH) Apr 1, 1957

ELIZABETH JANNIS SMITH [6004] (1918 – 1992) aka "Lib", daughter of James and Gretchen (Lung) Smith, married Joseph Engelbert Kreutzpeintner with whom she was mother of (4).   **ELLSWORTH JOLLY SMITH** Eighth great grandson of progenitor Nicholas Kegg.   **EMMA JANE SMITH** [6005] (1887 – 1960) daughter of Thomas and Sarah (Bodle) Smith married twice; first to Charles Elwood Harris with whom she was mother of (2). Later, she married Henry Albert Spatz. Emma was a member of Redeemer English Lutheran Church, the Ladies Aid of the church and the Spanish-American War Veterans Auxiliary. **EMMONS ELIAS SMITH** [6006] (1925 – 2004) son of Harrison and Mary (Simon) Smith, married Audrey Patricia Long with whom he was father of (2). Emmons served in the United States Army, 271st Infantry. He had worked out of state as a laborer for several construction companies, before retiring. Emmons enjoyed hunting and playing baseball with the Broad Top Old Timers. He was a member of the Saxton Sportsmen's Club; Veterans of Foreign Wars Post No. 4129, Saxton; Saxton Volunteer Fire Co.;   **EMMONS FORREST SMITH** Fifth great grandson of progenitor Nicholas Kegg.   **ERIN SMITH** Sixth great granddaughter of progenitor Nicholas Kegg.   **ETHAN SMITH** Seventh great grandson of progenitor Nicholas Kegg. **EUGENE MCHUGH SMITH** aka "Max" Sixth great grandson of progenitor Nicholas Kegg.   **FERN M. SMITH** [6007] (1887 – 1969) daughter of Joseph and Lottie (May) Smith, married Myron Walton Thornburg with whom she was mother of (1).   **FORREST L SMITH** [6007A] (1917 – 2004) son of Harrison and Mary (Simon) Smith married Olive Mae Maust with whom he was father of (1). Forrest served in the U.S. Army during World War II as Master Sergeant for the 353rd Engineer Construction Battalion in the Asiatic Pacific Theater, supervising construction projects, specifically airplane runways, and received the Asiatic-Pacific Theater Ribbon with 1 bronze star, the Philippine Liberation Ribbon, the Good Conduct Medal, and the World War II Victory Medal. He was a member of Operating Engineers Union Local No. 66 Pittsburgh and worked on many construction projects as a crane operator setting steel. Forrest enjoyed deer and turkey hunting, baseball and mechanic work. He was a great auto racing fan, having raced at the former Penn National Raceway in Everett.   **FRANCIS F. SMITH** [6008] (1912 – 1989) aka "Star", son of Charles and Helen (Heffner) Smith, married Vergie Margaret Foor with whom he was father of (3). Francis retired after 25 years as an equipment operator for James E Kilcoin Supply Co. He was a former Snake Spring Township supervisor. **G. TODD SMITH** Fifth great grandson of progenitor Nicholas Kegg.   **GAIL ELIZABETH SMITH** [6009] (1948 – 1996) daughter of Clarence and Ariene (Mowry) Smith, married Dewey D. Ingram with whom she was mother of (1). Gail was employed as a nurse at Stow-Glen. Gail was a member of Hudson Community Chapel, where she served as a Sunday school teacher.   **GAIL LEE SMITH** Sixth great granddaughter of progenitor Nicholas Kegg.   **GARON R. SMITH** Sixth great grandson of progenitor Nicholas Kegg.   **GARY L. SMITH** Sixth great grandson of progenitor Nicholas Kegg.   **GEORGE ESSINGTON SMITH** [6010] (1874 – 1944) son of Henry and Elizabeth (Kegg) Smith, married Etta V. Redinger with whom he was father of (1).   **GEORGE F. SMITH** (born abt. 1908) son of Charles and Helen (Heffner) Smith.   **GERALD LYNN SMITH** Fifth great grandson of progenitor Nicholas Kegg. **GERTRUDE SMITH** [6011] (1916 – 1989) daughter of James and Gretchen (Lung) Smith, married Charles E. Stiffler.   **GIAO L. SMITH** Sixth great granddaughter of progenitor Nicholas Kegg. **GREGG DEAN SMITH** [6012] (1955 – 1955) son of Thomas and Bonnie (Truex) Smith.   **GREGORY KIPP SMITH** (1954 – 2014) aka "Gregg", son of Robert and Charlotte (Kennel) Smith, married Phyllis Brooks.   **GWENDOLYN JO SMITH** Sixth great granddaughter of progenitor Nicholas Kegg. **HANNA SMITH** Seventh great granddaughter of progenitor Nicholas Kegg.   **HANNAH SMITH** Seventh great granddaughter of progenitor Nicholas Kegg.   **HAROLD ANDREW SMITH** Seventh great grandson of progenitor Nicholas Kegg. **HAROLD BENJAMIN SMITH** [6012A] aka "Zeke" (1911 – 1987) son of Scott and Daily (Yoder) Smith married Ethel K. Hayes with whom he was father of (7).

[6004] obituary clipping contributed by Al Wopshall Find A Grave Memorial# 58614891 [6005] p.2 Ft Wayne Journal Gazette (IN) Oct 8, 1960 obtained by D. Sue Dible [6006] USGenWeb Project obituary transcribed by Sharon Culp [6007] p.C8 - The Plain Dealer (OH) Dec 4, 1969 [6007A] p.8 - Bedford Inquirer (PA) May 14, 2004 contributed by Bob Rose [6008] Bedford County Historical Society (PA), book 72, page 166, obtained by D. Sue Dible [6009] p.B11 - Akron Beacon Journal (OH) July 28, 1996 [6010] Cumberland Times (MD) Oct. 23, 1944 [6011] Elkhart Truth (IN) Jul 31, 2000 [6012] p.2 Elkhart Truth (IN) Nov 29, 1955, obtained by D. Sue Dible [6012A] p.B5- Elkhart Truth (IN) June 23, 1987, contributed by D. Sue Dible

Zeke retired from F.W. Means in South Bend and was a U.S. Navy veteran of World War II. He was a life member of the Veterans of Foreign Wars and Disabled American Veterans and had served as past commander of the Military Order of Cooties. He was a member of the Father's Auxiliary. **HAROLD EUGENE SMITH** (6012B) (1953 – 2016) son of Dennis and Janet (James) Smith married Pamela Mae Slachta with whom he was father of (2). Harold was a retiree of Penn DOT. He loved the outdoors and was an avid gold panner, hunter, and fisherman. Harold also enjoyed collecting shark teeth and coins. His pursuits also included world travel and metal recovery from discarded electronics. He was a member of Safari Club International. **HAROLD FRED SMITH** Fifth great grandson of progenitor Nicholas Kegg. **HARRY DONALD (DEAN) SMITH** (6013) (1917 – 2002) aka "Don", son of Lemuel and Edith (Wilger) Dean Smith, married Sara Mae Rahn with whom he was father of (1). Harry was a retired Harrisburg area Realtor and appraiser. He was a veteran of World War II, a graduate of Officer Candidate School in Fort Monmouth, N.J., and served as a captain in the U.S. Army from 1941 to 1946. He served in New Guinea and Japan. He was a member of Stevens Memorial United Methodist Church in Harrisburg where he had been past president of Hershey Sunshine Class, chairman of the board of trustees and chairman of the Christmas Giving Program. He also was a member of Williamsport United Methodist Church. He was past president of the Greater Harrisburg Board of Realtors, served as a trustee of Community General Osteopathic Hospital of Harrisburg from 1967 to 1989, was a 32nd degree Mason, a member of Harrisburg Consistory and the National Sojourners, a past member of the Executive Club of Central Pennsylvania, a past volunteer of the American Cancer Society, a member of the American Heart Association, a past member of the Zembo Shrine and past chairman of building drives for Community General Osteopathic Hospital. **HELEN JANE SMITH** Fifth great granddaughter of progenitor Nicholas Kegg. **HELEN MARGARET SMITH** (6013A) aka "Margaret" (1917 – 1996) daughter of Charles Frederick and Helen (Heffner) Smith married Ellis Jasper Foor with whom she was mother of (9). Helen had worked as a cook at the Washington Coffee Shop and the Hillcrest Inn. **HENRY CARLOS SMITH** (abt 1908 -?) son of Edward and Grace (Whalley) Smith. **HENRY JAY SMITH** (6014) (1914 – 1975) son of Scott and Daily (Yoder) Smith married Phoebe Viola Millican with whom he was father of (3). **HORACE CLINTON SMITH** (6015) (1916 – 1956) son of James and Dorothy (Livingston) Smith, married Mary Francis Snyder with whom he was father of (5). Horace was well known throughout Bedford County as a carpenter. He was a member of the Loyal Order of Moose 453 of College Park, Md. **HOWARD K. SMITH**, (1884 -?) son of Henry and Elizabeth (Kegg) Smith. **HUNTER MATTHEW SMITH** Seventh great grandson of progenitor Nicholas Kegg. **INFANT SMITH** (1906 – 1906) son of Charles and Helen (Heffner) Smith. **INFANT SMITH** son of Richard and Dede (Beegle) Smith. **IRIS ELTON SMITH** (6016) (1889 – 1942) son of Thomas and Sarah (Bodle) Smith married twice; first to Lenora Desailes Eldridge Saddler. Later, he married Dehlia Yoder with whom he was father of (6). **IRL ROBERT SMITH** Sixth great grandson of progenitor Nicholas Kegg. **ISABELLE MCKELVAY SMITH** (6017) (1921 – 1963) daughter of Harrison and Mary (Simon) Smith married twice; first to Franklin Charles Hofacker with whom she was mother of (2). Later, she married Lewis S. Pepple with whom she was mother of (2). **ISAIAH ALLEN SMITH** Seventh great grandson of progenitor Nicholas Kegg. **JACK LEWIS SMITH** (1918 – 1973) son of John and Jessie (Kennedy) Smith married Norah Bell Browne with whom he was father of (1). **JAMES SMITH** Fifth great grandson of progenitor Nicholas Kegg. **JAMES D. SMITH** Fifth great grandson of progenitor Nicholas Kegg. **JAMES EDWIN SMITH** (6018) (1941 – 2022) son of Miles and Helen Louise (Kerr) Smith married Rosemary Yeh-Lih Sun. Later he married Henedine Corpuz. **JAMES JOLLIE ELLIS SMITH** (6019) (1893 – 1966) aka "Jim", son of Thomas and Sarah (Bodle) Smith, married Gretchen Inez Lung with whom he was father of (4). James was employed as a kiln burner for Medusa Portland Cement Co. **JAMES P. SMITH** Fifth great grandson of progenitor Nicholas Kegg.

(6012B) Wetzel & Son Funeral Home obituary Willow Grove, PA contributed by D. Sue Dible (6013) Hagerstown Herald-Mail (MD) June 23, 2002 (6013A) Bedford County Historical Society (PA), book 79, page 63 contributed by D. Sue Dible (6014) Sarasota Herald Tribune (FL) Dec 5, 2017 (6015) Bedford County Genealogical Society obituary obtained by D. Sue Dible (6016) p.2 Elkhart Truth (IN) Jan 21, 1942, obtained by D. Sue Dible (6017) p. 3290 Duke Clark obituary Collection (6018) Roanoke Times (VA) Apr. 13, 2022 (6019) The Toledo Blade (OH) July 15, 1966, obtained by D. Sue Dible

JAMES ROSS SMITH (6020) (1890 – 1953) son of Lewis and Sarah (Ditch) Smith, married Dorothy Pearl Livingston with whom he was father of (5) in addition to a foster daughter. **JAMES ROSS SMITH** Fifth great grandson of progenitor Nicholas Kegg. **JAMIE SMITH** Sixth great granddaughter of progenitor Nicholas Kegg. **JAN SMITH** Sixth great granddaughter of progenitor Nicholas Kegg. **JANET SMITH** Fifth great granddaughter of progenitor Nicholas Kegg. **JANET SMITH** Sixth great granddaughter of progenitor Nicholas Kegg. **JANICE LEE SMITH** Sixth great granddaughter of progenitor Nicholas Kegg. **JANINE ANNETTE SMITH** (6020A) (1952 – 2000) daughter of Sgt. Noel and Ruth (Donavan) Smith married Gary Lee Lallathin with whom she was mother of (4). **JARED TY SMITH** Sixth great grandson of progenitor Nicholas Kegg. **JASON SMITH** Sixth great grandson of progenitor Nicholas Kegg. **JASON AARON SMITH** Seventh great grandson of progenitor Nicholas Kegg. **JASON SCOTT SMITH** Sixth great grandson of progenitor Nicholas Kegg. **JAYSON ROSS SMITH** Fifth great grandson of progenitor Nicholas Kegg. **JEANETTE SMITH** Sixth great granddaughter of progenitor Nicholas Kegg. **JEANINE JO SMITH** Fifth great granddaughter of progenitor Nicholas Kegg. **JEANNINE SUE SMITH** Fourth great granddaughter of progenitor Nicholas Kegg. Janine was employed at the Ohio State University **JEFF SMITH** Fifth great grandson of progenitor Nicholas Kegg. **JEFF SMITH** Sixth great grandson of progenitor Nicholas Kegg. **JEFFREY LEE SMITH** Sixth great grandson of progenitor Nicholas Kegg. **JEFFREY W. SMITH** Seventh great grandson of progenitor Nicholas Kegg. **JEFFREY WILLIAM SMITH** Fifth great grandson of progenitor Nicholas Kegg. **JENNIFER SMITH** Eighth great granddaughter of progenitor Nicholas Kegg. **JERROD SMITH** Seventh great grandson of progenitor Nicholas Kegg. **JERRY SMITH** Fifth great grandson of progenitor Nicholas Kegg. **JERRY LEE SMITH** (6020B) (1941 – 1999) son of Francis and Vergie (Foor) Smith married Patricia Hershberger with whom he was father of (4). Jerry was employed as a field assessor at the Blair County Courthouse and was owner/operator of Jerry Smith Insurance, Lakemont. He enjoyed country music, golf, and football, especially the Pittsburgh Steelers and University of Pittsburgh teams. He was a member of the Lakemont Lions Club, where he served as past president; Portage Lodge, Free and Accepted Masons, Hollidaysburg; and the Jalla Shrine ushers. He also coached girls' softball and boys' baseball. **JESSICA SMITH** Seventh great granddaughter of progenitor Nicholas Kegg. **JESSICA DAWN SMITH** (6021) (1986 – 2001) daughter of David and Karen (Smith) Diehl was a member of her high school honor society. **JESSICA E. SMITH** Sixth great granddaughter of progenitor Nicholas Kegg. **JILL SMITH** Seventh great granddaughter of progenitor Nicholas Kegg. **JIM SMITH** aka "Smitty" Sixth great grandson of progenitor Nicholas Kegg. **JOEL SMITH** Seventh great grandson of progenitor Nicholas Kegg. **JOHN C. SMITH** Sixth great grandson of progenitor Nicholas Kegg. **JOHN EDWARD SMITH** (1919 – 1919) son of Scott and Daily (Yoder) Smith. **JOHN L. SMITH** (1891 – 1939) son of Thomas and Sarah (Bodle) Smith. **JOHN PAUL SMITH** (6022) (1946 – 1952) son of Harold and Ethel (Hayes) Smith, died in the fire that destroyed the families trailer home. Firemen found the boy's body in his bedding after the flames had subsided. His pet dog was there with him. **JONATHAN KENNEDY SMITH** Fifth great grandson of progenitor Nicholas Kegg. **JORDAN SMITH** Seventh great grandson of progenitor Nicholas Kegg. **JORDYN SMITH** Seventh great grandson of progenitor Nicholas Kegg. **JOSEPH HARPER SMITH** (6023) (1915 – 1994) son of Charles and Helen (Heffner) Smith married twice; first to Violet Jean Harper and later, to Ona Mallow. Joseph retired from Reliance Steel Mill in Pittsburgh. **JOSEPH KENNETH SMITH** (6024) (1920 – 2004) son of James and Dorothy (Livingston) Smith, married Vivian McEldowney with whom he was father of (1). **JOSIAH SMITH** Eighth great grandson of progenitor Nicholas Kegg **JOSHUA LEE SMITH** Seventh great grandson of progenitor Nicholas Kegg. **JOSHUA SAMUEL SMITH** Seventh great grandson of progenitor Nicholas Kegg **JOYCE MAXINE SMITH** Fifth great granddaughter of progenitor Nicholas Kegg. **J.R. SMITH** Seventh great grandson of progenitor Nicholas Kegg.

(6020) Bedford Gazette (PA) April 20, 1953 (6020A) Advocate (OH) Aug. 27, 2019 (6020B) Altoona Mirror (PA) Feb 22, 1999, contributed by D. Sue Dible (6021) Public Opinion (Chambersburg, PA) Oct 17, 2001 (6022) p.1,2,8, Elkhart Truth (IN) Mar 7, 1952, obtained by D. Sue Dible (6023) Bedford County Historical Society (PA), book 77 page 150 obtained by D. Sue Dible (6024) Altoona Mirror (PA) Feb 26, 2016

JUDITH SMITH Fifth great granddaughter of progenitor Nicholas Kegg. **JULIAN SMITH** Eighth great grandson of progenitor Nicholas Kegg. **JULIE SMITH** Sixth great granddaughter of progenitor Nicholas Kegg. **JULIE LYNN SMITH** Fifth great granddaughter of progenitor Nicholas Kegg. **JUSTAN SMITH** Seventh great granddaughter of progenitor Nicholas Kegg. **KAREN SUE SMITH** aka "Katie" Fifth great granddaughter of progenitor Nicholas Kegg. **KATHLEEN SMITH** Sixth great granddaughter of progenitor Nicholas Kegg. **KATHLEEN CAROLE SMITH** Fourth great granddaughter of progenitor Nicholas Kegg. **KATHRYN ASHLEY SMITH** Seventh great granddaughter of progenitor Nicholas Kegg. **KATHRYN IRENA SMITH** [6025] (1927 – 2005) daughter of Iris and Dehlia (Yoder) Smith, married Glenn Ervin Bingaman with whom she was mother of (4). Kathryn retired after 22 years as an inspector in the packing department at Vincent Bach Manufacturing. **KENDYLL SMITH** Seventh great granddaughter of progenitor Nicholas Kegg. **KENNETH F. SMITH** aka "Ken", Fifth great grandson of progenitor Nicholas Kegg. **KENNETH R. SMITH** Fifth great grandson of progenitor Nicholas Kegg. **KONNER MATTHEW SMITH** Seventh great grandson of progenitor Nicholas Kegg. **LACE SMITH** Seventh great granddaughter of progenitor Nicholas Kegg. **LARRY SMITH** aka "Buck" Fifth great grandson of progenitor Nicholas Kegg. **REV. LARRY P. SMITH** Sixth great grandson of progenitor Nicholas Kegg. **LAURA JEAN SMITH** Sixth great granddaughter of progenitor Nicholas Kegg. **LAURINDA GAIL SMITH** Sixth great granddaughter of progenitor Nicholas Kegg. **LEANN K. SMITH** Seventh great granddaughter of progenitor Nicholas Kegg. **LEROY C. SMITH** Fifth great grandson of progenitor Nicholas Kegg. **LEVI SMITH** (born abt. 1873) son of Henry and Elizabeth (Kegg) Smith. **LINDA ALICE SMITH** Fifth great granddaughter of progenitor Nicholas Kegg. **LINDSAY SMITH** Fifth great granddaughter of progenitor Nicholas Kegg. **LISA SMITH** Sixth great granddaughter of progenitor Nicholas Kegg. **LISA DAWN SMITH** Sixth great granddaughter of progenitor Nicholas Kegg. **LISA MARIE SMITH** Sixth great granddaughter of progenitor Nicholas Kegg. **LORI SMITH** Sixth great granddaughter of progenitor Nicholas Kegg. **LLOYD DONALD SMITH** [6025A] aka "Smitty" (1946 – 2015) son of Ralph and Hazel (Morris) Smith married twice, first to Theresa J. Fickes with whom he was father of (1). Later, he married Norma Jean Villareal. Smitty served in the United States Marine Corp in the Vietnam War, where he proudly earned both the Republic of Vietnam Cross of Valentry and the Vietnam Campaign Medal. He was a employed throughout his lifetime as a service writer for various auto dealerships, and most recently as an insurance estimator for various body shops in Texas, until retiring. An avid fisherman, Smitty spent as much time as he could out in the Gulf fishing, and when you sat down to reminisce about the good ole days, you could find yourself lost in hours of talk. **LUCILLE MARGURITE SMITH** [6026] (1914 – 1982) daughter of James and Gretchen (Lung) Smith married four times; first to Franklin J. Deeds with whom she was mother of (1). She married Cleon John Richards and later married Mr. Marsh. Lastly, she married Hal Graham. **LUCY ANN SMITH** [6027] (1898 – 1984) daughter of Thomas and Sarah (Bodle) Smith, married Clarence Charles Pfenning with whom she was mother of (9). Lucy was retired from Howe Military School and was a member of Lima Presbyterian Church. **LYNETTE ELLEN SMITH** Fifth great granddaughter of progenitor Nicholas Kegg. **MARGARET IRENE SMITH** [6027A] (1928 – 1994) daughter of Harold and Mae (Diehl) Smith married Calvin Walter Beegle with whom she was mother of (11). **MARILYN GENE SMITH** aka "Jean", Fifth great granddaughter of progenitor Nicholas Kegg. **MARILYN LOUISE SMITH** Sixth great granddaughter of progenitor Nicholas Kegg. **MARJORIE ELLEN SMITH** (1929 – 1946) daughter of John and Jessie (Bussard) Smith. **MARK THOMAS SMITH** Sixth great grandson of progenitor Nicholas Kegg.

[6025] p.A6 - The Truth (Elkhart, IN) Sept 08, 2005 [6025A] Bedford Gazette (PA) March 9, 2015, contributed by Bob Rose [6024] Altoona Mirror (PA) Feb 26, 2016 [6025] p.A6 - The Truth (Elkhart, IN) Sept 08, 2005 [6025A] Bedford Gazette (PA) March 9, 2015, contributed by Bob Rose [6026] p.19 Toledo Blade (OH) Feb 6, 1982, obtained by D. Sue Dible [6027] gen.nobleco.lib.in.us/Obituaries. [6027A] Bedford Inquirer (PA) Sep 9, 1994, contributed by Duke Clark

MARTHA E. SMITH (6027B) (1883 – 1947) daughter of Thomas and Sarah (Bodle) Smith married Jacob H. Shafer with whom she was mother of (8). **MARTIN SMITH** aka "Marty" Sixth great grandson of progenitor Nicholas Kegg. **MARY BETH SMITH** Fifth great granddaughter of progenitor Nicholas Kegg. **MARY JOAN SMITH** Fifth great granddaughter of progenitor Nicholas Kegg. **MATTHEW SMITH** Fifth great grandson of progenitor Nicholas Kegg. **MATTHEW IRA SMITH** Sixth great grandson of progenitor Nicholas Kegg. **MEREDITH MARIE SMITH** Seventh great granddaughter of progenitor Nicholas Kegg. **MICHAEL B. SMITH** Sixth great grandson of progenitor Nicholas Kegg. **MICHAEL D. SMITH** Fifth great grandson of progenitor Nicholas Kegg. **MICHAEL FRANCIS SMITH** (6027C) (1928 – 1985) son of Iris and Dehlia (Yoder) Smith married Shirley Holderman with whom he was father of (8). Michael was a retired painter and veteran of U.S. Army serving in World War II. He was a member of the Moose and Veterans of Foreign Wars in Salinas. **MICHAELA MAE SMITH** Fifth great granddaughter of progenitor Nicholas Kegg. **MOLLY SMITH** Seventh great granddaughter of progenitor Nicholas Kegg. **MONICA SMITH** Seventh great granddaughter of progenitor Nicholas Kegg. **MORGAN SMITH** Seventh great granddaughter of progenitor Nicholas Kegg. **NANCY BERTHA SMITH** (6028) (1877 – 1942) daughter of Henry and Elizabeth (Kegg) Smith, married John S. Snyder with whom she was mother of (3). Nancy was a member of the Church of the Brethren. **NANCY CARROLL SMITH** (1940 – 2001) daughter of William and Genevieve (Hoover) Smith married Mr. Vandemark. **NANCY L. SMITH** Fifth great granddaughter of progenitor Nicholas Kegg. **NOEL SHERWOOD SMITH, III** aka "Butch" (1953 – 2006) son of Noel and Ruth (Donavan) Smith married Janice Fay Thornton with whom he was father of (3). Noel retired from the Newark City Schools and was a drummer in several local bands in his earlier years and was a music, art, car and sports enthusiast. **NOEL SHERWOOD SMITH JR.** (1926 – 1995) son of Noel and Mildred (Johnson) Smith married twice; first to Ruth Ann Donavan with whom he was father of (4). Later, he married Rose Ann (McKee) Dunlap. Sgt. Smith was a veteran of World War II. Awarded the Silver Star and Purple Heart. **NOEL SHERWOOD SMITH IV** Seventh great grandson of progenitor Nicholas Kegg. **OTIS SMITH** Fifth great grandson of progenitor Nicholas Kegg. **OTIS EDWIN SMITH** (6028A) (1924 – 2018) son of James and Dorothy (Livingston) Smith. married Margaret Hunt with whom he was father of (4). **PAM SMITH** Fifth great granddaughter of progenitor Nicholas Kegg. **PAMELA SMITH** Fifth great granddaughter of progenitor Nicholas Kegg. **PAMELA SUE SMITH** (6029) (1958 – 1970) daughter of Jerry and Patricia (Hershberger) Smith was fatally injured in an automobile accident near Ashland, VA. Pamela was a member of St. Mary's Roman Catholic Church. **PARKER E. SMITH** Seventh great grandson of progenitor Nicholas Kegg. **PARKER SMITH** Ninth great grandson of progenitor Nicholas Kegg. **PAT SMITH** Fifth great granddaughter of progenitor Nicholas Kegg. **PATRICIA KAY SMITH** Fifth great granddaughter of progenitor Nicholas Kegg. **PATRICIA KERR SMITH** (1951 – 1966) daughter of Miles and Helen (Kerr) Smith. **PERRY V. SMITH** Sixth great grandson of progenitor Nicholas Kegg. **PHILIP J. SMITH** Sixth great grandson of progenitor Nicholas Kegg. **RACHEL SMITH** Seventh great granddaughter of progenitor Nicholas Kegg. **RAELYNN SMITH** Seventh great granddaughter of progenitor Nicholas Kegg. **RALPH L. SMITH** (6030) (1915 – 1978) aka "Pete", son of James and Gretchen (Lung) Smith married twice; first to Violet Louwella Edwards with whom he was father of (2). Pete retired from Medusa Cement Co., where he had been employed for 30 years as a welder. **RALPH LEROY SMITH** (6031) (1936 – 1978) aka "Buz", son of Ralph and Violet (Edwards) Smith, married Maryanna E. Liske with whom he was father of (4). **RANDALL LIVINGSTON SMITH** Fifth great grandson of progenitor Nicholas Kegg. **RAYMOND R. SMITH** (6032) (1925 – 2008) son of Iris and Dehlia (Yoder) Smith married Marilyn M. Miller with whom he was father of (1). Proud WWII and Korean War Veteran, Raymond served his country in the United States Marine Corps.

(6027B) p.2- Elkhart Truth (IN) May 8, 1947, contributed by D. Sue Dible (6027C) p.16- Elkhart Truth (IN) June 27, 1985, contributed by D. Sue Dible (6028, 6029) Bedford County Genealogical Society (PA) obituary obtained by D. Sue Dible (6028A) Roy W Barber Funeral Home (MD) obituary contributed by D. Sue Dible (6030) Toledo Blade (OH) Library obituary obtained by D. Sue Dible (6031) Toledo Blade (OH) May 8, 1978 (6032) p.A49 - Newsday (Long Island, NY) Feb 12, 2008

RAYMOND TIMOTHY SMITH Fifth great grandson of progenitor Nicholas Kegg. **REBECCA E. SMITH** Fifth great granddaughter of progenitor Nicholas Kegg. **REBECCA LYNN SMITH** Sixth great granddaughter of progenitor Nicholas Kegg. **RHODA IRENE SMITH** [6033] (1876 – 1941) daughter of Lin and Martha (Cessna) Smith, married John Edgar Ott with whom she was mother of (2). **RICHARD EARL SMITH** (1923 – 2007) son of Simon and Bertha (Snavely) Smith. **ROBERT SMITH** Fifth great grandson of progenitor Nicholas Kegg. **ROBERT SMITH** Fifth great grandson of progenitor Nicholas Kegg. **ROBERT CHARLES SMITH** [6034] (1932 – 1990) son of Willis and Lisbeth (Anderson) Smith, married Bernadette V. Antkowiak with whom he was father of (4). **ROBERT D. SMITH** Sixth great grandson of progenitor Nicholas Kegg. **ROBERT EUGENE SMITH** (1924 – 1994) son of Simon and Bertha (Snavely) Smith. **ROBERT LEE SMITH** [6035] (1941 – 2022) son of Harry and Letha (Venable) Smith married Nancy Koons with whom he was father of (2). Robert was employed as a machinist at Colfor Manufacturing. He was a Christian by faith. Robert enjoyed cars, trucks and his John Deere tractor. **ROBERT IRIS SMITH** [6035A] aka "Bob" (1930 – 2008) son of Iris and Dehlia (Yoder) Smith married twice, first to Charlotte Maurine Kennel with whom he was father of (6) later, he married Theresa Clare Gorney. Bob was a Korean veteran. He was employed for 30 years by Carnation Milk, 15 years for Dave Martin Sand and Supplies, and eight years for Freightliner. **ROBERT LEE SMITH** [6035B] (1930 – 1963) son of Harold and Mae (Diehl) Smith. Robert was a veteran of WWII. **ROGER SMITH** Sixth great grandson of progenitor Nicholas Kegg. **ROSS L SMITH** [6035C] (1922 – 2010) son of James and Dorothy (Livingston) Smith married Mildred Josephine Hunt with whom he was father of (4). Ross served in the United States Army – Air Force during World War II. He worked as a building contractor most of his life having owned and operated Ross L. Smith Construction until his retirement. Ross was a member of the Carpenter Union Local #1590. **ROY LEE SMITH** (1949 – 1949) son of Dennis and Janet (James) Smith. **RYAN LANE SMITH** Seventh great grandson of progenitor Nicholas Kegg. **SAMUEL DEWEY SMITH** [6035D] (1901 – 1975) son of Thomas and Sarah (Bodle) Smith married Lissie Stayner. **SANDRA DAY SMITH** Sixth great granddaughter of progenitor Nicholas Kegg. **SANDRA MARIE SMITH** Fifth great granddaughter of progenitor Nicholas Kegg. **SANDY SMITH** Sixth great granddaughter of progenitor Nicholas Kegg. **SARAH SMITH** Sixth great granddaughter of progenitor Nicholas Kegg. **SARAH JANE SMITH** [6036] (1924 – 2018) daughter of Iris and Dehlia (Yoder) Smith, married Charles Edward Lanning Mapes with whom she was mother of (7). Sarah was a member of the Women of the Moose Lodge 662 in Dunnellon. **SCOTT K. SMITH** Sixth great grandson of progenitor Nicholas Kegg. **SCOTT WINFIELD SMITH** [6037] (1881 – 1921) son of Thomas and Sarah (Bodle) Smith, married Daily Yoder with whom he was father of (5). **SHANNON L. SMITH** Sixth great granddaughter of progenitor Nicholas Kegg. **SHARON VIRGINIA SMITH** [6037A] (1949 – 2016) daughter of Thomas and Virginia (Dadisman) Smith married John L. Trapp with whom she was mother of (2). A teacher, foster mother, and a well-known community activist, she touched the lives of countless individuals and was loved by many. While living in Martinsburg, W.Va., she worked at the Shenandoah Women's Center; she was the executive director of Bethany House, a shelter for homeless women and children, for a decade, during which she founded Community Networks, Inc., a non-profit adult education and employment assistance program for homeless women and those in need; she opened a shelter for individuals suffering from HIV and AIDS; and in 2002 founded The Rose of Sharon House, a day care facility and after school program for clients served by Community Networks, Inc., and Bethany House. She volunteered with C-CAP, Berkeley County Loaves and Fishes, West Virginia Legal Services, and many other community organizations. During her youth, she enjoyed a myriad of interests; becoming a Rainbow Girl in conjunction with the Masons in Cumberland, a member of a drill team that performed during the half-time show of the Cotton Bowl, and lived in Colon, Panama, for a time. She was a resident

---

[6033] p.2 - Bedford Gazette (PA) Feb 18, 1941 [6034] p.C7 Pittsburgh Press (PA) Nov 28, 1990 [6035] Salem News (OH) April 2, 2022, obtained by D. Sue Dible [6035A] p. B4 - The San Diego Union-Tribune (CA) Aug 22, 2008 [6035B] Book 11, p. 4098, Bedford County Historical Society obituary contributed by D. Sue Dible [6035C] Altoona Mirror (PA) Oct 28, 2010 [6035D] p.28- Elkhart Truth (IN) Dec 31, 1975 [6036] Roberts Funeral Home (FL) [6037] Gospel Herald Obituaries Volume XIV, Number 31 - November 3, 1921 - p. 607 [6037A] Cumberland Times (MD) Aug 5, 2016

of Alaska for several years, living in Adak, Kodiak, and Anchorage; during which time, she was a foster mother to three Aleut children, a substitute house parent for foster children, an animal shelter volunteer, taught at a community service preschool, and operated an in-home daycare. She had a passion for helping others, traveled extensively, adored music and dancing, enjoyed antiquing and collecting postcards. **SHAWN MICHAEL SMITH** Eighth great grandson of progenitor Nicholas Kegg. **SHELBY SMITH** Seventh great granddaughter of progenitor Nicholas Kegg. **SHERRY SMITH** Sixth great granddaughter of progenitor Nicholas Kegg. **SIMON EARL SMITH** [6038] (1892 – 1945) son of Lewis and Sarah (Ditch) Smith, married Bertha Loraine Snavely with whom he was father of (2). Earl was a veteran of World War I and a former resident of Altoona. **SONIA KAY SMITH** Fifth great granddaughter of progenitor Nicholas Kegg. **STACY SMITH** Seventh great granddaughter of progenitor Nicholas Kegg. **STANLEY IRVIN (SMITH) MULL** [6039] (1947 – 2021) son of Irvin Elwood and Mabel (Fisher) Smith and his adoptive parents, Roy and Pauline (Harding) Mull. He married Kathy, whom he was father of (2). A former member of the Coast Guard, Stanley was a carpenter by trade and an avid hunter and fisherman who enjoyed tying flies and reloading. He also loved spending time with family. **STEPHANIE SMITH** Sixth great granddaughter of progenitor Nicholas Kegg. **STEVE SMITH** Fifth great grandson of progenitor Nicholas Kegg. **STEVEN PAUL SMITH** Fifth great grandson of progenitor Nicholas Kegg. **SUSAN K. SMITH** Sixth great granddaughter of progenitor Nicholas Kegg. **SUSAN MATILDA SMITH** (1884 – 1957) daughter of Thomas and Sarah (Bodle) Smith married John J. Baker with whom she was mother of (4). **SUZANN SMITH** [6039A] aka "Suzie" (1959 – 2018) daughter of Francis and Vergie (Foor) Smith married Melvin C. Clapper with whom she was mother of (2). Suzie worked in retail for G.C. Murphy's, Ames, and Wal-Mart. She also worked as a waitress for Perkins restaurant, in Breezewood. She enjoyed puzzles, sudoku, swimming, playing cards and spending time with her family. **TAMMY SMITH** Seventh great granddaughter of progenitor Nicholas Kegg. **TARA NICOLE SMITH** Seventh great granddaughter of progenitor Nicholas Kegg. **TAYLOR SMITH** Seventh great grandson of progenitor Nicholas Kegg. **TERRY SMITH** Fifth great grandson of progenitor Nicholas Kegg. **TERRY SMITH** Fifth great grandson of progenitor Nicholas Kegg. **TERRY SMITH** Fifth great grandson of progenitor Nicholas Kegg. **TERRY SMITH** Sixth great grandson of progenitor Nicholas Kegg. **TERRY J. SMITH** Fifth great grandson of progenitor Nicholas Kegg. **THEODORE MONROE SMITH** Fifth great grandson of progenitor Nicholas Kegg. **THERESA MARIE SMITH** Sixth great granddaughter of progenitor Nicholas Kegg. **THOMAS EARL SMITH** Sixth great grandson of progenitor Nicholas Kegg. **THOMAS ELTON SMITH** [6039B] (1957 – 2005) son of Michael and Shirley (Holderman) Smith married Cheryl Krumrie. Thomas was employed by Gaska Tape. **THOMAS EUGENE SMITH** [6040] (1925 – 2006) son of Charles and Ethel (Speicher) Smith, married Virginia Opal Dadisman with whom he was father of (1). Thomas retired from C&P Telephone Co., as a telephone technician. He was a World War II veteran, serving in the U.S. Navy. Thomas was a 32nd Degree Mason and a member of the Cumberland Consistory Scottish Rite. **TONY SMITH** Sixth great grandson of progenitor Nicholas Kegg. **TRAVIS SMITH** Seventh great grandson of progenitor Nicholas Kegg. **TROY DONALD SMITH** Sixth great grandson of progenitor Nicholas Kegg. **TROY L. SMITH** Sixth great grandson of progenitor Nicholas Kegg. **TWYLA SMITH** Sixth great granddaughter of progenitor Nicholas Kegg. **TYLER SMITH** Seventh great grandson of progenitor Nicholas Kegg. **TYLER SMITH** Seventh great grandson of progenitor Nicholas Kegg. **VERA PEARL SMITH** [6041] (1911 – 1967) daughter of George and Etta (Redinger) Smith was a child welfare worker in the Keyser, office of the West Virginia Department of Welfare. **VICTORIA J. SMITH** aka "Vicki", Fifth great granddaughter of progenitor Nicholas Kegg. **VICTORIA L. SMITH** Fifth great granddaughter of progenitor Nicholas Kegg. **VINCE SMITH** Seventh great grandson of progenitor Nicholas Kegg. **VIRGIL SMITH** Fifth great grandson of progenitor Nicholas Kegg. **WANDA SMITH** Fifth great granddaughter of progenitor Nicholas Kegg. **WILLIAM SMITH** aka "Billy", Sixth great grandson of progenitor Nicholas Kegg.

[6038] p.2 - Bedford Gazette (PA) Aug 17, 1945 [6039] Tribune Review (Greensburg, PA) July 6, 2021 [6039A] Timothy A Berkebile Funeral Home, Inc [6039B] p.A6 - The Truth (Elkhart, IN) Sep 4, 2005 [6040] Morning Herald (MD) Apr 9, 2006 [6041] p.15 - Cumberland News (MD) Feb 2, 1967

WILLIAM CARL SMITH (1909 – 1944) son of Charles and Helen Heffner Smith, married Catherine Koseyk Briggs was killed in Germany during WWII. **WILLIAM EARL SMITH** [6042] (1918 – 1973) son of James and Dorothy (Livingston) Smith, married Genevieve Hoover with whom he was father of (3). William was in the construction business and was the former owner of the Little Jack's Corner Restaurant. **WILLIAM HENRY SMITH** aka "Babba" Fifth great grandson of progenitor Nicholas Kegg. **WILLIAM W. SMITH** [6042A] (1936 – 1998) son of George and Edith (Calhoun) Smith married Peggy Ann Strayer with whom he was father of (2). William was a truck driver for 30 years and drove for Consolidated Freightways of Carlisle for eight years before retiring. He was a member of Bedford Masonic Lodge #320 F&AM and Teamsters Local #776 in Harrisburg. **WILLIS SMITH** Fifth great grandson of progenitor Nicholas Kegg. **WILLIS H. SMITH** (1909 – 1993) son of Charles and Helen (Heffner) Smith, married Lisbeth Caroline Marie Anderson with whom he was father of (2). **XAVIER SMITH** Eighth great grandson of progenitor Nicholas Kegg. **YVONNE SMITH** Sixth great granddaughter of progenitor Nicholas Kegg. **ZACHARY R. SMITH** Seventh great grandson of progenitor Nicholas Kegg. **ZELE SMITH** Seventh great granddaughter of progenitor Nicholas Kegg.

SMOUSE

ANDREW SMOUSE Seventh great grandson of progenitor Nicholas Kegg.
NATHAN SMOUSE Seventh great grandson of progenitor Nicholas Kegg.

SMOTHERS

WILLIAM SMOTHERS Eighth great grandson of progenitor Nicholas Kegg.

SMOYER

CORY SMOYER Seventh great grandson of progenitor Nicholas Kegg.
JOSEPH WILSON SNAPP Fourth great grandson of progenitor Nicholas Kegg.

SNAPP

DANA ELIZABETH SNAPP Fifth great granddaughter of progenitor Nicholas Kegg.
JOSEPH WILSON SNAPP Fifth great grandson of progenitor Nicholas Kegg.

SNAVELY

BESSIE WILLETTA SNAVELY (1871 – 1943) daughter of William and Mary Jane (Dean) Snavely, married Carroll McClellan Beem with whom she was mother of (3). **BONNIE ANN SNAVELY** Fourth great granddaughter of progenitor Nicholas Kegg. **JESSIE B. SNAVELY** (1863 – 1894) daughter of William and Mary Jane (Dean) Snavely, married George S. Sneer with whom she was mother of (1). **KATHERINE O. SNAVELY** (1874 - 1955) aka "Kittie", daughter of William and Mary Jane (Dean) Snavely, married George W. Thum with whom she was mother of (1). Later she married Floyd Dean Archer. **LEAH MAY SNAVELY** daughter of William and Mary Jane (Dean) Snavely died in infancy. **LULU DELL SNAVELY** (1867 – 1871) daughter of William and Mary Jane (Dean) Snavely. **NELLIE E. SNAVELY** [6043] (1866 – 1942) daughter of William and Mary Jane (Dean) Snavely married twice; first to Henry Clay McFall with whom she was mother of (2). Later, she married Frank H. Smiley. **WILLIAM ALEXANDER SNAVELY** [6044] (1879 – 1951) son of William and Mary Jane (Dean) Snavely, married Hallie L. (Gregg) Bell. William was a retired timekeeper.

[6042] Bedford County Genealogical Society (PA) obituary obtained by D. Sue Dible [6042A] Bedford Inquirer (PA) Jan 8, 1999, contributed by Duke Clark [6043] Chicago Tribune (IL) Oct 21, 1942 [6044] p.19 San Diego Union (CA) Oct 29, 1951

SNEER

MAUREE B. SNEER [6045] (1892 – 1963) daughter of George and Jessie (Snavely) Sneer, married Ewing Hamilton Scott with whom she was mother of (2).

SNELL

ARDITH MABELLE SNELL (1923 – 2004) daughter of George and Laura (Scharmen) Snell, married Earl Lemar Doler with whom she was mother of (6). **BOB SNELL** Seventh great grandson of progenitor Nicholas Kegg. **CHAD SNELL** Fifth great grandson of progenitor Nicholas Kegg. **CYNTHIA LOUISA SNELL** Fifth great granddaughter of progenitor Nicholas Kegg. **DAWN SNELL** Seventh great granddaughter of progenitor Nicholas Kegg. **ELSIE SNELL** Fourth great granddaughter of progenitor Nicholas Kegg. **FLOYD S. SNELL** (1922 – 1925) son of George and Laura (Scharmen) Snell. **GEORGE KEITH SNELL** [6046] (1921 – 2002) son of George and Laura (Scharmen) Snell married three times; first to Jean Ardis Worden. He married Betty L. Wildie and later, married Elizabeth Doty. George was a member of the Port St. Lucie Yacht Club and a former member of the Commodores Club, where he served on the board of trustees. **HAROLD NELSON SNELL** Sixth great grandson of progenitor Nicholas Kegg. **IDAS T. SNELL** Sixth great grandson of progenitor Nicholas Kegg. **JAMES F. SNELL** (1935 – 1936) son of George and Laura (Scharmen) Snell. **JASON SNELL** Seventh great grandson of progenitor Nicholas Kegg. **JOHN ALBERT SNELL** (1943 – 1994) son of Joseph and Evelyn (Streight) Snell married Sandra Lynn with whom he was father of (4). John served in the US Air Force. **KEESHAWNA LYNN SNELL** Seventh great granddaughter of progenitor Nicholas Kegg. **KELLY SNELL** Seventh great granddaughter of progenitor Nicholas Kegg. **KENNETH LEE SNELL** Sixth great grandson of progenitor Nicholas Kegg. **KRISSY SNELL** Seventh great granddaughter of progenitor Nicholas Kegg. **LISA ANN SNELL** Seventh great granddaughter of progenitor Nicholas Kegg. **MARYANN SNELL** Sixth great granddaughter of progenitor Nicholas Kegg. **ROBERT SNELL** Fifth great grandson of progenitor Nicholas Kegg. **ROBERT IRVING SNELL** [6047] (1927 – 2002) son of George and Laura (Scharmen) Snell married twice; first to Vivian M. Lautner with whom he was father of (4). Later, he married Ruth Elizabeth (Lamb) Jaquish. Robert was a veteran of World War II, serving in the U.S. Army. He was a member of the American Legion in Englewood, Fla. Robert was also a member of the Michigan Farm Bureau, the Rotonda Golf and Country Club, and he was a charter member of Sunshine Medical Group Golf Association of Englewood, Fla. Robert retired after farming for 48 years. He also formed and operated Northwestern Real Estate with his son-in-law. **STEPHEN G. SNELL** Seventh great grandson of progenitor Nicholas Kegg. **STERLING SNELL** Eighth great grandson of progenitor Nicholas Kegg. **TIFFANY SNELL** Seventh great granddaughter of progenitor Nicholas Kegg. **VICTORIA SNELL** Seventh great granddaughter of progenitor Nicholas Kegg. **WILLIAM SNELL** Fifth great grandson of progenitor Nicholas Kegg. **WINIFRED THELMA SNELL** aka "Winnie", Fourth great granddaughter of progenitor Nicholas Kegg.

SNOEYINK

AUSTIN SNOEYINK Sixth great grandson of progenitor Nicholas Kegg.
CALEB SNOEYINK Sixth great grandson of progenitor Nicholas Kegg.

SNYDER

ANNA BROWN SNYDER Fifth great granddaughter of progenitor Nicholas Kegg.
ARLAN NIAL SNYDER (1932 – 1932) son of Samuel and Cornelia (Hockenberry) Snyder.

[6045] p.7 The Des Moines Register (IA) Oct 15, 1915 [6046] p.C4 - Stuart News/Port St. Lucie News (FL) June 25, 2002 [6047] Traverse City Record-Eagle (MI) Jan 20, 2002

BARBARA ANN SNYDER Sixth great granddaughter of progenitor Nicholas Kegg. **CHARLES F. SNYDER** Seventh great grandson of progenitor Nicholas Kegg. **CHARLIE SNYDER** Seventh great grandson of progenitor Nicholas Kegg. **CHARLES OWEN SNYDER** [6047A] aka Chuck" (1950 – 1969) son of Edgar and Ruth (Calhoun) Snyder was fatally injured in Quong Nam Province of Vietnam where he was serving with the United States Marine Corps. **CHARLOTTE MONTGOMERY SNYDER** [6047B] (1937 – 1997) daughter of Herbert and Charlotte (Vickers) Snyder, married Jerry Parker Frisby with whom she was mother of (3). Charlotte was a member of Montgomery United Methodist Church. **CHRISTINA L. SNYDER** Seventh great granddaughter of progenitor Nicholas Kegg. **DORIS JEAN SNYDER** Sixth great granddaughter of progenitor Nicholas Kegg. **DORIS MARIE SNYDER** Sixth great granddaughter of progenitor Nicholas Kegg. **DUSTY SNYDER** Seventh great grandson of progenitor Nicholas Kegg. **EDGAR J. SNYDER** (1948 – 1948) son of Edgar and Ruth (Calhoun) Snyder. **EUGENE DEAN SNYDER** Sixth great grandson of progenitor Nicholas Kegg. **GEORGE GLENN SNYDER** (1912 – 1914) son of John and Nancy (Smith) Snyder. **GREGORY SNYDER** Eighth great grandson of progenitor Nicholas Kegg. **HELEN PAULINE SNYDER** [6048] (1901 – 1947) daughter of William and Blanche (Diehl) Snyder had been an invalid for over twenty years, during which time her disposition was always sweet and gentle, with never a word of complaint. **HERBERT AUSTIN SNYDER** [6049] (1913 – 1972) aka "Herb", son of Herbert and Naomi (Cessna) Snyder married twice; first to Charlotte E. Vickers with whom he was father of (1). Later, he married Lillian Anna Brown with whom he was father of (4). Herb was the plant foreman for Union Carbide Metals Corp. at Alloy with 36 years' service. **HERBERT WALTON SNYDER** Fifth great grandson of progenitor Nicholas Kegg. **IRENE MAUDE SNYDER** (1897 – 1976) daughter of William and Blanche (Diehl) Snyder, married Wallace Dewey Smith. **JANET LEE SNYDER** Seventh great granddaughter of progenitor Nicholas Kegg. **JEAN SNYDER** (1954 – 1954) daughter of Ross and Emma Carol (Casteel) Snyder. **JOHN THOMAS SNYDER** Fifth great grandson of progenitor Nicholas Kegg. **JOHN THOMAS SNYDER** Sixth great grandson of progenitor Nicholas Kegg. **JOHN WILLIAM SNYDER** [6049A] (1939 – 1998) son of Edgar and Ruth (Calhoun) Snyder married Ryth M. Fetters with whom he was father of (4). John was an employee of Valley Quarries Co. of Chambersburg. He served in the U S Army as a SP4 (t) E-4 in Headquarters Co. 19th Engineering Battalion (C) from 1959-1962. He was a member of VFW Post 2088, Everett and the Everett Honor Guard. **JOYCE LOUISE SNYDER** Sixth great granddaughter of progenitor Nicholas Kegg. **JULIA RENEE SNYDER** Sixth great granddaughter of progenitor Nicholas Kegg. **KATHLEEN SNYDER** (born abt.1899) aka "Dollie", daughter of William and Blanche (Diehl) Snyder. **LINDA DARLENE SNYDER** [6049B] (1945 – 1997) daughter of Edgar and Ruth (Calhoun) Snyder married Rollin Treece with whom she was mother of (3). **LINDA RUTH SNYDER** Fifth great granddaughter of progenitor Nicholas Kegg. **LOIS A. SNYDER** Sixth great granddaughter of progenitor Nicholas Kegg. **NANCY JANE SNYDER** [6049C] (1943 – 2023) daughter of Samuel and Cornelia Olive (Hockenberry) Snyder married Allan Edward Semanek with whom she was mother of (2). Over her career Nancy worked as a teacher at Prontos Beauty School in Altoona and also owned and operated her own beauty salon in Bedford. She later managed the Johnny Appleseed Restaurant, the All American 76 Truck Stop Restaurant and lastly, Perkins Restaurant. Nancy was a member of the Daughters of the American Revolution organization, the Bedford County Historical Society and was a gifted painter and avid antique collector. She had great interests in music, sewing and classic stories. She was also a very good cook, which she learned from her mother who was the cook at the grade school in Snake Spring Valley. **PATRICIA A. SNYDER** Seventh great granddaughter of progenitor Nicholas Kegg. **PAUL JAMES SNYDER** [6050] (1941 – 1986) son of Edgar and Ruth (Calhoun) Snyder, married June Emery with whom he was father of (3). Paul was a member of the Stevens Chapel United Methodist Church.

[6047A] Bedford Inquirer (PA) Apr 17, 1969, contributed by D. Sue Dible [6047B] GenealogyBuff [6048] p.2 - Bedford Gazette (PA) Oct. 30, 1947 [6049] p.10A - Charleston Daily Mail (WVA) Jan 20, 1972 [6049A] Bedford County Historical Society (PA), book 81, p. 128 contributed by D. Sue Dible [6049B] Bedford County Genealogocal Society obituary clipping contributed by D. Sue Dible [6049C] Bedford Gazette (PA) Feb 10, 2023 [6050] Bedford County Genealogical Society (PA) Obituary obtained by D. Sue Dible

PAULA JEAN SNYDER Seventh great granddaughter of progenitor Nicholas Kegg.
REBECCA JANE SNYDER Fifth great granddaughter of progenitor Nicholas Kegg.
ROBERT SNYDER aka "Hunk", Sixth great grandson of progenitor Nicholas Kegg.
RONI SNYDER Seventh great granddaughter of progenitor Nicholas Kegg.
RUTH SNYDER [6050A] (1918 – 2003) daughter of Herbert and Naomi (Cessna) Snyder married Elmer H. Lanthorn with whom she was mother of (3). Ruth was always radiating God's love in her own special caring ways.
SAMUEL FLOYD SNYDER (1912 – 1982) son of John and Nancy (Smith) Snyder, married Cornelia Olive Hockenberry with whom he was father of (3).
SHARON E. SNYDER Seventh great granddaughter of progenitor Nicholas Kegg.
VERDA M. SNYDER [6051] (1907 – 1991) daughter of John and Nancy (Smith) Snyder, married Roy Elias Creps with whom she was mother of (4). Verda was a member of the Snake Spring Valley Church of the Brethren, where she had previously served as a deaconess.
WILLIAM A. SNYDER Seventh great grandson of progenitor Nicholas Kegg.

SOLANO

KALEN BRYCE SOLANO Seventh great grandson of progenitor Nicholas Kegg.
LYNDSAY SOLANO Seventh great granddaughter of progenitor Nicholas Kegg.

SOLHAN

SABRINA SOLHAN Eighth great granddaughter of progenitor Nicholas Kegg.

SOLIDAY

ALEXANDRA NICOLE SOLIDAY Eighth great granddaughter of progenitor Nicholas Kegg.
DANIELLE LEIGH SOLIDAY Eighth great granddaughter of progenitor Nicholas Kegg.

SOLLENBERGER

BENJAMIN JAMES SOLLENBERGER Sixth great grandson of progenitor Nicholas Kegg.
LACEY PEARL SOLLENBERGER Sixth great granddaughter of progenitor Nicholas Kegg.
WILLIAM THEODORE SOLLENBERGER Sixth great grandson of progenitor Nicholas Kegg.

SOLOMON

EMMALINE SOLOMON aka "Emmie", Seventh great granddaughter of progenitor Nicholas Kegg.
OLIVER SOLOMON aka "Ollie", Seventh great grandson of progenitor Nicholas Kegg.

SONES

ABIGAIL SONES Seventh great granddaughter of progenitor Nicholas Kegg.

SONTAG

KARL E. SONTAG Fifth great grandson of progenitor Nicholas Kegg.
MICHELE A. SONTAG Fifth great granddaughter of progenitor Nicholas Kegg.
SUZANNE K. SONTAG Fifth great granddaughter of progenitor Nicholas Kegg.

[6050A] Charleston Daily Mail (WVA) Dec 5, 2003 [6051] Bedford Gazette (PA) March 15, 1991, obtained by Carol Eddleman

SORG

CHARLES RICHARD SORG Sixth great grandson of progenitor Nicholas Kegg.

SOSEBEE

COURTNEY SOSEBEE Seventh great granddaughter of progenitor Nicholas Kegg.
SAMANTHA SOSEBEE Seventh great granddaughter of progenitor Nicholas Kegg.

SOTIROKOS

BLAINE EDWARD SOTIROKOS aka "Eddie" Sixth great grandson of progenitor Nicholas Kegg.
EARNEST GEORGE SOTIROKOS aka "Earnie" Sixth great grandson of progenitor Nicholas Kegg.

SOUCY

ADDISON R. SOUCY Seventh great granddaughter of progenitor Nicholas Kegg.

SOUDERS

ALICE JEAN SOUDERS (1953 – 1953) daughter of Robert and Alma (Kegg) Souders.
SARAH ELLEN SOUDERS Fourth great granddaughter of progenitor Nicholas Kegg.
SAMUEL CLAIR SOUDERS 4th great grandson of progenitor Nicholas Kegg.
SUSAN ROBE SOUDERS [6051A] (1951 – 1994) daughter of Robert and Alma (Kegg) Souders, married Craig A. Steele with whom she was mother of (3). Susan was a homemaker.

SOUSLIN

JENNIFER SOUSLIN Sixth great granddaughter of progenitor Nicholas Kegg.

SPADE

CHAD SPADE Seventh great grandson of progenitor Nicholas Kegg.
JODI LYNN SPADE Seventh great granddaughter of progenitor Nicholas Kegg.

SPAFFORD

AARON JAMES SPAFFORD (1971 – 1982) son of Kenneth and Donna (Julius) Spafford.
ADAM D. SPAFFORD Sixth great grandson of progenitor Nicholas Kegg.
JEREMY SPAFFORD Sixth great grandson of progenitor Nicholas Kegg.
JUSTIN SPAFFORD Sixth great grandson of progenitor Nicholas Kegg.

SPARKS

AARON SPARKS Sixth great grandson of progenitor Nicholas Kegg. **CHRISTOPHER R. SPARKS** Sixth great grandson of progenitor Nicholas Kegg. **HEATHER ELIZABETH SPARKS** Seventh great granddaughter of progenitor Nicholas Kegg. **JASON DAVID SPARKS** [6052] (1975 – 1990) aka "Jay Bird", son of David and Janice (Graham) Sparks. Jason was a student at the Seventh day Adventist

---

[6051A] p.2 – Huntingdon Daily News (PA) Oct 28, 1994 [6052] Record Searchlight (CA) June 14, 1990

School in Redding. He was a member of the Pathfinders group at the school. **JOEL SPARKS** Sixth great grandson of progenitor Nicholas Kegg. **PATRICIA S. SPARKS** Fifth great granddaughter of progenitor Nicholas Kegg. **PHILLIP TODD SPARKS** Sixth great grandson of progenitor Nicholas Kegg. **RICHARD L. SPARKS** Fifth great grandson of progenitor Nicholas Kegg.

SPAW

KIMBERLY ANN SPAW Sixth great granddaughter of progenitor Nicholas Kegg.

SPEAR

ANNA LOIS SPEAR [6052A] (1932 – 2013) daughter of Elvin and Florence (Elder) Spear married twice, first to Thomas Ray Miller with whom she was mother of (3), later she married Robert E. Crater. Anna was employed for 17 years at Miami Deposit Bank of Yellow Springs, Ohio and 20 years at national City Bank of Palmetto, Florida. She was a member of First Christian Church and Home City Chapter of O.E.S. Anna was a wonderful quilter and made quilts for each grandchild. But most of all she loved her family. **GREGORY ALLEN SPEAR** Sixth great grandson of progenitor Nicholas Kegg. **JAKE SPEAR** Seventh great grandson of progenitor Nicholas Kegg. **JAY SPEAR** Sixth great grandson of progenitor Nicholas Kegg. **JAYCE SPEAR** Seventh great grandson of progenitor Nicholas Kegg. **JENNY SPEAR** Seventh great granddaughter of progenitor Nicholas Kegg. **JOHN JACOB SPEAR** [6052B] (1927 – 2019) son of Elvin and Florence (Elder) Spear married Janet Lou Clark with whom he was father of (4). John worked for Florida Power and Light in Sarasota, Fl.; While there he worked from the ground up and was employed by them for 35 years until he retired. His dream was to be a cattleman and after retirement he did just that by moving to Ona and starting his ranch. **JOHN RAYMOND SPEAR** [6052C] aka "Jackie" son of John and Janet (Clark) Spear married Georgia Ann Bryant with whom he was father of (2). Jackie loved and trusted Jesus to take care of him and his family. He was a member and an usher at Faith Life Church, as well as a general building contractor and cattle rancher. Jackie always gave anything to help others. **PHILIP RAY SPEAR** [6052D] (1947 – 2009) son of Robert and Ruth (Taylor) Spear was a retired software analyst from the Federal Reserve Bank in Dallas, Texas. He was an Air Force veteran of the Vietnam Conflict and was a member of the VFW #4464 and the Patriot Masonic Lodge. **JOLEE SPEAR** Seventh great granddaughter of progenitor Nicholas Kegg. **LEO SPEAR** Eighth great grandson of progenitor Nicholas Kegg. **MEGAN ANNA SPEAR** Seventh great granddaughter of progenitor Nicholas Kegg. **OLIVE LOUISE SPEAR** [6053] (1915 – 1985) daughter of Elvin and Florence (Elder) Spear, married Cloyd Charles Caldwell. Olive was a member of the first Christian Church, Keystone Class, and the women's Circle Ruth Counsel. **ROBERT LEWIS SPEAR** [6054] (1923 – 1981) son of Elvin and Florence (Elder) Spear, married Ruth Leah Taylor with whom he was father of (3). Robert was an employee of Ohio Edison Co. for more than 30 years. He served overseas with the U.S. Army in 1945-46. He was a member of St. Mark United Methodist Church. He was a past patron of the Home City Chapter of the Order of the Eastern Star No 258 and a member of St. Andrew's Masonic Lodge No. 619 F and AM.; the Royal Arch Masons, Shawnee Chapter No. 237; the Ancient and Accepted Scottish Rite, Valley of Dayton; and the Palestine Commandery No. 33 Knights Templar. **ROBERTA LYNN SPEAR** Sixth great granddaughter of progenitor Nicholas Kegg. **RUTH EMMA SPEAR** [6055] (1929 – 2008) daughter of Elvin and Florence (Elder) Spear, married Charles Ross Dickinson with whom she was mother of (4). Ruth had worked as a bookkeeper for Roger's Jewelers, Springfield Bank, Stradling Tool Rental and the Paul Deer Farm. She was a member of Grace Evangelical Lutheran Church, taught Sunday School, was a Cub Scout Den Mother, and a 4-H Sewing Club Advisor, and participated in the YMCA Summer Tennis Clinic and the parental organizations at Reid Elementary

---

[6052A] Springfield News-Sun (OH) Sept. 16, 2013 [6052B] Robarts Funeral Home (FL) [6052C] Herald Tribune (FL) Feb 27, 2019 [6052D] www.mydailytribune.com [6053] Springfield News-Sun, (OH) Nov. 11, 1985, obtained by D. Sue Dible

and Middle Schools and Shawnee High School. **SAMUEL ROBERT SPEAR** Seventh great grandson of progenitor Nicholas Kegg. **SARAH BELLE SPEAR** [6056] (1916 – 2000) aka "Sally", daughter of Elvin and Florence (Elder) Spear, married Harry R. Oberly with whom she was mother of (1).

SPECHT

KENNETH F. SPECHT Fifth great grandson of progenitor Nicholas Kegg.

SPEICHER

CECIL RAYMOND SPEICHER (1915 – 2010) son of Virgil and Gladys (Sidders) Speicher married Bernice Drusillc Keech with whom he was father of (2). **CORA EDITH SPEICHER** [6057] (1877 – 1899) daughter of John and Emma (Kegg) Speicher received her education in a little schoolhouse on the east side of the Allegheny Mountain three miles west of New Baltimore, in Somerset County and afterwards in the Berlin and Meyersdale Normals. She taught several terms successfully. Her influence for good was not only noticeable in the school room, but also in the home and in the church. During the winter of 1897 and 1898 she did not only have her schoolwork, but also had to care for her sick mother and the management of the household duties of a large family. **DANIEL GARNER SPEICHER** (1883 – 1906) son of John and Emma (Kegg) Speicher. **EDNA LAVERNE SPEICHER** [6057A] (1921 – 2020) daughter of John and Binnie (Koontz) Speicher married Benjamin Frannklin Van Scoyoc with whom she was mother of (5). Edna was a homemaker. Due to the Covid-19 Pandemic there were no funeral services. **GENEVIEVE BELLE SPEICHER** (1894 – 1982) daughter of John and Emma (Kegg) Speicher, married Joseph Antone Stocking. **GEORGE F. SPEICHER** Sixth great grandson of progenitor Nicholas Kegg. **HOWARD FRANKLIN SPEICHER** [6058] (1887 – 1993) son of John and Emma (Kegg) Speicher married twice; first to Annie Marteeny with whom he was father of (1). Later, he married Margaret Gray. Howard was a member of Meyersdale Church of the Brethren, senior citizens and RSVP. **JANIE SPEICHER** Sixth great granddaughter of progenitor Nicholas Kegg. **JASON M. SPEICHER** Seventh great grandson of progenitor Nicholas Kegg. **JESS HAROLD SPEICHER** [6058A] (1908 – 1988) son of Royal and Barbara (McVicker) Speicher married Clifford Glenn with whom he was father of (2). Jess was employed as training director for Pure Oil Dealers. **JOHN PATTERSON SPEICHER** [6059] (1890 – 1975) son of John and Emma (Kegg) Speicher, married Binnie P. Koontz with whom he was father of (1). John was a retired manager of National Radiator Company, veteran of World War I, a former member of Everett Barracks of World War I Veterans Association and member of New Paris United Methodist Church.
KAREN SUE SPEICHER Sixth great granddaughter of progenitor Nicholas Kegg.
KATE CHRISTINE SPEICHER Seventh great granddaughter of progenitor Nicholas Kegg.
KEVIN DAVID SPEICHER Seventh great grandson of progenitor Nicholas Kegg.
KIMBERLY ANN SPEICHER Seventh great granddaughter of progenitor Nicholas Kegg.
MERLE SPEICHER [6060] (1913 – 2003) son of Howard and Annie (Marteeny) Speicher, married Della Mae Bisel. **NICHOLAS ELSWORTH SPEICHER** [6061] (1878 – 1927) son of John and Emma (Kegg) Speicher. **ROBERT GLENN SPEICHER** Fifth great grandson of progenitor Nicholas Kegg.
TIM ALLEN SPEICHER Sixth great grandson of progenitor Nicholas Kegg.
VELMA ROBERTA SPEICHER [6062] (1918 – 2003) daughter of Virgil and Gladys (Sidders) Speicher married Guy M. Gordon with whom she was mother of (3). Velma worked at the Ben Franklin store for 10 years, and with the Girl Scouts for several years. Velma dedicated her life to taking care of her family.
VIOLA SPEICHER (1889 – 1889) daughter of John and Emma (Kegg) Speicher.

[6054] Library obituary clipping obtained by D. Sue Dible [6055] Richards, Raff & Dunbar Memorial Home, OH [6056] p.16 - Springfield News-Sun (OH) Dec 6, 2000, obtained by D. Sue Dible [6057] newspaper obituary clipping obtained by Bob Rose [6057A] Bedford Gazette (PA) April 22, 2020, contributed by Bob Rose [6058] Daily American (PA) Dec 7, 1993, Meyersdale Library obituary transcribed by Denise Phillips [6058A] p.5 - Fort Pierce News Tribune (FL) Apr 15, 1952 [6059] Meyersdale Republic (PA) May 22, 1975, transcribed by Denise Phillips [6060] Daily American (PA) Oct 14, 2003, transcribed by Denise Phillips [6061] p.14 San Francisco Chronicle (CA) May 14, 1927 [6062] Bush News Tribune (CO) April 16, 2003

WAYNE SPEICHER Sixth great grandson of progenitor Nicholas Kegg.
WESLEY SPEICHER Sixth great grandson of progenitor Nicholas Kegg.
WILLIAM KARL SPEICHER Fifth great grandson of progenitor Nicholas Kegg.

SPENCE

TEAH SPENCE Sixth great granddaughter of progenitor Nicholas Kegg.
TESSAH C. SPENCE Sixth great granddaughter of progenitor Nicholas Kegg.

SPENCER

AUDRA LEE SPENCER Sixth great granddaughter of progenitor Nicholas Kegg.
DEBORAH SPENCER Fifth great granddaughter of progenitor Nicholas Kegg.
DENNIS SPENCER Sixth great grandson of progenitor Nicholas Kegg.
ERIC SPENCER Sixth great grandson of progenitor Nicholas Kegg.
ERIN R. SPENCER Sixth great granddaughter of progenitor Nicholas Kegg.
KEVIN RAY SPENCER Fifth great grandson of progenitor Nicholas Kegg.
LAURA L. SPENCER Seventh great granddaughter of progenitor Nicholas Kegg.
REBECCA SPENCER Fifth great granddaughter of progenitor Nicholas Kegg.
RICHARD SPENCER Sixth great grandson of progenitor Nicholas Kegg.
RICHARD LEE SPENCER Fifth great grandson of progenitor Nicholas Kegg.
ZEB SPENCER Sixth great grandson of progenitor Nicholas Kegg.

SPETTLE

GREGORY L. SPETTLE Seventh great grandson of progenitor Nicholas Kegg.

SPICER

BRETT SPICER Seventh great grandson of progenitor Nicholas Kegg.

SPIERENBURG

ELI SPIERENBURG Seventh great grandson of progenitor Nicholas Kegg.

SPISAK

CAROL AUDREY SPISAK Sixth great granddaughter of progenitor Nicholas Kegg.
JAMES SPISAK Sixth great grandson of progenitor Nicholas Kegg.
KATHLEEN SPISAK Sixth great granddaughter of progenitor Nicholas Kegg.
MARY P. SPISAK Sixth great granddaughter of progenitor Nicholas Kegg.

SPOERRY

CINDY JO SPOERRY Sixth great granddaughter of progenitor Nicholas Kegg.
FLOYD D. SPOERRY Sixth great grandson of progenitor Nicholas Kegg.
PENNY L. SPOERRY Sixth great granddaughter of progenitor Nicholas Kegg.
HENRY W. SPOERRY Sixth great grandson of progenitor Nicholas Kegg.

SPONSLER

TARA LYNN SPONSLER Sixth great granddaughter of progenitor Nicholas Kegg.

SPRAGUE

JACOB SPRAGUE, aka "Jake", Seventh great grandson of progenitor Nicholas Kegg.

SPRENGER

ALEXIS SPRENGER Seventh great granddaughter of progenitor Nicholas Kegg. **AMBER SPRENGER** Seventh great granddaughter of progenitor Nicholas Kegg. **AMY SPRENGER** Sixth great granddaughter of progenitor Nicholas Kegg. **BRENT SPRENGER** Sixth great grandson of progenitor Nicholas Kegg. **KATIE SPRENGER** Seventh great granddaughter of progenitor Nicholas Kegg. **TODD SPRENGER** Sixth great grandson of progenitor Nicholas Kegg. **TORREY SPRENGER** Sixth great grandson of progenitor Nicholas Kegg.

SPROW

NICK SPROW Seventh great grandson of progenitor Nicholas Kegg.
TONY SPROW Seventh great grandson of progenitor Nicholas Kegg.

SQUIRE

RYAN SQUIRE Eighth great grandson of progenitor Nicholas Kegg.

STACK

PATRICK STACK Sixth great grandson of progenitor Nicholas Kegg.
PAULA STACK Sixth great granddaughter of progenitor Nicholas Kegg.

STACKHOUSE

JASON ALEXANDER STACKHOUSE Sixth great grandson of progenitor Nicholas Kegg.
PETER ARRON STACKHOUSE Sixth great grandson of progenitor Nicholas Kegg.

STAETTER

EMILEE STAETTER Sixth great granddaughter of progenitor Nicholas Kegg.

STAILEY

BENJAMIN STAILEY Eighth great grandson of progenitor Nicholas Kegg. **CHARLIE STAILEY** Seventh great grandson of progenitor Nicholas Kegg. **JAMIE STAILEY** Seventh great grandson of progenitor Nicholas Kegg. **JULIA STAILEY** Eighth great granddaughter of progenitor Nicholas Kegg. **MELISSA STAILEY** Seventh great granddaughter of progenitor Nicholas Kegg.

STAILY

MITCHELL J. STAILY Sixth great grandson of progenitor Nicholas Kegg.
ZANE K. STAILY Sixth great grandson of progenitor Nicholas Kegg.

STANGE

LLOYD STANGE Fifth great grandson of progenitor Nicholas Kegg.
PHILLIP STANGE Fifth great grandson of progenitor Nicholas Kegg.
ROY STANGE Fifth great grandson of progenitor Nicholas Kegg.

STANKER

DAVID STANKER Seventh great grandson of progenitor Nicholas Kegg.
HOLLY STANKER Seventh great granddaughter of progenitor Nicholas Kegg.
JESSICA STANKER Seventh great granddaughter of progenitor Nicholas Kegg.

STANLEY

JANNIE ILENE STANLEY [6062A] aka "Ilene" (1936 – 2016) daughter of James and Arlene (Laird) Stanley married Charles Dwain Tull with whom she was mother of (5). Ilene was a farm wife and worked on the farm. She also was a healthcare worker at a nursing home. She was a faithful member of the Assembly of God Church.

WANDA LORRAINE STANLEY [6062B] (1920 – 1991) daughter of William and Winnie (Laird) Stanley, married Robert Earl Gannan with whom she was mother of (2). Wanda was a homemaker and a member of the Blue Ridge Christian Union Church.

STANTON

GUY STEWART STANTON Fourth great grandson of progenitor Nicholas Kegg.
HOLLY THERESA STANTON Fifth great granddaughter of progenitor Nicholas Kegg.
JULIE ANN STANTON Fifth great granddaughter of progenitor Nicholas Kegg.
ROBIN MARIE STANTON Fifth great granddaughter of progenitor Nicholas Kegg.
SARA R. STANTON, aka "Sally", Fourth great granddaughter of progenitor Nicholas Kegg.
THOMAS WINSTON STANTON Fourth great grandson of progenitor Nicholas Kegg.
WILLIAM TURNER STANTON [6063] aka "Bill" (1932 – 2004) son of Guy and Almira (Turner) Stanton married Darlene Francis Green with whom he was father of (3). Bill was a cattle breeder and also served as a milk tester for the Dairy Herd Improvement Association in Howard County for 43 years. His family also produced maple syrup in western Maryland.

STAPEL

BRENDA STAPEL Seventh great granddaughter of progenitor Nicholas Kegg.
DALE D. STAPEL Seventh great grandson of progenitor Nicholas Kegg.

STARBUCK

AUSTIN GARRETT STARBUCK Seventh great grandson of progenitor Nicholas Kegg.
LARRY DEAN STARBUCK Sixth great grandson of progenitor Nicholas Kegg.
LONNIE RAY STARBUCK Sixth great grandson of progenitor Nicholas Kegg.
MARCIE JOANN STARBUCK Seventh great granddaughter of progenitor Nicholas Kegg.
MARISSA LIN STARBUCK Seventh great granddaughter of progenitor Nicholas Kegg.
MATRINA RENEE STARBUCK Seventh great granddaughter of progenitor Nicholas Kegg.
MALANIE KAY STARBUCK Seventh great granddaughter of progenitor Nicholas Kegg.
SETH RAY STARBUCK Seventh great grandson of progenitor Nicholas Kegg.

[6062A] News-Press Now (IA) Apr 20, 2016 [6062B] St. Joseph News-Press/Gazette (MO) Nov 11, 1991 [6063] Howard County Times (MD) Dec 17, 2004

STARK

JEANNE STARK Fifth great granddaughter of progenitor Nicholas Kegg. **LARRY ALVIN STARK** (1938 – 2007) son of Everard and Lucile (Abbott) Stark was a veteran of Vietnam. Larry was a fifth great grandson of progenitor Nicholas Kegg. **MARGARET KATHLEEN STARK** Sixth great granddaughter of progenitor Nicholas Kegg. **RAY E. STARK** Fifth great grandson of progenitor Nicholas Kegg. **ROBERT EVERETT STARK** Sixth great grandson of progenitor Nicholas Kegg. **ROBERT M. STARK** Fifth great grandson of progenitor Nicholas Kegg.

STARLING

ASHLEE MAE STARLING Seventh great granddaughter of progenitor Nicholas Kegg.

STARLIPER

BRADLEY ALLEN STARLIPER Seventh great grandson of progenitor Nicholas Kegg.

STARR

ANN MARIE STARR Seventh great granddaughter of progenitor Nicholas Kegg. **GEORGE STARR** Sixth great grandson of progenitor Nicholas Kegg. **JOHN ROBERT STARR**, aka "Bob", Sixth great grandson of progenitor Nicholas Kegg. **JUSTIN STARR** Seventh great grandson of progenitor Nicholas Kegg. **LISA KAY STARR** Seventh great granddaughter of progenitor Nicholas Kegg. **VALERIE STARR** Sixth great granddaughter of progenitor Nicholas Kegg.

STATES

BETSEY STATES Sixth great granddaughter of progenitor Nicholas Kegg.
EMILY STATES Sixth great granddaughter of progenitor Nicholas Kegg.
JENNIFER D. STATES Sixth great granddaughter of progenitor Nicholas Kegg.
JOHN D. STATES Sixth great grandson of progenitor Nicholas Kegg.

STATLER

NATALIE L. STATLER Sixth great granddaughter of progenitor Nicholas Kegg.

STAYER

ARVILLA SUSAN STAYER [6063A] (1913 – 1989) daughter of Edward and Emma (Fickes) Stayer married twice, first to Chester William Thompson with whom she was mother of (1) later, she married Frederick Miller Blattenberger. **BERTHA A STAYER** [6063B] (1898 – 1951) daughter of Edward and Emma (Fickes) Stayer married Marshall Earl Foore with whom she was mother of (3). Bertha was a member of the Six Mile Run Church of God and was very active in church functions. She was very diligent in her Christian responsibilities. **CAROL DIANA STAYER** [6063C] (1947 – 2011) daughter of Ernest and Doris (McCleaf) Stayer married Rick Essen with whom she was mother of (1). **CLARENCE LLOYD STAYER** [6063D] (1897 – 1947) son of Edward and Emma (Fickes) Stayer, married Julia Gertrude Shaffer with whom he was father of (3). **DAPHNE KAY STAYER** Seventh great granddaughter of progenitor Nicholas Kegg. **HAROLD L. STAYER** Sixth great grandson of progenitor Nicholas Kegg. **HAROLD LLOYD STAYER** [6063E] aka "Freddy" (1942 – 2013) son of

---

[6063A] Bedford County Genealogical Society obituary obtained and contributed by D. Sue Dible [6063B] p.11 - Daily News (PA) Oct 1, 1951 [6063C] St. Louis Post-Dispatch (MO) Aug 1, 2011 [6063D] p.6 - Bedford Gazette (PA) April 24, 1947 contributed by Bob Rose [6063E] Bedford Gazette (PA) Dec 23, 2013 contributed by Bob Rose

Clarence and Julia (Shaffer) Stayer married Wanda Darlene Wilt with whom he was father of (3). Harold served in the U.S. Army with the 404th MP Company. He was self-employed as a welder for 30 years. Harold was a member of the Bedford Masonic Lodge No. 320 F&AM and enjoyed tinkering.

JOHN EDWARD STAYER (1933 – 1933) son of Ray C. and Ethel (Mowry) Stayer.

JOHN ROSS STAYER [6064] (1930 – 1981) son of Clarence and Julia (Shaffer) Stayer.

JOYCE LYNN STAYER [6064A] (1951 – 2019) daughter of Ernest and Doris (McCleaf) Stayer married John O. Bartholow with whom she was mother of (2). Joyce worked as a House Parent for Scotland School of Veterans Children for eight years. She was a member of United Church of Christ, VFW Lady's Auxiliary and American Legion in Shippensburg. In her spare time, Joyce enjoyed travelling across the U.S. and internationally with John, boating and water skiing at Lake Raystown and feeding wildlife at her and John's cabin. She was known to her family and friends as an extremely caring, giving, smiley person.

JULIE MARIE STAYER Sixth great granddaughter of progenitor Nicholas Kegg.

KEVIN R. STAYER Sixth great grandson of progenitor Nicholas Kegg.   **MARY A. STAYER** [6064B] (1901 – 1975) daughter of Edward and Emma (Fickes) Stayer married Roy Conda Casteel with whom she was mother of (3). Mary was a member of St. James Lutheran Church and the Ladies Aid of the church.

NANCY STAYER (1934 – 1934) daughter of Ray C. and Ethel (Mowry) Stayer.

PAUL JOSEPH STAYER [6065] (1935 – 1939) son of Clarence and Julia (Shaffer) Stayer was jolted from his position on top of a load of lumber when his father started to pull the load with a tractor. Paul fell to the ground and the back wheels of the wagon ran over his body.   **RAY C. STAYER** [6065A] (1905 – 1982) son of Edward and Emma (Fickes) Stayer married Ethel T. Mowry with whom he was father of (3). Ray was the former owner of Bedford Hotel and Motel. He was a member of St. John's United Church of Christ, Bedford Blue Lodge No. 320, Valley of Harrisburg Consistory, Jaffa Temple, Altoona, Shawnee Forest No. 167 Tall Cedars of Lebanon, and Bedford Moose Lodge No. 480.   **RYLEA STAYER** Seventh great granddaughter of progenitor Nicholas Kegg.   **STANLEY RAY STAYER** aka "Stan" Sixth great grandson of progenitor Nicholas Kegg.

STEACH

DENNIS JAMES STEACH Fifth great grandson of progenitor Nicholas Kegg.   **LARRY J. STEACH** Sixth great grandson of progenitor Nicholas Kegg.   **LORELLE STEACH** Sixth great granddaughter of progenitor Nicholas Kegg.   **MICHELE STEACH** Sixth great granddaughter of progenitor Nicholas Kegg.   **PATRICIA ANN STEACH** [6065B] (1937 – 2015) daughter of Grant and Ruth (Bollman) Steach married John B. Mobus with whom she was mother of (5). Patty was a very dedicated and a very well liked employee at the First National Bank, Everett, for more than 30 years until her retirement. She was a member of the Bedford Springs Chapter No.41 Order of the Eastern Star and a former member of the Junior Women's Club in Everett. She had an infectious laugh and a positive outlook on life, never saying anything negative about anyone. She loved vacations to the Outer Banks with her family. Patty was a fan of the Pittsburgh Steelers, as well as the Pitt Panthers and enjoyed watching NASCAR Racing.

ROBERT ARTHUR STEACH Fifth great grandson of progenitor Nicholas Kegg.

ROBERT A. STEACH Sixth great grandson of progenitor Nicholas Kegg.   **SHAUNA L. STEACH** Sixth great granddaughter of progenitor Nicholas Kegg.   **THOMAS W. STEACH** [6065C] aka "Buck" (1945 – 2006) son of Grant and Ruth (Bollman) Steach married twice; first to Connie Cornell with whom he was father of (2). Later, he married Missy Hillegass. Buck was an avid hunter, horseman, NASCAR and dirt track fan. He was a member of the Everett Legion Post No. 8 and was employed at Kennametal for 38 years. Buck served in the U.S. Army as a sergeant in the Vietnam War. He received the Vietnam Service Medal, Vietnam Campaign Medal, and the Bronze Star Medal. Buck was an expert rifleman (M-16), and a sharpshooter (M-14).

[6064] Bedford County Historical Society (PA), book 11, page 4218 obtained by D. Sue Dible [6064A] Bedford Gazette (PA) April 23, 2019 contributed by Bob Rose [6064B] Bedford County Genealogical Society obituary obtained by D. Sue Dible [6065] Bedford County Historical Society (PA), book 86, page 108 obtained by D. Sue Dible [6065A] p.5 – Bedford Inquirer (PA) July 9, 1982 [6065B] Bedford Gazette (PA) Oct 27, 2015, contributed by Bob Rose [6065C] Bedford Inquirer (PA) Dec 22, 2006, contributed by Bob Rose

STECKEL

ROBERT DALE STECKEL aka "Bob", Sixth great grandson of progenitor Nicholas Kegg.

STEDWILL

LISA ANNE STEDWILL Sixth great granddaughter of progenitor Nicholas Kegg.
MARGARET ELIZABETH STEDWILL [6065D] (1927 – 2016) daughter of Edgar and Lena (Bowers) Stedwill married Harley Joe Hubble with whom she was mother of (4). Margaret retired as the Dean of the School of Nursing at Hocking College. She earned her Nursing degree from The Ohio State University and later earned a Master of Education from Ohio University and a Masters of Nursing from Wright State University. She was a member of Sigma Theta Tau, the International Honor Society of Nursing. **MARY SUSAN STEDWILL** Sixth great granddaughter of progenitor Nicholas Kegg.
ROLAND SCOTT STEDWILL Fifth great grandson of progenitor Nicholas Kegg.

STEELE

ARON STEELE Seventh great grandson of progenitor Nicholas Kegg. **BOBBIE LEE STEELE** Seventh great granddaughter of progenitor Nicholas Kegg. **BRIAN L. STEELE** Seventh great grandson of progenitor Nicholas Kegg. **DENISE ANN STEELE** Seventh great granddaughter of progenitor Nicholas Kegg. **HELENA MAE STEELE** Fifth great granddaughter of progenitor Nicholas Kegg. **HIRAM STEELE** [6066] (1877 – 1896) son of Johnson and Mary (Parent) Steele.
INFANT STEELE [6067] (1905 – 1905) daughter of Knode and Lizzie (Renner) Steele.
JOHN STEELE [6068] (1883 – 1934) son of Johnson and Mary (Parent) Steele, married Edith Subkowski. John was employed as a meat cutter with the Wilkins Packing company and was a member of Beacon Light Spiritualist church. **KNODE STEELE** [6069] (1881 – 1970) son of Johnson and Mary (Parent) Steele married twice; first to Lizzir Renner with whom he was father of (2). Later, he married Edith Hardy. Knode was employed by the Biscuit Co. in St. Joseph, Michigan. He was a member of the Masonic Lodge in St. Joseph, Mich., and the Fisherman's Bible Class in Fort Wayne.
LUKE STEELE Fifth great grandson of progenitor Nicholas Kegg.
MARK STEELE Fifth great grandson of progenitor Nicholas Kegg.
MARY CATHERINE STEELE [6070, 6071] (1889 – 1984) aka "Mamie", daughter of Johnson and Mary (Parent) Steele, married David Allen Dinius with whom she was mother of (1).
MATTHEW STEELE Fifth great grandson of progenitor Nicholas Kegg.
MICHELLE LEE ANN STEELE [6071A] aka "Shellbell" (1979 – 2002) daughter of Robert and Robbie (Carson) Steele married Joseph Houseworth with whom she was mother of (1). Shellbell worked as a cashier at the Calico Texaco in Yermo for two years, and Top of the Hill and Lil's Saloon at Calico Ghost Town for eight years. Houseworth enjoyed quilting, sewing, making angels and "being a social butterfly." She was always willing to help anyone.
ROBERT J. STEELE Sixth great grandson of progenitor Nicholas Kegg.
ROBERT JOHN STEELE Fifth great grandson of progenitor Nicholas Kegg.
TODD D. STEELE Fifth great grandson of progenitor Nicholas Kegg.
VICTORIA MELISSALUANN STEELE Sixth great granddaughter of progenitor Nicholas Kegg.
WELCOME EDWARD STEELE (1911 – 1954) son of Knode and Lizzie (Dennis) Steele married Emma A Litlec and later married Mariana Connors.
WILLIAM B. STEELE [6072] (1885 – 1942) son of Johnson and Mary (Parent) Steele was a member of the Indiana Association of the Blind.

[6065D] Athens Messenger (OH) June 15, 2016 [6066] Fort Wayne News (IN) Sept 25, 1896 [6067] p.5 - Fort Wayne Journal Gazette July 20, 1905 [6068] p.2 - Fort Wayne Journal Gazette Oct 31,1934, obtained by D. Sue Dible [6069] Fort Wayne Journal Gazette (IN) June 10, 1970, obtained by D. Sue Dible [6070] p.2 Fort Wayne News (IN) Aug 13, 1915 [6071] Fort Wayne News (IN) Jan 6, 1957 [6071A] FindAGrave # 83113555 [6072] p. 5 Fort Wayne Journal Gazette Jan 9,1942, obtained by D. Sue Dible

STEFL

PATRICK STEFL Fifth great grandson of progenitor Nicholas Kegg.
WILLIAM ANTON STEFL Fifth great grandson of progenitor Nicholas Kegg.

STEGMAIER

JAMES MICHAEL STEGMAIER Fifth great grandson of progenitor Nicholas Kegg.

STEGMAN

SHEILA STEGMAN Fifth great granddaughter of progenitor Nicholas Kegg.
SHELLEY STEGMAN Fifth great granddaughter of progenitor Nicholas Kegg.

STEHLIK

CONNER STEHLIK Eighth great grandson of progenitor Nicholas Kegg.
KELSEY STEHLIK Eighth great granddaughter of progenitor Nicholas Kegg.
RYAN CHARLES STEHLIK Sixth great grandson of progenitor Nicholas Kegg.
TAYLOR STEHLIK Eighth great granddaughter of progenitor Nicholas Kegg.

STEIGERWALT

JENNIFER LYNN STEIGERWALT Sixth great granddaughter of progenitor Nicholas Kegg.

STEIN

JARED STEIN Sixth great grandson of progenitor Nicholas Kegg.
LAUREN STEIN Sixth great granddaughter of progenitor Nicholas Kegg.
MARTHA SUE STEIN aka "Marti" Fifth great granddaughter of progenitor Nicholas Kegg.
ROBERT ROY STEIN Fifth great grandson of progenitor Nicholas Kegg.

STEMEN

JUDITH MARIE STEMEN Fifth great granddaughter of progenitor Nicholas Kegg.
LESLIE A. STEMEN Fifth great granddaughter of progenitor Nicholas Kegg.
MATTHEW A. STEMEN Fifth great grandson of progenitor Nicholas Kegg.
TERESA JO STEMEN Fifth great granddaughter of progenitor Nicholas Kegg.

STEPHEN

DALLAS GENE STEPHEN Sixth great grandson of progenitor Nicholas Kegg.
MONICA STEPHEN Sixth great granddaughter of progenitor Nicholas Kegg.
VERONICA STEPHEN Sixth great granddaughter of progenitor Nicholas Kegg.

STEPHENS

JEFF STEPHENS Sixth great grandson of progenitor Nicholas Kegg.
SAVANAH STEPHENS Seventh great granddaughter of progenitor Nicholas Kegg.
SHANDA STEPHENS Sixth great granddaughter of progenitor Nicholas Kegg.
SHERRY STEPHENS Sixth great granddaughter of progenitor Nicholas Kegg.

STEPHENSON

BRIAN STEPHENSON Seventh great grandson of progenitor Nicholas Kegg.
CODY STEPHENSON Eighth great grandson of progenitor Nicholas Kegg. **ERIC STEPHENSON** Seventh great grandson of progenitor Nicholas Kegg. **GABRIELLA STEPHENSON** Nineth great granddaughter of progenitor Nicholas Kegg. **IAN MICHAEL STEPHENSON** Seventh great grandson of progenitor Nicholas Kegg. **SAMANTHA STEPHENSON** Eighth great granddaughter of progenitor Nicholas Kegg. **TRAYCI LYNN STEPHENSON** Seventh great granddaughter of progenitor Nicholas Kegg.

STEPLOWSKI

MICHAEL STEPLOWSKI Eighth great grandson of progenitor Nicholas Kegg.

STEPPE

CATHLEEN STEPPE Sixth great granddaughter of progenitor Nicholas Kegg.
SUSANNE RAE STEPPE Sixth great granddaughter of progenitor Nicholas Kegg.

STERLING

DYLAN STERLING [6073] (1992 – 2014) son of Robert and Kim (Foreman) Sterling loved composing electronic music and had dreams of becoming an electronic music producer. A highlight of his life was going to Shambhala (a famous 5-day electronic music festival in Salmo, BC). Dylan pursued an idea he had to become an entrepreneur as he worked for the Good Health Mart Brampton store where he was employed as the assistant manager. Dylan was an invaluable resource to his co-workers.
EDEN STERLING Sixth great grandson of progenitor Nicholas Kegg.
GLENN ALLEN STERLING [6074] (1923 – 2004) son of Robert and Loa (Keesy) Sterling married twice; first to Mary Dandakis with whom he was father of (1). Later, he married Alverda C. Crissman. Glenn retired from the Ford Motor Co., Sandusky, and prior to that worked at Norwalk Truck Lines.
IONA PEARL STERLING [6075] (1915 – 1992) daughter of Robert and Loa (Keesy) Sterling was a retired 44-year employee of the Mansfield Products Co (Westinghouse Electric Co) She was a member of First Church of the Brethren, its Covenant Group and the choir. **JOHN E. STERLING** Fifth great grandson of progenitor Nicholas Kegg. **JUSTIN STERLING** Sixth great grandson of progenitor Nicholas Kegg. **MONICA MARIE STERLING** Sixth great granddaughter of progenitor Nicholas Kegg. **ROBERT EARL STERLING III** [6075A] (1927 – 1965) son of Robert and Loa (Keesy) Sterling married Sara Jane Evans with whom he was father of (6). Robert had been a pattern maker at Fate Root eHath in Plymouth. He was a member of the Willard EUB Church and the Elks Lodge. **ROBERT SCOTT STERLING** [6075B] aka "Bob" (1957 – 2020) son of Robert and Sara Jane (Evans) Sterling married Kim Foreman with whom he was father of (3). Bob was larger than life, a force of nature and the person in a roomful of people who commanded attention. To be with Bob at his best was to be enveloped in laughter and love. Bob lived in Hamilton, Ohio after attending Ohio University, where he became involved in the city's community theater family. In this he followed in the footsteps of his mother, from whom he inherited a beautiful singing voice and a love of performance. Bob's adventuresome spirit then took him to New York City where he enrolled in the American Academy of Dramatic Arts. Bob's career took him and his family to Amsterdam, working for his friend Jerome Mol, with whom he worked off and on the rest of his life. Bob believed so much that if you open your heart to the universe, miracles will happen. And they did. He also believed that he was protected by his angels, those who had passed.

[6073] https://www.dylansterling.net/obtained by D. Sue Dible [6074] Sandusky Register (OH) Mar 26, 2004 [6075] Library obituary clipping obtained by D. Sue Dible

RONALD L. STERLING [6076] (1918 – 1953) son of Robert and Loa (Keesy) Sterling was a veteran of World War II. Ronald killed in a ditch cave-in on a road construction project near Ann Arbor, Michigan. **SALLY ANN STERLING** Fifth great granddaughter of progenitor Nicholas Kegg. **SHERYL JANE STERLING** Fifth great granddaughter of progenitor Nicholas Kegg. **SUSAN KAY STERLING** Fifth great granddaughter of progenitor Nicholas Kegg. **THOMAS ALLEN STERLING** [6076A] (1952 – 1997) son of Glenn and Mary (Dandakis) Sterling, married Kristine Susan Eaton with whom he was father of (2). Thomas worked as a pipefitter at Delphi Chassis Systems in Sandusky for more than 20 years. He owned and operated the Village Cafe and Pizzaria and M&M's Video, both in New London. He was a member of American Legion Broom Wood Post 292, VFW 4654, and Eagles Arie 2869, all of New London. **THOMAS GLENN STERLING** Sixth great grandson of progenitor Nicholas Kegg. **WILLIAM A. STERLING** Fifth great grandson of progenitor Nicholas Kegg.

STERN

BARRY LEE STERN Fifth great grandson of progenitor Nicholas Kegg.
BRENDA LORRAINE STERN Fifth great granddaughter of progenitor Nicholas Kegg.
TOMI CHAD STERN Fifth great grandson of progenitor Nicholas Kegg.

STERRETT

DAMON STERRETT Seventh great grandson of progenitor Nicholas Kegg.

STETZ

GEORGE M. STETZ Fifth great grandson of progenitor Nicholas Kegg.
JENNIFER MARIE STETZ Sixth great granddaughter of progenitor Nicholas Kegg.
MELANIE J. STETZ Sixth great granddaughter of progenitor Nicholas Kegg.
MICHAEL P. STETZ Sixth great grandson of progenitor Nicholas Kegg. **MICHELLE L. STETZ** Sixth great granddaughter of progenitor Nicholas Kegg. **PAUL J. STETZ** Fifth great grandson of progenitor Nicholas Kegg. **RICHARD STETZ** Fifth great grandson of progenitor Nicholas Kegg.

STEVENSON

DANIEL STEVENSON Seventh great grandson of progenitor Nicholas Kegg.
DUNCAN STEVENSON Seventh great grandson of progenitor Nicholas Kegg.

STEVEY

CLAYTON STEVEY Seventh great grandson of progenitor Nicholas Kegg.
KATRINA STEVEY Seventh great granddaughter of progenitor Nicholas Kegg.
LEROY STEVEY Seventh great grandson of progenitor Nicholas Kegg.

STEWART

EVALINE L. STEWART [6077] (1930 – 2014) daughter of Roy and Ruth (Knouf) Stewart, married Leland Dewitt Bohmont. **JACK G. STEWART** [6078] (1937 – 2004) son of Lester and Anna (Estep) Stewart, married Zelda G. Gensimore. Jack retired from Gwin, Dobson, Foreman Inc., Altoona, as a professional surveyor.

[6075A] p.3 Mansfield News Journal (OH) Sep 6, 1965 [6075B] A S Turner & Sons Funeral Home & Crematory (GA) [6076] p.10 Sandusky Register (OH) June 17, 1953 [6076A] p.3 C 1-2 Norwalk Reflector (OH) Sep 15, 1997, contributed by D. Sue Dible [6077] News-Leader (MO) Oct. 21, 2014 [6078] Altoona Mirror (PA) Sep 21, 2004

JOSEPHINE RUTHANNA STEWART [6079] (1919 – 1994) daughter of Roy and Ruth (Knouf) Stewart, married Harold H. Hoffman with whom she was mother of (6). Josephine was a charter member of American Legion Post 375 Auxiliary, and the Reorganized Church of Jesus Christ of Latter-day Saints. **MAMIE MARIE STEWART** [6079A] (1923 – 2006) daughter of Roy and Ruth (Knouf) Stewart, married Paul Forest Cain with whom she was mother of (1). Hybridizer and iris grower, Mamie was a member and historian of the Lincoln Iris Society. Member, United Methodist Church of Fairbury and Fairbury Garden Club. Co-owner of Alvo Grocery Store. Retired fireman and E.M.T. for Alvo Fire and Rescue. Life and charter member of the American Legion Auxiliary 375. Chaplain and life member of VFW Post 3113; life member of the Disabled American Veterans Auxiliary Chapter 7, Lincoln. **MARILYN JOIE STEWART** Sixth great granddaughter of progenitor Nicholas Kegg. **MARLENE W. STEWART** [6079B] (1926 – 2006) daughter of Roy and Ruth (Knouf) Stewart, married Laverne D. Amick with whom she was mother of (2). Marlene was employed at Goodyear Manufacturing for over 27 years. Member of Eastern Star (Chpt. 153), American Legion Aux. (Unit 375), & the D.A.V.A. (Chpt. 7). **SHAYLEI NICOLE STEWART** Eighth great granddaughter of progenitor Nicholas Kegg.

STICHTER

ADAM STICHTER Sixth great grandson of progenitor Nicholas Kegg. **ALMAN STICHTER** [6080] (1904 – 1907) son of Henry and Lucy (Kegg) Stichter. **BECKY STICHTER** Fifth great granddaughter of progenitor Nicholas Kegg. **CAROLYN STICHTER** Fourth great granddaughter of progenitor Nicholas Kegg. **CHARLOTTE STICHTER** Fifth great granddaughter of progenitor Nicholas Kegg. **CRYSTAL STICHTER** Fifth great granddaughter of progenitor Nicholas Kegg. **CYNTHIA STICHTER** Fifth great granddaughter of progenitor Nicholas Kegg. **DENNIS W. STICHTER** Fourth great grandson of progenitor Nicholas Kegg. **DONALD R. STICHTER** [6079C] (1931 – 2017) son of Gordon and Esther (Good) Stichter married Evelyn Louise Brown with whom he was father of (6). Donald farmed for 12 years then went into real estate and auctioneering. His last 20 years before retirement he was a bus driver for the Wa-Nee Schools. He was a member of Yellow Creek Mennonite Church and served for a term on the finance committee and with the Bible Memory Program. He also served on various service projects. His hobbies were restoring antique cars and tractors and he belonged to the Antique Car Restorers Club and 2 Cylinder Club. **EILEEN STICHTER** Fourth great granddaughter of progenitor Nicholas Kegg **ELSIE LEONA C. STICHTER** [6081] (1922 – 2001) daughter of Harvey and Grace (Culp) Stichter, married Walter W. Ramer with whom she was mother of (4). **ESTHER LEONA STICHTER** [6082] (1926 – 1958) daughter of Fred and Goldie (Hygema) Stichter, was an employee in the furniture factory. **FRANK STICHTER** Fifth great grandson of progenitor Nicholas Kegg. **FRED STICHTER** [6083] (1898 – 1998) son of Henry and Lucy (Kegg) Stichter married twice; first to Goldie Hygema with whom he was father of (1). Later, he married Bertha Naomi Yoder with whom he was father of (3). **GORDON H. STICHTER** [6084] (1905 – 1956) son of Henry and Lucy (Kegg) Stichter, married Esther Susan Good with whom he was father of (6). Gordon accepted Christ as his Savior in youth and was a member of the North Main Street Mennonite Church at the time of his death. He had a keen interest in missions and disaster and relief work and gave freely of his time to various projects as they arose. He was a member of the local Mission Committee and the Disaster and Service Committee. **GORDON JAMES STICHTER** Fifth great grandson of progenitor Nicholas Kegg. **HARVEY STICHTER** [6085] (1901 – 1948) son of Henry and Lucy (Kegg) Stichter, married Grace B. Culp with whom he was father of (3). In his youth Harvey united with the Mennonite Church, and for the last nineteen years of his life held his membership with the Yellow Creek congregation, near Goshen, Indiana. **HENRY LEE STICHTER** [6086] (1942 – 1942) son of Fred and

---

[6079] p. A5 - Mountain Democrat (CA) Oct 26, 1994 [6079A] p.4 - Lincoln Journal Star (NE) Feb 15, 2006 [6079B] Aspen Mortuary, Inc (NE) [6079C] Goshen News (IN) Apr 1, 2017 [6080] Missionary Church Gospel Herald [6081] p.13 - The Mennonite (KS) April 3, 2001 [6082] Gospel Herald - Vol LI, No. 48 - Dec 2, 1958 [6083] p.B5 - South Bend Tribune (IN) May 12, 1998 [6084] Gospel Herald Sep 1956 [6085] Gospel Herald May 1948 transcribed by John Ingold [6086] Wakarusa Tribune (IN) Mar 19, 1942 [6086A] Goshen News (IN) July 12, 2013 contributed by D. Sue Dible

Bertha (Yoder) Stichter. **JEREMIAH STICHTER** Sixth great grandson of progenitor Nicholas Kegg. **JOE STICHTER** Fifth great grandson of progenitor Nicholas Kegg. **KAREN STICHTER** Fifth great granddaughter of progenitor Nicholas Kegg. **KATHLEEN STICHTER** Fifth great granddaughter of progenitor Nicholas Kegg. **KENNETH E STICHTER** [6086A] (1939 – 2013) son of Gordon and Esther (Good) Stichter married Etolia B. Pruitt with whom he was father of (2). Ken was a small plane pilot. He saw much of Alaska and shared his love of flying with his family and friends. **KRIS STICHTER** Fifth great grandson of progenitor Nicholas Kegg. **LUKE STICHTER** Sixth great grandson of progenitor Nicholas Kegg. **MAGGIE LUCRETIA STICHTER** [6087] (1889 – 1981) daughter of Henry and Lucy (Kegg) Stichter married twice; first to Samuel W. Blosser with whom she was mother of (4). Later, she married J. Frank Miller. Maggie was a member of North Goshen Mennonite Church. **MAHLON H. STICHTER** [6088] (1891 – 1952) son of Henry and Lucy (Kegg) Stichter, married Sarah Homes with whom he was father of (1). Mahlon was of the Mennonite faith. **MELISSA STICHTER** Fifth great granddaughter of progenitor Nicholas Kegg. **MIKE STICHTER** Fifth great grandson of progenitor Nicholas Kegg. **PERRY H. STICHTER** (1895 – 1915) son of Henry and Lucy (Kegg) Stichter. **RALPH L. STICHTER** Fourth great grandson of progenitor Nicholas Kegg. **REBECCA BETHANY STICHTER** [6089] (1997 – 1999) daughter of Roger and Jane (Ingold) Stichter. **ROBERT EARL STICHTER** (1929 – 2016) son of Harvey and Grace (Culp) Stichter married Harriet Ann Schrock with whom he was father of (1). **ROGER LEE STICHTER** Fifth great grandson of progenitor Nicholas Kegg. **RUTH NAOMI STICHTER** [6090] (1915 – 1994) daughter of Mahlon and Sarah (Homes) Stichter, was a seamstress at Elkhart General Hospital and a clerk at Christian Light Book Store, Nappanee, until she retired. Ruth was a member of Bible Baptist Church for many years and was a Sunday school teacher. **STEVE STICHTER** Fifth great grandson of progenitor Nicholas Kegg. **SUSANNA STICHTER** Sixth great granddaughter of progenitor Nicholas Kegg. **TIM STICHTER** Fifth great grandson of progenitor Nicholas Kegg. **WILL STICHTER** Fifth great grandson of progenitor Nicholas Kegg.

STIEB

DALE PATRICK STIEB Sixth great grandson of progenitor Nicholas Kegg.
EUGENE CURTIS STIEB Sixth great grandson of progenitor Nicholas Kegg.
JACE STIEB Eighth great grandson of progenitor Nicholas Kegg.
JEREMY STIEB Seventh great grandson of progenitor Nicholas Kegg.

STIGERS

ANGELL L. STIGERS Sixth great granddaughter of progenitor Nicholas Kegg.
RUSH D. STIGERS Sixth great grandson of progenitor Nicholas Kegg.
VICKI DIANE STIGERS Sixth great granddaughter of progenitor Nicholas Kegg.

STILLWAGNER

CHARLES EDWARD STILLWAGNER III [6091] (1943 – 1983) son of Charles and Charlotte (Meyers) Stillwagner. Charles was a veteran of Vietnam.

STINNETT

EILEEN E. STINNETT [6092] (1922 – 1985) daughter of Clarence and Ethel (Keggs) Stinnett, married Paul Lowell Dunlap with whom she was mother of (2).

[6087] Missionary Church Gospel Herald [6088] p. 2 – Elkhart Truth (IN) Feb 19, 1952 [6089] p.7 – News-Sentinel (IN) May 21, 1999 [6090] p.B6 - South Bend Tribune (IN) Sept 20, 1994 [6091] The Republic (PA) April 14, 1983 [6092] Tampa Bay Times (FL) Jan 26, 1985

JENNIFER M. STINNETT Sixth great granddaughter of progenitor Nicholas Kegg.
MARILYN JANE STINNETT Fourth great granddaughter of progenitor Nicholas Kegg.

STINSON

DEANN STINSON Seventh great granddaughter of progenitor Nicholas Kegg. **JAMES STINSON** Seventh great grandson of progenitor Nicholas Kegg. **JASON ADAM STINSON** Seventh great grandson of progenitor Nicholas Kegg. **JOSEPH DEAN STINSON** Sixth adopted great grandson of progenitor Nicholas Kegg. **KATHERINE B. STINSON** aka "Kathie", Seventh great granddaughter of progenitor Nicholas Kegg. **ROBERT A. STINSON JR.** [6093] (1976 – 1991) son of Robert and Lorraine (Horton) Stinson would have been a freshman at Mitchell High School when he accidentally drowns. **ROBIN M. STINSON** Seventh great granddaughter of progenitor Nicholas Kegg. **SANDRA LOUISE STINSON**, aka "Sandy" Sixth great granddaughter of progenitor Nicholas Kegg. **SHELLY STINSON** Seventh great granddaughter of progenitor Nicholas Kegg.

STITH

ERIKA STITH Eighth great granddaughter of progenitor Nicholas Kegg.

STITHEM

CHARLOTTE STITHEM [6093A] aka "Charlie" (1948 – 2010) daughter of Albert and Frances (Knouf) Stithem was a Hutchinson newspaper carrier.
ERMA ALBERTA STITHEM Fifth great granddaughter of progenitor Nicholas Kegg.

STOBART

APRIL DAWN STOBART Sixth great granddaughter of progenitor Nicholas Kegg.
TONYA MARIE STOBART Sixth great granddaughter of progenitor Nicholas Kegg.
VALERIE LYNN STOBART Sixth great granddaughter of progenitor Nicholas Kegg.

STOERI

ALISON LOUISE STOERI Seventh great granddaughter of progenitor Nicholas Kegg.
ANDREW THOMAS STOERI Seventh great grandson of progenitor Nicholas Kegg.

STOGDALE

BRANDT STANLEY STOGDALE Sixth great grandson of progenitor Nicholas Kegg.
BROOKE STOGDALE Eighth great granddaughter of progenitor Nicholas Kegg.
CHERYL STOGDALE Sixth great granddaughter of progenitor Nicholas Kegg.
DEBRA STOGDALE Sixth great granddaughter of progenitor Nicholas Kegg.
DONNA LEE STOGDALE Sixth great granddaughter of progenitor Nicholas Kegg.
ELIZABETH ANN STOGDALE Fifth great granddaughter of progenitor Nicholas Kegg.
GILDA L. STOGDALE Sixth great granddaughter of progenitor Nicholas Kegg.
JAMES EDWARD STOGDALE Fifth great grandson of progenitor Nicholas Kegg.
JAMES STANTON STOGDALE [6093B] (1954 – 2016) son of James and Wanda (Condit) Stogdale married Deborah A. Grauel with whom he was father of (2). James was a roofer by trade.

[6093] Jackson County Banner (IN) July 4, 1991 [6093A] Hays Daily News (KS) Oct 19, 2010 [6093B] Gettysburg Times (PA) Dec 13, 2016

JOHN SPENCER STOGDALE Sixth great grandson of progenitor Nicholas Kegg.
KATHRINA GAIL STOGDALE Sixth great granddaughter of progenitor Nicholas Kegg.
MICHAEL E. STOGDALE Seventh great grandson of progenitor Nicholas Kegg.
ROBERT NICHOLAS STOGDALE Seventh great grandson of progenitor Nicholas Kegg.
STEVEN KYLE STOGDALE Seventh great grandson of progenitor Nicholas Kegg.
THOMAS ALLEN STOGDALE Sixth great grandson of progenitor Nicholas Kegg.
THOMAS STANLEY STOGDALE [6094] (1931 – 2018) son of Joseph and Olive (Clark) Stogdale, married Linda C. with whom he was father of (3).

STONE

BRADY STONE Seventh great grandson of progenitor Nicholas Kegg.
HAYDEN STONE Seventh great grandson of progenitor Nicholas Kegg.

STONECIPHER

MELISSA STONECIPHER aka "Missy", Sixth great granddaughter of progenitor Nicholas Kegg.
REBECCA STONECIPHER aka "Becca", Sixth great granddaughter of progenitor Nicholas Kegg.
STEPHANIE STONECIPHER Sixth great granddaughter of progenitor Nicholas Kegg.

STONER

PATRICIA A. STONER Sixth great granddaughter of progenitor Nicholas Kegg.

STONEROOK

DONALD L. STONEROOK Fourth great grandson of progenitor Nicholas Kegg.
DOROTHY MARIE STONEROOK aka "Dottie" Fourth great granddaughter of progenitor Nicholas Kegg. **GARRETT TODD STONEROOK** Fifth great grandson of progenitor Nicholas Kegg.
JASON STONEROOK Fifth great grandson of progenitor Nicholas Kegg.

STOSICK

HANK W. STOSICK Fifth great grandson of progenitor Nicholas Kegg.
THOMAS JOSEPH STOSICK Fifth great grandson of progenitor Nicholas Kegg.

STOUFFER

ALEX STOUFFER Sixth great grandson of progenitor Nicholas Kegg. **BARRY ROSS STOUFFER** Fifth great grandson of progenitor Nicholas Kegg. **DAVID BEN STOUFFER** Fifth great grandson of progenitor Nicholas Kegg. **ERIKA P STOUFFER** Sixth great granddaughter of progenitor Nicholas Kegg. **ERIN G. STOUFFER** Sixth great granddaughter of progenitor Nicholas Kegg.
HERBERT LEWIS STOUFFER [6095] (1934 – 2020) son of Herbert and Ida May (Kegg) Stouffer married and was father of (3). Herbert served in the United States Marine Corps which included 14 months in Korea where he was wounded twice during the conflict. Sgt. Stouffer wore the Purple Heart with Oak Leaf Cluster, American Presidential Unit Citation, National Defense Ribbon, Korean and UN Service Ribbons and the Korean Presidential Unit Citation. Thereafter, he served the Commonwealth of Pennsylvania, and retired as a Lieutenant with the Pennsylvania State Police after 25 years. Along the way, he graduated Cum Laude from Indiana University of Pennsylvania in 1980. In 1984, he retired to

---

[6094] The Washington Post (D.C.) March 6, 2018, obtained by D. Sue Dible [6095] Sun-Sentinel (FL) April 26, 2020, obtained by D. Sue Dible

Florida where he started another career serving 18 years as Chief of Security for Broward County Government. Herbert enjoyed the beach, bicycling, family gatherings, playing cards and caring for his dogs. Herbert often reflected on the fond memories he had being raised by his grandparents. He is remembered for his dedication to family, generosity, hard work ethic and zeal for living. **HOLLY J. STOUFFER** Sixth great granddaughter of progenitor Nicholas Kegg. **JEFFREY M. STOUFFER** Fifth great grandson of progenitor Nicholas Kegg. **MICHAEL A. STOUFFER** Sixth great grandson of progenitor Nicholas Kegg. **PAMELA ANN STOUFFER** Fifth great granddaughter of progenitor Nicholas Kegg. **SCOTT DAVID STOUFFER** 5th great grandson of progenitor Nicholas Kegg.
SHIRLEY M. STOUFFER [6095A] daughter of Herbert and Ida May (Kegg) Stouffer married Melvin George Rager with whom she was mother of (4) Endless generosity and perpetual smile were terms used to describe Shirley. She was formerly employed by U.S. Bank and Bali Bra Co. Shirley was a longtime member of the Bethany Presbyterian Church, where she served as a Deacon. She was also a member of the Orchard Card Club.

STOUT

CHRISTOPHER BENJAMIN STOUT Seventh great grandson of progenitor Nicholas Kegg.
MEGAN ELIZABETH STOUT Seventh great granddaughter of progenitor Nicholas Kegg.
MICHAEL BENJAMIN STOUT Seventh great grandson of progenitor Nicholas Kegg.

STOWE

JUSTIN T. STOWE Seventh great grandson of progenitor Nicholas Kegg.

STOY

GRACE ELIZABETH STOY Seventh great granddaughter of progenitor Nicholas Kegg.
JOHN THOMAS STOY Seventh great granddaughter of progenitor Nicholas Kegg.

STRALEY

BRIAN TYLER STRALEY Seventh great grandson of progenitor Nicholas Kegg.
JEREMY SCOTT STRALEY Seventh great grandson of progenitor Nicholas Kegg.
STEPHANIE STRALEY Seventh great granddaughter of progenitor Nicholas Kegg.

STRAUB

DOTTIE MAE STRAUB [6095B] (1948 – 2017) daughter of Oscar and Dorothy (Calhoun) Straub; Dottie had a way to win anyone over with her talented "saleslady-like" approach and bring you laughter while winning her requests. She loved to collect and read the Bedford Gazette newspapers and enjoyed recalling and sharing the events to remind everyone she knew what was current in Bedford. She remembered holidays, birthdates, and anniversaries, and always selected cards that suited her friends and family. Her love for puppies was a support for her, as well as a very caring brother, family and caretakers. Her goodhearted, caring personality made it difficult to notice her special needs. Dottie occupied her time working at the Bedford County Workshop.
JOSEPH C. STRAUB Seventh great grandson of progenitor Nicholas Kegg.
JOSEPH C. STRAUB Sixth great grandson of progenitor Nicholas Kegg.
JOSEPH MICHAEL STRAUB Eighth great grandson of progenitor Nicholas Kegg.

[6095A] Tribune-Democrat (PA) Nov 13, 2006 [6095B] Bedford Gazette (PA) Oct 20, 2017, contributed by Bob Rose

KAYLA SUE STRAUB Eighth great granddaughter of progenitor Nicholas Kegg.
KELLY ELIZABETH STRAUB Eighth great granddaughter of progenitor Nicholas Kegg.
SUSAN JANE STRAUB Sixth great granddaughter of progenitor Nicholas Kegg.

STRAWSER

JERRET ROY STRAWSER Seventh great grandson of progenitor Nicholas Kegg.

STRAYER

BROCK STRAYER Seventh great grandson of progenitor Nicholas Kegg. **CAROL STRAYER** Sixth great granddaughter of progenitor Nicholas Kegg. **CATHY STRAYER** Sixth great granddaughter of progenitor Nicholas Kegg. **PHILLIP RAY STRAYER** Sixth great grandson of progenitor Nicholas Kegg. **TYLER STRAYER** Seventh great grandson of progenitor Nicholas Kegg.

STREAM

BRANDON STREAM Seventh great grandson of progenitor Nicholas Kegg.

STREET

ABIGAIL LOU STREET Seventh great granddaughter of progenitor Nicholas Kegg.
GRACE LOUISE STREET Seventh great granddaughter of progenitor Nicholas Kegg.
JOHN SHELBY STREET Seventh great grandson of progenitor Nicholas Kegg.
MATTHEW AMARIAH STREET Seventh great grandson of progenitor Nicholas Kegg.

STREETS

SARAH ELIZABETH STREETS Eighth great granddaughter of progenitor Nicholas Kegg.

STREIGHT

ADAM STREIGHT Seventh great grandson of progenitor Nicholas Kegg. **BARBARA LYNN STREIGHT** Sixth great granddaughter of progenitor Nicholas Kegg. **BELIA STREIGHT** Eighth great granddaughter of progenitor Nicholas Kegg. **CLARENCE ELVIN STREIGHT** [6096] (1896 – 1959) son of John and Rosa (Bussard) Streight, married Wilma Dolly Forrest with whom he was father of (6). Clarence was a member of the Steadman - Keenan Post of the American Legion in Brunswick. **CLARENCE E. STREIGHT JR.** [6096A] (1925 – 1960) son of Clarence and Wilma (Forrest) Streight married twice, first to Virginia Martin with whom he was father of (3), later he married Cora Sue Plowman with whom he was father of (1). Clarence was a World War II veteran and worked as a meat cutter for the Swift and Company plant in Washington D.C. **DAWN MICHELLE STREIGHT** Seventh great grandson of progenitor Nicholas Kegg. **DEBORAH LYNN STREIGHT** Seventh great granddaughter of progenitor Nicholas Kegg. **DON MICHAEL STREIGHT** Sixth great grandson of progenitor Nicholas Kegg. **ELSIE I. STREIGHT** [6097] (1894 – 1983) daughter of John and Rosa (Bussard) Streight, married Milford Calhoun with whom she was mother of (4). Elsie was a lifetime member of Mt. Union United Church of Christ at Mench Town, where she served as superintendent of Children's Sunday school, and was a Sunday school teacher. She taught school in Bedford County and taught weekly religious education in the Everett school system. She attended Juanita College, was a member of the Huntingdon, Bedford, Fulton Area Senior Citizens, the Everett Happy Senior Citizens, and had been employed by Lion Manufacturing Company in Everett.

[6096] p.4 – The Post (MD) Sept 18, 1959 [6097] Duke Clark Obituary clipping collection [6096A] Frederick Post (MD) July 19, 1960

ETTA ELEANOR STREIGHT [6098] (1898 – 1987) aka "Ertie", daughter of John and Rosa (Bussard) Streight married twice; first to Hugh Carl Poling with whom she was mother of (1). Later, she married John Derkach with whom she was mother of (1). Ertie was a homemaker all her life. **EVELYN M. STREIGHT** [6098A] (1922 – 2016) daughter of Clarence and Wilma (Forrest) Streight married Joseph John Snell with whom she was mother of (6). Evelyn was employed at the Woolco (Red Grille) and the Dollar Store in the Mac Dade Mall. Evelyn served as a member on the Ladies Auxiliary, American Legion Post 507 in Norwood for many years. **FLO STREIGHT** (1899 – 1899) daughter of John and Rosa (Bussard) Streight. **GLORIA STREIGHT** Fifth great granddaughter of progenitor Nicholas Kegg. **HARRY VERNON STREIGHT** [6099] (1892 – 1988) son of John and Rosa (Bussard) Streight, married Maud M. Hesrick with whom he was father of (8). Harry was a former machinist at the Aro Equipment Corporation. **HELEN MARIE STREIGHT** [6099A] (1922 – 2008) daughter of Harry and Maud (Hesrick) Streight married Brankle Lee Brumley with whom she was mother of (2). Helen was employed by Campbell Soup Supply Co., Napoleon, for 15 years. **IDA MAY STREIGHT** (1901 – 1901) daughter of John and Rosa (Bussard) Streight. **JODY ANN STREIGHT** Seventh great granddaughter of progenitor Nicholas Kegg. **JOHN B. STREIGHT** [6099B] aka "J.B." (1936 – 2016) son of Clarence and Wilma (Forrest) Streight married Patricia Lou Moreland with whom he was father of (1). John had been employed at Safeway Inc., and later at Giant Foods, Inc., in the shipping and receiving department. JB was a member of Fraternal Order of Eagles Aerie 1136 in Brunswick and a former member of the Moose Lodge 1582 in Brunswick. He enjoyed good food, dancing, and fishing and he also played the harmonica and organ. **JUDY D. STREIGHT** Fifth great granddaughter of progenitor Nicholas Kegg. **JULSIE STREIGHT** Eighth great granddaughter of progenitor Nicholas Kegg. **LORETTA A. STREIGHT** Sixth great granddaughter of progenitor Nicholas Kegg. **LYSA STREIGHT** Seventh great granddaughter of progenitor Nicholas Kegg. **MICK STREIGHT** Eighth great grandson of progenitor Nicholas Kegg. **ORVILLE BRADLEY STREIGHT** Sixth great grandson of progenitor Nicholas Kegg. **ORVILLE F. STREIGHT** [6100] (1921 – 1944) son of Clarence and Wilma (Forrest) Streight was among the first of the World War II victims removed from European cemeteries and returned to family. First reported as killed in action, Orville died of a heart attack in his sleep at Butenbach, Belgium. His company officer, Capt. William Feaster, notified the parents of the circumstances of his death several weeks after his demise. The officer said Pfc. Streight had not been ill prior to the fatal attack. **RICKY MARTIN STREIGHT** Sixth great grandson of progenitor Nicholas Kegg. **RUTH LOUISE STREIGHT** [6101] (1919 – 1993) daughter of Harry and Maud (Hesrick) Streight was mother of (1). Later, she married twice; first to Harold Lynn Gordon with whom she was mother of (1). Lastly, she married Joseph Filler Miller. **STEVEN ORVILLE STREIGHT** [6101A] (1960 – 2016) son of Clarence and Cora Sue (Plowman) Streight married Melissa Louise Backus with whom he was father of (1). Steven worked for Acme Paper Company for 18 years and was a dedicated, well loved and respected employee. He loved to travel home for family gatherings, hunting, relaxing and visiting the place he loved. He was a true lover of boating, spending many hours fishing the waters of VA and NC. Steven had a passion for fast muscle cars and collected several beautiful mustangs throughout his life. Engines of any kind were his regular tinker toys. He was always fiddling with engines from cars to lawn mowers. He loved to start his garden each spring and work it until bearing fruit of his labor, a passion that he enjoyed sharing with others. His 6'5" stature, blonde hair, ocean blue eyes, contagious smile and gentle character were some of the many qualities. **TIFFANY N. STREIGHT** Seventh great granddaughter of progenitor Nicholas Kegg.

STEPHENS

DRAVEN STEPHENS Eighth great grandson of progenitor Nicholas Kegg.
GAGE STEPHENS Eighth great grandson of progenitor Nicholas Kegg.
TRYSTIN STEPHENS Eighth great granddaughter of progenitor Nicholas Kegg.

[6098] p.A5- The News (Frederick, MD) Mar 2, 1987 [6098A] The Daily Times (PA) Apr. 5, 2016 [6099] p.3 - The Bryan Times (OH) Jan 2, 1988 [6099A] p. 5A - The Cresent News (OH) Dec. 3, 2008 [6099B] The Frederick News-Post (MD) Sept. 28, 2016 [6100] Frederick Post (MD) Oct 27, 1947 [6101] Tampa Tribune (FL) Aug 31, 1993 [6101A] J.T. Morriss & Son Incorporated (VA)

STRICKLAND

DAVID STRICKLAND Fifth great grandson of progenitor Nicholas Kegg.
JEAN STRICKLAND [6102] (1932 – 2003) daughter of Clarence and Doris (Cline) Strickland, married Raymond Lee Caspers with whom she was mother of (3).
RUTH STRICKLAND Fifth great granddaughter of progenitor Nicholas Kegg.

STRINGFIELD

ROBERT CHARLES STRINGFIELD Sixth great grandson of progenitor Nicholas Kegg.

STROZ

ATLAS WRENN STROZ Seventh great grandson of progenitor Nicholas Kegg.
SOPHIA GRACE STROZ Seventh great granddaughter of progenitor Nicholas Kegg.

STUCKEY

ALBERT STUCKEY [6103] (1850 – 1928) son of Simon and Caroline (Border) Stuckey, married Frances Houston with whom he was father of (2). **ALLIE BETH STUCKEY** Sixth great granddaughter of progenitor Nicholas Kegg. **ANN MARTIN STUCKEY** Fifth great granddaughter of progenitor Nicholas Kegg. **ANNA CARRIE STUCKEY** [6104, 6105] (1885 – 1957) daughter of Charles and Mary (Diehl) Stuckey, married Bernard Morgan Clarke with whom she was mother of (6).
ARTHUR EARL STUCKEY [6106] (1899 – 1918) son of Augustus and Fanny (Gleason) Stuckey.
AUGUSTUS A. STUCKEY [6107] (1863 – 1901) son of Simon and Caroline (Border) Stuckey, married Fanny L. Gleason with whom he was father of (4). Augustus was a man full of enterprise and manliness. His ability as a businessman was that of superiority over others. When the final summons came that he must go, he raised both hands and said: "God bless us all." He was willing to go and said the worst of all was "Leaving his family" He bid them all goodbye and said: "For them not to feel so bad as it would not be long before they would all be there just the same." **AVIS STUCKEY** [6108] (1856 – 1943) aka "Avia", daughter of Simon and Caroline (Border) Stuckey, married Charles Wesley Main with whom she was mother of (2). **BARBARA ELLEN STUCKEY** [6109] (1832 – 1918) daughter of Simon and Mary Ann (Kegg) Stuckey, married Josiah F. Shoemaker with whom she was mother of (11).
BETTY CAROL STUCKEY [6109A] (1929 – 2009) daughter of William and Gladys (Sloan) Stuckey married David D. Reichert with whom she was mother of (3). Betty worked on the farm with her husband and also owned and operated a beauty salon out of her home for about 20 years. She was a member of the First Presbyterian Church in Minatare and enjoyed traveling. **BRADLEY ANDERSON STUCKEY** Sixth great grandson of progenitor Nicholas Kegg. **CAREY LYNN STUCKEY** Sixth great granddaughter of progenitor Nicholas Kegg. **CAROL JUANITA STUCKEY** Fifth great granddaughter of progenitor Nicholas Kegg. **CARLOS GEORGETTE STUCKEY** Fifth great granddaughter of progenitor Nicholas Kegg. **CHARLENE STUCKEY** Fifth great granddaughter of progenitor Nicholas Kegg. **CHARLES STUCKEY** (1833 – 1874) son of Simon and Mary Ann (Kegg) Stuckey.
CHARLES EDWARD STUCKEY [6110] (1859 – 1938) son of David and Catherine (Hetrick) Stuckey, married Mary Olive Diehl with whom he was father of (3). Charles was a carpenter by trade.
CHARLES STANLEY DIEHL STUCKEY [6111] (1887 – 1969) son of Charles and Mary (Diehl) Stuckey, married Myrtle May Patch with whom he was father of (2). Corporal Stuckey was wounded while serving in France during WWI.

[6102] Omaha World-Herald (NE) Jan 15, 2003, obtained by D. Sue Dible [6103] Hutchinson News (KS) July 3, 1928 [6104] p.4 - Bedford Gazette (PA) Apr 2, 1909 [6105] The Cumberland News (MD) Nov 23, 1961 [6106] p.4 Omaha World Herald July 8, 1921 [6107] Custer County Republican (NE) June 6, 1901 [6108] Find A Grave memorial # 118206094 Added by: Talbot Fisher [6109] Bedford Gazette (PA) Apr 19, 1918 [6109A] Gering Courier (NE) March 5, 2009 [6110] The Cumberland News (MD) Nov 1, 1938 [6111] Find A Grave memorial # 20133395 Added by: Darla

CHARLES VIRGIL STUCKEY [6112] (1884 – 1946) aka "Chas", son of Simon and Mary Virginia (Smith) Stuckey, married Dixie Virginia Arnold. Chas was employed as a clerk in the P. R. R. offices at Johnstown.   **CLARENCE LEROY STUCKEY** [6113] (1913 – 1949) son of Charles and Myrtle (Patch) Stuckey, married Mary Rak with whom he was father of (4).   **DAVID FRANKLIN STUCKEY** [6114] (1883 – 1908) son of Charles and Mary (Diehl) Stuckey, was employed on the threshing machine owned and operated by Michael Diehl and was an industrious and sober minded young man, making many friends in the community in which he lived throughout his life. He united with the Friend's Cove Reformed church in 1899 and was a consistent member.   **DAVID H. STUCKEY** [6115] (1836 – 1864) son of Simon and Mary Ann (Kegg) Stuckey, married Catherine A. Hetrick with whom he was father of (2). A Corporal in A Company of the 184th Pennsylvania Infantry, David died of a vitamin deficiency known as Scorbutus, in Andersonville, Georgia during the Civil War.   **DORIS MARIE STUCKEY** (1912 – 2002) daughter of William and Gladys (Sloan) Stuckey married Martin K. Ouderkirk with whom she was mother of (1). Later, she married Paul Leroy Tompsett with whom she was mother of (3) and lastly, married and divorced Milton Franklin Driggers.   **ELLEN BORDER STUCKEY** [6116, 1617] (1854 – 1921) aka "Ella", daughter of Simon and Carol (Border) Stucky married twice; first to David S. Brilhart with whom she was mother of (3). Later, she married Peter Melvin Gilcrist.   **ELLWOOD STUCKEY** (1851 – 1894) son of Simon and Caroline (Border) Stuckey, married Clara Ann Shinn.   **EVA AVIS STUCKEY** (1892 – 1986) daughter of Augustus and Fanny (Gleason) Stuckey, married Fred Elmer Simpson.   **EVA MILDRED STUCKEY** (1899 – 1961) daughter of William and Maud (Wilson) Stuckey, married Joseph Hume McCormack with whom she was mother of (1) Later, she married Phillip Benjamin Robinson with whom she was mother of (1).   **FAY ALICE STUCKEY** (1925 – 1925) daughter of William and Gladys (Sloan) Stuckey.   **FRANK ALBERT STUCKEY** [6117A] aka "Zeke" (1921 – 2007) son of George and Helen (Fearl) Stuckey married Norma Lee Anderson with whom he was father of (3). Zeke was retired chairman of the former Stuckey Lumber and Supply Co. He belonged to First Presbyterian Church. He was a member of the Hutchinson Chamber of Commerce Board, Kansas Cosmosphere and Space Center Board, Hutchinson Community College Endowment Association Board, Economic Development Council Board, Home Builders Association Board, Living Land Foundation Board, Hutchinson Chapter of Rotary International, Bob Johnson Youth Center Board, Maplewood Girls Home Board, American Legion Lysle Rishel Post No. 68, Southern Economic Development Council, Volunteer of the year in Kansas Industrial Development Association, Eagle Scout Troop "1", Hutchinson, and has tutored math for many years at both Winans and Lincoln Elementary schools. He served in the U.S. Navy Air Corps during World War II from 1942 to 1946.   **FRANK ANDERSON STUCKEY** Fifth great grandson of progenitor Nicholas Kegg.   **GAYLE ELLEN STUCKEY** Fifth great granddaughter of progenitor Nicholas Kegg.   **GEORGE BORDER STUCKEY** [6118] (1900 – 1986) son of William and Maud (Wilson) Stuckey, married Katherine Gracie Runkle with whom he was father of (3). George was employed in Altona as a farmer for many years and taught at Galesburg and Winola high schools. He was also a member of the Altona Lions Club and Altona Senior Citizens.   **GEORGE FEARL STUCKEY** [6119] (1923 – 1998) son of George and Helen (Fearl) Stuckey, married Mary Sampson with whom he was father of (3). A veteran of World War II, George was co-founder of Stuckey Lumber & Supply Co.   **GEORGE GRANT STUCKEY** [6120] (1868 – 1947) son of George and Catherine (Hetrick) Stuckey, married Matilda Barnes with whom he was father of (1). George had been an inspector for the Bigley & May Co.   **GEORGE HARR STUCKEY** (1890 – 1956) son of Albert and Frances (Houston) Stuckey married Helen Fearl with whom he was father of (4). George was a letterman on one of Phog Allen's earliest basketball teams, University of Kansas. He was proprietor of Stuckey Lumber and Supply Co.   **GEORGE WASHINGTON STUCKEY** [6121] (1834 – 1899) son of Simon and Mary Ann (Kegg) Stuckey married twice; first to Mary Ellen Diehl with whom he was father of (4). Later, he married Catherine A. Hetrick with whom he was father of (1). George was born on what was known for nearly a

---

[6112] Bedford Gazette (PA) Jun 3, 1910 [6113] p.24 - Plain Dealer (OH) Sept 8, 1949 [6114] p.5 - Bedford Gazette (PA) Sep 11, 1908 [6115] Bedford Gazette (PA) June 5, 1908 [6116] Herald (Lathrop, MO) Dec 9, 1881 [6117] Plattsburg Leader (MO) May 8, 1896 [6117A] Hutchinson News (KS) Apr 19, 2007 [6118] p.C18 Journal Star (Peoria, Illinois) Nov 23, 1986 [6119] p.10A Wichita Eagle (KS) Sept 2, 1998 [6120] p. 22 - Johnstown Tribune (PA) May 26, 1947, obtained by Michael S. Caldwell [6121] Bedford Gazette (PA) July 28, 1899

century as the Stuckey farm. It was here on this farm that "Uncle Wash," as he was familiarly called, spent the younger and happier days of his life in that humble, yet profitable profession, farming. During the period in which he lived in Rainsburg he received a common school education. He lived with his father until he thought it time to establish a home of his own. On the twenty-first of September 1864, George enlisted in Company F, 107th regiment, Pennsylvania volunteers, under the command of John A. Tompkins, captain. His company joined the Army of the Potomac. He was a gallant soldier, always in front and never seemed to fear the dangers of warfare. He took part in several hard-fought battles and came out uninjured. He lay in one of the southern hospitals for a while, suffering from eczema. He was discharged in June 1865, near Washington D.C. **GERALDINE FAYE STUCKEY** [6121A] (1935 – 2020) daughter of Paul and Ruby (Smith) Stuckey married Palmer Schledewitz. Later she married Charley Frank Matthaei with whom she was mother of (2). **GLADINA STUCKEY** [6122] (1918 – 2003) daughter of William and Gladys (Sloan) Stuckey married twice; first to Walter Earl Zweifel with whom she was mother of (1). Later, she married William Ivan Schultz with whom she was mother of (1). Gladina was a homemaker and farmed side-by-side with her husband. She was a very hard worker all of her life and preferred being in the field, rather than the house. She lived her entire life in the Gering, Morrill and Sunflower communities. **GLEASON AUGUSTA STUCKEY** aka "Glea" (1894 – 1987) daughter of Augustus and Fanny (Gleason) Stuckey married three times Royal Edward Munn with whom she was mother of (3). Later, to Roy Alex Henderson Thompson with whom she was mother of (3). Last she married John Walter Craig with whom she was mother of (1). **GRACE MADARA STUCKEY** [6123] (1912 – 1998) daughter of Charles and Myrtle (Patch) Stuckey, married Albert C. Ferguson. Grace worked as an Avon representative for many years. **GREGORY PAUL STUCKEY** Sixth great grandson of progenitor Nicholas Kegg. **HAROLD BARNES STUCKEY** [6124, 6125] (1901 – 1973) son of George and Matilda (Barnes) Stuckey, married Mary Ellen Huzzard. Harold purchased the tobacco store and pool parlor from Howard Hill. Howard owned and operated the confectionary store on Richard Street. **HOWARD WILSON STUCKEY** (1894 – 1949) son of William and Maud (Wilson) Stuckey, married Lydia Erma Martin with whom he was father of (3). **IDA MAE STUCKEY** [6126] (1865 – 1890) daughter of Simon and Caroline (Border) Stuckey, married Chauncey Joseph McMaster. **JACK JENELL STUCKEY** (1923 – 1978) son of William and Gladys (Sloan) Stuckey. **JACOB STUCKEY** (1841 – 1842) son of Simon and Mary Ann (Kegg) Stuckey. **JAMIE DEE STUCKEY** Fourth great granddaughter of progenitor Nicholas Kegg. **JANE STUCKEY** Fifth great granddaughter of progenitor Nicholas Kegg. **JEFFREY STUCKEY** Sixth great grandson of progenitor Nicholas Kegg. **JOHN PHILLIP STUCKEY** Fifth great grandson of progenitor Nicholas Kegg. **JOHN WILLIAM STUCKEY** [6126A] (1922 – 1969) son of Howard and Lydia (Martin) Stuckey married Madelyn Elizabeth Phillips with whom he was father of (5). John was a Phoenix Dentist who died when his twin-engine plane plunged into the side of a mountain in the San Tan range. **JOSEPHINE STUCKEY** [6126B] aka "Jody" (1928 – 2012) daughter of George and Helen (Fearl) Stuckey married James Murph Drewry with whom she was mother of (3). Jody worked for DeGolyer and MacNaughton in Dallas and was later the Office Manager for her husband's dental practice. She loved to play tennis, socialize with friends, cook for family, and play bridge. Jody always made every day special for her family. **KELLY ANNETTE STUCKEY** Sixth great granddaughter of progenitor Nicholas Kegg. **KENNETH DEE STUCKEY** (1942 – 1996) son of Paul and Ruby (Smith) Stuckey. Kenneth worked as an over the road truck driver for various trucking companies. **LADD LEWIS STUCKEY** [6127] (1942 – 1943) son of Clarence and Mary (Rak) Stuckey. **LOUISE GERTRUDE STUCKEY** [6128] (1910 – 2002) daughter of William and Gladys (Sloan) Stuckey married twice; first to Harlan William Gibbens with whom she was mother of (3). Later, she married Claude William Swanger. Louise was a teacher for Tillamook School District. She was a member of the Moose Lodge.

[6121A] Newcomer - East Metro Chapel (CO) [6122] Star Herald (NE) Oct 1, 2003 [6123] Warren-Trumbull County Public Library obituary obtained by D. Sue Dible [6124] Bedford Gazette (PA) Feb 14, 1953/*From the files of the Gazette for February 10, 1933* [6125] Bedford County Historical Society obituary obtained by D. Sue Dible [6126] "Historical Encyclopedia of Illinois" Chicago: Munsell Pub. Co., 1899 [6126A] p.2- Tucson Daily Citizen (AZ) May 29, 1969 [6126B] Grace Gardens Funeral Home (TX) [6127] Plain Dealer (Cleveland, OH) Feb 10, 1943, obtained by Mary K Ward [6128] p.B6 San Diego Union-Tribune (CA) Dec 4, 2002

LYN C. STUCKEY Fifth great granddaughter of progenitor Nicholas Kegg. **MARGARET ANN STUCKEY** (1859 – 1888) daughter of Simon and Caroline (Border) Stuckey, married William D. Cook. **MARGARET CATHERINE STUCKEY** [6128A] (1828 – 1903) daughter of Simon and Mary Ann (Kegg) Stuckey married twice, first to Peter Morgart Cessna with whom she was mother of (7), later to Samuel Stuckey. Margaret was a loyal Christian and had a loving circle of friends. **MARGARET HELEN STUCKEY** [6129] (1897 – 1973) daughter of William and Maud (Wilson) Stuckey, married Pierce M. Whiting with whom she was mother of (2). **MARY AMANDA STUCKEY** (1846 – 1900) daughter of Simon and Mary Ann (Kegg) Stuckey, married William Ditch with whom she was mother of (8). **MARY JANE STUCKEY** [6130] (1858 – 1939) daughter of George and Mary Ellen (Diehl) Stuckey, married Francis Robert Shuck Biddle with whom she was mother of (11). Mary Jane was a member of Trinity Reformed Church at Friend's Cove. **MARY LEA STUCKEY** Fifth great granddaughter of progenitor Nicholas Kegg. **MARY LOUISE STUCKEY** Fifth great granddaughter of progenitor Nicholas Kegg. **MELVIN LEROY STUCKEY** Fifth great grandson of progenitor Nicholas Kegg. **NANCY STUCKEY** Fifth great granddaughter of progenitor Nicholas Kegg. **NANCY E. STUCKEY** Fourth great granddaughter of progenitor Nicholas Kegg. **OLIVER NEWTON STUCKEY** [6131] (1920 – 1939) son of William and Gladys (Sloan) Stuckey, married Darlene Marie Drake with whom he was father of (1). **PATRICIA ANN STUCKEY** [6132] (1939 – 2001) aka "Pat" daughter of Clarence and Mary (Rak) Stuckey married twice; first to James Raymond Thompson with whom she was mother of (2). Later, she married Raymond Dean White with whom she was mother of (1). Pat was a former manager of Bass Kennels. **PAUL AUSTIN STUCKEY** [6133] (1916 – 1994) son of William and Gladys (Sloan) Stuckey, married Ruby Faye Smith with whom he was father of (4). **PEARL MABLE STUCKEY** [6133A] (1888 – 1941) daughter of Albert and Frances (Houston) Stuckey married Wallace Everett Pratt with whom she was mother of (3). Pearl was the first president of the Women's Student Government association and was largely instrumental in getting the movement for self-government among women students at the University of Kansas. **RACHAEL STUCKEY** (born abt.1860 infant) daughter of George and Mary Ellen (Diehl) Stuckey. **RACHAEL VIRGINIA STUCKEY** (1916 – 1916) daughter of Howard and Lydia (Martin) Stuckey. **RICHARD A. STUCKEY** [6133B] (1917 – 2010) son of Charles and Elsie (Harclerode) Stuckey. **SAMUEL ALAN STUCKEY** Fifth great grandson of progenitor Nicholas Kegg. **SAMUEL STUCKEY** (infant) son of George and Helen (Fearl) Stuckey. **SANDRA KAY STUCKEY** [6133C] (1939 – 2001) daughter of Oliver and Darlene (Drake) Stuckey married John L. Page with whom she was mother of (2). Sandra had been a self-employed beautician until her retirement. She enjoyed playing bingo, fishing and working crossword puzzles. **SARAH STUCKEY** [6134] (1861 – 1947) daughter of George and Mary Ellen (Diehl) Stuckey married twice; first to Winfield Scott Fisher with whom she was mother of (6). Later she married Abram J. Pittman. Sarah was affiliated with the Reformed church of McConnellsburg. **SIMON LINCOLN STUCKEY** [6135, 6136] (1861 – 1945) son of David and Catherine (Hetrick) Stuckey married twice; first to Mary Virginia Smith with whom he was father of (2). Later, he married Sarah Brandt. Simon was a farmer until he entered the bakery business. He was a member of the Republican Party and attended the Reformed Church of Rainsburg. **SIMON N. STUCKEY** (abt 1861 infant) son of George and Mary Ellen (Diehl) Stuckey. **SOPHIA STUCKEY** [6137] (1843 – 1920) daughter of Simon and Mary Ann (Kegg) Stuckey, married Andrew Jackson Pennell with whom she was mother of (4). **SUSAN LEE STUCKEY** [6137A] (1948 – 2012) daughter of Frank and Norma (Anderson) Stuckey married Robert Joseph Sully. After receiving her master's degree from the School of International Training, Brattleboro, Vt., Susan spent the next five years in Japan, teaching children English as a foreign language. When she returned to the United States, Susan worked in international business relations with several different international companies. **TAYLOR STUCKEY** Sixth great grandson of progenitor Nicholas Kegg.

[6128A] Bedford Gazette (PA) June 12, 1903 [6129] p.16 Galesburg Register-Mail (IL) Jan 5, 1974 [6130] obituary clipping obtained by Glenn Biddle [6131] p.2 Idaho Statesman (ID) Sep 8, 1939 [6132] The Orlando Sentinel (FL) Oct 4, 2001 [6133] Star Herald (NE) July 3, 2006 [6133A] p.8- The Jeffersonian Gazette (KS) Nov 13, 1912 [6133B] Timothy A. Berkebile Funeral Home (PA) [6133C] Quad-City Times (IA) Nov 27, 2001 [6134] p.2 - Bedford Gazette (PA) April 10, 1947, obtained by Bob Rose [6135] p.613 - Juanita Valley History [6136, 6137] Bedford County Historical Society obituary obtained by D. Sue Dible [6137A] Hutchinson News (KS) March 30, 2012

THOMAS EDWARD STUCKEY Sixth great grandson of progenitor Nicholas Kegg. **VIRGINIA MAE STUCKEY** [6138] (1892 – 1959) daughter of Samuel and Lulu (Shinn) Stuckey, married Robert Montgomery Harrington with whom she was mother of (2). Robert was working his way through the University of Missouri by waiting on the tables. Virginia's parents had objections to the marriage of their daughter and Robert who had been sweethearts for two years. After postponing the wedding repeatedly, the two arranged to meet at the Kansas-Missouri football game, and it was decided there that the wedding would be put off no longer. Virginia was taking music lessons in Kansas City on Saturday mornings, so it was arranged that they elope from there to Independence where the two were married. **WAYNE CRAIG STUCKEY** Fifth great grandson of progenitor Nicholas Kegg. **WILLIAM B. STUCKEY** [6139] (1937 – 2012) son of Clarence and Mary (Rak) Stuckey, married Betty Jane Butcher with whom he was father of (2). **WILLIAM CARL STUCKEY** [6139A] (1890 – 1965) son of Augustus and Fanny (Gleason) Stuckey married Gladys Belinda Sloan with whom he was father of (9). A farmer, William was a member of the Modern Woodmen of America and had served on various committees and boards. **WILLIAM CHARLES STUCKEY** [6139B] aka "Bill" (1913 – 1993) son of William and Gladys (Sloan) Stucky married twice, first to Leila Mae James with whom he was father of (1). Later he married Dorothy Scheer with whom he was father of (2). Bill served in the armed forces during World War II. He was honorably discharged Oct. 24, 1945. He was a member of the Army National Guard from 1947 to 1955. He was a life member of the Veterans of Foreign Wars and farmed in Cedar Canyon. **WILLIAM DAVID STUCKEY** Sixth great grandson of progenitor Nicholas Kegg. **WILLIAM H. STUCKEY** [6140] (1886 – 1938) son of Simon and Mary Virginia (Smith) Stuckey, married Mary Agnes Thompson. William had been employed for 31 years by the P. R. R., his run being from Pittsburgh to Altoona. He was returning home from work about 2 o'clock in the morning when he suffered a heart attack on a streetcar and died as he was entering a hospital. **WILLIAM HENRY STUCKEY** [6141] (1841 – 1917) son of Simon and Mary Ann (Kegg) Stuckey, married Margaret Kegg. William enlisted in Company C., Capt. Compher, 101st Pa. Volunteers in 1861. After three years hard service he was honorably discharged and returned to the old homestead and engaged in farming. In 1884 he moved to Everett, where he was engaged in draying. William never aspired to public life but being public spirited, he served the town in several important positions. He was a devout Christian and a member of the Reformed Church for many years. Was a charter member of the Rainsburg Lodge of I.O.O.F.

STUDNIARZ

WILLIAM STUDNIARZ aka "Billy", Seventh great grandson of progenitor Nicholas Kegg.

STULL

BAYLEE KEITH STULL Seventh great grandson of progenitor Nicholas Kegg.
STEVEN STULL Seventh great grandson of progenitor Nicholas Kegg.

STULTZ

DONALD LEE STULTZ [6141A] (1945 – 1977) son of Samuel and Margaret (Turner) Stultz married Lucy Virginia (Haddix) Delasko. A Navy Veteran, Donald was employed by Drywall Associates Inc. of Newport News and attended Providence Mennonite Church. **GREGORY JOSEPH STULTZ** [6141B] (1952 – 1974) son of Joseph and Marjorie (Bollman) Stultz was employed as an equipment operator for the Regal Construction Company in Washington, D.C. **JEFFREY WILLIAM STULTZ** Sixth great grandson of progenitor Nicholas Kegg. **JENNIFER LYNN STULTZ** Sixth great granddaughter of progenitor Nicholas Kegg. **JOSEPH STULTZ** Sixth great grandson of progenitor Nicholas Kegg.

[6138] p.1 Kansas City Star (MO) Dec 3, 1912 [6139] The Ledger (Lakeland, FL) Jan 27, 2012 [6139A] The Ansley Herald (NE) March 11, 1965 [6139B] Find A Grave Memorial #152227401 [6140] Johnstown Tribune Democrat obituary clipping (PA) obtained by D. Sue Dible [6141] The Bedford Gazette (PA) May 25, 1917 [6141A] Newport News Daily Press (VA) Mar 16, 1977 [6141B] obituary newspaper clipping contributed by Bob Rose

LISA SHAWN STULTZ Sixth great granddaughter of progenitor Nicholas Kegg. **MELISSA A. STULTZ** Sixth great granddaughter of progenitor Nicholas Kegg. **ROBERT E. STULTZ** Sixth great grandson of progenitor Nicholas Kegg. **CHERYL DAWN STULTZ** [6142] aka "Sheri" (1949 – 2022) daughter of Joseph and Marjorie (Bollman) Stultz married Gary Lynn Greenawalt with whom she was mother of (2). Sheri married two more times, to Tyler Dobson and later to John Dunkle. Sheri was an accomplished musician and teacher. Throughout the years she taught many students the skill along with the love and appreciation for music, with many continuing to use their talents still to this day. In addition, Sheri was owner and operator, along with being a former employee, of Bollman Charter Service. She had many roles there throughout the years; from office work and travel agent, to setting up tours, and even escorting many tours and school groups all over the United States and Canada.

STUMBAUGH

ANDREA STUMBAUGH Seventh great granddaughter of progenitor Nicholas Kegg.
ELIZABETH STUMBAUGH Seventh great granddaughter of progenitor Nicholas Kegg.
LANCE STUMBAUGH Seventh great grandson of progenitor Nicholas Kegg.
PAUL F. STUMBAUGH Sixth great grandson of progenitor Nicholas Kegg.
SHELLEY DANIEL STUMBAUGH Sixth great grandson of progenitor Nicholas Kegg.

STURTZ

BETTY MAXINE STURTZ [6143] (1920 – 2014) daughter of Albert and Jessie (Rouzer) Sturtz married twice; first to Francis Leo Palmer with whom she was mother of (2). Later, she married Allen Fitch. Betty retired from C & P Telephone Company.

STYER

RYAN KEITH STYER Sixth great granddaughter of progenitor Nicholas Kegg.
SHAWN WAYNE STYER Sixth great grandson of progenitor Nicholas Kegg.

STYNCHULA

ELIJAH STYNCHULA Seventh great grandson of progenitor Nicholas Kegg.
MCKENNAH STYNCHULA Seventh great granddaughter of progenitor Nicholas Kegg.

SUASA

TRAVIS GABRIEL SUASA Sixth great granddaughter of progenitor Nicholas Kegg.

SUDER

HOMER SEWELL SUDER (1892 – 1893) son of Albert and Laura (Kegg) Suder.
INFANT SUDER [6144] (died 1897) child of Albert and Laura (Kegg) Suder succumbed to cholera infanturn.

SUFRONKO

BRANDON SUFRONKO Seventh great grandson of progenitor Nicholas Kegg.
DALE MAX SUFRONKO [6145] (1962 – 2009) son of George and Barbara (Dixon) Sufronko.

[6142] Bedford Gazette (PA) Nov 14, 2022 [6143] Sturtevant Funeral Home & Crematory (VA) [6144] p.5 - Evening Times (MD) July 22.1897 [6145] Athens Messenger (OH) July 15, 2009

DAVID EDWARD SUFRONKO Sixth great grandson of progenitor Nicholas Kegg. **GINA SUE SUFRONKO** Seventh great granddaughter of progenitor Nicholas Kegg. **KYLE DAVID SUFRONKO** Seventh great grandson of progenitor Nicholas Kegg. **PAUL V SUFRONKO** [6146] (1965 – 2020) son of George and Barbara (Dixon) Sufronko, married Kim Conkel with whom he was father of (1). Paul was always dependable and was a hard worker. He worked for 18 years as a cemetery sexton for the York Township Cemeteries, and he formerly worked for several years as a supervisor at Rocky Shoes & Boots.

SULLIVAN

BILLIE SAMUEL SULLIVAN Sixth great grandson of progenitor Nicholas Kegg.
MERLIE NICOLE SULLIVAN Sixth great granddaughter of progenitor Nicholas Kegg.

SUMMERS

ALEXIS LEE SUMMERS Seventh great granddaughter of progenitor Nicholas Kegg.
JANE LEA SUMMERS aka "Jani", Seventh great granddaughter of progenitor Nicholas Kegg.
MATTHEW MICHAEL SUMMERS Seventh great grandson of progenitor Nicholas Kegg.

SUNDEY

FRANK GEORGE SUNDEY Fifth great grandson of progenitor Nicholas Kegg.
FREDERICK JOSEPH SUNDEY (1948 – 1993) aka "Rick", son of Ralph and Virginia (Kegg) Sundey married twice; first to Marie S. Mayo and later, to Leonora Tarroyo. **OLIVIA L. SUNDEY** Sixth great granddaughter of progenitor Nicholas Kegg. **RACHEL SUNDEY** Sixth great granddaughter of progenitor Nicholas Kegg. **RAYMOND RALPH SUNDEY** Fifth great grandson of progenitor Nicholas Kegg. **ROSALIND SUNDEY** Sixth great granddaughter of progenitor Nicholas Kegg.

SUNDIN

EMMA SUNDIN Sixth great granddaughter of progenitor Nicholas Kegg.

SURRENA

AMY L. SURRENA Sixth great granddaughter of progenitor Nicholas Kegg. **JASON SURRENA** Sixth great grandson of progenitor Nicholas Kegg. **EDWIN LEE SURRENA** [6146A] aka "Ed" (1946 – 2019) son of Wayne and Alene (Beegle) Surrena married Ann Robinson with whom he was father of (2). Ed began his career at Bashline Company and then moved on to the Pennsylvania State Police Academy, retiring after 25 years of service. Ed was a member of the Brady Paul Lodge #54 and a member of the National Guard for approximately six years. He was an avid golfer, fisherman, and hunter with a deep appreciation for classic cars (especially his 1965 red GTO). Ed was a Pittsburgh sports enthusiast.

SUSZKO

BRENT SUSZKO Seventh great grandson of progenitor Nicholas Kegg.
JOEL SUSZKO Seventh great grandson of progenitor Nicholas Kegg.

SUTER

NATASHA ANN SUTER Seventh great granddaughter of progenitor Nicholas Kegg.

[6146] Athens Messenger (OH) Jan 28, 2020 [6146A] The Herald (Sharon, PA) July 8, 2019

SUTTER

CHRISTOPHER SUTTER Sixth great grandson of progenitor Nicholas Kegg.
EMILY SUTTER Sixth great granddaughter of progenitor Nicholas Kegg.

SUTTERLIN

BROGAN GAINES SUTTERLIN Sixth great grandson of progenitor Nicholas Kegg.
FRANK WALTER SUTTERLIN Fifth great grandson of progenitor Nicholas Kegg.
FRANK WILLIAM JOE SUTTERLIN Fourth great grandson of progenitor Nicholas Kegg.
JON CHRISTOPHER SUTTERLIN Fourth great grandson of progenitor Nicholas Kegg.
MCKENNA MARIE SUTTERLIN Sixth great granddaughter of progenitor Nicholas Kegg.
REBECCA MICHELE SUTTERLIN Fifth great granddaughter of progenitor Nicholas Kegg.
WILLIAM CHRISTOPHER SUTTERLIN Fifth great grandson of progenitor Nicholas Kegg.

SUTTLES

JOE D. SUTTLES Sixth great grandson of progenitor Nicholas Kegg.

SUTTON

CAROL SUTTON Fifth great granddaughter of progenitor Nicholas Kegg. **ERIC TIKI SUTTON** Sixth great grandson of progenitor Nicholas Kegg. **HEATHER SUTTON** Sixth great granddaughter of progenitor Nicholas Kegg. **LANCE K. SUTTON** Fifth great grandson of progenitor Nicholas Kegg. **LINDA SUTTON** Fifth great granddaughter of progenitor Nicholas Kegg.

SWAILES

ROBERT A. SWAILES Sixth great grandson of progenitor Nicholas Kegg.
RYAN P. SWAILES Sixth great grandson of progenitor Nicholas Kegg.

SWALLOWS

KENNETH LEE SWALLOWS Seventh great grandson of progenitor Nicholas Kegg.

SWANGER

AMY SWANGER Sixth great granddaughter of progenitor Nicholas Kegg.
CAROL DIANE SWANGER Sixth great granddaughter of progenitor Nicholas Kegg.
DANIEL LEE SWANGER Sixth great grandson of progenitor Nicholas Kegg.
DENISE MARIE SWANGER Sixth great granddaughter of progenitor Nicholas Kegg.

SWANK

ALISA L. SWANK (1960 – 1960) daughter of William and Janis (Brown) Swank.
ALLEN L. SWANK Sixth great grandson of progenitor Nicholas Kegg.
CHRISTEN A. SWANK (1965 – 1965) daughter of William and Janis (Brown) Swank.
DORIS MARIE SWANK [6147] (1912 – 2004) daughter of Walter and Ivah (Laird) Swank, married Alfred Amil Adolphsen. Doris grew up attending rural school and graduated from the Shannon City High

---

[6147] Lenox Time Table (IA) July 28, 2004 obtained by Julia Johnson

School with the Class of 1929. Aspiring to teach school, she attended an extension of Iowa State Teachers College and taught four terms of rural school. Although they were never able to have children of their own, Doris' friends and relatives were an inspiration to her, she always had a deep concern for them, being especially close to her nieces and nephews. Doris was a long-time member and faithful attendant of the Lenox United Methodist Church, the Mayflower Club, Jolly Neighbor's Club and V.I.C. and U.M.W.
DOROTHY HAZEL SWANK [6148] (1913 – 2004) daughter of Walter and Ivah (Laird) Swank, married Floyd Garfield Lee with whom she was mother of (3); Dorothy graduated from Shannon City High School, then, attended an extension of Iowa State Teachers College in preparation for teaching in rural schools. After completing the course, she still was too young to teach school, so she worked at the Union County Home near Creston. Dorothy was a homemaker and worked in area nursing homes.
EVA MAXINE SWANK [6148A] (1921 – 2017) daughter of Walter and Ivah (Laird) Swank married twice; first to Gerald Barton Curtis with whom she was mother of (3). Later, she married Charlie Dee Lindgren. Eva worked as a rural schoolteacher for three years; later she was employed at Jefferson Bank and Trust. Eva took pride in her home as a homemaker throughout her life. **GARY DEAN SWANK** Fifth great grandson of progenitor Nicholas Kegg. **HELEN LAUREEN SWANK** [6149] (1915 – 1957) daughter of Walter and Ivah (Laird) Swank, married Paul Arie Weeda with whom she was mother of (2). **JOHN J. SWANK** Sixth great grandson of progenitor Nicholas Kegg. **LARRY LEE SWANK** (1937 – 2005) son of William and Doris (Johnson) Swank married Joyce A Sandidge. Larry was a Vietnam veteran having served in the U. S. Navy. **NANCY ANN SWANK** Fifth great granddaughter of progenitor Nicholas Kegg. **SHIRLEY A. SWANK** Fifth great granddaughter of progenitor Nicholas Kegg. **SHIRLEY LYNNE SWANK** Fifth great granddaughter of progenitor Nicholas Kegg. **WALTER EARL SWANK** [6150] (1919 – 1988) son of Walter and Ivah (Laird) Swank married twice; first to Letha Webster with whom he was father of (1). Later, he married Mary V. Garrett with whom he was father of (2). W. Earl was employed at John Deere Harvester Works in East Moline. **WILLIAM BYRLE SWANK** (1910 – 1993) son of Walter and Ivah (Laird) Swank, married Doris Amanda Johnson with whom he was father of (3). **WILLIAM BYRLE SWANK** Fifth great grandson of progenitor Nicholas Kegg. **WILLIAM C. SWANK** Sixth great grandson of progenitor Nicholas Kegg.

SWANSON

ELLEN E. SWANSON Sixth great granddaughter of progenitor Nicholas Kegg.
SARAH SWANSON Sixth great granddaughter of progenitor Nicholas Kegg.

SWARTS

LEWIS RICHARD SWARTS Seventh great grandson of progenitor Nicholas Kegg.
STEVEN NORBERT SWARTS Seventh great grandson of progenitor Nicholas Kegg.

SWARTZ

BARBARA SWARTZ Sixth great granddaughter of progenitor Nicholas Kegg.
CATHERINE ANN SWARTZ Sixth great granddaughter of progenitor Nicholas Kegg.
LINDA SWARTZ Sixth great granddaughter of progenitor Nicholas Kegg.
RONALD SWARTZ aka "Ronnie" Sixth great grandson of progenitor Nicholas Kegg.

SWARTZWELDER

BARBARA A. SWARTZWELDER Seventh great granddaughter of progenitor Nicholas Kegg

---

[6148] Creston News-Advertiser (IA) Dec 16, 2004 [6148A] The Default Newspaper (CO) Dec. 21, 2017 [6149] Creston News-Advertiser (IA) Nov 21, 1983 [6150] (IL) newspaper obituary clipping obtained by Pallas Houser

JOHN CLYDE SWARTZWELDER Fifth great grandson of progenitor Nicholas Kegg. **KAYE SWARTZWELDER** Sixth great granddaughter of progenitor Nicholas Kegg. **MELANIE SWARTZWELDER** Sixth great granddaughter of progenitor Nicholas Kegg. **NORMAN LEE SWARTZWELDER** [6151] (1939 – 2007) son of Richard and Sara (Perdew) Swartzwelder, married Anna Kay Kyong with whom he was father of (3). Norman was a retired supervisor for the C&P Telephone Company with 31 years of service. He was a U.S. Army veteran and a member of the Melvin United Methodist Church. **RICHARD EUGENE SWARTZWELDER** Seventh great grandson of progenitor Nicholas Kegg. **ROBERT LEE SWARTZWELDER** Seventh great grandson of progenitor Nicholas Kegg. **SALLY SWARTZWELDER** Sixth great granddaughter of progenitor Nicholas Kegg.

SWEARINGEN

JACKSON SWEARINGEN Seventh great grandson of progenitor Nicholas Kegg.
SYDNEY SWEARINGEN Seventh great granddaughter of progenitor Nicholas Kegg.

SWEET

ALAXENDER SWEET Seventh great grandson of progenitor Nicholas Kegg.
ZACHARY SWEET Seventh great grandson of progenitor Nicholas Kegg.

SWEGER

JASON M. SWEGER Seventh great grandson of progenitor Nicholas Kegg.
WAYNE SWEGER Seventh great grandson of progenitor Nicholas Kegg.

SWEITZER

BRANDON SWEITZER Eighth great grandson of progenitor Nicholas Kegg.
SAMANTHA SWEITZER Eighth great granddaughter of progenitor Nicholas Kegg.

SWERLEIN

JACK SWERLEIN [6152] (1937 – 1955) adopted son of James and Lois (Elder) Swerlin died on the operating table after the accidental discharge of his .22 rifle. A Hollow-nose bullet struck him near his right ear, particles of the bullet splitting off and lodging in his brain. Had it been a hard bullet the wound might not have been fatal. Jack had just returned home after being discharged from the air force. Jack and two neighbor boys decided to test their marksmanship. They stood on the edge of the lawn in front of the house and were firing at clods of earth from a newly plowed field. Jack had his bolt-action rifle strapped to his right arm. The other boys were using a shotgun. As one of the boys fired the shotgun, he handed it across to the other. Jack cautioned them to watch the safety. He had just uttered the words when his own rife hanging from the arm strap discharged. Jack fell to the ground. One of the boys ran to the house to summon Mr. and Mrs. Swerlein. The father reached the boy's side in time to hear him subconsciously mumble again, "watch the safety". Jack was taken to Lansing Hospital by ambulance. At the hospital he was given blood transfusions and was placed under an oxygen tent while surgeons prepared to operate. They were operating when Jack's life expired.

SWIFT

JESSICA FRANCES SWIFT Seventh great granddaughter of progenitor Nicholas Kegg.

[6151] p.14 - Cumberland Times News (MD) Jan 4, 2007 [6152] p.1 - Ingham County News (MI) Oct 27, 1955, obtained by D. Sue Dible

JOHN R. SWIFT Sixth great grandson of progenitor Nicholas Kegg.
JOSHUA ROBERT SWIFT Seventh great grandson of progenitor Nicholas Kegg.
SHARON E. SWIFT Sixth great granddaughter of progenitor Nicholas Kegg.

SWIKOSKI

ALLISON R. SWIKOSKI Sixth great granddaughter of progenitor Nicholas Kegg. **ANTHONY ROMAN SWIKOSKI** Sixth great grandson of progenitor Nicholas Kegg. **CARSON SWIKOSKI** Seventh great grandson of progenitor Nicholas Kegg. **CATHERINE SUE SWIKOSKI** Sixth great granddaughter of progenitor Nicholas Kegg. **CLAYTON S. SWIKOSKI** Sixth great grandson of progenitor Nicholas Kegg. **DAVID JOHN SWIKOSKI** [6153] (1948 – 2012) son of John and Loretta (Kegg) Swikoski, married Carolyn Joy with whom he was father of (2). David proudly served his country in the United States Army and then the United States Navy for several years. He enjoyed woodworking and having coffee with his friends at the local restaurant. **DOMINIQUE SWIKOSKI** Seventh great grandson of progenitor Nicholas Kegg. **JAMES VINCENT SWIKOSKI** [6154] (1949 – 1993) son of John and Loretta (Kegg) Swikoski, married Nona Bernice Bard with whom he was father of (3). James was fishing with his brother in St. Martin's Bay near St. Ignace, Michigan. The water was rough, and the boat became swamped. James drowned and, his brother Martin died of exposure after floating with a life preserver for a number of hours after the propeller of their boat became tangled in fishing nets owned and maintained by Floyd A. Paquin, Jr. who had been appointed a captain by the Sault Ste. Marie Tribe of Chippewa Indians for the purpose of regulating tribal fishing in the Great Lakes. **JAMEY LEE SWIKOSKI** Sixth great grandson of progenitor Nicholas Kegg. **JEFFIFER L. SWIKOSKI** Sixth great granddaughter of progenitor Nicholas Kegg. **JOHN SWIKOSKI** Sixth great grandson of progenitor Nicholas Kegg. **MARTIN JAMES SWIKOSKI** (1975 – 1993) aka "Marty", son of John and Loretta (Kegg) Swikoski. **MARY A. SWIKOSKI** Fifth great granddaughter of progenitor Nicholas Kegg. **RICHARD ROMAN SWIKOSKI** Fifth great grandson of progenitor Nicholas Kegg.

SWINEHART

ANDREW SWINEHART Seventh great grandson of progenitor Nicholas Kegg. **DAN SWINEHART** Sixth great grandson of progenitor Nicholas Kegg. **DARIAN SWINEHART** Eighth great grandson of progenitor Nicholas Kegg. **JORDIAN SWINEHART** Eighth great granddaughter of progenitor Nicholas Kegg. **NANCY SWINEHART** Sixth great granddaughter of progenitor Nicholas Kegg.

SWINGER

ALINA SWINGER Seventh great granddaughter of progenitor Nicholas Kegg. **BRENDAN J. SWINGER** Sixth great grandson of progenitor Nicholas Kegg. **DAVID SWINGER** Fifth great grandson of progenitor Nicholas Kegg. **DAVID SWINGER** Seventh great grandson of progenitor Nicholas Kegg. **DAVID R. SWINGER** Sixth great grandson of progenitor Nicholas Kegg. **DRAKE SWINGER** Seventh great grandson of progenitor Nicholas Kegg. **GREGORY SWINGER** Fifth great grandson of progenitor Nicholas Kegg. **IVY SWINGER** Seventh great granddaughter of progenitor Nicholas Kegg. **JACE SWINGER** Seventh great grandson of progenitor Nicholas Kegg. **JIMMIE MICHAEL SWINGER** Fifth great grandson of progenitor Nicholas Kegg. **KEITH A. SWINGER** [6155] (1988 – 2005) son of David and Kimberly (Plummer) Swinger was employed by Tri-County Drywall Corp. Keith was an avid outdoorsman and an excellent woodworker. **MADI SWINGER** Seventh great granddaughter of progenitor Nicholas Kegg. **MARGARET ANN SWINGER** aka "Peggy" Fifth great granddaughter of progenitor Nicholas Kegg.

[6153] Mortensen Funeral Home, MI [6154] <http://statecasefiles.justia.com/documents/michigan/court-of-appeals> [6155] Johnstown Tribune-Democrat (PA) July 3, 2005

MICHAEL JOSEPH SWINGER Sixth great grandson of progenitor Nicholas Kegg.
RANDY SWINGER Fifth great grandson of progenitor Nicholas Kegg.
RILYNN SWINGER Seventh great granddaughter of progenitor Nicholas Kegg.
TRAVIS E. SWINGER [6156] (1983 – 2005) son of David and Kimberly (Plummer) Swinger, was engaged to Krystal L. Zaffuto with whom he was father of (1). Travis was employed by Johnstown Welding Corp. He was a member of Brookside Sportsmen.
VICKY SWINGER Fifth great granddaughter of progenitor Nicholas Kegg.

SWINK

RACHEL LYNN SWINK Sixth great granddaughter of progenitor Nicholas Kegg.

SWINTZ

BRITTANY SWINTZ Seventh great granddaughter of progenitor Nicholas Kegg.
JENNIFER SWINTZ Seventh great granddaughter of progenitor Nicholas Kegg.

SWOPE

HELEN MARIE SWOPE Seventh great granddaughter of progenitor Nicholas Kegg.
LYDIA D. SWOPE Seventh great granddaughter of progenitor Nicholas Kegg.
RUSSELL SWOPE Ninth great grandson of progenitor Nicholas Kegg.
TINA J. SWOPE Seventh great granddaughter of progenitor Nicholas Kegg.

SWORD

ADDISON SWORD Eighth great grandson of progenitor Nicholas Kegg.
SAMANTHA SWORD Eighth great granddaughter of progenitor Nicholas Kegg.

SYKES

KATHY SYKES Fifth great granddaughter of progenitor Nicholas Kegg.
ROBIN SUZANNE SYKES Fifth great granddaughter of progenitor Nicholas Kegg.
NANCY LEE SYKES Fifth great granddaughter of progenitor Nicholas Kegg.

SYMONS

TRISTAN SYMONS Eighth great grandson of progenitor Nicholas Kegg.

SZWEC

RAYCE JAMES SZWEC [6157] (1992 – 2020) son of Stephen and Kimberly (Spaw) Szwec. Rayce always said, "A True Fisherman never buys bait, they Catch it."
RAYNE SZWEC Seventh great grandson of progenitor Nicholas Kegg.

SZYNSKI

MICHAEL SZYNSKI Seventh great grandson of progenitor Nicholas Kegg.

[6156] Johnstown Tribune-Democrat (PA) May 1, 2005 [6157] Herald Tribune (FL) Oct. 3, 2020

TABLER

BRANDE TABLER Seventh great granddaughter of progenitor Nicholas Kegg.
BRANDEN MATTHEW TABLER Sixth great grandson of progenitor Nicholas Kegg.
DUSTIN CHRISTOPHER TABLER Sixth great grandson of progenitor Nicholas Kegg.
HUNTER ASHTON TABLER Seventh great grandson of progenitor Nicholas Kegg.

TAKORES

DYLAN LAWRENCE TAKORES Seventh great grandson of progenitor Nicholas Kegg.
ERIN TAKORES Seventh great granddaughter of progenitor Nicholas Kegg.
LAUREN CHRISTINE TAKORES Seventh great granddaughter of progenitor Nicholas Kegg.

TALBOTT

ARIA KATHERINE TALBOTT Eighth great granddaughter of progenitor Nicholas Kegg.
ELORA ANN TALBOTT Eighth great granddaughter of progenitor Nicholas Kegg.
LIAM RYAN TALBOTT Eighth great grandson of progenitor Nicholas Kegg.

TALCOTT

CONSTANCE TALCOTT Fourth great granddaughter of progenitor Nicholas Kegg.
DORA JEAN TALCOTT aka "Dody", Fourth great granddaughter of progenitor Nicholas Kegg.
FREDERICK L. TALCOTT Fourth great grandson of progenitor Nicholas Kegg.
MARJORIE J. TALCOTT aka "Marjie", Fourth great granddaughter of progenitor Nicholas Kegg.

TALLEY

DANIEL TALLEY Sixth great grandson of progenitor Nicholas Kegg.
ROBERT WESLEY TALLEY Sixth great grandson of progenitor Nicholas Kegg.

TALLMAN

DAVID B. TALLMAN Sixth great grandson of progenitor Nicholas Kegg. **JOSEPH TALLMAN** Sixth great grandson of progenitor Nicholas Kegg. **LACIE ELIZABETH TALLMAN** Sixth great granddaughter of progenitor Nicholas Kegg. **LUWANA R. TALLMAN** Fifth great granddaughter of progenitor Nicholas Kegg. **MARK TALLMAN** Sixth great grandson of progenitor Nicholas Kegg. **PAULA RUTH TALLMAN** Fifth great granddaughter of progenitor Nicholas Kegg. **REBECCA LEE TALLMAN** Fifth great granddaughter of progenitor Nicholas Kegg. **RUTH TALLMAN** Sixth great granddaughter of progenitor Nicholas Kegg. **SHARON M. TALLMAN** Sixth great granddaughter of progenitor Nicholas Kegg.

TAMM

ALBERT EMIL TAMM [6158] (1945 – 2021) son of Albert and Dorothea (May) Tamm married Verna Lynne Hunnecutt with whom he was father of (8). Albert joined the United States Marine Corps and proudly served until his honorable discharge in 1977. He enjoyed playing poker, collecting coins and key chains, reminiscing and most importantly, spending time with his family.
ALBERT TAMM III Sixth great grandson of progenitor Nicholas Kegg.

[6158] Buresh Funeral Homes (MI)/ Tribute Archive obtained by D. Sue Dible

ANDREA JOY TAMM Sixth great granddaughter of progenitor Nicholas Kegg. **BRIAN MATTHEW TAMM** Sixth great grandson of progenitor Nicholas Kegg. **CHERYL LYNN TAMM** Sixth great granddaughter of progenitor Nicholas Kegg. **CYNTHIA TAMM** Sixth great granddaughter of progenitor Nicholas Kegg. **DANIEL RICHARD TAMM** Sixth great grandson of progenitor Nicholas Kegg. **DAVID RAY TAMM** [6159] (1956 – 2007) son of Frederick and Patricia (Barrows) Tamm, married Myra Denise Wise with whom he was father of (1). David was employed by Scheller Corp., Chesterfield Twp. **DEBRA TAMM** Sixth great granddaughter of progenitor Nicholas Kegg. **DEBI TAMM** Sixth great granddaughter of progenitor Nicholas Kegg. **DOUGLAS TAMM** Sixth great grandson of progenitor Nicholas Kegg. **EMIL TAMM** Sixth great grandson of progenitor Nicholas Kegg. **FREDERICK TAMM** Sixth great grandson of progenitor Nicholas Kegg. **FREDERICK CARL TAMM** [6160] (1931 – 2008) son of Albert and Dorothea (May) Tamm married twice; first to Patricia Ann Barrows with whom he was father of (3). Later, he married Paulette Ricca with whom he was father of (5). **HELENA TAMM** Sixth great granddaughter of progenitor Nicholas Kegg. **JAMES GLEN TAMM** aka "Jim", Sixth great grandson of progenitor Nicholas Kegg. **JENNIFER TAMM** Sixth great granddaughter of progenitor Nicholas Kegg. **JEREMY TAMM** Seventh great grandchild of progenitor Nicholas Kegg. **JESSICA TAMM** Seventh great granddaughter of progenitor Nicholas Kegg. **JOSEPH TAMM** Sixth great grandson of progenitor Nicholas Kegg. **JUDE MAXWELL TAMM** [6161] (2012 – 2017) son of Richard Tamm and Crystal Hughes attended Hymera Elementary School. .**KALEY TAMM** Seventh great granddaughter of progenitor Nicholas Kegg. **KAREN TAMM** Sixth great granddaughter of progenitor Nicholas Kegg. **KATHY TAMM** Sixth great granddaughter of progenitor Nicholas Kegg. **MARK TAMM** Sixth great grandson of progenitor Nicholas Kegg. **MISTY TAMM** Sixth great granddaughter of progenitor Nicholas Kegg. **PAULINE JANE TAMM** Sixth great granddaughter of progenitor Nicholas Kegg. **ROBERT M. TAMM** Sixth great grandson of progenitor Nicholas Kegg. **ROBERT MAY TAMM** [6162] (1937 – 2003) son of Albert and Dorothea (May) Tamm, married Ellen Irene Vagts with whom he was father of (5). **TAMMY RENEE TAMM** Sixth great granddaughter of progenitor Nicholas Kegg. **TEEGAN TAMM** Seventh great granddaughter of progenitor Nicholas Kegg. **TRENT TAMM** Seventh great grandson of progenitor Nicholas Kegg. **WILLIAM TAMM** Sixth great grandson of progenitor Nicholas Kegg. **WILLIAM HENRY TAMM** [6163] (1932 – 1995) son of Albert and Dorothea (May) Tamm, married Helen Wayne McKenzie with whom he was father of (6).

TANGER

BRIANNE NICOLE TANGER Sixth great granddaughter of progenitor Nicholas Kegg.
MANDY DANIELLE TANGER Sixth great granddaughter of progenitor Nicholas Kegg.

TANNEHILL

ALEX THOMAS TANNEHILL Seventh great grandson of progenitor Nicholas Kegg.
AMY PATRICIA TANNEHILL Seventh great granddaughter of progenitor Nicholas Kegg.

TAPP

RACHEL TAPP Sixth great granddaughter of progenitor Nicholas Kegg.
STEPHANNIE JETT TAPP Sixth great granddaughter of progenitor Nicholas Kegg.

TARTER

DENISE VIOLA TARTER [6163A] aka "Boots" (1955 – 2014) daughter of Harold and Frantie (Laird)

[6159] Detroit News (MI) Oct 24, 2007 [6160] Detroit News (MI) Feb 22, 2008 [6161] Tribune Star (IN) Oct 23, 2017 [6162] Detroit Free Press (MI) Nov 2, 2003 [6163] Detroit Free Press (MI) Feb 16, 1995

Tarter, married Randy Rexwinkle with whom she was mother of (1). Boots was a thoughtful and selfless person that always put others before herself. From unique and customized gifts that she would somehow manage to always perfectly match to their recipient, to her ability to remember small details about someone that would allow her to say or do something that meant the world to someone else. Boots was having the time of her life in Alaska, living out other people's vacations from fishing in the summer, hunting Musk Ox in the winter, to making a point of driving to the end of as many roads as she could in the last frontier. Denise was a devoted wife, loving mother, a phenomenal grandmother, an excellent friend, and above all else, an amazing human being.

TATE

AMANDA TATE Sixth great granddaughter of progenitor Nicholas Kegg. **CHANDLER TATE** Sixth great grandson of progenitor Nicholas Kegg. **KEVIN TATE** Sixth great grandson of progenitor Nicholas Kegg. **OLIVIA TATE** Sixth great granddaughter of progenitor Nicholas Kegg. **SPENCER TATE** Sixth great grandson of progenitor Nicholas Kegg.
TIMOTHY ALAN TATE aka "Alan" Fifth great grandson of progenitor Nicholas Kegg.

TAVERNIER

SCOTT ALLAN TAVERNIER Sixth great grandson of progenitor Nicholas Kegg.
SUSAN RENEE TAVERNIER Sixth great granddaughter of progenitor Nicholas Kegg.

TAYLOR

ADRIAN CALVIN TAYLOR [6164] (2003 – 2004) son of Joshua and Tracy (Swifney) Taylor. **AUSTIN TAYLOR** Seventh great grandson of progenitor Nicholas Kegg. **BARRY NEIL TAYLOR** Fifth great grandson of progenitor Nicholas Kegg. **BROOKLYN IRENE TAYLOR** [6164A] (2016 – 2016) daughter of Vernon and Brianna (Risner) Taylor. **CHERI ANITA TAYLOR** Sixth great granddaughter of progenitor Nicholas Kegg. **EDDIE WARREN TAYLOR** Eighth great grandson of progenitor Nicholas Kegg. **ELDON T. TAYLOR** Seventh great grandson of progenitor Nicholas Kegg. **ELDON TYLER TAYLOR** [6165] (1983 – 2022) son of Georgine Taylor and Shane Ramsey. Eldon was raised in the home of his maternal grandparents, Lyda 'Mam' (Warsing) and the late Eldon 'Pap' Taylor, both of whom he loved and cared for. Tyler shared his Pap's love of hunting, shooting, and especially fishing. He was one of the first ever TMO members, and was the 2013 Points Champion, 2016 TMO Classic Champion, and has several regular season and big bass tournament wins to his credit. **GEORGINE TAYLOR** [6165A] (1964 – 2004) daughter of Eldon and Lyda (Warsing) Taylor, was united with Shane Ramsey with whom she was mother of (1). She married Marty L. Robinson. She was mother of (2). Georgine was employed for over nine years as a waitress at the Howard Johnson Restaurant in Breezewood. She then worked as a cashier at the BP in Breezewood, later working in the gift shop at the Family House Restaurant. **GRACIE FAYE TAYLOR** Seventh great granddaughter of progenitor Nicholas Kegg. **HANNAH ROSE TAYLOR** Eighth great granddaughter of progenitor Nicholas Kegg. **JILL SHANNON TAYLOR** Sixth great granddaughter of progenitor Nicholas Kegg. **JOHN MINNICH TAYLOR** Fifth great grandson of progenitor Nicholas Kegg. **JONATHAN P. TAYLOR** Seventh great grandson of progenitor Nicholas Kegg. **JONATHAN SHANE TAYLOR** Sixth great grandson of progenitor Nicholas Kegg. **JOSHUA DAMON TAYLOR** Sixth great grandson of progenitor Nicholas Kegg. **KAREN MINNICH TAYLOR** (1944 – 1945) daughter of William and Grace (Minnich) Taylor. **LACEY TAYLOR** Seventh great granddaughter of progenitor Nicholas Kegg. **LARRY TAYLOR** Seventh great grandson of progenitor Nicholas Kegg. **MELISSA KAY TAYLOR** Sixth great granddaughter of progenitor Nicholas Kegg.

[6163A] p.7B- Grand Junction Daily Sentinel (CO) July 26, 2014 [6164] Muskegon Chronicle (MI) Mar 30, 2004 [6164A] Engle-Shook Funeral Home & Crematory, Tiffin (OH) contributed by D. Sue Dible [6165] Bedford Gazette (PA) Jan 22, 2022 [6165A] Bedford Inquirer (PA) July 23, 2004, contributed by Bob Rose

MICHELLE ELISE TAYLOR Sixth great granddaughter of progenitor Nicholas Kegg. **MIKE TAYLOR** Sixth great grandson of progenitor Nicholas Kegg. **PAUL TAYLOR** Sixth great grandson of progenitor Nicholas Kegg. **SHILOH TAYLOR** Seventh great grandson of progenitor Nicholas Kegg. **TROY CHRISTOPHER TAYLOR** Eighth great grandson of progenitor Nicholas Kegg. **VERNON EUGENE TAYLOR** [6165B] (1973 – 2011) son of Vernon and Lois (Timmons) Taylor, married Crystal Fox with whom he was father of (2). Vernon was a truck driver. Vernon was happiest when he was doing something outdoors, whether it be hunting, fishing, gardening or just working in the yard. He cherished the time he spent with his family, knowing it was too short. **VERNON EUGENE TAYLOR** aka "Vern", Eighth great grandson of progenitor Nicholas Kegg. **WILLIAM STATLER TAYLOR** Fifth great grandson of progenitor Nicholas Kegg. **WILLIAM STATLER TAYLOR** Sixth great grandson of progenitor Nicholas Kegg.

TEAL

ROARY TEAL Seventh great grandson of progenitor Nicholas Kegg.
TYLER REESE TEAL Seventh great granddaughter of progenitor Nicholas Kegg.

TEEL

MEGAN CARISSA TEEL Seventh great granddaughter of progenitor Nicholas Kegg.

TENBROECK

CATHERINE TENBROECK Sixth great granddaughter of progenitor Nicholas Kegg.

TENNIHILL

CLARENCE TENNIHILL [6166] (1911 – 1969) son of Orren and Martha (Cagg) Tennihill, had worked at the National Cash Register Co. in Dayton until being forced to retire by ill health. **GILBERT E. TENNIHILL** [6167] (1917 – 1972) son of Orren and Martha (Cagg) Tennihill, married Betty Van Bibber. **MARGARET TENNIHILL** [6168] (1920 – 1975) daughter of Orren and Martha (Cagg) Tennihill married twice; first to Howard Ross Linscott with whom she was mother of (5). Later, she married Ralph H. Dugle. Margaret was a member of the First United Presbyterian Church of Logan, Order of the Eastern Star, Twig III of the Hocking Valley Community Hospital Auxiliary, and was a past member of Logan Emblem Club 263. **ROLLAND LEO TENNIHILL** [6169, 6170] (1923 – 1985) aka "Joe", son of Orren and Martha (Cagg) Tennihill, married Bernice Lucille Hardbarger. Rolland was awarded the Bronze Star medal in Viet Nam. Sergeant Major Tennihill was serving with Headquarters Company, 228th Assault Support Helicopter Battalion, 1st Cavalry Division. Joe was a former employee of General Electric, Logan, he was a member of Christ Christian Fellowship Church, Lithopolis.

TERPENING

EDWARD H. TERPENING [6170A] (1921 – 2010) son of Edward and Margaret (Howard) Terpening, married Sylvia Irene Richardson. Edward was a WWII Navy veteran and worked as a vocational rehabilitation counselor supervisor at the state government level. Ed was raised by and very fond of his maternal grandmother Stella Howard of Everett, He was a past commander of Bedford American Legion, former president of the Easter Seal Society, a member of the Everett Masonic Lodge #524 F. & A.M. and Bedford Moose Lodge #480. He was a former Federal Banking Examiner for FDIC, and a former director

---

[6165B] Stombaugh-Batton Funeral Home (OH) [6166] p.8 Logan Daily News (OH) Dec 27, 1969 [6167] p.8 Logan Daily News (OH) Jan 22, 1972 [6168] p.2 Logan Daily News (OH) Oct 9, 1975 [6169] p.8 Logan Daily News (OH) Aug 3, 1966 [6170] p.14-Lancaster-Eagle Gazette (OH) Sept 4, 1985 [6170A] Timothy A. Berkebile Funeral Home (PA)

of Friends Cove Mutual Insurance Company.

THIES

ALICE ELIZABETH THIES [6170B] (1919 – 2009) daughter of Elmer and Amy (Kerr) Thies married Karl Bachmann with whom she was mother of (2). Alice was a graduate of Cortland College in New York. She retired from Clarence Central Schools in New York after many years as a teacher. She was a member of the Resurrection Lutheran Church in Lebanon. **BRIAN COKER THIES** Fifth great grandson of progenitor Nicholas Kegg. **CHARLES ELMER THIES** Fourth great grandson of progenitor Nicholas Kegg. **CORINNE THIES**, aka "Cori", Sixth great granddaughter of progenitor Nicholas Kegg. **DOROTHY ELMERNA THIES** [6171] (1921 – 2011) daughter of Elmer and Amy (Kerr) Thies married twice; first to Dean Harper. Later, she married Thomas L. Kelly with whom she was mother of (2). **EARL THIES** Fifth great grandson of progenitor Nicholas Kegg. **MARK THIES** Fifth great grandson of progenitor Nicholas Kegg. **WADE M. THIES** Fifth great grandson of progenitor Nicholas Kegg.

THIESHEN

DAVID H. THIESHEN Sixth great grandson of progenitor Nicholas Kegg.
EARNEST H. THIESHEN Fifth great grandson of progenitor Nicholas Kegg.
SEAN A. THIESHEN Sixth great grandson of progenitor Nicholas Kegg.

THIGPEN

ANDREW THIGPEN Seventh great grandson of progenitor Nicholas Kegg. **GARRISON THIGPEN** Eighth great grandson of progenitor Nicholas Kegg. **GAVIN THIGPEN** Eighth great grandson of progenitor Nicholas Kegg. **JERAMY THIGPEN** Seventh great grandson of progenitor Nicholas Kegg. **NICHOLAS S. THIGPEN** Seventh great grandson of progenitor Nicholas Kegg. **RACHEL THIGPEN** Seventh great granddaughter of progenitor Nicholas Kegg.

THOMAS

AMANDA DEE THOMAS Seventh great granddaughter of progenitor Nicholas Kegg. **ANDRIA THOMAS** Eighth great granddaughter of progenitor Nicholas Kegg. **ANGELIQUE MARIE THOMAS** Seventh great granddaughter of progenitor Nicholas Kegg. **BRENDON ALEXANDER THOMAS** Eighth great grandson of progenitor Nicholas Kegg. **BROOKS ALLEN THOMAS** Seventh great grandson of progenitor Nicholas Kegg. **DREU THOMAS** Seventh great grandson of progenitor Nicholas Kegg. **JEREMIAH ELIAS THOMAS** aka "Jeremy" Seventh great grandson of progenitor Nicholas Kegg. **JOAN KATHRYN THOMAS** [6171A] (1936 – 2016) daughter of Howard and Kathryn (Saylor) Thomas married David Lee Phillip with whom she was mother of (3). Before retiring, Joan was a cashier at various places throughout the City of Medina. She loved her family and had a fondness for babies and puppies. **JORDAN MICHAEL THOMAS** Seventh great grandson of progenitor Nicholas Kegg. **JUSTINA THOMAS** Eighth great granddaughter of progenitor Nicholas Kegg. **KAREN THOMAS** Fifth great granddaughter of progenitor Nicholas Kegg. **KATHRYN DALE THOMAS** Fifth great granddaughter of progenitor Nicholas Kegg. **KIRA ANNE THOMAS** Eighth great granddaughter of progenitor Nicholas Kegg. **MALACHI ALLEN THOMAS** Eighth great grandson of progenitor Nicholas Kegg. **MARGARET THOMAS** (1913 – 2001) daughter of Theodore and Grace (Graham) Thomas, married William Douglas Maclean with whom she was mother of (4).

[6170B] The Western Star (OH) April 2, 2009 [6171] Plain Dealer (OH) Dec. 15, 2011 [6171A] Waite Funeral Home (OH)

MAX THOMAS Fifth great grandson of progenitor Nicholas Kegg. **MITCHELL THOMAS** Eighth great grandson of progenitor Nicholas Kegg. **ROY JIM THOMAS** (1951 – 1955) son of Jim and Lorna (Woodson) Thomas. **SHAWN MICHAEL THOMAS** Eighth great grandson of progenitor Nicholas Kegg. **THEO THOMAS** [6172] (1911 – 1969) daughter of Theodore and Grace (Graham) Thomas, married Frank Joseph Anthony Defebio with whom she was mother of (3). Theo was a taxi driver when she came into national prominence after removing two of her sons from public schools in North Carolina in 1950 to protest the state's compulsory school attendance law. After Theo fought the pupil placement requirements through courts, the Supreme Court in 1958 rejected her appeal that the law was unconstitutional. Theo frequently protested in Washington D.C. by sleeping on the District Building front steps and during the day carried a sign stating "I am starving to death" as she picketed the building in an attempt to obtain welfare aid.

THOMPSON

AMANDA THOMPSON Seventh great granddaughter of progenitor Nicholas Kegg. **BONNIE MARNO THOMPSON** [6173] (1929 – 1997) daughter of Harold and Esther (Cagg) Thompson married twice; first to Paul Mock with whom she was mother of (1). Later, she married J. W. Carpenter. Bonnie was self-employed in the auto salvage business and was a Methodist church member. **CARL ALVIN THOMPSON** Fifth great grandson of progenitor Nicholas Kegg. **CHARLES A. THOMPSON** (1928 – 2006) son of Roy and Gleason (Stuckey) Thompson married Nancy J. Williams. **CONNIE JO THOMPSON** Fifth great granddaughter of progenitor Nicholas Kegg. **DEANNA KAY THOMPSON** Fifth great granddaughter of progenitor Nicholas Kegg. **DIANA RAE THOMPSON** Sixth great granddaughter of progenitor Nicholas Kegg. **DONALD ROBERT THOMPSON** Fifth great grandson of progenitor Nicholas Kegg. **ELISSE THOMPSON** Seventh great granddaughter of progenitor Nicholas Kegg. **FLORENCE AGNES THOMPSON** (1914 – 1991) daughter of Tellie and Ethel (Tuohy) Thompson married Michael Fellows. **FLORENCE M. THOMPSON** [6174] (1883 – 1943) daughter of John and Luella (Laird) Thompson, married Alonzo Philipp Schoepflin with whom she was mother of (1). **GAIL LEE THOMPSON** (1957 – 2011) daughter of James and Patricia (Stuckey) Thompson married three times; first to Guadalupe Lara Hiracheta, then to Gregory Duff Keys. Later, she married Sid-Ali Mounedji. **GLENN EDWARD THOMPSON** Sixth great grandson of progenitor Nicholas Kegg. **GOLDIE THOMPSON** (1900 – 1940) daughter of John and Luella (Laird) Thompson married twice; first to Milo Percy Hards with whom she was mother of (2). Later, she married Horace Joseph Traynor. **HAROLD IRVING THOMPSON** [6175] (1931 – 1936) son of Harold and Esther (Cagg) Thompson sustained internal injuries when the light delivery truck driven by his father hurtled from the pike. The family was on its way to Athens when Thompson lost control of the car on a curve. The truck overturned, hurling the occupants to the ground killing his father and brother Richard. **HAROLD S. THOMPSON** (1934 – 1960) aka "Toddie" son of Harold and Esther (Cagg) Thompson married Minnie Joan Lowe. **HAZEL THOMPSON** [6176] (1898 – 1965) daughter of John and Luella (Laird) Thompson married twice; first to Frank Leroy Wallace with whom she was mother of (4). Later, she married Theodore Crew Blazek. **HEATHER THOMPSON** Seventh great granddaughter of progenitor Nicholas Kegg. **HOLLY MARIE THOMPSON** Seventh great granddaughter of progenitor Nicholas Kegg. **INFANT THOMPSON** (1958 – 1958) daughter of Kenneth and Cora (Miller) Thompson. **IRENE MYRTLE THOMPSON** [6177] (1928 – 2005) daughter of Harold and Esther (Cagg) Thompson, married Raymond Coldrion Barnett with whom she was mother of (1). Irene retired from co-owning a carpet cleaning business. She was a member of the Tremont Methodist Church. **JAMES THOMPSON** Seventh great grandson of progenitor Nicholas Kegg. **JAMES LEE THOMPSON** [6178] (1923 – 1958) son of Telly and Ethel (Tuohy) Thompson was a veteran of WWII. James was a member of the Steam Fitters and Refrigeration Union No. 342 of Oakland and Oakland

---

[6172] p.28 Evening Star (DC) June 13, 1969 [6173] Daily Journal (MS) Nov 24, 1997 [6174] p.12 Denver Post (CO) Sep 27, 1902 [6175] The Times Recorder (Zanesville, OH) July 7, 1936 [6176] familysearch.org/IDAHO, SOUTHERN COUNTIES OBITUARIES, 1943-2013 [6177] Daily Journal (MS) Oct 24, 2005 [6178] Oakland Tribune (CA) July 22, 1958

Revival Tabernacle. **JENNIE MAY THOMPSON** [6179] (1884 – 1972) daughter of John and Luella (Laird) Thompson married three times; first to Charles S. Donaldson with whom she was mother of (1). She married Sam Schrottmann and later married Victor Henry Flood. **JERI LINN THOMPSON** [6179A] (1954 – 2017) daughter of John and Jean (Garver) Thompson married twice, first to Larry Lee Schohl and later to Stanley Zabolotney with whom she was mother of (1). A graduate of the University of Alabama. Jeri was a member of The Chapel, F.O.E. Riders Group and volunteered for CASA. She most enjoyed working with people and animals. **JOHN C. THOMPSON** Fifth great grandson of progenitor Nicholas Kegg. **JOHN HENDERSON PENROD THOMPSON** [6179B] (1924 – 2012) son of Roy and Gleason (Stuckey) Thompson married Mary Elizabeth Griffith with whom he was father of (3). John was a retired miner and farmer. **JOSEPH A. THOMPSON** (1886 -?) son of John and Luella (Laird) Thompson. **JOSEPH E. THOMPSON** [6180] (1959 – 2021) son of Carl and Betty Jane (Davis) Thompson was the father of (2). Later, he married Terri Smith. Joe was a hard worker. He worked as a warehouseman for Target Distribution and First Stop Shop in Altoona. Joe was a kind-hearted and easy-going guy who touched the lives of many. He was quite the gardener that enjoyed giving the fruits and vegetables of his labor to others. Joe was most proud of being a PIAA baseball (41 years) and volleyball official. His greatest achievement was having umpired two boys' baseball state championship games. **JUANITA THOMPSON** (1919 - 1974) daughter of Tellie and Ethel (Tuohy) Thompson, married Billy Hall Dunn with whom she was mother of (1). **KAITLYN THOMPSON** Eighth great granddaughter of progenitor Nicholas Kegg. **KAREN THOMPSON** Seventh great granddaughter of progenitor Nicholas Kegg. **KAREN L. THOMPSON** [6181] (1950 – 2020) daughter of Carl and Betty Jane (Davis) Thompson married Larry Shippey with whom she was mother of (1). Karen was a kindhearted person who frequently helped with church activities. She enjoyed her cats and was loved by all who knew her. **KATHY ANN THOMPSON** Fifth great granddaughter of progenitor Nicholas Kegg. **KENADIE THOMPSON** Eighth great granddaughter of progenitor Nicholas Kegg. **KITTY LEE THOMPSON** Fifth great granddaughter of progenitor Nicholas Kegg. **LEAPHA WOLESKA THOMPSON** (1894 – 1984) daughter of John and Luella (Laird) Thompson, married Samuel Bergeman with whom she was mother of (2). **LEON J. THOMPSON** (1890 – 1946) son of John and Luella (Laird) Thompson, married Celia Johnson with whom he was father of (2). **LOGAN THOMPSON** Eighth great grandson of progenitor Nicholas Kegg. **LONNIE MELVIN THOMPSON** Fifth great grandson of progenitor Nicholas Kegg. **MAJEL EDNA THOMPSON** (1925 – 1925) daughter of Harold and Esther (Cagg) Thompson. **MISTI THOMPSON** Seventh great granddaughter of progenitor Nicholas Kegg. **PATRICIA JANET THOMPSON** Sixth great granddaughter of progenitor Nicholas Kegg. **PATTI GAIL THOMPSON** Fifth great granddaughter of progenitor Nicholas Kegg. **PENNY THOMPSON** Sixth great granddaughter of progenitor Nicholas Kegg. **RICHARD LEROY THOMPSON** Sixth great grandson of progenitor Nicholas Kegg. **RICHARD OLAF THOMPSON** (1936 – 1936) son of Harold and Esther (Cagg) Thompson. **SCOTT ALLEN THOMPSON** (1960 – 2010) son of James and Patricia (Stuckey) Thompson married Tina Denise Fultz. **SHARON THOMPSON** Sixth great granddaughter of progenitor Nicholas Kegg. **SHEILA BETH THOMPSON** Seventh great granddaughter of progenitor Nicholas Kegg. **STEPHEN THOMPSON** Seventh great grandson of progenitor Nicholas Kegg. **STEVEN LEE THOMPSON** [6181A] (1950 – 1975) son of Kenneth and Cora (Miller) Thompson married Theresa Marie Will with whom he was father of (1). Steven was an industrial engineer employed by Kennametal Inc., Bedford. Steven was a member of the Certified Engineers Association; the Penn State University Alumni; and a member of St. Thomas Catholic Church, Bedford. **SUSAN ELIZABETH THOMPSON** Fifth great granddaughter of progenitor Nicholas Kegg. **TELLIE ARTHUR THOMPSON** [6182] (1889 – 1938) son of John and Luella (Laird) Thompson, married Ethel Agnes Tuohy with whom he was father of (5). **VELMA BERNICE THOMPSON** [6182A] (1917 – 1999) daughter of Tellie and Ethel (Tuohy) Thompson married Orson Harris Hill with whom she was mother of (3). Velma was the owner of a floral business and hot dog stand.

[6179] Newman Grove Reporter (NE) Oct 19, 1955 [6179A] Fort Wayne Newspapers (IN) March 2, 2017 [6179B] Great Falls Tribune (MT) Mar. 24, 2012 [6180] Bedford Gazette (PA) Aug 18, 2021 [6181] Timothy A. Berkebile Funeral Home Inc., PA [6181A] p.3 - Bedford Inquirer (PA) Aug 22, 1975 [6182] Oakland Tribune (CA) Sept 2, 1938 [6182A] Contra Costa Times (Walnut Creek, CA) May 1, 1999

WALTER LAVERNE THOMPSON (6182B) (1911 – 1996) son of Tellie and Ethel (Tuohy) Thompson married Maria Tommasa Ambrose with whom he was father of (2). Walter was retired from a long career with Cal-Trans San Luis Obispo. **WAYNE THOMPSON** Sixth great grandson of progenitor Nicholas Kegg.

THOMSON

JULIA THOMSON Sixth great granddaughter of progenitor Nicholas Kegg.
KATIE THOMSON Sixth great granddaughter of progenitor Nicholas Kegg.
MARGARET THOMSON Sixth great granddaughter of progenitor Nicholas Kegg.
PRESSON THOMSON Sixth great grandson of progenitor Nicholas Kegg.

THORN

ALIA THORN Seventh great granddaughter of progenitor Nicholas Kegg.

THORNBURG

ADAM J. THORNBURG Fifth great grandson of progenitor Nicholas Kegg.
JACQUE M. THORNBURG Fourth great grandson of progenitor Nicholas Kegg.
JACQUE WILBUR THORNBURG (6183) (1909 – 1979) son of Myron and Fern (Smith) Thornburg, married Eileen Loretta Bolger with whom he was father of (2).
JAMES ROY THORNBURG Fourth great grandson of progenitor Nicholas Kegg.
NICOLE M. THORNBURG Fifth great granddaughter of progenitor Nicholas Kegg.
TYLER THORNBURG Fifth great grandson of progenitor Nicholas Kegg.

THORNSBERRY

HALEY BROOKE THORNSBERRY Seventh great granddaughter of progenitor Nicholas Kegg.
JACOB THORNSBERRY Seventh great grandson of progenitor Nicholas Kegg.

THUM

AARON GUSTAVE THUM Sixth great grandson of progenitor Nicholas Kegg. **GEORGE WILLIAM THUM** (1904 – 1977) son of George and Katherine (Snavely) Thum, married Marjorie (Bjorklund) Rose with whom he was father of (1). George was a member of King of Kings Lutheran Church, Maitland, and a former resort proprietor in Crivitz. **GEORGE WILLIAM THUM** Sixth great grandson of progenitor Nicholas Kegg. **JACOB EPHRAIM THUM** Sixth great grandson of progenitor Nicholas Kegg. **JOEL LUCAYA THUM** Sixth great grandson of progenitor Nicholas Kegg. **THOMAS GARTH GUSTOF THUM** (1954 – 2015) son of George and Marjorie (Bjorklund) Thum married Joanne Ellen Davis.

THUMMA

PARKER THUMMA Eighth great grandson of progenitor Nicholas Kegg.

THURMOND

LAWRENCE ALLEN THURMOND aka "A. J.", Seventh great grandson of progenitor Nicholas Kegg.

(6182B) familysearch.org California, Oakland, Alameda County, Newspaper Record Collection Film Number 004265898 (6183) p.11C - The Plain Dealer (OH) July 20, 1979

TIEDEMAN

CARTER JAMES TIEDEMAN [6184] (2005 – 2012) son of Christopher and Emily (Farrer) Tiedeman. Carter was a fighter his entire life. His smile and passion for life inspired everyone who met him. He was an angel on earth who is now with his heavenly father.   **CHRISTOPHER ALLEN TIEDEMAN** Sixth great grandson of progenitor Nicholas Kegg.   **ELLA TIEDEMAN** Seventh great granddaughter of progenitor Nicholas Kegg.   **JOSHUA TIEDEMAN** Sixth great grandson of progenitor Nicholas Kegg.   **NATHANIEL TIEDEMAN** Seventh great grandson of progenitor Nicholas Kegg.   **STEPHANIE TIEDEMAN** Sixth great granddaughter of progenitor Nicholas Kegg.

TIDWELL

DEBORAH ANN TIDWELL Sixth great granddaughter of progenitor Nicholas Kegg.
KRISTINA LYNNE TIDWELL Sixth great granddaughter of progenitor Nicholas Kegg.
RICHARD WAYNE TIDWELL Sixth great grandson of progenitor Nicholas Kegg.

TILLERY

PATSY JEAN TILLERY Fifth great granddaughter of progenitor Nicholas Kegg.

TIMBY

MARTHA JANE TIMBY (1917 – 2008) daughter of William and Edna (Laird) Timby married Charles Oscar Dabney with whom she was mother of (3).   **MARY ELAINE TIMBY** [6185] (1916 – 1925) daughter of William and Edna (Laird) Timby had always been a child of unusually good health and strong vitality. Suddenly she was stricken with an illness which at first was not considered serious but within two days her condition grew worse. It was deemed advisable by attending physicians to take her to the hospital at Des Moines. By the time she reached the hospital her condition was such that specialists called in consultation announced that there was nothing medical science could do and that it was impossible for her to live for more than a few hours.   **WILLIAM TIMBY** (1919 – 1920) aka "Little Billy", son of William and Edna (Laird) Timby.

TIMMONS

CINDY TIMMONS Sixth great granddaughter of progenitor Nicholas Kegg.   **JOHN LAFAYETTE TIMMONS** (1922 – 1922) son of Robert and Maybelle (Woodward) Timmons.   **KEVIN TIMMONS** Seventh great grandson of progenitor Nicholas Kegg.   **PATRICK TIMMONS** Seventh great grandson of progenitor Nicholas Kegg.   **PEARL J. TIMMONS** [6186] (1926 – 1942) son of Robert and Maybelle (Woodward) Timmons worked as a farm hand.   **RILLA LUCILE TIMMONS** [6187] (1932 – 1935) daughter of Robert and Maybelle (Woodward) Timmons had been playing on the rear porch of the home and was not missed until sometime after her fatal plunge. A neighbor recovered the body from the cistern. The father is in a CCC camp at Portsmouth. In a frantic effort to save her life the city fireman were summoned to use their respirators. At the summons of Kenton patrolmen Dr. J.F. Holtsmuller of Forest, Hardin County coroner was summons and pronounced a verdict of accidental death by drowning.

TINDALL

WESTON HURLEY TINDALL Sixth great grandson of progenitor Nicholas Kegg.

[6184] Glancy Funeral Home (IN) [6185] Mount Ayr Record-News contributed by Sharon R. Becker [6186] The Zanesville Signal (OH) July 8, 1942
[6187] Kenton Daily Democrat (OH) Jan 21, 1935, obtained by D. Sue Dible

TINDLE

CANDACE LYNN TINDLE Sixth great granddaughter of progenitor Nicholas Kegg.
PENNY SUE TINDLE Sixth great granddaughter of progenitor Nicholas Kegg.

TIRPAK

DOMINICK TIRPAK Ninth great grandson of progenitor Nicholas Kegg.

TISDEL

BEN TISDEL Sixth great grandson of progenitor Nicholas Kegg. **PATRICIA TISDEL** Fifth great granddaughter of progenitor Nicholas Kegg. **RICHARD PHILIP TISDEL** [6187A] aka "Rich" (1943 – 1999) son of Peres and Helen (Laird) Tisdel married Francie Cady with whom he was father of (2). The Vietnam War was raging, and Rich joined the Navy's Judge Advocate General (JAG) Corps, and was commissioned as a Lieutenant J.G. He was stationed first in Newport, R.I. then in San Francisco, Calif. before relocating with his family to Canberra, Australia in 1971. Rich spent the next three years looking after the legal needs of American soldiers in Australia on R&R from Vietnam, as well as working occasionally at the Navy's "Operation Deep Freeze" New Zealand base, which until recently provided logistical support to the United States Antarctic Program. an attorney, a dreamer, an adventurer, and in all things, a prankster extraordinaire. Humor fizzes through the stories of his life. It is impossible for those who knew him to dwell too long upon his death, for the memories of all his antics cannot be repressed. And the memories bring laughter, perhaps the best of all the gifts he left behind. Rich was the senior attorney at Tisdel, Hockersmith and Burns, P.C., the major law firm in Ouray County. Rich served as Ouray County attorney for 20 years and was very involved in the many development issues as Ouray went from a mining and agriculture area into growth and tourism. In 1997 his peers in the 7th Judicial District Bar Association honored him with the Award for Professionalism. The touchstones of his career were honesty, integrity, an absolute intolerance of bigotry, especially in his own community and an ability to recognize and nurture that in people which is good. Rich sang in the Ouray Presbyterian Church choir and performed in the Totally Talentless Trio (TTT), as well as Musical Saw sing-a-longs. Rich had a true knack with friendship and could put people immediately at ease with his easy warmth and humor.
SAMANTHA TISDEL Sixth great granddaughter of progenitor Nicholas Kegg.

TITUS

BARBARA TITUS Fifth great granddaughter of progenitor Nicholas Kegg.
BRADFORD TITUS 5th great grandson of progenitor Nicholas Kegg.
CAROL TITUS Fifth great granddaughter of progenitor Nicholas Kegg.
JANET TITUS Fifth great granddaughter of progenitor Nicholas Kegg.

TODIA

DEBORAH D. TODIA Sixth great granddaughter of progenitor Nicholas Kegg.
LAURA A TODIA Sixth great granddaughter of progenitor Nicholas Kegg.
ROBERT K. TODIA Sixth great grandson of progenitor Nicholas Kegg.

TODD

DUANE A. TODD Sixth great grandson of progenitor Nicholas Kegg.
GARY L. TODD Sixth great grandson of progenitor Nicholas Kegg.

[6187A] Montrose Press (CO) April 19, 1999

TOELLER

BROOKE TOELLER Sixth great granddaughter of progenitor Nicholas Kegg.
DONALD DALE TOELLER Fifth great grandson of progenitor Nicholas Kegg.
GARY RICHARD TOELLER Fifth great grandson of progenitor Nicholas Kegg.
WHITNEY TOELLER Sixth great granddaughter of progenitor Nicholas Kegg.

TOLAN

DEBBIE TOLAN Sixth great granddaughter of progenitor Nicholas Kegg.
DON RUSSELL TOLAN [6188] (1940 – 2006) son of Russell and Georgia (Mayer) Tolan, married Katie Dolzall with whom he was father of (1). Don was an Air Force veteran who spent 30 years as a customer service agent for TWA and later American Airlines.

TOLLE

JODY ELIZABETH TOLLE Sixth great granddaughter of progenitor Nicholas Kegg.
JOHN EDWARD TOLLE Sixth great grandson of progenitor Nicholas Kegg.

TOLLEFSON

ERIC S. TOLLEFSON Fifth great grandson of progenitor Nicholas Kegg.
KIRSTEN E. TOLLEFSON Fifth great granddaughter of progenitor Nicholas Kegg.

TOM

JANICE EMILY TOM [6189] (1960 – 2006) daughter of Petro and Phyllis (Kegg) Tom married Mr. Perry.

TOMASETTI

DEBRA SUZANNE TOMASETTI Fifth great granddaughter of progenitor Nicholas Kegg.
MICHELE L. TOMASETTI aka "Mickey Jay" Fifth great granddaughter of progenitor Nicholas Kegg.
PAULA J. TOMASETTI aka "Penny" Fifth great granddaughter of progenitor Nicholas Kegg.

TOMKO

ALEX TOMKO Seventh great grandson of progenitor Nicholas Kegg.
ANTONELA TOMKO Seventh great granddaughter of progenitor Nicholas Kegg.
KATE TOMKO Seventh great granddaughter of progenitor Nicholas Kegg.

TOMPSETT

GENE EDGAR TOMPSETT [6189A] (1936 – 2018) son of Paul and Doris (Stuckey) Tompsett married twice, first to Jolane Ella Funk and later to Carolyn Louise (Jones) McPheeters.
LEE ELDEN TOMPSETT Fifth great grandson of progenitor Nicholas Kegg.
TERESA RENEE TOMPSETT Sixth great granddaughter of progenitor Nicholas Kegg.
VERONA TOMPSETT Sixth great granddaughter of progenitor Nicholas Kegg.

[6188] The Indianapolis Star (IN) Apr. 2, 2006 [6189] The Indianapolis Star (IN) Mar. 16, 2006

TOMS

CAROLYN LEAH TOMS Sixth great granddaughter of progenitor Nicholas Kegg.
JAY CARTE TOMS Sixth great grandson of progenitor Nicholas Kegg.
MADISON L. TOMS Sixth great grandson of progenitor Nicholas Kegg.

TONER

CHRISTOPHER TONER Sixth great grandson of progenitor Nicholas Kegg.
MATTHEW ALAN TONER Sixth great grandson of progenitor Nicholas Kegg.
STANLEY PHILLIP TONER aka "Stan" Fifth great grandson of progenitor Nicholas Kegg.

TONY

EMILY TONY Seventh great granddaughter of progenitor Nicholas Kegg. **KATHY TONY** Sixth great granddaughter of progenitor Nicholas Kegg. **RANDY C. TONY** Sixth great grandson of progenitor Nicholas Kegg. **STEVEN J. TONY** [6189B] (1952 – 2015) son of John and Wilma (Keller) Tony married Katherine Ruth Fuquay with whom he was father of (1). Steve was a tireless advocate for people with disabilities. He served his community in many ways through his work on various commissions and committees. He was the recipient of several awards for his hard work to improve the lives of others. Steve was employed in various capacities at ADEC for 27 years. He did private consulting for companies and individuals on issues of accessibility for the disabled. **VICKI TONY** Sixth great granddaughter of progenitor Nicholas Kegg.

TORTOREA

HUNTER TORTOREA Seventh great grandson of progenitor Nicholas Kegg.

TOWNE

ERIK TOWNE Seventh great grandson of progenitor Nicholas Kegg.
JAY LELAND TOWNE Sixth great grandson of progenitor Nicholas Kegg.

TOWNSEND

BARBARA JANE TOWNSEND Fourth great granddaughter of progenitor Nicholas Kegg.
CHARLES FRANKLIN TOWNSEND Fifth great grandson of progenitor Nicholas Kegg.
RODNEY A. TOWNSEND Fifth great grandson of progenitor Nicholas Kegg.

TRACEY

HAVEN TRACEY Sixth great granddaughter of progenitor Nicholas Kegg.
MELANIE TRACEY Sixth great granddaughter of progenitor Nicholas Kegg.

TRACY

BRYAN GARTH TRACY Seventh great grandson of progenitor Nicholas Kegg.
CAROLYN JEANNE TRACY Sixth great granddaughter of progenitor Nicholas Kegg.

[6189A] Register-Guard (OR) Jan 18, 2018 [6189B] p.6A Elkhart Truth (IN) Apr 5, 2015, contributed by D. Sue Dible

GERALD LEE TRACY [6189C] aka "Jerry" (1944 – 2005) son of Melvin and Vera (Coffman) Tracy married Marsha Knowlton with whom he was father of (1). Jerry served in the Air Force and was a former Boeing engineer. **PAMELA LYNNE TRACY** Sixth great granddaughter of progenitor Nicholas Kegg. **RICHARD KARL TRACY** Sixth great grandson of progenitor Nicholas Kegg. **SHARA DANIELLE TRACY** Seventh great granddaughter of progenitor Nicholas Kegg.

TRAIL

AMY LOUISE TRAIL [6190] (1965 – 2010) daughter of Robert and Delores (Lamanna) Trail, had been the manager at the former Super 8 Hotel at the Interchange, and prior to that, had worked as a travel agent. **DEBRA J. TRAIL** Fifth great granddaughter of progenitor Nicholas Kegg. **HEATHER LOUISE TRAIL** [6191] (1921 – 2022) daughter of Robert and Marie Kay (Shaffer) Trail was mother of (1). Heather was employed as a cook and bartender. **JAMES H. TRAIL** [6191A] (1925 – 1946) son of Glenn and Marie (Biddle) Trail married Edith Arlene Miller. James had been employed as a caterpillar driver before his induction into the Army. He received basic training in the M.P. Corps at Newport News, Va., going overseas in December 1944 with the 42nd Infantry division. In January he was awarded the Combat Infantryman Badge in recognition of his performance in ground combat against the enemy. He was wounded Feb 26, 1945, at Strasbourg, Germany, and was later awarded both the Purple Heart and the Silver Star. **JAMES H. TRAIL** [6192] (1974 – 2022) son of Robert and Marie (Shaffer) Trail married Christina Press with whom he was father of (1). James was self-employed as a commercial flooring installer. **JOSH TRAIL** Seventh great grandson of progenitor Nicholas Kegg. **LACY J. TRAIL** Sixth great granddaughter of progenitor Nicholas Kegg. **LINDA KAY TRAIL** Sixth great granddaughter of progenitor Nicholas Kegg. **MARY LOIS TRAIL** Fourth great granddaughter of progenitor Nicholas Kegg. **RICHARD GEISER TRAIL** (1928 – 1990) son of Glenn and Marie (Biddle) Trail married Lois Jean Way with whom he was father of (1). **ROBERT ANTHONY TRAIL** [6193] (1951 – 1993) aka "Butch", son of Robert and Delores (Lamanna) Trail married twice; first to Marie Kay Shaffer with whom he was father of (2). Later, he married Penny L. Adams with whom he was father of (1). Butch was manager of the Dollar General Store in Everett. He previously served in the U.S. Army and for 13 years managed Wolf Furniture in Bedford. **ROBERT C. TRAIL** [6194] (1924 – 1992) son of Glenn and Marie (Biddle) Trail, married Delores V. Lamanna with whom he was father of (4). Robert was a retired truck driver. He was an Army veteran of World War II, during which he served in the European Theater. Robert was very active in the Boy Scouts of America for many years. He was also a past member of both the veterans of Foreign Wars of Bedford, Post 7527, and Bedford American Legion, Post 113. **SHIRLEY JOAN TRAIL** Fourth great granddaughter of progenitor Nicholas Kegg.

TRAPP

JENNY L. TRAPP Sixth great granddaughter of progenitor Nicholas Kegg.
TESANNA K. TRAPP Sixth great granddaughter of progenitor Nicholas Kegg.

TRAVER

EUGENE WILLIAM TRAVER (1902 – 1985) son of Leonard and Eva (Border) Traver, married Pearl Helen Allen with whom he was father of (1). **ROBERT CLAIRE TRAVER** (1916 – 1979) aka "Bob", son of Leonard and Eva (Border) Traver, married Lenora A. Thompson. **RONALD DOUGLAS TRAVER** [6194A] (1936 – 2006) son of Eugene and Pearl (Allen) Traver married twice; first to Carol Joyce Malmgreen and later to Jacquelin Costello

---

[6189C] Kansas City Star (MO) Jan 7, 2005 [6190] p.8 - Bedford Inquirer (PA) Dec 31, 2010, obtained by Bob Rose [6191] Bedford Gazette (PA) July 5, 2022 [6191A] p.3- Huntingdon Daily News (PA) Aug 22, 1946 [6192] Bedford Gazette (PA) August 31, 2022, obtained by Bob Rose [6193] Bedford Gazette (PA) Dec 30, 1993 [6194] Bedford Gazette (PA) Jan 28, 1992

TREECE

BRIAN K. TREECE Seventh great grandson of progenitor Nicholas Kegg.

RICHARD JAMES TREECE [6194B] aka "Rick" (1963 – 2005) son of Rollin and Linda (Snyder) Treece married Erin Dawn Holt. Rick served in the U.S. Navy from 1982 to 1986 as a boiler technician and fireman's mate aboard the USS Concord, having served in Beirut and throughout the Mediterranean. After his service with the Navy, he was employed as a boiler operator at Blue Triangle Hardwoods in Everett, and then worked as a welder at Grove Manufacturing in Shady Grove, Pa., JLG in Fort Littleton, Pa., and then at Letterkenney Army Depot, Chambersburg, Pa. Rick was an outdoorsman who enjoyed hunting and fishing, riding ATV.

SHERRI LEE TREECE [6194C] (1965 – 2020) daughter of Rollin and Linda (Snyder) Treece married John E. Hershberger with whom she was mother of (2). Later, she married Brett Wayne Miller. Sherri enjoyed spending time with her daughters, grandson, and special pet cat "Harper." She also loved playing bingo.

TREES

ADAM JOSEPH TREES Fifth great grandson of progenitor Nicholas Kegg.
RYAN JAMES TREES Fifth great grandson of progenitor Nicholas Kegg.

TRESSLER

DANIELLE LYNN TRESSLER Seventh great granddaughter of progenitor Nicholas Kegg.
THOMAS RONALD TRESSLER Seventh great grandson of progenitor Nicholas Kegg.

TRIMNER

BRINN TRIMNER Eighth great granddaughter of progenitor Nicholas Kegg.
BRISTOL TRIMNER Eighth great grandson of progenitor Nicholas Kegg.
GEOFFREY TRIMNER Seventh great grandson of progenitor Nicholas Kegg.

TRIPLETT

JACQUELYN JOAN TRIPLETT Fifth great granddaughter of progenitor Nicholas Kegg.

TRIPP

DELORAS ANN TRIPP [6195] (1944 – 2017) daughter of Walter and Dorothy (Crouse) Tripp, married Dale Devier Stapel with whom she was mother of (2). Deloras was a member of the Red Hat Society.
DIANE M. TRIPP [6196] (1943 – 2014) daughter of Walter and Dorothy (Crouse) Tripp, married David L. Kooi. Diane loved her dog, Perrie, casino trips, shopping, dining out with her husband David.
GERALDINE DOROTHY TRIPP Sixth great granddaughter of progenitor Nicholas Kegg.
TAMMY TRIPP Seventh great granddaughter of progenitor Nicholas Kegg.

TRITT

JACQUI TRITT Seventh great granddaughter of progenitor Nicholas Kegg.

[6194A] Oregonian (OR) May 30, 1956 [6194B] The Daily Mail (MD) Feb 17, 2005 [6194C] Bedford Gazette (PA) June 6, 2020, contributed by Bob Rose [6195] Ever Rest Funeral Home Muskegon, MI [6196] Muskegon Chronicle (MI) June 4, 2014

TROPF

EMILY GRACE TROPF Sixth great granddaughter of progenitor Nicholas Kegg.
KRISTEN TROPF Sixth great granddaughter of progenitor Nicholas Kegg.

TROUTMAN

BESSIE A. TROUTMAN [6197] (1897 – 1949) daughter of Emanuel and Mary (McDaniel) Troutman, married George Calvin Homan. **EMILY M. H. TROUTMAN** [6198] (1889 – 1911) daughter of Emanuel and Mary (McDaniel) Troutman, married Lynn Davis with whom she was mother of (1). **ESTELLA GUSSIE TROUTMAN** [6199] (1890 – 1961) aka "Gussie" daughter of Emanuel and Mary (McDaniel) Troutman, married Nelson Henry Hann with whom she was mother of (6). Stella was a member of the Wesleyan Methodist Church of Niles, Ohio. **JOEL F. TROUTMAN** (1894 – 1918) son of Emanuel and Mary (McDaniel) Troutman. **TIMOTHY P. TROUTMAN** Eighth great grandchild of progenitor Nicholas Kegg.

TROWER

SHEILA RAE TROWER Seventh great granddaughter of progenitor Nicholas Kegg.

TROWNSON

CARL P. TROWNSON Fifth great grandson of progenitor Nicholas Kegg.
DEBORAH K. TROWNSON Fifth great granddaughter of progenitor Nicholas Kegg.
MICHELE L. TROWNSON Fifth great granddaughter of progenitor Nicholas Kegg.
TONYA NICOLE TROWNSON Sixth great granddaughter of progenitor Nicholas Kegg.

TROYER

ANTHONY BRIAN TROYER Seventh great grandson of progenitor Nicholas Kegg.
ISAAC MONROE TROYER Seventh great grandson of progenitor Nicholas Kegg.
JOSHUA RODNEY TROYER Seventh great grandson of progenitor Nicholas Kegg.
JULIE TROYER Sixth great granddaughter of progenitor Nicholas Kegg.
MICHAEL EUGENE TROYER [6200] (1960 – 2018) son of Eli and Mary (Shafer) Troyer.
RANDOLPH SCOTT TROYER Seventh great grandson of progenitor Nicholas Kegg.
SHERRY L. TROYER (1946 – 1946) daughter of Eli and Mary (Shafer) Troyer.

TRUEAX

BRETT LEIGH TRUEAX Sixth great granddaughter of progenitor Nicholas Kegg.
TANNER BEAU TRUEAX Sixth great grandson of progenitor Nicholas Kegg.

TUCKER

ALEX JOSEPH TUCKER Seventh great grandson of progenitor Nicholas Kegg. **ARTHUR SMITH TUCKER JR.** [6200A] aka "Archie" (1948 – 2012) son of Arthur and Lucy (Marabain) Tucker. Archie was a counselor and avid horseback rider at Red Raider Camp. Archie was a quiet, kind man who graduated from Brooklyn Law School. Even when he had little, always gave some of what he had to charity,

---

[6197] Bedford Gazette (PA) Nov 18, 1949 [6198] Bedford Gazette (PA) May 26, 1911 [6199] Altoona Mirror (PA) Sep 12, 1961, Find A Grave memorial # 59233368 Created by: Sky [6200] Peeples-Rhoden Funeral Home (SC) obtained by D. Sue Dible [6200A] The Plain Dealer (OH) Dec 9, 2012

particularly The Salvation Army. He spent several years near the end of his life assisting patients with mental and physical disabilities. As a longtime Clevelander, he loved, and suffered with, the Browns and Indians. **AUGUSTINE JOHN TUCKER** Fifth great grandson of progenitor Nicholas Kegg. **BRIAN TUCKER** Fifth great grandson of progenitor Nicholas Kegg. **CLINT TUCKER** Fifth great grandson of progenitor Nicholas Kegg. **ERNIE TUCKER** [6200B] aka "Joe" (1969 – 2009) son of William and Patricia (Cunningham) Tucker married Veronique Pavic with whom he was father of (1). Joe was a veteran of the U.S. Navy. **FRANCIS CARLILE TUCKER** [6201, 6202] (1915 – 1996) son of Francis and Emma (Boose) Tucker, married Emma Elizabeth Scott. He served in the Armed Forces as a medical officer in India and China. Francis was a medical missionary. When he returned to the U.S., he was Pathologist and Director of the Laboratory at St. Luke's Hospital in Cedar Rapids, Iowa from 1950 to 1958. From 1958 to 1981 he was Pathologist and Director of the Laboratory at Deaconess Hospital (later Freeport Memorial) in Freeport, Illinois, serving as Chief of Staff from 1967-68. **LEWIS SCOTT TUCKER** Sixth great grandson of progenitor Nicholas Kegg. **SARA WAITSTILL TUCKER** Fourth great granddaughter of progenitor Nicholas Kegg. **TARVEZ TUCKER** Fourth great granddaughter of progenitor Nicholas Kegg. **TIA FRANCES TUCKER** (1950 – 2010) daughter of Augustine and Nancy (Pratt) Tucker married and divorced Timothy Obrien. **WENDY ELLEN TUCKER** Sixth great granddaughter of progenitor Nicholas Kegg. **WILLIAM JENKINS TUCKER** (1946 – 1966) son of Augustine and Nancy (Pratt) Tucker. **WILLIAM KIRKBY TUCKER** Fourth great grandson of progenitor Nicholas Kegg.

TULL

AMANDA DIANE TULL [6202A] (1979 – 2018) daughter of Ivan and Ruth (Groves) Tull married Sylvester Cobb. She was the mother of (4). Amanda enjoyed doing crossword puzzles, playing computer games, and most of all spending time with family. **ANTHONY TULL** Eighth great grandson of progenitor Nicholas Kegg. **CHARLES WILLIAM TULL** aka "Little Willie" (1971 – 1977) son of Charles and Jannie (Stanley) Tull. **IVAN DWAIN TULL** (1955 – 1984) son of Charles and Jannie (Stanley) Tull married Ruth Darlene Groves with whom he was father of (2). **JAY TULL** Seventh great grandson of progenitor Nicholas Kegg. **JEREMIAH TULL** Ninth great grandson of progenitor Nicholas Kegg. **JOHN DAVID TULL** [6202B] (1964 – 1980) son of Charles and Jannie (Stanley) Tull had just completed his freshman year at Mount Ayr Community high school where he was a member of Future Farmers of America. The family reported John missing and the Mount Ayr volunteer fire department helped in the search. John's body was found in a farm pond northeast of Mount Ayr. **PAUL TULL** Seventh great grandson of progenitor Nicholas Kegg.

TURGEON

CHRISTOPHER LEE TURGEON Sixth great grandson of progenitor Nicholas Kegg.
MARK F. TURGEON Sixth great grandson of progenitor Nicholas Kegg.

TURNER

ADAM TURNER Seventh great grandson of progenitor Nicholas Kegg.
ALLEN GABRIEL TURNER Fifth great grandson of progenitor Nicholas Kegg.
ALMIRA MARIE TURNER [6203] (1908 – 1993) daughter of James and Mary (Frost) Turner, married Guy Stewart Stanton with whom she was mother of (4). Almira operated The Maples, a maple sugar production farm for 50 years. Mrs. She was a member of St. John's Episcopal Church, Frostburg and the Mars Hill Homemakers Club. She was a graduate of Catherman's Business School.

[6200B] The Plain Dealer (OH) Oct 25, 2009 [6201] the archive holdings of Oberlin College [6202] p.19 Register Star (Rockford, IL) Dec 31, 1996 [6202A] Chauvin Funeral Home (LA) [6202B] Mount Ayr Record-News (IA) June 12, 1980 contributed by Sharon R. Becker [6203] The Republic (PA) Oct 28, 1993, transcribed by Patty Millich and Alice James

ALTA LUELLA TURNER [6204] (1889 – 1987) daughter of Benjamin and Sarah (Fike) Turner, married William Ellwood Kendall with whom she was mother of (2). **AMANDA TURNER** (1857 – 1871) daughter of Lewis and Maria (Egolf) Turner. **ANDREW J. TURNER** (1841 – 1861) son of Andrew and Anna (Kegg) Turner. **ANNA MARIA TURNER** [6205] (1834 – 1902) aka "Marie", daughter of Andrew and Anna (Kegg) Turner, married William Jackson Kerr with whom she was mother of (6). Marie was noble and had a gracious disposition. She was always kind to the poor. She would rather give than receive. Her last words were "I am ready and willing to go". **ANNA MARY TURNER** [6206] (1852 – 1935) daughter of Lewis and Mary (Egolf) Turner, married John Rufus Boose with whom she was mother of (9). **ANNA RUTH TURNER** [6206A] (1935 – 2015) daughter of Joshua and Sarah (Garlitz) Turner married Robert F. Lloyd with whom she was mother of (4). **ANNIE MARY TURNER** [6207] (1859 – 1934) daughter of Joshua and Almira (Corley) Turner, married Norman B. Durst with whom she was mother of (5). **BENJAMIN FRANKLIN TURNER** [6208] (1863 – 1952) aka "Frank", son of Lewis and Mary (Egolf) Turner, married Sarah Fike with whom he was father of (4). Frank was a farmer. **BERTHA PEARL TURNER** [6209] (1898 – 1966) daughter of Henry and Anna (Hillegass) Turner, married Delbert Earl Hillegass with whom she was mother of (7). **BETTY C. TURNER** [6209A] (1925 – 2011) daughter of Weaver and Margaret (Pyle) Turner married Arvil Charles Garlitz with whom she was mother of (2). Betty retired from the GC Murphy's Company and later worked at the FSU bookstore. Betty was blessed throughout her life with God's love, family and friends. She traveled to 48 of the 50 states and Europe. **BONNIE LEE TURNER** Fifth great granddaughter of progenitor Nicholas Kegg. **BRADLEY DAVID TURNER** Sixth great grandson of progenitor Nicholas Kegg. **BRETT SAMUEL TURNER** Sixth great grandson of progenitor Nicholas Kegg. **BRIAN C. TURNER** Sixth great grandson of progenitor Nicholas Kegg. **CAROL ANN TURNER** Fifth great granddaughter of progenitor Nicholas Kegg. **CAROLINE TURNER** [6210] (1861 – 1943) aka "Carrie", daughter of Lewis and Maria (Egolf) Turner, married Lewis J. Ort with whom she was mother of (5). **CATHERINE TURNER** [6211] (1830 – 1911) daughter of Andrew and Anna (Kegg) Turner, married George Kerr with whom she was mother of (9). **CHARLES G. TURNER** Fifth great grandson of progenitor Nicholas Kegg. **CHARLES WEAVER TURNER** [6212] (1932 – 2004) son of Weaver and Margaret (Pyle) Turner, married Marilyn Justine Saunders. Charles served in the U.S. Air Force. **CHARLES WEAVER TURNER** Fifth great grandson of progenitor Nicholas Kegg. **CHARLES WILLIAM TURNER** Fifth great grandson of progenitor Nicholas Kegg. **CHARLES WILLIAM TURNER** [6213] (1930 – 2008) aka "Bill", son of Joshua and Sarah (Garlitz) Turner, married Ruth Beatrice Winner with whom he was father of (5). Bill was a roads construction worker for IA Construction. He was a member of the Old St. Ann's Shrine and Local 37, Operating Engineers Union. **CHERYL ELIZABETH TURNER** Fifth great granddaughter of progenitor Nicholas Kegg. **CHRISTINE MARIE TURNER** Fifth great granddaughter of progenitor Nicholas Kegg. **CLARENCE ELMER TURNER** (1888 – 1918) son of Henry and Anna (Hillegass) Turner. **DAMON TURNER** Seventh great grandson of progenitor Nicholas Kegg. **DARLENE K. TURNER** Fifth great granddaughter of progenitor Nicholas Kegg. **DAVID MICHAEL TURNER** [6213A] (1946 – 2010) son of James and Laura (Durst) Turner married Dottie Moses with whom he was father of (1) Dave earned a Master's of Science degree in Business Management from Frostburg State College, after which he served as Adjunct Professor in the Master's of Business Management program until accepting a position at Goodyear in Akron. He was employed in the Financial Analysis Dept. at Kelly Springfield Tire and Rubber Company Corporate Headquarters in Cumberland when he entered the Army Corp of Engineers at Ft. Belvoir, Va., as a Second Lieutenant. He was then stationed at the Army Map Service in Bethesda until leaving the service at the rank of Captain. Later Dave became an ordained

---

[6204] p.B13-Rockford Morning Star (IL) June 9, 1967 [6205] Bedford Gazette (PA) July 25, 1905 [6206] Titusville Herald (PA) Dec 16, 1935 [6206A] Durst Funeral Home (MD) [6207] The Republic (Meyersdale, PA) Aug 30, 1934 [6208] p.5A - Rockford Morning Star (IL) April 8, 1952 [6209] Washington Post clipping/Historical Newspapers 1851-2003 [6209A] Cumberland Times-News (MD) Feb 18, 2011 [6210] The Cumberland News (MD) Dec 28, 1943 [6211] Bedford Gazette (PA) Jan 27, 1911 [6212] Daily Press (Newport News, VA) Feb 12, 1956

priest at St. Peter's Episcopal Church. David was a member of the Viet Nam Veterans of America Chapter 172, Cumberland. Mr. Turner liked to spend time in the woods and working on his cabin. He enjoyed cross country skiing and served as a cross country ski coach for Allegany County Special Olympics for several years. **DEBORAH TURNER** aka "Debbie", Fifth great granddaughter of progenitor Nicholas Kegg. **DEBORAH MARIE TURNER** Fifth great granddaughter of progenitor Nicholas Kegg. **DEBRA M. TURNER** Fifth great granddaughter of progenitor Nicholas Kegg. **DONALD G. TURNER** Sixth great grandson of progenitor Nicholas Kegg. **DONALD HARTWELL TURNER** [6213B] (1931 – 2002) son of William and Hazel (Hartwell) Turner married Barbara Marion Wentworth with whom he was father of (4). A professor at Willamette University College of Law for 30 years, Donald served as deputy district attorney for Wasco County in 1960 and as district attorney from 1961 to 1971. He was President of the Oregon District Attorney's Association in 1966. Donald taught criminal law, criminal procedure, evidence and scientific proof. He loved coaching the Moot Court Teams and served as Marion County juvenile referee from 1988 to 1992. He was a voracious reader all his life and was especially fond of history books. He enjoyed playing chess and won many chess tournaments including the Oregon Championship in 1964. He loved children and directed OMSI (Oregon Museum of Science and Industry) chess tournaments for many years. He was a patron of the Ashland Shakespeare Festival and attended for nearly 50 years. **DONNA M. TURNER** Fourth great granddaughter of progenitor Nicholas Kegg. **DOUGLAS TURNER** Sixth great grandson of progenitor Nicholas Kegg. **ELEANOR SARAH TURNER** [6214] (1909 – 1993) daughter of Ezra and Mary (Calhoun) Turner, married Herbert W. Jess. Eleanor worked for the Clark County auditor's office during World War II and as a salesclerk for several years for Meier & Frank Co. in Portland. **ELIZABETH ANN TURNER** (1855 – 1858) daughter of Lewis and Maria (Egolf) Turner. **ELMER CLARENCE TURNER** [6215] (1918 – 1990) son of Charles and Marie (Hardy) Turner, married Rosemary Shaffer. **EMILY TURNER** Seventh great granddaughter of progenitor Nicholas Kegg. **EMMA JANE TURNER** (1854 – 1855) daughter of Lewis and Maria (Egolf) Turner. **EUGENE PAUL TURNER** (1900 – 1972) son of John and Matilda (Shoemaker) Turner. **FLORA BELL TURNER** [6216] (1869 – 1955) daughter of Lewis and Maria (Egolf) Turner, married Caleb F. Way. **FRANK P. TURNER** [6217] (1899 – 1980) son of George and Maude (Pope) Turner, married Edith McDonald. Frank was a member of Mount Zion United Methodist Church, Woodmen of the World Camp 41, Grantsville, Md., and was a Golden Age Eagle with Aerie 295 Fraternal Order of Eagles, Cumberland. **FRANK RAY TURNER** [6218] (1937 – 1993) son of Joshua and Sarah (Garlitz) Turner. **GABE TURNER** Sixth great grandson of progenitor Nicholas Kegg. **GARY DALE TURNER** Fifth great grandson of progenitor Nicholas Kegg. **GARY R. TURNER** Fifth great grandson of progenitor Nicholas Kegg. **GEORGE TURNER** Sixth great grandson of progenitor Nicholas Kegg. **GEORGE ALBERT TURNER** (1884 – 1920) son of Henry and Anna (Hillegass) Turner. **GEORGE CHARLES TURNER** [6219] (1872 – 1941) son of Joshua and Almira (Corley) Turner, married Maude Pope with whom he was father of (3). **GEORGE EARL TURNER** (1917 – 1929) son of Joshua and Sarah (Garlitz) Turner. **GEORGE L. TURNER** [6220] (1889 – 1954) son of John and Matilda (Shoemaker) Turner, married Julia Kathryn Helbok. **GEORGE W. TURNER** [6221] (1948 – 2001) son of George and Barabara Turner, married and was father of (3). Later, he married Terri L. Dennis with whom he was father of (1). George was a veteran of Vietnam having served as a Master Sgt. In the U.S. Army. **GERALD TURNER** Fourth great grandson of progenitor Nicholas Kegg. **GRACE MARY TURNER** [6222] (1890 – 1982) daughter of John and Matilda (Shoemaker) Turner married three times; first to Thomas Francis Hanley with whom she was mother of (2). Grace married James Bess and later, married Ernest Benson McMahon. **GRANT TURNER** Sixth great grandson of progenitor Nicholas Kegg. **GRIFFIN TURNER** Seventh great grandson of progenitor Nicholas Kegg. **HARRY EDWARD TURNER** (1924 – 1924) son of Charles

[6213] Newman Funeral Homes, MD [6213A] Cumberland Times News (MD) Feb 16, 2010 [6213B] Dalles Chronicle (OR) Feb 19, 2002 [6214] p.B2 - Oregonian (Portland, OR) Jul 13, 1993 [6215] News-Messenger (OH) July 23, 2014 [6216] p.14 Pittsburgh Post-Gazette (PA) June 25, 1955 [6217] The Republic (Meyersdale, PA) transcribed by John C. Oester [6218] The Baltimore Sun (MD) March 28, 1993 [6219] The Republic (Meyersdale, PA) Dec 11, 1941 [6220] p.4M-The Orgonian (OR) May 22, 1954 [6221] GenLookups.com/Michigan Obituary and Death Notice Archive – p.942 [6222] p.D13 - Bakersfield Californian (PA) Mar. 5, 1982, obtained by D. Sue Dible

and Marie (Hardy) Turner. **HARVEY ELLIS TURNER** (1892 – 1893) son of Henry and Anna (Hillegass) Turner. **HAZEL ESTER TURNER** [6223] (1894 – 1974) daughter of Benjamin and Sarah (Fike) Turner married twice; first to William Raymond Bowers with whom she was mother of (1). Later, she married Nello Joseph Hardacre with whom she was mother of (1). **HELEN TURNER** [6223A] (1935 – 2016) daughter of Weaver and Margaret (Pyle) Turner married twice, first to Daniel Lee Rafferty with whom she was mother of (4), Later, she married John C. Martin. Helen had worked at Kings Department Store. She was a member of Saint Michael's Catholic Church and a member of the Ladies of the Frostburg Moose. **HENRY TURNER** (1910 – 1910) son of James and Mary (Frost) Turner. **IDA REBECCA TURNER** (1865 – 1940) daughter of Lewis and Maria (Egolf) Turner. **ISABELLE EILEEN TURNER** Fourth great granddaughter of progenitor Nicholas Kegg. **JAMES TURNER** Sixth great grandson of progenitor Nicholas Kegg. **JAMES C. TURNER** Fifth great grandson of progenitor Nicholas Kegg. **JAMES HENRY TURNER** [6224] (1863 – 1934) son of Joshua and Almira (Corley) Turner, married Mary (Frost) Turner with whom he was father of (8). **JAMES MARK TURNER** [6225] (1897 – 1952) aka "Bud", son of John and Matilda (Shoemaker) Turner, married Erna Elizabeth Kefsky with whom he was father of (1). Bud was a veteran of World War I, having served in the U. S. Army. **JAMES RICHARD TURNER** [6225A] (1921 – 1980) son of Joshua and Sarah (Garlitz) Turner, married Laura Durst with whom he was father of (4). James was a veteran of World War II, and a member of the American Legion Post 24, Frostburg, the FO Eagles Aerie 1273, Frostburg and the Grantsville Business Association. He was a retired coal and timberman. **JEFFREY JAMES TURNER** Fifth great grandson of progenitor Nicholas Kegg. **JENNIE VIRGINIA TURNER** [6226] (1867 – 1953) daughter of Joshua and Almira (Corley) Turner, married Eugene Weaver with whom she was mother of (2). **JESS TURNER** Fourth great grandson of progenitor Nicholas Kegg. **JESSIE TURNER** Sixth great granddaughter of progenitor Nicholas Kegg. **JOE M. TURNER** Fifth great grandson of progenitor Nicholas Kegg. **JOHN TURNER** aka "Johnny", Sixth great grandson of progenitor Nicholas Kegg. **JOHN E. TURNER** Fifth great grandson of progenitor Nicholas Kegg. **JOHN MARK TURNER** Fifth great grandson of progenitor Nicholas Kegg. **JOHN RANDOLPH TURNER** [6227] (1860 – 1911) son of Lewis and Maria (Egolf) Turner, married Matilda Agnes Shoemaker with whom she was mother of (5). **JOHN S. TURNER** Fourth great grandson of progenitor Nicholas Kegg. **JORDAN TURNER** Sixth great grandson of progenitor Nicholas Kegg. **JOSEPH TURNER** Sixth great grandson of progenitor Nicholas Kegg. **JOSEPH DANIEL TURNER** [6228] (1925 – 2005) son of Silas and Jessie (Larue) Turner, married Betty J. Biddington with whom he was father of (6). Joseph served in the U.S. Army in Europe at the conclusion of World War II. He was employed as a welder with Fruehof and retired from A-1 Welding. Joseph also was an antique dealer with his wife with J. & B. Antiques. **JOSHUA TURNER** Sixth great grandson of progenitor Nicholas Kegg. **JOSHUA TURNER** [6229] (1832 – 1915) son of Andrew and Anna (Kegg) Turner, married Almira M. Corley with whom he was father of (8). **JOSHUA HAMMOND TURNER** [6230] (1894 – 1942) son of James and Mary (Frost) Turner, married Sarah Adell Garlitz with whom he was father of (10). **JOSHUA J. TURNER** [6231] (1925 – 1989) son of Joshua and Sarah (Garlitz) Turner, married Gladys V. Anderson with whom he was father of (3). Joshua was a retired school bus driver for the Garrett County Board of Education and was a Navy veteran of World War II. **JOYCE ELAINE TURNER** Fourth great granddaughter of progenitor Nicholas Kegg. **JULIANA TURNER** (1838 – 1874) daughter of Andrew and Anna (Kegg) Turner, married Henry Hillegass with whom she was mother of (7). **KATHLEEN SARAH TURNER** [6231A] aka "Kit" (1928 – 2009) daughter of Joshua and Sarah (Garlitz) Turner married twice, first to James Vincent Matt with whom she was mother of (2). **KENNETH R. TURNER** Fifth great grandson of progenitor Nicholas Kegg. **KEVIN W. TURNER** Sixth great grandson of progenitor Nicholas Kegg. **KITTY TURNER** (1888 – 1888) daughter of John and Matilda (Shoemaker) Turner.

[6223] p.A 8- Rockford Morning Star (IL) July 16, 1974 [6223A] Cumberland Times-News (MD) Jan 31, 2016 [6224] rootsweb.ancestry/md.garret obituaries [6225] p.6M - The Orgonian (OR) Jan 19, 1952 [6225A] The Republic (PA) Feb 28, 1980, contributed by John C. Oester [6226] The Republic (Meyersdale, PA) Jan 29, 1953 [6227] Weekly Rogue River Courier (OR) Feb 24, 1911 [6228] Lorain County News (OH) Jan 7, 2005 [6229] usgenwebarchives transcribed by Charles Often [6230] p.11- Cumberland Evening Times, May 20,1942 [6231] p.13 Cumberland Times News (MD) Oct 17, 1989 [6231A] Cumberland Times News (MD) Mar 13, 2009

KOTI TURNER Sixth great grandson of progenitor Nicholas Kegg. **KRISTIN ANN TURNER** Sixth great granddaughter of progenitor Nicholas Kegg. **LANA K. TURNER** [6232] (1951 – 1975) daughter of Robert and Mildred (Dye) Turner. **LAURA ANNA TURNER** [6233] (1915 – 1995) daughter of William and Emma (Blocher) Turner, married Daniel Elwood Klotz with whom she was mother of (2). **LAURA BELLE TURNER** [6234] (1861 – 1937) daughter of Joshua and Almira (Corley) Turner, married Norval Mason Layman. **LAURA BELLE TURNER** [6235] (1890 – 1984) daughter of Silas and Annie (Miller) Turner, married Harry Lawrence Haugh with whom she was mother of (1). **LEWIS A. TURNER** [6236] (1828 – 1903) son of Andrew and Anna (Kegg) Turner, married Maria Egolf with whom he was father of (11). Lewis founded Pine Hill in the southern part of Berlin Township. A post office was established, and Lewis was the first postmaster. Lewis also engaged in the mercantile business which was known as Turner's store and proved very successful. After a few years he engaged in manufacturing and purchasing barrel staves, commonly called shook, at that time one of the principal industries of this section. He gave employment to a large number of workmen, but finally met with financial reverses, owing to the rascality of commission merchants to whom he consigned the product of his shops. It is said that he lost 18,000 on a single consignment of barrel staves shipped to Havana. Mr. Turner was active in politics and in 1871 was elected associate judge for a term of five years. **LORRAINE R. TURNER** Fifth great granddaughter of progenitor Nicholas Kegg. **LUKAS TURNER** Seventh great grandson of progenitor Nicholas Kegg. **LYNDA LEE TURNER** Fifth great granddaughter of progenitor Nicholas Kegg. **MARGARET TURNER** (1896 – 1896) daughter of James and Mary (Frost) Turner. **MARGARET GRACE TURNER** [6237] (1923 – 2010) daughter of James and Erma (Kefsky) Turner married twice; first to Earnest Schaen with whom she was mother of (1). Later, she married Earl R. Olson with whom she was mother of (1). Margaret and husband Earl built several houses together, doing most of the work themselves. Her pride was the house and small horse farm they built in 1963, where she remained until her death. Although she was a stay-at-home mom, she filled her time raising gardens, horses, livestock, tropical fish, and Siamese cats. As a seamstress, she sewed riding clothes and royalty outfits for horse organizations. She was the perfect horse show mom, towing a custom horse trailer behind her 1961 Pontiac. **MARGARET L. TURNER** (born abt. 1925) daughter of Charles and Marie (Hardy) Turner married twice, first to Samuel Willis Stultz with whom she was mother of (2). Later she married Elmer Nathaniel Spangler. **MARK D. TURNER** Fifth great grandson of progenitor Nicholas Kegg. **MARK T. TURNER** Sixth great grandson of progenitor Nicholas Kegg. **MARTIN LUTHER TURNER** (1895 – 1920) son of Henry and Anna (Hillegass) Turner was employed as an inspector for the National Radiator Co., Johnstown, PA **MARY TURNER** Fifth great granddaughter of progenitor Nicholas Kegg. **MARY ELIZA TURNER** [6237A] (1927 – 2018) daughter of Thomas and Nancy (Wright) Turner. Mary worked as a secretary for Beall Elementary School and retired from Alliant Techsystems (ABL) with 29 years of service. Later, she worked as a part-time employee for the Bon-Ton department store. **MARY L. TURNER** Fifth great granddaughter of progenitor Nicholas Kegg. **MARY MAY TURNER** [6238] (1923 – 2013) daughter of Joshua and Sarah (Garlitz) Turner, married Henry Thomas Russell with whom she was mother of (1). **MICHAEL TURNER** Fifth great grandson of progenitor Nicholas Kegg. **MICHAEL L. TURNER** [6238A] (1956 – 2012) son of Charles and Faye (Meyers) Turner. Michael was employed at Ball & Kerr. When Ball & Kerr went out of business Michael moved back to Westernville where he lived with his parents. **MICHAEL PAUL TURNER** Sixth great grandson of progenitor Nicholas Kegg. **MINERVA TURNER** [6239] (1865 – 1944) daughter of Lewis and Maria (Egolf) Turner, married Joseph Brubaker Musser with whom she was mother of (6). **MINNIE VIOLET TURNER** [6240] (1891 – 1927) daughter of Henry and Anna (Hillegass) Turner, married William Franklin Beneigh with whom she was mother of (1). **NANCY TURNER** Fifth great granddaughter of progenitor Nicholas Kegg. **NANCY JEAN TURNER** Fifth great granddaughter of progenitor Nicholas Kegg. **NANCY REBECCA TURNER** (1886 – 1907) daughter of Henry and Anna

---

[6232] p.8 Cumberland News (MD) Mar 5, 1975 [6233] p.15 - Cumberland Times (MD) Apr 11, 1986 [6234] The Republic (Meyersdale, PA) March 27, 1947 transcribed by Richard Boyer [6235] p.3B-Rockford Register Star (IL) May 29, 1984 [6236] The Bedford Gazette (PA) May 1, 1903 [6237] Columbian (Vancouver, WA) Apr 1, 2010 [6237A] Durst Funeral Home (MD) [6238] Chester County Press (PA) Jul 3, 2013 [6238A] Mills Funeral Home (NY) [6239] The Pittsburgh Press (PA) March 25, 1944 [6240] Find A Grave memorial# 72401013 obituary Contributed by Brian J. Ensley

(Hillegass) Turner. **OSCAR LEROY TURNER** (1930 – 2003) son of Charles and Marie (Hardy) Turner. **PAMELA LYNN TURNER** Sixth great granddaughter of progenitor Nicholas Kegg. **PATRICK TURNER** Sixth great grandson of progenitor Nicholas Kegg. **PAUL THOMAS TURNER** Fifth great grandson of progenitor Nicholas Kegg. **RALPH D. TURNER** (1901 – 1904) son of Benjamin and Sarah (Fike) Turner. **ROBERT DWIGHT TURNER** [6241] (1907 – 1993) aka "Dwight", son of Benjamin and Sarah (Fike) Turner, married June L. Harrington with whom he was father of (2). Dwight was a lifelong farmer and served on the board of directors of Carroll County Farm Bureau, Sinnissippi Mental Health Center and Rolling Hills Progress Cemetery. **ROBERT J. TURNER** Fifth great grandson of progenitor Nicholas Kegg. **ROBERT M. TURNER** (1927 -1934) son of Silas and Jessie (Larue) Turner. **ROBERT MICHAEL TURNER** [6241A] (1932 – 2015) son of Joshua and Sarah (Garlitz) Turner, married Mildred Irene Dye with whom he was father of (3). For many years Robert was the Engineer for the Town of Midland and a self-employed contractor. He owned Turner Apartments, Midland. He was also a lifetime member of the Midland Volunteer Fire Department and the Midland Sportsmans Club "The Patch". He loved the time he spent at his winter home in Florida but equally enjoyed the countless hours he spent at his camp in Hyndman, Pa., which his grandchildren will always know as Pappy Turner's River. In his spare time, he found his passion in cooking and grilling. He also enjoyed playing cards at the fire hall and The Patch and hunting on Old Dans Rock and Avilton. **RONALD R. TURNER** [6241B] (1947 – 2014) son of Joshua and Gladys V. Anderson, married Jeanne Stark with whom he was father of (1). Ron was a Navy veteran. He later graduated from Frostburg State University. He became a CPA and operated his own accounting practice in Keyser, W.Va. After retiring from accounting, he began a new career as General Manager of Jenkins Collision Center in Clarysville. **RUTH TURNER** Fifth great granddaughter of progenitor Nicholas Kegg. **RUTH MARIE TURNER** (1925 – 1979) daughter of Charles and Marie (Hardy) Turner, married and was mother of (1). **SADIE ELANE TURNER** [6242] (1928 – 2001) daughter of Weaver and Margaret (Pyle) Turner. **SAMUEL B. TURNER**, (1858 –?) son of Lewis and Maria (Egolf) Turner. **SARA CELINA TURNER** [6243] (1918 – 2011) aka "Sally", daughter of William and Emma (Blocher) Turner, married John Vincent Blocher with whom she was mother of (3). Sally was a partner in Turner's Diary Farm where she worked both in the operation of the dairy and later in life as the bookkeeper/secretary. She was also a waitress for Hill Top Restaurant from 1964-1979 and Penn Alps from 1980-1997. Sally was a loving and caring individual. She had an infectious personality, an enthusiasm for living, a strong work ethic and a quiet strength. She lived her live with dignity and joy. Sally was a member of St. Ann Catholic Church and enjoyed reading, bingo and traveling. **SARAH C. TURNER** [6244] (1857 – 1919) daughter of Joshua and Almira (Corley) Turner, married Thomas Wright Frost. Sarah was a member of the official board of the First Methodist Episcopal Church and was president of the Ladies Aide Society. She was past worthy grand matron of the Maryland Assembly, Order of the Eastern Star, and was past matron of the Frostburg Chapter. **SARAH CATHERINE TURNER** (1897 – 1977) daughter of George and Maude (Pope) Turner. **SARAH ELLEN TURNER** [6245] (1898 – 1944) daughter of James and Mary (Frost) Turner, married Daniel Joshua Hummel with whom she was mother of (5). **SCOTT TURNER** Sixth great grandson of progenitor Nicholas Kegg. **SHERRY TURNER** Fifth great granddaughter of progenitor Nicholas Kegg. **SHIRLEY TURNER** Fourth great granddaughter of progenitor Nicholas Kegg. **SHIRLEY J. TURNER** [6245A] (1937 – 2010) daughter of Charles and Marie (Hardy) Turner, married Eugene Clark Hadix with whom she was mother of (1). Shirley enjoyed playing bingo and pinochle. **SILAS ELY TURNER** [6246] (1855 – 1932) son of Joshua and Almira (Corley) Turner, married Annie Alice Miller with whom he was father of (1). Silas was a retired farmer and life-long resident of Whiteside County. **SILAS ELY TURNER** [6247] (1905 – 1977) son of James and Mary (Frost) Turner, married Jessie Marie Larue with whom he was father of (4). Silas retired from Kelly Springfield Tire Company where he had been an employee with 43 years of service.

[6241] p.8A - Rockford Register Star (IL) Oct 25, 1993 [6241A] Cumberland Times-News (MD) June 30, 2015 [6241B] Cumberland Times News (MD) Dec 24, 2014 [6242] p.16 Cumberland Times (MD) Jan 22, 2001 [6243] Cumberland Times-News (MD) Oct 4, 2011 [6244] p.14 - Cumberland Evening Times, Dec 15, 1919 [6245] The Republic (Meyersdale, PA) Dec 21, 1944, transcribed by Richard Boyer [6245A] Tribune Democrat (PA) Feb 16, 2010 [6246] p.5 - Rockford Morning Star (IL) July 19, 1932 [6247] p.8 - Cumberland News (MD) Jan 15, 1977

STEVE TURNER Fifth great grandson of progenitor Nicholas Kegg. **SULLIVAN TURNER** Seventh great grandson of progenitor Nicholas Kegg. **SUSAN ALMIRA TURNER** [6248] (1919 – 1992) aka "Polly", daughter of Joshua and Sarah (Garlitz) Turner married twice; first to Marvin Willard Warnick with whom she was mother of (1). Later she married Mr. Wyatt. **SUSAN MYRA TURNER** [6248A] (1949 – 2004) daughter of Joshua and Gladys (Anderson)Turner, married Gary Willliam Kamp. Susan was former co-owner of Fuel City and Chestnut Ridge Gas and Liquors, with her husband. Previously, she had been a dispatcher for the Maryland State Police for 10 years. Susie was a homemaker and enjoyed gardening. **THELMA MARIE TURNER** [6248B] (1922 – 1984) daughter of Charles and Marie (Hardy) Turner, married Dalton Warren Hillegass with whom she was mother of (10). Thelma was an evangelizer for her faith, she was highly regarded for extending hospitality to traveling representatives of the Watchtower Society and to those in the local Jehovah's Witnesses congregation for her generosity. Thelma dedicated her life to volunteer work, enjoyed gardening, flowers, especially roses, and her cats. **THOMAS TURNER** Fifth great grandson of progenitor Nicholas Kegg. **THOMAS FROST TURNER** [6249] (1902 – 1976) son of James and Mary (Frost) Turner, married Nancy Wright with whom he was father of (4). Thomas was a retired carpenter and a member of the Carpenters' Union, Local 1029. **THOMAS J. TURNER** [6250] (1930 – 1955) son of Thomas and Nancy (Wright) Turner, married Joyce Kidwell. Thomas had been employed in Baltimore. He served three years in the paratroopers. **THOMAS SCOTT TURNER** Fifth great grandson of progenitor Nicholas Kegg. **TRACEY TURNER** Sixth great granddaughter of progenitor Nicholas Kegg. **TRACY LYNN TURNER** Fifth great granddaughter of progenitor Nicholas Kegg. **TRENT R. TURNER** Sixth great grandson of progenitor Nicholas Kegg. **TROY TURNER** Sixth great grandson of progenitor Nicholas Kegg. **VESTA VICTORIA TURNER** (1900 – 1960) daughter of Ezra and Mary (Calhoun) Turner, married William Thomas Evan Pugh. **WEAVER CHARLES TURNER** [6251] (1901 – 1963) son of George and Maude (Pope) Turner, married Margaret Pyle with whom he was father of (4). Weaver was employed in the engineering department of the Amcelle Plant of the Celanese Fibers Company and was a member of Mt. Zion Church and LOOM 348, Frostburg. **WILDEN TURNER** aka "Willie" Seventh great grandson of progenitor Nicholas Kegg. **WILLIAM EZRA DAVID TURNER** [6252] (1902 – 1982) son of Ezra and Mary (Calhoun) Turner married three times; first to Hazel Alice Hartwell with whom he was father of (1). He married Effie Murial Lynn and later, married Mary with whom he was father of (1). **WILLIAM H. TURNER** [6253] (1911 – 1970) son of William and Emma (Blocher) Turner was the operator of Turners Dairy, affiliated with Potomac Farms Dairy of Cumberland and owned a large dairy farm on U.S. Route 40 at the home place. **WILLIAM J. TURNER** Fifth great grandson of progenitor Nicholas Kegg. **WILLIAM LEWIS TURNER** [6254] (1869 – 1956) son of Joshua and Almira (Corley) Turner, married Emma Missouri Blocher with whom he was father of (3). **WINIFRED ANN FROST TURNER** [6255] (1911 – 1997) aka "Doris", daughter of James and Mary (Frost) Turner, married Byard A. McKenzie with whom she was mother of (1). Doris was a member of the Old St. Ann's Shrine, Avilton, and Christian Mothers.

TUSHA

VICTOR TUSHA Seventh great grandson of progenitor Nicholas Kegg.

TUTTLE

BROOKE E. TUTTLE [6255A] (1935 – 2011) son of Raymond and Florence (Sholl) Tuttle, married Barbara Boyer with whom he was father of (2). After graduating from Ohio State, Brooke served as a

---

[6248] The Evening Sun (Baltimore, MD) Jan 22, 1992 [6248A] Newman Funeral Homes (MD) [6248B] p.3- Bedford Inquirer (PA) Dec 19, 2003 contributed by Bob Rose [6249] Meyersdale Republic (PA) Jan 11, 1979, transcribed by John C. Oester [6250] Cumberland Evening Times (MD) June 15, 1955 [6251] p.18 - Cumberland Times (MD) Jan 13, 1963 [6252] p. D 8 - The Sunday Oregonian, Nov 28, 1982 [6253] p.24 – Cumberland Times (MD) March 29, 1970 [6254] p.4 - Cumberland Times (MD) Oct 31, 1927 [6255] Cumberland Times-News (MD) Oct. 31,1997 [6255A] Indianapolis Star (IN) Dec. 4, 2011

Captain in the U.S. Army where he served as General's aide. Upon leaving the Army, he joined Cummins, Inc. During his 29-year career at Cummins, Brooke re-located a manufacturing plant from Seymour, IN, to Cookeville TN, where he then served as General Manager of Cummins' Fleetguard filtration business. He also served as an international consultant to the US State Department advising Slovakia and Italy on how to attract foreign investment Later, Brooke taught Economics at Ivy Tech and Indiana University/Purdue University Columbus, where he was an adjunct professor for 20 years. He received the "Excellence in Teaching" award from IUPUC in 1990 and 2010. In August 2010 he received the Alumni Achievement Award from Delta Tau Delta Fraternity in Washington, DC, which is given to alumni whose achievements have brought honor and prestige to the fraternity. He also received the Columbus, Indiana Chamber of Commerce Community Service Award and the Sagamore of the Wabash Award. Brooke was always active and involved in community affairs. He served as president of Rotary Club International, the Columbus Foundation for Youth, and the Columbus Girls Club. He also served as Moderator for Leadership Bartholomew County, a Big Brother, and a Boy's Club basketball coach. He was a Deacon at the First Presbyterian Church and served on the IUPUC Board of Advisors and the Visitor's Center Board. **DEBRA TUTTLE** Seventh great granddaughter of progenitor Nicholas Kegg. **JASON DEAN TUTTLE** Sixth great grandson of progenitor Nicholas Kegg. **JEFFREY SCOTT TUTTLE** Sixth great grandson of progenitor Nicholas Kegg. **KATHERINE L. TUTTLE** Sixth great granddaughter of progenitor Nicholas Kegg. **PHILLIP EDWARD TUTTLE** (1934 – 1989) son of Raymond and Florence (Sholl) Tuttle, married Suzanne Marie Bricker with whom he was father of (3). **PHILLIP E. TUTTLE** Sixth great grandson of progenitor Nicholas Kegg. **SARAH ELIZABETH TUTTLE** Seventh great granddaughter of progenitor Nicholas Kegg. **STEPHANIE TUTTLE** Seventh great granddaughter of progenitor Nicholas Kegg. **STEWART E. TUTTLE** Sixth great grandson of progenitor Nicholas Kegg.

TUTWILER

LARRY TUTWILER Sixth great grandson of progenitor Nicholas Kegg.
PAUL TUTWILER Sixth great grandson of progenitor Nicholas Kegg.

TVRDY

JAMIE TVRDY Sixth great granddaughter of progenitor Nicholas Kegg.
JAROD S. TVRDY Sixth great grandson of progenitor Nicholas Kegg.

TWIGG

SUSAN APRIL TWIGG Seventh great granddaughter of progenitor Nicholas Kegg.

TYUKODI

PAYTON TYUKODI Eighth great granddaughter of progenitor Nicholas Kegg.
RACHAEL MARLI TYUKODI Eighth great granddaughter of progenitor Nicholas Kegg.

UDISCHAS

ALEXIS UDISCHAS Eighth great granddaughter of progenitor Nicholas Kegg.
ASHLEIGH UDISCHAS Eighth great granddaughter of progenitor Nicholas Kegg.
BRANDON MICHAEL UDISCHAS Eighth great grandson of progenitor Nicholas Kegg.
CHARLES EDWARD UDISCHAS Seventh great grandson of progenitor Nicholas Kegg.
DONNA JANE UDISCHAS Seventh great granddaughter of progenitor Nicholas Kegg.
EDWARD KEITH UDISCHAS Seventh great grandson of progenitor Nicholas Kegg.

FAITH UDISCHAS Eighth great granddaughter of progenitor Nicholas Kegg.
JON ERIC UDISCHAS Seventh great grandson of progenitor Nicholas Kegg.
MICKAELA J. UDISCHAS Eighth great granddaughter of progenitor Nicholas Kegg.

UDOUTCH

AARON UDOUTCH Sixth great grandson of progenitor Nicholas Kegg.
CHRISTOPHER DAVID UDOUTCH (1980 – 1980) son OF Steven and Kathleen (Bennett) Udoutch.
DANIEL F. UDOUTCH Fifth great grandson of progenitor Nicholas Kegg.
DEREK ANDREW UDOUTCH Sixth great grandson of progenitor Nicholas Kegg.
DOROTHY LOU UDOUTCH (1936 – 1938) daughter of Frank and Mary (Owens) Udoutch.
FRANCIS J. UDOUTCH Fourth great grandson of progenitor Nicholas Kegg.
HAYDEN UDOUTCH Sixth great granddaughter of progenitor Nicholas Kegg.
JENNIFER LYNN UDOUTCH Sixth great granddaughter of progenitor Nicholas Kegg.
JOEL UDOUTCH Sixth great grandson of progenitor Nicholas Kegg.
KENDALL ELIZABETH UDOUTCH Sixth great granddaughter of progenitor Nicholas Kegg.
LAURIE A. UDOUTCH Fifth great granddaughter of progenitor Nicholas Kegg.
LINDA UDOUTCH Fifth great granddaughter of progenitor Nicholas Kegg.
LISA K. UDOUTCH Fifth great granddaughter of progenitor Nicholas Kegg.
PATRICIA ANNE UDOUTCH [6255B] aka "Pat" (1932 – 2016) daughter of Frank and Mary (Owens) Udoutch married John James Castranio with whom she was mother of (4). Pat graduated as valedictorian from Altoona's Mercy Hospital School of Nursing. She completed graduate studies in ophthalmology and coronary care. She was named Cary Woman of the Year. An ardent member of the Cary Band Boosters, Pat traveled with the band to the Tournament of Roses Parade and the Fêtes de Genève in Switzerland. She was a member of the VFW Auxiliary, Cary Library Board of Trustees from 1974 to 1984, and Wake County Library Commission in the 1980s, also serving as the chairman in 1984. To the people in her life, she was the one who always listened with a sympathetic ear to the troubles of others, who provided expert medical advice at any time when asked, who made chicken soup and meatballs for friends who needed comfort, and who always remembered others with a card or a phone call. **REESE UDOUTCH** Sixth great granddaughter of progenitor Nicholas Kegg. **SARAH UDOUTCH** Sixth great granddaughter of progenitor Nicholas Kegg. **STEVEN M. UDOUTCH** Fifth great grandson of progenitor Nicholas Kegg.

UDOVICH

JOHN LOUIS UDOVICH Seventh great grandson of progenitor Nicholas Kegg.

ULERY

CHRISTINA JEANETTE ULERY Seventh great granddaughter of progenitor Nicholas Kegg.

ULRICH

ANNE JACQUELINE ULRICH Sixth great granddaughter of progenitor Nicholas Kegg.
CORY ELISE ULRICH Sixth great granddaughter of progenitor Nicholas Kegg.
EMILY JAYNE ULRICH Sixth great granddaughter of progenitor Nicholas Kegg.
EVELYN JUDITH ULRICH Sixth great granddaughter of progenitor Nicholas Kegg.
MEGHAN LEIGH ULRICH Sixth great granddaughter of progenitor Nicholas Kegg.
SADIE BETH ULRICH Sixth great granddaughter of progenitor Nicholas Kegg.

[6255B] The News & Observer (NC) June 15, 2016

UNDERHILL

CORBIN RAY UNDERHILL Eighth great grandchild of progenitor Nicholas Kegg.

UNDERWOOD

BERTHA JO UNDERWOOD Fifth great granddaughter of progenitor Nicholas Kegg. **BRANDON LEE UNDERWOOD** Sixth great grandson of progenitor Nicholas Kegg. **BRYAN ANDREW UNDERWOOD** Sixth great grandson of progenitor Nicholas Kegg. **DAVID UNDERWOOD** Sixth great grandson of progenitor Nicholas Kegg. **DAVID R. UNDERWOOD** Fifth great grandson of progenitor Nicholas Kegg. **ERNEST BARTLETT UNDERWOOD** [6256] (1916 – 1989) son of Robert and Bertha (Graham) Underwood married twice; first to Evelyn A. Brasill with whom he was father of (4). Later, he married Josephine Pruitt with whom he was father of (3). Ernest attended Forest Lake Academy in Apopka, Fla. He was a former owner of Underwood Trucking Feed and Seed Business in Rhea County, Tenn., and owned Collegedale Discount Motors. He was president of Collegedale Central Exxon and a past member of Collegedale Seventh-day Adventist Church. **ERNESTINE UNDERWOOD** Fifth great granddaughter of progenitor Nicholas Kegg. **HAROLD ERNEST UNDERWOOD** Fifth great grandson of progenitor Nicholas Kegg. **JOSEPH BARTLETT UNDERWOOD** aka "J.B." Fifth great grandson of progenitor Nicholas Kegg. **KAITLIN UNDERWOOD** Sixth great granddaughter of progenitor Nicholas Kegg. **KATHY UNDERWOOD** Fifth great granddaughter of progenitor Nicholas Kegg. **LARRY UNDERWOOD** Fifth great grandson of progenitor Nicholas Kegg. **MELVIN GRAHAM UNDERWOOD** [6256A] (1921 – 2009) son of Archie and Hazel (Graham) Underwood married Julia Cline with whom he was father of (2). Melvin served as a Surgical Technician in the US Army for 3 years. He was awarded the Victory and Good Conduct medals. After being honorably discharged, he returned to Paradise Valley Hospital and finished his degree in nursing. During his lifetime he worked at San Diego County, San Bernardino County, Patton State, and Dewitt State Hospitals. He also worked at the Veterans Home of California, Napa State Hospital, and retired from Stockton Developmental Center. He enjoyed cars and owned over a hundred cars during this lifetime. He was also fond of spending many hours reading the local newspaper and taking his granddaughters to the park. **PAULINE HILDA UNDERWOOD** [6257] (1915 – 2002) daughter of Archie and Hazel (Graham) Underwood, married Bowman Andrew Deal with whom she was mother of (2). Pauline was an administrative secretary to the president of South-eastern California Conference of Seventh Day Adventists and to the president of Pacific Union College of Seventh Day Adventists. **RALPH LEE UNDERWOOD** [6258] (1946 – 2010) son of Ernest and Evelyn (Brasill) Underwood, married Beverly Sue Gentry. **RAYMOND A. UNDERWOOD** Fifth great grandson of progenitor Nicholas Kegg. **SIENNA LEIGH UNDERWOOD** Seventh great granddaughter of progenitor Nicholas Kegg.

UNGER

CALEB UNGER Seventh great grandson of progenitor Nicholas Kegg.

UNICE

JOSH K. UNICE Sixth great grandson of progenitor Nicholas Kegg.

USLICK

DAVID ANDERSON USLICK Sixth great grandson of progenitor Nicholas Kegg.
LAUREN MARIE USLICK Sixth great granddaughter of progenitor Nicholas Kegg.

[6256] Chattanooga Historical Society obituary clipping obtained by D. Sue Dible [6256A] LodiNews (CA) Jan 9, 2010 [6257] The Desert Sun (Palm Springs, FL) May 10, 2002 [6258] Chattanooga Times Free Press July 30, 2010

MICHELLE LOUISE USLICK Sixth great granddaughter of progenitor Nicholas Kegg.

VALENTINE

JENNA M. VALENTINE [6259] (1987 – 2021) daughter of Jeff and Jeanette (Miller) Valentine married Keith A. Hinish with whom she was mother of (2). Jenna was employed at McDonalds in Everett and Breezewood for several years, she later assisted her husband with their farming operation. She was proud of being a stay-at-home mom and a homemaker. She enjoyed going on drives to get ice cream with the family and time spent with family. **JENNESSA VALENTINE** Sixth great granddaughter of progenitor Nicholas Kegg.

VAN BLAIR

CARTER VAN BLAIR Seventh great grandson of progenitor Nicholas Kegg.
LEXI VAN BLAIR Seventh great granddaughter of progenitor Nicholas Kegg.

VAN BUSKIRK

CHRISTINE VAN BUSKIRK Fifth great granddaughter of progenitor Nicholas Kegg.
CRAIG PRESTON VAN BUSKIRK Fifth great grandson of progenitor Nicholas Kegg.
JEFFREY PRESCOTT VAN BUSKIRK Fifth great grandson of progenitor Nicholas Kegg.
RALPH PRESCOTT VAN BUSKIRK (1927 – 2004) son of Ralph and Caroline (Knouf) Van Buskirk married twice; first to Betty Jane Drake with whom he was father of (3). Later, he married Anna M. Pinon.

VAN CAMP

CHRISTIN LEE VAN CAMP Seventh great granddaughter of progenitor Nicholas Kegg.

VAN DEUSEN

CHRISTINA VAN DEUSEN Fifth great granddaughter of progenitor Nicholas Kegg.
COURTLAND VAN DEUSEN Fifth great grandson of progenitor Nicholas Kegg.
EDWARD VAN DEUSEN Fifth great grandson of progenitor Nicholas Kegg.
LAWRENCE VAN DEUSEN Fifth great grandson of progenitor Nicholas Kegg.

VAN HOOSE

LISA K. VAN HOOSE Seventh great granddaughter of progenitor Nicholas Kegg.
LORETTA VAN HOOSE Seventh great granddaughter of progenitor Nicholas Kegg.

VAN SCOYOC

ADAM M. VAN SCOYOC Sixth great grandson of progenitor Nicholas Kegg.
BENJAMIN VAN SCOYOC III 5th great grandson of progenitor Nicholas Kegg.
BRIAN VAN SCOYOC Seventh great grandson of progenitor Nicholas Kegg.
DEBORAH JOAN VAN SCOYOC Fifth great granddaughter of progenitor Nicholas Kegg.
JOHN RICHARD VAN SCOYOC (1942 – 1959) son of Benjamin and Edna (Speicher) Van Scoyoc.

[6259] Bedford Gazette (PA) May 11, 2021

MARY BETH VAN SCOYOC [6259A] aka "Betsy" (1949 – 2007) daughter of Benjamin and Edna (Speicher) Van Scoyoc married Albert Lee Bruck with whom she was mother of (4). Betsy was a Cambria-Rowe Business College graduate. She worked as a housekeeper for the Best Western. Prior to that, she was a payroll clerk at Fort Bedford Hotel. She was also a Troop Leader for the Girl Scouts in Hyndman for many years. **MIRA VAN SCOYOC** Seventh great granddaughter of progenitor Nicholas Kegg. **PAIGE VAN SCOYOC** Seventh great granddaughter of progenitor Nicholas Kegg.
SUSAN GAYLE VAN SCOYOC [6259B] (1948 – 2017) daughter of Benjamin and Edna (Speicher) Van Scoyoc married James L. Estep. Susan was coordinator for the Center for Independent Living for 20 years. She was a member of Bethany Lutheran Church, Altoona, and she loved reading, her pets and working on the Kindle.

VANANKEREN

SHANNON VANANKEREN Sixth great granddaughter of progenitor Nicholas Kegg.

VANARSDALE

SCOTT VANARSDALE Sixth great grandson of progenitor Nicholas Kegg.

VANAUKEN

DAVID BRENDON VANAUKEN Sixth great grandson of progenitor Nicholas Kegg.
PAMELA SUE VANAUKEN Sixth great granddaughter of progenitor Nicholas Kegg.

VANCE

CYNTHIA LYNN VANCE Sixth great granddaughter of progenitor Nicholas Kegg.
JULIA A. VANCE Sixth great granddaughter of progenitor Nicholas Kegg.
TIMOTHY KEITH VANCE Sixth great grandson of progenitor Nicholas Kegg.

VANDEBUNTE

EVELYN RUTH VANDEBUNTE Ninth great granddaughter of progenitor Nicholas Kegg.
OLIVIA VANDEBUNTE Ninth great granddaughter of progenitor Nicholas Kegg.

VANDENBURG

DAVID W. VANDENBURG Sixth great grandson of progenitor Nicholas Kegg.
MALINDA VANDENBURG Sixth great granddaughter of progenitor Nicholas Kegg.
MICHAEL R. VANDENBURG Sixth great grandson of progenitor Nicholas Kegg.
RITA JACKS VANDENBURG Sixth great granddaughter of progenitor Nicholas Kegg.
VICKY SUE VANDENBURG Sixth great granddaughter of progenitor Nicholas Kegg.

VANDERAA

AMY VANDERAA Seventh great granddaughter of progenitor Nicholas Kegg.
KIA MICHELLE VANDERAA Seventh great granddaughter of progenitor Nicholas Kegg.
MIA TAMERA VANDERAA Seventh great granddaughter of progenitor Nicholas Kegg.

[6259A] Cumberland Times-News (MD) Dec 3, 2007 [6259B] Altoona Mirror (PA) June 17, 2017, contributed by D. Sue Dible

VANDERLAAN

MARK ALLEN VANDERLAAN [6260] (1954 – 1993) son of Glenn and Marilynn (Routsong) Vanderlaan. Mark was a member of the Big Island AIDS Project and the Religious Science Church.
MARY MARGARET VANDERLAAN Fifth great granddaughter of progenitor Nicholas Kegg.

VANDERLYN

COURTNEY VANDERLYN Eighth great granddaughter of progenitor Nicholas Kegg.
JAMES F. VANDERLYN Eighth great grandson of progenitor Nicholas Kegg.
JAMES KEITH VANDERLYN Seventh great grandson of progenitor Nicholas Kegg.
KRISTEN E. VANDERLYN Eighth great granddaughter of progenitor Nicholas Kegg.
SUSAN J. VANDERLYN Seventh great granddaughter of progenitor Nicholas Kegg.

VANDERPOOL

AMY NICOLE VANDERPOOL Seventh great granddaughter of progenitor Nicholas Kegg.
ANDREW J. VANDERPOOL Sixth great grandson of progenitor Nicholas Kegg.
CHRISTINA RENAY VANDERPOOL Seventh great granddaughter of progenitor Nicholas Kegg.
CHRISTOPHER LEE VANDERPOOL Sixth great grandson of progenitor Nicholas Kegg.
DEVAN JUSTICE VANDERPOOL Seventh great grandson of progenitor Nicholas Kegg.
JESSICA MICHELLE VANDERPOOL Seventh great granddaughter of progenitor Nicholas Kegg.
KELLIE D. VANDERPOOL Seventh great granddaughter of progenitor Nicholas Kegg.
LAURIE ANN VANDERPOOL Sixth great granddaughter of progenitor Nicholas Kegg.
MARLEE A VANDERPOOL Sixth great granddaughter of progenitor Nicholas Kegg.
MICHAEL VANDERPOOL Seventh great grandson of progenitor Nicholas Kegg.
MICHAEL TODD VANDERPOOL Sixth great grandson of progenitor Nicholas Kegg.
RODNEY KEITH VANDERPOOL Sixth great grandson of progenitor Nicholas Kegg.
STACEY KRISTINE VANDERPOOL Sixth great granddaughter of progenitor Nicholas Kegg.

VANDIVER

DAVID VANDIVER Eighth great grandson of progenitor Nicholas Kegg.

VANLANDINGHAM

AUSTIN C. VANLANDINGHAM Sixth great grandson of progenitor Nicholas Kegg.
TAWNYA VANLANDINGHAM Sixth great granddaughter of progenitor Nicholas Kegg.

VANNUYS

ALLISON VANNUYS Sixth great granddaughter of progenitor Nicholas Kegg.
CAROLYN VANNUYS Fifth great granddaughter of progenitor Nicholas Kegg.
LEAH VANNUYS Sixth great granddaughter of progenitor Nicholas Kegg.
WALTER C. VANNUYS aka "Boo", Fifth great grandson of progenitor Nicholas Kegg.

VANPELT

KATHRYN VANPELT Seventh great granddaughter of progenitor Nicholas Kegg.

[6260] The Honolulu Advertiser (HA) April 15, 1993

VANWAGNER

KERRI JO VANWAGNER Sixth great granddaughter of progenitor Nicholas Kegg.
LARAMIE LYNN VANWAGNER 6th great granddaughter of progenitor Nicholas Kegg.
TIMOTHY DUANE VANWAGNER Sixth great grandson of progenitor Nicholas Kegg.

VARGO

KALLI VARGO Seventh great granddaughter of progenitor Nicholas Kegg. **KRIS JAMES VARGO** [6260A] son of Albert and Shirley (Saylor) Vargo married Tamara Elchynski with whom he was father of (3). Founder of The Vargo Company, Kris was an intelligent and successful businessman. He graduated from Coventry High School and Hiram College. Kris was an avid baseball fan and was recently inducted into his alma mater, the Hiram College Athletics' Hall of Fame. He was a huge Cleveland sports fan who enjoyed cheering for the Browns, Indians and Cavaliers. He enjoyed hunting, golfing. **MICHAEL JON VARGO** Sixth great grandson of progenitor Nicholas Kegg. **RACHAEL VARGO** Seventh great granddaughter of progenitor Nicholas Kegg. **TEVEN VARGO** Seventh great grandson of progenitor Nicholas Kegg. **TIM VARGO** Sixth great grandson of progenitor Nicholas Kegg.

VARNER

ERIC VARNER Seventh great grandson of progenitor Nicholas Kegg.
RICHARD DUANE VARNER Sixth great grandson of progenitor Nicholas Kegg.

VAUGHAN

BRUCE VAUGHAN Fifth great grandson of progenitor Nicholas Kegg. **CHRISTINA MARY VAUGHAN** [6260B] daughter of James and Jacquelyn (Long) Vaughan married twice, first to Gregory Allen Corbett with whom she was mother of (1). Later, she married Anthony John Skufca with whom she was mother of (1). **COLLEEN VAUGHAN** Fifth great granddaughter of progenitor Nicholas Kegg. **EOFFREY C. VAUGHAN** Seventh great grandson of progenitor Nicholas Kegg. **JEANNE VAUGHAN** Fifth great granddaughter of progenitor Nicholas Kegg. **MARJORIE ELLEN VAUGHAN** Fifth great granddaughter of progenitor Nicholas Kegg. **PAMELA SUE VAUGHAN** Fifth great granddaughter of progenitor Nicholas Kegg. **VIRGIL EDWARD VAUGHAN** [6261] (1954 – 1991) son of Virgil and Harriet (Meyers) Vaughan. Virgil was assistant scout master of Berlin Boy Scouts Troop 135. He was a member of Trinity United Church of Christ, Berlin; Berlin VFD, berlin Sportsman, and Mountain Field and Stream.

VAUGHN

DAVID J. VAUGHN Sixth great grandson of progenitor Nicholas Kegg. **DAVID R. VAUGHN** Seventh great grandson of progenitor Nicholas Kegg. **DONALD LEE VAUGHN** [6262] (1960 – 2013) son of Charles Donald and June (Minear) Vaughn. **HEATHER VAUGHN** Seventh great granddaughter of progenitor Nicholas Kegg. **MICHAEL WAYNE VAUGHN** [6263] (1963 – 2020) aka "Mike" son of Charles Donald and June (Minear) Vaughn was a funny, gracious, family man who was cherished by many. Mike loved old cars, fishing, and music. As a Machinist by trade, one of his favorite things to do was make little figurines from left over wire.

[6260A] Burton Wintergreen Funeral Home (PA) [6260B] Columbus Dispatch (OH) Aug 31, 2014 [6261] Daily American (PA) April 24, 1991 [6262] San Diego Union Tribune (CA) March 30, 2013 [6263] El Cajon Mortuary and Cremation Service (CA) obtained by D. Sue Dible

VAUSE

CARLY VAUSE Seventh great granddaughter of progenitor Nicholas Kegg.
SHELBY VAUSE Eighth great granddaughter of progenitor Nicholas Kegg.
TAYLOR REESE VAUSE Eighth great grandson of progenitor Nicholas Kegg.
TREY VAUSE Seventh great grandson of progenitor Nicholas Kegg.

VEEDER

MARY MILDRED VEEDER (1921 – 1990) daughter of Robert and Mary (McDermott) Veeder, married Hiram Pearl Edwards with whom she was mother of (3).

VEIK

BRENDA VEIK Seventh great granddaughter of progenitor Nicholas Kegg.
ERIC ALAN VEIK Seventh great grandson of progenitor Nicholas Kegg.

VEIL

BRIANNA LYNN VEIL Sixth great granddaughter of progenitor Nicholas Kegg.
CHERI CHEVON VEIL (1979 – 1982) daughter of Thomas and Audrey (Kegg) Veil.
GAUGE VEIL Seventh great grandson of progenitor Nicholas Kegg.
SHAUN THOMAS VEIL Sixth great grandson of progenitor Nicholas Kegg.

VENABLE

LETHA ELINOR VENABLE [6264] (1916 – 1998) daughter of Charles and Mabel (Kegg) Venable, married Harry L. Smith with whom she was mother of (2). Letha was employed by the J. C. Penney Co. of Salem for 17 years. She graduated from Goshen High School in 1935. She retired as catalog department supervisor in 1985. She was a member of Goshen Harmony Club, Salem Senior Citizen's and J. C. Penney Girls. Letha was secretary-treasurer of the Windsor Square Condominium Association. She attended Salem First Friends Church in Salem and was also a member of the Encourager's Sunday School Class.   **RUTH E. VENABLE** [6264A] daughter of Charles and Mabel (Kegg) Venable married Ronald C. Hoopes with whom she was mother of (2). Ruth spent many years working at the Methodist Wesley Foundation in Tempe, where she became "Mom" to hundreds of ASU students throughout the years.

VENEZIA

ADRIANA VENEZIA Seventh great granddaughter of progenitor Nicholas Kegg.
DANIEL VENEZIA Sixth great grandson of progenitor Nicholas Kegg.   **DANIEL VENEZIA JR.** Seventh great grandson of progenitor Nicholas Kegg.   **DEREK VENEZIA** Seventh great grandson of progenitor Nicholas Kegg.   **JOSEPH G. VENEZIA** Sixth great grandson of progenitor Nicholas Kegg.   **MICHAEL JOHN VENEZIA** Sixth great grandson of progenitor Nicholas Kegg.
OLIVIA VENEZIA Seventh great granddaughter of progenitor Nicholas Kegg.
SCOTT R. VENEZIA [6265] (1980 – 2014) son of Robert and Therese (Greene) Venezia. Scott was an electrician for Venezia Electric in Billerica. He took great pride and joy of his installation of Christmas lights in Billerica center. He had a love for animals. He was an avid sports fan.

[6264] Alliance Review (OH) June 25, 1998, obtained by D. Sue Dible [6264A] East Valley Tribune (AZ) Nov 21, 2004 [6265] Boston Herald (Mass) Jan 11, 2014

VERCAMEN

KIM MICHELLE VERCAMEN Fifth great granddaughter of progenitor Nicholas Kegg.
PAUL REID VERCAMEN Fifth great grandson of progenitor Nicholas Kegg.
REBECCA MICHELLE VERCAMEN Sixth great granddaughter of progenitor Nicholas Kegg.
TONYA BERNICE VERCAMEN Sixth great granddaughter of progenitor Nicholas Kegg.

VICKERS

AMY VICKERS Seventh great granddaughter of progenitor Nicholas Kegg. **CATHERINE BELLE VICKERS** Seventh great granddaughter of progenitor Nicholas Kegg. **CHARLOTTE M. VICKERS** Sixth great granddaughter of progenitor Nicholas Kegg. **DAWN MARIE VICKERS** Sixth great granddaughter of progenitor Nicholas Kegg. **FLORENCE ANN VICKERS** [6265A] (1957 – 2014) daughter of Lawrence and Mary (Moler) Vickers. Florence received a four-year degree from Shepherd College, and received her master's degree from West Virginia University. She was a member of the Eastern Star, and an active member of CEO's, and was a 4-H Extension Agent and teacher. In addition, she worked at Locust Grove Farm with her family and was a caregiver for her parents. **JOHN L. VICKERS** Sixth great grandson of progenitor Nicholas Kegg. **KENDALL AVA VICKERS** Eighth great granddaughter of progenitor Nicholas Kegg. **LARNIE VICKERS** Seventh great grandson of progenitor Nicholas Kegg. **LAWRENCE ELMER VICKERS** [6265B] aka "Elmer" (1929 – 2016) son of Lawrence and Charlotte (Grose) Vickers, married Mary Catherine Moler with whom he was father of (4). Lawrence was a lifelong dairy farmer having owned and operated with his family, Locust Grove Farm, His day was not complete unless he made it to the barn, or the "Boys" updated him of their progress. Having attended Sheperd College, Elmer was very active with the Milk Coop. serving many years. Member of the Jefferson County Farm Bureau; Jefferson County Fair Board, receiving the honor of Director Emeritus, FHA, and was a WV 4-H All Star. **LAWRENCE ELMER VICKERS** Sixth great grandson of progenitor Nicholas Kegg. **MARY BETH VICKERS** Seventh great granddaughter of progenitor Nicholas Kegg. **MATTHEW JOHN VICKERS** Seventh great grandson of progenitor Nicholas Kegg. **TERRI LYNN VICKERS** Sixth great granddaughter of progenitor Nicholas Kegg. **TY LAWRENCE VICKERS** Eighth great grandson of progenitor Nicholas Kegg.

VILLARD

CODY VILLARD Seventh great grandson of progenitor Nicholas Kegg.
JOHN VILLARD Seventh great grandson of progenitor Nicholas Kegg.

VINING

ANTHONY VINING Sixth great grandson of progenitor Nicholas Kegg. **DAVID M. VINING** [6265C] (1956 – 2021) son of Paul and Patricia (Repp) Vining married Carol Shaw with whom he was father of (2). David owned Vining Slaughter Haus for 12 years and he worked in the family business for over 40 years. He was a member of the Sons of the America Legion squadron 160 and the Loyal Order of the Moose. **JOE VINING** Sixth great grandson of progenitor Nicholas Kegg. **PAULA VINING** Sixth great granddaughter of progenitor Nicholas Kegg. **SHANNON ANN VINING** (1990 – 1990) daughter of David and Carol (Shaw) Vining. **STEVEN VINING** Sixth great grandson of progenitor Nicholas Kegg. **SUSANNA VINING** Seventh great granddaughter of progenitor Nicholas Kegg.

[6265A] Melvin T. Strider Colonial Funeral Home (WVA) [6265B] Spirit of Jefferson (WV) Aug 10, 2016, contributed by D. Sue Dible [6265C] The Huntington County TAB (IN) Jan 7, 2021

VINSON

PATRICIA VINSON Fifth great granddaughter of progenitor Nicholas Kegg.
SHIRLEY VINSON Fifth great granddaughter of progenitor Nicholas Kegg.

VISNIC

LAUREN MAE VISNIC Seventh great granddaughter of progenitor Nicholas Kegg.
PIERCE VISNIC Eighth great grandson of progenitor Nicholas Kegg.
STEPHEN RICHARD VISNIC Seventh great grandson of progenitor Nicholas Kegg.

VITA

RICKY VITA Sixth great grandson of progenitor Nicholas Kegg.

VLASATY

DONNA REGINA VLASATY [6266] (1938 – 2011) daughter of Emery and Elizabeth (Green/e) Vlasaty married Angelo Karas with whom she was mother of (1). Later she married Mr. Goracke. Donna was a homemaker. **KENNETH C. VLASATY** Fifth great grandson of progenitor Nicholas Kegg. **MARGARET A. VLASATY** Fifth great granddaughter of progenitor Nicholas Kegg. **NANCY ANN VLASATY** Sixth great granddaughter of progenitor Nicholas Kegg. **PATRICIA L. VLASATY** Fifth great granddaughter of progenitor Nicholas Kegg. **ROBERT CHARLES VLASATY** [6267] (1941 – 2016) son of Emery and Elizabeth (Green/e) Vlasaty married June Phyllis Wilson with whom he was father of (2). Robert was Lieutenant Fire Fighter in Newport, Rhode Island. **ROBERT CHARLES VLASATY JR.** Sixth great grandson of progenitor Nicholas Kegg.

VOLLBRECHT

CARSON VOLLBRECHT Eighth great grandson of progenitor Nicholas Kegg.
KYLEE VOLLBRECT Eighth great granddaughter of progenitor Nicholas Kegg;

VOLLRATH

ABBY VOLLRATH Eighth great granddaughter of progenitor Nicholas Kegg.
KHRISTI LYNN VOLLRATH Seventh great granddaughter of progenitor Nicholas Kegg.
NEIL D. VOLLRATH Seventh great grandson of progenitor Nicholas Kegg.
RYAN VOLLRATH Eighth great grandson of progenitor Nicholas Kegg.

VORBECK

MITCH VORBECK Seventh great grandson of progenitor Nicholas Kegg.

VORHAUER

ADAM ROGER VORHAUER Sixth great grandson of progenitor Nicholas Kegg.
TRISHA EILEEN VORHAUER Sixth great granddaughter of progenitor Nicholas Kegg.

[6266] Roselawn Memorial Park (KS) obituary obtained by D. Sue Dible [6267] Dignity Memorial (St. Lucie, FL)

VOSSEN

BRIAN WAYNE VOSSEN Eighth great grandson of progenitor Nicholas Kegg.
CORRIN BLAIR VOSSEN Eighth great granddaughter of progenitor Nicholas Kegg.
SHERELE VOSSEN Eighth great granddaughter of progenitor Nicholas Kegg.

WADE

HARRISON WADE Seventh great grandson of progenitor Nicholas Kegg.
KELLI DANISE WADE Sixth great granddaughter of progenitor Nicholas Kegg.
ROBERT DOUGLAS WADE (6267A) aka "Robbie" (1967 – 2016) son of Dannal and Cheryl (Cagg) Wade married Heidi Diana Dean with whom he was father of (1).

WADLE

SAVANNA GRACE WADLE Eighth great granddaughter of progenitor Nicholas Kegg.

WAGAR

CLARENCE LEE WAGAR (6268) (1943 – 1999) son of Eugene and Elsie (Rice) Wagar married and was father of (1).   **PENNY LYNN WAGAR** Sixth great granddaughter of progenitor Nicholas Kegg.

WAGENKNECHT

JULIE ANN WAGENKNECHT Seventh great granddaughter of progenitor Nicholas Kegg.

WAGGERMAN

ARLEEN VIOLET WAGGERMAN (1932 – 1992) daughter of Raymond and Luceill (Nelson) Waggerman, married Henry Wallace Koym with whom she was mother of (2).   **BETTY RAECIEL WAGGERMAN** (6268A) (1927 – 2014) daughter of Raymond and Luceill (Nelson) Waggerman married Vernon R. Neely with whom she was mother of (3).   **BRIAN DAVID WAGGERMAN** Sixth great grandson of progenitor Nicholas Kegg.   **CHARLES H. WAGGERMAN** Sixth great grandson of progenitor Nicholas Kegg.   **CHARLES WILLIAM WAGGERMAN** (1928 – 2012) aka "Billie", son of Earle and Luella (Yoder) Waggerman married twice; first to Nancy Magelene Stone with whom he was father of (2). Later, he married Katheryn E. Johns.   **CHRISTOPHER CHARLES WAGGERMAN** Seventh great grandson of progenitor Nicholas Kegg.   **EARL ELMER WAGGERMAN** (1925 – 1997) son of Earle and Luella (Yoder) Waggerman, married Janet Louise Butler with whom he was father of two known sons.   **EDITH ROSEANNE WAGGERMAN** (6268B) (1930 – 2011) daughter of Earl and Luella (Yoder) Waggerman married twice, first to Paul Daniel Kirksey with whom she was mother of (2) and later to Donald Dye. A young widow, Edith was a hardworking, self-sufficient, devoted mother, raising her two daughters on her own until her marriage to Donald. Don and Edith formed quite a team running their business together and taking care of the family. Edith was a gifted artist and brilliant seamstress. She was a member of the Loyal Order of Moose, Lodge 468 for eight years.   **IMOGENE ROSE WAGGERMAN** Fourth great granddaughter of progenitor Nicholas Kegg.   **JEFFERY NEAL WAGGERMAN** (1974 – 1988) son of Jimmie and Michelle (Hall) Waggerman.   **.JIMMIE NEAL WAGGERMAN** (6268C) son of Charles and Nancy (Stone) Waggerman, married Michelle M. Hall with whom he was father of (2). He later married Janet Schwitters and Joyce Harris. An Army veteran, Jimmie

---

(6267A) Dayton Daily News (OH) Mar. 12, 2016 (6268) p.D8 - South Bend Tribune (IN) Dec 19, 1999 (6268A) Bimarck Tribune (ND) May 7, 2014 (6268B) Times Herald (CA) March 3, 2011 (6268C) p.12 The Recorder Herald (ID) Oct 12, 2006

attended Porter Ville Horse Shoeing School and received a Certification as a horse Ferrier and later worked for the Twin Peaks Ranch. He also worked for the US forest Service as a trail blazer. When the ranch sold, he started working for Clyde Chaffin at Steel and Ranch in Salmon and later for Cooper's Ready Mix Plant and purchased the Septic Pumping and portable rest room business from Cooper. **LOLA MAE WAGGERMAN** [6269] (1932 – 2016) daughter of Earle and Luella (Yoder) Waggerman, married Gerald Earl Stolz. **SAMUEL HARRISON WAGGERMAN** [6270] (1928 – 2017) son of Earle and Luella (Yoder) Waggerman, married Loween Iris Dahl with whom he was father of (2). **SANDRA L. WAGGERMAN** Sixth great granddaughter of progenitor Nicholas Kegg. **STEPHANIE RENE WAGGERMAN** Sixth great granddaughter of progenitor Nicholas Kegg. **TIMOTHY E. WAGGERMAN** Sixth great grandson of progenitor Nicholas Kegg.

WAGONER

CYNTHIA LYNN WAGONER Sixth great granddaughter of progenitor Nicholas Kegg.
MICHELE A. WAGONER Sixth great granddaughter of progenitor Nicholas Kegg.
RICHARD WAGONER Sixth great grandson of progenitor Nicholas Kegg.

WAKEFIELD

ADDIE WAKEFIELD Seventh great granddaughter of progenitor Nicholas Kegg.
JAMES JOHN WAKEFIELD Fifth great grandson of progenitor Nicholas Kegg.
JON T. WAKEFIELD Sixth great grandson of progenitor Nicholas Kegg.
KIMBERLY ANN WAKEFIELD Fifth great granddaughter of progenitor Nicholas Kegg.
LANE WAKEFIELD Seventh great grandchild of progenitor Nicholas Kegg.
SCOTT WAKEFIELD Sixth great grandson of progenitor Nicholas Kegg.
NASH WAKEFIELD Seventh great grandson of progenitor Nicholas Kegg.
THAD WAKEFIELD Sixth great grandson of progenitor Nicholas Kegg.
THOMAS WILLIAM WAKEFIELD Fifth great grandson of progenitor Nicholas Kegg.
QUINN WAKEFIELD Seventh great grandson of progenitor Nicholas Kegg.

WAKEFOOSE

JOEL WAKEFOOSE Sixth great grandson of progenitor Nicholas Kegg.
SARAH WAKEFOOSE Sixth great granddaughter of progenitor Nicholas Kegg.

WAKLEY

KORBIN XAVIER WAKLEY Eighth great grandson of progenitor Nicholas Kegg.

WALBRIDGE

SAM WALBRIDGE Eighth great grandson of progenitor Nicholas Kegg.

WALCUTT

BARRY WALCUTT Fifth great grandson of progenitor Nicholas Kegg.
HOLLY WALCUTT Fifth great granddaughter of progenitor Nicholas Kegg.
MICHAEL WALCUTT Fifth great grandson of progenitor Nicholas Kegg.

[6269] TimesHeraldOnline Apr. 8, 2016 [6270] Crawford-Bowers Funeral Home, TX

WALBOURNE

LIAM WALBOURNE Seventh great grandson of progenitor Nicholas Kegg.
LILY WALBOURNE Seventh great granddaughter of progenitor Nicholas Kegg.

WALE

BARBARA CYNTHIA WALE Sixth great granddaughter of progenitor Nicholas Kegg.
ELMER GEORGE WALE (1921 – 1998) son of Lieut Garland and Shirley (Cagg) Wale, married Barbara Jean Ketcham with whom he was father of (1). Later, he married Charlyne Mary Davis Caffey. Elmer was a former state highway policeman.

WALKER

BRANDON WALKER Eighth great grandson of progenitor Nicholas Kegg. **BRIAN WALKER** Seventh great grandson of progenitor Nicholas Kegg. **CATHERINE WALKER** Fifth great granddaughter of progenitor Nicholas Kegg. **DEBORAH WALKER** Fifth great granddaughter of progenitor Nicholas Kegg. **GREGORY HUDSON WALKER** Seventh great grandson of progenitor Nicholas Kegg. **JAMES P. WALKER** Sixth great grandson of progenitor Nicholas Kegg. **JENNIFER WALKER** Seventh great granddaughter of progenitor Nicholas Kegg. **JOAN BOOSE WALKER** [6270A] (1921 – 2011) daughter of Leland and Vida (Boose) Walker married twice, first to William J. Geary with whom she was mother of (2) later, she married Gerald Kraus. Joan was a graduate of Carnegie Tech and the University of Pittsburgh. Joan was a teacher at St. Ursula School and for the Pine Richland School District, member of the Glenshaw Garden Club, Glenshaw Century Club and the DAR. She also volunteered at Carnegie Museum in School Programs, and at North Hills Passavant Hospital, and enjoyed playing bridge. **JOHN HERBERT WALKER** Fifth great grandson of progenitor Nicholas Kegg. **KARIS WALKER** Sixth great granddaughter of progenitor Nicholas Kegg. **LAUREN WALKER** Seventh great granddaughter of progenitor Nicholas Kegg. **MICHAEL WAYNE WALKER** [6270B] aka "Shorty" (1953 – 2011) son of Royal and Kathleen (James) Walker married Marlene Carol Patrick with whom he was father of (2). Michael was a retired machinist and currently was an express truck driver for Pepsi Bottling Ventures in Salisbury. He enjoyed riding his Harley- Davidson Super Glide and was an avid Baltimore Ravens fan. **NICK WALKER** Seventh great grandson of progenitor Nicholas Kegg. **PAMELA WALKER** Fifth great granddaughter of progenitor Nicholas Kegg. **PATRICIA WALKER** [6270C] (1929 – 2017) daughter of Leland and Vida (Boose) Walker married James John Arthur with whom she was mother of (3). Patricia was the former president of the Somerset Welfare League in which her mother Vida B. Walker founded in 1938. She did volunteer work for the DAR (Daughters of the American Revolution) where she was past regent. **PATTY WALKER** Sixth great granddaughter of progenitor Nicholas Kegg. **RYAN P. WALKER** Sixth great grandson of progenitor Nicholas Kegg. **SHAUNA NICOLE WALKER** Sixth great granddaughter of progenitor Nicholas Kegg. **SONIA WALKER** Sixth great granddaughter of progenitor Nicholas Kegg. **STACEY WALKER** Seventh great granddaughter of progenitor Nicholas Kegg. **STELLA WALKER** Eighth great granddaughter of progenitor Nicholas Kegg. **TIMOTHY L. WALKER** Fifth great grandson of progenitor Nicholas Kegg. **VALARIE WALKER** Seventh great granddaughter of progenitor Nicholas Kegg.

WALKLEY

JUDITH ANN WALKLEY Fifth great granddaughter of progenitor Nicholas Kegg.
NANCY LEE WALKLEY 5th great granddaughter of progenitor Nicholas Kegg.

[6270A] Pittsburgh Post-Gazette (PA) Dec 24, 2011 [6270B] Bradshaw & Sons Funeral Home (MD) [6270C] Daily American (Somerset, PA) Sept 11, 2017

WALLACE

CLARK ALLISON WALLACE [6270D] (1915 – 2008) son of Frank and Hazel (Thompson) Wallace married Jean Provo with whom he was father of (6). The day after Clark turned 17, he joined the United States Navy. Following boot camp he was assigned to the battleship USS Oklahoma where he served the ensuring 6 years and his brother Roy was also aboard for part of the time. In 1938 the Oklahoma was sent to Barcelona, Spain to pick up refugees from the Spanish Civil War and that was to be Clark's final voyage at sea aboard the famed vessel, which was later sunk on December 7, 1941 at Pearl Harbor. Clark re-enlisted for shore duty and was assigned to Pensacola, Florida. There he was accepted into flight training as an enlisted man and he received "his wings" on December 6, 1941. Stopping by home in Denver on his way to his new station at San Diego, CA he learned of the Pearl Harbor attack, and he immediately reported for duty at San Diego. Clark flew numerous missions overseas during World War II and was especially proud of the 155 missions he flew during the Berlin Airlift at the end of the war in Europe. His military duty was completed when he served aboard the USS Eldorado. In 1954 he settled on the Peninsula where he began logging for Ray Provo's logging operation and this later became Peterson-Wallace Logging Co. When he retired, he worked part time for Roy Oman's lumber yards on the Peninsula. Clark was a very faithful and devoted member of Saint Mary's Catholic Church of Seaview where he enjoyed many friendships. Clark was also a devoted family man and in past years enjoyed building and flying (and sometimes crashing) radio-controlled aircraft. Clark was a member of Ilwaco Post 48 of the American Legion where he was a past commander and past adjutant. **DANIEL WALLACE** Sixth great grandson of progenitor Nicholas Kegg. **DAVID CLARKE WALLACE** (1937 – 2002) son of Clark and Jean (Provo) Wallace married Nancy Kay Gove with whom he was a father. David was a U.S. Navy veteran having served in Vietnam. **DAVID CLARKE WALLACE JR.** Seventh great grandson of progenitor Nicholas Kegg. **ERIC SCOTT WALLACE** Seventh great grandson of progenitor Nicholas Kegg. **FRANK LEROY WALLACE** (1917 – 1995) son of Frank and Hazel (Thompson) Wallace, married Helen Lee Beasley. **JOYCE ELOISE WALLACE** (1922 – 1977) daughter of Frank and Hazel (Thompson) Wallace, married Charles W. Johnson with whom she was mother of (1). **KIM ELAINE WALLACE** Seventh great granddaughter of progenitor Nicholas Kegg. **MAGGIE WALLACE** Eighth great granddaughter of progenitor Nicholas Kegg. **MICHAEL WALLACE** Sixth great grandson of progenitor Nicholas Kegg. **PATRICIA WALLACE** Sixth great granddaughter of progenitor Nicholas Kegg. **RICHARD JAMES WALLACE** Sixth great grandson of progenitor Nicholas Kegg. **OBIN SMITH WALLACE** Seventh great grandchild of progenitor Nicholas Kegg. **SHIRLEY ELIZABETH WALLACE** (1920 – 1995) daughter of Frank and Hazel (Thompson) Wallace married William Miles Hopkins with whom she was mother of (3). **STEPHEN WALLACE** Sixth great grandson of progenitor Nicholas Kegg.

WALLING

BARBARA JEAN WALLING [6270E] (1942 – 2017) daughter of Francis and Vesta (Davis) Walling married Mr. Cook with whom she was mother of (2). She later married Byron Hugh Sistler with whom she was mother of (1). Barbara assisted her husband Byron in running his genealogical publishing business, Byron Sistler and Associates.

WALSH

DELLA RAE WALSH Eighth great granddaughter of progenitor Nicholas Kegg.

WALTER

NATHANIEL WALTER Sixth great grandson of progenitor Nicholas Kegg.

[6270E] Hoopston Chronicle (IL) Mar 9, 2017

REBECCA JO WALTER Sixth great granddaughter of progenitor Nicholas Kegg.

WALTERS

ANTHONY WALTERS Seventh great grandson of progenitor Nicholas Kegg. **BETH A. WALTERS** Seventh great granddaughter of progenitor Nicholas Kegg. **BRENDA LEE WALTERS** [6271] (1966 – 2021) daughter of Robert and Patty (Mellott) Walters married Darren Roy Hanlin. Brenda was employed as a purchasing agent for an electric company. **CHANDLER WALTERS** Seventh great granddaughter of progenitor Nicholas Kegg.

WALTMAN

INFANT WALTMAN (1906 – 1906) Fourth great grandson of progenitor Nicholas Kegg.

WALTMIRE

CODY DANIEL WALTMIRE Sixth great grandson of progenitor Nicholas Kegg. **TANNER LEWIS WALTMIRE** Sixth great grandson of progenitor Nicholas Kegg.

WALTON

GEORGE E. WALTON [6272] (1927 – 1988) son of George and Carmoleta (Cagg) Walton, married Mary J. Murray. George was a veteran of WWII having served in the U. S. Navy. **JEAN CATHERINE WALTON** [6272A] (1933 – 2014) daughter of George and Carmelita (Cagg) Walton married Dempsey T. Sharp with whom she was mother of (3). Jean was employed by the Board of Education and after returning to Nelsonville in 1979, she set a true example by completing her associate degree in nursing at Hocking Technical College at the age of 51. Thereafter, she worked for the State of Ohio for several years as an RN. She was an expert cook and baker, and a professional grade seamstress. She was a loving and giving individual who touched the lives of all who knew her. **JOELLEN WALTON** Fifth great granddaughter of progenitor Nicholas Kegg.

WALZ

KYLIE WALZ Seventh great granddaughter of progenitor Nicholas Kegg.

WAMPLER

AURORA GWENDALYN WAMPLER Seventh great granddaughter of progenitor Nicholas Kegg. **DOLLIE ELAYNE WAMPLER** Fifth great granddaughter of progenitor Nicholas Kegg. **DURWARD EARL WAMPLER** [6272B] aka "Woody" (1945 – 2017) son of James and Violet (Graham) Wampler married Sylvia Cordova with whom he was father of (3). Woody joined the Army where he served in the Vietnam War. After returning home he worked as a cook in several states. Later, he started his life long career as an auto mechanic. He loved to go fishing and bowling, He was a volunteer firefighter for the City of Tucumcari for 20 years. Woody always had a smile on his face, he had such a big heart he would give you the shirt off of his back if you needed it. He opened his house to his nephews and raised them as his own. Woody loved life, and a good joke. **MARCOS E. WAMPLER** Sixth great grandson of progenitor Nicholas Kegg. **MICHAEL R. WAMPLER** Sixth great grandson of progenitor Nicholas Kegg. **MIRANDA WAMPLER** Sixth great granddaughter of progenitor Nicholas Kegg. **TITUS LEX WAMPLER** Seventh great grandson of progenitor Nicholas Kegg.

[6271] Merritt Funeral Home Spring Hill, Florida [6272] Athens County, OH Obit book obtained by D. Sue Dible [6272A] Athens Messenger (OH) May 24, 2014 [6272B] Eastern New Mexico News Aug. 2, 2017

WANDEL

DAWN WANDEL Sixth great granddaughter of progenitor Nicholas Kegg.
ELIZABETH WANDEL aka "Beth" Sixth great granddaughter of progenitor Nicholas Kegg.
SHELLY WANDEL Sixth great granddaughter of progenitor Nicholas Kegg.

WANLESS

JOSEPH S. WANLESS (1982 – 1982) son of Robert and Elenora (Crissman) Wanless.

WARD

BENJAMIN ZACHARY WARD Seventh great grandson of progenitor Nicholas Kegg. **DEMERRILL BETH WARD** Sixth great granddaughter of progenitor Nicholas Kegg. **JEREMY WARD** [6273] Sixth great grandson of progenitor Nicholas Kegg. **JOHN CARTER WARD** [6273] (1939 – 2021) son of Herman and Edith (Grose) Ward married Joan Ann (Rauchschwalbe) ward with whom he was father of (2). John worked for the United States Postal Service for many years. He was a self-taught small engine mechanic and enjoyed repairing lawn mowers for his many friends and neighbors. John enjoyed hunting, fishing, and practicing taxidermy. **JOHN CARTER WARD II** Sixth great grandson of progenitor Nicholas Kegg. **JOHN CARTER WARD III** Seventh great grandson of progenitor Nicholas Kegg. **LARISSA WARD** Eighth great granddaughter of progenitor Nicholas Kegg. **NANCY JOAN WARD** [6274] daughter of John and Joan Ann (Rauchschwalbe) Ward married Gerhard Braatz. Nancy was employed by MCI. **OLIVER REILEY WARD** Sixth great grandson of progenitor Nicholas Kegg. **REBECCA KATHLEEN WARD** Eighth great granddaughter of progenitor Nicholas Kegg. **SPENCER CAMERON WARD** Seventh great grandson of progenitor Nicholas Kegg. **TATE ALLEN WARD** Seventh great grandson of progenitor Nicholas Kegg. **TRISIAN ELIZABETH WARD** Seventh great granddaughter of progenitor Nicholas Kegg.

WARE

ALEXIS WARE Sixth great granddaughter of progenitor Nicholas Kegg. **ANTON WARE** Sixth great grandson of progenitor Nicholas Kegg. **CAROLINE JULIA WARE** [6275] (1950 – 2020) daughter of Lester Morris and Mildred Caroline (Knouf) Ware became another statistic in the global catastrophe of this COVID-19 pandemic disease. She was graced with a peaceful transition, not the prolonged suffering of so many taken by COVID. Caroline knew the joys of life along with the sorrows. She loved the adventure of food, and every meal was a source of happiness. Knowing that pizza was a favorite. Caroline was an exemplary example of truly loving and non-judgmental. **DANIEL LESTER WARE** Fifth great grandson of progenitor Nicholas Kegg. **INFANT WARE** daughter of Caroline Ware, adopted at birth by parents who give thanks to Caroline for the gift of life.

WAREHIME

ADA WAREHIME Seventh great granddaughter of progenitor Nicholas Kegg.

WARNER

BAYLEE WARNER Seventh great granddaughter of progenitor Nicholas Kegg.
JACK Q. WARNER Seventh great grandson of progenitor Nicholas Kegg.
JOAN CAROL WARNER Fourth great granddaughter of progenitor Nicholas Kegg.

[6273] Hines-Rinaldi Funeral Home (MD) [6274] The Frederick News-Post (MD) Sep. 15, 1998 [6275] Walla Walla Union-Bulletin (WA) Aug 2, 2020

JUDITH ANNE WARNER [6276] (1931 – 2018) daughter of Gordon and Maybelle (Scharmen) Warner, married Merrill Ray Spencer with whom she was mother of (3). Judy was a teacher in the Royal Oak School District. She was a long-time, active member of Royal Oak Missionary Church, serving as a deaconess and choir member. She led the Pioneer Girls' Club for many years, teaching young girls to follow Jesus, have fun, camp, sing ridiculous songs, and make a portable stove out of cardboard, wax and a tuna can. She later served as the church librarian and gardener. She found great joy in leading neighborhood Bible studies wherever she lived. Judy was a skilled seamstress, she taught all her children to use her sewing machine, even letting them turn old jeans into marble bags. Her attention to detail and precision allowed her to graduate from sewing skirts and tops for the kids to a beautiful hand-beaded bridal gown and bridesmaid dresses. Her skill and drive to create helped her children learn not to be afraid to dive into a new project of any nature. **JUNE EMMA WARNER** Fourth great granddaughter of progenitor Nicholas Kegg. **KYLE WARNER** Seventh great grandson of progenitor Nicholas Kegg.

WARNICK

DURAE ANNE WARNICK Sixth great granddaughter of progenitor Nicholas Kegg. **KIMI KAI WARNICK** Sixth great granddaughter of progenitor Nicholas Kegg. **MARVIN WILLARD WARNICK** [6277] (1940 – 2020) aka "Marzie" son of Marvin and Susan (Turner) Warnick married Cappi Swoboda with whom he was father of (4). Later he married Laurie Ellen. Marzie spent most of his career in bread sales at the Schmidt Baking Company. He was also the owner and operator of his karaoke company, "All In Fun". **ROBYN WARNICK** Sixth great granddaughter of progenitor Nicholas Kegg. **SEAN PAUL WARNICK** Sixth great grandson of progenitor Nicholas Kegg.

WARNOCK

CAITLIN WARNOCK Sixth great granddaughter of progenitor Nicholas Kegg.
GRADY WARNOCK Sixth great grandson of progenitor Nicholas Kegg.

WARREN

ASHTON WARREN Eighth great grandson of progenitor Nicholas Kegg. **CHASITY WARREN** Eighth great granddaughter of progenitor Nicholas Kegg. **GAIL L. WARREN** Seventh great granddaughter of progenitor Nicholas Kegg. **JACKI LYNN WARREN** Seventh great granddaughter of progenitor Nicholas Kegg. **KELLY SUSAN WARREN** [6278] (1960 -2020) daughter of Jack and Marylynn (Arrants) Warren was always in motion. Kelly was both energetic and accident prone. In 8th grade, Kelly got hooked on running. As an 80 lb 4'1" High school freshman she was knocked down and stepped on at her first cross country meet. She got up and finished second. She went on to become captain of the track and cross-country teams. She won a scholarship to Spokane C.C. She is in the Hall of Fame at both schools. She ran countless 5 and 10 k races and several marathons over the decades. Kelly loved to travel. She explored Northern Europe, Hawaii and North America. She loved to jump into her red jeep and hit the back roads and blue highways. Checking out the sights, fairs, festivals and funky restaurants. Kelly worked in insurance, manufacturing, flower delivery and at the Library for the Blind. But her favorite job was at the Department of Natural Resources. That's where she got to use her encyclopedic knowledge of Washington State. Volunteering was a big part of Kelly's retirement. She worked art fairs, plant and airplane festivals and anywhere she could be of use. An avid reader, Kelly knew the location of every Little Free Library in the city. **KRISTIAAN WARREN** Sixth great granddaughter of progenitor Nicholas Kegg. **STEVE WARREN** Seventh great granddaughter of progenitor Nicholas Kegg.

[6276] Kinsey-Garrett Funeral Homes, Inc., MI [6277] Baltimore Sun (MD) Nov. 6, 2020, obtained by D. Sue Dible [6278] Evergreen Funeral Home & Cemetery, WA

WARSING

ALICE GEORGINE WARSING Fifth great granddaughter of progenitor Nicholas Kegg.
ELSIE WARSING Fifth great granddaughter of progenitor Nicholas Kegg.
JOHN NELSON WARSING Fifth great grandson of progenitor Nicholas Kegg
JULIA WARSING Fifth great granddaughter of progenitor Nicholas Kegg.
LYDA WARSING Fifth great granddaughter of progenitor Nicholas Kegg.
MARGARET WARSING Fifth great granddaughter of progenitor Nicholas Kegg.
MARTHA WARSING Fifth great granddaughter of progenitor Nicholas Kegg.
MILDRED WARSING Fifth great granddaughter of progenitor Nicholas Kegg.
PATRICIA WARSING Fifth great granddaughter of progenitor Nicholas Kegg.
SUSAN WARSING Fifth great granddaughter of progenitor Nicholas Kegg.

WASHABAUGH

DONALD E. WASHABAUGH Sixth great grandson of progenitor Nicholas Kegg.
KAYLA DANIELLE WASHABAUGH Seventh great granddaughter of progenitor Nicholas Kegg.
LORI ANN WASHABAUGH Sixth great granddaughter of progenitor Nicholas Kegg.
LYNN ALISON WASHABAUGH Sixth great granddaughter of progenitor Nicholas Kegg.
NICHOLAS WASHABAUGH Seventh great grandson of progenitor Nicholas Kegg.

WASHBURN

CHLOE WASHBURN Sixth great granddaughter of progenitor Nicholas Kegg.

WASKO

BRANDON WASKO Sixth great grandson of progenitor Nicholas Kegg.
STACEY WASCO Sixth great granddaughter of progenitor Nicholas Kegg.

WASSAMIRE

ASHLEY MARIE WASSAMIRE Seventh great granddaughter of progenitor Nicholas Kegg.

WATERS

AMANDA WATERS Sixth great granddaughter of progenitor Nicholas Kegg.
BRITTANY WATERS Sixth great granddaughter of progenitor Nicholas Kegg.
KAITLYN WATERS Sixth great granddaughter of progenitor Nicholas Kegg.
NICHOLAS WATERS Sixth great grandson of progenitor Nicholas Kegg.

WATKIN

MICHAEL R. WATKIN Seventh great grandson of progenitor Nicholas Kegg.

WATKINS

D. J. WATKINS Seventh great grandson of progenitor Nicholas Kegg.   **DOMINIC WATKINS** Seventh great grandson of progenitor Nicholas Kegg.   **JASON WATKINS** Seventh great grandson of progenitor Nicholas Kegg.   **JAYSON WATKINS** Seventh great grandson of progenitor Nicholas Kegg.   **JEFFREY WATKINS** Sixth great grandson of progenitor Nicholas Kegg.

KAYDEN WATKINS Seventh great grandson of progenitor Nicholas Kegg. **KHLOE WATKINS** Seventh great granddaughter of progenitor Nicholas Kegg. **NATHANIEL COLBY WATKINS** Sixth great grandson of progenitor Nicholas Kegg.

WATSON

DYLAN JAMES WATSON [6280] (1993 – 2016) son of Randy Allsup and Christie Watson was found dead after crashing his truck into the trailer of a semi turning onto a highway. Dylan was working in an apprentice program with Local 234 as a heavy machine operator. He loved being outdoors. He was an avid shooter, where he spent many days hunting and fishing with family and friends. He lived his short life to the fullest. His greatest attribute was his ability to make friends with anyone in any situation, never meeting a stranger. **JAMES ROBERT WATSON** [6281] (1921 – 2004) aka "Jim," son of James and Bessie (Galvin) Watson, married Dorothy Uriz with whom he was fathr of (1). Jim served in the U.S. Marine Corps during World War II. He was a self-employed Realtor for 50 years, with Jim Watson Real Estate, and had previously owned Jim Watson Furniture store in Marysville for several years. Before going into business, he was a football coach and P.E. instructor at the College of the Pacific. He played one season, 1945, in the NFL with the Washington Redskins. He was a charter member and president of Kiwanis Club of Marysville and a member of the Beale Military Affairs Association and the University of the Pacific Alumni Association. He was the recipient of several awards including Kiwanian of the Year, the United Way Pedro Award and the American Red Cross Three Rivers Chapter Humanitarian Award. **JIMETTE KATHLEEN WATSON** [6282] (1946 – 1999) daughter of James and Dorothy (Uriz) Watson, married Ronald Laverne Ward. **WILLIAM ANTHONY WATSON** [6283] (1926 – 1944) son of James and Bessie (Galvin) Watson a senior student in the Marysville Union High School, died as the result of an automobile wreck.

WATTIGNY

CODY WATTIGNY Eighth great grandson of progenitor Nicholas Kegg.
STEPHANIE WATTIGNY Eighth great granddaughter of progenitor Nicholas Kegg.

WATTS

CARLYN WATTS Seventh great granddaughter of progenitor Nicholas Kegg.
COURTNEY WATTS Seventh great granddaughter of progenitor Nicholas Kegg.

WATTSON

SAMANTHA E. WATTSON Sixth great granddaughter of progenitor Nicholas Kegg.

WAY

GEORGE HARRY WAY [6283A] (1921 – 1950) son of Harry and Beatrice (Diehl) Way. George enlisted in the U. S. Army January 13, 1949. He trained at Fort Knox, Ky., and Ft. Lewis, Wash., and was sent overseas in August 1950. The parents received their last letter from the PFC soldier 138th REG., August 27, 1950. He was reported killed in action by a Defense Department cablegram November 29, 1950.
LOIS JEAN WAY Fifth great granddaughter of progenitor Nicholas Kegg.
MISTY DAWN WAYBRIGHT [6283B] (1984 – 2002) daughter of John and Tara (Hershberger) Waybright enjoyed playing softball and basketball. Misty was an artist and wrote poetry.

[6280] Johnson Family Funeral Home & Cremation Services, IA [6281] Appeal Democrat (CA) May 11, 2004 [6282] The Sacramento Bee (CA) Jan 14, 1968 [6283] Lincoln News Messenger (CA) March 2, 1944. Transcribed by KKM [6283A] p.1 & 2 - Bedford Gazette (PA) August 31, 1951

WAYBRIGHT

RANDY WAYBRIGHT Seventh great grandson of progenitor Nicholas Kegg.

WEAR

ALANNAH WEAR Seventh great granddaughter of progenitor Nicholas Kegg. **ALEX CONOR WEAR** (1992 – 1992) son of Michael and Doris (Price) Wear. **CATHERINE WEAR** aka "Cathy" Fifth great granddaughter of progenitor Nicholas Kegg. **CODY WEAR** Seventh great grandson of progenitor Nicholas Kegg. **DOROTHY JEAN WEAR** aka "Dottie" Fifth great granddaughter of progenitor Nicholas Kegg. **DOUGLAS S. WEAR** Sixth great grandson of progenitor Nicholas Kegg. **FLORABELLE AMANDA WEAR** Sixth great granddaughter of progenitor Nicholas Kegg. **JANE E. WEAR** Fifth great granddaughter of progenitor Nicholas Kegg. **JEFFREY C. WEAR** Sixth great grandson of progenitor Nicholas Kegg. **JOHN WAYNE WEAR** Sixth great grandson of progenitor Nicholas Kegg. **LELAND WALTER WEAR** Sixth great grandson of progenitor Nicholas Kegg. **MARK ALAN WEAR** Sixth great grandson of progenitor Nicholas Kegg. **MATTHEW ALVAN WEAR** Sixth great grandson of progenitor Nicholas Kegg. **SAMUEL DOWNING WEAR** Sixth great grandson of progenitor Nicholas Kegg. **WENDELL B. WEAR** Fifth great grandson of progenitor Nicholas Kegg.

WEAVER

AMY WEAVER Fifth great granddaughter of progenitor Nicholas Kegg. **CHARLES WEAVER** Sixth great grandson of progenitor Nicholas Kegg. **DEBBIE WEAVER** Sixth great granddaughter of progenitor Nicholas Kegg. **DIXIE LEE WEAVER** Sixth great granddaughter of progenitor Nicholas Kegg. **FRANK P. WEAVER** Sixth great grandson of progenitor Nicholas Kegg. **HANNA JANE WEAVER** Seventh great granddaughter of progenitor Nicholas Kegg. **HARRISON S. WEAVER** Seventh great grandson of progenitor Nicholas Kegg. **JAMES EUGENE WEAVER** [6283C] (1928 – 2001) son of Thomas and Mabel (Hinchman) Weaver married Eleanor Jean Rinehart with whom he was father of (3). James was a U.S. Marine Corps veteran and a member of the Marine Corps League. For many years, he worked in the Morgantown community as a car salesman. He began his career with Layman Motors, later was employed with Richter Volkswagen, Oldsmobile, and then retired from Larry Smith Buick. During his career, he was involved in many local civic groups in the Morgantown area. **JASON WEAVER** Sixth great grandson of progenitor Nicholas Kegg. **JEB WEAVER** Sixth great grandson of progenitor Nicholas Kegg. **JIM WEAVER** Sixth great grandson of progenitor Nicholas Kegg. **JOHN S. WEAVER** Sixth great grandson of progenitor Nicholas Kegg. **JOSH DUANE WEAVER** Sixth great grandson of progenitor Nicholas Kegg. **JULIANNE R. WEAVER** Seventh great granddaughter of progenitor Nicholas Kegg. **KASEY LANCE WEAVER** Seventh great grandson of progenitor Nicholas Kegg. **KEVIN LEE WEAVER** Sixth great grandson of progenitor Nicholas Kegg. **KOLBY LEVI WEAVER** Seventh great grandson of progenitor Nicholas Kegg. **LAURA WEAVER** Fifth great granddaughter of progenitor Nicholas Kegg. **LILA KRISTIN WEAVER** Sixth great granddaughter of progenitor Nicholas Kegg. **LINDSEY WEAVER** Sixth great granddaughter of progenitor Nicholas Kegg. **LYNDA WEAVER** Fifth great granddaughter of progenitor Nicholas Kegg. **MADISYN LYNNE WEAVER** Seventh great granddaughter of progenitor Nicholas Kegg. **MAX ROBERT WEAVER** Sixth great grandson of progenitor Nicholas Kegg. **MICHAEL WEAVER** Fifth great grandson of progenitor Nicholas Kegg. **MILDRED ELIZABETH WEAVER** [6284] (1966 – 2002) daughter of Donald and Mildred (Warsing) Weaver was employed as a claim's processor for First Health in Moon Township. She was engaged to marry Timothy Culley when she sustained injuries in an automobile accident that took her life.

[6283B] Johnstown Tribune Democrat (PA) May 14, 2002 [6283C] Dominion Post (WV) Dec 5, 2003 [6284] Pittsburgh Post-Gazette (PA) July 24, 2002

NICHOLAS L. WEAVER Fifth great grandson of progenitor Nicholas Kegg.
PATRICK WEAVER Fifth great grandson of progenitor Nicholas Kegg.
PRESTON JACK WEAVER Seventh great grandson of progenitor Nicholas Kegg.
ROBERT H. WEAVER Fifth great grandson of progenitor Nicholas Kegg.
RUSSELL L. WEAVER Fifth great grandson of progenitor Nicholas Kegg.
SAMANTHA ROMA WEAVER Sixth great granddaughter of progenitor Nicholas Kegg.
SARAH CATHERINE WEAVER (1906 – 1944) daughter of Eugene and Jennie (Turner) Weaver
SCOTT DEAN WEAVER Seventh great grandson of progenitor Nicholas Kegg.
SHAWN WEAVER Sixth great grandson of progenitor Nicholas Kegg.
SPENCER DALE WEAVER Seventh great grandson of progenitor Nicholas Kegg.
SUSAN M. WEAVER Sixth great granddaughter of progenitor Nicholas Kegg.
THOMAS FROST WEAVER Fifth great grandson of progenitor Nicholas Kegg.
THOMAS FROST WEAVER (1901 – 1976) son of Eugene and Jennie (Turner) Weaver, married Mabel Balyss Hinchman with whom he was father of (4).
TOM J. WEAVER Sixth great grandson of progenitor Nicholas Kegg.

WEAVERLING

BARRY S. WEAVERLING Sixth great grandson of progenitor Nicholas Kegg.
CHASE THOMAS WEAVERLING Eighth great grandson of progenitor Nicholas Kegg.
LARRY A. WEAVERLING Sixth great grandson of progenitor Nicholas Kegg.
MICHAEL J. WEAVERLING Sixth great grandson of progenitor Nicholas Kegg.
RANDALL THOMAS WEAVERLING Seventh great grandson of progenitor Nicholas Kegg.
THOMAS CHRISTOPHER WEAVERLING Seventh great grandson of progenitor Nicholas Kegg.
TIMOTHY CHARLES WEAVERLING Seventh great grandson of progenitor Nicholas Kegg.

WEBB

AARON WEBB Eighth great grandson of progenitor Nicholas Kegg.
ALYSSA WEBB Ninth great granddaughter of progenitor Nicholas Kegg.
BRODY AUSTIN WEBB Seventh great grandson of progenitor Nicholas Kegg.
CHASE WEBB Seventh great grandson of progenitor Nicholas Kegg.
HAYDAN WEBB Seventh great grandson of progenitor Nicholas Kegg.
JASON M. WEBB aka "Jay" Sixth great grandson of progenitor Nicholas Kegg.
JEREMY JOSEPH WEBB Sixth great grandson of progenitor Nicholas Kegg.
LEXIS WEBB Ninth great granddaughter of progenitor Nicholas Kegg.
MADISON WEBB aka "Maddie", Ninth great granddaughter of progenitor Nicholas Kegg.
OLIVIA WEBB Seventh great granddaughter of progenitor Nicholas Kegg.
TAYLOR WEBB Eighth great granddaughter of progenitor Nicholas Kegg.

WEBER

KAITLYN A. WEBER Sixth great granddaughter of progenitor Nicholas Kegg.
TYLER S. WEBER Sixth great grandson of progenitor Nicholas Kegg.

WEDEL

DELLA WEDEL Seventh great granddaughter of progenitor Nicholas Kegg.
ZOEY ARDEN WEDEL Seventh great granddaughter of progenitor Nicholas Kegg.

WEDGE

COLE WEDGE Seventh great grandson of progenitor Nicholas Kegg.
KENNA WEDGE Seventh great granddaughter of progenitor Nicholas Kegg.

WEDLOCK

AISLYN DENAE WEDLOCK Eighth great granddaughter of progenitor Nicholas Kegg.
BRIAN WEDLOCK Seventh great grandson of progenitor Nicholas Kegg.

WEEDA

BRIAN K. WEEDA Sixth great grandson of progenitor Nicholas Kegg. **GARY DEAN WEEDA** Sixth great grandson of progenitor Nicholas Kegg. **KEITH DEAN WEEDA** Fifth great grandson of progenitor Nicholas Kegg. **KENNETH PAUL WEEDA** [6284A] aka "Kenny" (1936 – 2022) son of Paul and Helen (Swank) Weeda, married Marilyn Minnick with whom he was father of (5). Growing up, Kenny enjoyed riding horses and helping his dad farm. Kenny loved farming and spent the rest of his life raising cattle and hogs. Specifically, purebred Simmental cattle and bulls. One of Kenny's hobbies was showing cattle and helping his kids with 4-H projects. The family kept busy showing cattle, traveling to cattle shows on the weekends. Kenny enjoyed watching both his children and grandchildren grow and teaching them the farm life. One year, they had 17 bottle calves that brought delight to his grandchildren. **MARY ANN WEEDA** Sixth great granddaughter of progenitor Nicholas Kegg. **MICHELLE LEA WEEDA** Sixth great granddaughter of progenitor Nicholas Kegg. **PAUL WEEDA** Sixth great grandson of progenitor Nicholas Kegg. **SANDRA LYNN WEEDA** aka "Sandy", Sixth great granddaughter of progenitor Nicholas Kegg. **TERRY PAUL WEEDA** Sixth great grandson of progenitor Nicholas Kegg.

WEEKLEY

CHERI WEEKLEY Sixth great granddaughter of progenitor Nicholas Kegg
HEIDI WEEKLEY Sixth great granddaughter of progenitor Nicholas Kegg.

WEEKS

BARBARA MAE WEEKS [6285] (1921 – 2001) daughter of Luther and Frances (Sidders) Weeks married Robert Thompson. Later, she married Victor Carl Fisher with whom she was mother of (2). **CAROL ANN WEEKS** Sixth great granddaughter of progenitor Nicholas Kegg. **DAVID LEE WEEKS** Sixth great grandson of progenitor Nicholas Kegg. **DAVID WEEKS** Seventh great grandson of progenitor Nicholas Kegg. **DEBRA WEEKS** Seventh great granddaughter of progenitor Nicholas Kegg. **DENNIS W WEEKS** Sixth great grandson of progenitor Nicholas Kegg. **DONNA WEEKS** Seventh great granddaughter of progenitor Nicholas Kegg. **EDWARD RICHARD WEEKS** [6286] (1918 – 2003) aka "Dick", son of Luther and Frances (Sidders) Weeks married Anna Elaine McPherson with whom he was father of (8). Dick owned and operated AA Plumbing and Heating. **EVAN WEEKS** Seventh great grandson of progenitor Nicholas Kegg. **GARY CHARLES WEEKS** Sixth great grandson of progenitor Nicholas Kegg. **KEVIN WEEKS** Seventh great grandson of progenitor Nicholas Kegg. **LARRY CURTIS WEEKS** Sixth great grandson of progenitor Nicholas Kegg. **MERWIN DAROLD WEEKS** Sixth great grandson of progenitor Nicholas Kegg. **MERWIN RONALD WEEKS** [6287] (1916 – 2003) aka "Buck", son of Luther and Frances (Sidders) Weeks married Charlette Lilli White with whom

---

[6284A] Mount Ayr Record News (IA) May 18, 2022, obtained by D. Sue Dible [6285] The Kansas City Times (MO) Dec 7, 1982 [6286] Idaho Statesman (ID) Jan. 4, 2010 [6287] Find A Grave Memorial # 119835039 obituary.

he was father of (2). Buck operated B & H Furniture. Following the 1947 tornado, Buck built houses for the Red Cross and later operated Buck's Grocery. He owned and operated Buck's Electric for a time, until he was employed by the Town of Fort Supply. Together with his son Buck owned and operated Weeks' Furniture for a time until selling. Buck was an avid bowler and was a lifetime member of the Bowling Hall of Fame. **MICHAEL WEEKS** Seventh great grandson of progenitor Nicholas Kegg. **RANDY MARK WEEKS** (1955 – 1957) son of Edward and Anne (McPherson) Weeks fell into an irrigation canal and drown. **RICHARD WESLEY WEEKS** [6288] (1939 – 2015) aka "Dickie" son of Edward and Anne (McPherson) Weeks married Bonnie Montgomery with whom he was father of (3). Later he married Meta Martin. Having served in the U.S. Marine Corp., Dickie worked as a plumber all over the Pacific Northwest and Alaska. He was an avid outdoorsman and spent much of his free time hunting, fishing, and playing cribbage and blackjack. **RONALD DWIGHT WEEKS** [6289] (1936 – 2020) aka "R.D.", son of Merwin and Charlette (White) Weeks married Verda Rosendale with whom he was father of (4). Later, he married Patricia Patton. R. D. worked as a route salesman in Kansas and Oklahoma, and he also sold real estate in Wichita, Kansas. R.D. retired from Lance Inc. in Bethany, Oklahoma. **SCOTT WEEKS** Seventh great grandson of progenitor Nicholas Kegg. **SHANNON WEEKS** Sixth great granddaughter of progenitor Nicholas Kegg. **SHELLEY WEEKS** Seventh great granddaughter of progenitor Nicholas Kegg. **STONEY LEE WEEKS** [6290] (1970 – 2021) aka "Stoneman" son of Larry and Mary Ann (Sayko) Weeks was father of (3). Anyone who ever knew Stoney knew he had the biggest heart; his joy was in helping others. It didn't matter the hour nor the expense, Stoney was only a phone call away. In Garden City he was nothing short of a local hero. Stoney was born with Cystic Fibrosis, despite his struggles he still enjoyed life to the fullest. During adolescence Stoney had many friends, this carried into adulthood. Throughout the day people were knocking on his door coming to visit. There was never a dull moment when hanging with The Stoneman. His contagious laughter and humor kept even the most difficult moments lighthearted. After his barn fire, when calling the hospital friends would be greeted with "Thank you for calling the barbecued burn center this is Stoney." Depending on the day or season you could find him working at the top of a tree, on a backhoe or in a snowplow. Stoney enjoyed camping, fishing, hunting, spending time with friends and occasionally gambling. He was a collector of things such as Budweiser memorabilia. For many years Stoney helped manage the family business Tammy's Riverside Park (a mobile home park). Despite having the potential to make money we often saw little profit because Stoney could not turn anyone away, even if they couldn't pay. **TERRI WEEKS** Seventh great grandchild of progenitor Nicholas Kegg.

WEHRLE

CLEORA ETHEL WEHRLE (1909 – 1990) daughter of Chris and Lillie (Laird) Wehrle, married Otto Bennett Hutchison with whom she was mother of (1). **FERN MILDRED LAVON WEHRLE** [6291] (1902 – 1978) daughter of Chris and Lillie (Laird) Wehrle, married Sherman Rex Sickels with whom she was mother of (8). When a young woman Fern confessed her faith in Christ and was baptized by Minister Julius Clark of the Church of Christ. Fern and her husband spent their lives together farming. **FRANK MERLIND WEHRLE** [6292] (1907 – 1986) son of Chris and Lillie (Laird) Wehrle, married Hazel Waive Cole. Frank was a farmer. **WILMA MAUDE WEHRLE** [6293] (1921 – 1985) daughter of Chris and Lillie (Laird) Wehrle, married Clarence Robert Owens with whom she was mother of (2).

WEICHT

CORY WEICHT Seventh great grandson of progenitor Nicholas Kegg.
GABRIEL JOSHUA WEICHT Eighth great grandson of progenitor Nicholas Kegg.
EMMA WEICHT Eighth great granddaughter of progenitor Nicholas Kegg.

[6288] Idaho Statesman (ID) Feb. 19, 2015 [6289] Enid Buzz (OK) Feb 11, 2020 [6290] Idaho Statesman (ID) Nov. 21, 2021 [6291] Mount Ayr Record-News (IA) Apr 1978, contributed by Sharon R. Becker [6292] GenealogyBuff Ringgold County, Iowa Obituary Collection - 40 [6293] Leon Journal-Reporter (IA) Aug 22, 2007

ISAAC WEICHT Seventh great grandson of progenitor Nicholas Kegg.
IVY LORAINE WEICHT Eighth great granddaughter of progenitor Nicholas Kegg.
JOSHUA E. WEICHT Seventh great grandson of progenitor Nicholas Kegg.
LILLIAN JANELLE WEICHT aka "Lily," Eighth great granddaughter of progenitor Nicholas Kegg.
LINDA J. WEICHT Fifth great granddaughter of progenitor Nicholas Kegg.
NAOMI WEICHT Seventh great granddaughter of progenitor Nicholas Kegg.
PEGGY J. WEICHT Fifth great granddaughter of progenitor Nicholas Kegg.
RICHARD J. WEICHT Fifth great grandson of progenitor Nicholas Kegg.
VICTOR L. WEICHT Fifth great grandson of progenitor Nicholas Kegg.

WEIDLEY

JOHN WEIDLEY Seventh great grandson of progenitor Nicholas Kegg.
JOHN WEIDLEY Eighth great grandson of progenitor Nicholas Kegg.
MICHELE WEIDLEY Seventh great granddaughter of progenitor Nicholas Kegg.
RACHEL WEIDLEY Eighth great granddaughter of progenitor Nicholas Kegg.

WEIMAN

ANDY WEIMAN Sixth great grandson of progenitor Nicholas Kegg.

WEIMER

AMY WEIMER Seventh great granddaughter of progenitor Nicholas Kegg.
ANGELA C. WEIMER Sixth great granddaughter of progenitor Nicholas Kegg.
HEATHER WEIMER Seventh great granddaughter of progenitor Nicholas Kegg.
STACIE MARIE WEIMER Sixth great granddaughter of progenitor Nicholas Kegg.

WEINDLING

JESSICA WEINDLING Sixth great granddaughter of progenitor Nicholas Kegg.
STEPHEN WEINDLING Sixth great grandson of progenitor Nicholas Kegg.

WEIR

VIOLA H. WEIR (1865 – 1933) daughter of John and Mary (Kegg) Weir, married Thomas J. Korns.

WEIS

ALLISON RENEE WEIS Eighth great granddaughter of progenitor Nicholas Kegg.
ASHLEY NICOLE WEIS Eighth great granddaughter of progenitor Nicholas Kegg.
CHRISTINA WEIS Seventh great granddaughter of progenitor Nicholas Kegg.
DONALD EUGENE WEIS Seventh great grandson of progenitor Nicholas Kegg.

WEISENBERGE

JINNIE LEA WEISENBERGE Sixth great granddaughter of progenitor Nicholas Kegg
RENNIE M. WEISENBERGE Sixth great granddaughter of progenitor Nicholas Kegg.

WEISS

HARRY DAVID WEISS Seventh great grandson of progenitor Nicholas Kegg.
SARAH ANN WEISS Seventh great granddaughter of progenitor Nicholas Kegg.

WEISSER

ALEX WEISSER Sixth great grandson of progenitor Nicholas Kegg.

WELD

EVAN ROBERT WELD Sixth great grandson of progenitor Nicholas Kegg.
HUNTER LEE WELD Sixth great grandson of progenitor Nicholas Kegg.
SIERRA RENEA WELD Sixth great granddaughter of progenitor Nicholas Kegg.

WELLER

PHILIP VANALSTYNE WELLER Sixth great grandson of progenitor Nicholas Kegg.

WELLING

JOHN T. WELLING Sixth great grandson of progenitor Nicholas Kegg.
MARK D. WELLING Sixth great grandson of progenitor Nicholas Kegg.
ROBERT L. WELLING Sixth great grandson of progenitor Nicholas Kegg.
SANDRA J. WELLING Sixth great granddaughter of progenitor Nicholas Kegg.

WELLMAN

BARRY WELLMAN Sixth great grandson of progenitor Nicholas Kegg.
BILL WELLMAN Sixth great grandson of progenitor Nicholas Kegg.
STACEY WELLMAN Sixth great granddaughter of progenitor Nicholas Kegg.
VALERIE WELLMAN Sixth great granddaughter of progenitor Nicholas Kegg.

WELLS

ANITA WELLS Sixth great granddaughter of progenitor Nicholas Kegg. **ANNAMARIE WELLS** Seventh great granddaughter of progenitor Nicholas Kegg. **BETTY JOAN WELLS** [6293A] (1929 – 2008) daughter of Richard and Mabel (Ross) Matheny Wells married twice, first to Joseph Misleh with whom she was mother of (3). Later, she married Troy Bell. Betty's world revolved around the many daycare children she cared for. They were her passion, and she gave many a loving head start in life. Her other passion was a gift to the community. **BRENDA JOYCE WELLS** Fifth great granddaughter of progenitor Nicholas Kegg. **BRIAN WELLS** Sixth great grandson of progenitor Nicholas Kegg. **CAILIN WELLS** Sixth great granddaughter of progenitor Nicholas Kegg. **CHARLES ELLSWORTH WELLS** [6293B] aka "Chuck" (1905 – 1981) son of George and Sylvia (Russell) Wells married twice, first to Glenna Mumford Brown and later to Julia Bertha Flannigan. Chuck was the owner and operator of the Oasis on Lagonda Avenue. **CHARLES NEAL WELLS** [6294] (1929 – 1963) son of Willis and Pauline (Crevison) Wells, married Virginia Marie Holub with whom he was father of (3). **CHRISTOPHER B. WELLS** Sixth great grandson of progenitor Nicholas Kegg. **CINDY ROSE WELLS** Sixth great granddaughter of progenitor Nicholas Kegg.

[6293A] Northwest Florida Daily News (FL) Apr 20, 2008 [6293B] Library obituary clipping contributed by D. Sue Dible [6294] p.38- Plain Dealer (OH) April 26, 1963

DARLENE M. WELLS Sixth great granddaughter of progenitor Nicholas Kegg. **DEBORAH WELLS** Sixth great granddaughter of progenitor Nicholas Kegg. **DIANNA WELLS** (1957 – 1957) daughter of Larry and Sandra (Shaffer) Wells. **DUANE MARTIN WELLS** [6294A] (1953 – 2020) son of Willis and Shirley (Decarlo) Wells married Sharon R. Cerny with whom he was father of (1). Duane began his professional life as a racing mechanic, then transitioned into the Building & Contracting industry as a painter. Hard working, and always busy on multiple projects. He had a passion for remodeling his homes and rebuilding cars. Pet lover and Great Dane devotee **DWIGHT MARVIN WELLS** [6295] (1956 – 1994) son of Willis and Shirley (Decarlo) Wells. Dwight worked as a mechanic and in lawn Maintenance. **EDWARD STANLEY GARVIN WELLS** [6296] (1958 – 1996) son of Richard and Darlene (Knight) Wells worked with the Southwest Washington Health District to create a syringe exchange program to help prevent the spread of the HIV virus. Edward had attended community colleges in Vancouver and Seattle, earning his degree from The Evergreen State College. In the early 1990s he lived in Seattle and worked as a lab technician at Providence Medical Center. An advocate for HIV/AIDS programs at the local and state levels, Edward served with the Southwest Washington HIV/AIDS Consortium in the final months of his life. Edward was a Jimmy Buffet and Bette Midler fan. He was also an active computer bulletin board user. **GAYLE WELLS** Sixth great granddaughter of progenitor Nicholas Kegg. **GERALD LEE WELLS** [6297] (1936 – 2019) son of Willis and Pauline (Crevison) Wells married twice; first to Laura Jane Gedeon with whom he was father of (5). Later, he married Annette M. Cox. **GERALDINE WELLS**, aka "Gerry" Fifth great granddaughter of progenitor Nicholas Kegg. **GORDON ADRIEN WELLS** (1924 – 1924) son of Willis and Pauline (Crevison) Wells. **GREGORY WELLS** Sixth great grandson of progenitor Nicholas Kegg. **IBEN KENNETH WELLS** (1904 -?) son of Denton and Mollie (Spring) Wells. **JACOB WELLS** Seventh great grandson of progenitor Nicholas Kegg. **JANICE MAE WELLS** Fifth great granddaughter of progenitor Nicholas Kegg. **JOAN MARIE WELLS** [6298] (1925 – 2005) daughter of Willis and Pauline (Crevison) Wells, married Newton R. Chalfont with whom she was mother of (2). **JOHN WELLS** Sixth great grandson of progenitor Nicholas Kegg. **JUDITH MARIE WELLS** (1942 – 2000) daughter of Ralph and Mabel (Beegle) Wells, married Thomas Carroll with whom she was mother of (1). **KATHY WELLS** Sixth great granddaughter of progenitor Nicholas Kegg. **KERRY J. WELLS** Sixth great granddaughter of progenitor Nicholas Kegg. **KRISTEN WELLS** Sixth great granddaughter of progenitor Nicholas Kegg. **LAURA BELLE WELLS** [6299] (1921 – 1985) daughter of Willis and Pauline (Crevison) Wells, married Richard Seeley Jackson with whom she was mother of (5). **LINDA WELLS** Fifth great granddaughter of progenitor Nicholas Kegg. **LISA WELLS** Sixth great granddaughter of progenitor Nicholas Kegg. **MARILYN JUNE WELLS** [6300] (1932 – 1995) daughter of William and Marguerite (Leeth) Wells, married John C. Boyer with whom she was mother of (5). **MICHAEL RICHARD WELLS** Sixth great grandson of progenitor Nicholas Kegg. **NICHOLAS WELLS** Seventh great grandson of progenitor Nicholas Kegg. **PALINA JEANNE WELLS** (1922 – 1922) daughter of Willis and Pauline (Crevison) Wells. **PAMELA WELLS** Sixth great granddaughter of progenitor Nicholas Kegg. **RICHARD ALLEN WELLS** Seventh great grandson of progenitor Nicholas Kegg. **RICHARD JUNIOR WELLS** [6300A] (1930 – 1977) son of Richard and Mabel (Ross) Wells, married Darlene Kay (Knight) Garvin with whom he was father of (4). Private First-Class Richard J. Wells, United States Army, was held as a Prisoner of War after he was captured during the Korean War on 4 November 1950 and was held until his release on 27 August 1953 after the signing of the Armistice. Richard was a retired staff sergeant who served 20 years in the U.S. Air Force. After he retired from the service, he was the owner and real estate broker of the Wells Family Realty Co. **RICHARD STYLES WELLS** [6301] (1908 – 1958) son of Denton and Mollie (Spring) Wells married twice; first to Mabel Agnes (Ross) Matheny with whom he was father of (2). Later, he married Beulah Elizabeth Casey. Richard was a retired chef. He was employed at several Cleveland hotels before going into the Army in World War II.

[6294A] The Plain Dealer (OH) May 17, 2020, obtained by D. Sue Dible [6295] Tampa Bay Times (FL) June 1, 1994 [6296] The Columbian (Vancouver, WA) Feb 13, 1996 [6297] The Plain Dealer (OH) July 21, 2019, obtained by D. Sue Dible [6298] p.B5 - The Plain Dealer (OH) Oct 25, 2005, obtained by D. Sue Dible [6299] p. 5, col. 1-Kenton Times (OH) Oct 9, 1985, obtained by D. Sue Dible [6300] News-Journal (Mansfield, OH) Nov 28, 1995 [6300A] p.5- Findlay Courier (OH) Oct 15, 1977, contributed by D. Sue Dible

ROSALIND WELLS Fifth great granddaughter of progenitor Nicholas Kegg. **RUSSELL WELLS** Sixth great grandson of progenitor Nicholas Kegg. **SHAFFER WELLS** Seventh great grandson of progenitor Nicholas Kegg. **SHIRLEY WELLS** (1932 – 1981) daughter of Willis and Pauline (Crevison) Wells. **STEPHEN DOUGLAS WELLS** Sixth great grandson of progenitor Nicholas Kegg. **TERRI WELLS** Sixth great grandchild of progenitor Nicholas Kegg. **TIMOTHY LEE WELLS** Sixth great grandson of progenitor Nicholas Kegg. **WILLIAM C. WELLS** Sixth great grandson of progenitor Nicholas Kegg. **WILLIAM H. WELLS** aka "Billy", Fifth great grandson of progenitor Nicholas Kegg. **WILLIAM W. WELLS** [6302] (1911 – 1976) son of Denton and Mollie (Spring) Wells married twice; first to Marguerite Belle Leeth with whom he was father of (2). Later, he married Nora Faye Ernsberger. William was a retired general foreman for the Mansfield Tire and Rubber Co. and a member of the 25 Year Club at Mansfield Tire. He was a member of the First United Methodist Church. **WILLIS DUANE WELLS** [6303] (1934 – 2010) son of Willis and Pauline (Crevison) Wells, married Shirley Lillian DeCarlo with whom he was father of (3).

WELP

BROCK WELP Eighth great grandson of progenitor Nicholas Kegg.
CAMDEN WELP Eighth great grandson of progenitor Nicholas Kegg.
LANDRIE WELP Eighth great grandson of progenitor Nicholas Kegg.

WENDT

BABY WENDT [6304] (1964 – 1964) son of James and Patricia (Lafferty) Wendt.
BONNIE SUE WENDT Fifth great granddaughter of progenitor Nicholas Kegg.

WENSING

EDWARD MICHAEL WENSING Fifth great grandson of progenitor Nicholas Kegg.
JACOB WENSING Sixth great grandson of progenitor Nicholas Kegg.
SEAN M. WENSING Fifth great grandson of progenitor Nicholas Kegg.
SHELBY WENSING Sixth great granddaughter of progenitor Nicholas Kegg.
TYLER WENSING aka "Ty", Sixth great grandson of progenitor Nicholas Kegg.
VINCENT WENSING Sixth great grandson of progenitor Nicholas Kegg.

WERDER

ANN WERDER Sixth great granddaughter of progenitor Nicholas Kegg.
MARY LYNN WERDER Sixth great granddaughter of progenitor Nicholas Kegg.
PAMELA WERDER Sixth great granddaughter of progenitor Nicholas Kegg.

WERT

GARY WAYNE WERT Fifth great grandson of progenitor Nicholas Kegg.
INFANT WERT (1938 – 1938) daughter of Carl and Vivian (Boissenet) Wert.
MARK EDWARD WERT Fifth great grandson of progenitor Nicholas Kegg.
MICHAEL D. WERT Fifth great grandson of progenitor Nicholas Kegg.
STEVEN LYNN WERT Fifth great grandson of progenitor Nicholas Kegg.

[6301] p.2 - Lima News (OH) Oct 15, 1958 [6302] Library obituary clipping obtained by D. Sue Dible [6303] St. Petersburg Times (FL) Oct 9, 2010 [6304] Rootsweb Archiver PABLAIR Area Obits

WERTZ

CHARLES MCCLAY WERTZ [6305, 6306] (1860 – 1941) son of Henry and MaryAnn (May) Wertz married twice; first to Eva Esther Bushey with whom he was father of (2). Later, he married Alida Jane Sheeley Hawk. **EDWIN IRVIN WERTZ** [6307] (1911 – 1913) son of Dr. Irvin and Jane (Gaines) Wertz. **FRANKLIN WERTZ** [6307] (1858 – 1892) son of Henry and MaryAnn (May) Wertz roamed the West working as a carpenter. Later he went into railroading. On Sept. 12, 1889 Frank was in a train accident and was badly injured. **GREGORY B. WERTZ** Sixth great grandson of progenitor Nicholas Kegg. **IRVIN MAY WERTZ** [6308, 6309] (1873 – 1937) son of Henry and and MaryAnn (May) Wertz married twice; first to Jane Price Gaines with whom he was father of (2). Later, he married Ruth D. Barnhart with whom he was father of (1). Dr. Wertz graduated from Dickinson College, Carlisle, Pa., and the University of Maryland medical school. In 1904 Irvin was assistant clinical pathologist in the Maryland General Hospital, Baltimore, Md. and began practicing medicine in 1907. He was elected mayor of Hagerstown in 1933, for a 4-year term. **LAURA ELIZABETH WERTZ** [6310] (1855 – 1912) daughter of Henry and MaryAnn (May) Wertz, married Emanuel Rose with whom she was mother of (3). On the day preceding her death Laura was in a livelier mood then general and visited 10 or 12 of her neighbors. She was in her usual health on retiring at 2 o'clock her husband noticed that she was breathing heavily. He had trouble arousing her. She spoke a few words, then became unconscious and remained in that condition until 4 o'clock when she passed away. **RANDOLPH WERTZ** (1860 -?) son of Henry and MaryAnn (May) Wertz. **SARAH JANE WERTZ** [6310A] (1914 – 2009) daughter of Irvin and Jane (Gaines) Wertz married Frank William Sutterlin with whom she was mother of (2). Sarah received her master's degree in social work at Columbia University in New York. She pursued her profession in child welfare. Sarah served on several boards of directors. **WILLIAM HOWARD WERTZ** [6311] (1866 – 1918) son of Henry and MaryAnn (May) Wertz married Alta Marie and was employed as a blacksmith for Eclipse Stove Co.

WESSELL

JAMES VAUGHN WESSELL Sixth great grandson of progenitor Nicholas Kegg.
JAMES VAUGHN WESSELL Fifth great grandson of progenitor Nicholas Kegg.
LINDA R. WESSELL Fifth great granddaughter of progenitor Nicholas Kegg.

WESSLING

DIEDRICH THOMAS WESSLING Seventh great grandson of progenitor Nicholas Kegg.
DORLEEN WESSLING Seventh great granddaughter of progenitor Nicholas Kegg.
KYLE WESSLING Seventh great grandson of progenitor Nicholas Kegg.

WEST

BRIAN LESLIE WEST [6311A] (1963 – 2011) son of Douglas and Imogene (Waggerman) West married Kari Ann Levenson. **CHRISTOPHER BLAKE WEST** [6311B] (1976 – 1995) son of Steve and Shirley (Rathburn) West. Christopher was a "good Samaritan" trying to help an injured man into his house on New Year's Eve and was shot to death by the man's frightened son. **CODY JO WEST** Sixth great grandson of progenitor Nicholas Kegg. **COLETTE MARIE WEST** Sixth great granddaughter of progenitor Nicholas Kegg. **DEBORAH ANN WEST** Sixth great granddaughter of progenitor Nicholas Kegg. **HELEN J. WEST** Fifth great granddaughter of progenitor Nicholas Kegg.

[6305] Daily Globe (OH) Dec 5, 1927, obtained by D. Sue Dible [6306] Daily Globe (OH) Jan 15, 1951, obtained by D. Sue Dible [6307] The Mail (Hagerstown, MD) June 13, 1913, transcribed by Sanebee [6308] p. 666 - Williams, Thomas J.C.; History of Washington County, Maryland Runk & Titsworth, 1906 [6309] p.10 - Frederick Post (MD) Feb 24, 1937 [6310] Bedford Gazette (PA) March 22, 1912 obtained by Bob Rose [6310A] Bristol Herald Courier (VA) May 17, 2009 [6311] Willard Times (OH) Oct 24, 1918 obtained by R. Reed [6311A] Victoria Advocate (TX) March 28, 2011 [6311B] The Ellensburg Daily Record (WA) Jan 2, 1995/The News Tribune (WA) Jan 4, 1995

JOAN ALICE WEST [(6312)] (1939 – 2017) daughter of Harry and Edith (Ferrell) West married Robert Dale Herman with whom she was mother of (6). Later she married Charles William Cadle. **SANDRA GAYLE WEST** Fifth great granddaughter of progenitor Nicholas Kegg. **SCOTT ALAN WEST** Fifth great grandson of progenitor Nicholas Kegg. **WILLIAM WEST** Sixth great grandson of progenitor Nicholas Kegg. **WILLIAM ROGER WEST** (1941 – 1941) son of Harry and Edith (Ferrell) West. **WILLIAM ROGER WEST** [(6313)] (1943 – 2020) aka "Bill", son of Harry and Edith (Ferrell) West married Mary Ann Hobbs with whom he was father of (3). Bill retired from Huss Inc., where he had been employed as a Terminal Manager.

WESTCOAT

TODD P. WESTCOAT Sixth great grandson of progenitor Nicholas Kegg.

WESTERVELT

BARBARA LYNN WESTERVELT [(6313A)] (1934 – 1999) daughter of Howard and Helen (Bradley) Westervelt married Myles Ramon Miller with whom she was mother of (2). **NANCY L. WESTERVELT** [(6313B)] (1938 – 2013) daughter of Howard and Helen (Bradley) Westervelt married James Adams with whom she was mother of (2). Nancy was an employee of Prudential Life Insurance Company and a longtime employee of the Perrysburg Public Schools as an assistant to the school psychologist. **WESLEY B. WESTERVELT** Fifth great grandson of progenitor Nicholas Kegg.

WESTFALL

CRAIG LEE WESTFALL Seventh great grandson of progenitor Nicholas Kegg.
JOEL HOWARD WESTFALL Eighth great grandson of progenitor Nicholas Kegg.
LORINDA JO WESTFALL Seventh great granddaughter of progenitor Nicholas Kegg.

WESTPHAL

GRACIE WESTPHAL Eighth great granddaughter of progenitor Nicholas Kegg.
MCKENZIE WESTPHAL Eighth great granddaughter of progenitor Nicholas Kegg.

WETZEL

ANNA WETZEL Seventh great granddaughter of progenitor Nicholas Kegg.
BENJAMIN WETZEL Seventh great grandson of progenitor Nicholas Kegg.

WEYANT

ANATONIA R. WEYANT Seventh great granddaughter of progenitor Nicholas Kegg.
BARBARA KAY WEYANT Sixth great granddaughter of progenitor Nicholas Kegg.
BRAIDEN WEYANT Eighth great grandson of progenitor Nicholas Kegg.
CATHERINE WEYANT aka "Kate", Sixth great granddaughter of progenitor Nicholas Kegg.
CHARLES J. WEYANT Fifth great grandson of progenitor Nicholas Kegg.
DONNA WEYANT Sixth great granddaughter of progenitor Nicholas Kegg.
KIRK M. WEYANT Sixth great grandson of progenitor Nicholas Kegg.
LAURA DIANN WEYANT Fifth great granddaughter of progenitor Nicholas Kegg.

[(6312)] Asheville Citizen-Times (NC) Jan. 18, 2017 [(6313)] Family Choice Funeral & Cremations (Virginia Beach, VA) [(6313A)] El Paso Times (TX) May 23, 2006 [(6313B)] The Blade (OH) Jan. 26, 2013

MARGARET JANE WEYANT aka "Peggy", Fifth great granddaughter of progenitor Nicholas Kegg.
MARTIN EUGENE WEYANT Sixth great grandson of progenitor Nicholas Kegg.
TERRY WEYANT Sixth great grandson of progenitor Nicholas Kegg.
TRENTON DAVID WEYANT Eighth great grandson of progenitor Nicholas Kegg.

WHALEY

BROOKE LASER WHALEY Seventh great granddaughter of progenitor Nicholas Kegg.
KIRSTEN GAYLE WHALEY Seventh great granddaughter of progenitor Nicholas Kegg.

WHEELAND

MICHAEL THOMAS WHEELAND Fifth great grandson of progenitor Nicholas Kegg.
NANCEE JOY WHEELAND Fifth great granddaughter of progenitor Nicholas Kegg.

WHERRY

ANNA WHERRY Seventh great granddaughter of progenitor Nicholas Kegg.
CAROLE WHERRY Sixth great granddaughter of progenitor Nicholas Kegg.
LILY WHERRY Seventh great granddaughter of progenitor Nicholas Kegg.
MARK B. WHERRY Sixth great grandson of progenitor Nicholas Kegg.
THOMAS MATTHEW WHERRY Sixth great grandson of progenitor Nicholas Kegg.

WHETSEL

MARCIA KAY WHETSEL [6313C] (1950 – 2008) daughter of Thomas and Dorothy (Streight) Whetsel, married Dennis Coup with whom she was mother of (1). Marcia retired from the City of Akron's Licensing and Assessments Department after 31 years' service.

WHETSTONE

BERNARD DALE WHETSTONE [6314] (1939 – 2020) aka "Flintstone" son of Lester and Fannie (Hoover) Whetstone married Dorothy Benz with whom he was father of (4). Flintstone started driving race cars at the age of 13 and retired when he turned 70. He loved to fish and hunt. Flintstone was employed as a truck driver and mechanic for W.G. McClellan Trucking. **BETTY LOUISE WHETSTONE** [6315] (1928 – 1984) daughter of Lester and Fannie (Hoover) Whetstone was a member of the Woodbury Church of the Brethren. **BRIAN G. WHETSTONE** Sixth great grandson of progenitor Nicholas Kegg. **CHRISTOPHER TODD WHETSTONE** Fourth great grandson of progenitor Nicholas Kegg. **DARLEEN WHETSTONE** (1948 – 1948) daughter of Marshall and Florence (Walter) Whetstone. **DARYL JAY WHETSTONE** Fourth great grandson of progenitor Nicholas Kegg. **DEBORAH KAY WHETSTONE** Fifth great granddaughter of progenitor Nicholas Kegg. **DENISE SHARON WHETSTONE** Fifth great granddaughter of progenitor Nicholas Kegg. **DIANNA JANE WHETSTONE** Fourth great granddaughter of progenitor Nicholas Kegg. **EDGAR CLAIR WHETSTONE** [6316] (1904 – 1908) son of Levi and Sue (Guyer) Whetstone. **EDNA ROMAINE WHETSTONE** [6317] (1923 – 2001) daughter of Lester and Fannie (Hoover) Whetstone, married George Henry Hall with whom she was mother of (9). **ELSIE MILDRED WHETSTONE** [6318] (1919 – 1983) aka "Sissy", daughter of Lester and Fannie (Hoover) Whetstone was a member of the Woodbury Church of the Brethren. **FREDA PAULINE WHETSTONE** Third great granddaughter of progenitor Nicholas Kegg. **HAILIE WHETSTONE** Seventh great granddaughter of progenitor Nicholas Kegg.

[6313C] Akron Beacon Journal (OH) Nov 27, 2008 [6314] Altoona Mirror (PA) Dec 26, 2020 [6315] Bedford County Genealogical Society (PA) obtained by D. Sue Dible [6316] p.8 -The Bedford Gazette (PA) Nov 13, 1908 [6317] p.13 – Altoona Mirror (PA) Nov 24, 2001

HANNAH WHETSTONE Seventh great granddaughter of progenitor Nicholas Kegg.   **HEATHER WHETSTONE** Seventh great granddaughter of progenitor Nicholas Kegg.   **JOEL E. WHETSTONE** Sixth great grandson of progenitor Nicholas Kegg.   **JOSH WHETSTONE** Fifth great grandson of progenitor Nicholas Kegg.   **KYRESTEN WHETSTONE** Fifth great granddaughter of progenitor Nicholas Kegg.   **L. E. WHETSONE** Fourth great grandson of progenitor Nicholas Kegg.   **LESTER MELVIN WHETSTONE** [6319] (1918 – 1932) son of Lester and Fannie (Hoover) Whetstone was a member of the sophomore class of the Martinsburg High school and the Boy Scouts when he was stricken with appendicitis and was admitted to the hospital. He died several days following an operation.   **LEVI BRINTON WHETSTONE** [6320] (1865 – 1907) son of Josiah and Hester (Kegg) Whetstone, married Sue Guyer with whom he was father of (4). Levi was kindhearted, honest and energetic, self-forgetful in the welfare of family and friends.   **LORA KAY WHETSTONE** Sixth great granddaughter of progenitor Nicholas Kegg.   **MARC A. WHETSTONE** Fourth great grandson of progenitor Nicholas Kegg.   **MARK WHETSTONE** Fifth great grandson of progenitor Nicholas Kegg.   **MARSHALL GALEN WHETSTONE** [6320A] aka "Doc" (1921 – 2014) son of Lester and Fannie (Hoover) Whetstone married Florence Jane Walter with whom he was father of (3). Marshall was the owner of Galen Whetstone Trucking of Woodbury; he owned his tractor and trailer, leasing them to New Enterprise Stone & Lime Co. for more than 20 years; he hauled and delivered ice. Doc served in U.S. Army during World War II as an ambulance driver, 1320th SCU Med Detachment; he was recipient of the Good Conduct Medal, American Theater Ribbon and the World War II Victory Ribbon. He was a member of the Roaring Spring Lions Club, enjoyed making pancakes, and working at the chicken barbecues and ox roasts; former member of Cove Lions Club where he served as president. Doc enjoyed hunting, fishing and was a 40-year volunteer for the American Red Cross, Bedford County; was a stock car owner and driver; he organized Saxton Speedway and helped build the Heston Speedway; owned Gayland Speedway, Everett, from 1972-73. "Doc" was a recipient of many awards for racing and community service. **MARY EDNA WHETSTONE** [6321] (1920 – 1991) daughter of Benjamin and Ella (Diehl) Whetstone, married Joseph Ward Stewart with whom she was mother of (1). Mary had worked with her husband for many years at the former Joseph W. Stewart Funeral Home in Everett.   **PAULA S. WHETSTONE** Fourth great granddaughter of progenitor Nicholas Kegg.   **PLEASY PHYLLIS WHETSTONE** [6322] (1926 – 2012) daughter of Charles and Ruth (Provins) Whetstone, married Earl P. Stonerook with whom she was mother of (3). Pleasy assisted in the daily operation of the family dairy farm near Martinsburg, but she was also actively employed as a nurse's aide at Nason Hospital, Roaring Spring, and then as a private-duty nurse's aide in Blair County. She was a lifelong member of Martinsburg Mennonite Church. Pleasy enjoyed bowling, flower gardening and music.   **RICHARD LEWIS WHETSTONE** [6322A] (1949 – 2016) son of Chester and Bonnie (Whetstone) Cagg, married Judy E. Mitchell with whom he was father of (1). Richard was employed as a truck driver for forty-five years. Richard worked for many trucking companies and for the last thirteen years he worked for Landstar Trucking and received the silver level of safety award. He was part Cherokee Indian from the Wolf Clan and he was proud of his heritage. He enjoyed attending rendezvous and pow wows. He was an avid outdoorsman who enjoyed hunting and fishing, guns, riding Harleys, four wheelers and spending time with his family.   **ROBIN WHETSTONE** [6323] (1963 – 2014) daughter of Bernard and Dorothy (Benz) Whetstone, married Curtis L. Queen with whom she was mother of (3).   **RUTH ELEANOR WHETSTONE** [6324] (1924 – 1987) daughter of Lester and Fanny (Hoover) Whetstone, married Donald S. Imler with whom she was mother of (3).   **SAMUEL S. WHETSTONE** [6325] (1859 – 1916) son of Josiah and Hester (Kegg) Whetstone, married Rebecca Diehl. Samuel was a good citizen and had been an efficient employee of the Bedford Springs Co., for many years.   **SONDRA CAROL WHETSTONE** Fifth great granddaughter of progenitor Nicholas Kegg.   **TERRY WHETSTONE** Fourth great grandson of progenitor Nicholas Kegg.

[6318] Morrison Cove Herald (PA) obtained by D. Sue Dible [6319] Find A Grave Memorial# 147256710 obituary obtained by D. Sue Dible [6320] The Bedford Gazette (PA) May 24,1907 [6320A] Bedford Gazette (PA) March 14, 2014 contributed by Bob Rose [6321] The Bedford Gazette (PA) March 26, 1991 transcribed by Carol Eddleman [6322] Altoona Mirror (PA) Dec 22, 2012 [6322A] Vasa Funeral Chapels and Crematory (WY) [6323] Altoona Mirror (PA) Sep 17, 2014 [6324] Bedford County Genealogical Society obituary (PA) obtained by D. Sue Dible [6325] The Bedford Gazette (PA) Aug 4, 1916

TIMOTHY WHETSTONE Fifth great grandson of progenitor Nicholas Kegg
TIMOTHY B. WHETSTONE Fourth great grandson of progenitor Nicholas Kegg.

WHIPKEY

DOUGLAS EARL WHIPKEY Sixth great grandson of progenitor Nicholas Kegg. **HEAVEN CATHLEEN WHIPKEY** Eighth great grandchild of progenitor Nicholas Kegg. **KEVIN WHIPKEY** Seventh great grandson of progenitor Nicholas Kegg. **MALCOLM KEITH WHIPKEY** Sixth great grandson of progenitor Nicholas Kegg. **ROBERT E. WHIPKEY** [6326] (1979 – 2005) son of Douglas and Catherine (Newland) Whipkey, married Trisha Dufford with whom he was father of (1). Robert was a dock worker at PJAX Trucking in Gibsonia. He was a member of the Winfield Township Volunteer Fire Co. and enjoyed NASCAR, camping, fishing, and hunting. **SCOTT WHIPKEY** Seventh great grandson of progenitor Nicholas Kegg. **STACEY WHIPKEY** Seventh great granddaughter of progenitor Nicholas Kegg.

WHISEL

ADAM WHISEL Seventh great grandson of progenitor Nicholas Kegg.
GAVIN WHISEL Eighth great grandson of progenitor Nicholas Kegg.
GEORGIANA WHISEL Eighth great granddaughter of progenitor Nicholas Kegg.
JARED W. WHISEL Eighth great grandson of progenitor Nicholas Kegg.
NOLAN WHISEL Eighth great grandson of progenitor Nicholas Kegg.

WHITAKER

ANNA WHITAKER Seventh great granddaughter of progenitor Nicholas Kegg.
BENNETT WHITAKER Seventh great grandson of progenitor Nicholas Kegg.
KALA WHITAKER Eighth great granddaughter of progenitor Nicholas Kegg.
KATE WHITAKER Seventh great granddaughter of progenitor Nicholas Kegg.
LIAM WHITAKER Seventh great grandson of progenitor Nicholas Kegg.

WHITCOMB

KENNETH WHITCOMB Seventh great grandson of progenitor Nicholas Kegg.

WHITE

ALEXANDER WHITE Seventh great grandson of progenitor Nicholas Kegg. **ADDISON MARIE WHITE** Seventh great granddaughter of progenitor Nicholas Kegg. **CATHY WHITE** Sixth great granddaughter of progenitor Nicholas Kegg. **CHRISTOPHER WHITE** Sixth great grandson of progenitor Nicholas Kegg [6327] (1942 – 1975) son of Louis and Irma (Bordner) White. **DENISE WHITE** Sixth great granddaughter of progenitor Nicholas Kegg. **DENNIS A. WHITE** Sixth great grandson of progenitor Nicholas Kegg. **DOLORES EVELYN WHITE** [6328] (1927 – 1998) daughter of Louis and Irma (Bordner) White married twice; first to Ernest J. Mouser with whom she was mother of (3). Later, she married Ernest Dewey Riddle with whom she was mother of (1). Dolores was a homemaker and enjoyed gardening, canning, and cooking. **ERNEST ARNOLD WHITE** Fifth great grandson of progenitor Nicholas Kegg. **GLENN EDWARD WHITE** Sixth great grandson of progenitor Nicholas Kegg. **GLENN VANCE WHITE** [6329] (1938 – 2009) son of Louis and Irma

---

[6326] Butler Eagle (PA) Sept. 13, 2005 [6327] Arizona Daily Star (Tucson, AZ) Feb 18, 1975 [6328] p.9 San Miguel Basin Forum (CO) July 23, 1998, obtained by D. Sue Dible [6329] Arizona Daily Star (AZ) Mar 13, 2009

Ardelthea Bordner married twice; first to Alice Emily Baldwin with whom he was father of (2). He married a second time and was father of (2). **HILLARIE WHITE** Sixth great granddaughter of progenitor Nicholas Kegg. **JACQUELINE WHITE** Seventh great granddaughter of progenitor Nicholas Kegg. **JAMES WHITE** Seventh great grandson of progenitor Nicholas Kegg. **JEFFREY STEPHEN WHITE** [6330] (1960 – 1984) son of Joseph and Fredrica (Fisher) White. **JIMMY WHITE** Sixth great grandson of progenitor Nicholas Kegg. **JOE WHITE** Sixth great grandson of progenitor Nicholas Kegg. **JOHN WHITE** Sixth great grandson of progenitor Nicholas Kegg. **JOHN HENRY DAVID WHITE** Sixth great grandson of progenitor Nicholas Kegg. **JOSEPHINE WHITE** Seventh great granddaughter of progenitor Nicholas Kegg. **KATHLEEN RUTH WHITE** (1924 – 1984) daughter of Louis and Irma (Bordner) White married twice; first to John Abraham Kerns with whom she was mother of (1). Later, she married Russell Eugene Fetherolf with whom she was mother of (7). **KATHY WHITE** Sixth great granddaughter of progenitor Nicholas Kegg. **KENZLEIGH WHITE** Eighth great granddaughter of progenitor Nicholas Kegg. **LAWRENCE WHITE** Sixth great grandson of progenitor Nicholas Kegg. **LISA WHITE** Sixth great granddaughter of progenitor Nicholas Kegg. **LOIS WHITE** Sixth great granddaughter of progenitor Nicholas Kegg. **LOUIS E. WHITE** [6330A] aka "Buddy" (1932 – 2016) son of Louise and Irma (Bordner) White married Barbara Schirtzinger with whom he was father of (3). Louis served our country as a part of the United States Army. He was a retired Greyhound Driver. Louis enjoyed playing euchre and was an avid golfer. **LYNN WHITE** Sixth great granddaughter of progenitor Nicholas Kegg. **MARK WHITE** Sixth great grandson of progenitor Nicholas Kegg. **MICHAEL DANIEL WHITE** [6331] (1958 – 1980) son of Joseph and Fredrica (Fisher) White served with the U.S. Navy. He was employed at Letterkenny Army Depot. **MIKE WHITE** Sixth great grandson of progenitor Nicholas Kegg. **PHYLLIS IRENE WHITE** [6331A] (1930 – 2006) daughter of Louise and Irma (Bordner) White married Roger Lee Fetherolf with whom she was mother of (4). **TERRENCE MICHAEL WHITE** Sixth great grandson of progenitor Nicholas Kegg. **TIFFANY WHITE** Sixth great granddaughter of progenitor Nicholas Kegg. **TINA WHITE** Sixth great granddaughter of progenitor Nicholas Kegg. **VICKY LEE WHITE** [6332] (1960 – 2018) daughter of Glenn and Alice (Baldwin) White, married Gregory J. Hammond with whom she was mother of (2). She was "momma V" to a lot of people.

WHITED

BARBARA GALE WHITED Sixth great granddaughter of progenitor Nicholas Kegg. **BARRON GENE WHITED** Seventh great grandson of progenitor Nicholas Kegg. **ELAINE RUTH WHITED** Sixth great granddaughter of progenitor Nicholas Kegg. **JACQUELYN LOUISE WHITED** [6333] aka "Jackie" (1946 – 2018) daughter of Robert and Bette (Calhoun) Whited married Gary Gene Geyer. **MALCOLM OWEN WHITED** [6334] (1945 – 2009) son of Malcolm and Arvilla (Foore) Whited, married Martha Eileen Heath with whom he was father of (1). Malcolm worked for the Sheet Metal Union Workers, Local 19 in Philadelphia. He primarily worked in the York area. Previously he worked out of the carpenter's union. Mr. Whited was of the Protestant faith. He was a member of the Tunnel Hill Gun Club and enjoyed hunting and fishing. **MALCOLM OWEN WHITED** Seventh great grandson of progenitor Nicholas Kegg.

WHITELEY

DAVID WHITELEY Sixth great grandson of progenitor Nicholas Kegg.
MEGAN WHITELEY Seventh great granddaughter of progenitor Nicholas Kegg.

[6330] Public Opinion (Chambersburg, PA) Dec 8, 1984 [6330A] The Columbus Dispatch (OH) Aug. 2, 2016 [6331] Public Opinion (Chambersburg, PA) Feb 14, 1980 [6331A] Vinton County Coutier (OH) Sep 7, 2008 [6332] Newcomer Funeral Home Grove City, Ohio [6333] Pittsburgh Post-Gazette (PA) Nov 15, 2018 [6334] York Daily Record (PA) Dec 5, 2009.

WHITING

DIANNE KAY WHITING Fifth great granddaughter of progenitor Nicholas Kegg.
JOANNE LEE WHITING Fifth great granddaughter of progenitor Nicholas Kegg.
MARTHA JANET WHITING [6335] (1915 – 2000) daughter of Pierce and Margaret (Stuckey) Whiting, married Wayne D. Leinbach with whom she was mother of (2). Martha worked for Prairie Farms Creamery in Galesburg; the Illinois School for the Deaf in Jacksonville; and later worked for Galesburg Research Hospital and Peoria State Hospital in Bartonville. She attended Western Illinois University in Macomb. She was a member of the Senior Citizens of Altona.
MORSE WILLIAM WHITING [6336] (1917 – 1977) son of Pierce and Margaret (Stuckey) Whiting, married Verla Hieser with whom he was father of twins. Morse was a land appraiser for the Veterans Land Program, a WWII veteran, member of the Austin Moose Lodge, member of the Austin American Legion Post 83 and a member of the VFW Post 2010 in Cameron.

WHITSETT

STEPHANIE HEATHER WHITSETT Sixth great granddaughter of progenitor Nicholas Kegg.

WHITTAKER

TONY DALE WHITTAKER Seventh great grandson of progenitor Nicholas Kegg.
PAUL CHARLES WHITTAKER Seventh great grandson of progenitor Nicholas Kegg.

WHITWORTH

JEFFREY O. WHITWORTH Sixth great grandson of progenitor Nicholas Kegg.
LORI WHITWORTH Sixth great granddaughter of progenitor Nicholas Kegg.

WICKER

DEBRA SUE WICKER Sixth great granddaughter of progenitor Nicholas Kegg.
DONNA J. WICKER Sixth great granddaughter of progenitor Nicholas Kegg.
MARSHA K. WICKER Sixth great granddaughter of progenitor Nicholas Kegg.
NANCY WICKER Sixth great granddaughter of progenitor Nicholas Kegg.

WIEGAND

LANDYN WIEGAND Seventh great grandson of progenitor Nicholas Kegg.

WIGFIELD

AMANDA WIGFIELD Seventh great granddaughter of progenitor Nicholas Kegg. **BRENDA DIANE WIGFIELD** aka "Wiggy" 6th great granddaughter of progenitor Nicholas Kegg. **CAROLYN F. WIGFIELD** Fifth great granddaughter of progenitor Nicholas Kegg. **CYNTHIA ANN WIGFIELD** [6336A] (1954 – 2003) daughter of William and Stella (Dively) Wigfield married Danny J. Byers with whom she was mother of (3). Cindy worked as a slither operator for Conalco Aluminum Company in Monroe County, Ohio, and also enjoyed flying, having once owned her own plane. She enjoyed coaching softball and her children's leagues. **DEBRA M. WIGFIELD** Seventh great granddaughter of progenitor Nicholas Kegg. **DENNIS MARK WIGFIELD** Sixth great grandson of progenitor Nicholas Kegg.

[6335] p.B5 Peoria Journal Star (IL) July 15, 2000 [6336] p.14 Cameron Herald (TX) July 11, 1977

DORIS KAY WIGFIELD [6337] (1927 – 2000) daughter of Otis and Maude (Kagarise) Wigfield, married Charles A. Irvin with whom she was mother of (3). Doris retired from Methodist Hospital in Philadelphia where she had been employed as a registered nurse. She was a 1948 graduate of Methodist Hospital School of Nursing and served in the Army Nursing Cadet Corps. Doris had been a Sunday school teacher in Media and in Orchard Park, N.Y. **EDWARD C. WIGFIELD** Sixth great grandson of progenitor Nicholas Kegg. **ELAINE WIGFIELD** [6338] (1912 – 1974) daughter of Philip and Martha (Calhoun) Wigfield, married Hershel Bixler Hershberger with whom she was mother of (1). Elaine was a graduate of Catherman's Business College, Cumberland, Maryland, and was a registered nurse, having graduated from Miner's Hospital, Spangler, Pennsylvania. She had been employed at the First National Bank and Trust Company in Bedford, the Washington Coffee Shop, Howard Johnson's Restaurant at Midway, and worked for many years as a nurse in Dr. Sipes Hospital in Everett. **HAROLD ORVIS WIGFIELD** [6338A] (1924 – 1943) son of Orvis and Lula (Williams) Wigfield had been missing since Oct 29, 1944, when an airplane dropped into the ocean near the Bahama Islands, was then believed to have lost his life at that time along with the entire crew of ten. The first word came Nov 2, when the plane was reported missing, and the Dept conducted a search for some time. On Feb 1, 1945, his mother received the following written message- Regret to inform you it has now been determined that your son, Staff Sergeant Harold O. Wigfield, who was previously reported missing, was killed on 29 Oct (1944) in North American area as a result of an aircraft accident. The Secretary of War desires that I extend his deep sympathy to you. Harold was a radio operator U.S. Army Air Forces 704th Bomber Squadron, 446th Bomber Group. His name appears on the Tablets of The Missing at East Coast Memorial in New York City. **JAMES WILLIAM WIGFIELD** [6338B] (1958 – 1999) son of William and Stella (Dively) Wigfield married Lori Foor with whom he was father of (2). James had been employed as a manager in the asbestos removal business. He had served in the U. S. Marine Corps. He was also a member of the Improved Order of the Redman Wambic Tribe 507 in Everett. **LISA WIGFIELD** Sixth great granddaughter of progenitor Nicholas Kegg. **MARY ALICE WIGFIELD** [6338C] (1935 – 2012) daughter of Ottis and Maude (Kagarise) Wigfield, married Donald Eugene Washabaugh with whom she was mother of (3). Mary was employed as a purchasing agent at the National Institutes of Health in Bethesda, MD. She enjoyed reading the Bible, gardening, interior decorating, collecting antiques, traveling, and the beach. **MATTHEW WILLIAM WIGFIELD** [6338D] (1981 – 2006) son of James and Lori (Foor) Wigfield. Matthew was employed by Mineral Springs Bottling Company and the Penn State Blue Course. Matt attended State College Assembly of God. He especially enjoyed the out-of-doors and loved to go hiking and camping. He also enjoyed baseball and basketball. **ORVIS W. WIGFIELD** [6339] (1900 – 1967) son of Philip and Martha (Calhoun) Wigfield, married Lula Mae Williams with whom he was father of (2). Orvis operated the Wigfield Family Shoe Store in Everett and sold shoes and general merchandise for 15 years. **OTTIS E. WIGFIELD** [6340] (1902 – 1970) son of Philip and Martha (Calhoun) Wigfield, married Maude Lucille Kagarise with whom he was father of (4). Ottis was a member of Everett United Methodist Church. **PHYLLIS ANN WIGFIELD** [6340A] (1928 – 2003) daughter of Ottis and Maude (Kagarise) Wigfield married Russell Harvey Lee with whom she was mother of (2). Phyllis had been employed in the Everett Area School District for 28 years before her retirement from the Central office. **REBECCA WIGFIELD** Seventh great granddaughter of progenitor Nicholas Kegg. **SUSETTE WIGFIELD** Sixth great granddaughter of progenitor Nicholas Kegg. **TARA M. WIGFIELD** Seventh great granddaughter of progenitor Nicholas Kegg. **TERRY WIGFIELD** Sixth great grandson of progenitor Nicholas Kegg. **TRAVIS J. WIGFIELD** Seventh great grandson of progenitor Nicholas Kegg. **VICKIE JO WIGFIELD** Sixth great granddaughter of progenitor Nicholas Kegg. **WILLIAM W. WIGFIELD** [6341] (1928 – 1987) son of Orvis and Lula (Williams) Wigfield, married Stella A. Dively with whom he was father of (2). William had served in the U.S. Navy during the

---

[6336A] p.3 - Bedford Inquirer (PA) April 11, 2003, contributed by Bob Rose [6337] p. 3 - Bedford Inquirer (PA) July 28, 2000 [6338] Bedford County (PA) obituary clipping from Duke Clark collection p. 1955 [6338A] Bedford County Historical Society obituary contributed by D. Sue Dible [6338B] Bedford Inquirer (PA) Feb 12, 1999, contributed by Duke Clark [6338C] Frederick News Post (MD) Dec 9, 2012 [6338D] Centre Daily Times (PA) June 26, 2006 [6339, 6340] Bedford Gazette (PA) Duke Clark Obituary collection p. 4515 [6340A] p.3 - Bedford Inquirer (PA) Dec 12, 2003, contributed by Bob Rose [6341] Bedford Inquirer (PA) Mar 20, 1987, obtained by Duke Clark

Korean Conflict on the USS Midway. He had been employed by the Breezewood Telephone Co. for 22 years where he had worked as an assistant manager for maintenance of the central office equipment.

WIGGINS

CHARLES WIGGINS Ninth great grandson of progenitor Nicholas Kegg.
HEATHER R. WIGGINS Sixth great granddaughter of progenitor Nicholas Kegg.
JACK WIGGINS Ninth great grandson of progenitor Nicholas Kegg.
SAM WIGGINS Ninth great grandson of progenitor Nicholas Kegg.

WILBER

SAMANTHA WILBER Seventh great granddaughter of progenitor Nicholas Kegg.

WILCOX

JOYCE MARIE WILCOX [6341A] (1935 – 1997) daughter of Lee and Velma (Hershiser) Wilcox, married Paul M. Myers with whom she was mother of (3). Joyce was an elementary school teacher for 16 years, teaching in the Monroeville, Norwalk and Willard school districts and at Christie Lane School and Workshop. She was also a former Pink Lady volunteer at Fisher-Titus. She was a member of the Norwalk First united Methodist Church, where she was active with the Church Circle, and the Disciple Bible Study. **PATRICIA ANN WILCOX** aka "Patty" Sixth great granddaughter of progenitor Nicholas Kegg. **ROGER LEE WILCOX** [6341B] (1937 – 2018) son of Lee and Velma (Hershiser) Wilcox married Esther Bauer with whom he was father of (1). Roger was the owner and operator of Wilcox Garage, a business which his father started in 1937. He worked and ran wreckers in his early youth years, and continued to work alongside his father for many years until the business was turned over to him in 1972. He continued to run the business until he turned it over to his grandsons in 2014. Roger was an active member of Trinity Lutheran Church and was a past member of the Willard Fire Department.
RUTH ELAINE WILCOX Fifth great granddaughter of progenitor Nicholas Kegg.

WILDER

HOWARD CALVIN WILDER [6342] (1927 – 1993) aka "Bud", son of William and Mabel (Saylor) Wilder, married Constance Joan Mayfield. Bud was a veteran of World War II having served in the U. S. Navy. **KATHLEEN SUZANNE WILDER** Sixth great granddaughter of progenitor Nicholas Kegg.
LINDSAY SUZANNE WILDER Seventh great granddaughter of progenitor Nicholas Kegg.
PATRICIA LYNN WILDER Sixth great granddaughter of progenitor Nicholas Kegg.
SHEILA ANN WILDER Fifth great granddaughter of progenitor Nicholas Kegg.
WILLIAM DAVID WILDER Sixth great grandson of progenitor Nicholas Kegg.
WILLIAM THOMAS WILDER [6342A] aka "Bill" (1925 – 2012) son of William and Mabel (Saylor) Wilder married Juanita O'Nile Stump with whom he was father of (3). Bill worked for Goodyear Tire Company where he piloted the Goodyear Blimp. In 1957 became a pilot with Eastern Airlines where he flew for 28 years and served on the Safety Committee in Washington D.C.. His biggest love was for his family where he always made time to play or work with his children and grandchildren and all young people who came into his life. Bill was a sports enthusiast having been on a swim team, life guard, manager of a swim park and played semi pro football. He still played baseball at age 70 and enjoyed the game of golf above all others. Bill was guided by a life under God and served in positions in his churches.

[6341A] p.4- Norwalk Reflector (OH) Jan 23, 1997, contributed by D. Sue Dible [6341B] News Journal (OH) Sep. 29, 2018 [6342] p.C11 Akron Beacon Journal (OH) Dec 12, 1993, obtained by D. Sue Dible [6342A] Miami Herald (FL) Oct 24, 2012, contributed by D. Sue Dible

WIECZOROWSKI

AMY WIECZORSKI Sixth great granddaughter of progenitor Nicholas Kegg.
PETER WIECZOROWSKI Sixth great grandson of progenitor Nicholas Kegg.

WILES

JACK WILES Eighth great grandson of progenitor Nicholas Kegg.
LUKE DOUGLAS WILES Eighth great grandson of progenitor Nicholas Kegg.
MAX WILES Eighth great grandson of progenitor Nicholas Kegg.

WILEY

CRAIG PATRICK WILEY Sixth great grandson of progenitor Nicholas Kegg.
GERRY WILEY Fourth great grandson of progenitor Nicholas Kegg.
JASON TODD WILEY Sixth great grandson of progenitor Nicholas Kegg.
MARLENE WILEY Fourth great granddaughter of progenitor Nicholas Kegg.
SIDNEY KENT WILEY [6342B] aka "Kent" (1939 – 2015) son of Walter and Ruth (Scheller) Wiley married Karen M. Smith with whom he was father of (2). A member of the Colorado National Guard unit when it was activated during the Pueblo Crisis. He was sent to Korea where he proudly served his country. Upon his return to the United States, he began working seasonally for Colorado State Parks at Bonny Reservoir in eastern Colorado. After retiring, he kept busy with going to the gym to work out and socialize, cooking for friends and family, riding ATVs, watching Denver Bronco games, photography, and hanging out at his cabin in the mountains.

WILGER

HARRY GILBERT WILGER (1897 – 1898) son of Frank and Viola (Kegg) Wilger.

WILHELM

BECKY WILHELM Sixth great granddaughter of progenitor Nicholas Kegg. **GEORGE ALFRED WILHELM** [6342C] (1935 – 2009) son of John and Margaret (Clark) Wilhelm, married Carlee Davis with whom he was father of (3). George was a fireman at Chillum-Adelphi Fire Department, and then later Prince George's Co. Firefighters. **KAREN LEE WILHELM** [6342D] (1957 – 2017) daughter of George and Carlee (Davis) Wilhelm married Harold Bradley Gardner. Karen did accounts payable for Central Truck Center in Landover, MD. **SUSAN WILHELM** Sixth great granddaughter of progenitor Nicholas Kegg.

WILKINS

CYNTHIA WILKINS aka "Cindy" Ninth great granddaughter of progenitor Nicholas Kegg.

WILKINSON

BRIAN WILKINSON Sixth great grandson of progenitor Nicholas Kegg. **DEBRA ANN WILKINSON** Sixth great granddaughter of progenitor Nicholas Kegg. **GORDON WILKINSON** Fifth great grandson of progenitor Nicholas Kegg. **JAY ARTHUR WILKINSON** [6343] (1944 – 2006) son of John and Orva (Meredith) Wilkinson, married Eileen Cecile Kramer with whom he was father of (1). Jay

---

[6342B] Gazette (CO) Dec. 1, 2015 [6342C] Cumberland Times-News (MD) May 12, 2009 [6342D] GASCH's Funeral Home (Hyattsville, MD) [6343] Asbury Park Press (NJ) Dec 6, 2006

was a man of many interests. A graduate of Sterling College, Sterling, Kansas, with a bachelor's degree in History/Physical Education. Jay served as an educator for the Toms River School District for 35 years, having retired in 2002. He spent 22 years as a physical education teacher at Intermediate School East. Mr. Wilkinson was one of the founding coaches of the Monmouth/Ocean Intermediate School Wrestling League and for over 20 years served as a highly successful wresting coach at Intermediate East. His students knew him as a tough, but fair teacher and coach with compassion and a dry sense of humor. In 1987, Mr. Wilkinson earned his master's degree in Labor Relations from Rutgers University, New Brunswick. He was then elected president of the Toms River Education Association, a role he served for 13 years until his retirement. In addition, he was a negotiation consultant for the New Jersey Education Association and was a delegate to over 10 National Education Association Conventions. Additionally, be belonged to the OOCEA and over the years served on many committees. He was active in the community, serving on the Toms River Youth Advisory Commission, a former member of the Toms River Business Improvement District and the Ocean County Historical Society. He had also been involved with the United Way Christmas Tree Fundraiser. Additionally, Jay worked many jobs while on summer recess, his favorite, serving as a police officer in the Seaside Heights Police Department for over a decade. He was an avid reader, loved going to the movies, watching Jeopardy and spending hours on the golf course. He was a long time Philadelphia sports fan, especially rooting for the Eagles and Phillies. **JEAN ELLYNE WILKINSON** aka "Jeanne", Fourth great granddaughter of progenitor Nicholas Kegg. **JOHN WILKINSON** Fifth great grandson of progenitor Nicholas Kegg. **ROBERT LAWRENCE WILKINSON** [6344] (1931 – 1954) son of John and Mardell (Hershiser) Wilkinson, married Dorothy Stallings. After graduating from Attica High school, he served 20 months in the Army, 10 of them in Korea. He had been attending Tiffin Business College and would have been graduated Friday evening. Mr. Wilkinson who is an electrical contractor in Willard and was returning from work when the accident occurred. Robert was killed instantly in a two-car head-on collision. He was a member of the Attica Methodist church, Blue Lodge of the Masonic order, Order of Eastern Star and American Legion. **RONALD WILKINSON** Fifth great grandson of progenitor Nicholas Kegg. **SANDRA LEE WILKINSON** Sixth great granddaughter of progenitor Nicholas Kegg. **SHARON ELAINE WILKINSON** Sixth great granddaughter of progenitor Nicholas Kegg. **STEVEN EDWARD WILKINSON** Sixth great grandson of progenitor Nicholas Kegg.

WILL

PATTI A. WILL Seventh great granddaughter of progenitor Nicholas Kegg.
SANDIE C. WILL Seventh great granddaughter of progenitor Nicholas Kegg.

WILLARD

DOROTHELLE MAOLA WILLARD [6344A] (1919 – 2018) daughter of Dr. Edwin and Ethel (Combs) Willard married Robert E. Fites with whom she was mother of (2). Dorothelle attended secondary school in Seattle and received the freshman trustee scholarship to Mills College, from whence she was graduated in '39.

WILLEY

RANDI J. WILLEY Seventh great granddaughter of progenitor Nicholas Kegg.

WILLFORD

JAYSON PHILLIP WILLFORD Seventh great grandson of progenitor Nicholas Kegg.

[6344] Mansfield News Journal (OH) May 17, 1954 [6344A] The ParishScope July 8-15, 2018 Vol 327.

JOSHUA CHARLES WILLFORD Seventh great grandson of progenitor Nicholas Kegg.
KRISTI LYNNE WILLFORD Seventh great granddaughter of progenitor Nicholas Kegg.

WILLIAMS

AARON LEE WILLIAMS Eighth great grandson of progenitor Nicholas Kegg. **AMBER LYNN WILLIAMS** Seventh great granddaughter of progenitor Nicholas Kegg. **ANN WILLIAMS** Sixth great granddaughter of progenitor Nicholas Kegg. **ANN PATRICE WILLIAMS** Sixth great granddaughter of progenitor Nicholas Kegg. **ARTHUR A. WILLIAMS** Fifth great grandson of progenitor Nicholas Kegg. **ASHLEY WILLIAMS** Eighth great granddaughter of progenitor Nicholas Kegg. **ASHLEY WILLIAMS** Eighth great granddaughter of progenitor Nicholas Kegg. **BERNARD M. WILLIAMS** [6345] (1911 – 1971) son of Bernard and Stella (Calhoun) Williams, married Mildred R. Stoner with whom he was father of (2). Bernard was a member of the John Wesley United Methodist church and vice president of the Wesleyan Sunday School class. He had been associated with C. E. Darner and Sons and the Maryland General Realty Co. **BEVERLY REBECCA WILLIAMS** [6345A] aka "Becky" (1956 – 2010) daughter of Jay and Bonita (Smith) Williams was a kind, respectful and often hilarious woman who enjoyed singing songs of all musical genres during PJ's karaoke night. "She was just a really sweet lady," said a PJ's employee who added she could still hear Becky singing her favorite song, Billy Joel's "Just the Way You Are," Becky was murdered, having suffered a brutal death. Her body was discovered in a condemned house on a rundown street. **BRITTANY WILLIAMS** Seventh great granddaughter of progenitor Nicholas Kegg. **CARSON WILLIAMS** Eighth great grandson of progenitor Nicholas Kegg. **CASEY WILLIAMS** Seventh great granddaughter of progenitor Nicholas Kegg. **CECELIA WILLIAMS** Eighth great granddaughter of progenitor Nicholas Kegg. **CHARLES LAVERNE WILLIAMS** [6346] (1931 – 2010) son of Allen and Clara (Kegg) Williams married twice; first to June B. Clark with whom he was father of (3). Later, he married Stephanie Louise Keller McIntyre. **CHASE WILLIAMS** Seventh great grandson of progenitor Nicholas Kegg. **CONNER WILLIAMS** Eighth great grandson of progenitor Nicholas Kegg. **CONSTANCE KAY WILLIAMS** aka "Connie" Sixth great granddaughter of progenitor Nicholas Kegg. **DAWN WILLIAMS** Seventh great granddaughter of progenitor Nicholas Kegg. **DEBRA WILLIAMS** Sixth great granddaughter of progenitor Nicholas Kegg. **DEBRA L. WILLIAMS** Sixth great granddaughter of progenitor Nicholas Kegg. **DEREK LEE WILLIAMS** Sixth great grandson of progenitor Nicholas Kegg. **DIANA WILLIAMS** aka "Dee", Fifth great granddaughter of progenitor Nicholas Kegg. **DUSTIN WILLIAMS** Fifth great grandson of progenitor Nicholas Kegg. **EDWARD EARL WILLIAMS** [6347] (1917 – 1984) son of Edward and Amelia Williams married Alma Florence Zobel with whom he was father of (2). **EDWARD JOHN WILLIAMS** [6348] (1882 – 1967) son of John and Joanna (Beaver) Williams married Amelia Louise Muehlauser with whom he was father of (2). Edward was an electrician employed by Republic Steel Co. **EDWIN ERNEST WILLIAMS** [6349] (1919 – 1991) son of Ernest and Edith (Kegg) Williams married Sally Marie Aulds with whom he was father of (2). Edwin was a Navy veteran of WWII. **EDWINA LOUISE WILLIAMS** [6350, 6351] (1943 – 2022) daughter of Edwin and Sally Marie (Aulds) Williams married five times.; first to William Louis Pederson with whom she was mother of (1). Later she married Bobby Gladden, Charles Milton Polson, Theodore Jack Lube and Kenneth Wayne Schneider. **ERIN WILLIAMS** Seventh great granddaughter of progenitor Nicholas Kegg. **ERIN MAUREEN WILLIAMS** Seventh great granddaughter of progenitor Nicholas Kegg. **FENLEY WILLIAMS** Eighth great grandson of progenitor Nicholas Kegg. **GAIL WILLIAMS** Sixth great granddaughter of progenitor Nicholas Kegg. **GILBERT GERALD WILLIAMS** aka "Jerry" Fifth great grandson of progenitor Nicholas Kegg. **HOWARD BENSON WILLIAMS** (1891 – 1939) son of John and Joanna (Beaver) Williams.

[6345] p.11 - Daily Mail (Hagerstown, MD.) Feb. 2, 1971 [6345A] Go upstate(Spartansburg, SC) April 27, 2010 [6346] Creps-Abels Funeral Home in Eldora, IA obtained by D. Sue Dible [6347] Johnstown Democrat-Tribune (PA) April 21, 1984, obtained by D. Sue Dible [6348] Canton Repository (OH) Dec 25, 1967, obtained by D. Sue Dible. [6349] East Oregonian (OR) March 14, 2019 [6350] Herald and News (Klamath Falls, OR) March 25, 1962 [6351] Glasgow Funeral Home (Montana)

JACK S. WILLIAMS Fourth great grandson of progenitor Nicholas Kegg. **JACQUELINE MARIE WILLIAMS** Sixth great granddaughter of progenitor Nicholas Kegg. **JAMES WILLIAMS** Seventh great grandson of progenitor Nicholas Kegg. **JASON NEAL WILLIAMS** Eighth great grandson of progenitor Nicholas Kegg. **JEFF WILLIAMS** Sixth great grandson of progenitor Nicholas Kegg. **JEFFREY WILLIAMS** Seventh great grandson of progenitor Nicholas Kegg. **JESSIE CARRIE WILLIAMS** (born abt.1894) daughter of James and Emma (Kegg) Williams, married James Joseph Davidson with whom she was mother of (5). **JON WILLIAMS** Sixth great grandson of progenitor Nicholas Kegg. **KATELYN RENEE WILLIAMS** Seventh great granddaughter of progenitor Nicholas Kegg. **KATHLEEN E. WILLIAMS** Fifth great granddaughter of progenitor Nicholas Kegg. **KELSEY WILLIAMS** Seventh great granddaughter of progenitor Nicholas Kegg. **KEVIN PATRICK WILLIAMS** Seventh great grandson of progenitor Nicholas Kegg. **KYLE WILLIAMS** Sixth great grandson of progenitor Nicholas Kegg. **LARRY WILLIAMS** Sixth great grandson of progenitor Nicholas Kegg. **LEAH WILLIAMS** Seventh great granddaughter of progenitor Nicholas Kegg. **LISA G. WILLIAMS** Sixth great granddaughter of progenitor Nicholas Kegg. **LISA J. WILLIAMS** [6351A] (1958 – 2012) daughter of R. Richard and Peggy J. (Weicht) Williams married Bryan C. Zimmerman with whom she was mother of (3). Lisa was previously employed at UPMC Bedford Memorial Hospital as a switchboard attendant and later worked at Builders Surplus as a salesclerk. She was a family-oriented person who enjoyed being home, gardening, cooking and reading. **LOGAN WILLIAMS** Seventh great grandson of progenitor Nicholas Kegg. **LYNN WILLIAMS** Sixth great granddaughter of progenitor Nicholas Kegg. **MARK A. WILLIAMS** Sixth great grandson of progenitor Nicholas Kegg. **MARY A. WILLIAMS** (born abt. 1884) daughter of John and Joanna (Beaver) Williams. **MEGAN WILLIAMS** Seventh great granddaughter of progenitor Nicholas Kegg. **NANCY MAY WILLIAMS** Fourth great granddaughter of progenitor Nicholas Kegg. **NORMAN C. WILLIAMS** Fourth great grandson of progenitor Nicholas Kegg. **ORVILLE WILLIAMS** Seventh great grandson of progenitor Nicholas Kegg. **PAUL WILLIAMS** Fifth great grandson of progenitor Nicholas Kegg. **PAUL ALAN WILLIAMS** Seventh great grandson of progenitor Nicholas Kegg. **RAYMOND JOSEPH WILLIAMS** (1923 -2010) son of George and Zelma (Baker) Williams. **RICHARD E. WILLIAMS** [6353] (1953 – 2017) son of Ssgt Edward and Alma (Zobel) Williams. Richard was an avid fan of history and guns. **RICHARD WAYNE WILLIAMS** Fourth great grandson of progenitor Nicholas Kegg. **ROBERT A. WILLIAMS** (1894 – 1971) son of James and Emma (Kegg) Williams. **ROBERT HERCHEL WILLIAMS** son of Edward and Amelia (Muehlhauser) Williams. **ROBERTA WILLIAMS** [6354] (1913 – 2004) daughter of Bernard and Stella (Calhoun) Williams, married Thomas Brace Lovett with whom she was mother of (2). Roberta was a graduate of Lock Haven University and taught primary education in the Pennsbury School District for over 15 years. She was an original member of the Faith Reformed Church, an active seniors group member, a volunteer at Pennsbury Manor. **ROGER WILLIAMS** Sixth great grandson of progenitor Nicholas Kegg. **ROGER MONROE WILLIAMS** Sixth great grandson of progenitor Nicholas Kegg. **RON WILLIAMS** Sixth great grandson of progenitor Nicholas Kegg. **RYAN S. WILLIAMS** Seventh great grandson of progenitor Nicholas Kegg. **SANDRA LEE WILLIAMS** [6355] (1944 – 2001) daughter of Edward and Alma (Zobel) Williams married Stephen Robert Devine with whom she was mother of (5). **SHERRY DENISE WILLIAMS** Sixth great granddaughter of progenitor Nicholas Kegg. **STEVE WILLIAMS** Seventh great grandson of progenitor Nicholas Kegg. **TAYLOR WILLIAMS** Seventh great grandchild of progenitor Nicholas Kegg. **THELMA EDITH WILLIAMS** [6355A] (1920 – 2015) daughter of Ernest and Edith (Kegg) Williams married Harold Herbert Mort with whom she was mother of (4). Thelma loved family and large family dinners. She loved flowers and gardening. She could catch a fish before Pappy was out of the truck and loved hunting. She loved animals and of course her dog Tobey.

[6351A] Akers Funeral Home (PA) contributed by D. Sue Dible [6353] The Washington Post (DC) April 26, 2017, obtained by D. Sue Dible [6354] p.7C - Bucks County Courier Times (PA) Oct 29, 2004. [6355] Johnstown Democrat-Tribune (PA) March 6, 2001, obtained by D. Sue Dible [6355A] Siskiyou Daily News (CA) Sep 17, 2015

THEODORE ROY WILLIAMS aka "Teddy" Sixth great grandson of progenitor Nicholas Kegg. **TIMOTHY P. WILLIAMS** Seventh great grandson of progenitor Nicholas Kegg. **VICKIA V. WILLIAMS** Fourth great granddaughter of progenitor Nicholas Kegg. **WADE E. WILLIAMS** Seventh great grandson of progenitor Nicholas Kegg.

WILLIAMSON

GEORGE MILLER WILLIAMSON JR. [6356] (1955 – 1964) son of George and Patricia (Howard) Williamson was a member of the St. John's Lutheran Church Sunday School in Belleville, and he attended the Day Care Center at the Seventh Ward School in Lewistown.

WILLIARD

ZACHARY H. WILLIARD Seventh great grandson of progenitor Nicholas Kegg.
ZACHARY H. WILLIARD Eighth great grandson of progenitor Nicholas Kegg.

WILLIE

ALEX WILLIE Seventh great grandson of progenitor Nicholas Kegg.
SARAH WILLIE Seventh great granddaughter of progenitor Nicholas Kegg.

WILLIS

BRENDA S. WILLIS Sixth great granddaughter of progenitor Nicholas Kegg.
MICHAEL R. WILLIS Fifth great grandson of progenitor Nicholas Kegg.
RONALD LEE WILLIS Sixth great grandson of progenitor Nicholas Kegg.
TERRY L. WILLIS Sixth great granddaughter of progenitor Nicholas Kegg.
WYATT WILLIS Seventh great grandson of progenitor Nicholas Kegg.

WILLS

CLAIRE WILLS Seventh great granddaughter of progenitor Nicholas Kegg.
JAELYN WILLS Seventh great granddaughter of progenitor Nicholas Kegg.

WILSHER

ROBERT WILSHER Sixth great grandson of progenitor Nicholas Kegg.
ROBIN LEE WILSHER Sixth great granddaughter of progenitor Nicholas Kegg.

WILSON

ANDREA SUE WILSON Fifth great granddaughter of progenitor Nicholas Kegg. **CHRISTOPHER C. WILSON** Sixth great grandson of progenitor Nicholas Kegg. **CYNTHIA MAUREEN WILSON** [6357] (1948 – 2004) daughter of Kenneth and Ruth (Biddle) Wilson, married Richard W. Lins. Cynthia had worked at UPMC Bedford Memorial Hospital as a medical secretary. She was a member of the Trinity Lutheran Church in Bedford, Bedford Women of the Moose, American Trap Shooters Association, and the Bedford County Sportsmen's Club. **CYNTHIA LEE WILSON** aka "Cindy" Sixth great granddaughter of progenitor Nicholas Kegg. **ELEANORA LEE WILSON** [6358] (1951 – 2013) daughter of Jack and Audrey (Kegg) Wilson.

[6356] p.2-Daily News (Huntingdon, PA) Jan 10, 1964 [6357] Bedford Inquirer (PA) July 30, 2004, obtained by Bob Rose [6358] Greenfield Daily Reporter (IN) Feb 2013

JACKLYN SUE WILSON [6358A] (1944 – 2008) daughter of Jack and Lilian (Huddy) Wilson married twice, first to Robert Allison Mohney with whom she was mother of (3). Later she married Mark W. Zapert. **LEE WILSON** Fifth great granddaughter of progenitor Nicholas Kegg. **RICHARD CALVIN WILSON** Fifth great grandson of progenitor Nicholas Kegg. **RICHARD DOUGLAS WILSON** Sixth great granddaughter of progenitor Nicholas Kegg. **SHELLEY LYNN WILSON** Fifth great granddaughter of progenitor Nicholas Kegg. **STEPHEN ROBERT WILSON** [6359] (1951 – 2014) son of Kenneth and Ruth (Biddle) Wilson, served in the U.S. Navy for 7 years. **SYLVIA KAY WILSON** Fifth great granddaughter of progenitor Nicholas Kegg. **WENDY ANN WILSON** Sixth great granddaughter of progenitor Nicholas Kegg.

WINEBRENNER

BRENT DAVID WINEBRENNER Sixth great grandson of progenitor Nicholas Kegg.
ERIC WINEBRENNER Sixth great grandson of progenitor Nicholas Kegg.

WINEGAR

MAGGIE FAYE WINEGAR Seventh great granddaughter of progenitor Nicholas Kegg.

WINGARD

DOROTHY JANE WINGARD [6359A] (1929 – 2023) daughter of Henry and Esther Pearl (McDaniel) Wingard married Rev. Jacob Maurice Brumbaugh with whom she was mother of (3). Dorothy led an active life that always reflected her Christian principals. She was a dedicated prayer-warrior for family and friends in addition to being a talented musician (marimba, piano, and choir), farmers wife, gardener, seamstress and 4-H Leader. Dorothy was a dedicated homemaker and especially was active in church as a Pastors wife at Cramer U.M.C. where she served as choir director. She was previously an active contributing member of Park Ave U.M.C. She served as caretaker for many over the years and was a talented cook and baker. Dorothy served and worked for many local businesses and organizations over her lifetime **VIONA LOUISE WINGARD** [6359B] aka "Nona" (1924 – 2020) daughter of Rev. Henry and Esther Pearl (McDaniel) Wingard married Donald Henry Fyock with whom she was mother of (1).

WINEGARDNER

MACKENZI WINEGARDNER Sixth great granddaughter of progenitor Nicholas Kegg.
MADISON WINEGARDNER Sixth great granddaughter of progenitor Nicholas Kegg.

WININGER

JOHN TYLER WININGER [6360] (1952 – 1955) son of John and Sherry (Stephens) Wininger received part of his mother's liver in an operation. The spirited, happy child suddenly became ill and died within hours from septic shock caused by a massive infection. **KATELYN WININGER** Seventh great granddaughter of progenitor Nicholas Kegg. **KYLE WININGER** Seventh great grandson of progenitor Nicholas Kegg. **RYA WININGER** Seventh great granddaughter of progenitor Nicholas Kegg.

WINKLER

JOSEPH ALAN WINKLER Fifth great grandson of progenitor Nicholas Kegg.

[6358A] Columbus Dispatch (OH) Apr. 13, 2008 [6359] Timothy A. Berkebile Funeral Home, PA [6359A] The Tribune Democrat (PA) Feb 15, 2023 [6359B] Johnstown Tribune-Democrat (PA) July 16, 2020 [6360] Mount Ayr Record-News (IA) April 20, 1955, obtained by Sharon R. Becker

WIRE

BOBBIE WIRE Fifth great granddaughter of progenitor Nicholas Kegg. **BONNIE JEAN WIRE** [6360A] (1927 – 2010) daughter of Lloyd and Belle (Garver) Wire married Professor Robert Milton Northrop with whom she was mother of (3). Bonnie was a former teacher in the Ann Arbor Public school system. **CAROLYN D. WIRE** Fifth great granddaughter of progenitor Nicholas Kegg. **DAN FORREST WIRE** Fifth great grandson of progenitor Nicholas Kegg. **JAMES ALFRED WIRE** [6360B] (1916 – 2009) son of Lloyd and Belle (Garver) Wire married Gwendolyn Marquerite Parrish with whom he was father of (2). James was a Conservation Officer for 29 years, receiving both state and federal awards. In 1965, he was presented the National Wildlife Conservationist of the Year by First Lady, Lady Byrd Johnson. **JAMES R. WIRE** Fifth great grandson of progenitor Nicholas Kegg. **LLOYD ROBERT WIRE** [6360C] aka "Bob" (1918 – 1981) son of Lloyd and Belle (Garver) Wire married Sally Black with whom he was father of (4). A local civic and union leader, Lloyd was one of the founders of the Northside Neighborhood Association and was on its board of directors. He also founded the Sandbag Coalition. He was a member of the Three Rivers Greenway Consortium, Fort Wayne Future Citizens Advisory Council to the Fort Wayne Community Schools and a lifelong member of the Athletic League. He was appointed by Mayor Winfield Moses Jr. to the Citizens Advisory Committee Council on Flood Plain Management. He was a Democratic precinct committeeman, ward chairman and fund-raiser. He also was the Democratic nominee for the 2nd District city councilman's seat in 1975 and had been elected delegate to several state conventions. During Mayor Ivan Lebamoff's administration, Mr. Wire was a member of the Fort Wayne Board of Public Safety. Lloyd was a Navy veteran of World War II. **MARJORIE LOUISE WIRE** [6361, 6362] (1923 – 1980) daughter of Lloyd and Belle (Garver) Wire married twice; first to Frank Joseph Herzog with whom she was mother of (2). Later, she married Daniel William Miller with whom she was mother of (1). **SUZANNE WIRE** Fifth great granddaughter of progenitor Nicholas Kegg. **TIM ARTHUR WIRE** Fifth great grandson of progenitor Nicholas Kegg.

WIRTH

BENJAMIN PHILIP WIRTH Seventh great grandson of progenitor Nicholas Kegg.
JASON DOUGLAS WIRTH Seventh great grandson of progenitor Nicholas Kegg.

WISCHMEIER

AMANDA WISCHMEIER Seventh great granddaughter of progenitor Nicholas Kegg.
CASIE LEE WISCHMEIER Seventh great grandson of progenitor Nicholas Kegg.

WISDA

DIANA M. WISDA Seventh great granddaughter of progenitor Nicholas Kegg.

WISE

DEBORAH ANN WISE Fifth great granddaughter of progenitor Nicholas Kegg. **DONALD H. WISE** [6363] (1911 – 2000) son of Harry and Blanche (McQuown) Wise married twice; first to Minerva Kate McMurray. Later, he married Naomi Ruth Morgan with whom he was father of (1). Donald retired as a machinist from Marion Power Shovel where he worked for many years. **EVALENA WISE** [6364] (1868 – 1935) daughter of Hiram and Christena (Kegg) Wise was a well-known and popular lady. For several years she was a clerk in the post office and had a wide circle of friends.

[6360A] Ann Arbor News (MI) April 20, 2010 [6360B] Fort Wayne News Sentinel (IN) May 16, 2009 [6360C] Fort Wayne Journal Gazette (IN) library clipping contributed by D. Sue Dible [6361] Brazzell Funeral Home, IN [6362] p.10A - News-Sentinel (IN) Sept 16, 1994 [6363] Marion Star (OH) Dec 27, 2000 [6364] Forest Review (OH) May 23, 1935, obtained by D. Sue Dible

HARRY DALE WISE [6365] (1881 – 1958) son of Hiram and Christena (Kegg) Wise, married Blanche McQuown with whom he was father of (1). **JENNIE WISE** (1870 – 1874) daughter of Hiram and Christena (Kegg) Wise. **KEITH DEVON WISE** (1954 – 1954) son of Sherman and Margaret (Pfenning) Wise. **TULLIS DANIEL WISE** (1875 – 1951) son of Hiram and Christena (Kegg) Wise, married Mary Belle Bowman with whom he was father of (1).

WISELEY

COURTNEY WISELEY Seventh great granddaughter of progenitor Nicholas Kegg.
RACHEL WISELEY Seventh great granddaughter of progenitor Nicholas Kegg.

WISEMAN

CORAL DORIS WISEMAN Seventh great granddaughter of progenitor Nicholas Kegg.

WITHERITE

BETSY JO WITHERITE Fifth great granddaughter of progenitor Nicholas Kegg.
CAROL ANN WITHERITE [6366] (1942 – 1944) daughter of Harold and Hazel (Gump) Witherite.
RANDALL HAROLD WITHERITE Fifth great grandson of progenitor Nicholas Kegg.

WITHERS

JEAN DELORES WITHERS (1926 – 2012) daughter of Thomas and Agnes (Nanna) Withers married twice, first to David Frederick Wheeland with whom she was mother of (2). Later, she married James Oliver Cox. **MARGARET MAY WITHERS** [6367] (1924 – 1931) six-year-old daughter of Thomas and Agnes (Nanna) Withers passed away after a brief illness of pneumonia. **SANDRA DIANE WITHERS** [6367A] aka "Sandy" (1936 – 2020) daughter of Thomas and Agnes (Nanna) Withers married David Emerson Grindle with whom she was mother of (2). Sandy retired after more than 25 years from Ashland City School's where she was a Library Aide. Sandy loved to be involved in the many activities of her family, friends, and community including study club, pinochle club, garden club, Ashland Symphony Orchestra Women's League and the Salvation Army Board to a name a few. She had a special fondness for the ladies in both her coffee and tennis group that met and enjoyed fellowship together. **THOMAS M. WITHERS** [6367B] (1931 – 2019) son of Thomas and Agnes (Nanna) Withers married Jeanne Clifford with whom he was father of (3). Tom proudly served in the United States Army during the Korean Conflict. He worked for more than 30 years for the Hoover Company in administration. Tom went to work for ServiceMaster for an additional 10 years as a building manager in New York City prior to his retirement. Throughout his life, Tom enjoyed fishing, golfing and working crossword puzzles. He was an avid coffee drinker, who loved the Indians, Browns, Buckeyes and Boston Celtics.

WITHROW

BARBARA ANN WITHROW Fifth great granddaughter of progenitor Nicholas Kegg.
DAVID RUSH WITHROW Fifth great grandson of progenitor Nicholas Kegg.
DIANE WITHROW Fifth great granddaughter of progenitor Nicholas Kegg.

WITT

ARTHUR WITT Sixth great grandson of progenitor Nicholas Kegg.

[6365] p.10 - Marion Star (OH) Feb 24, 1973, obtained by D. Sue Dible [6366] p.3 - Huntingdon Daily News (PA) Feb 5, 1944 [6367] Port Clinton Ohio Progressive Times (OH) Feb 5, 1931 [6367A] Ashland Times-Gazette (OH) June 18, 2020 [6367B] The Plain Dealer (OH) July 31, 2019

CAMBRIA MARIE WITT Seventh great granddaughter of progenitor Nicholas Kegg. **CATHY WITT** Sixth great granddaughter of progenitor Nicholas Kegg. **CONNIE WITT** Spouse of sixth great grandson of progenitor Nicholas Kegg. **EDWARD BRYAN WITT** [6368] (1961 – 1992) son of Paul and Rose (Catanese) married Elizabeth Jane Bray with whom he was father of (1). Edward was formerly the officer manager of Delta Industries in Grantsville. **JESSICA WITT** Seventh great granddaughter of progenitor Nicholas Kegg. **PAUL W. WITT** Seventh great grandson of progenitor Nicholas Kegg. **PAUL W. WITT** Sixth great grandson of progenitor Nicholas Kegg. **ROBERT WITT** Seventh great grandson of progenitor Nicholas Kegg. **SUZAN MARIE WITT** Sixth great granddaughter of progenitor Nicholas Kegg. **THOMAS LEE WITT** [6369] (1958 – 2004) aka "Tom" son of Paul and Rose (Catanese) Witt, married Sandra Burton with whom he was father of (1).

WITTEL

JASON M. WITTEL Seventh great grandson of progenitor Nicholas Kegg.
JESSE M. WITTEL Seventh great grandson of progenitor Nicholas Kegg.

WITTENDORF

FRANK WITTENDORF Sixth great grandson of progenitor Nicholas Kegg.

WITTMAIER

AMELIA WITTMAIER Eighth great granddaughter of progenitor Nicholas Kegg.
PENELOPE WITTMAIER aka "Penny" Eighth great granddaughter of progenitor Nicholas Kegg.

WIZER

ALISON WIZER Sixth great granddaughter of progenitor Nicholas Kegg.
SAM RAHLDG WIZER Sixth great grandson of progenitor Nicholas Kegg.

WOGAN

DANIEL WOGAN Fifth great grandson of progenitor Nicholas Kegg.
JEFFREY WOGAN Fifth great grandson of progenitor Nicholas Kegg.
STEPHEN WOGAN Fifth great grandson of progenitor Nicholas Kegg.

WOJAHN

KELSI WOJAHN Seventh great granddaughter of progenitor Nicholas Kegg.

WOLF

ALICE HESTER WOLF [6369A] (1930 – 1981) daughter of Arlington and Minnie (Lingenfelter) Wolf married Warren Emerson Clapper with whom she was mother of (2). Alice was employed was head cashier for K-Mart in the Altoona and Washington stores. **ANNABELLE RUTH WOLF** [6370] (1927 – 1974) aka Butch", daughter of Arlington and Minnie (Lingenfelter) Wolf, married Francis Ferman Barroner with whom she was mother of (3). **ARLINGTON ISAAC WOLF** [6371] (1910 – 1989) aka "Arlie", son of Daniel and Hester (Harclerode) Wolf, married Minnie Mabel Lingenfelter with whom he

---

[6368] p.26 Cumberland Times News (MD) Aug 20, 1992 [6369] Cumberland Times News (MD) Oct 21, 2004 [6369A] Altoona Mirror (PA) Sep 28, 1981, contributed by D. Sue Dible [6370] Sorge Funeral Home, PA [6371] Bedford County Historical Society (PA), book 117, page 35 obtained by D. Sue Dible

was father of (5). Arlie retired as a self-employed appliance Repairman. He was a member of the First United Methodist Church, Hollidaysburg, where he was a member of the men's Bible class. Arlie was also a member of the Railroad Historical Society. **DANIEL HOWARD WOLF** Fourth great grandson of progenitor Nicholas Kegg. **DONALD DAVID WOLF** [6372] (1929 – 1938) son of Donald and Wlima (Keiper) Wolf, died of tetanus. Lockjaw developed from what was believed to be a throat infection. It was later determined the infection had been caused by a splinter of wood in the knee obtained while playing on floor Donald David Wolf was a member of the Church of the Brethren Sunday school. He attended the fourth grade of the Hlllcrest School. **DONALD LEIDY WOLF** [6373] (1908 – 1978) son of Daniel and Hester (Harclerode) Wolf, married Wilma Lorreta Keiper with whom he was father of (3). Donald was a graduate of Pennsylvania State University School of Architecture, class of 1931. He retired from Dana Corporation where he had been employed as a tool designer for 24 years. **JAMES FREDERICK WOLF** aka "Jimmy", Fourth great grandson of progenitor Nicholas Kegg. **JEFFREY LEE WOLF** [6374] (1971 – 1997) son of Daniel and Sarah (Allen) Wolf was a graduate of Berks Vocational-Technology Center, East Campus, where he studied carpentry, he was a mixer driver for Allied Concrete. Before that he was a light technician for Zeus Light & Sound Co. Jeffrey was also a firefighter and had been a member of the Amity (Berks County) Fire Company for many years. He was a guitar player for the Ramones Tribute band and a member of the Reading Motorcycle Club and the Blacksmith's Shop of Amity. **RANDALL K. WOLF** aka "Randy" Fifth great grandson of progenitor Nicholas Kegg. **ROBERT K. WOLF** Fourth great grandson of progenitor Nicholas Kegg. **THOMAS DANIEL WOLF** Fourth great grandson of progenitor Nicholas Kegg. **WILLIAM A WOLF** aka "Billy" Fourth great grandson of progenitor Nicholas Kegg.

WOLFE

BONNIE LEE WOLFE Fifth great granddaughter of progenitor Nicholas Kegg.
CATHY A. WOLFE Fifth great granddaughter of progenitor Nicholas Kegg.
GEORGE BARTON WOLFE Fifth great grandson of progenitor Nicholas Kegg.
HEATHER RENEE WOLFE Seventh great granddaughter of progenitor Nicholas Kegg.
JAMES M. WOLFE Fifth great grandson of progenitor Nicholas Kegg.
LINDA LOU WOLFE Fifth great granddaughter of progenitor Nicholas Kegg.
MITCHELL WOLFE Seventh great grandson of progenitor Nicholas Kegg.

WOLFHOPE

SARAH WOLFHOPE Sixth great granddaughter of progenitor Nicholas Kegg.

WOLFSON

AMANDA WOLFSON Seventh great granddaughter of progenitor Nicholas Kegg.
ZACHARY WOLFSON Seventh great grandson of progenitor Nicholas Kegg.

WOLTER

DAVIN WOLTER Seventh great grandson of progenitor Nicholas Kegg.

WONDERLY

ANDREW JAMES WONDERLY Seventh great grandson of progenitor Nicholas Kegg. **BEULAH FAYE WONDERLY** [6375] (1911 – 2001) daughter of Harvey and Pearl (Coffman) Wonderly married

---

[6372] p.2 Altoona Tribune (PA) Sep 14, 1938 [6373] Bedford County Historical Society (PA), book 12 page 4719 obtained by D. Sue Dible [6374] The Morning Call (PA) June 12, 1997 [6375] Appeal Democrat (CA) Sep 25, 2001

twice; first to Leslie Albertus Kimerer with whom she was mother of (2). Later, she married Charles Martin Kimerer. Beulah was a member of the First Presbyterian Church of Colusa and served as former president of the Rebecca Lodge. **DAVID ADAM WONDERLY** Seventh great grandson of progenitor Nicholas Kegg. **ERIC JAMES WONDERLY** Seventh great grandson of progenitor Nicholas Kegg. **GERALD LYNELL WONDERLY** [6375A] (1933 – 1991) son of Ralph and Mildred (Wiseman) Wonderly, married Gloria Garloff with whom he was father of (2). A navy veteran, Gerald spent his tour of duty in the Pacific aboard the destroyer Black as electronics technician third class. Gerald was a communication technician for American Telephone and Telegraph for 36 years. He was an avid photographer and loved gardening. He also raised goldfish. **GLENN ALVIN WONDERLY** Fifth great grandson of progenitor Nicholas Kegg. **JACOB CLINTON WONDERLY** Seventh great grandson of progenitor Nicholas Kegg. **KEITH A. WONDERLY** Sixth great grandson of progenitor Nicholas Kegg. **KENNETH G. WONDERLY** Sixth great grandson of progenitor Nicholas Kegg. **KENNETH L. WONDERLY** Sixth great grandson of progenitor Nicholas Kegg. **LEONA M. WONDERLY** (1913 – 1987) daughter of Harvey and Pearl (Coffman) Wonderly married Volney Nicholas Vinson. Later, she married and divorced Edwin Clarence Skoglund. **PAUL ALAN WONDERLY** Seventh great grandson of progenitor Nicholas Kegg. **RALPH OTIS WONDERLY** [6376] (1908 – 1998) son of Harvey and Pearl (Coffman) Wonderly, married Mildred Faye Wiseman with whom he was father of (2). **RUSSELL R. WONDERLY** Sixth great grandson of progenitor Nicholas Kegg.

WONSETLER

AUBREY ELIZABETH WONSETLER Seventh great granddaughter of progenitor Nicholas Kegg. **DAVID MICHAEL WONSETLER** Sixth great grandson of progenitor Nicholas Kegg. **JOSEPH WAYNE WONSETLER** Sixth great grandson of progenitor Nicholas Kegg. **KAREN JENETTE WONSETLER** aka "Karrie" Seventh great granddaughter of progenitor Nicholas Kegg. **KIMBERLY LYNN WONSETLER** Seventh great granddaughter of progenitor Nicholas Kegg. **NATHAN JOSEPH WONSETLER** Seventh great grandson of progenitor Nicholas Kegg.

WOOD

DARREN T. WOOD Sixth great grandson of progenitor Nicholas Kegg.
DAVID E. WOOD Sixth great grandson of progenitor Nicholas Kegg.
DONNA M. WOOD Sixth great granddaughter of progenitor Nicholas Kegg.

WOODARD

ALICE LOUISE WOODARD Fifth great granddaughter of progenitor Nicholas Kegg. **CAROL SUE WOODARD** Fifth great granddaughter of progenitor Nicholas Kegg. **DENNIS JAY WOODARD** aka "Denny", Fifth great grandson of progenitor Nicholas Kegg. **DURWARD HUDDY WOODARD** aka "Woody", Fourth great grandson of progenitor Nicholas Kegg. **ELIZABETH AGNES WOODARD** aka "Betty" Fifth great granddaughter of progenitor Nicholas Kegg. **FRANCES ANN WOODARD** [6376A] (1934 – 2000) daughter of Durwood and Frances (Kreiter) Woodard married twice, first to Patrick Grady with whom she was mother of (3) and later to Ralph Grattan. Frances was a teacher of gifted students with the Sheffield/Sheffield Lake School System, a program she pioneered. Frances was a Martha Holden Jennings Scholar (an educational honor for exceptional teachers). She was a World Finalist Coach for Olympics of the Mind and a member of the National Education Association. **JOHN STARR WOODARD** Fifth great grandson of progenitor Nicholas Kegg. **KENNETH EDWIN WOODARD** (1919 – 1987) son of Sylvester and Agnes (Huddy) Woodard, married Rachel LaVan Steenrod with whom he was father of (4).

[6375A] Sacramento Bee (CA) Jan 17, 1958 [6376] The Sacramento Bee (CA) Oct 17, 1996

MARY JANE WOODARD (6377) (1938 – 1973) daughter of Durwood and Frances (Kreiter) Woodard married Ralph Merwin Brown.   **MICHAEL KEN WOODARD** (1942 – 1999) son of Kenneth and Rachel (La Van Steenrod) Woodard, married Patricia Anne Barnette.   **NICHOLAS S. JEWELL WOODARD** aka "Jewell" Fifth great grandson of progenitor Nicholas Kegg.   **STEVEN WAYNE WOODARD** Fifth great grandson of progenitor Nicholas Kegg.   **WAYNE ARTHUR WOODARD** (6378) (1915 – 1982) son of Sylvester and Agnes (Huddy) Woodard, married Virginia Eileen Green with whom he was father of (1). Later he married Janet Eloise Starr with whom he was father of (2).

WOODBURY

ROBIN E. WOODBURY Fifth great granddaughter of progenitor Nicholas Kegg.

WOODLING

DANIEL MARK WOODLING (6379) (2005 – 2005) son of Michael and Julie (Koontz) Woodling.   **MAVERICK WOODLING** Eighth great grandson of progenitor Nicholas Kegg.

WOODRING

ASHLEY WOODRING Seventh great granddaughter of progenitor Nicholas Kegg.   **CONNER WOODRING** Seventh great grandson of progenitor Nicholas Kegg.   **DALE ROBERT CECIL WOODRING** (6379A) aka "Woody" (1955 – 2002) son of Robert and Mary Anne (Lewis) Woodring. Dale worked as a sales representative at Dick's Homecare, Altoona. He was active in the Pittsburgh Steel Wheelers, appearing in commercials with the Pittsburgh Steelers promoting the National Wheel Chair Games. Mr. Woodring was an accomplished wrestler and football player, having attended Lock Haven State University on a sports scholarship. His hobbies included lifting weights and riding his four-wheeler. However, his real joy was spending time with his family.   **DAVID W. WOODRING** Sixth great grandson of progenitor Nicholas Kegg.   **DEBBIE K. WOODRING** Sixth great granddaughter of progenitor Nicholas Kegg.   **JENI MARIE WOODRING** Seventh great granddaughter of progenitor Nicholas Kegg.   **JODI LYNN WOODRING** Seventh great granddaughter of progenitor Nicholas Kegg.   **PHYLLIS L. WOODRING** Sixth great granddaughter of progenitor Nicholas Kegg.

WOODS

DANIEL SCOTT WOODS Eighth great grandson of progenitor Nicholas Kegg.   **DAVID PORTER WOODS** (6380) (1952 – 1995) son of Joseph and Bessie (Porter) Woods, was an artist known for his woodworking talent. David showed an aptitude for working with his hands, and as an adult he made furniture, cabinets and other items. He was most proud of decorations he had hung at the Insect Museum at the Smithsonian Institution in Washington.   **EDDIE WOODS** Sixth great grandson of progenitor Nicholas Kegg.   **ELIZABETH PIRIE WOODS** Fifth great granddaughter of progenitor Nicholas Kegg.   **JEAN BALINDA WOODS** Sixth great granddaughter of progenitor Nicholas Kegg.   **JESSICA LINDSEY WOODS** aka "Jess", Sixth great granddaughter of progenitor Nicholas Kegg.   **JIMMY WOODS** Sixth great grandson of progenitor Nicholas Kegg.   **JOSEPH L. WOODS** Sixth great grandson of progenitor Nicholas Kegg.   **MARY JANNEY WOODS** Fifth great granddaughter of progenitor Nicholas Kegg.   **SEAN PATRICK WOODS** Sixth great grandson of progenitor Nicholas Kegg.   **VICKY WOODS** Sixth great granddaughter of progenitor Nicholas Kegg.   **WILLIAM BROPHY WOODS** Sixth great grandson of progenitor Nicholas Kegg.

(6376A) Logan Daily News (OH) May 10, 2000 (6377) Logan Daily News (OH) Feb 27, 1958 (6378) Detroit Free Press (MI) Sep 19, 1982 (6379) Bedford County Historical Society Pioneer Library (PA), book 96, p.235 obtained by D. Sue Dible (6379A) p.9 - Altoona Mirror (PA) May 28, 2002 (6380) p.4B - The Sun (MD) - Aug 26, 1995

WOODSON

ARLINE MABEL WOODSON [6381] (1910 – 1990) daughter of Roy and Edna (Dwigans) Woodson, married Francis Bernard Roberts with whom she was mother of (3). **ASHLEY MARIE WOODSON** Seventh great granddaughter of progenitor Nicholas Kegg. **BARRY RICHARD WOODSON** Sixth great grandson of progenitor Nicholas Kegg. **CARRIE WOODSON** Sixth great granddaughter of progenitor Nicholas Kegg. **CORALINE WOODSON** Eighth great granddaughter of progenitor Nicholas Kegg. **DENISE WOODSON** Sixth great granddaughter of progenitor Nicholas Kegg. **GABRIEL WOODSON** Eighth great grandson of progenitor Nicholas Kegg. **GARY D. WOODSON** Fifth great grandson of progenitor Nicholas Kegg. **LARRY LEROY WOODSON** [6383] (1937 – 1987) son of Bernard and Edythe (Christensen) Woodson married Arlene Williams with whom he was father of (2). Larry served four years with the United States Navy. He followed the carpenter trade and lately was getting interested in raising sheep. He loved the outdoors and especially enjoyed golf. **MARCIA WOODSON** Fifth great granddaughter of progenitor Nicholas Kegg. **NORMA FAE WOODSON** [6386] (1925 – 1998) daughter of Roy and Edna (Dwigans) Woodson married twice; first to James Robert Kidd with whom she was mother of (2). Later, she married Edward Edwin Barlow. Norma was a homemaker. **PRESLEY WOODSON** Seventh great granddaughter of progenitor Nicholas Kegg. **REBECCA PAIGE WOODSON** Seventh great granddaughter of progenitor Nicholas Kegg. **RICHARD WOODSON** aka "Dick" Fifth great grandson of progenitor Nicholas Kegg. **RICHARD L. WOODSON** Sixth great grandson of progenitor Nicholas Kegg. **RITA M. WOODSON** Fifth great granddaughter of progenitor Nicholas Kegg. **TANNER WOODSON** Seventh great grandson of progenitor Nicholas Kegg. **TYLER WOODSON** Seventh great grandson of progenitor Nicholas Kegg. **VALERIE WOODSON** Sixth great granddaughter of progenitor Nicholas Kegg. **VICKI WOODSON** Sixth great granddaughter of progenitor Nicholas Kegg.

WOODWARD

ALEXIS WOODWARD Sixth great granddaughter of progenitor Nicholas Kegg. **BRAYDEN WOODWARD** Sixth great grandson of progenitor Nicholas Kegg. **GARY JOHN WOODWARD** [6387] (1963 – 1987) son of Gerald and Joan (Deno) Woodward, married Sandra Statile. Gary was an avid rodeo enthusiast and professional bull rider. He belonged to the American Rodeo Association and the Professional Cowboys Rodeo Association. He also enjoyed hunting and fishing. Gary was employed as a machinist with the American Tissue Co. **GEORGE F. WOODWARD** (born abt. 1909) son of Jay and Clarissa (Callahan) Woodward. **GERALD THOMAS WOODWARD** Sixth great grandson of progenitor Nicholas Kegg. **JAY C. WOODWARD** (1911 – 1911) son of Jay and Clarissa (Callahan) Woodward. **MICKYLE WOODWARD** Seventh great granddaughter of progenitor Nicholas Kegg. **MOLLY ROSE WOODWARD** Seventh great granddaughter of progenitor Nicholas Kegg. **ROSA BELLE WOODWARD** [6388] (1881 – 1963) daughter of James and Catherine (Kegg) Woodward, married Everet Elwood Crevison with whom she was mother of (4). Rosa was Postmistress at Athol, NY until she retired in 1941. She was a member of the First Methodist church and the WSCS and a 27-year member of Queens Village chapter, Order of Eastern Star at Warrensburg, NY.

WOOLF

JAMES AARON WOOLF Sixth great grandson of progenitor Nicholas Kegg.

[6381] Free Press (IA) Sep 3, 1986, obtained by D. Sue Dible [6383] Stuart Herald (IA) Feb 20, 1987, obtained by D. Sue Dible [6386] The Des Moines Register (IA) Feb 10, 1998 [6387] The Post-Star (Glens Falls, New York) Nov 23, 1987. [6388] p.5 - Kenton Times (OH) Jan. 15, 1963, obtained by D. Sue Dible

WORDEN

LANDON WORDEN Seventh great grandson of progenitor Nicholas Kegg.
LANE WORDEN Seventh great grandson of progenitor Nicholas Kegg.
LINZEY WORDEN Seventh great granddaughter of progenitor Nicholas Kegg
LUKE WORDEN Seventh great grandson of progenitor Nicholas Kegg.

WORGAN

BOLDEN SAMUEL WORGAN Sixth great grandson of progenitor Nicholas Kegg.
DAVID BOLDEN WORGAN Fifth great grandson of progenitor Nicholas Kegg.
DIANE WORGAN Fifth great granddaughter of progenitor Nicholas Kegg.
MADISON WORGAN Sixth great granddaughter of progenitor Nicholas Kegg.
NANCY WORGAN Fifth great granddaughter of progenitor Nicholas Kegg.
SOPHIA A. WORGAN Sixth great granddaughter of progenitor Nicholas Kegg.

WRIGHT

AVA WRIGHT Eighth great granddaughter of progenitor Nicholas Kegg.
CHAD WRIGHT Fifth great grandson of progenitor Nicholas Kegg.
CHARLIE WRIGHT Seventh great grandson of progenitor Nicholas Kegg.
CINDY WRIGHT Fifth great granddaughter of progenitor Nicholas Kegg.
EDWIN A. WRIGHT [6389] (1913 – 1987) son of Albert and Florence (Graham) Wright, married Julie Elizabeth Hansen. Edwin was a retired carpenter.
ELIOT WRIGHT Eighth great grandson of progenitor Nicholas Kegg.
GLENN D. WRIGHT Fifth great grandson of progenitor Nicholas Kegg.
JUSTIN WRIGHT Eighth great grandson of progenitor Nicholas Kegg.
KEITH VICTOR WRIGHT Fifth great grandson of progenitor Nicholas Kegg.
LEILA HAZEL WRIGHT [6390] (1909 – 1941) daughter of Albert and Florence (Graham) Wright, married Walter Milton Corwin with whom she was mother of (3).
LINCOLN WRIGHT Seventh great grandson of progenitor Nicholas Kegg.
MATTHEW WRIGHT Eighth great grandson of progenitor Nicholas Kegg.
MORGAN WRIGHT Seventh great grandson of progenitor Nicholas Kegg.
ROBERT ELLSWORTH WRIGHT [6390A] aka "Bob" (1926 – 2012) son of Stanley and Ruth (McDaniel) Wright, married Betty Louise Blades with whom he was father of (4).
SANDRA WRIGHT Fifth great granddaughter of progenitor Nicholas Kegg.
SUE KATHERINE WRIGHT Fifth great granddaughter of progenitor Nicholas Kegg.

WRIGLEY

ANDREW WRIGLEY Sixth great grandson of progenitor Nicholas Kegg.
DAVID WRIGLEY Sixth great grandson of progenitor Nicholas Kegg.
JENNIFER WRIGLEY Sixth great granddaughter of progenitor Nicholas Kegg.

WYANT

ANDIE WYANT Eighth great grandson of progenitor Nicholas Kegg. **BLAINE E. WYANT** [6391] (1938 – 2008) aka "Cowboy", son of Harold and Laura (Fisher) Wyant, married Donna McQuade with whom he was father of (5). Blaine was a U.S. Army veteran. He retired from Bethlehem Steel Johnstown

---

[6389] p.A6-Pierce County Herald (WA) May 12, 1987, obtained by D. Sue Dible [6390] The San Bernardino County Sun (CA) Oct 8, 1941 [6390A] Daily Courier (Prescott, AZ) July 1, 2018 [6391] Daily American (PA) Sep 27, 2008, transcribed by Barry and Betty Christy

after 37 years. Blaine was a member of Berlin Brethren Church and New Baltimore Sportsmen's Club. He was a former member of Somerset Co. Saddle Club and Berlin American Legion Home. **COLE WYANT** Eighth great grandson of progenitor Nicholas Kegg. **DAVID H. WYANT** Fifth great grandson of progenitor Nicholas Kegg. **DIANNE CAROL WYANT** Fifth great granddaughter of progenitor Nicholas Kegg. **DONNA MAE WYANT** Fifth great granddaughter of progenitor Nicholas Kegg. **EDWARD WYANT** Sixth great grandson of progenitor Nicholas Kegg. **HAROLD WYANT** Sixth great grandson of progenitor Nicholas Kegg. **JAMES E. WYANT** Sixth great grandson of progenitor Nicholas Kegg. **KATHY WYANT** Sixth great granddaughter of progenitor Nicholas Kegg. **KAYLA WYANT** Eighth great granddaughter of progenitor Nicholas Kegg. **KRISTOPHER LEE WYANT** Seventh great grandson of progenitor Nicholas Kegg. **LINDA WYANT** Fifth great granddaughter of progenitor Nicholas Kegg. **MACKENZIE MARIE WYANT** [6391A] aka "Kenzie" (1996 – 2014) daughter of Kristopher and Heather (Ritter) Wyant. Kenzie graduated from Yough High School and was employed as a waitress for Kerber's Dairy. **NANCY WYANT** Sixth great granddaughter of progenitor Nicholas Kegg.

WYCKOFF

ALBERT WESLEY WYCKOFF [6392] (1893 – 1967) son of John and Emma (Calkins) Wyckoff, married Golda May White. During the latter part of World War I, Albert was employed by a livery company in Kansas City, Mo., traveling the Southwest as a horse buyer and seller under government contract. He spent several years in Texas and Oklahoma and in later years enjoyed telling of his many interesting experiences in the Southwest during the last days of the frontier west. In his early twenties, Albert returned to this area to work for Swift & Co. in St. Joseph, Mo., where he had previously worked as a messenger. He later transferred to the Swift owned St. Louis Independent Packing Co., where he stayed until his retirement in 1958. He spent his remaining years with his family in St. Louis but took every opportunity to return to Iowa for visits with his relatives and old friends. He valued his friendships highly and always enjoyed these visits. He loved to talk and loved a joke and somehow, he touched all who knew him with the great kindness of his heart. **ALISON WYCKOFF** Sixth great granddaughter of progenitor Nicholas Kegg. **ALYSSA ROSE WYCKOFF** Seventh great granddaughter of progenitor Nicholas Kegg. **ANITA MADGE WYCKOFF** (1889 – 1972) daughter of Frank and Amanda (Comell) Wyckoff, married John William Norman with whom she was mother of (9). **ARTHUR ELMER WYCKOFF** [6393] (1898 – 1960) son of Louis and Elsina (Rabourn) Wyckoff, married Essica Gladys Shehan with whom he was father of (2). Arthur was well known as a mechanic. **ASHLEY WYCKOFF** Eighth great granddaughter of progenitor Nicholas Kegg. **BARBARA JANE WYCKOFF** [6393A] (1921 – 2005) daughter of Bert and Edith (Greelee) Wyckoff, married Lowell Robert Hubbard with whom she was mother of (3). Barbara was employed as a teller with Commerce Bank for 13 years. **BERT CLYDE WYCKOFF** [6393B] (1878 – 1951) son of John and Barbara (Laird) Wyckoff, married Edith Ann Greelee with whom he was father of (11). Bert was a rural mail carrier out of the Bedford post office for a number of years and was later a city carrier in St. Joseph until he retired. He was prominent in musical circles in Bedford, being a member of the Bedford band, of which he was director for a time. Bert was a member of the Methodist church, National Association of Letter Carriers, Spanish American War Veterans camp, and was a 32nd degree Mason. **BERT CHRIS WYCKOFF** [6393C] "Bertie" (1933 – 2010) son of John and Hildreth (Rhoades) Wyckoff, married Suzanne Jane Gausz with whom he was father of (4). Bert earned the rank of Eagle Scout as a young man and went on to serve his country during the Korean and Cold Wars. Bert worked as a software engineer from the industry's early years for many different government contractors till his retirement. **BERTHA ETTA WYCKOFF** [6394] (1870 – 1878) daughter of John and Barbara (Laird) Wyckoff. **BEULAH BELL WYCKOFF** (1919 – 1919) daughter of Louis and Elsina (Rabourn) Wyckoff. **BONNIE VESPER WYCKOFF** [6395] (1921 – 2012)

[6391A] Greensburg Tribune Review (PA) Oct 29, 2014 [6392] p.6 Bedford Times-Press (IA) Apr 27, 1967, transcribed by Julie Johnson [6393] p8 Bedford Times-Press (IA) Feb 18, 1960, transcribed by Julie Johnson [6393A] St. Joseph News-Press (MO) March 15, 2005 [6393B] The Gazette (CO) Apr 7, 2010 [6393C] Bedford Times-Press (IA) Mar 1, 1951 contributed by Julie Johnson IAGenweb [6394] p.3 Taylor County Republican (IA) June 27, 1878, transcribed by Julia Johnson [6395] Wyoming Tribune Eagle (WY) August 3, 2012 daughter of Louis and Elsina (Rabourn) Wyckoff, married Don S. Weil with whom she was mother of (6). Bonnie was employed as a clerk for Montgomery Ward. **BRENDA WYCKOFF** Fifth great granddaughter of progenitor Nicholas Kegg. **BRENT WYCKOFF** [6396] (1959 – 2019) son of Donald and Olivia (Smith) Wyckoff, married Michelle Cunningham with whom he was father of (2). Brent worked at JLL Commercial Real Estate as Chief Assistant Engineer. He loved to ride his Harley and had a big heart for all his animals. **BRITTANY WYCKOFF** Eighth great granddaughter of progenitor Nicholas Kegg. **BRYANNA WYCKOFF** Seventh great granddaughter of progenitor Nicholas Kegg. **CARL ALVIN WYCKOFF** (1896 – 1968) son of Louis and Minnie Etta (Greenlee) Wyckoff. **CARMEN WYCKOFF** Fifth great granddaughter of progenitor Nicholas Kegg. **CAROLYN ANN WYCKOFF** Fifth great granddaughter of progenitor Nicholas Kegg. **CARRIE FAYE WYCKOFF** [6397] (1914 – 2000) aka "Fay" daughter of Louis and Elsina (Rabourn) Wyckoff married William Albert Pullen with whom she was mother of (5). Fay's family was the most important part of her life. She worked together with her husband managing an oil company with an adjoining cafe. Fay enjoyed reading, cross stitching, and making quilts, which she loved giving to family members. **CHARLIE EDWARD WYCKOFF** Eighth great grandson of progenitor Nicholas Kegg. **CHRISTOPHER WYCKOFF** Sixth great grandson of progenitor Nicholas Kegg. **CLARA LUANNE WYCKOFF** [6398] (1937 – 2021) aka "Luanne" daughter of Fred and Erma (Kysar) Wyckoff married Frank Elliott with whom she was mother of (4). Later she married Luke Lukat. Luanne loved working crossword puzzles, reading, walking, swimming, watching movies, and playing pool. Luanne also enjoyed traveling by bus and Amtrak. Luanne was a life member of the VFW Auxiliary. **CRAIG LAVERNE WYCKOFF** Sixth great grandson of progenitor Nicholas Kegg. **DAVID LYNN WYCKOFF** Fifth great grandson of progenitor Nicholas Kegg. **DIANE ELAINE WYCKOFF** Fifth great granddaughter of progenitor Nicholas Kegg. **DILLION WYCKOFF** Seventh great grandson of progenitor Nicholas Kegg. **DON AUBREY WYCKOFF** (1894 – 1966) son of Frank and Amanda (Comell) Wyckoff was a veteran of WWI where he served in the 313 French Mortar Battery Co. E. 88 Div.; **DONALD DEAN WYCKOFF** [6399] (1922 – 1996) son of Moran and Mabel (Harris) Wyckoff, married Mary Alice Larkin with whom he was father of (2). **DONALD LAVERNE WYCKOFF** [6399A] aka "Buddy" (1922 – 2014) son of Arthur and Essica (Shehan) Wyckoff married Olive Julia Smith with whom he was father of (5). Buddy served in the U.S. Navy during WWII. He worked for several railroad companies and retired from Rock Island. **DONN ELDON WYCKOFF** Sixth great grandson of progenitor Nicholas Kegg. **DOROTHY ILENE WYCKOFF** [6400] (1915 – 1990) daughter of Bert and Edith (Greelee) Wyckoff, married Leonard Wayne McKnight with whom she was mother of (10). **DORRIS IRENE WYCKOFF** (1915 – 1916) daughter of Bert and Edith (Greelee) Wyckoff. **ELDON JUNIOR WYCKOFF** [6401] (1920 – 1996) son of Moran and Bessie (Harris) Wyckoff married Edwina Witherspoon with whom he was father of (2). MSGT Wyckoff US Army Air Corps was a veteran of WWII. **ERIC B. WYCKOFF** Sixth great grandson of progenitor Nicholas Kegg. **ERNEST S. WYCKOFF** [6402] (1869 – 1887) aka "Ernie", son of Joseph and Emma (Laird) Wyckoff. **ESPER MAY WYCKOFF** (1912 – 1994) daughter of Louis and Elsina (Rabourn) Wyckoff married Clarence H. Smith. **ETHAN WYCKOFF** Seventh great grandson of progenitor Nicholas Kegg. **EVA ELSIE WYCKOFF** Third great granddaughter of progenitor Nicholas Kegg. **FRANK ALBERT WYCKOFF** [6403] (1865 – 1926) son of Joseph and Emma (Laird) Wyckoff married twice; first to Amanda J. Comell with whom he was father of (3). Later, he married Elizabeth (Saltzman) Schlappia. **FRANK EDWARD WYCKOFF** [6404] (1905 – 1907) son of Bert and Edith (Greelee) Wyckoff had been ill for several weeks with catarrhal pneumonia, and for days before the end came, its condition was critical. However, at times it rallied, bringing sweet hopes to the loving anxious parents and on Tuesday its condition was such that the father felt safe to leave and attend to his regular avocation as rural carrier; when the summons came, he had the added sorrow of not being by the side of his little one. Three times have these grief-stricken parents been

---

[6396] Des Moines Register (IA) May 26, 2019 [6397] Bedford Times-Press (IA) April 12, 2000 [6398] Nelson-Boylan-LeRette Funeral Chapel, Inc., IA [6399] The Kansas City Star (MO) Jan 21, 1995 [6399A] Iowa Living Magazine July 10, 2014 [6400] Savannah Reporter and Andrew County Democrat (MO) Sep 20, 1990 [6401] The Kansas City Star (MO) Jan 7, 2005 [6402] The Ringgold Record (IA) 1887 transcribed by Sharon R. Becker [6303] Mount Ayr Record-News (IA) 1926 transcribed by Sharon R. Becker [6404] Times-Republican (IA) June 6, 1907 transcribed by Julia Johnson

called upon to bear this greatest sorrow that can come to father and mother. Three children have come to make happy their home, to make life brighter, to make their home circle complete and more precious, and each, after tarrying a little while have gone back to Him who gave them. A few years ago, their first-born was called, and only a few weeks ago, they followed to the grave all that was mortal of another precious babe. Frank was the only one left to them and as his little body is laid away, it seems to his loving parents as though a pall of eternal night had fallen, shutting out all sunshine and happiness from their lives. **FRED WYCKOFF** (1891 – 1966) son of Frank and Amanda (Comell) Wyckoff, was a veteran of WWI. **FRED EDWARD WYCKOFF** [6405, 6406] (1908 – 1987) son of Louis and Elsina (Rabourn) Wyckoff married twice; first to Helen Mildren Wooten with whom he was father of (4). Later, he married Erma Coryl Kysar with whom he was father of (7). **GARY WYCKOFF** Fifth great grandson of progenitor Nicholas Kegg. **GLEN DREXEL WYCKOFF** [6407] (1901 – 1956) son of Louis and Elsina (Rabourn) Wyckoff, married Letha Beatrice Pace with whom he was father of (3). **HANNAH WYCKOFF** Eighth great granddaughter of progenitor Nicholas Kegg. **HELEN ESTHER WYCKOFF** [6408] (1913 – 1994) daughter of Bert and Edith (Greelee) Wyckoff married twice; first to Kersey Clinton Clarke with whom she was mother of (2). Later, she married Winfield Scott Eshnaur with whom she was mother of (2). Helen and her husband Winfieldowned Capco Canvas Company in West Palm Beach, Florida. **HENRY EDWARD WYCKOFF** [6409] (1924 – 1997) son of Moran and Mabel (Harris) Wyckoff, married Evelyn Mae Jones with whom he was father of (2). Henry was a veteran of World War II having served in the U. S. Army Air Forces. **INFANT WYCKOFF** (1896 – 1896) child of Louis and Minnie Etta (Greenlee) Wyckoff. **JACK OWEN WYCKOFF** [6410] (1932 – 2011) son of Fred and Helen (Wooten) Wyckoff, married Evon A. Moore. Jack worked primarily as a mechanic but also drove the school bus for many years. **JANINE MICHELE WYCKOFF** Sixth great granddaughter of progenitor Nicholas Kegg. **JARED WYCKOFF** Seventh great grandson of progenitor Nicholas Kegg. **JEAN LOUISE WYCKOFF** [6411] (1945 – 2017) aka "Louise" daughter of Fred and Erma (Kysar) Wyckoff married Keith Platt with whom she was mother of (2). Louise was a very intelligent, upbeat, optimistic person. She enjoyed making crafts, sewing, crochet, painting and drawing, song writing, piano playing, yardwork, birds, casinos, and reading. **JEFFREY WYCKOFF** Sixth great grandson of progenitor Nicholas Kegg. **JEFFREY W. WYCKOFF** Sixth great grandson of progenitor Nicholas Kegg. **JERRY ALLAN WYCKOFF** Sixth great grandson of progenitor Nicholas Kegg. **JERRY ALLEN WYCKOFF** [6412] (1931 – 1999) son of Fred and Helen (Wooten) Wyckoff, married Shirley J. Keough with whom he was father of (4). Jerry was employed as a long-haul truck driver for many years. **JESSE LEE WYCKOFF** Seventh great grandson of progenitor Nicholas Kegg. **JOANNE KATHRYN WYCKOFF** [6413] (1935 – 2020) daughter of Fred and Helen (Wooten) Wyckoff married Ellis H. Scofield with whom she was mother of (2). Joanne had a variety of interests and enjoyed listening to country music, going to rodeos, watching car racing on TV and at the Adams County Speedway. In her early years, she drove in the demolition derby in Bedford, Iowa. She also enjoyed reading and doing puzzle books. Some of her favorite activities included crocheting, quilting and sewing. Joanne won awards for her afghans, quilts and crocheted doll clothes. **JOE DEAN WYCKOFF** [6414] (1933 – 2020) son of Fred and Helen (Wooten) Wyckoff married Evelyn Arlene Harig with whom he was father of (3). When Joe was 17 years old, he went into the U.S. Navy serving 3 years on the USS Boxer, which was a large Aircraft Carrier during the Korean War. **JOHN WYCKOFF** Sixth great grandson of progenitor Nicholas Kegg. **JOHN K. WYCKOFF** [6414A] aka "Pat" (1931 – 2022) son of John and Hildreth Irene (Henderson) Wyckoff, married Doris A. Ottinger with whom he was father of (3). Pat served in the U.S. Army in a MASH unit during the Korean War. Later, he worked for and retired from Wire Rope. Running was a passion of his. Pat ran 26 marathons and many other shorter races. **JOHN KENNETH WYCKOFF** [6415] (1910 – 1991) son of Bert and Edith (Greelee) Wyckoff, married Hildreth Irene

---

[6405] St. Joseph News-Press (MO) March 16, 1937 [6406] Nelson-Boylan-LeRette Funeral Chapel, IA [6407] p.6 Bedford Times-Press (IA) Oct 12, 1972, transcribed by Julie Johnson [6408] Palm Beach Post (FL) Nov 11, 1994 [6409] Kansas City Star (MO) Sept 12, 2004 [6410] News-Press Now (MO) Sep 7, 2011 [6411] The Red Oak Express (IA) Apr. 25, 2017 [6412] Oakland Tribune (CA) Aug 29, 1999 transcribed by Nancy Hart Servin [6413] Clarinda Herald-Journal (IA) April 2, 2020 [6414] Olinger Funeral, Cremation & Cemetery-Crown Hill, CO [6414A] St. Joseph News-Press (MO) May 24, 2022, obtained by D. Sue Dible [6415] St. Joseph News-Press (MO) June 9, 1992

Henderson Rhoades with whom he was father of (3). **JOHN WESLEY WYCKOFF** [6416] (1872 – 1951) son of John and Barbara (Laird) Wyckoff married twice; first to Emma Calkins with whom he was father of (1). Later, he married Lucile Yerty Vandeman. John was a retired carpenter for Swift & Co.; **JOSEPH ALVA WYCKOFF** [6416A] (1910 – 1981) son of Louis and Mary (Rabourn) Wyckoff, married Doris Elizabeth David with whom he was father of (2). Joseph was employed by Cudahy Packing Co. in Bedford for 23 years and was custodian at Bedford High School for 14 years. Joseph was known as being kind and considerate **JUDY WYCKOFF** Fifth great granddaughter of progenitor Nicholas Kegg. **JULIA CAROLYN WYCKOFF** [6417] (1939 – 2004) daughter of Fred and Erma (Kysar) Wyckoff married twice; first to Russell Raymond Lewis with whom she was mother of (3). Later, she married Darold Jerry Smith with whom she was mother of (2). Julia enjoyed gardening, floral arranging and bird watching. **LANA WYCKOFF** Fifth great granddaughter of progenitor Nicholas Kegg. **LARRY WYCKOFF** [6417A] aka "Fuzzy" (1942 – 2006) son of Eldon and Edwina (Witherspoon) Wyckoff had a Ph. D in Anthropology and served four years in the Navy. He was a co-owner of The Glass Barn, Inc. Fuzzy volunteered for many activities and organizations such as Bridging the Gap, The Sherwood Center, and United Way Day of Caring. He was father of (1). **LARY WYCKOFF** Fifth great grandson of progenitor Nicholas Kegg. **LAURA WYCKOFF** Fifth great granddaughter of progenitor Nicholas Kegg. **LEE ARCHER WYCKOFF** [6418] (1918 – 1923) son of Louis and Mary Elsina (Rabourn) Wyckoff was sick only a few weeks. The little one made a brave fight for life, but his little body was too weak, and he went back to the Great Master who gave. **LEILA EDNA WYCKOFF** [6419] (1891 – 1908) daughter of Louis and Minnie Etta (Greenlee) Wyckoff was sick but a few days and then the friends thought but little about it, as she was so uncomplaining, but this is a verification of the old adage, "In the midst of life we are in death." This young girl was the picture of health and bid fair to live to a good old age, but she is no more. **LENA EDNA WYCKOFF** [6420] (1907 – 1907) daughter of Bert and Edith (Greelee) Wyckoff was apparently healthy and hearty. Lena appeared to have caught a cold, but it was not thought to be seriously ill, and the loving parents had no thought that the angel of death was hovering nigh. Thursday morning Mr. Wyckoff arose and went to the bedside of his wife who was sleeping with the babe upon her arm. He awoke Mrs. Wyckoff, and bent over to see the little one, when he discovered that it was dead. Sometime during the night, the messenger had come, and the soul of Little Lenna had gone, pure, white and undefiled, back to Him who gave it. **LEROY DALLAS WYCKOFF** [6421] (1905 – 1987) son of Louis and Mary Elsina (Rabourn) Wyckoff married Blanche Estelle Whitlock. **LINDA WYCKOFF** Fifth great granddaughter of progenitor Nicholas Kegg. **LISA S. WYCKOFF** Sixth great granddaughter of progenitor Nicholas Kegg. **LLOYD HAROLD WYCKOFF** [6421A] (1924 – 1983) son of Glen and Letha (Pace) Wyckoff, married Cha Hui Kim. Lloyd was a retired Army Staff sergeant and a member of Korean Community Presbyterian Church; **LOLA LUCILE WYCKOFF** [6421B] (1925 – 2006) daughter of Glen and Letha (Pace) Wyckoff, married Loy Donald McNutt with whom she was mother of (5). Lola was a homemaker. She served as PTA President at James School KC. Lola enjoyed gardening, crafts and was an all-around Good Samaritan. **LORI LYNN WYCKOFF** Sixth great granddaughter of progenitor Nicholas Kegg. **LOUIS ELMER WYCKOFF** [6422] (1866 – 1937) son of John and Barbara (Laird) Wyckoff married twice; first to Minnie Etta Greenlee with whom he was father of (4). Later, he married Mary Elsina Rabourn with whom he was father of (14). Louis was very well known in this community. He worked faithfully and well at his trade his entire life. He was known for his excellent workmanship, his dependability and his honesty. **LYNNDA A. WYCKOFF** Sixth great granddaughter of progenitor Nicholas Kegg. **MARK WYCKOFF** Sixth great grandson of progenitor Nicholas Kegg. **MARTHA J WYCKOFF** (1919 – 1997) daughter of Bert and Edith (Greelee) Wyckoff, married Alfred Thomas Carpenter with whom she was mother of (1). **MARY ADELIA WYCKOFF** (1864 – 1864) daughter of John and Barbara (Laird) Wyckoff.

[6416] p.5 Bedford Times-Press (IA) Dec 6, 1951 transcribed by Julia Johnson [6416A] p.4- Bedford Times-Press (IA) Nov 26, 1981 contributed by Julie Johnson IAGenweb [6417] Pioneer Press (WI) Jan. 7, 2004 [6417A] Kansas City Star (MO) Jan 25, 2006, obtained by D. Sue Dible [6418] Bedford Free Press (IA) May 17, 1923, transcribed by Julia Johnson [6419] Bedford Free Press (IA) Sep 10, 1908, transcribed by Julia Johnson [6420] p.3 Bedford Times-Republican (IA) Apr 25, 1907, transcribed by Julia Johnson [6421] The Des Moines Register (IA) Oct 13, 1987 [6421A] p.43- State (Columbia, South Carolina) Apr 24, 1983 [6421B] Examiner (Independence - Blue Springs - Grain Valley, MO) July 7, 2006 [6422] p.7 Bedford Times-Press (IA) Nov 25, 1937, transcribed by Julia Johnson

MARY ELIZABETH WYCKOFF [6423] (1912 – 1913) daughter of Bert and Edith (Greelee) Wyckoff had pneumonia and was sick only a day.   **MASON EDWARD WYCKOFF** [6424, 6425] (2014 – 2016) son of Dillion and Stephanie (Erickson) Wyckoff called himself, "Me Me", his father called him Edward, and grandpa called him everything. He was full of energy, surrounded himself with stuffed animals, especially cows, loved to fly a kite, and watch his YouTube videos which he called, "his games." He was a loveable little boy who was murdered by his mother. A custody battle caused erratic behavior in the mentally unstable mother who took her own life.   **MORAN ELDON WYCKOFF** [6426] (1893 – 1984) son of Louis and Minnie Etta (Greenlee) Wyckoff married twice; first to Bessie Elizabeth Harris with whom he was father of (1). Later, he married Mabel C. Harris, with whom he was father of (2). Moran was a millwright for the Volney Felt Co. before he retired in 1963. He was an Army veteran of World War I and a member of the Veterans of Foreign Wars.   **NELLIE BEATRICE WYCKOFF** (1927 – 2001) daughter of Glen and Letha (Pace) Wyckoff, married Charles Otis Lemert with whom she was mother of (1). **NELLIE MARIE WYCKOFF** [6427] (1884 – 1959) daughter of Oren and Alice (Kegg) Wyckoff, married Floyd Wesley Keiser with whom she was mother of (2).   **NINA ESTELLA WYCKOFF** [6428] (1917 – 2008) daughter of Louis and Mary Elsina (Rabourn) Wyckoff married Melvin Eugene Gaule with whom she was mother of (5).   **ORPHA LOLA WYCKOFF** (1898 – 1950) daughter of Samuel and Minnie (Whisler) Wyckoff.   **PATRICIA D. WYCKOFF** Sixth great granddaughter of progenitor Nicholas Kegg.   **PAUL STANLEY WYCKOFF** (1908 – 1979) son of Bert and Edith (Greelee) Wyckoff, married Mildred Violet Cleveland. **REX RAYMOND WYCKOFF** [6429] (1923 – 2013) son of Louis and Mary Elsina (Rabourn) Wyckoff married Eva Lavonne Churchill with whom he was father of (4). Family is what Rex valued the most. Rex was employed as a mail carrier for the United States Post office and after retirement enjoyed traveling the country on his motorcycle collecting state patches to sew on his cycling vest. Rex enjoyed being very active with the American Legion. He helped with a variety of their activities but was most passionate about the Avenue of the Flags. In 2010, Rex had the opportunity to go on the Honor Flight to Washington D.C. to visit the Veterans Memorial. Rex also was very active with the Bedford Fire Department, obtaining a 50-year award for his services.   **RHONDA LANE WYCKOFF** [6430] (1951 – 1979) daughter of Donald and Olive (Smith) Wyckoff left her apartment to jogg and was found two days later near some railroad tracks. Investigators said she had been stabbed three times in the chest and had a 14-inch gash in her abdomen. They said she apparently was sexually assaulted after she was killed. Detective Carl Kent said the killing may be related to a series of rapes and beatings in northwest Houston.   **RICHARD ERIC WYCKOFF** (1946 – 2008) son of Donald and Olive (Smith) Wyckoff married and was father of (1).   **RICHARD LEE WYCKOFF** Sixth great grandson of progenitor Nicholas Kegg.   **ROBERT J. WYCKOFF** Sixth great grandson of progenitor Nicholas Kegg.   **ROSE ALMA WYCKOFF** [6431] (1915 – 1960) daughter of Louis and Mary Elsina (Rabourn) Wyckoff married twice; first to Harold Dueling with whom she was mother of (2). Later, she married James Clifford Cortner with whom she was mother of (3). Rose was a member of the Christian church in Clearfield outlived her brother Arthur by six hours.   **ROSS ALLEN WYCKOFF** [6432] (1915 – 1994) son of Louis and Mary Elsina (Rabourn) Wyckoff married Emma Marie Spreng with whom he was father of (1). Ross retired from Delavan Corp.   **ROWENA LOUISE WYCKOFF** [6432A] (1921 – 2013) daughter of Arthur and Essica (Shehan) Wyckoff, married Gus Clay Shimer with whom she was mother of (3). Rowena played the piano and guitar by ear. She enjoyed singing and yodeling. Everyone was always welcome in her home, and she would often invite her guests to stay and share a meal with the family. Rowena worked at Cudahy Packing Company, the Highway Café, the Junction Café, O'Bryan Brothers and cleaned homes. She loved caring for and helping others.   **RUTH FAYE WYCKOFF** (1892 – 1941) daughter of Joseph and Emma (Laird) Wyckoff, married Glenn Otto Scott with whom she was mother of (3).   **SAMUEL C. WYCKOFF** (1870 – 1951) son of Joseph and Emma (Laird)

[6423] Times-Republican (IA) Jan 13, 1913, transcribed by Julia Johnson [6424] Des Moines Register (IA) July 25, 2016 [6425] Des Moines Register (IA) July 26, 2016 [6426] Bedford Times-Press (IA) Aug 9, 1984, transcribed by Marty & Harley [6427] The Los Angeles Times (CA) Dec 30, 1959 [6428] The Des Moines Register (IA) April 13, 2008 [6429] Find A Grave memorial# 121529406 Created by: Matthew Whelan [6430] p.2 Brownsville Herald (TX) Aug 30, 1979 [6431] p.8 Bedford Times-Press (IA) Feb 18, 1960, transcribed by Julia Johnson [6432] The Des Moines Register (IA) Feb 9, 1994 [6432A] Clarinda Herald-Journal (IA) Apr 18, 2013

Wyckoff, married Minnie May Whisler with whom he was father of (1). **SCOTT WYCKOFF** Sixth great grandson of progenitor Nicholas Kegg. **SCOTT WYCKOFF** Seventh great grandson of progenitor Nicholas Kegg. **SHARON JEANNE WYCKOFF** [6433] (1946 – 2008) daughter of Eldon and Edwina (Witherspoon) Wyckoff married Mr. Eastep with whom she was mother of (4). **SUSAN KAY WYCKOFF** Fifth great granddaughter of progenitor Nicholas Kegg. **TAMMY WYCKOFF** Sixth great granddaughter of progenitor Nicholas Kegg. **THELMA MORAY WYCKOFF** (1903 – 1904) daughter of Bert and Edith (Greelee) Wyckoff. **WENDY WYCKOFF** Sixth great granddaughter of progenitor Nicholas Kegg.

WYCUFF

JEANA MARIE WYCUFF Seventh great granddaughter of progenitor Nicholas Kegg.

WYLIE

ALAN KEITH WYLIE Sixth great grandson of progenitor Nicholas Kegg. **CATHY WYLIE** Sixth great granddaughter of progenitor Nicholas Kegg. **CHRISTOPHER DAVID WYLIE** Seventh great grandson of progenitor Nicholas Kegg. **CLAYTON RUSSELL WYLIE** [6433A] aka "Russ" (1933 – 2013) son of Charles and Helen (Zong) Wylie, married Anne Edwards Woods with whom he was father of (2). Russ was a retired Navy Captain with 31 years of service. He served in Vietnam and Grenada where he was awarded two Legion of Merit awards and received many awards by other allies. He was an attaché to the U.S. Embassy in Caracas, Venezuela; Trinidad Tobago; Barbados and Grenada. Russ loved golf, reading, traveling and was a great sports fan. **JEAN WYLIE** Fifth great granddaughter of progenitor Nicholas Kegg. **KEITH WARREN WYLIE** Fifth great grandson of progenitor Nicholas Kegg. **LAURA WYLIE** Sixth great granddaughter of progenitor Nicholas Kegg. **NOELLE ELIZABETH WYLIE** [6434, 6435] aka "Elle" (1992 – 2018) daughter of Alan and Alyson (Frutchey) Wylie excelled academically in High School where she participated in basketball, volleyball, chorus, and dance. Elle had a competitive spirit and did her best in everything. She earned a Bachelor of Arts degree in psychology and dreamed of becoming a nurse. Elle was a ray of sunshine to all who knew her, and she saw the best in everyone. Bubbly and social, she liked all things pink, bling, and sparkle. Elle's greatest joy in life was her son. Playing with her baby brought her so much joy. She was a devoted mother and worked very hard to make a happy life for her young son. **PEGGY WYLIE** Sixth great granddaughter of progenitor Nicholas Kegg.

WYMAN

CALEB WYMAN Seventh great grandson of progenitor Nicholas Kegg.

WYSOCKI

KIERAN WYSOCKI Eighth great grandson of progenitor Nicholas Kegg.

YACOB

RHONDA YACOB Fifth great granddaughter of progenitor Nicholas Kegg.
SHERON KAY YACOB [6436] (1950 – 2002) daughter of George and Joyce (Kochel) Yacob married twice; first to Jackie Keaton with whom she was mother of (1). Later, she married Larry Joseph Heydinger. Sheron was an employee at the Home Savings & Loan in Willard. She was a member of the First United Methodist Church in Willard, where she was in the church choir.

[6433] The Kansas City Star (MO) May 23, 2008 [6433A] Village-News (FL) Nov 29, 2013 [6434] Daily News (CA) Sep. 21, 2018 [6435] Red Bluff Daily News (CA) Oct 4, 2018 [6436] New Washington Herald (OH) July 18, 2002

YARNELL

MELANIE YARNELL Sixth great granddaughter of progenitor Nicholas Kegg.

YATES

ELIZABETH ANN YATES aka "Beth" Fifth great granddaughter of progenitor Nicholas Kegg.
JANE ELLEN YATES Fifth great granddaughter of progenitor Nicholas Kegg.

YATMAN

BRENT NICHOLAS YATMAN Sixth great grandson of progenitor Nicholas Kegg.
CHRISTE E. YATMAN Sixth great granddaughter of progenitor Nicholas Kegg.
MARK EUGENE YATMAN Sixth great grandson of progenitor Nicholas Kegg.

YEARICK

SETH P. YEARICK Seventh great grandson of progenitor Nicholas Kegg.

YERINGTON

ANDREW ANTHONY CLAY YERINGTON (2000 – 2000) son of Jeffrey and Rachel (Lowery) Yerington. **JEFFREY LYNN YERINGTON** Eighth great grandson of progenitor Nicholas Kegg. **JEFFREY LYNN YERINGTON** Seventh great grandson of progenitor Nicholas Kegg. **LILLY ANN RENEE YERINGTON** Eighth great granddaughter of progenitor Nicholas Kegg. **MATTHEW TIMOTHY YERINGTON** Eighth great grandson of progenitor Nicholas Kegg.

YINGLING

CODY JAMES YINGLING Eighth great grandson of progenitor Nicholas Kegg.
COLE MICHAEL YINGLING Eighth great grandson of progenitor Nicholas Kegg.

YODER

ANDREW RAY YODER [6437, 6438, 6439] (1972 – 2021) son of Cromer and Nancy Jo (Easton) Yoder married Gail Lynette Brant with whom he was father of (1). A Navy veteran, Andrew was a regional manager for Quality Farm & Fleet and Tractor Supply for over 10 years. He won many awards for his stores. Andrew enjoyed spending time with his family, grilling out, and watching South Park. **CARL E. YODER** (1919 – 1920) son of Samuel and Ethel (Nelson) Yoder. **CAROL LEE YODER** Fifth great granddaughter of progenitor Nicholas Kegg. **DANIEL JAMES YODER** [6439A] (1915 – 2001) son of Samuel and Ethel (Nelson) Yoder married Cecelia Bell Richardson with whom he was father of (2). During World War II, Daniel worked as a technician for Beech Aircraft. He worked most of his life as a carpenter and builder where he owned Yoder Construction and Yoder Real Estate. He constructed many homes in the Blackwell area and other buildings including the Church of Christ in 1954 and the Roberts Funeral Home chapel in 1965. **DAVID LEONARD YODER** Fifth great grandson of progenitor Nicholas Kegg. **DAVID SAMUEL YODER** [6440] (1917 – 1976) son of Samuel and Ethel (Nelson) Yoder, married Ruthena Elizabeth Miller with whom he was father of (1). David was called to active duty with the 45th Division early in 1942 a communications wire chief and took part in the invasions of Sicily,

---

[6437] Herald Tribune (FL) Mar. 18, 2021 [6438] gofundme [6439] Herald Tribune (FL) Mar. 15, 2006 [6439A] Blackwell Journal Tribune (OK) Apr 13, 2001, contributed by D. Sue Dible [6440] Blackwell Journal Tribune (OK) May 20, 1976, obtained by D. Sue Dible

Anzio, Rome, Central Europe and the Rhineland. Mr. Yoder was awarded the Purple Heart, the EAME Service ribbon and Good Conduct and American Defense ribbons. He was discharged in 1945 after 51/2 years' service. He entered the construction business and worked with his father, and brother. Later he was employed at Blackwell Zinc, the Blackwell school system and was associated with Northern Oklahoma College. He was a member of Chikaskia Masonic Lodge 109 and was 32nd degree Mason and was a past worthy patron of the Order of Eastern Star. In the First Christian Church, where David was a member, he served as deacon and Boy Scout leader. **DEVON ALAN RAY YODER** [6441] (1995 – 2016) son of Andrew and Gail (Brant) Yoder was an amazing young soul who loved life, was loved by everyone who knew him, and was always the life of the party. **JOSEPH GILMORE YODER** [6442] (1911 – 1961) son of Samuel and Ethel (Nelson) Yoder married twice; first to Doris Babcock. Later, he married Cora Elizabeth Bourne with whom he was father of (1). Joseph was found dead in the wreckage of his car seven miles east and three north of Medford. Highway Patrolman Skipper Smith estimated that he had been killed about three hours before. The tragedy was discovered by Jimmy Waldroup of Medford, who drove by and saw the wreckage. Trooper Smith reported that the 1959 Rambler was traveling north, the vehicle going out of control on the country road, smashing through a fence into a pasture and overturning in a small creek some 150 feet away. Joseph's car went into a slide of 49 feet, traveled down the ditch for 60 feet before going through the fence and plunging downhill across the pasture and over a series of small embankments before plunging 10 feet across the creek and turning on the right side before coming to rest in the creek bottom. Smith said that his investigation showed that the car the air three times for distances of 33, 54 and 31 feet. It traveled out of control for a distance of 493 feet. The highway trooper reported that Yoder suffered head and chest injuries, and possibly a broken neck. His wristwatch was stopped a 1:28 p.m. which was fixed as the time of the accident. **LILLIAN E. YODER** [6443] (1909 – 2007) daughter of Samuel and Ethel (Nelson) Yoder, married Alfred William Schambron with whom she was mother of (1). **LUELLA MAY YODER** [6444] (1907 – 1991) daughter of Samuel and Ethel (Nelson) Yoder, married Earl Elmer Waggerman with whom she was mother of (5). Luella owned and operated Nob Hill Market on San Pablo Avenue in Richmond from 1960 to 1974.

YOKUM

AMBER REBECCA YOKUM Sixth great granddaughter of progenitor Nicholas Kegg.
DEVANY NICOLE YOKUM Sixth great granddaughter of progenitor Nicholas Kegg.

JILL REBECCA YOKUM Fifth great granddaughter of progenitor Nicholas Kegg.
REBECCA LYNN YOKUM Sixth great granddaughter of progenitor Nicholas Kegg.
SAMUEL TODD YOKUM Fifth great grandson of progenitor Nicholas Kegg.
SHARON ANN YOKUM Fifth great granddaughter of progenitor Nicholas Kegg.
WANDA JANE YOKUM Fifth great granddaughter of progenitor Nicholas Kegg.
WESLEY BRIAN YOKUM Sixth great grandson of progenitor Nicholas Kegg.
WILLIAM KEITH YOKUM Fifth great grandson of progenitor Nicholas Kegg.
WYATT TODD YOKUM Sixth great grandson of progenitor Nicholas Kegg.

YONTOSH

JILLIAN RENEE YONTOSH Seventh great granddaughter of progenitor Nicholas Kegg.
RYAN YONTOSH Seventh great grandson of progenitor Nicholas Kegg.
RYLAN ROSE YONTOSH Eighth great granddaughter of progenitor Nicholas Kegg.
ZACHARY YONTOSH Seventh great grandson of progenitor Nicholas Kegg.

[6441] Herald Tribune (FL) Apr. 21, 2016 [6442] Blackwell Journal-Tribune (OK) July 24, 1961 [6443] Blackwell Journal-Tribune (OK) Jan 3, 1929 [6444] p.A4 - Vallejo Times Herald (CA) Dec 11, 1991 obtained by D. Sue Dible

YORK

CLARENCE JAMES YORK Fifth great grandson of progenitor Nicholas Kegg.
DOLLIE JEANNE YORK Fifth great granddaughter of progenitor Nicholas Kegg.

YOST

BRIAN THOMAS YOST Sixth great grandson of progenitor Nicholas Kegg. **CATHERINE YOST** Fifth great granddaughter of progenitor Nicholas Kegg. **DONNA JUNE YOST** Fifth great granddaughter of progenitor Nicholas Kegg. **LESTER HARRY YOST** (1922 – 2002) son of Lester and Mary (Imler) Yost married Genevieve Catherine Miller with whom he was father of (3). **ROBERT YOST** Fifth great grandson of progenitor Nicholas Kegg.

YOUNG

ADISYN YOUNG Eighth great granddaughter of progenitor Nicholas Kegg. **ALVA JEAN YOUNG** aka "Jeanie", Fifth great granddaughter of progenitor Nicholas Kegg. **ASHLEN YOUNG** Eighth great granddaughter of progenitor Nicholas Kegg. **AVA ALEXANDRA YOUNG** Eighth great granddaughter of progenitor Nicholas Kegg. **BILLIE YOUNG** Sixth great granddaughter of progenitor Nicholas Kegg. **BOBBIE YOUNG** Sixth great granddaughter of progenitor Nicholas Kegg. **BRAE YOUNG** Eighth great granddaughter of progenitor Nicholas Kegg. **BRIDGET SUE YOUNG** [6445] (1992 – 1992) daughter of Herman and Sheri (Fredritz) Young. **BRITTANY LYNN MARIA YOUNG** (1987 – 1988) daughter of Michael and Patricia (Nodich) Young. **CHANDLER YOUNG** Seventh great grandson of progenitor Nicholas Kegg. **DALE YOUNG** Fifth great grandson of progenitor Nicholas Kegg. **DAMIEN YOUNG** Seventh great grandson of progenitor Nicholas Kegg. **DAVID LEROY YOUNG** Fifth great grandson of progenitor Nicholas Kegg. **EMMAUS HAVEN YOUNG** Seventh great grandson of progenitor Nicholas Kegg. **GRACIE YOUNG** Sixth great granddaughter of progenitor Nicholas Kegg. **HANNAH YOUNG** Eighth great granddaughter of progenitor Nicholas Kegg. **JEFFREY YOUNG** Sixth great grandson of progenitor Nicholas Kegg. **JUDITH YOUNG** Sixth great granddaughter of progenitor Nicholas Kegg. **KIMBERLY DAWN YOUNG** Sixth great granddaughter of progenitor Nicholas Kegg. **LINDA ELLEN YOUNG** Sixth great granddaughter of progenitor Nicholas Kegg. **LUCAS YOUNG** Seventh great grandson of progenitor Nicholas Kegg. **MARC ALAN YOUNG** Sixth great grandson of progenitor Nicholas Kegg. **MARY ELLEN YOUNG** [6446] (1929 – 2016) daughter of Virgil and Goldie (Robinson) Young, married Maynard Evan Hurd with whom she was mother of (4). Mary served as York Twp. fiscal officer for many years, attended Nelsonville Church of the Nazarene, was formerly active in various civic organization, and was a Republican Central Committeeman for more than 40 years. **MICHAELA YOUNG** Seventh great granddaughter of progenitor Nicholas Kegg. **RITA JOYCE YOUNG** Sixth great granddaughter of progenitor Nicholas Kegg. **ROBERT VANCE YOUNG** [6447] (1922 – 1969) son of Virgil and Grace (Whitlatch) Young, married Rita Mae Bird with whom he was father of (6). Robert was employed in plant production at Libbey-Owens-Ford since 1946. He was a veteran of the U.S. Air Force in WWII and a member of the United Glass and Ceramic Workers of North America, AFL-CIO. **STEVEN DALE YOUNG** (1957 – 1965) son of Dale and Betty (McKnight) Young. **SUSAN YOUNG** Sixth great granddaughter of progenitor Nicholas Kegg. **VICTORIA LYNNE YOUNG** aka "Vicki" Sixth great granddaughter of progenitor Nicholas Kegg. **VIRGIL HASTINGS YOUNG** (1897 – 1978) son of Harley and Laura (Jones) Young married three times; first to Grace Lee Whitlatch with whom he was father of (1). He married Goldie Vergene Robinson with whom he was father of (2). Later, he married Ana Avonell Taylor.

[6445] Fostoria, Ohio Library obituary clipping obtained by D. Sue Dible [6446] Athens Messenger (OH) Apr. 28, 2016 [6447] Toledo Blade (OH) Dec 29, 1969, obtained by D. Sue Dible

YOUNKER

DYLAN YOUNKER Seventh great grandson of progenitor Nicholas Kegg.
NATALIE YOUNKER Seventh great granddaughter of progenitor Nicholas Kegg.

YU

HELEN YU Seventh great granddaughter of progenitor Nicholas Kegg

YUNETZ

JANICE M. YUNETZ Fifth great granddaughter of progenitor Nicholas Kegg.
JEFFREY YUNETZ Sixth great grandson of progenitor Nicholas Kegg.
JEFFREY S. YUNETZ Fifth great grandson of progenitor Nicholas Kegg.
JOSEPH K. YUNETZ Fifth great grandson of progenitor Nicholas Kegg.

YURECHKO

KATHY YURECHKO Sixth great granddaughter of progenitor Nicholas Kegg.

ZABEL

CELESTE NICOLE ZABEL Seventh great granddaughter of progenitor Nicholas Kegg.
FRANK ZABEL Seventh great grandson of progenitor Nicholas Kegg.
JESSE ZABEL Seventh great grandson of progenitor Nicholas Kegg.

ZABOLOTNEY

KIRA L. ZABOLOTNEY Sixth great granddaughter of progenitor Nicholas Kegg.

ZARANKO

RILEY GRACE ZARANKO Sixth great granddaughter of progenitor Nicholas Kegg.

ZEIGLER

BRANDON HARVEY ZEIGLER Sixth great grandson of progenitor Nicholas Kegg.
DORRIT RENEE ZEIGLER Seventh great granddaughter of progenitor Nicholas Kegg.
ELIOT EMANUEL ZEIGLER Seventh great grandson of progenitor Nicholas Kegg.
EMILY JENNIFER ZEIGLER Sixth great granddaughter of progenitor Nicholas Kegg.
MARTIN HARVEY ZEIGLER Seventh great grandson of progenitor Nicholas Kegg.
MATTHEW JOSEPH ZEIGLER Sixth great grandson of progenitor Nicholas Kegg.
MICHAEL ZEIGLER Sixth great grandson of progenitor Nicholas Kegg.
NATHANIEL JOSIAH ZEIGLER Seventh great grandson of progenitor Nicholas Kegg.
ROSE KATHERINE ZEIGLER Seventh great granddaughter of progenitor Nicholas Kegg.

ZELLER

CHARLENE ZELLER Fifth great granddaughter of progenitor Nicholas Kegg.
CHESTER ZELLER Fifth great grandson of progenitor Nicholas Kegg.
DALE A. ZELLER Fourth great grandson of progenitor Nicholas Kegg.

DENISE ZELLER Fifth great granddaughter of progenitor Nicholas Kegg.
DEVORAH ZELLER Fifth great granddaughter of progenitor Nicholas Kegg.
JACQUELINE R. ZELLER Fourth great granddaughter of progenitor Nicholas Kegg.
MARVIN LEE ZELLER JR. Fifth great grandson of progenitor Nicholas Kegg.
SCOTT ZELLER Fifth great grandson of progenitor Nicholas Kegg.

ZELLERS

BRAYDEN ZELLERS Eighth great grandson of progenitor Nicholas Kegg.
KAMI ZELLERS Seventh great granddaughter of progenitor Nicholas Kegg.
SHANE ZELLERS Seventh great grandson of progenitor Nicholas Kegg.

ZELLMAN

JOSEPH AUGUST ZELLMAN Seventh great grandson of progenitor Nicholas Kegg.

ZENDER

BRADON ARNOLD ZENDER Seventh great grandson of progenitor Nicholas Kegg.
CONNER ZENDER Seventh great grandson of progenitor Nicholas Kegg.
IAN PATRICK ZENDER Seventh great grandson of progenitor Nicholas Kegg.
REILLY ZENDER Seventh great granddaughter of progenitor Nicholas Kegg.

ZENTACK

TERESSA ZENTACK Sixth great granddaughter of progenitor Nicholas Kegg.

ZICKAFOOSE

ANDREW MICHAEL ZICKAFOOSE Seventh great grandson of progenitor Nicholas Kegg.
JOHN JOSEPH ZICKAFOOSE Seventh great grandson of progenitor Nicholas Kegg.

ZIMMER

LUKE HOWARD ZIMMER Seventh great grandson of progenitor Nicholas Kegg.

ZIMMERMAN

AMANDA ZIMMERMAN Seventh great granddaughter of progenitor Nicholas Kegg.
BRANDI ZIMMERMAN Seventh great granddaughter of progenitor Nicholas Kegg.
BRANDON ZIMMERMAN Eighth great grandson of progenitor Nicholas Kegg.
DEVIN ZIMMERMAN Eighth great grandson of progenitor Nicholas Kegg.
ELIZABETH REBECCA ZIMMERMAN Eighth great granddaughter of progenitor Nicholas Kegg.
HANNAH ZIMMERMAN Seventh great granddaughter of progenitor Nicholas Kegg.
SARAH S. ZIMMERMAN Eighth great granddaughter of progenitor Nicholas Kegg.

ZINK

ANGELA LYNN ZINK Seventh great granddaughter of progenitor Nicholas Kegg.
DANIEL MICHAEL ZINK Sixth great grandson of progenitor Nicholas Kegg.
DANIEL MICHAEL ZINK JR. Seventh great grandson of progenitor Nicholas Kegg.

MARY KATHERINE ZINK Sixth great granddaughter of progenitor Nicholas Kegg.
THOMAS EDWARD ZINK (1956 – 2021) son of Charles and Gloria (Benton) Zink married Donna Parr with whom he was father of (1).
THOMAS EDWARD ZINK JR. Seventh great grandson of progenitor Nicholas Kegg.

ZONG

DORIS LILLIAN ZONG [6449] (1913 – 1996) daughter of Frank and Ruby (Coffman) Zong, married Earl Harvey Kutscher with whom she was mother of (3). **HELEN ZULA ZONG** [6450] (1911 – 1998) daughter of Frank and Ruby (Coffman) Zong, married Charles R. Wylie with whom she was mother of (3). **ILA M. ZONG** [6451] (1915 – 1995) daughter of Frank and Ruby (Coffman) Zong married Olin William Brinegar with whom she was mother of (1). during World War II, Ila was employed by the United States Air Corps as a civilian. She later became a supervisor for Sears in California. After retirement, Ila was a member of the First United Methodist Church in Hebron; O.E.S. Chapter No. 31 of Hebron; Belvidere Women's Club; Bible Club of Hebron; also, a member of various bridge clubs of Hebron.

ZULFIC

KAMERON ZULFIC Fifth great grandson of progenitor Nicholas Kegg.

ZUMDAHL

BENJAMIN LYLE ZUMDAHL Sixth great grandson of progenitor Nicholas Kegg.
LAURA ELIZABETH ZUMDAHL Sixth great granddaughter of progenitor Nicholas Kegg.
LEAH CHRISTIAN ZUMDAHL Sixth great granddaughter of progenitor Nicholas Kegg.

ZUVELLA

KYLE MICHAEL ZUVELLA Sixth great grandson of progenitor Nicholas Kegg.
SHANE PAUL ZUVELLA Sixth great grandson of progenitor Nicholas Kegg.

ZUVICH

BENJAMIN ZUVICH Eighth great grandson of progenitor Nicholas Kegg.
MATTHEW ZUVICH Eighth great grandson of progenitor Nicholas Kegg.

ZWEIFEL

KENT SCOTT ZWEIFEL [6452] (1961 – 2021) son of Robert and Deanna (Luenenborg) Zweifel had various jobs including farming, working at Great Western Sugar, but his favorite job was driving as a long-haul trucker for many years. He loved driving from coast to coast and took great pride in his career.
LIBBY L. ZWEIFEL Sixth great granddaughter of progenitor Nicholas Kegg.
LISA MARIE ZWEIFEL Sixth great granddaughter of progenitor Nicholas Kegg.
ROBERT EARL ZWEIFEL Fifth great grandson of progenitor Nicholas Kegg.
RORY ROY ZWEIFEL Sixth great grandson of progenitor Nicholas Kegg.

[6449] Lincoln Journal Star (NE) Sep 27, 1996 [6450] The Daily Herald (Provo, Utah) Nov 28, 1998 [6451] Hebron Journal Register (NE) Feb 22, 1995 [6452] The Star-Herald (NE) Apr. 27, 2021

Note From the Author

Hundreds of Surnames A-Z, remind me of a conversation with Roy Kegg who made me laugh when he said, "It doesn't matter if the last name is not Kegg. If it walks like a Kegg and talks like a Kegg. It must be a Kegg". Every individual has a little bit of everyone who had gone before. It is interesting to line up photographs of your parents, grandparents and great grandparents and see the characteristics that have been passed down through the genetic line to you. The Mark of Nicholas Kegg is intended to preserve the history of the Kegg family tree. All the information that the older people remember goes to waste if it is not shared.

www.ingramcontent.com/pod-product-compliance
Lightning Source LLC
Chambersburg PA
CBHW080533300426
44111CB00017B/2711